The Chartered Management Institute

DICTIONARY OF BUSINESS AND MANAGEMENT

D1464133

The Chartered Management Institute

DICTIONARY OF BUSINESS AND MANAGEMENT

BLOOMSBURY

A BLOOMSBURY REFERENCE BOOK
Created from the Bloomsbury Business Database
www.ultimatebusinessresource.com

© Bloomsbury Publishing Plc 2004
Management terms © Chartered Management Institute 2002

All rights reserved; no part of this publication may be reproduced, stored in a retrieval system, or transmitted by any means, electronic, mechanical, photocopying or otherwise, without the prior written permission of the Publisher.

No responsibility for loss caused to any individual or organisation acting or refraining from action as a result of the material in this publication can be accepted by Bloomsbury Publishing or the authors.

First published in 2004 by
Bloomsbury Publishing Plc
38 Soho Square
London W1D 3HB

British Library Cataloguing in Publication Data
A CIP record for this book is available from the British Library.

ISBN 0 7475 7200 3

Design by Fiona Pike, Pike Design, Winchester
Typeset by RefineCatch Limited, Bungay, Suffolk
Printed by Clays Ltd, St Ives plc

Contents

User's Guide

The Chartered Management Institute *Dictionary of Business and Management* provides clear, jargon-free definitions to more than 6,500 international business and management terms. Updated and expanded from the flagship edition of *BUSINESS: The Ultimate Resource™*, the Dictionary has been compiled by an international team of expert researchers and business information specialists. It is an up-to-date, practical resource that will help the user understand both basic and complex terms business terms from around the world. Easy-to-use and full of helpful information, it aims to define the world of business.

TOPIC AREAS
The terms have been drawn from eight key topic areas, and each term labelled accordingly. The topic areas have been abbreviated for ease of use, and they appear in the Dictionary as follows:

E-commerce	*E-com*
Economics	*Econ*
Finance, Banking, and Accounting	*Fin*
General Management	*Gen Mgt*
HR & Personnel	*HR*
Marketing	*Mkting*
Operations and Production	*Ops*
Statistics	*Stats*

The topic areas help to give extra context to each term, especially when it can have more than one meaning depending on the situation in which it is used. For example:

churn rate 1. *Fin* a measure of the frequency and volume of trading of stocks and bonds in a brokerage account **2.** *Gen Mgt* the rate at which new customers try a product or service and then stop using it

ORDER OF TERMS
All terms are listed in strict alphabetical order, apart from when a term is part of a phrase. In these cases, the definition is shown at the most valid element of the phrase. For example:

ball
take the ball and run with it *Gen Mgt* to take an idea and implement it (*slang*)

STANDARD AND EXTENDED DEFINITIONS
Each term in the Dictionary has been given a clear, jargon-free definition. For example:

keyword *E-com* a word used by a search engine to help locate and register a website. Companies need to think very carefully about the keywords they place in their *meta-tags* and in web pages in order to attract relevant search-engine traffic.

However, mini-essays are used at more complex terms to help explain a concept in greater depth:

Boston Box *Gen Mgt* a model used for analysing a company's potential by plotting **market share** against growth rate. The Boston Box was conceived by the Boston Consulting Group in the 1970s to help in the process of assessing in which businesses a company should invest and of which it should divest itself. A business with a high market share and high growth rate is a **star**, and one with a low market share and low growth rate is a **dog**. A high market share with low growth rate is characteristic of a *cash cow*, which could yield significant but short-term gain, and a low market share coupled with high growth rate produces a **question mark company**, which offers a doubtful return on investment. To be useful, this model requires accurate assessment of a business's strengths and weaknesses, which may be difficult to obtain.

WORKED EXAMPLES

In addition to the mini-essays, at terms which explain financial ratios, we show a fully worked example of how the ratio functions. These examples are indicated by the EXAMPLE icon:

bond yield *Fin* the annual return on a bond (the rate of interest) expressed as a percentage of the current market price of the bond. Bonds can tie up investors' money for periods of up to 30 years, so knowing their yield is a critical investment consideration.

EXAMPLE Bond yield is calculated by multiplying the face value of the bond by its stated annual rate of interest, expressed as a decimal. For example, buying a new ten-year £1,000 bond that pays 6% interest will produce an annual yield amount of £60:

$$1,000 \times 0.060 = 60$$

The £60 will be paid as £30 every six months. At the end of ten years, the purchaser will have earned £600, and will also be repaid the original £1,000. Because the bond was purchased when it was first issued, the 6% is also called the 'yield to maturity'.

This basic formula is complicated by other factors. First is the 'time-value of money' theory: money paid in the future is worth less than money paid today. A more detailed computation of total bond yield requires the calculation of the present value of the interest earned each year. Second, changing interest rates have a marked impact on bond trading and, ultimately, on yield. Changes in interest rates cannot affect the interest paid by bonds already issued, but they do affect the prices of new bonds.

CROSS-REFERENCES

Cross-reference are used in the Dictionary to link terms that are closely related, or which expand on information given in another entry. For example, at this entry:

accountability *Gen Mgt* the allocation or acceptance of *responsibility* for actions

the concept of 'responsibility' is referred to, and highlighted in bold italics to show that it has an entry in its own right:

responsibility *Gen Mgt* the duty to carry out certain activities and be accountable for them to others

Terms that are defined at another word (as part of an associated concept), or which are less preferred versions of a standard term, are cross-referred to the term whose definition contains the information you need. For example:

pull strategy *Mkting see **push and pull strategies***

BIOGRAPHICAL ENTRIES

The Dictionary also includes many biographical entries, which detail the lives, careers, and influence of international business writers, educators, and practitioners. These entries are found at the surname of the person profiled. For example:

Kotler, Philip (*b.* 1931) *Gen Mgt* US academic. Acknowledged as an expert in **marketing** theory, which he has made a major business function and academic discipline, and which he explained in *Marketing Management* (first published 1980).

Mini-essays have been included for the world's most influential business thinkers. For example:

Drucker, Peter (*b.* 1909) *Gen Mgt* US academic. Recognised as the father of management thinking. His earlier works studied management practice, while later he tackled the complexities and the management implications of the post-industrial world. *The Practice of Management* (1954), best known perhaps for the introduction of *management by objectives*, remains a classic. He also anticipated other management themes such as the importance of marketing (see *marketing management*) and the rise of the *knowledge worker*.

ABBREVIATIONS

Business English is full of abbreviations and acronyms, and the Dictionary features many of these. Where the abbreviation is the most commonly used version of a term or phrase, the abbreviation's full form is given at that entry:

B2B *abbr E-com* business-to-business: relating to an advertising or marketing programme aimed at businesses doing business with other businesses as opposed to consumers. The term is most commonly used in reference to commerce or business that is conducted over the Internet between commercial enterprises.

In cases where the full form of an abbreviation is the most commonly known form of the concept, the expanded form is shown at the entry for the abbreviation:

EDC *abbr E-com* electronic data capture

Variant names of a word or phrase are also shown in the Dictionary:

points plan *HR* a method of *job evaluation* that uses a points scale for rating different criteria. *Also known as **point-factor system***

For more information about *BUSINESS: The Ultimate Resource™* and other related titles, please visit:
www.ultimatebusinessresource.com

To register for free electronic upgrades, please go to
www.ultimatebusinessresource.com/register,
type in your e-mail address, and key in your password: **Drucker**

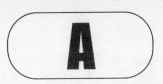

AAA¹ *abbr* **1.** *E-com* authentication, authorisation, and accounting: the software security verification procedures that acknowledge or validate an e-commerce user or message **2.** *Fin* American Accounting Association

AAA² *Fin* the prime maximum safety rating given by Standard & Poor's, one of the two best known bond-rating agencies

AAMOF *abbr Gen Mgt* as a matter of fact (*slang*)

AARF *abbr Fin* Australian Accounting Research Foundation

AAS *abbr Fin* Australian Accounting Standard

AASB *abbr Fin* Australian Accounting Standards Board

AAT *abbr Fin* Association of Accounting Technicians

abandonment option *Fin* the option of terminating an investment before the time that it is scheduled to end

abandonment value *Fin* the value that an investment has if it is terminated at a particular time before it is scheduled to end

ABB *abbr Fin* activity-based budgeting

ABC *abbr Fin* activity-based costing

Abilene paradox *Gen Mgt* a theory stating that some decisions that seem to be based on consensus are in fact based on misperception and lead to courses of action that defeat original intentions. The Abilene paradox was proposed by Jerry Harvey in 1974 following a trip made by his family to the town of Abilene. One person suggested the visit as he felt the others needed entertainment, and the others agreed as they all believed that everyone else wanted to go. On their return, everyone admitted that they would rather have stayed at home. Harvey used this experience to illustrate the mismanagement of agreement, and of **decision-making** in organisations when apparent consensus is actually founded on poor communication. The Abilene paradox shows similarities to the **attribution theory of leadership**.

ABN *abbr Fin* Australian Business Number: a numeric code that identifies an Australian business for the purpose of dealing with the Australian Tax Office and other government departments. ABNs are part of the new tax system that came into operation in Australia in 1998.

abnormal loss *Fin* any losses which exceed the normal loss allowance. Abnormal losses are generally costed as though they were completed products.

abnormal spoilage *Fin* the unexpectedly high level of shrinkage that has contributed to an **abnormal loss**

above-the-line 1. *Fin* used to describe entries in a company's profit and loss accounts that appear above the line separating those entries that show the origin of the funds that have contributed to the profit or loss from those that relate to its distribution. Exceptional and extraordinary items appear above the line. *See also* **below-the-line** *(sense 2)* **2.** *Fin* in macroeconomics, used to describe a country's revenue transactions. *See also* **below-the-line** *(sense 3)* **3.** *Mkting* relating to marketing expenditure on advertising in media such as press, radio, television, cinema, and the World Wide Web, on which a commission is usually paid to an agency

ABS *abbr Fin* Australian Bureau of Statistics

absenteeism *HR* the problem of employees taking short-term, unauthorised **leave** from work, resulting in lost **productivity** and increased costs. Absenteeism is usually sickness-related. Other causes may include a lack of **motivation**, domestic difficulties, or poor management.

There is no such thing as great talent without great willpower.   *Honoré de Balzac*

absorbed account *Fin* an account that has lost its separate identity by being combined with related accounts in the preparation of a financial statement

absorbed business *Gen Mgt* a company that has been merged into another company

absorbed costs *Fin* the indirect costs associated with manufacturing, for example, insurance or property taxes

absorbed overhead *Fin* overhead attached to products or services by means of **absorption rates**

absorption costing *Fin* an accounting practice in which fixed and variable costs of production are absorbed by different cost centres. Providing all the products or services can be sold at a price that covers the allocated costs, this method ensures that both fixed and variable costs are recovered in full. However, should sales be lost because the resultant price is too high, the organisation may lose revenue that would contribute to its overheads. *See also* **marginal costing**

absorption rate *Fin see* **overhead absorption rate**

abusive tax shelter *Fin* a tax shelter that somebody claims illegally to avoid or minimise tax

ACA *abbr Fin* Australian Communications Authority

ACCA *abbr Fin* **1.** Association of Chartered Certified Accountants **2.** associate of the Association of Chartered Certified Accountants

ACCC *abbr Fin* Australian Competition and Consumer Commission: an independent statutory body responsible for monitoring trade practices in Australia. It was set up in November 1995 as a result of the merger of the Trade Practices Commission and the Prices Surveillance Authority.

accelerated cost recovery system *Fin* a system used in the United States for computing the depreciation of some

assets acquired before 1986 in a way that reduces taxes. *Abbr* **ACRS**

accelerated depreciation *Econ, Fin* a system used for computing the depreciation of some assets in a way that assumes that they depreciate faster in the early years of their acquisition. *Also known as* **declining balance method**

acceptable quality level *Ops* the level at which an output of manufactured components is considered to be of satisfactory quality. Acceptable quality level is usually expressed with the number of defective items shown as a proportion of the total output. Today, owing to a general increase in competitive pressure, the only acceptable quality level is **zero defects**, so the term is rarely used.

acceptance *Fin* the signature on a bill of exchange, indicating that the drawee (the person to whom it is addressed) will pay the face amount of the bill on the due date

acceptance bonus (*US*) *HR* a **bonus** paid to a new **employee** on acceptance of the job. An acceptance bonus can be a feature of a **golden hello** and is designed both to attract and to retain staff.

acceptance credit *Fin* a line of credit granted by a bank to an importer against which an exporter can draw a bill of exchange. After acceptance by the bank, the bill can either be sold in the market or held until maturity.

acceptance house *Econ, Fin* an institution that accepts financial instruments and agrees to honour them should the borrower default

acceptance region *Stats* the set of values in a test statistic for which the null hypothesis can be accepted

acceptance sampling *Ops* a **quality control** decision-making technique used in a manufacturing environment, in which acceptance or rejection of a batch of parts is decided by testing a sample of the batch. The sample is checked against established standards and, if it meets those standards, the whole batch is deemed acceptable.

accepting bank *Fin* the bank that accepts a bill of exchange drawn under a *documentary credit*

acceptor *Fin* the person to whom a signed bill of exchange is addressed

access bond (*S Africa*) *Fin* a type of mortgage that permits borrowers to take out loans against extra capital paid into the account, home-loan interest rates being lower than interest rates on other forms of credit

ACCI *abbr Fin* Australian Chamber of Commerce and Industry

account 1. *Fin* a business arrangement involving the exchange of money or credit in which payment is deferred, or a record maintained by a financial institution itemising its dealings with a particular customer **2.** *Mkting* a client of an advertising or PR agency

accountability *Gen Mgt* the allocation or acceptance of *responsibility* for actions

accountability concept *Fin* management accounting presents information measuring the achievement of the objectives of an organisation and appraising the conduct of its internal affairs in that process. In order that further action can be taken, based on this information, it is necessary at all times to identify the responsibilities and key results of individuals within the organisation.

accountancy *Fin* the practice of accounting

accountancy bodies *Fin* professional institutions and associations for accountants

accountancy profession *Fin* professional bodies of accountants that establish and regulate training entry standards, professional examinations, and ethical and technical rules and guidelines. These bodies are organised on national and international levels.

accountant *Fin* a professional person who maintains and checks the business records of a person or organisation and prepares forms and reports for financial purposes

accountant's letter *Fin* a written statement by an independent accountant that precedes a financial report, describing the scope of the report and giving an opinion on its validity

account day *Fin* the day on which an executed order is settled by the delivery of securities, payment to the seller, and payment by the buyer. This is the final day of the *accounting period*.

account debtor *Fin* a person or organisation responsible for paying for a product or service

account director *Mkting* a senior person within an advertising agency responsible for overall policy on a client's advertising account

account executive *Mkting* an employee of an organisation such as a bank, public relations firm, or advertising agency who is responsible for the business of a particular client

accounting cost *Fin* the cost of maintaining and checking the business records of a person or organisation and the preparation of forms and reports for financial purposes

accounting cycle *Fin* the regular process of formally updating a firm's financial position by recording, analysing, and reporting its transactions during the accounting period

accounting equation *Fin* a formula in which a firm's assets must be equal to the sum of its liabilities and the owners' equity. *Also known as* **balance sheet equation**

accounting exposure *Econ, Fin* the risk that foreign currency held by a company may lose value because of exchange rate changes when it conducts overseas business

accounting insolvency *Econ, Fin* the condition that a company is in when its liabilities to its creditors exceed its assets

accounting period *Fin* an amount of time in which businesses may prepare internal accounts so as to monitor progress on a weekly, monthly, or quarterly basis. Accounts are generally prepared for external purposes on an annual basis.

accounting principles *Fin* the rules that apply to accounting practices and provide guidelines for dealing appropriately with complex transactions

accounting profit *Fin* the difference between total revenue and explicit costs

accounting rate of return *Fin* the ratio of profit before interest and taxation to the percentage of capital employed at the end of a period. Variations include using profit after interest and taxation, equity capital employed, and average capital for the period.

accounting ratio *Fin* an expression of accounting results as a ratio or percentage, for example, the ratio of *current assets* to *current liabilities*

accounting reference date *Fin* the last day of a company's *accounting reference period*

accounting reference period *Fin* the period for which a company makes up its accounts. This period is normally, although not necessarily, 12 months. Also used for taxation where it represents the period for which corporation tax is calculated.

accounting system *Fin* the means, including staff and equipment, by which an organisation produces its accounting information

accounting year *Fin* the annual *accounting period*

account reconciliation *Fin* **1.** a procedure for ensuring the reliability of accounting records by comparing balances of transactions **2.** a procedure for comparing the register of a chequebook with an associated bank statement

account sales *Fin* a statement rendered to a consignor of merchandise by the consignee, giving particulars of sales, the quantity remaining unsold, gross proceeds, expenses incurred, consignee's commission, and net amount due to the consignor

accounts payable *Fin* the amount that a company owes for goods or services obtained on credit

accounts receivable *Fin* the money that is owed to a company by those who have bought its goods or services and have not yet paid for them

accounts receivable ageing *Fin* a periodic report that classifies outstanding receivable balances according to customer and month of the original billing date

accounts receivable factoring (*US*) *Fin* the buying of accounts receivable at a discount with the aim of making a profit from collecting them

accounts receivable financing *Econ, Fin* a form of borrowing in which a company uses money that it is owed as collateral for a loan it needs for business operations

accounts receivable turnover *Econ, Fin* a ratio that shows how long the customers of a business wait before paying what they owe. This can cause cash-flow problems for small businesses.
EXAMPLE The formula for accounts receivable turnover is straightforward. Simply divide the average amount of receivables into annual credit sales:

Sales / Receivables = Receivables turnover
If, for example, a company's sales are £4.5 million and its average receivables are £375,000, its receivables turnover is:

$$4,500,000 / 375,000 = 12$$

A high turnover figure is desirable, because it indicates that a company collects revenues effectively, and that its customers pay bills promptly. A high figure also suggests that a firm's credit and collection policies are sound. In addition, the measurement is a reasonably good indicator of cash flow, and of overall operating efficiency.

The meek shall inherit the earth but not the mineral rights. *J. Paul Getty*

accreditation of prior learning *HR* a process through which formal recognition for the achievements of past learning and experiences may be obtained. Accreditation of prior learning may be used to support the award of a vocational qualification.

accredited investor *Fin* an investor whose wealth or income is above a particular amount. It is illegal for an accredited investor to be a member of a private limited partnership.

accreted value *Fin* the value of a bond if interest rates do not change

accretion *Fin* the growth of a company through additions or purchases of plant or value-adding services

accrual *Fin* a charge that has not been paid by the end of an accounting period but must be included in the accounting results for the period. If no invoice has been received for the charge, an estimate must be included in the accounting results.

accrual basis *Fin see* **accrual method**

accrual bond *Fin see* **zero coupon bond**

accrual concept *Fin* the idea that income and expense items must be included in financial statements as they are earned or incurred. *See also* **cash accounting**

accrual method *Fin* an accounting method that includes income and expense items as they are earned or incurred irrespective of when money is received or paid out. *Also known as* **accrual basis**

accrual of discount *Fin* the annual gain in value of a bond owing to its having been bought originally for less than its par value

accrue *Fin* to include an income or expense item in the transaction records at the time it is earned or incurred

accrued expense *Fin* an expense that has been incurred within a given accounting period but not yet paid

accrued income *Fin* income that has been earned but not yet received

accrued interest *Fin* the amount of interest earned by a bond or similar investment since the previous interest payment

accruing *Fin* added as a periodic gain, for example, as interest on an amount of money

accumulated depreciation *Fin* the cumulative annual depreciation of an asset that has been claimed as an expense since the asset was acquired. *Also known as* **aggregate depreciation**

accumulated dividend *Fin* the amount of money in dividends earned by a stock or similar investment since the previous dividend payment

accumulated earnings tax *or* **accumulated profits tax** *Fin* the tax that a company must pay because it chose not to pay dividends that would subject its owners to higher taxes

accumulating shares *Fin* ordinary shares issued by a company equivalent to and in place of the net dividend payable to ordinary shareholders

accumulation unit *Fin* a unit of a unit trust that retains dividend income instead of distributing it to individual investors

accuracy *Stats* the degree to which data conforms to a recognised standard value

ACH *abbr E-com* automated clearing house

achievement test *HR* a type of *psychometric test* which measures what a person already knows and can do at the time of testing. The two most common types of achievement tests measure verbal reasoning and mathematical ability. There are many test preparation books available. As well as explaining how the questions are structured, they offer test strategies and sample tests. As with other psychometric tests, it has been proven that people perform better at these tests when they are well-rested, in good physical shape, and slightly hungry.

acid-test ratio *Fin* an accounting ratio used to measure an organisation's liquidity. The most common expression of the ratio is:

(Current assets – Inventory) / Current liabilities = Acid-test ratio

If, for example, current assets total £7,700, inventory amounts to £1,200 and current liabilities total £4,500, then:

(7,700 – 1,200) / 4,500 = 1.44

A variation of this formula ignores inventories altogether, distinguishes assets as cash, receivables, and short-term investments, then divides the sum of the three by the total current liabilities, or:

Cash + Accounts receivable + Short-term investments / Current liabilities = Acid-test ratio

If, for example, cash totals £2,000, receivables total £3,000, short-term investments total £1,000, and liabilities total £4,800, then:

(2,000 + 3,000 + 1,000) / 4,800 = 1.25

In general, the ratio should be 1:1 or better. It means a company has a unit's worth of easily convertible assets for each unit of its current liabilities.

Ackoff, Russell Lincoln (*b.* 1919) *Gen Mgt* US academic. Pioneer of operations research and systems thinking, whose publications include *Ackoff's Fables: Irreverent Reflections on Business and Bureaucracy* (1991).

ACM *abbr Gen Mgt* Australian Chamber of Manufactures

acquiescence bias *Stats* the bias produced when respondents in a survey give positive answers to two mutually conflicting questions

acquirer *or* **acquiring bank** *E-com* a financial institution, commonly a bank, that processes a merchant's credit card authorisations and payments, forwarding the data to a credit card association, which in turn communicates with the issuer. *Also known as* **clearing house**, **processor**

acquisition *Gen Mgt see* **merger**

acquisition accounting *Fin* the standard accounting procedures that must be followed when one company merges with another

acquisition rate *Gen Mgt* a measure of the ability of marketing programmes to win new business

ACRS *abbr Fin* accelerated cost recovery system

action-centred leadership *Gen Mgt* a *leadership* model developed by *John Adair* that focuses on what leaders actually have to do in order to be effective. The action-centred leadership model is illustrated by three overlapping circles representing the three key activities undertaken by leaders: achieving the task, building and maintaining the team, and developing the individual.

action learning *HR* learning by sharing real problems with others, as opposed to theoretical classroom learning. Action learning was introduced in the mid-1940s by *Reg Revans*, who expressed it as: Learning = Programmed knowledge + the ability to ask insightful Questions, or L = P + Q. The technique works best when people in small groups tackle real work-based problems with a view to solving them. Action learning differs from *experiential learning*, which can apply to an individual alone.

action research *Gen Mgt* research in which the researcher takes an involved role as a participant in planning and implementing change. Action research was originated by *Kurt Lewin*, and it involves conducting experiments by making changes while simultaneously observing the results.

active asset *Fin* an asset that is used in the daily operations of a business

active fund management *Fin* the managing of a unit trust by making judgments about market movements instead of relying on automatic adjustments such as indexation. *See also* **passive investment management**

active listening *HR* a technique for improving understanding of what is being said by taking into account how something is said and the non-verbal signs and *body language* that accompany it. This technique requires receptive awareness and response on the part of the listener. Six principles form the core of active listening: encourage people to express opinions; clarify perceptions of what is said; restate essential points and ideas; reflect the speaker's feeling and opinions; summarise the content of the message to check validity; acknowledge the opinion and contribution of the speaker. It is used particularly in counselling.

active portfolio strategy *Fin* the managing of an investment portfolio by making judgments about market movements instead of relying on automatic adjustments

activist fiscal policy *Fin* the policy of a government or national bank that tries to affect the value of its country's money by such measures as changing interest rates for loans to banks and buying or selling foreign currencies

activity-based budgeting *Fin* the allocation of resources to individual activities. Activity-based budgeting involves determining which activities incur costs within an organisation, establishing the relationships between them, and then deciding how much of the total *budget* should be allocated to each activity. *Abbr* **ABB**

activity-based costing *Fin, Gen Mgt* a method of calculating the cost of a business by focusing on the actual cost of activities, thereby producing an estimate of the cost of individual products or services.

An ABC cost-accounting system requires three preliminary steps: converting to an *accrual method* of accounting; defining cost centres and cost allocation; and determining process and procedure costs.

Businesses have traditionally relied on the cash basis of accounting, which recognises income when received and expenses when paid. ABC's foundation is the accrual-basis income statement. The numbers this statement presents are assigned to the various procedures performed during a given period. Cost centres are a company's identifiable products and services, but also include specific and detailed tasks within these broader activities. Defining cost centres will of course vary by business and method of operation. What is critical to ABC is the inclusion of all activities and all resources.

Once cost centres are identified, management teams can begin studying the activities each one engages in and allocating the expenses each one incurs, including the cost of employee services.

The most appropriate method is developed from time studies and direct expense allocation. Management teams who choose this method will need to devote several months to data collection in order to generate sufficient information to establish the personnel components of each activity's total cost.

Time studies establish the average amount of time required to complete each task, plus best- and worst-case performances. Only those resources actually used are factored into the cost computation; unused resources are reported separately. These studies can also advise management teams how best to monitor and allocate expenses which might otherwise be expressed as part of general overheads, or go undetected altogether. *Abbr* **ABC**

activity-based management *Gen Mgt* a management control technique that focuses on the resource costs of organisational activities and processes, and the improvement of quality, profitability, and customer value. This technique uses *activity-based costing* information to identify strategies for removing resource waste from operating activities. Main tools employed include: *strategic analysis*, *value analysis*, cost analysis, *life-cycle costing*, and *activity-based budgeting*.

activity driver *Gen Mgt see* **cost driver**

activity indicator *Econ* a statistic used to measure labour productivity or manufacturing output in an economy

activity sampling *Ops* a ***work measurement*** technique used to analyse the activities of employees, machines, or business operations. Activity sampling requires random observations of the amount of time spent on a given activity to be recorded over a fixed period. The results are used to predict the total time spent on each activity and to highlight areas in need of quality, efficiency, or effectiveness improvement. *Also known as **work sampling**, **ratio-delay study**, **random observation method***

ACTU *abbr Gen Mgt* Australian Council of Trade Unions

actuals *Fin* earnings and expenses that have occurred rather than being only projected, or commodities that can be bought and used, as contrasted with commodities traded on a futures contract

actual to date *Fin* the cumulative value realised by something between an earlier date and the present

actual turnover *Fin* the number of times during a particular period that somebody spends the average amount of money that he or she has available to spend during that period

actuarial age *Fin* the statistically derived life expectancy for any given chronological age, used, for example, to calculate the periodic payments from an annuity

actuarial analysis *Fin* a life expectancy or risk calculation carried out by an actuary

actuarial science *Fin, Stats* the branch of statistics used in calculating risk and life expectancy for the administration of pension funds and life assurance policies

actuary *Fin, Stats* a statistician who calculates probable lengths of life so that the insurance premiums to be charged for various risks can be accurately determined

ACU *abbr Fin* Asian Currency Unit

ad *E-com* a banner, button, pop-up screen, or other on-screen device calling attention to an e-commerce product or business

Adair, John Eric (*b*. 1934) *Gen Mgt* British academic. Best known for his three-circle model of ***leadership***, which is based on overlapping circles representing the task, the team, and the individual. Adair's model, otherwise known as ***action-centred leadership***, is described in the book of the same name (1973). Like ***Warren Bennis***, Adair, who has a military background, believes that leadership can be taught.

Adams, Scott (*b*. 1957) *Gen Mgt* US humorist. Creator of the ***Dilbert principle***, he satirises the many absurdities of business life through his cartoons.

adaptive control *Ops* a system of automatic monitoring and adjustment, usually by computer, of an industrial process. Adaptive control allows operating parameters to be changed continuously in response to a changing environment in order to achieve optimum performance.

adaptive measure *Stats* a means of choosing the most appropriate method for a statistical analysis

ad banner *E-com see **banner***

ad click *E-com see **click-through***

ad click rate *E-com see **click-through rate***

ADDACS *abbr Fin* Automated Direct Debit Amendments and Cancellation Service

added value 1. *Gen Mgt see **value added*** **2.** *Mkting* an increase in the attractiveness to customers of a product or a service achieved by adding something to it

address book *E-com* an e-mail software facility enabling people and businesses to store and manage e-mail addresses and contact information

address verification *E-com* a procedure used by the processor of a credit card to verify that a customer's ordering address matches the address in the customer's record

---

Avarice and luxury, those evils which have been the ruin of every great state. *Livy*

ADF *abbr Fin* Approved Deposit Fund

ad hoc research *Mkting* a single, one-off piece of research designed for a particular purpose, as opposed to continuous, regularly repeated, or syndicated research

ad impression *E-com see* **ad view**

adjusted book value *Fin* the value of a company in terms of the current market values of its assets and liabilities. *Also known as* **modified book value**

adjusted futures price *Fin* the current value of a futures contract to buy a commodity at a fixed future date

adjusted gross income *Fin* the amount of annual income that a person or company has after various adjustments for income or corporation tax purposes

adjusted present value *Fin* the value of a commodity when costs and advantages associated with taxes and borrowing are taken into consideration in addition to its market value

adminisphere *Gen Mgt* the part of an organisation that deals with administrative matters, often perceived negatively by employees because of the apparently unnecessary nature of decisions taken by its members (*slang*)

administration *Gen Mgt* the management of the affairs of a business, especially the planning and control of its operations

administration school *Gen Mgt see* **business administration**

administrative expenses *Fin* the cost of management, secretarial, accounting, and other services which cannot be related to the separate production, marketing, or research and development functions

administrivia *E-com* the often tedious tasks associated with maintaining a website, mailing list, or any other form of Internet resource (*slang*)

admissibility *Stats* the property of a procedure if, and only if, no other of its class exists that performs as well as it and better than it in at least one case

ADR *abbr Fin* American depository receipt: a document that indicates a US investor's ownership of stock in a foreign corporation

Adshel™ *Mkting* a type of bus shelter, specifically designed to carry advertising posters

ADSL *abbr E-com* asymmetrical digital subscriber line: a system that provides high-speed, high-bandwidth connections to the Internet. ADSL is asymmetric because it has more capacity for data received by a computer than for data to be sent from it. This uneven upload/download balance means that downloaded text and graphics appear quickly and that audio-visual elements are of better quality than when sent via a normal telephone line. ADSL was initially developed by Bellcore Labs in New Jersey in 1993 as a means of bringing bandwidth to homes and small businesses.

adspend *Mkting see* **advertising expenditure**

ad transfer *E-com see* **click-through**

ad valorem *Fin* a tax or commission, for example, Value Added Tax, that is calculated on the value of the goods or services provided, rather than on their number or size

Advance Corporation Tax *Fin* formerly, in the United Kingdom, a tax paid by a company equal to a percentage of its dividends or other distributions of profit to its shareholders. It was abolished in 1999.

advanced manufacturing technology *Gen Mgt, Ops* a high-technology development in computing and microelectronics, designed to enhance manufacturing capabilities. Advanced manufacturing technology is used in all areas of manufacturing, including design, control, fabrication, and assembly. This family of technologies includes *robotics*, *computer-aided design* (CAD), *computer-aided* *engineering* (CAE), **MRP II**, automated *materials handling* systems, *electronic data interchange* (EDI), computer-integrated manufacturing (CIM) systems, *flexible manufacturing systems*, and *group technology*. *Abbr* **AMT**

advance payment *Fin* an amount paid before it is earned or incurred, for example, a prepayment by an importer to an exporter before goods are shipped, or a cash advance for travel expenses

advance payment guarantee *or* **advance payment bond** *Fin* a guarantee that enables a buyer to recover an advance payment made under a contract or order if the supplier fails to fulfil its contractual obligations

adventure training *HR* activities undertaken out of doors and away from the everyday work environment with a view to developing the skills and abilities of participants. Adventure training often takes place at a residential outdoor activity centre and may include physically challenging activities such as climbing and abseiling or group exercises and games. The activities are designed to promote *experiential learning* in areas such as *interpersonal communication*, *problem-solving*, *decision-making*, and *teamwork*, and to develop self-confidence and *leadership* skills. Adventure training has its origins in the work of Kurt Hahn, the founder of Gordonstoun School, who developed the Outward Bound programme of outdoor activities during the second world war. Adventure training programmes for organisational personnel became popular during the late 1970s and 1980s, although some people have doubted their value and effectiveness. *Also known as* **outdoor training**, **outward bound training**

adverse balance *Fin* the deficit on an account, especially a nation's balance of payments account

adverse opinion *Fin* a statement in the auditor's report of a company's annual accounts indicating a fundamental disagreement with the company to such an extent that the auditor considers the accounts misleading

advertisement *Mkting* a public announcement by a company in a newspaper, on television or radio, or over the Internet, intended to attract buyers for a product or service

advertising *Mkting* the promotion of goods, services, or ideas, through paid announcements. Advertising aims to persuade or inform the general public and can be used to induce purchase, increase *brand awareness*, or enhance *product differentiation*. An advertisement has two main components: the message and the medium by which it is transmitted. Advertising forms just one part of an organisation's total marketing strategy.

advertising agency *Mkting* an organisation that, on behalf of clients, drafts and produces advertisements, places advertisements in the media, and plans *advertising campaigns*. Advertising agencies may also perform other marketing functions, including *market research* and consultancy.

advertising campaign *Mkting* a planned programme using *advertising* aimed at a particular target market or audience over a defined period of time for the purpose of increasing sales or raising awareness of a product or service

advertising department *Mkting* the department within an organisation that is responsible for advertising its products or services. The advertising department is also the name given to the section of a publishing house that co-ordinates the placing of advertisements in its magazines, newspapers, or other publications. It is involved in the sale of advertising space to clients.

advertising expenditure *Mkting* the amount spent by an organisation on advertising, usually per year. Advertising expenditure is analysed by breaking it down into the main advertising channels used by companies, such as newspapers, magazines, television, radio, cinema, and outdoor advertising. Expenditure can show the total spend nationally, by sector, by type and size of company, or may relate to one company's spend on advertising, including the proportion spent on its specific brands. *Also known as* ***adspend***

advertising manager *Mkting* an employee of a business who is responsible for planning and controlling its advertising activities and budgets

advertising media *Mkting* the communication channels used for advertising, including television, radio, the printed press, and outdoor advertising

advertising research *Mkting* research carried out before or after advertising to ensure or test its effectiveness

advertorial *Mkting* a combination of an *advertisement* and an article. The content of an advertorial is significantly influenced, and may even be entirely written, by the advertisers. Examples of advertorials include travel or leisure supplements in newspapers or magazines that are designed to attract advertisements from suppliers of relevant goods or services. A criticism of advertorials is that it is sometimes difficult to distinguish between an advertising article and ordinary journalistic articles, particularly when they appear in the same typeface as the other contents of the newspaper or magazine. To overcome this, some advertorials are headed 'Advertisement'. (*slang*)

advice note *Fin see* ***delivery note***

advice of fate *Fin* immediate notification from a drawer's bank as to whether a cheque is to be honoured or not. This special presentation of a cheque bypasses the normal clearing system and so saves time.

advid *Mkting* a video used to promote a product or service (*slang*)

ad view *E-com* the number of times a banner or other ad is downloaded and presumably seen on a web page. *Also known as* ***ad impression***, ***exposure***

AFAIK *abbr Gen Mgt* as far as I know (*slang*)

affiliate *Gen Mgt* a company that is controlled by another or is a member of a group, or either of two companies that owns a minority of the voting shares of the other

affiliate directory *E-com* a directory that indexes sites belonging to affiliate schemes. Affiliate directories offer information for companies seeking to subscribe to a scheme, as well as for those wanting to set up affiliate schemes of their own.

affiliate marketing *E-com* the use of *affiliate programmes*

affiliate partner *Mkting* a company that markets a product or service on the Internet for another company

affiliate programme *E-com* an advertising programme in which one merchant induces others to place his or her banners and buttons on their websites in return for a commission on purchases made by their customers. *Also known as* ***associate programme***

affinity card *Fin* a credit card issued to members of a particular group, for example, past students of a college, owners of a particular make of car, or supporters of a particular charity. The organisation may benefit from a donation upon issue or first use, and a small percentage of the card's subsequent turnover. Other cards give benefits such as air miles.

affluent society *Fin* a community in which material wealth is widely distributed

affluenza *Gen Mgt* feelings of unhappiness, stress, and guilt induced by the pursuit and possession of wealth (*slang*)

AFTA *abbr Fin* ASEAN Free Trade Area

after-acquired collateral *Fin* collateral for a loan that a borrower obtains after making the contract for the loan

after date *Fin see* ***bill of exchange***

after-sales service *Mkting* customer support following the purchase of a

---

True creativity often starts where language ends.   *Arthur Koestler*

product or service. In some cases, after-sales service can be almost as important as the initial purchase. The manufacturer, retailer, or service provider determines what is included in any warranty (or guarantee) package. This will include the duration of the warranty—traditionally one year from the date of purchase, but increasingly two or more years—maintenance and/or replacement policy, items included/excluded, labour costs, and speed of response. In the case of a service provider, after-sales service might include additional top-up training or helpdesk availability. Of equal importance is the customer's perception of the degree of willingness with which a supplier deals with a query or complaint, speed of response, and action taken. Underpinning any warranty is the additional statutory protection afforded to consumers by the Sale of Goods Acts and related legislation that require that all goods must be of merchantable quality.

after-tax *Fin* relating to earnings or income from which tax has already been deducted

AG *abbr Fin* Aktiengesellschaft: the German, Austrian, or Swiss equivalent of PLC

against actuals *Fin* relating to a trade between owners of futures contracts that allows both to reduce their positions to cash instead of commodities

age analysis of debtors *Fin* the amount owed by debtors, classified by age of debt

aged debt *Fin* a debt that is overdue by one or more given periods, usually increments of 30 days

aged debtor *Fin* a person or organisation responsible for an overdue debt

age discrimination *or* **ageism** *HR* unfavourable treatment in employment based on prejudice in relation to a person's age. While age discrimination affects people at all stages of their working lives, difficulties experienced in selection, development, and promotion can be particularly acute at the two extremes of the age spectrum. Countries such as Australia

and the United States have passed legislation to make it unlawful to discriminate on grounds of age.

agency *Gen Mgt* a relationship between two people or organisations in which one is empowered to act on behalf of the other in dealings with a third party

agency commission *Mkting* a percentage of advertising expenditure rebated to an advertising agency, media buyer, or client organisation by a media owner

agency mark-up *Mkting* a management fee charged by an advertising agency in addition to the cost of external services that it buys on behalf of a client

agency theory *Fin* a hypothesis that attempts to explain elements of organisational behaviour through an understanding of the relationships between principals (such as shareholders) and agents (such as company managers and accountants). A conflict may exist between the actions undertaken by agents in furtherance of their own self-interest, and those required to promote the interests of the principals. Within the hierarchy of firms, the same goal incongruence may arise when divisional managers promote their own self-interest over those of other divisions and of the company generally.

agenda *Gen Mgt* a list of topics to be discussed or business to be transacted during the course of a meeting, usually sent prior to the meeting to those invited to attend

agent *Gen Mgt* **1.** a person or organisation empowered to act on behalf of another when dealing with a third party **2.** *see* **executive**

agent bank (*ANZ*) *Fin* a bank that acts on behalf of a foreign bank, or a bank that participates in another bank's credit card programme, acting as a depository for merchants

age pension (*ANZ*) *Fin* a sum of money paid regularly by the government to people who have reached the age of retirement, currently 65 for men and 60 for women

---

Most Japanese corporations lack even an approximation of an organisation chart.
Kenichi Ohmae

aggregate demand *Econ* the sum of all expenditures in an economy that makes up its *GDP*, for example, consumers' expenditure on goods and services, investment in *capital stocks*, and government spending

aggregate depreciation *Fin see accumulated depreciation*

aggregate income *Fin* the total of all incomes in an economy without adjustments for inflation, taxation, or types of double counting

aggregate output *Econ* the total value of all goods and services produced in an economy

aggregate planning *Ops* medium-range *capacity planning*, typically covering a period of 3 to 18 months. Aggregate planning is used in a manufacturing environment and determines not only the overall output levels planned but the appropriate resource input mix to be used for related groups of products. Generally, planners focus on overall or aggregate capacity rather than on individual products or services. Aggregate planning can be used to influence demand as well as supply, in which case variables such as price, advertising, and the product mix are taken into account.

aggregate supply *Econ* the total of all goods and services produced in an economy

aggregator *(US) E-com, Mkting* an organisation that acts as an intermediary between producers and customers in an Internet business web. The aggregator selects products, sets prices, and ensures fulfilment of orders.

aggressive *Gen Mgt* relating to an investment strategy marked by willingness to accept high risk while trying to realise higher than average gains. Such a strategy involves investing in rapidly growing companies that promise capital appreciation but produce little or no income from dividends and de-emphasises income-producing instruments such as bonds.

aggressive growth fund *Fin* a unit trust that takes considerable risks in the hope of making large profits

agile manufacturing *Ops* a manufacturing philosophy that focuses on meeting the demands of customers by adopting flexible manufacturing practices. Agile manufacturing emerged as a reaction to *lean production*. It differs by focusing on meeting the demands of customers without sacrificing quality or incurring added costs. Based on the idea of *virtual organisation*, agile manufacturing aims to develop flexible, often short-term, relationships with suppliers, as market opportunities arise. Stock control is considered less important than satisfying the customer, and so *customer satisfaction* measures become more important than output measures. Agile manufacturing requires an adaptable, innovative, and empowered workforce.

agility *Gen Mgt* the organisational capability to be flexible, responsive, adaptive, and show initiative in times of change and uncertainty. Agility has origins in manufacturing and has been cited as a source of *competitive advantage* by many management gurus, including *Rosabeth Moss Kanter* and *Tom Peters*. One writer who has explored the concept of agility in greater depth is *Richard Pascale*, for whom the key to agility lies in what the organisation is, as opposed to what it does. Agility grew as a reaction against the slowness of bureaucratic organisations to respond to the demands of changing market conditions. The *virtual organisation* has been quoted as one extreme example of an agile organisation.

AGM *abbr Gen Mgt* annual general meeting, a yearly meeting at which a company's management reports the year's results and shareholders have the opportunity to vote on company business, for example, the appointment of directors and auditors. Other business, for example, voting on dividend payments and board- and shareholder-sponsored resolutions, may also be transacted. *US term **annual meeting***

agora *E-com* a marketplace on the Internet. The term comes from an ancient Greek word for 'market'.

agreement of sale *Gen Mgt* a written contract specifying the terms under which the buyer agrees to buy a property and the seller agrees to sell it

agricultural produce *Fin see biological assets*

AHI (*S Africa*) *Gen Mgt* Afrikaanse Handelsinstituut, the national chamber of commerce for Afrikaans businesses

aim *Gen Mgt see* **objective**

AIM *abbr Fin* Alternative Investment Market: the London market trading in shares of emerging or small companies not eligible for listing on the London Stock Exchange. It replaced the Unlisted Securities Market (USM) in 1995.

air bill *Fin* a US term for the documentation accompanying a package sent using an express mail service

AIRC *abbr HR* Australian Industrial Relations Commission

airtime *Mkting* the amount of time given to an advertisement on television, radio, or in cinemas

air waybill *Fin* a UK term for a receipt issued by an airline for goods to be freighted

AITC *abbr Fin* Association of Investment Trust Companies

Aktb *abbr Fin* Aktiebolaget, the Swedish equivalent of PLC

alignment *Gen Mgt* the process of building a corporate culture to achieve strategic goals

all equity rate *Fin* the interest rate that a lender charges because of the apparent risks of a project that are independent of the normal market risks of financing it

All Industrials Index *Fin* a subindex of the Australian All Ordinaries Index that includes all the companies from that index that are not involved in resources or mining

All Mining Index *Fin* a subindex of the Australian All Ordinaries Index that includes all the companies from that index that are involved in the mining industry

All Ordinaries Accumulation Index *Fin* a measure of the change in share prices on the Australian Stock Exchange, based on the All Ordinaries Index, but assuming that all dividends are reinvested

All Ordinaries Index *Fin* the major index of Australian share prices, comprising more than 300 of the most active Australian companies listed on the Australian Stock Exchange. *Abbr* **All Ords**

all-or-none underwriting (*ANZ*) *Fin* the option of cancelling a public offering of shares if the underwriting is not fully subscribed

All Resources Index *Fin* a subindex of the Australian All Ordinaries Index that includes all the companies from that index that are involved in the resources industry

alphabet theories of management *Gen Mgt* management theories named along the lines of *Douglas McGregor*'s *Theory X* and *Theory Y*. Alphabet theories of management include *Theory E*, *Theory J*, *Theory O*, *Theory W*, and *Theory Z*.

alpha geek *Gen Mgt* the person who knows most about computer technology in a company or department (*slang*)

alpha rating *Fin* the return a security or a portfolio would be expected to earn if the market's rate of return were zero. Alpha expresses the difference between the return expected from a stock or unit trust, given its *beta rating*, and the return actually produced. A stock or trust that returns more than its beta would predict has a positive alpha, while one that returns less than the amount predicted by beta has a negative alpha. A large positive alpha indicates a strong performance, while a large negative alpha indicates a dismal performance.

To begin with, the market itself is assigned a beta of 1.0. If a stock or trust has a beta of 1.2, this means its price is likely to rise or fall by 12% when the overall market rises or falls by 10%; a beta of 7.0 means the stock or trust price is likely to move up or down at 70% of the level of the market change.

In practice, an alpha of 0.4 means the stock or trust in question outperformed the market-based return estimate by 0.4%. An alpha of –0.6 means the return was 0.6% less than would have been predicted from the change in the market alone.

Both alpha and beta should be readily available upon request from investment firms, because the figures appear in standard performance reports. It is always best to ask for them, because calculating a stock's alpha rating requires first knowing a stock's beta rating, and beta calculations can involve mathematical complexities. *See also **beta rating***

alpha test *Gen Mgt* a test of a new or upgraded piece of computer software or hardware carried out by the manufacturer before it is released to the public

alpha value *Fin* a sum paid to an employee when he or she leaves a company that can be transferred to a concessionally taxed investment account such as an *Approved Deposit Fund*

alternate director *Fin* a person who is allowed to act for an absent named director of a company at a board meeting

alternative investment *Fin* an investment other than in bonds or shares of a large company or one listed on a stock exchange

Alternative Investment Market *Fin see **AIM***

alternative mortgage instrument *Fin* any form of mortgage other than a fixed-term amortising loan

amalgamation *Gen Mgt* the process of two or more organisations joining together for mutual benefit, either through a *merger* or *consolidation*

Amazon *E-com* to claim a significant portion of the market from a traditional retail business that failed to develop an effective e-business strategy. The term stems from the seemingly overnight success of online bookseller Amazon.com™. (*slang*)

ambit claim (*ANZ*) *Gen Mgt* a claim made to an arbitration authority for higher pay or improved conditions that is deliberately exaggerated because the claimants know that they will subsequently have to compromise

American depository receipt *Fin see **ADR***

American option *Fin* an option contract that can be exercised at any time up to and including the expiry date. Most exchange-traded options are of this style. *See also **European option***. *Also known as American-style option*

American Stock Exchange *Fin see **AMEX***

American-style option *Fin see **American option***

AMEX *abbr Fin* American Stock Exchange: a New York stock exchange listing smaller and less mature companies that those listed on the larger New York Stock Exchange (NYSE)

amortisation *Fin* **1.** a method of recovering (deducting or writing off) the capital costs of intangible assets over a fixed period of time.

EXAMPLE For tax purposes, the distinction is not always made between amortisation and depreciation, yet amortisation remains a viable financial accounting concept in its own right.

It is computed using the straight-line method of depreciation: divide the initial cost of the intangible asset by the estimated useful life of that asset. For example, if it costs £10,000 to acquire a patent and it has an estimated useful life of 10 years, the amortised amount per year is £1,000.

Initial cost / useful life = amortisation per year £10,000 / 10 = £1,000 per year

The amount of amortisation accumulated since the asset was acquired appears on the organisation's balance sheet as a deduction under the amortised asset.

While that formula is straightforward, amortisation can also incorporate a variety of non-cash charges to net earnings and/or asset values, such as depletion, write-offs, prepaid expenses, and deferred charges. Accordingly, there are many rules to regulate how these charges appear on financial statements. The rules are different in each country, and are occasionally changed, so it is necessary to stay abreast of them and rely on expert advice.

For financial reporting purposes, an intangible asset is amortised over a period of years. The amortisable life—'useful life'—of an intangible asset is the period over which it gives economic benefit.

Intangibles that can be amortised can include:

Copyrights, based on the amount paid either to purchase them or to develop them internally, plus the costs incurred in producing the work (wages or materials, for example). At present, a copyright is granted to a corporation for 75 years, and to an individual for the life of the author plus 50 years. However, the estimated useful life of a copyright is usually far less than its legal life, and it is generally amortised over a fairly short period.

Cost of a *franchise*, including any fees paid to the franchiser, as well legal costs or expenses incurred in the acquisition. A franchise granted for a limited period should be amortised over its life. If the franchise has an indefinite life, it should be amortised over a reasonable period not to exceed 40 years.

Covenants not to compete: an agreement by the seller of a business not to engage in a competing business in a certain area for a specific period of time. The cost of the not-to-compete covenant should be amortised over the period covered by the covenant unless its estimated economic life is expected to be less. Easement costs that grant a right of way may be amortised if there is a limited and specified life.

Organisation costs incurred when forming a corporation or a partnership, including legal fees, accounting services, incorporation fees, and other related services. Organisation costs are usually amortised over 60 months.

Patents, both those developed internally and those purchased. If developed internally, a patent's 'amortisable basis' includes legal fees incurred during the application process. A patent should be amortised over its legal life or its economic life, whichever is the shorter.

Trademarks, brands, and trade names, which should be written off over a period not to exceed 40 years.

Other types of property that may be amortised include certain intangible drilling costs, circulation costs, mine development costs, pollution control facilities, and reforestation expenditures.

Certain intangibles cannot be amortised, but may be depreciated using a straight-line approach if they have 'determinable' useful life. Because the rules are different in each country and are subject to change, it is essential to rely on specialist advice.

2. the repayment of the principal and interest on a loan in equal amounts over a period of time

amortise *Fin* to gradually reduce the value of an asset by systematically writing off its cost over a period of time, or to repay a debt in a series of regular instalments or transfers

amortised value *Fin* the value at a particular time of a financial instrument that is being amortised

AMPS *abbr Fin* auction market preferred stock

AMT *abbr Ops* advanced manufacturing technology

analysis of variance *Stats* the process of separating the statistical variance caused by a particular factor from that caused by other factors

analysis of variance table *Stats* a table that shows the total variation in the observations in a statistical data set

analytical review *Fin* the examination of ratios, trends, and changes in balances

I don't invest in anything I don't understand—it makes more sense to buy TV stations than oil wells.
Oprah Winfrey

from one period to the next, to obtain a broad understanding of the financial position and results of operations and to identify any items requiring further investigation

angel investor *E-com* an individual or group of individuals willing to invest in an unproven but well-researched e-business idea. Angel investors are typically the first port of call for Internet start-ups looking for financial backing, because they are more inclined to provide early funding than *venture capital* firms are. After investing in a company, angel investors take an advisory role without making demands.

angry fruit salad *E-com* a garish and unattractive visual interface on a computer (*slang*)

angular histogram *Stats* a histogram that represents data in a circular form

announcement *Fin* a statement that a company makes to provide information on its trading prospects that will be of interest to its existing and potential investors

annoyware *E-com* a shareware program that repeatedly interrupts normal functioning to remind users they are using an unregistered copy and will have to pay in order to continue (*slang*)

annual general meeting *Gen Mgt see* **AGM**

annual hours *HR* a *flexible working hours* practice in which working hours are averaged over a year. Employees are contracted to work a given number of hours per year rather than the traditional number of hours per week. Earnings are determined on a similar basis, but usually a fixed weekly or monthly salary is paid regardless of the number of hours worked. Hours are worked when demand dictates and therefore the need for *overtime* diminishes. Annual hours systems usually cover manual *shiftworkers*, rather than other parts of the workforce.

annual meeting (*US*) = *AGM*

annual percentage rate *or* **annualised percentage rate** *Fin see* **APR**

annual percentage yield *Fin* the effective or true annual rate of return on an investment, taking into account the effect of *compounding*. For example, an annual percentage rate of 6% compounded monthly translates into an annual percentage yield of 6.17%.

annual report *Fin* a document prepared each year to give a true and fair view of a company's state of affairs.

Annual reports are issued to shareholders and filed at Companies House in accordance with the provisions of company legislation. Contents include a profit and loss account and *balance sheet*, a *cash-flow statement*, directors' report, *auditor's report*, and, where a company has subsidiaries, the company's group accounts.

The financial statements are the main purpose of the annual report, and usually include notes to the accounts. These amplify numerous points contained in the figures and are critical for anyone wishing to study the accounts in detail.

annuity *Fin* a contract in which a person pays a lump-sum premium to an insurance company and in return receives periodic payments, usually yearly, often beginning on retirement.

There are several types of annuity. They vary both in the ways they accumulate funds and in the ways they disperse earnings. A fixed annuity guarantees fixed payments to the individual receiving it for the term of the contract, usually until death; a variable annuity offers no guarantee but has potential for a greater return, usually based on the performance of a stock or unit trust; a deferred annuity delays payments until the individual chooses to receive them; a hybrid annuity, also called a combination annuity, combines features of both the fixed and variable annuity.

annuity in arrears *Fin* an annuity whose first payment is due at least one payment period after the start date of the annuity's contract

---

anorexic organisation *Gen Mgt* an organisation that has become so small that it has lost the strength and depth to compete effectively. An anorexic organisation may have been through the process of extreme *downsizing* or *delayering*, probably with accompanying *redundancies*. (*slang*)

ANSI X.12 standard *E-com* an American National Standards Institute-supported protocol for the electronic interchange of business transactions. *Also known as X.12*

Ansoff, H. Igor (1918–2002) *Gen Mgt* Russian-born manager and academic. Established *strategic planning* as a management activity, developing a framework of tools and techniques by which strategic planning decisions could be made. He explained his approach in *Corporate Strategy* (1965). One of his most well known models is the *three Ss*. He later introduced the concept of *strategic management*.

anticipation note *Fin* a bond that a borrower intends to pay off with money from taxes due or money to be borrowed in a later and larger transaction

anticipatory hedging *Fin* hedging carried out before the transaction to which the hedge applies occurs

anticipointment *Gen Mgt* high public expectations of a new product, entertainment, or service that are subsequently disappointed (*slang*)

anti-dumping *Econ* intended to prevent the sale of goods on a foreign market at a price below their *marginal cost*

anti-site *E-com* a website devoted to attacking a company or organisation. Typically, an anti-site is set up by an aggrieved customer who has been unable to contribute his or her opinion to the company's website. Anti-sites are often intended to parody or replicate the site they are targeting. In some instances, an anti-site can beat the official site in the search engine rankings by generating more site visits. *Also known as hate site*

antitrust *Gen Mgt* relating to US legislative initiatives aimed at protecting trade and commerce from monopolistic business practices that restrict or eliminate competition. Antitrust laws also attempt to curb trusts and cartels and to keep them from employing monopolistic practices to make unfair profits.

ANZCERTA *abbr Fin* Australia and New Zealand Closer Economic Relations Trade Agreement

APEC *Fin* Asia-Pacific Economic Co-operation, a forum designed to promote trade and economic co-operation among countries bordering the Pacific Ocean. It was set up in 1989. Members include Australia, Indonesia, Thailand, the Philippines, Singapore, Brunei, and Japan.

applet *E-com* a small application, usually written in *Java*. Owing to their miniature size, applets can be set to download automatically when an Internet user visits a web page.

application form *HR* a form used in the *recruitment* process to enable a job candidate to supply information about his or her qualifications, skills, and experience. Employers may ask a candidate to complete an application form instead of, or as well as, providing a *curriculum vitae*. Application forms should be reviewed regularly to ensure that questions asked take account of current legislation, accepted good practice, and internal organisational developments. These questions should be job-related and avoid unjustifiable intrusion into a candidate's personal life.

application program interface *Gen Mgt* a computer program or piece of software designed to perform a function directly for a user, for example, a word processor, spellchecker, or spreadsheet

application server *E-com* an advanced type of server used to run programming languages that help websites to deliver dynamic information such as the latest news headlines, stock quotes, personalised information, or shopping baskets

---

Miracles can be made, but only by sweating.   *Giovanni Agnelli*

application service provider *E-com see ASP*

applied economics *Econ* the practical application of theoretical economic principles, especially in formulating national and international economic policies

appointment 1. *Gen Mgt* an engagement to meet at a particular place and time for a particular purpose **2.** *HR* the selection of somebody for a position or job

apportion *Fin* to spread revenues or costs over two or more cost units, centres, accounts, or time periods

appraisal *HR see performance appraisal*

appreciation *Fin* **1.** the value that certain assets, particularly land and buildings, accrue over time. Directors of companies are obliged to reflect this in their accounts. **2.** the increase in value of one currency relative to another

appropriation *Fin* a sum of money that has been allocated for a particular purpose

appropriation account *Fin* in trading and non-profit entities, a record of how the profit/loss or surplus/deficit has been allocated to distributions, reserves, or funds

Approved Deposit Fund (*ANZ*) *Fin* a concessionally taxed fund managed by a financial institution into which *Eligible Termination Payments* can be transferred from a superannuation fund. *Abbr* **ADF**

APR *abbr Fin* Annual or Annualised Percentage Rate of interest: the interest rate that would exist if it were calculated as simple rather than compound interest. EXAMPLE Different investments typically offer different compounding periods, usually quarterly or monthly. The APR allows them to be compared over a common period of time: one year. This enables an investor or borrower to compare like with like, providing an excellent basis for comparing mortgage or other loan rates. In the United Kingdom, lenders are required to disclose it.

APR is calculated by applying the formula:

$$\text{APR} = [1 + i/m]m - 1.0$$

In the formula, **i** is the interest rate quoted, expressed as decimal, and **m** is the number of compounding periods per year.

The APR is usually slightly higher than the quoted rate, and should be expressed as a decimal, that is, 6% becomes 0.06. When expressed as the cost of credit, other costs should be included in addition to interest, such as loan closing costs and financial fees.

*Also known as **annual percentage rate**, **effective annual rate**, **nominal annual rate***

APRA *abbr Fin* Australian Prudential Regulation Authority

aptitude test *HR* a measure of a person's natural ability or potential to learn a skill or set of skills. Abilities that are typically measured by aptitude tests include abstract, verbal, and numerical reasoning, because these give a rounded view of a person's general ability in relation to the workplace. Aptitude tests are a form of *psychometric test* and are administered by trained users.

arb *Gen Mgt* an *arbitrageur* (*slang*)

arbitrage *Fin* the buying and selling of foreign currencies, products, or financial securities between two or more markets in order to make an immediate profit by exploiting differences in market prices quoted

arbitrage pricing theory *Fin* a model of financial instrument and portfolio behaviour that provides a benchmark of return and risk for capital budgeting and securities analysis. It can be used to create portfolios that track a market index, estimate the risk of an asset allocation strategy, or estimate the response of a portfolio to economic developments.

arbitrageur *Fin* a firm or individual who purchases shares or financial securities to make a windfall profit

arbitration *Gen Mgt, HR* the settlement of a dispute by an independent third person, rather than by a court of law. Arbitration allows for claims or grievances to be settled quickly, cost-effectively, privately, and by somebody who is suitably qualified. A contract may include an arbitration clause to be invoked in the case of a dispute. *Mediation* is a related term.

arbitrator *Gen Mgt* an impartial person accepted by both parties in a dispute to hear both sides and make a judgment

area sampling *Stats* a form of sampling in which a region is subdivided and some of the divisions are then selected at random for a complete survey

area under a curve *Stats* a means of summarising the information from a series of statistical measurements made over a period of time such as a month

Argyris, Christopher (*b.* 1923) *Gen Mgt* US academic and consultant. Known for his work on *training* and *organisational learning*, specifically T-Groups (see *sensitivity training*), and single-loop and double-loop learning. Argyris's research is set out in *Organizational Learning* (1978), co-written with *Donald Schön*. Their work also produced the idea of a *learning organisation*, later developed by *Peter Senge*.

Argyris argues that organisations depend fundamentally on people, but too often stand in the way of people fulfilling their potential. The main thrust of his work has been to explore the relations between personality and the organisation and to suggest how these relations can best be made mutually beneficial.

arithmetic mean *Fin* a simple average calculated by dividing the sum of two or more items by the number of items

Arizmendietta, Jose Maria (1915–77) *Gen Mgt* Basque priest, more commonly known as Father Arizmendi. Co-founder of the *Mondragon co-operative* movement.

armchair economics *Gen Mgt* economic forecasting or theorising based on insufficient data or knowledge of a subject (*slang*)

arm's-length price *Fin* a price at which an unrelated seller and buyer agree to transact on an asset or a product

ARPAnet *E-com* the precursor to the Internet, an experimental network that linked scientists engaged in military research. It was developed by the US Defence Department in the late 1960s, and was originally intended to link together different computers spread out throughout the world.

arrow shooter *Gen Mgt* a person within an organisation who produces visionary new ideas (*slang*)

art director *Mkting* a person who is responsible for planning and designing the creative element for advertisements and other communications material

articles of association *Gen Mgt* an official document governing the running of a company, that is placed with the *Registrar of Companies*. The articles of association constitute a contract between the company and its members, set out the voting rights of shareholders and the conduct of shareholders' and directors' meetings, and detail the powers of management of the company. A *memorandum of association* is a related document.

articles of incorporation *Fin* in the United States, a legal document that creates a privately held company whose powers are governed by the general corporation laws of the state in which it was founded

articles of partnership *Fin* see *partnership agreement*

artificial intelligence *Gen Mgt* a branch of computer science concerned with the development of computer systems capable of performing functions that normally require human intelligence, for example, reasoning, problem-solving, learning from experience, and speech recognition. Artificial intelligence research combines elements of computer science and cognitive psychology. It is a controversial field because of the difficulty of defining its goals and

---

The finest eloquence is that which gets things done; the worst is that which delays them.
David Lloyd-George

disagreement over whether these goals are attainable. Much research has been done since the second world war, beginning with the theoretical work of Alan Turing during the 1940s. The term became known with the publication in 1961 of the paper *Steps towards Artificial Intelligence* by Marvin Minsky, co-founder with John McCarthy of the Artificial Intelligence Laboratory at Massachusetts Institute of Technology. Branches of artificial intelligence with applications in business and management include *expert systems* and *robotics*.

ASAP *abbr Gen Mgt* as soon as possible (*slang*)

ASEAN Free Trade Area *Fin* a conceptual regional free trade agreement supported by Singapore to foster trade within the region. *Abbr* **AFTA**

A share *Fin* **1.** a non-voting share in a company issued to raise additional capital without diluting control of the company **2.** in the United States, a type of mutual fund share that has a sales charge associated with it

A shares (*US*) *Fin* = *non-voting shares*

Asian Currency Unit *Fin* a book-keeping unit used for recording transactions made by approved financial institutions operating in the Asian Dollar market. *Abbr* **ACU**

ASIC *abbr Fin* Australian Securities and Investments Commission

ask *Fin* **1.** the bid price at which a dealer in stocks and shares, commodities, or financial securities is prepared to buy the stocks and shares, commodities, or securities **2.** (*US*) the price that a security is offered for sale, or the net asset value of a mutual fund plus any sales charges. *Also known as **asked price**, **offering price***

asked price *Fin see **ask** (sense 2)*

asking price *Fin* the price that a seller puts on something before any negotiation

ASP *abbr E-com* application service provider: a hosting service that will operate, support, manage, and maintain a company's software applications for a fee.

The advantages to an organisation of using an ASP are several. It can save time and money: rented applications can be cost-effective and (in theory) can be up and running more quickly than buying an application. It gives them access to the best and latest software without worrying about upgrades and costly installations. It can fill any IT skills shortage.

However, there are disadvantages too, including considerable risk: the ASP industry is still young, and many ASPs have gone out of business. Problems may also arise because many applications are simply not designed to be accessed over a network, especially the Internet, and speed of access is often slow.

assembly *Ops* the joining together of components to make a complete product

assembly line *Ops* a line of production in which a number of assembly operations are performed in a set sequence. The speed of movement of an assembly line has to be matched with the skills and abilities of the *workforce* and the complexity of the assembly process to be performed. The assembly line emerged from the ideas of *scientific management* and was popularised by a number of entrepreneurs, including *Henry Ford* in the car production industry.

assembly plant *Ops* the building in which an *assembly line* is housed

assessed loss *Fin* the excess of tax-deductible expenses over taxable income as confirmed by the South African Revenue Service. It may be carried forward and deducted in determining the taxpayer's taxable income in subsequent years of assessment.

assessed value *Fin* a value for something that is calculated by a person such as an investment advisor

assessment centre *HR* a process whereby a group of participants undertake a series of job-related exercises under observation, so that skills, competencies, and character traits can be assessed. Specially trained assessors evaluate each participant against predetermined criteria. Various methods of assessment may be used, including interviews, *psychometric tests*, group discussions, group problem-solving exercises, individual job-simulated tasks, and role plays. Assessment centres are used in selection for recruitment and promotion, and in training and development, and aim to provide an organisation with an assessment process that is consistent, free of prejudice, and fair.

assessment of competence *HR* the measurement of an employee's performance against an agreed set of standards for work-based activities. In the United Kingdom, assessment of competence is generally made against indicators of the successful achievement of a particular job function. There are four dimensions to assessment: the knowledge and understanding required to carry out a task; the *performance indicators* to be looked for; the scope or range of situations across which an employee is expected to perform; and any particular evidence requirements. *Vocational qualifications* for a wide range of jobs in the United Kingdom are based on a set of occupational standards that contain these elements. A wide variety of techniques or instruments exists to assess *competence*. These include specific work-based ability and *aptitude tests*, as well as traditional methods of *performance appraisal* and evaluation. Recent years have seen a dramatic rise in the use of direct observation at work by trained assessors, the collection of personal portfolios, and peer assessment techniques such as *360 degree appraisal*. All require the careful review of work behaviour against a set of indicators that have been clearly shown to be associated with successful performance.

asset *Fin, Gen Mgt* any tangible or intangible item to which a value can be assigned. Assets can be physical, such as machinery and consumer durables, or financial, such as cash and accounts receivable.

Assets are typically broken down into five different categories. Current assets include cash, cash equivalents, marketable securities, inventories, and prepaid expenses that are expected to be used within one year or a normal operating cycle. All cash items and inventories are reported at historical value. Securities are reported at market value. Non-current assets, or long-term investments, are resources that are expected to be held for more than one year. They are reported at the lower of cost and current market value, which means that their values will vary. Fixed assets include property, plants and facilities, and equipment used to conduct business. These items are reported at their original value, even though current values might well be much higher. Intangible assets include legal claims, patents, franchise rights, and accounts receivable. These values can be more difficult to determine. FR10, published by the Accounting Standards Board of the Institute of Chartered Accountants for England and Wales is essential reading for dealing with this issue. Deferred charges include prepaid costs and other expenditures that will produce future revenue or benefits.

asset allocation *Fin* an investment strategy that distributes investments in a portfolio so as to achieve the highest investment return while minimising risk. Such a strategy usually apportions investments among cash equivalents, shares in domestic and foreign companies, fixed-income investments, and property.

asset-backed security *Econ, Fin* a security for which the collateral is neither land nor land-based financial instruments

asset-based lending *Fin* the lending of money with the expectation that the proceeds from an asset or assets will allow the borrower to repay the loan

asset conversion loan *Fin* a loan that the borrower will repay with money raised by selling an asset

asset coverage *Fin* the ratio measuring a company's solvency and consisting of its net assets divided by its debt

---

asset demand *Econ* the amount of assets held as money, which will be low when interest rates are high and high when interest rates are low

asset financing *Fin* the borrowing of money by a company using its assets as collateral

asset for asset swap *Fin* an exchange of one bankrupt debtor's debt for that of another

asset management *Fin* an investment service offered by some financial institutions that combines banking and brokerage services

asset play *Fin* a purchase of a company's stock in the belief that it has assets that are not properly documented and therefore unknown to others

asset pricing model *Fin* a model used to determine the profit that an asset will yield

asset protection trust *Fin* a trust, often set up in a foreign country, used to make the trust's principal inaccessible to creditors

asset restructuring *Fin* the purchase or sale of assets worth more than 50% of a listed company's total or net assets

asset side *Fin* the side of a balance sheet that shows the economic resources a firm owns, for example, cash on hand or in bank deposits, products, or buildings and fixtures

assets requirements *Fin* the assets needed for a business to continue trading

asset-stripper *Fin* a company that acquires another company and sells its assets to make a profit without regard for the acquired company's future business success

asset-stripping *Fin* the purchase of a company whose market value is below its asset value, usually so that the buyer may sell the assets for immediate gain. The buyer usually has little or no concern for the purchased company's employees or other **stakeholders**, so the practice is generally frowned upon.

asset substitution *Fin* the purchase of assets that involve more risk than those a lender expected the borrower to buy

asset swap *Fin* an exchange of assets between companies so that they may divest parts no longer required and enter another product area

asset turnover *Fin* the ratio of a firm's sales revenue to its total assets, used as a measure of the firm's business efficiency.
  EXAMPLE   Asset turnover's basic formula is simply sales divided by assets:

Sales revenue / Total assets

Most experts recommend using average total assets in this formula. To determine this figure, total assets at the beginning of the year are added to total assets at the end of the year and divided by two. If, for instance, annual sales totalled £4.5 million, and total assets were £1.84 million at the beginning of the year and £1.78 million at the year end, the average total assets would be £1.81 million, and the asset turnover ratio would be:

4,500,000 / 1,810,000 = 2.49

A variation of the formula is:

Sales revenue / Fixed assets

If average fixed assets were £900,000, then asset turnover would be:

4,500,000 / 900,000 = 5

Asset turnover numbers are useful for comparing competitors within industries, and for growth companies to gauge whether or not they are growing revenue, for example, turnover, in healthy proportion to assets. Too high a ratio may suggest overtrading: too much sales revenue with too little investment. Conversely, too low a ratio may suggest undertrading and inefficient management of resources. A declining ratio may be indicative of a company that overinvested in plant, equipment, or other fixed assets, or is not using existing assets effectively.

asset valuation *Fin* the aggregated value of the assets of a firm, usually the capital assets, as entered on its balance sheet

---

asset value per share *Fin* a way of measuring the value of assets per share, to assist with investment and disinvestment decisions, usually for the benefit of equity shareholders. It is calculated as follows:

**Total assets less liabilities /
Number of issued equity shares**

assign *Fin* to transfer ownership of an asset to another person or organisation

assignable cause of variation *Ops* an evident reason for deviation from the norm. An assignable cause exists when variation within a process can be attributed to a particular cause that is a fundamental part of the process. Once identified, the assignable cause of the errors must be investigated and the process adjusted before other possible causes of variation are examined. Using the technique of *statistical process control*, control charts can be used to distinguish causes that are assignable from those that are random.

assigned risk *Fin* a poor insurance risk that a company is required by law to insure against

associate *Fin* a member of a stock exchange who does not have a seat on it

associate programme *E-com see affiliate programme*

Association of British Insurers *Fin* an association that represents over 400 UK insurance companies to the government, the regulators, and other agencies as well as providing a wide range of services to its members

assumable mortgage *Fin* a mortgage that the buyer of a property can take over from the seller

assumed bond *Fin* a bond for which a company other than the issuer takes over responsibility

assumption *Stats* the conditions under which valid results can be obtained from a statistical technique

assured shorthold tenancy *Gen Mgt* a tenancy for a fixed period of at least six months during which the tenant cannot be evicted other than by court order. Any new tenancy without a written agreement is an assured shorthold tenancy.

assured tenancy *Fin* a tenancy for an indefinite period in which the tenant cannot be evicted other than by court order

ASX *abbr Fin* Australian Stock Exchange

ASX 100 *Fin* a measure of the change in share prices on the *Australian Stock Exchange* based on changes in the stocks of the top 100 companies. Similar indexes include the ASX 20, ASX 50, ASX 200, and ASX 300.

asymmetrical digital subscriber line *E-com see ADSL*

asymmetrical distribution *Stats* a frequency or probability distribution of statistical data that is not symmetrical about a central value in the data

asymmetric taxation *Fin* a difference in tax status between parties to a transaction, typically making the transaction attractive to both parties because of taxes that one or both can avoid

asynchronous transmission *E-com* the transmission of data in which the end of the transmission of one unit denotes the start of the next, rather than transmission at fixed intervals

at best *Fin* an instruction to a stockbroker to buy or sell securities immediately at the best possible current price in the market, regardless of adverse price movements. It is equally applicable to the commodity or currency markets. *See also at limit*

at call *Fin* used to describe a short term loan that is repayable immediately upon demand

Athos, Anthony *Gen Mgt* US academic. *See Pascale, Richard Tanner*

at limit *Fin* an instruction to a stockbroker to buy or sell a security within certain limits, usually not to sell below or to buy above a set price. A time limit is stipulated by the investor and if there has been no transaction within that period, the instruction lapses. It is equally applicable to the commodity or currency markets. *See also* **at best**

ATM *Gen Mgt* an electronic machine from which bank customers can withdraw paper money using an encoded plastic card

ATO *abbr Fin* Australian Taxation Office

atom *Mkting* any traditional non-digital means of delivering information such as a newspaper, book, or magazine

atomise *Gen Mgt* to split a large organisation into smaller operating units

at sight *Fin see* **bill of exchange**

attachment 1. *E-com* a file that is attached to a standard text e-mail message **2.** *Fin* a process that enables a judgment creditor to secure dues from a debtor. A debtor's earnings and/or funds held at his or her bankers may be attached.

attendance *HR* presence at work, normally noted in an attendance register. The phenomenon of irregular attendance is referred to as **absenteeism**. One method of improving attendance is by paying an **attendance bonus**.

attendance bonus *(US) HR* a financial or non-financial incentive offered to employees by an employer to arrive for work on time

attention management *Gen Mgt* a method of ensuring that employees are focused on their work and on organisational goals. Attention management is similar to **time management**, as inattentiveness results in wasted time. An important factor in winning and sustaining attention is tapping into people's emotions.

at-the-money *Fin* used to describe an option with a strike price roughly equivalent to the price of the underlying shares

attitude *Gen Mgt* a mental position consisting of a feeling, emotion, or opinion evolved in response to an external situation. An attitude can be momentary or can develop into a habitual position that has a long-term influence on an individual's behaviour. Attempts can be made to modify attitudes that have a negative effect in the workplace, for example, through education and training. The **employee attitude survey** is one tool used to assess prevalent attitudes in the workforce.

attitude research *Gen Mgt* an investigation into people's beliefs regarding an organisation, its products or services, or its activities. Attitude research is used in marketing to ascertain opinions among consumers and the public in general. It is also used within organisations when **employee attitude surveys** are conducted.

attitude survey *Mkting* a piece of research carried out to assess the feelings of a target audience towards a product, brand, or organisation

attribute sampling *Ops* a random testing method for determining the quality of a finished product by inspecting a sample number of the items in each batch. The items selected are examined for a particular attribute, which is usually an abnormal or negative characteristic—for example, a sample of cars from one production run might be inspected for poor paintwork, and the number of sampled cars found with this attribute used to calculate the number of defective items in the whole batch.

attribution theory of leadership *Gen Mgt* the theory that leaders observe their followers' behaviour, attribute it to particular causes, and as a result respond in a particular way

auction *E-com, Fin* a sale of goods or property by competitive bidding on the spot, by mail, by telecommunications, or over the Internet

auction market preferred stock *Fin* stock in a company owned in the United Kingdom that pays dividends whose amounts track a money-market index. *Abbr* **AMPS**

AUD *abbr Fin* Australian dollar

We don't believe in market research for a new product unknown to the public. So we never do any.
Akio Morita

audience *Mkting* the total number of readers, viewers, or listeners who are exposed to an advertisement

audience research *Mkting* research carried out to measure the size or composition of the target audience for a piece of advertising

audit *Fin* an accountant's formal examination and verification of the accuracy and completeness of financial records, especially those of a business. An *internal audit* is conducted by an employee of the business, and an *external audit* is performed by an independent outsider.

audit committee *Fin* a committee of a company's board of directors, from which the company's executives are excluded, that monitors the company's finances

Auditing Practices Board *Fin* a body formed in 1991 by an agreement between the six members of the Consultative Committee of Accountancy Bodies, to be responsible for developing and issuing professional auditing standards in the United Kingdom and the Republic of Ireland

Auditor-General *Fin* an officer of an Australian state or territory government who is responsible for ensuring that government expenditure is made in accordance with legislation

auditor's report *Fin* a certification by an auditor that a firm's financial records give a true and fair view of its profit and loss for the period

audit trail *Gen Mgt* the records of all the sequential stages of a transaction. An audit trail may trace the process of a purchase, a sale, a customer complaint, or the supply of goods. Tracing what happened at each stage through the records can be a useful method of *problem-solving*. In financial markets, audit trails may be used to ensure fairness and accuracy on the part of the dealers.

aural signature *Mkting* a musical theme that is part of a company or product's brand identity

Aussie Mac *Fin* an informal name for a mortgage-backed certificate issued in Australia by the National Mortgage Market Corporation. The corporation has been issuing such certificates since 1985.

Austrade *Fin* Australian Trade Commission, a federal government body responsible for promoting Australian products abroad and attracting business to Australia. It currently has 108 offices in 63 countries.

Australia and New Zealand Closer Economic Relations Trade Agreement *Fin* an accord between Australia and New Zealand designed to facilitate the exchange of goods between the two countries. It was signed on 1 January 1983. *Abbr* **ANZCERTA**

Australian Accounting Standards Board *Fin* a body that is responsible for setting and monitoring accounting standards in Australia. It was established under Corporations Law in 1988, replacing the Accounting Standards Review Board. *Abbr* **AASB**

Australian Bureau of Statistics *Stats* an Australian federal government body responsible for compiling national statistics and conducting regular censuses. It was set up in 1906. *Abbr* **ABS**

Australian Chamber of Commerce and Industry *Fin* a national council of business organisations in Australia. It represents around 350,000 businesses and its members include state chambers of commerce as well as major national employer and industry associations. *Abbr* **ACCI**

Australian Chamber of Manufactures *Gen Mgt* a body representing Australian manufacturers, established in 1878. *Abbr* **ACM**

Australian Communications Authority *Fin* a government body responsible for regulating practices in the communications industries. It was set up in 1997 as a result of the merger of the Australian Telecommunications Authority and the

Spectrum Management Agency. *Abbr* **ACA**

Australian Council of Trade *Gen Mgt* Australia's national trade union organisation. It was founded in 1927 and is based in Melbourne. *Abbr* **ACTU**

Australian Industrial Relations Commission *HR* an administrative tribunal responsible for settling industrial disputes by conciliation and for setting and modifying industrial awards. It was established in 1988 to replace the Arbitration Commission and other specialist tribunals. *Abbr* **AIRC**

Australian Prudential Regulation Authority *Fin* a federal government body responsible for ensuring that financial institutions are able to meet their commitments

Australian Securities and Investments Commission *Fin* an Australian federal government body responsible for regulating Australian businesses and the provision of financial products and services to consumers. It was established in 1989, replacing the Australian Securities Commission. *Abbr* **ASIC**

Australian Stock Exchange *Fin* the principal market for trading shares and other securities in Australia. It was formed in 1987 as a result of the amalgamation of six state stock exchanges and has offices in most state capitals. *Abbr* **ASX**

Australian Taxation Office *Fin* a statutory body responsible for the administration of the Australian federal government's taxation system. It is based in Canberra and is also responsible for the country's superannuation system. *Abbr* **ATO**

authentication *E-com* a software security verification procedure to acknowledge or validate the source, uniqueness, and integrity of an e-commerce message to make sure data is not being tampered with. The verification is typically achieved through the use of an electronic signature in the form of a key or algorithm that is shared by the trading partners.

authorisation *Fin* the process of assessing a financial transaction, confirming that it does not raise the account's debt above its limit, and allowing the transaction to proceed. This would be undertaken, for example, by a credit card issuer. A positive authorisation results in an authorisation code being generated and the relevant funds being set aside. The available credit limit is reduced by the amount authorised.

authorised capital *Fin* the money made by a company from the sale of authorised ordinary and preference shares. It is measured by multiplying the number of authorised shares by their par value.

authorised share *Fin* a share that a company is authorised to issue

authorised share capital *Fin* the type, class, number, and amount of the shares which a company may issue, as empowered by its memorandum of association. *Also known as* **nominal share capital**, **registered share capital**

authorised signatory *Fin* the most senior issuer of authorisation certificates in an organisation, recognised by a signatory authority and designated in a signatory certificate

authority *Gen Mgt* the right to act or command. People willingly obey a person in authority, because they believe he or she has a legitimate entitlement to exercise power. *Max Weber* distinguishes three types of legitimate authority: rational-legal, derived from the office held; traditional, from custom, an ancient tradition of obedience; and charismatic, exerted by those whose exceptional abilities confer the right to lead. The third form is the basis for the *charismatic authority* leadership theory.

authority chart *Gen Mgt* a diagram showing the hierarchical lines of *authority* and reporting within an organisation. *Organisation charts* are similar.

authority-compliance management *Gen Mgt see* **Managerial Grid™**

A lawyer with his briefcase can steal more than a hundred men with guns.   Mario Puzo

automated clearing house *E-com* a payment network available to *POS* or *ATM* systems for interbank clearing and settlement of financial transactions. The network is also used for electronic fund transfers from a current or savings account.

Automated Direct Debit Amendments and Cancellation Service *Fin* in the United Kingdom, a *BACS* service that allows paying banks to inform direct debit payees of a change of instruction, for example, an amendment to the customer's account details or a request to cancel the instructions. *Abbr* **ADDACS**

automated handling *Ops* the use of computers to control the moving and positioning of materials in a warehouse or factory. Automated handling may involve the use of robots.

Automated Order Entry System *Fin* in the United States, a system that allows small orders to bypass the floor brokers and go straight to the specialists on the exchange floor

automated screen trading *Fin* an electronic trading system for the sale and purchase of securities. Customers' orders are entered via a keyboard, a computer system matches and executes the deals, and prices and deals are shown on monitors, thus dispensing with the need for face-to-face contact on a trading floor.

automated storage and retrieval systems *Ops* the use of computerised vehicles to store, select, and move pallets around a large warehouse

automated teller machine *Fin see* **ATM**

automatic assembly *Ops* a computerised *production control* technique used in the production of manufactured goods to balance output of production with demand. All factors affecting production performance are input when setting the operating parameters of an automatic assembly system, including sales information and production *capacity*.

automatic debit (*US*) *Fin* = *standing order*

automatic guided vehicle system *Ops* a transportation system consisting of driverless electric vehicles that follow a predetermined track, used for the distribution of materials around a plant

automatic rollover *Fin* on the London Money Market, the automatic reinvestment of a maturing fixed term deposit for a further identical fixed term, an arrangement that can be cancelled at any time

automation *Ops* the self-controlling operation of machinery that reduces or dispenses with human communication or control when used in normal conditions. Automation was first introduced in the late 1940s by the Ford Motor Company. *Also known as* **mechanisation**

autonomation *Ops* a production system in which workers are allowed, and machines are equipped with a mechanism, to stop production if a defect in a product is detected during the production process. Autonomation became known through the *Toyota production system*. The concept evolved from braking devices on machines that automatically stop if a problem occurs. Within Toyota, the concept has been carried forward so that all machines are equipped with various safety devices to prevent defective products, and production workers are allowed to stop the production line if a problem occurs. The problem is then properly explored in order to find a solution and to ensure that everyone understands the underlying reasons for the problem. In the long term, this creates a more efficient production line.

autonomous work group *HR* a small group of people who are empowered to manage themselves and the work they do on a day-to-day basis. The members of an autonomous work group are usually responsible for a whole process, product, or service, and not only carry out the work but also design and manage it. *Also known as* **self-directed team**, *self-managed team, self-managed work team, self-managing team*

Auto Pact *Fin* the informal name for the Agreement Concerning Automotive Products between Canada and the United States, by which duties were reduced on imported cars for US car makers assembling vehicles in Canada. Subsequent provisions of the North American Free Trade Agreement reduced its effect.

autoresponder *E-com* an e-mail software application that enables Internet users to send automated e-mails when they are not able to respond to incoming e-mail. Some autoresponse software enables a degree of personalisation, for example, by incorporating the recipient's name in the responding message.

availability float *Fin* money that is available to a company because cheques that it has written have not yet been charged against its accounts

available hours *Fin* the number of hours for which a worker or machine is available to work.

EXAMPLE In a simple case for a worker this could be as follows for a four-week period:

	Hours	
Number of contractual hours	40	
Overtime hours	20	
Absence:		
Public holidays	7	
Annual holidays	28	
Certified sickness	14	
Other absence	1	(50)
Available hours	110	

average *Stats* the arithmetic mean of a sample of observations

average accounting return *Fin* the percentage return realised on an asset, as measured by its book value, after taxes and depreciation

average collection period *Fin* the mean time required for a firm to liquidate its accounts receivable, measured from the date each receivable is posted until the last payment is received.

Its formula is:

Accounts receivable / Average daily sales = Average collection period

For example, if accounts receivable are £280,000, and average daily sales are 7,000, then:

280,000 / 7,000 = 40

average cost of capital *Fin* the average of what a company is paying for the money it borrows or raises by selling stock

average deviation *Stats* the spread of a sample of observations

average nominal maturity *Fin* the average length of time until a unit trust's financial instruments mature

average option *Fin* an option whose value depends on the average price of a commodity during a particular period of time

Average Weekly Earnings *Stats* a measure of wage levels in the Australian workforce that is calculated regularly by the *Australian Bureau of Statistics*. The measure is considered one of Australia's key economic indicators. *Abbr* **AWE**

Average Weekly Ordinary Time Earnings *Stats* a measure of wage levels in the Australian workforce that excludes overtime payments, published by the *Australian Bureau of Statistics*

avoidable costs *Fin* the specific costs of an activity or sector of a business which would be avoided if that activity or sector did not exist

award *HR* **1.** the terms of employment set by an industrial court or tribunal for a particular occupation **2.** a decision handed down by a court of arbitration

award wage *(ANZ)* *HR* a rate of pay set by an industrial court or tribunal for a particular occupation

AWE *abbr Stats* Average Weekly Earnings

axis *Stats* a reference line used in geometry to locate a point in space or in a plane

---

Men their rights and nothing more; women their rights and nothing less. **Susan B. Anthony**

B2B *abbr* *E-com* business-to-business: relating to an advertising or marketing programme aimed at businesses doing business with other businesses as opposed to consumers. The term is most commonly used in reference to commerce or business that is conducted over the Internet between commercial enterprises.

B2B advertising *Mkting* advertising that is aimed at buyers for organisations rather than domestic consumers

B2B agency *Mkting* an advertising agency that specialises in planning, creating, and buying advertising aimed at buyers for organisations rather than domestic consumers

B2B auction *E-com* a Web marketplace that provides a mechanism for negotiating prices and bidding for services. Web-based B2B auctions reverse the traditional auction formula in which the aim is to help the seller get the best price. B2B Web auctions involve suppliers competing with one another by bidding down the price of their service. This inevitably benefits the buyer, as instead of having to bid higher for a particular service or product he or she can wait till the suppliers have bid themselves down to a reasonable price. Typically, online auctions require companies to follow a registration process in order to take part. During this process, users have to provide their credit-card information and shipping preferences as well as agree to the site's code of conduct. Some sites also manage secure auctions, which restrict potential bidders to specific firms or individuals (www.businessauctions.com is one example).

B2B commerce *E-com* the business conducted between companies, rather than between a company and individual consumers

B2B exchange *Gen Mgt see* **exchange**

B2B marketing *E-com* the planning, promotion, and distribution of goods or services for use by businesses rather than individual consumers

B2B Web exchange *E-com see* **exchange**

B2C *abbr* *E-com* business-to-consumer: relating to an advertising or marketing programme aimed at businesses doing business directly with consumers as opposed to other businesses. The term is most commonly used in reference to commerce or business that is conducted over the Internet between a commercial enterprise and a consumer.

B4N *abbr* *Gen Mgt* bye for now (*slang*)

BAA *abbr* *Fin* British Accounting Association

back duty *Fin* tax relating to a past period that has not been paid due to the taxpayer's failure to disclose relevant information through negligence or fraud. If back duty is found to be payable, the relevant authorities may instigate an investigation and penalties or interest may be charged on the amount.

back-end loading *Fin* the practice of charging a redemption fee or deferred sales charge if the holder of an investment decides to sell it. This is used as a discouragement to selling. *See also* **front-end loading**

backflush costing *Fin* a method of costing, associated with a *JIT* production system, which applies cost to the output of a process. Costs do not mirror the flow of products through the production process, but are attached to output produced (finished goods stock and cost of sales), on the assumption that such backflushed costs are a realistic measure of the actual costs incurred.

backlink checking *E-com* a means of finding out which web pages are linking to a specific website. Many **search engines** enable users to conduct backlink searches by entering the name of a website into the search box preceded by a special command (for example, 'link':). AltaVista and HotBot are two of the most popular search engines to offer this facility. The backlink checking process can be automated by using a service such as LinkPopularity-.com, which enables users to search for linking sites at various search engines at once. Backlink checking enables e-business and website managers to keep track of their own and their competitors' online popularity.

backlog *Ops* the build-up of unfulfilled orders for a product or process that is behind schedule. A backlog can result from bad scheduling, production delays, an unanticipated demand for a product or process, or where the capacity of the process is not able to keep up with demand. Some large products, for example, aircraft and ships, have to be built to a backlog of orders as it is not feasible to supply them on demand.

backlog depreciation *Fin* the additional depreciation required when an asset is revalued to make up for the fact that previous depreciation had been calculated on a now out-of-date valuation

back office *Fin, Gen Mgt* the administrative staff of a company who do not have face-to-face contact with the company's customers

back pay *HR* pay that is owed to an employee for work carried out before the current payment period and is either overdue or results from a backdated pay increase

back-to-back loan *Fin* an arrangement in which two companies in different countries borrow offsetting amounts in each other's currency and each repays it at a specified future date in its domestic currency. Such a loan, often between a company and its foreign subsidiary, eliminates the risk of loss from exchange rate fluctuations.

back-to-school sale (*US*) *Gen Mgt* a shop sale that is timed to coincide with the return of children to school after the summer holidays (*slang*)

back-up *Fin* a period in which bond yields rise and prices fall, or a sudden reversal in a stock market trend

back-up facility *Gen Mgt* a secondary system, record, or contract intended to take the place of another that fails

back-up withholding *Fin* withholding tax that a payer sends to the Internal Revenue Service in the United States so that somebody receiving income cannot avoid all taxes on that income

backward integration *Ops* the building of relationships with *suppliers* in order to secure the supply of *raw materials*. Backward integration can involve taking control of supply companies and is a feature of Japanese *keiretsu*. It is the opposite of *forward integration*.

backward scheduling *Ops* a *production scheduling* technique for planning work on the basis of when the completed work is due. By using backward scheduling, managers are able to assign work to particular workstations so that the overall task is completed exactly when it is due. The technique allows potential bottlenecks and idle time for particular workstations to be identified in advance.

BACS *Fin* an electronic bulk clearing system generally used by banks and building societies for low-value and/or repetitive items such as standing orders, direct debits, and automated credits such as salary payments. It was formerly known as the Bankers Automated Clearing Services.

BADC *abbr Fin* Business Accounting Deliberation Council of Japan

bad debt *Fin* a debt that is unlikely to be repaid because a company or customer has become insolvent

bad debt reserve *Fin* an amount of money that a company sets aside to cover bad debts

bad debts ratio *Fin* a way of calculating the significance of bad debts as a proportion of credit sales:

Bad debts × 100 / Turnover on credit

College professors are suspect because whenever emotion is in control, anti-intellectualism prevails.
Gordon Allport

To calculate the significance of bad debts as a proportion of debtors, however:

Bad debts × 100 / Total debtors at a point in time

bad debts recovered *Fin* money formerly classified as *bad debts* and therefore written off that has since been recovered either wholly or in part

badwill *Fin* negative goodwill (*slang*)

bailment *Fin* the delivery of goods from the owner to another person on the condition that they will eventually be returned

bait and switch *Mkting* a marketing practice whereby customers are encouraged to enter a shop by an advertisement for one product and are then persuaded to buy another more expensive product (*slang*)

balance *Fin* **1.** the state of an account, for example, a debit or a credit balance, indicating whether money is owed or owing **2.** in double-entry bookkeeping, the amount required to make the debit and credit figures in the books equal

balance billing *Fin* the practice of requesting payment from a receiver of a service such as medical treatment for the part of the cost not covered by the person's insurance

balanced budget *Econ* a budget in which planned expenditure on goods and services and debt income can be met by current income from taxation and other central government receipts

balanced design *Stats* an experimental design in which the same number of observations is used for each combination of the experimental factors

balanced fund *Fin* a unit trust that invests in a variety of types of companies and financial instruments to reduce the risk of loss through poor performance of any one type

balanced investment strategy *Fin* a strategy of investing in a variety of types of companies and financial instruments to reduce the risk of loss through poor performance of any one type

balanced line *Ops* an *assembly line* in which the cycle time for all the workstations is equal. A balanced line is achieved by allocating the right amount of work and the correct amount of operators and machinery to produce a given flow of product over a set period, taking into account the fact that each workstation will have a different capacity and that each process involved has a different cycle time.

balanced quantity *Ops* an *inventory* measure of the quantity of materials and parts required by a workstation to achieve a planned level of output

balanced scorecard *Gen Mgt* a system that measures and manages an organisation's progress towards strategic objectives. Introduced by *Robert Kaplan* and *David Norton* in 1992, the balanced scorecard incorporates not only financial indicators but also three other perspectives: customer, internal business, and learning/innovation. The scorecard shows how these measures are interlinked and affect each other, enabling an organisation's past, present, and potential performance to be tracked and managed.

balance off *Fin* to add up and enter the totals for both sides of an account at the end of an accounting period in order to determine the balance

balance of payments *Econ* a list of a country's credit and debit transactions with international financial institutions and foreign countries in a specific period

balance of payments on capital account *Fin* a system of recording a country's investment transactions with the rest of the world during a given period, usually one year. Among the included transactions are the purchase of physical and financial assets, intergovernmental transfers, and the provision of economic aid to developing nations.

balance of payments on current account *Fin* a system of recording a country's imports and exports of goods

---

It does seem the more you get the more you spend. It is rather like being on a golden treadmill.
Charles Allsop

and services during a period, usually one year

balance of trade *Econ* the difference between a country's exports and imports of goods and services

balance sheet *Fin* a financial report stating the total assets, liabilities, and owner's equity of an organisation at a given date, usually the last day of the accounting period. The format of a company's balance sheet is strictly defined by the 1985 Companies Act. The debit side of the balance sheet states assets, while the credit side states liability and equity, and the two sides must be equal, or balance.

EXAMPLE Assets include cash in hand and cash anticipated (receivables), inventories of supplies and materials, properties, facilities, equipment, and whatever else the company uses to conduct business. Assets also need to reflect depreciation in the value of equipment such as machinery that has a limited expected useful life.

Liabilities include pending payments to suppliers and creditors, outstanding current and long-term debts, taxes, interest payments, and other unpaid expenses that the company has incurred.

Subtracting the value of aggregate liabilities from the value of aggregate assets reveals the value of owners' equity. Ideally, it should be positive. Owners' equity consists of capital invested by owners over the years and profits (net income) or internally generated capital, which is referred to as 'retained earnings'; these are funds to be used in future operations.

As an example:

ASSETS	£
Current:	
Cash	8,200
Securities	5,000
Receivables	4,500
Inventory & supplies	6,300
Fixed:	
Land	10,000
Structures	90,000
Equipment (less depreciation)	5,000
Intangibles/other	
TOTAL ASSETS	129,000

LIABILITIES	£
Payables	7,000
Taxes	4,000
Misc.	3,000
Bonds & notes	25,000
TOTAL LIABILITIES	39,000
SHAREHOLDERS' EQUITY (stock, par value × shares outstanding)	80,000
RETAINED EARNINGS	10,000
TOTAL LIABILITIES AND SHAREHOLDERS' EQUITY	129,000

balance sheet audit *Fin* a limited audit of the items on a company's balance sheet in order to confirm that it complies with the relevant standards and requirements. Such an audit involves checking the value, ownership, and existence of assets and liabilities and ensuring that they are correctly recorded.

balance sheet equation *Fin* see *accounting equation*

balance sheet total *Fin* in the United Kingdom, the total of assets shown at the bottom of a balance sheet and used to classify a company according to size

balancing figure *Fin* a number added to a series of numbers to make the total the same as another total. For example, if a debit total is higher than the credit total in the accounts, the balancing figure is the amount of extra credit required to make the two totals equal.

ball

carry the ball *Gen Mgt* to have responsibility for a project (*slang*)

drop the ball *Gen Mgt* to avoid your responsibilities (*slang*)

take the ball and run with it *Gen Mgt* to take an idea and implement it (*slang*)

balloon loan *Fin* a loan repaid in regular instalments with a single larger final payment

balloon payment *Fin* the final larger payment on a balloon loan

ballpark *Gen Mgt* an informal term for a rough, estimated figure. The term was derived from the approximate assessment of the number of spectators that might be made on the basis of a glance around at a sporting event.

BALO *Fin* Bulletin des annonces légales obligatoires: a French government publication that includes financial statements of public companies

banded pack *Mkting* a product pack that has an additional product or promotional offer attached to it

bandwidth *E-com* the capacity of fibre-optic cables that carry information to and from the Internet. The higher the bandwidth, the faster information will pass through a cable, and therefore the faster information can be downloaded or uploaded via the Internet.

bang for the buck (*US*) *Gen Mgt* a return on investment (*slang*)

bangtail *Mkting* an order form for a new product that is attached by a perforated join to an envelope flap (*slang*)

bank *Fin* a commercial institution that keeps money in accounts for individuals or organisations, makes loans, exchanges currencies, provides credit to businesses, and offers other financial services

bank bill *Fin* **1.** a bill of exchange issued or accepted by a bank **2.** (*US*) a banknote

bank card *Fin* a plastic card issued by a bank and accepted by merchants in payment for transactions. The most common types are **credit cards** and **debit cards**. Bank cards are governed by an internationally recognised set of rules for the authorisation of their use and the clearing and settlement of transactions.

bank certificate *Fin* a document, often requested during an audit, that is signed by a bank official and confirms the balances due or from a company on a specific date

bank charge *Fin* an amount charged by a bank to its customers for services provided, for example, for servicing customer accounts or arranging foreign currency

transactions or letters of credit, but excluding interest

bank confirmation *Fin* verification of a company's balances requested by an auditor from a bank

bank credit *Fin* the maximum credit available to an individual from a particular bank

bank discount *Fin* the charge made by a bank to a company or customer who pays a note before it is due

bank discount basis *Fin* the expression of yield that is used for US treasury bills, based on a 360-day year

bank draft *Fin* see *banker's draft*

bank-eligible issue *Fin* US Treasury obligations that commercial banks may buy

banker *Fin* somebody who owns or is a senior executive of a bank

banker's acceptance *Fin* see *banker's credit*

banker's cheque *Fin* see *banker's draft*

banker's credit *Fin* a financial instrument, typically issued by an exporter or importer for a short term, that a bank guarantees. *Also known as* **banker's acceptance**

banker's draft *Fin* a bill of exchange payable on demand and drawn by one bank on another. Regarded as being equivalent to cash, the draft cannot be returned unpaid. *Also known as* **bank draft**, **banker's cheque**

bankers' hours *Fin* short hours of work. The term refers to the relatively short time that a bank is open in some countries. (*slang*)

banker's order *Fin* an instruction by a customer to a bank to pay a specific amount at regular intervals, usually monthly or annually, until the order is cancelled

banker's reference *Fin* a written report issued by a bank regarding a particular customer's creditworthiness

---

Dr ___ well remembered that he had a salary to receive, and only forgot that he had a duty to perform.
Edward Gibbon

bank fee *Fin* a charge included in most lease transactions that is either paid in advance or is included in the gross capitalised cost. The fee usually covers administrative costs such as the costs of obtaining a credit report, verifying insurance coverage, and checking the lease documentation.

Bank for International Settlements *Fin see* **BIS**

bank giro *Fin see* **giro** *(sense 1)*

bank guarantee *Fin* a commitment made by a bank to a foreign buyer that the bank will pay an exporter for goods shipped if the buyer defaults

bank holding company *Fin* a company that owns one or more banks as part of its assets

banking insurance fund *Fin* in the United States, a fund maintained by the Federal Deposit Insurance Corporation to provide deposit insurance for banks other than savings and savings and loan banks

Banking Ombudsman *Fin* an official of the Australian or New Zealand government responsible for dealing with complaints relating to banking practices

banking passport *Fin* a document used to provide somebody with a false identity for banking transactions in another country

banking syndicate *Fin* a group of investment banks that jointly underwrite and distribute a new security offering

banking system *Fin* a network of commercial, savings, and specialised banks that provide financial services including accepting deposits, loans and credit, and providing money transmission and investment facilities

bank investment contract *Fin* a contract that specifies what a bank will pay its investors

bankmail *Fin* an agreement by a bank not to finance any rival's attempt to take over the same company that a particular customer is trying to buy

Bank of England *Fin* the central bank of the United Kingdom, established in 1694. Originally a private bank, it became public in 1946 and increased its independence from government in 1997 when it was granted sole responsibility for setting base interest rates.

bank overdraft *Fin* borrowings from a bank on a current account, repayable on demand. The maximum permissible overdraft is normally agreed with the bank prior to the facility being made available, and interest, calculated on a daily basis, is charged on the amount borrowed, and not on the agreed maximum borrowing facility.

bank reconciliation *Fin* a detailed statement reconciling, at a given date, the cash balance in an entity's cash book with that reported in a bank statement.

EXAMPLE

Bank Reconciliation Statement
Cash book balance

	£	£
Cash book balance o/d		(1,205)
Bank charges not in cash book	(110)	
Dividends collected by the bank, not in cash book	113	3
Updated cash book balance		**(1,202)**
Cheques drawn, not presented to bank	4,363	
Cheques received, not yet credited by bank	(1,061)	3,302
Bank statement balance		**2,100**

bank reserve ratio *Fin* a standard established by a central bank governing the relationship between the amount of money that other banks must keep on hand and the amount that they can lend. By raising and lowering the ratio, the central bank can decrease or increase the money supply.

bank reserves *Fin* the money that a bank has available to meet the demands of its depositors

---

Live together like brothers and do business like strangers.   *Arab proverb*

bankroll *Fin* the money used as finance for a project

bankrupt *Fin* a person who has been declared by a court of law as unable to meet his or her financial obligations

bankruptcy *Fin* the condition of being unable to pay debts, with liabilities greater than assets. There are two types of bankruptcy: involuntary bankruptcy, where one or more creditors bring a petition against the debtor; and voluntary bankruptcy, where the debtor files a petition claiming inability to meet debts.

bank statement *Fin* a record, sent by a bank to its customer, listing transactions since the date of the previous statement

bank term loan *Fin* a loan from a bank that has a term of at least one year

banner *or* **banner ad** *E-com* an online interactive ad, often using graphic images and sound as well as text, placed on a web page that is linked to an external advertiser's website. The banner typically is sized so as to appear at the top or bottom of the web page. *Also known as* **ad banner**

banner advertising *Mkting* the use of rectangular advertisements or logos across the width of a page on a website. Organisations frequently place such ads on a third party's website in order to attract users to visit their own.
    Debate still continues on whether banner advertising is an efficient and cost-effective way of promoting a website. However, prices for banner advertising have dropped significantly in recent years, and it can be effective if the website is visited by people whose profile accurately matches the advertiser's target market. Banner ads are particularly useful for raising awareness when a new website, product, or service is being launched.

banner exchange *E-com* an advertising programme in which one merchant induces others to place his or her banners and buttons on their websites in return for similarly displaying theirs

bar *or* **outside the bar** *Fin* one million pounds sterling (*slang*)

bar chart *Gen Mgt* the presentation of data in the form of a graph, using blocks or bars of colour or shading. A bar chart is especially useful for showing the impact of one factor against another, for example, income over time, or customer calls against sales.

bar coding *Ops* the process of attaching a machine-readable code to a product, package, container, or sub-assembly, and using a scanner to relate its location to the product characteristics. Bar codes have uses in **stock control** and order picking and are used to validate every single transaction from packaging through to customer delivery.

barefoot pilgrim (*US*) *Fin* an unsophisticated investor who has lost everything trading in securities (*slang*)

bargain *Fin* a transaction on a stock market (*slang*)

bargaining chip *Fin* something that can be used as a concession or inducement in negotiation

bargain tax date *Fin* the date of a transaction on a stock market

Barnard, Chester (1886–1961) *Gen Mgt* US business executive. President of the New Jersey Bell Telephone Company, whose book, *The Functions of the Executive* (1938), looked at the relationship of the individual to the organisation and at *organisation structure*. Barnard's observations also covered the topics of *communication*, *authority*, and organisational *core values*.

Barnevik, Percy (*b.* 1941) *Gen Mgt* Swedish business executive. Formerly chief executive, and now chairman, of Asea Brown Boveri, where he reduced *bureaucracy*, decentralised resources and *authority*, introduced a *matrix management* structure, and ran a global expansion strategy.

barometer stock *Fin* a widely held security such as a blue chip that is regarded as an indicator of the state of the market

barren money *Fin* money that is unproductive because it is not invested

barrier option *Fin* an option that includes automatic trading in other options when a commodity reaches a specified price

barrier to entry *Gen Mgt* a factor preventing a company from entering a market. A barrier to entry may be created, for example, by the fact that current companies in that market have patents so that goods cannot be copied, or by the high cost of advertising needed to gain any *market share*. There may be strong *brand loyalty* to an existing product, or a large company may be able to produce goods very cheaply, whereas a small newcomer would have to charge higher prices. If too many barriers to entry exist, then competition within that market will be limited.

barrier to exit *Gen Mgt* a factor preventing a company from leaving a market in which it is currently doing business. A barrier to exit makes it difficult for a company to abandon an unprofitable product or service because of factors such as possession of specialist equipment only suited to the manufacture of one product, high costs of retraining the workforce in different skills, or the detrimental effect of withdrawing one product from a range on the rest of the product family. There may also be legal considerations or trade union agreements that prevent closure of a factory or redundancies.

barter *Fin* the direct exchange of goods between two parties without the use of money as a medium

Bartlett, Christopher (*b.* 1943) *Gen Mgt* Australian-born academic. Professor at Harvard Business School, and co-author with *Sumantra Ghoshal* of *Managing Across Borders* (1989).

BAS *abbr Gen Mgt* Business Activity Statement

base
touch base *Gen Mgt* to make contact with a person or group after a time of absence. To touch base is important for *teleworkers*, *homeworkers*, or *sales representatives* who work away from a main office. They may touch base by taking part in a *team briefing* or other real or virtual meeting, which enables them to renew contact and establish meaningful communication. (*slang*)

base currency *Fin* the currency used for measuring the return on an investment

base date *Econ* the reference date from which an index number such as the *retail price index* is calculated

base interest rate *Fin* in the United States, the minimum interest rate that investors will expect for investing in a non-Treasury security

base pay (*US*) *HR* = *basic pay*

base rate *Fin* the interest rate at which the Bank of England lends to other banks and which they in turn charge their customers

base rate tracker mortgage *Fin* a mortgage whose interest rate varies periodically, usually annually, so as to remain a specified amount above a particular standard rate

base year *Econ* the year from which an index is calculated

basic pay *HR* a guaranteed sum of money given to an employee in payment for work, disregarding any fringe benefits, allowances, or extra rewards from an *incentive scheme*. US term *base pay*

basic wage *HR* the minimum rate of pay set by an industrial court or tribunal for a particular occupation

basic wage rate *Fin* the wages paid for a specific number of hours work per week, excluding overtime payments and any other incentives

basis of apportionment *Fin* a physical or financial unit used to apportion costs equitably to cost centres

---

He that wants money, means, and content, is without three good friends.
William Shakespeare

basis point *Fin* one hundredth of 1%, used in relation to changes in bond interest rates. Thus a change from 7.5% to 7.4% is 10 basis points.

basis risk *Fin* the risk that price variations in the cash or futures market will diminish revenue when a futures contract is liquidated, or the risk that changes in interest rates will affect re-pricing interest-bearing liabilities

basket case *Fin* a company or individual considered to be in such dire circumstances as to be beyond help (*slang*)

basket of currencies *Fin* a group of selected currencies used in establishing a standard of value for another unit of currency

batch *Fin* a group of similar articles which maintains its identity throughout one or more stages of production and is treated as a cost unit

batch costing *Fin* a form of specific order costing in which costs are attributed to batches of products

batch-level activities *Fin* activities which vary directly with the number of batches of output produced, and which are independent of the number of units within a batch. Set up costs are batch-level activities. *See also* **hierarchy of activities**

batch production *Ops* a production system in which a process is broken down into distinct operations that are completed on a batch or group of products before moving to the next production stage. As batch sizes can vary from very small to extremely large quantities, batch production offers greater flexibility than other production systems.

bath
take a bath (*US*) *Fin* to suffer a serious financial loss (*slang*)

baud *Fin* a unit used to measure speed of data transmission, equal to one data unit per second

Bayesian theory *Stats* a statistical theory and method for drawing conclusions about the future occurrence of a given parameter of a statistical distribution by calculating from prior data on its frequency of occurrence. The theory is useful in the solution of theoretical and applied problems in science, industry, and government, for example, in econometrics and finance.

Bayes' theorem *Stats* a probability theorem that allows statisticians continually to revise the probability of an event according to new evidence

BBS *abbr E-com* bulletin board system: a system enabling Internet users to read and post messages in newsgroups. *See also* **discussion board**

BCA *abbr Gen Mgt* Business Council of Australia

bcc *abbr E-com* blind carbon copy: a function that enables a user to send an e-mail message to any number of e-mail addresses while concealing each recipient's e-mail address. The bcc box is widely used for distributing press releases, newsletters, and other mass mailings via e-mail. If there is no desire to conceal names, the *cc* address line can be used.

BCCS *abbr Fin* Board of Currency Commissioners

BCNU *abbr Gen Mgt* be seeing you (*slang*)

bean counter (*slang*) **1.** *Gen Mgt* a person of low rank within an organisation who has no real influence on the decision-making process **2.** *Fin* a derogatory term for an accountant, especially one who works in a large organisation

bear *Fin* somebody who anticipates unfavourable business conditions, especially somebody who sells stocks or commodities expecting their prices to fall, often with the intention of buying them back cheaply later. *See also* **bull**

bearer bond *Fin* a bond that is not registered on the books of the issuer and is therefore payable only to the party that presents it for payment

bearer instrument *Fin* a financial instrument such as a cheque or bill of exchange that entitles the person who presents it to receive payment

bearer security *Fin* a share or bond that is owned by the person who possesses it. For example, a eurobond can change hands without registration and so protect the owner's anonymity.

bear hug *Gen Mgt* an attempt to get the board of a company that is a target acquisition to recommend an offer to its shareholders. A bear hug may include the acquiring company offering to buy shares in the target at a premium. In a **reverse bear hug**, the board of the company to be acquired demonstrates its willingness to recommend an offer, usually on particular conditions. (*slang*)

bearish *Fin* relating to unfavourable business conditions or selling activity in anticipation of falling prices. *See also* **bullish**

bear market *Fin* a market in which prices are falling and in which a dealer is more likely to sell securities than to buy them. *See also* **bull market**

bear raid *Fin see* **raid**

bear spread *Fin* a combination of purchases and sales of options for the same commodity or stock with the intention of making a profit when the price falls. *See also* **bull spread**

bear tack *Fin* a downward movement in the value of a stock, part of the market, or the market as a whole

bed
get into bed with somebody *HR* to begin a business association with an individual or organisation (*slang*)
put something to bed *Gen Mgt* to dismiss an idea or put an end to a project (*slang*)

bed and breakfast deal *Fin* a transaction in which somebody sells shares at the end of one trading day and repurchases them at the beginning of the next. This is usually done to formally establish the profit or loss accrued to these shares for tax or reporting purposes.

Beer, Stafford (*b.* 1926) *Gen Mgt* British industrialist. Organisation systems thinker associated with cybernetics. Also a writer, his approach was first laid out in *Cybernetics and Management* (1959).

before-tax profit margin *Fin* the amount by which net income before tax exceeds expenditure

beginning inventory (*US*) *Fin* = **opening stock**

behavioural accounting *Fin* an approach to the study of accounting that emphasises the psychological and social aspects of the profession in addition to the more technical areas

behavioural implications *Fin* the ways in which humans affect, and are affected by, the creation, existence, and use of accounting information

behavioural interview *HR see* **interviewing**

behavioural modelling *HR* **1.** a process of capturing and encoding unconscious human expertise to make it transferable to others **2.** a skills training technique that seeks to imitate models and maintain learned behaviours

behavioural science *HR* academic disciplines such as sociology and psychology that relate to the study of the way in which humans conduct themselves. In the field of management, the behavioural sciences are used to study *organisation behaviour*.

behaviourist theories of leadership *Gen Mgt* a school of thought that defines *leadership* by leaders' actions, rather than by their personality characteristics or their sources of *power*. Behaviourist theories were developed in the 1970s as disillusionment with situational theory grew. There are many different behaviourist theories. One of the most prominent—the *Managerial Grid*™—was developed by *Robert Blake* and *Jane Mouton* as a tool to enable leaders to understand their own behaviour patterns. *Rensis Likert* also conducted research in this area, focusing

---

We cannot hide behind our boundaries, or hold onto the belief that we can survive alone.
Meg Wheatley

on how behaviour adapts to take account of people and situations.

Behn, Hernand (1880–1933) *Gen Mgt* US industrialist. Founder, with his brother *Sosthenes Behn*, of the conglomerate International Telephone and Telegraph (ITT) in 1920.

Behn, Sosthenes (1882–1957) *Gen Mgt* US industrialist. Founder, with his brother *Hernand Behn*, of the conglomerate International Telephone and Telegraph (ITT) in 1920. Under Behn's leadership, ITT expanded from the United States into Europe and South America. When Behn retired from ITT in 1956, most of its turnover came from its overseas interests. Under the leadership of *Harold Geneen*, ITT then developed into a massive diverse multinational incorporating hotels, car hire, frozen foods, potato crisps, and confectionery. The history of ITT is detailed in *Sovereign State—The Secret History of ITT* (1973).

Belbin, R. Meredith (*b.* 1926) *Gen Mgt* British academic and consultant. Acknowledged as the father of team-role theory, which identifies nine useful roles necessary for a successful team of managers. Belbin's approach to *team building* and *teamwork* was described in *Management Teams: Why They Succeed or Fail* (1981). Other models of team relationships include the Team Management System, developed by *Charles Margerison* and *Dick McCann*.

bell cow *Fin* a product that sells well and makes a reasonable profit (*slang*)

bells and whistles (*slang*) **1.** *Fin* special features attached to a derivatives instrument or securities issue that are intended to attract investors or reduce issue costs **2.** *Mkting* unnecessary but desirable peripheral features of a product

bellwether *Fin* a security whose price is viewed by investors as an indicator of future developments or trends

belly
go belly up (*US*) *Fin* to fail financially or go bankrupt (*slang*)

below-the-line **1.** *Fin* used to describe entries in a company's profit and loss account that show how the profit is distributed, or where the funds to finance the loss originate. *See also* **above-the-line** *(sense 2)* **2.** *Fin* in macroeconomics, used to describe a country's capital transactions. *See also* **above-the-line** *(sense 3)* **3.** *Mkting* relating to the proportion of marketing expenditure allocated to non-advertising activities such as public relations, sales promotion, printing, presentations, sponsorship, and salesforce support

benchmark *Gen Mgt* a point of reference or standard against which to measure performance. Originally used for a set of computer programs to measure the performance of a computer against similar models, benchmark is now used more generally to describe a measure identified in the context of a **benchmarking** programme against which to evaluate an organisation's performance in a specific area.

benchmark accounting policy *Fin* one of a choice of two possible policies within an International Accounting Standard. The other policy is marked as an 'allowed alternative', although there is no indication of preference.

benchmarking *Mkting* a systematic process of comparing the activities and work processes of an organisation or department with those of outstanding organisations or departments in order to identify ways to improve performance. Benchmarking was first developed by the Xerox Corporation in the late 1970s in order to learn from the achievements of Japanese competitors and was described by a Xerox manager, Robert C. Camp, in his book *Benchmarking: The Search for Industry Best Practices That Lead to Superior Performance* (1989).The use of benchmarking has become widespread and individual organisations have developed distinct approaches towards it. Benchmarking programmes commonly include the following stages: identifying the area requiring benchmarking and the process to use, collecting and analysing the data, implementing changes, and monitoring and reviewing improvements. Benchmarking is used in business appraisal, often as part of a *total quality management* or *business process re-engineering* programme.

Types of benchmarking include: internal benchmarking, a method of comparing one operating unit or function with another within the same industry; functional benchmarking, in which internal functions are compared with those of the best external practitioners of those functions, regardless of the industry they are in; competitive benchmarking, in which information is gathered about direct competitors, through techniques such as reverse engineering; and strategic benchmarking, a type of competitive benchmarking aimed at strategic action and organisational change.

benchmark interest rate *Fin* the lowest interest rate that US investors will accept on securities other than Treasury bills

beneficial owner *Fin* somebody who receives all the benefits of a stock such as dividends, rights, and proceeds of any sale but is not the registered owner of the stock

beneficiary bank *Fin* a bank that handles a gift such as a bequest

benefit *Fin* something that improves the profitability or efficiency of an organisation or reduces its risk, or any non-monetary reward given to employees, for example, paid holidays or employer contributions to pensions

benefit in kind *HR* a *benefit* other than cash received by employees as part of their total *compensation package*

benefits plan *HR* a Canadian government programme for the employment of Canadian citizens and for providing Canadian manufacturers, consultants, contractors, and service companies with opportunities to compete for projects

Bennis, Warren (*b.* 1925) *Gen Mgt* US academic. Guru of *leadership* theory, who has also carried out work in the areas of

small *group dynamics*, change in social systems, and T-Groups (see *sensitivity training*). Bennis wrote his first article on leadership in 1959, and subsequently carried out extensive research in the United States into common leadership factors. His findings are reported in *Leaders: The Strategies for Taking Charge* (1985). He was influenced by the theories of *Douglas McGregor*.

bequest *Fin* a gift that has been left to somebody in a will

Berhad *Fin* a Malay term for 'private'. Companies can use 'sendiran berhad' or 'Sdn Bhd' in their name instead of 'plc'. *Abbr* **Bhd**

Berners-Lee, Tim (*b.* 1955) *Gen Mgt* British computer scientist. Creator of the World Wide Web and director of the World Wide Web Consortium, the world coordinating body for developing the Web. Berners-Lee is concerned that the growth of the Web should benefit all, rather than make money for the few. His experiences and thoughts are recorded in *Weaving the Web: The Original Design and Ultimate Destiny of the World Wide Web* (1999).

Berne Union *Fin see International Union of Credit and Investment Insurers*

best-in-class *Gen Mgt* leading a market or industrial sector in efficiency. A best-in-class organisation exhibits exemplary *best practice*. Such an organisation is clearly singled out from the pack and is recognised as a leader for its procedures for dealing with the acquisition and processing of materials, and the delivery of end products or services to its customers. The concept of best in class is closely allied with *total quality management*, and one tool that can help in achieving this status is *benchmarking*.

best practice *Gen Mgt* the most effective and efficient method of achieving any objective or task. What constitutes best practice can be determined through a process of *benchmarking*. An organisation can move towards achieving best practice, either across the whole organisation or in a specific area, through **continuous improvement**. In production-based organisations, **world class manufacturing** is a related concept. More generally, a market or sector leader may be described as **best-in-class**.

best value *Gen Mgt* a UK government initiative intended to ensure cost efficiency and effectiveness in the delivery of public services by local authorities. The best value initiative was announced in early 1997 to replace compulsory competitive tendering (CCT), and pilot schemes in selected local authorities began in April 1998. The Local Government Act 1999 requires councils, as part of the best value process, to review all services over a five-year period, setting standards and performance indicators for each service, comparing performance with that of other bodies, and undertaking consultation with local taxpayers and service users.

beta *Fin* a numerical measure of the change in value of something such as a stock

beta coefficient *Fin* an indication of the level of risk attached to a share. A high beta coefficient indicates that a share is likely to be more sensitive to market movements.

beta factor *Fin* The measure of the volatility of the return on a share relative to the market. If a share price were to rise or fall at double the market rate, it would have a beta factor of 2.0. Conversely, if the share price moved at half the market rate, the beta factor would be 0.5. The beta factor is defined mathematically as a share's covariance with the market portfolio divided by the variance of the market portfolio.

beta rating *Fin* a means of measuring the volatility (or risk) of a stock or fund in comparison with the market as a whole.

The beta of a stock or fund can be of any value, positive or negative, but usually is between +0.25 and +1.75. Stocks of many utilities have a beta of less than 1. Conversely, most high-tech NASDAQ-based stocks have a beta greater than 1; they offer a higher rate of return but are also risky.

Both alpha and beta ratings should be readily available upon request from investment firms, because the figures appear in standard performance reports. It is always best to ask for them, because beta calculations can involve mathematical complexities. *See also* **alpha rating**

beta software *E-com* a version of a software product that is almost ready for release but needs more testing. It is possible to download beta software on the Internet free, as software companies like to test their products on members of the public before they are put on the market.

beta test *E-com* a test of a new or upgraded piece of computer software or hardware carried out by a few chosen customers before it is released to the public

BFH *Fin* Bundesfinanzhof: in Germany, the supreme court for issues concerning taxation

Bhd *abbr Fin* Berhad

BHP *abbr Gen Mgt* Broken Hill Proprietary Company Ltd: Australia's largest manufacturing company. Also known as **Big Australian**.

bias *Stats* inaccuracy or deviation in inferences, results, or a statistical method

bid *Fin* an offer to buy all or a majority of the capital shares of a company in an attempted takeover, or the highest price a prospective bidder is prepared to pay

bid-ask quote *Fin* a statement of the prices that are being offered and asked for a security or option contract

bid-ask spread *Fin* the difference between the buying and the selling prices of a traded commodity or a financial instrument

bid bond *Fin* a guarantee by a financial institution of the fulfilment of an international tender offer

---

bidding war *Fin* a competition between prospective buyers who successively offer more than each other for the same stock or security

bid form *Fin* in the United States, a form containing details of an offer to underwrite municipal bonds

bid-offer spread *Fin* the difference between the highest price that a buyer is prepared to offer and the lowest price that a seller is prepared to accept

bid price *Fin* the price a stock exchange dealer will pay for a security or option contract

bid-to-cover ratio *Fin* a number that shows how many more people wanted to buy US Treasury bills than actually did buy them

bid up *Fin* to bid for something merely to increase its price, or to make successive increases to the bid price for a security so that unopened orders do not remain unexecuted

Big Australian *(ANZ) Gen Mgt see* **BHP**

Big Bang *Fin* radical changes to practices on the London Stock Exchange implemented in October 1986. Fixed commission charges were abolished, leading to an alteration in the structure of the market, and the right of member firms to act as market makers as well as agents was also abolished. *(slang)*

big bath *Fin* the practice of making a particular year's poor income statement look even worse by increasing expenses and selling assets. Subsequent years will then appear much better in comparison. *(slang)*

Big Board *Fin* the New York Stock Exchange *(slang)*. *See also* **Little Board**

big business *Gen Mgt* powerful business interests or companies in general. The term is particularly used when referring to *large-sized businesses* or *multinational businesses*.

Big Four *(ANZ) Fin* Australia's four largest banks: the Commonwealth Bank of Australia, Westpac Banking Corporation, National Australia Bank, and ANZ Bank

Big GAAP *Fin* the *Generally Accepted Accounting Principles* that apply to large companies *(slang)*

big picture *Gen Mgt* an informal term for a broad perspective on an issue that encompasses its surrounding context and long-term implications

big swinging dick *Fin* a very successful financial trader *(slang)*

bilateral facility *Fin* a loan by one bank to one borrower

bilateral monopoly *Econ* a market in which there is a single seller and a single buyer

bilateral trade *Econ* trade between two countries who give each other specific privileges such as favourable import quotas that are denied to other trading partners

bill *Fin* **1.** an invoice **2.** to send an invoice

bill broker *Fin* somebody who buys and sells promissory notes and bills of exchange

bill discount *Fin* the interest rate that the Bank of England charges banks for short-term loans. This establishes a de facto floor for the interest rate that banks charge their customers, usually a fraction above the discount rate.

bill discounting rate *Fin* the amount by which the price of a US Treasury bill is reduced to reflect expected changes in interest rates

billing cycle *Fin* a period of time, often one month, between successive requests for payment

bill of entry *Fin* a statement of the nature and value of goods to be imported or exported, prepared by the shipper and presented to a customs house

bill of exchange *Fin* an unconditional order in writing from one person (the drawer) to another (the drawee and signatory), requiring the drawee to pay on demand a sum to a specified person (the payee) or bearer. It is now usually used in overseas trade and the drawee may be a bank as opposed to an importer.

The supplier or drawer usually submits the bill with the relative shipping documents. It is then anticipated by the drawee either as the agreed or implied method of payment. On receipt, the drawee either makes the required payment, or if payment is to be made at a future date, indicates acceptance by signing it.

Wording on the bill will state when payment has to be made, for example, '60 days after date, we promise to pay. . .' means 60 days after the date of the bill; '60 days after sight, we promise to pay. . .' means 60 days after acceptance; and **at sight** means the bill is payable upon presentation.

Once accepted, a bill of exchange is a negotiable instrument. The drawer can therefore obtain the money it represents by selling it to a financial institution at a discount. In the United Kingdom, the complex statutory law relating to these instruments is found in the Bills of Exchange Act (1882).

bill of goods *Fin* a consignment of goods, or a statement of their nature and value

bill of lading *Fin* a statement of the nature and value of goods being transported, especially by ship, along with the conditions applying to their transport. Drawn up by the carrier, this document serves as a contract between the owner of the goods and the carrier.

bill of materials *Fin* a specification of the materials and parts required to make a product

bill of sale *Fin* a document confirming the transfer of goods or services from a seller to a buyer

bill payable *Fin* a bill of exchange or promissory note payable

bill receivable *Fin* a bill of exchange or promissory note receivable

binary thinker *Gen Mgt* somebody who thinks only in absolute, black-and-white terms (*slang*)

bin card *Fin* a record of receipts, issues, and balances of the quantity of an item of stock handled by a store

bingo card *Mkting* a postcard advertisement for a product that is bound into a publication and can be returned to the manufacturer for additional information on the product (*slang*)

biodata *HR* **1.** information taken from an *application form*, *curriculum vitae*, or questionnaire concerning an employee's or potential employee's background and experience that is objectively scored by recruiters to predict job performance **2.** a potted biography placed in a periodical article or conference paper

biological assets *Fin* farm animals and plants classified as assets. International Accounting Standards require that they are recorded on balance sheets at market value. Once they have been slaughtered or harvested, the assets become **agricultural produce**.

biometrics *E-com* the study of measurable biological characteristics, or in computer security, authentication techniques that use characteristics such as speech, fingerprints, or scans of the human eye

biomimicry *Gen Mgt* the use in business of processes that imitate natural ones to reduce waste and limit impact on the environment

biorhythm *HR* any recurring biological cycle thought to affect the physical or mental state of a person, particularly patterns of digestion, sleep, and fatigue

BiRiLiG *Fin* Bilanzrichtliniengesetz: the 1985 German accounting directives law

birth-death ratio *Stats* the ratio of the number of births to the number of deaths in a population over a period of time such as 10 years

BIS *abbr Fin* Bank for International Settlements: a bank that promotes co-operation between central banks, provides facilities for international financial operations, and acts as agent or trustee in international financial settlements. The

17-member board of directors consists of the governors of the central banks of Belgium, Canada, France, Germany, Italy, Japan, the Netherlands, Sweden, Switzerland, the United Kingdom, and the United States.

bit *E-com* **1.** a binary digit number (0 or 1), the smallest unit of computerised data **2.** an item of information or knowledge

bivariate data *Stats* data in which two variables are involved in each subject

bivariate distribution *Stats* a form of distribution involving two random variables

black
in the black *Fin* making profit, or having more assets than debt (*slang*)

black-box engineering *Ops* the manufacturing of a component in which the supplier has total control over the design and content of the component and the purchaser knows only its external and physical specifications. The term black-box engineering is derived from the fact that the component in question appears as a black box on the design drawings for the purchaser.

black chip (*S Africa*) *Gen Mgt* a company that is owned or managed by black people, or is controlled by black shareholders

black economic empowerment (*S Africa*) *Gen Mgt* the promotion of black ownership and control of South Africa's economic assets

black economy *Econ* economic activity that is not declared for tax purposes and is usually carried out in exchange for cash

black hole *Gen Mgt* a project that consumes unlimited amounts of resources without yielding any profit (*slang*)

black knight *Gen Mgt see* **knight**

black market *Gen Mgt* an illegal *market*, usually for goods that are in short supply. Black market trading breaks government regulations or legislation and is particularly prevalent during times of shortage, such as rationing, or in industries that are very highly regulated, such as pharmaceuticals or armaments. *Also known as* **shadow market**

black market economy *Fin* a system of illegal trading in officially controlled goods, or an illicit secondary currency market that has rates markedly different from those in the official market

Black Monday *Fin* either of two Mondays, 29 October 1929 or 19 October 1987, that were marked by the largest stock market declines of the 20th century. Although both market crashes originated in the United States, they were immediately followed by similar market crashes around the world.

black money *Econ* money circulating in the *black economy* in payment for goods and services

Black Tuesday *Fin* 29 October 1929, when values of stocks fell precipitously

Blake, Robert (*b*. 1918) *Gen Mgt* US psychologist. Collaborated with *Jane Mouton* on the development of *The Managerial Grid*™ (1964), a framework for understanding managerial behaviour.

blamestorming *Gen Mgt* group discussion as to the reasons why a project has failed or is late and who is to blame for it. The term is modelled on 'brainstorming'. (*slang*)

blame-time *Gen Mgt* the moment in an organisation when blame for the failure of a project or task is publicly allocated (*slang*)

Blanchard, Kenneth (*b*. 1939) *Gen Mgt* US academic. Best known for his concept of one-minute management. *The One Minute Manager* (1982), co-written with *Spencer Johnson*, became a bestseller in the tradition of management self-help books alongside those by *Dale Carnegie* and *Stephen Covey*.

blanket bond *Fin* an insurance policy that covers a financial institution for losses caused by the actions of its employees

One of the greatest pains to a human being is the pain of a new idea. Walter Bagehot

bleed *Mkting* an area of a piece of printed material that extends beyond given margins or its edges

blended rate *Fin* an interest rate charged by a lender that is between an old rate and a new one

blind carbon copy *Gen Mgt see bcc*

blind certificate *E-com* a *cookie* from which the user's name is omitted so as to protect his or her privacy while making collected data available for marketing studies

blind entry *Fin* **1.** (*ANZ*) a document issued by a supplier that stipulates the amount charged for goods or services as well as the amount of GST payable **2.** a bookkeeping entry that records a debit or credit but fails to show other essential information

blind offer *Mkting* an inconspicuous offer buried in the body copy of a print advertisement, often used to determine the degree of reader attention to the advertisement

blind pool *Fin* a limited partnership in which the investment opportunities the general partner plans to pursue are not specified

blindside *Mkting* to attack somebody in a way that he or she cannot anticipate (*slang*)

blind trust *Fin* a trust that manages somebody's business interests, with contents that are unknown to the beneficiary. People assuming public office use such trusts to avoid conflicts of interest.

block diagram *Stats* a diagram that represents statistical data by rectangular blocks

blocked account *Fin* a bank account from which funds cannot be withdrawn for any of a number of reasons, for example, bankruptcy proceedings, liquidation of a company, or government order when freezing foreign assets

blocked currency *Fin* a currency that people cannot easily trade for other currencies because of foreign exchange control

blocked funds *Fin* money that cannot be transferred from one place to another, usually because of *exchange controls* imposed by the government of the country in which the funds are held

block grant *Fin* money that the government gives to local authorities to fund local services

blockholder *Fin* an individual or institutional investor who holds a large number of shares of stock or a large monetary value of bonds in a given company

block investment (*ANZ*) *Fin* the purchase or holding of a large number of shares of stock or a large monetary value of bonds in a given company

block release *HR* an arrangement whereby an employer permits an employee to be away from work to attend an educational institution for a period of time, usually several weeks

block trade *Fin* a sale of a large round number of stocks or amount of bonds

blow-in *Mkting* advertising in the form of cards bound inside magazines or newspapers (*slang*)

blow-off top *Fin* a rapid increase in the price of a financial stock followed by an equally rapid drop in price (*slang*)

bludge (*ANZ*) *Gen Mgt* to shirk work or responsibility, or live off the earnings of others

blue chip *Gen Mgt* relating to the highest-quality and lowest-risk ordinary equity shares or to high-quality established stable companies. The term is derived from the game of poker, in which blue is the highest value chip.

blue-chip stocks *Fin* ordinary shares of stock in a company that is considered to be well established, highly successful, and reliable, and is traded on a stock market

blue-collar job *HR* a position that involves mainly physical labour. With the decline in manufacturing and an increase in harmonisation agreements, the term blue-collar is now rarely used. Blue-collar refers to the blue overalls traditionally worn in factories in contrast to the white shirt and tie supposedly worn by an office worker, known as a *white-collar worker*.

blue-collar worker *HR* somebody whose job involves mainly physical labour

blue hair (*US*) *Mkting* used in advertising and marketing to refer to elderly women customers (*slang*)

blueshirt (*US*) *Gen Mgt* an employee of the computer company IBM (*slang*)

blue-sky ideas *Gen Mgt* extremely ambitious, idealistic, or unrealistic proposals, apparently unconfined by conventional thinking (*slang*)

blue-sky law *Fin* a US state law that regulates investments to prevent investors from being defrauded

blue-sky securities *Fin* stocks and bonds that have no value, being worth the same as a piece of 'blue sky' (*slang*)

blur *Gen Mgt* a period of transition for a business in which changes occur at great speed and on a large scale

board *Gen Mgt see* **board of directors**

board dismissal *Gen Mgt* the dismissal and removal from power of an entire **board** or **board of directors**

Board of Currency Commissioners *Fin* the sole currency issuing authority in Singapore, established in 1967. *Abbr* **BCCS**

Board of Customs and Excise *Fin* in the United Kingdom, the government department responsible for administering and collecting indirect taxes, such as customs and excise duties and Value Added Tax. It also prepares UK overseas trade statistics.

board of directors *Gen Mgt* the people selected to sit on an authoritative standing committee or governing body, taking responsibility for the management of an organisation. Members of the board of directors are officially chosen by shareholders, but in practice they are usually selected on the basis of the current board's recommendations. The board usually includes major shareholders as well as directors of the company. *Also known as* **board**

Board of Inland Revenue *Fin* in the United Kingdom, the government department responsible for the administration and collection of the main direct taxes, such as income tax. Its duties include appointing tax inspectors, advising on new legislation, and providing statistical information. *Also known as* **Inland Revenue**

board of trustees *Gen Mgt* a committee or governing body that takes responsibility for managing, and holds in trust, funds, assets, or property belonging to others, for example, charitable or pension funds or assets

boardroom *Gen Mgt* a room in which board meetings are held. A boardroom may be a room used only for board meetings or can be a multi-use room that becomes a boardroom for the duration of a board meeting.

boardroom battle *Gen Mgt* a conflict or power struggle between individual board members or between groups of board members

board seat *Gen Mgt* a position of membership of a board, especially a **board of directors**

board secretary *Gen Mgt see* **company secretary**

body corporate *Fin* an association, such as a company or institution, that is legally authorised to act as if it were one person

body language *HR* the combination of often subconscious gestures, postures, and facial expressions that send out messages about a person's feelings and emotions. Body language is an important aspect of **non-verbal communication**.

---

body of creditors *Fin* the creditors of a company or individual treated as a single creditor in dealing with the debtor

body of shareholders *Fin* the shareholders of a company treated as a single shareholder in dealing with the company

BOGOF *Mkting* buy one get one free, a sales promotion technique in which consumers are offered two products for the price of one

bogus degree *HR* a qualification awarded by an organisation of questionable or unrecognised standing, usually capitalising on the naivety of overseas students and the reputation of the education system of the host country. A bogus degree is normally offered by an organisation that has adopted a similar sounding name to a university of good standing.

boilerplate (*US*) *Gen Mgt* a standard version of a contract that can be used interchangeably from contract to contract (*slang*)

bona fide *Fin* used to describe a sale or purchase that has been carried out in good faith, without collusion or fraud

bona vacantia *Fin* the goods of a person who has died intestate and has no traceable living relatives. In the United Kingdom, these goods become the property of the state.

bond *Fin* **1.** a promise to repay with interest on specified dates money that an investor lends a company or government **2.** a certificate issued by a company or government that promises repayment of borrowed money at a set rate of interest on a particular date.

Short-term bonds mature in up to three years, intermediate-term bonds in three to ten years, and long-term bonds in more than ten years, with 30 years generally being the upper limit. Longer-term bonds are considered a higher risk because interest rates are certain to change during their lifetime. They tend to pay higher interest rates to attract investors and reward them for the additional risk.

Bonds are traded on the open market, just like stocks. They are reliable economic indicators, but perform in the reverse direction to interest rates: if bond prices are rising, interest rates and stock markets are likely to be falling, while if interest rates have gone up since a bond was first issued, prices of new bonds will fall. **3.** (*ANZ*) a sum of money paid as a deposit, especially on rented premises **4.** (*S Africa*) a mortgage bond

bond anticipation note *Fin* a loan that a government agency receives to provide capital that will be repaid from the proceeds of bonds that the agency will issue later

bond covenant *Fin* part of a bond contract whereby the lender promises not to do certain things, for example, borrow beyond a particular limit

bonded warehouse *Fin* a warehouse that holds goods awaiting duty or tax to be paid on them

bond equivalent yield *Fin* the interest rate that an investor would have to receive on a bond to profit as much as from investment in another type of security. *Also known as* **equivalent bond yield**

bond fund *Fin* a unit trust that invests in bonds

bondholder *Fin* an individual or institution owning bonds issued by a government or company and entitled to payments of the interest as due and return of the principal when the bond matures

bond indenture *Fin* a document that specifies the terms of a bond

bond indexing *Fin* the practice of investing in bonds in such a way as to match the yield of a designated index

bond issue *Fin* additional shares of stock in a company given by the company to existing shareholders in proportion to their prior holding

bond quote *Fin* a statement of the current market price of a bond

bond swap *Fin* an exchange of some bonds for others, usually to gain tax advantage or to diversify a portfolio

---

A man of action forced into a state of thought is unhappy until he can get out of it.
John Galsworthy

bond value *Fin* the value of an asset or liability recorded in the accounts of an entity

bond-washing *Fin* the practice of selling a bond before its dividend is due and buying it back later in order to avoid paying tax

bond yield *Fin* the annual return on a bond (the rate of interest) expressed as a percentage of the current market price of the bond. Bonds can tie up investors' money for periods of up to 30 years, so knowing their yield is a critical investment consideration.

EXAMPLE Bond yield is calculated by multiplying the face value of the bond by its stated annual rate of interest, expressed as a decimal. For example, buying a new ten-year £1,000 bond that pays 6% interest will produce an annual yield amount of £60:

$$1,000 \times 0.060 = 60$$

The £60 will be paid as £30 every six months. At the end of ten years, the purchaser will have earned £600, and will also be repaid the original £1,000. Because the bond was purchased when it was first issued, the 6% is also called the 'yield to maturity'.

This basic formula is complicated by other factors. First is the 'time-value of money' theory: money paid in the future is worth less than money paid today. A more detailed computation of total bond yield requires the calculation of the present value of the interest earned each year. Second, changing interest rates have a marked impact on bond trading and, ultimately, on yield. Changes in interest rates cannot affect the interest paid by bonds already issued, but they do affect the prices of new bonds.

bonus *HR* a financial incentive given to employees in addition to their *basic pay* in the form of a one-off payment or as part of a *bonus scheme*

bonus dividend *Fin* a one-off extra dividend in addition to the usual twice-yearly payment

bonus issue *Fin* additional shares of stock in a company given by the company to existing shareholders in proportion to their prior holding

bonus offer *Mkting* a sales promotion technique offering consumers an additional amount of product for the basic price

bonus scheme *HR* a form of *incentive scheme* under which a *bonus* is paid to employees in accordance with rules concerning eligibility, performance targets, time period, and size and form of payments. A bonus scheme may apply to some or all employees and may be determined on organisation, business unit, or individual performance, or on a combination of these. A bonus payment may be expressed as a percentage of salary or as a flat-rate sum.

bonus shares *Fin* **1.** *see scrip issue* **2.** in the United Kingdom, extra shares paid by the government as a reward to founding shareholders who did not sell their initial holding within a certain number of years

book-building *Fin* the research done among potential institutional investors to determine the optimum offering price for a new issue of stock

book cost *Fin* the price paid for a stock, including any commissions

book-entry *Fin* an accounting entry indicated in a record somewhere but not represented by any document

book inventory *Fin* the number of items in stock according to accounting records. This number can be validated only by a physical count of the items.

bookkeeper *Fin* a person who is responsible for maintaining the financial records of a business

bookkeeping *Fin* the activity or profession of recording the money received and spent by an individual, business, or organisation

bookkeeping barter *Fin* the direct exchange of goods between two parties without the use of money as a medium, but using monetary measures to record the transaction

---

Labour is the superior of capital and deserves much the higher consideration.
Abraham Lincoln

bookmark[1] *E-com* a web-browser software tool that enables users to select and store pages they are likely to return to, so that they can be accessed quickly and conveniently. On Microsoft Internet Explorer (the most popular web browser) this function is referred to as 'Favorites'.

bookmark[2] *Gen Mgt* to make a mental note to remember somebody or something for future reference (*slang*)

book of account *Fin* the ledgers and journals used in the preparation of financial statements

book of prime/original entry *Fin* a chronological record of a business's transactions arranged according to type, for example, cash or sales. The books are then used to generate entries in a double-entry bookkeeping system.

books of prime entry *Fin* a first record of transactions, such as sales or purchases, from which either detail or totals, as appropriate, are transferred to the ledgers

book-to-bill ratio *Fin* a ratio of the value of orders that a company has received to the amount for which it has billed its customers

book transfer *Fin* a transfer of ownership of a security without physical transfer of any document that represents the instrument

book value *Fin* the value of a company's stock according to the company itself, which may differ considerably from the market value. *Also known as* ***carrying amount***, ***carrying value***
EXAMPLE It is calculated by subtracting a company's liabilities and the value of its debt and preference shares from its total assets. All of these figures appear on a company's balance sheet. For example:

	£
Total assets	1,300
Current liabilities	−400
Long-term liabilities, preference shares	−250
Book value	**= 650**

Book value per share is calculated by dividing the book value by the number of shares in issue. If our example is expressed in millions of pounds and the company has 35 million shares outstanding, book value per share would be £650 million divided by 35 million:

650 / 35 = £18.57 book value per share
Book value represents a company's net worth to its shareholders. When compared with its market value, book value helps reveal how a company is regarded by the investment community. A market value that is notably higher than book value indicates that investors have a high regard for the company. A market value that is, for example, a multiple of book value suggests that investors' regard may be unreasonably high.

book value per share *Fin* the value of one share of a stock according to the company itself, which may differ considerably from the market value

Boolean search *E-com* a search allowing the inclusion or exclusion of documents containing certain words through the use of operators such as AND, NOT, and OR

boomerang worker *HR* an employee who returns to work for a previous employer (*slang*)

boot camp (*US*) *HR* an ***induction*** or orientation programme for new employees, designed to push recruits to their limits. Boot camps are modelled on the basic training of the US Marine Corps and aim to immerse new employees in the ***corporate culture*** of the employer, as well as transferring knowledge about technical skills.

bootstrapping *Gen Mgt* the early stages of setting up a new business, when a lot of effort is required (*slang*)

border crosser *HR* a multiskilled employee who is able to move from job to job within a company (*slang*)

borderless world *E-com* the global economy considered as having had barriers to international trade removed by use of the Internet

---

There is no end to what you can accomplish if you don't care who gets the credit.
Florence Luscomb

border tax adjustment *Fin* the application of a domestic tax on imported goods while exempting exported goods from the tax in an effort to make the exported goods' price competitive both nationally and internationally

borrowing costs *Fin* expenses, for example, interest payments, incurred from taking out a loan or any other form of borrowing. In the United States, such costs are included in the total cost of the asset whereas in the United Kingdom, and in International Accounting Standards, this is optional.

bosberaad (*S Africa*) *Gen Mgt* **1.** a *think tank*, *strategy*, or long-term planning meeting. *Also known as* **lekgotla 2.** a meeting of leaders at a remote place to avoid distractions. The word means literally 'bush summit'.

boss *Gen Mgt* the person in charge of a job, process, department, or organisation, more formally known as a *manager* or *supervisor*

Boston Box *Gen Mgt* a model used for analysing a company's potential by plotting *market share* against growth rate. The Boston Box was conceived by the Boston Consulting Group in the 1970s to help in the process of assessing in which businesses a company should invest in and of which it should divest itself. A business with a high market share and high growth rate is a *star*, and one with a low market share and low growth rate is a *dog*. A high market share with low growth rate is characteristic of a *cash cow*, which could yield significant but short-term gain, and a low market share coupled with high growth rate produces a **question mark company**, which offers a doubtful return on investment. To be useful, this model requires accurate assessment of a business's strengths and weaknesses, which may be difficult to obtain.

Boston Consulting Group matrix *Fin* a representation of an organisation's product or service offerings which shows the value of product sales (depicted by the area of a circle) expressed in relation to the growth rate of the market served and the market share held. The objective of the matrix is to assist in the allocation of funds to projects.

bottleneck *Ops* a limiting factor on the rate of an operation. A workstation operating at its maximum *capacity* becomes a bottleneck if the rate of production elsewhere in the plant increases, but throughput at that workstation cannot be increased to meet demand. An understanding of bottlenecks is important if the efficiency and capacity of an *assembly line* are to be increased. The techniques of *fishbone charts*, **Pareto charts**, and *flow charts* can be used to identify where and why bottlenecks occur.

bottom fisher *Fin* an investor who searches for bargains among stocks that have recently dropped in price (*slang*)

bottom line 1. *Fin* the net profit or loss that a company makes at the end of a given period of time, used in the calculation of the earnings-per-share business ratio **2.** *Gen Mgt* work that produces net gain for an organisation

bottom-of-the-harbour scheme (*ANZ*) *Fin* a tax avoidance strategy that involves stripping a company of assets then selling it a number of times so that it is hard to trace

bottom out *Fin* to reach the lowest level in the downward trend of the market price of securities or commodities before the price begins an upward trend again

bottom-up *Fin* relating to an approach to investing that seeks to identify individual companies that are fundamentally sound and whose shares will perform well regardless of general economic or industry-group trends

bottom-up approach *Gen Mgt* a consultative *leadership* style that promotes *employee participation* at all levels in *decision-making* and *problem-solving*. A bottom-up approach to leadership is associated with *flat organisations* and the *empowerment* of employees. It can encourage *creativity* and flexibility and is the opposite of a *top-down approach*.

bottom-up budgeting *Fin* see *participative budgeting*

bought-in goods *Ops* components and sub-assemblies that are purchased from an outside supplier instead of being made within the organisation

bounce *Fin* to refuse payment of a cheque because the account for which it is written holds insufficient money (*slang*) *Also known as* **dishonour**

bounced cheque *Fin* a draft on an account that a bank will not honour, usually because there are insufficient funds in the account

bourse *Fin* a European stock exchange, especially the one in Paris

boutique investment house *Fin* see *niche player*

box
think outside the box *Gen Mgt* to think imaginatively about a problem (*slang*)

box spread *Fin* an arbitrage strategy that eliminates risk by buying and selling the same thing

Boyatzis, Richard Eleftherios (*b*. 1946) *Gen Mgt* US academic. One of the key movers of the *competence* movement. His book, *The Competent Manager* (1982), acknowledged *David McClelland*'s earlier work.

BPR *abbr Gen Mgt* business process re-engineering

bracket creep (*US*) *Fin* the way in which a gradual increase in income moves somebody into a higher tax bracket

Brady bond *Fin* a bond issued by an emerging nation that has US Treasury bonds as collateral

braindrain *Gen Mgt* the overseas migration of specialists, usually highly qualified scientists, engineers, or technical experts, in pursuit of higher salaries, better research funding, and a perceived higher quality of working life

brainiac *HR* a highly intelligent and creative employee who is also unpredictable and eccentric (*slang*)

brainstorming *Gen Mgt* a technique for generating ideas, developing *creativity*, or *problem-solving* in small groups, through the free-flowing contributions of participants. The concept of brainstorming was originated by A. F. Osborn and described in his book *Applied Imagination: Principles and Practices of Creative Thinking* (1957). To encourage the free flow of ideas, brainstorming sessions operate according to a set of guidelines, and the production and evaluation of ideas are kept separate. Several variations of brainstorming and related techniques have emerged such as **brainwriting**, where ideas are written down by individuals, and *buzz groups*.

brainwriting *Gen Mgt* see **brainstorming**

branch accounts *Fin* the *books of account* or *financial statements* for the component parts of a business, especially those that are located in a different region or country than the main enterprise

branch office *Fin* a bank or other financial institution that is part of a larger group and is located in a different part of a geographical area from the parent organisation

branch tax *Fin* a South African tax imposed on non-resident companies that register a branch rather than a separate company

brand *Mkting* the distinguishing proprietary name, symbol, or *trademark* that differentiates a particular product, or service, from others of a similar nature

brand awareness *Mkting* the level of *brand recognition* that consumers have of a particular brand and its specific product category. Brand awareness examines three levels of recognition: whether the brand name is the first to come to mind when a consumer is questioned about a particular product category; whether the brand name is one of several that come to mind when a consumer is questioned about a particular product category; and

---

Despair is the prize one pays for setting oneself an impossible aim. Graham Greene

whether or not a consumer has heard of a particular brand name.

brand building *Mkting* the establishment and improvement of a brand's identity, including giving the brand a set of values that the consumer wants, recognises, identifies with, and trusts. Values developed in the process of brand building include psychological, physical, and functional properties that consumers desire and should always identify a property that is unique to that brand.

brand champion *Mkting* an employee of an organisation who is responsible for the development, performance, and communication of a particular brand

brand equity *Mkting* the estimated value of a *brand*

brand extension *Mkting* the exploitation, diversification, or stretching of a brand to revive or reinvigorate it in the marketplace. Products developed in the brand extension process may be directly recognisable derivatives or may look and feel completely different.

brand image *Mkting* the perception that consumers have of a brand. Brand image is usually carefully developed by the brand owner through marketing campaigns or product positioning. Occasionally, the image of a brand may develop spontaneously through customer responses to a product. The image of a brand can be seriously tarnished through inappropriate advertising or association with somebody or something that has fallen from public favour.

branding *Mkting* a means of distinguishing one firm's products or services from another's and of creating and maintaining an image that encourages confidence in the quality and performance of that firm's products or services

brand leader *Mkting* the brand with the largest *market share*

brand life cycle *Mkting* the three phases through which brands pass as they are introduced, grow, and then decline. The three stages of the brand life cycle are: the introductory period, during which the brand is developed and is introduced to the market; the growth period, when the brand faces competition from other products of a similar nature; and, finally, the maturity period in which the brand either extends to other products or its image is constantly updated. Without careful *brand management*, the maturity period can lead to decline and result in the brand being withdrawn. Similar stages can be observed in the *product life cycle*.

brand loyalty *Mkting* a long-term customer preference for a particular product or service. Brand loyalty can be produced by factors such as customer satisfaction with the performance or price of a specific product or service, or through identifying with a *brand image*. It can be encouraged by *advertising*.

brand management *Mkting* the marketing of one or more proprietary products. Brand managers (see *product management*) have responsibility for the promotion and marketing of one or more commercial brands. This includes setting targets, advertising, and retailing, and coordinating all related activities to achieve those targets. In the case of multiple brand management, consideration needs be given to questions relating to the treatment of the brands as equal or as having some differentiating value. This may affect the amount of resources committed to each brand.

brand manager *Mkting see brand management*

brand positioning *Mkting* the development of a brand's position in the market by heightening customer perception of the brand's superiority over other brands of a similar nature. Brand positioning relies on the identification of a real strength or value that has a clear advantage over the nearest competitor and is easily communicated to the consumer.

brand recognition *Mkting* a measurement of the ability of consumers to recall their experience or knowledge of a particular brand. Brand recognition forms part of *brand awareness*.

brand value *Mkting* the amount that a brand is worth in terms of income, potential income, reputation, prestige, and market value. Brands with a high value are regarded as considerable assets to a company, so that when a company is sold, a brand with high value may be worth more than any other consideration.

brand wagon *Mkting* the trend towards using branding in marketing concepts and techniques (*slang*)

brandwidth *Mkting* the degree to which a brand of product or service is recognised (*slang*)

Branson, Sir Richard (*b*. 1950) *Gen Mgt* British entrepreneur. Chairman of the Virgin Group, whose dominant *corporate strategy* has been to enter a variety of industries and challenge the existing leaders, using his flair for publicity. This *diversification* strategy is balanced by that of limiting *risk*. Branson's approach is explained in *Losing My Virginity: The Autobiography* (1998).

BRB *abbr Gen Mgt* be right back (*slang*)

breach of contract *Gen Mgt* a refusal or failure to carry out an obligation imposed by a *contract*

breadth-of-market theory *Fin* the theory that the health of a market is measured by the relative volume of items traded that are going up or down in price

breakeven *Mkting* the point at which revenue equals costs

breakeven analysis *Gen Mgt* a method for determining the point at which fixed and variable production costs are equalled by sales revenue and where neither a profit nor a loss is made. Usually illustrated graphically through the use of a *breakeven chart*, breakeven analysis can be used to aid *decision-making*, set product prices, and determine the effects of changes in production or sales volume on costs and profits.

breakeven chart *Gen Mgt* a management aid used in conjunction with *breakeven analysis* to calculate the point at which fixed and variable production costs are met by incoming revenue. Lines are plotted to indicate expected sales revenue and production costs. The point at which lines intersect marks the *breakeven point* where no profit or loss is made.

breakeven point *Fin* the point or level of financial activity at which expenditure equals income, or the value of an investment equals its cost so that the result is neither a profit nor a loss

breaking-down time *Fin* the period required to return a workstation to a standard condition after completion of an operation

breakout 1. *Fin* a rise in a security's price above its previous highest price, or a drop below its former lowest price, taken by technical analysts to signal a continuing move in that direction **2.** *Gen Mgt* a summary or breakdown of data that has been collected

breakthrough strategy *Gen Mgt* a strategy that achieves significant new results

break-up value *Fin* the combined market value of a firm's assets if each were sold separately as contrasted with selling the firm as an ongoing business. Analysts look for companies with a large break-up value relative to their market value to identify potential takeover targets.

Brech, Edward Francis Leopold (*b*. 1909) *Gen Mgt* British manager, writer, and historian. A publiciser and developer of the theories of *Henri Fayol* and *Frederick Winslow Taylor*, in common with *Lyndall Urwick*. Brech's *Principles and Practice of Management* (1953), sets down a structural and functional approach to management. In the 1990s, Brech completed a history of British management.

Bretton Woods *Econ* an agreement signed at a conference at Bretton Woods in

---

the United States in July 1944 that set up the *IMF* and the *IBRD*

bribery *HR* the act of persuading somebody to exercise his or her business judgment in your favour by offering cash or a gift and thereby gaining an unfair advantage. Many organisations have *codes of conduct* that expressly forbid the soliciting or payment of bribes.

brick
hit the bricks (*US*) *Gen Mgt* to go out on strike (*slang*)

bricks-and-mortar *E-com* relating to a traditional business not involved in e-commerce and incurring the cost of physical structures such as warehouses

bricolage *E-com* the opportunistic way in which the Web is put together, with Web designers being able to take *GIFs*, formats, and links from elsewhere on the Web to create new pages

bridge financing *Fin* borrowing that the borrower expects to repay with the proceeds of later larger loans. *See also* ***takeout financing***

bridge loan (*US*) *Fin* = ***bridging loan***

bridging *Fin* the obtaining of a short-term loan to provide a continuing source of financing in anticipation of receiving an intermediate- or long-term loan. Bridging is routinely employed to finance the purchase or construction of a new building or property until an old one is sold.

bridging loan *Fin* a temporary loan providing funds until further money is received, for example, for buying one property while trying to sell another. *US* term ***bridge loan***

brief *Mkting* a document or set of instructions issued to somebody as guidance in developing a marketing or advertising proposal. A brief should be as comprehensive as possible, covering all aspects of the project: background, objectives, research, media, competitors, product information, and the target audience at which it is aimed. If possible, the objectives should be measurable, so the success

or otherwise of the project can be assessed.

briefing group *HR see* ***team briefing***

Briggs, Katherine Cook (1875–1968) *Gen Mgt* US researcher. Inventor, together with her daughter, ***Isabel Briggs-Myers***, of the *Myers-Briggs type indicator*.

Briggs-Myers, Isabel (1897–1980) *Gen Mgt* US researcher. Inventor, together with her mother, ***Katherine Cook Briggs***, of the *Myers-Briggs type indicator*.

brightsizing *HR* the reduction of staff numbers within a company by making the mostly recently recruited employees redundant, an unintentional byproduct of which being that often the most highly capable or qualified employees are lost (*slang*)

bring forward *Fin* to carry a sum from one column or page to the next

Brisch system *Ops* a coding system developed principally for the engineering industry by E. G. Brisch and Partners in which a code is assigned to every item of resources, including materials, labour, and equipment.

British Accounting Association *Fin* in the United Kingdom, the main professional accounting body, founded in 1947. As well as promoting accounting education and research, it also organises conferences and publishes *The British Accounting Review*.

broadband *E-com* a class of transmission system that allows large amounts of data to be transferred at high speed

broadbanding *HR* the reworking of the pay hierarchy into fewer, wider *pay scales*. Broadbanding provides a more flexible reward structure that is more in tune with the *flat organisation*. Pioneered by GEC in the United States, the introduction of broadbanding can provide a method for pay increases and *career development*, even without a formal career ladder, and consequently can help improve *motivation*.

brochure *Fin* a booklet or pamphlet that contains descriptive information or advertising, for example, in relation to a product or property for sale, or an available service

brochureware *E-com* a website that is the online equivalent of a printed brochure providing information about products and services. The term is most often used in a derogatory way to refer to electronic advertising for planned but non-existent products.

broker¹ *Gen Mgt* to act as an agent in arranging a deal, sale, or contract

broker² *Fin* a person who acts as a financial agent in arranging a deal, sale, or contract

brokerage *Fin* **1.** a company whose business is buying and selling stocks and bonds for its clients **2.** the business of being a broker **3.** a fee paid to somebody who acts as a financial agent for somebody else

brokered market *Fin* a market in which brokers bring buyers and sellers together

broker loan rate *Fin* the interest rate that banks charge brokers on money that they lend for purchases on margin

Brown, Wilfred (1908–85) *Gen Mgt* British business executive. Chairman and managing director of the Glacier Metal Company who introduced *works councils* as an attempt at *industrial democracy*. During Brown's leadership, the Glacier Metal Company was used as the basis for the *Glacier studies*, carried out by *Elliot Jaques* of the Tavistock Institute of Human Relations.

brownfield site *Gen Mgt* an industrial site, usually located in an urban area, that is abandoned, inactive, or underutilised because of real or perceived environmental contamination

brown goods *Mkting* electrical consumer goods used primarily for home entertainment, for example, televisions, radios, and hi-fis

browser *E-com* a piece of software that allows people to access the Internet and World Wide Web. Internet Explorer and Netscape Navigator are the most commonly used browsers.

B share (*ANZ*) *Fin* a share in a unit trust that has no front-end sales charge but carries a redemption fee, or back-end load, payable only if the share is redeemed. This load, called a CDSC, or contingent deferred sales charge, declines every year until it disappears, usually after six years.

BTI *abbr Fin* Business Times Industrial index

BTW *abbr Gen Mgt* by the way (*slang*)

bubble economy *Econ* an unstable boom based on speculation in shares, often followed by a financial crash. This happened, for example, in the 1630s in the Netherlands and in the 1720s in England.

bucket shop *Fin* a firm of brokers or dealers that sells shares of questionable value

bucket trading *Fin* an illegal practice in which a stockbroker accepts a customer's order but does not execute the transaction until it is financially advantageous to the broker but at the customer's expense

budget *Fin* a plan specifying how a company's or department's resources will be spent or allocated during a particular period

budget account *Fin* a bank account set up to control a person's regular expenditures, for example, the payment of insurance premiums, mortgage, utilities, or telephone bills. The annual expenditure for each item is paid into the account in equal monthly instalments, bills being paid from the budget account as they become due.

budgetary *Fin* relating to a detailed plan of financial operations, with estimates of both revenue and expenditures for a specific future period

budgetary control *Fin* the establishment of budgets relating the responsibilities of executives to the requirements of a policy, and the continuous comparison of actual with budgeted results, either to secure by individual action the objectives of that policy or to provide a basis for its revision

budget centre *Fin* a section of an entity for which control may be exercised and budgets prepared

budget committee *Fin* the group within an organisation responsible for drawing up budgets that meet departmental requirements, ensuring they comply with policy, and then submitting them to the board of directors

budget cost allowance *Fin* the budgeted cost ascribed to the level of activity achieved in a budget centre in a control period. It comprises variable costs in direct proportion to volume achieved and fixed costs as a proportion of the annual budget. *Also known as* **flexed budget**

budget deficit *Fin* the extent by which expenditure exceeds revenue. *Also known as* **deficit**

budget director *Fin* the person in an organisation who is responsible for running the budget system

budgeted capacity *Fin* an organisation's available output level for a budget period according to the budget. It may be expressed in different ways, for example, in machine hours or standard hours.

budgeted revenue *Fin* the income that an organisation expects to receive in a budget period according to the budget

budget lapsing *Fin* withdrawal of unspent budget allowance due to the expiry of the budget period

budget management *Fin* the comparison of actual financial results with the estimated expenditures and revenues for the given time period of a budget and the taking of corrective action as necessary

budget manual *Fin* a detailed set of documents providing guidelines and information about the budget process. A budget manual may include: a calendar of budgetary events; specimen budget forms; a statement of budgetary objective and desired results; a listing of budgetary activities; original, revised, and approved budgets; and budget assumptions regarding inflation, interest rates etc.

budget period *Fin* the period for which a budget is prepared and used, which may then be subdivided into control periods

budget slack *Fin* the intentional overestimation of expenses and/or underestimation of revenues in the budgeting process

budget surplus *Fin* the extent by which revenue exceeds expenditure. *Also known as* **surplus**

buffer inventory *Ops* the products or supplies of an organisation maintained on hand or in transit to stabilise variations in supply, demand, production, or lead time

buffer stock *Fin* a stock of materials, or of work in progress, maintained in order to protect user departments from the effect of possible interruptions to supply

Buffett, Warren (*b.* 1930) *Gen Mgt* US investment banker. Chairman and CEO of Berkshire Hathaway, a vehicle for investing his vast wealth realised from a unique and successful share-purchase strategy. Buffett, dubbed the 'sage of Omaha', is much admired by **Bill Gates**.

building society *Fin* a financial institution that offers interest-bearing savings accounts, the deposits being reinvested by the society in long-term loans, primarily mortgage loans for the purchase of property

bull *Fin* somebody who anticipates favourable business conditions, especially somebody who buys particular stocks or commodities in anticipation that their prices will rise, often with the expectation of selling them at a large profit at a later time. *See also* **bear**

bulldog (*US, Canada*) *Gen Mgt* to attack a problem relentlessly (*slang*)

The most reliable way to anticipate the future is by understanding the past.   **John Naisbitt**

bulletin board *E-com* a computer-based forum used by an interest group to allow members to exchange e-mails, chat online, and access software. *Also known as* **newsgroup**

bulletin board system *E-com see* **BBS**

bullet loan *Fin* a loan that involves specified payments of interest until maturity, when the principal is repaid

bullish *Fin* conducive to or characterised by buying stocks or commodities in anticipation of rising prices in a market. *See also* **bearish**

bull market *Fin* a market in which prices are rising and in which a dealer is more likely to be a buyer than a seller. *See also* **bear market**

bullshit bingo *Gen Mgt* a game that involves counting how frequently words of incomprehensible jargon are used (*slang*)

bull spread *Fin* a combination of purchases and sales of options for the same commodity or stock intended to produce a profit when the price rises. *See also* **bear spread**

bullying *HR see* **workplace bullying**

bump up *Gen Mgt* to upgrade somebody to a higher class of service than has been paid for, for example in an aeroplane or hotel (*slang*)

bundle *Mkting* to group together two or more products or services into a single package that is then offered to the consumer at one price, for example, by providing software with a personal computer

bundling *Mkting* the practice of grouping together two or more products or services into a single package that is then offered to the consumer at one price

Bundy (*ANZ*) *HR* a timing system that records the arrival and departure of employees at their place of work

Bundy off (*ANZ*) *HR* to clock off from work

Bundy on (*ANZ*) *HR* to clock on for work

bureaucracy *Gen Mgt* an **organisation structure** with a rigid hierarchy of **personnel**, regulated by set rules and procedures. **Max Weber** believed that a bureaucracy was technically the most efficient form of organisation. He described a bureaucracy as an organisation structured around official functions that are bound by rules, each function having its own specified competence. The functions are structured into offices, which are organised into a hierarchy that follows technical rules and norms. Managers in a bureaucracy possess a rational-legal type of **authority** derived from the office they hold. Bureaucracies have been criticised for eradicating inspiration and **creativity** in favour of impersonality and the mundaneness and regularity of corporate life. This was best described in **William Whyte**'s *The Organization Man*, published in 1956, in which the individual was taken over by the bureaucratic machine in the name of efficiency. A more recent and humorous interpretation of life in a bureaucracy has been depicted by **Scott Adams** in *The Dilbert Principle* (1996). The term bureaucracy has gradually become a pejorative synonym for excessive and time-consuming paperwork and administration. Bureaucracies fell subject to **delayering** and **downsizing** from the 1980s onwards, as the flatter organisation became the target structure to ensure swifter market response and organisational flexibility.

Burns, James MacGregor (*b.* 1918) *Gen Mgt* US political scientist. Noted in the business sphere for identifying two approaches to leadership, the **transactional theory of leadership** and the **transformational theory of leadership**, described in his book *Leadership* (1978), which has an historical, social, and political perspective.

bush telegraph *Gen Mgt* a method of communicating information or rumours swiftly and unofficially by word of mouth or other means

Business Accounting Deliberation Council *Fin* in Japan, a committee controlled by the Ministry of Finance that is responsible for drawing up regulations regarding the consolidated financial statements of listed companies

Business Activity Statement *Fin* a standard document used in Australia to report the amount of *GST* and other taxes paid and collected by a business. *Abbr* **BAS**

business administration *Gen Mgt* **1.** a form of *management*. Business administration is used as a synonym for management, notably in government or the public sector. This use has developed from the **administration school** of thought established by *Henri Fayol*, which defines management activities as a set of processes. He argued that to manage was to plan, organise, co-ordinate, command, and control. These principles were put into exemplary practice by *Alfred Sloan Jr* at General Motors and are often seen as characteristic of large *bureaucracies*. **2.** the establishment and maintenance of *procedures*, records, and regulations in the pursuit of a commercial activity. Business administration involves the conduct of activities leading to, and resulting from, the delivery of a product or service to the customer. Administration is often seen as paperwork and form-filling, but it reaches wider than that to encompass the co-ordination of all the procedures that enable a product or service to be delivered, together with the keeping of records that can be checked to identify errors or opportunities for improvement.

business card *Fin* a small card printed with somebody's name, job title, business address, and contact numbers or e-mail address

business case *Gen Mgt* the essential value to the organisation of a proposal. A business case is made through the preparation and presentation of a business plan and is used to prevent *blue-sky ideas* taking root without justifiable or provable value to an organisation.

business cluster *Gen Mgt* a group of small firms from similar industries that team up and act as one body. Creating a business cluster enables firms to enjoy economies of scale usually only available to bigger competitors. Marketing costs can be shared and goods can be bought more cheaply. There are also networking advantages, in which small firms can share experiences and discuss business strategies.

business combinations (*US*) *Fin* acquisitions or mergers involving two or more enterprises

business continuity *Gen Mgt* the uninterrupted maintenance of business activities. Ensuring business continuity requires a proactive process of identifying essential business functions within an organisation and threats to those functions. Plans and procedures may then be put in place to ensure that key functions can continue whatever the circumstances. Plans may be drawn up, for example, for *contingency*, *disaster*, and *risk management*, or for *total loss control*.

Business Council of Australia *Gen Mgt* a national association of chief executives, designed as a forum for the discussion of matters pertaining to business leadership in Australia. *Abbr* **BCA**

business cycle *Econ* a regular pattern of fluctuation in national income, moving from upturn to downturn in about five years

business efficiency *Gen Mgt* a situation in which an organisation maximises benefit and profit, while minimising effort and expenditure. Maximisation of business efficiency is a balance between two extremes. Managed correctly, it results in reduced costs, waste, and duplication. *Max Weber*, who developed the concept of the *bureaucracy*, believed that efficiency was the goal of all bureaucratic organisations, which were designed to run like smooth machines. The greater the efficiency, the more impersonal, rational, and emotionally detached a bureaucracy becomes. The flatter organisations more prevalent today attempt to be more customer-responsive than efficient in this sense, and the notion of such an ordered and impersonal efficiency has lost favour in an era when *creativity* and *innovation* are valued as a *competitive advantage*.

business entity concept *Fin* the concept that financial accounting information relates only to the activities of the business entity and not to the activities of its owner(s)

business ethics *Gen Mgt* a system of moral principles applied in the commercial world. Business ethics provide guidelines for acceptable behaviour by organisations in both their strategy formulation and day-to-day operations. An ethical approach is becoming necessary both for corporate success and a positive *corporate image*. Issues that have raised the profile of business ethics include the Guinness, Maxwell, Polly Peck, and Barings scandals in the United Kingdom, high profits and high executive salaries, and the reports by Sir Anthony Nolan on disclosure of information and standards in public life and **Sir Adrian Cadbury** on *corporate governance*. Following the publication of these reports and pressure from consumers for more ethical and responsible business practices, many organisations are choosing to make a public commitment to ethical business by formulating *codes of conduct* and operating principles. In doing so, they must translate into action the concepts of personal and corporate accountability, *corporate giving*, corporate governance, and *whistleblowing*. Also known as *morality in business*

business excellence *Gen Mgt see excellence*

business excellence model *Gen Mgt see EFQM Excellence Model*

business failure *Gen Mgt* an organisation that has gone bankrupt. A business that is at risk of failure may be saved by *turnaround management*, which identifies and deals with the reasons for decline. Also known as *failure*

business game *Gen Mgt* a type of *simulation game* in which a model of a business situation is explored competitively for the purpose of learning

business gift *Mkting* a present, usually from a supplier to a customer, often used to maintain good relations. Business gifts may range from a pen to a hamper and are often a form of *merchandising*. The acceptance of a business gift is often governed by an organisation's *code of conduct* and is often forbidden on the grounds that business gifts, particularly high-value ones, may be seen as an attempt to bribe.

business intelligence *Gen Mgt* any information that can be of strategic use to a business

business interruption insurance *Fin* a policy indemnifying an organisation for loss of profits and continuing fixed expenses when some insurable disaster, for example, a fire, causes the organisation to stop or reduce its activities. *Also known as* **consequential loss policy**

business name *Fin* in the United Kingdom, the legal term for the name under which an organisation operates

business objective *Gen Mgt* a goal that an organisation sets for itself, for example, profitability, sales growth, or return on investment. These goals are the foundation upon which the strategic and operational policies adopted by the organisation are based.

business plan *Gen Mgt* a document describing the current activities of a business, setting out its aims and objectives and how they are to be achieved over a set period of time. A business plan may cover the activities of an organisation or a group of companies, or it may deal with a single department within the organisation. In the former case, it is sometimes referred to as a corporate plan. The sections of a business plan usually include a market analysis describing the target market, customers, and competitors, an operations plan describing how products and services will be developed and produced, and a financial section providing profit, budget, and cash flow forecasts, annual accounts, and financial requirements. Businesses may use a business plan internally as a framework for implementing strategy and improving performance or externally to attract investment or raise capital for development plans. A business plan may form part of the overall planning process, or *corporate planning*, within an organisation and be used for the implementation of corporate strategy.

business process re-engineering *Gen Mgt, Ops* the initiation and control of the change of *processes* within an organisation, in order to derive *competitive advantage* from improvement in the quality of products. Business process re-engineering was popularised by *Michael Hammer*. It requires a review and imaginative analysis of the processes currently used by the organisation. BPR, therefore, has similarities to *benchmarking*, as this review of processes can reveal critical points where significant improvements in *quality* can be made. Business process re-engineering was at the height of its popularity in the early- to mid-1990s. It has been criticised as one of the root causes of the bouts of *downsizing* and *delayering* that have affected many parts of industry. It has also received a negative press because few BPR projects have delivered the benefits expected of them. *Abbr* **BPR**

business property relief *Fin* in the United Kingdom, a reduction in the amount liable to inheritance tax on certain types of business property

business rates *Fin* in the United Kingdom, a tax on businesses calculated on the value of the property occupied. Although the rate of tax is set by central government, the tax is collected the local authority.

business risk *Fin* the uncertainty associated with the unique circumstances of a particular company, for example, the introduction of a superior technology, as they might affect the price of that company's securities

business school *Gen Mgt* a higher education institution that offers undergraduate and postgraduate courses in business-related subjects. Business schools provide courses of varying length and level, up to the *Master of Business Administration*. They cater for full-time students, but also offer part-time and *distance learning* to those already in employment. Subject coverage is broad, and courses cover all areas of business administration, management, technology, finance, and interpersonal skills.

business segment *Fin* a distinguishable part of a business or enterprise that is subject to a different set of risks and returns than any other part. Listed companies are required to declare in their annual reports certain information, for example, sales, profits, and assets, for each segment of an enterprise.

business strategy *Fin* a long-term approach to implementing a firm's business plans to achieve its business objectives

Business Times Industrial index *Fin* an index of 40 Singapore and Malaysian shares. *Abbr* **BTI**

business-to-business *E-com see* **B2B**

business-to-consumer *E-com see* **B2C**

business transfer relief *Fin* the tax advantage gained when selling a business for shares in stock of the company that buys it

business unit *Gen Mgt* a part of an organisation that operates as a distinct function, department, division, or standalone business. Business units are usually treated as a separate *profit centre* within the overall, owning business.

business web *E-com see* **b-web**

bust-up proxy proposal *Fin* an overture to a company's shareholders for a *leveraged buyout* in which the acquirer sells some of the company's assets in order to

---

Marketing takes a day to learn. Unfortunately, it takes a lifetime to master.   *Philip Kotler*

repay the debt used to finance the take-over

busymeet *Gen Mgt* a business meeting (*slang*)

butterfly spread *Fin* a complex option strategy based on simultaneously purchasing and selling calls at different exercise prices and maturity dates, the profit being the premium collected when the options are sold. Such a strategy is most profitable when the price of the underlying security is relatively stable.

button *E-com* an online interactive ad, smaller than the traditional *banner*, placed on a web page and linked to an external advertiser's site. Buttons are usually square in shape, represented to look like a push button, and located down the left or right edge of the page.

buy and hold *Fin* an investment strategy based on retaining securities for a long time

buy and write *Fin* an investment strategy involving buying stock and selling options to eliminate the possibility of loss if the value of the stock goes down

buy-back *Fin* the repurchase of bonds or shares, as agreed by contract

buy-down *Fin* the payment of principal amounts that reduce the monthly payments due on a mortgage

buyer *Fin* 1. somebody who is in the process of buying something or who intends to buy something 2. somebody whose job is to choose and buy goods, merchandise, services, or media time or space for a company, factory, shop, or advertiser

buyer expectation *Gen Mgt see customer expectation*

buyer's guide *Mkting* a document that offers information on a range of related products, usually from a number of different organisations

buyer's market *Fin* a situation in which supply exceeds demand, prices are relatively low, and buyers therefore have an advantage

buy in *Fin* to buy stock in a company so as to have a controlling interest. This is often done by or for executives from outside the company.

buying economies of scale *Fin* a reduction in the cost of purchasing raw materials and components or of borrowing money due to the increased size of the purchase

buying manager *Ops see purchasing manager*

buy on close *Fin* a purchase at the end of the trading day

buy one get one free *Mkting see BOGOF*

buy on opening *Fin* a purchase at the beginning of the trading day

buy or make *Ops see purchasing versus production*

buy out *Gen Mgt* 1. to purchase the entire stock of, or controlling financial interest in, a company 2. to pay somebody to relinquish his or her interest in a property or other enterprise

buy-out 1. *Gen Mgt* the purchase and *takeover* of an ongoing business. It is more formally known as an acquisition (see *merger*). If a business is purchased by managers or staff, it is known as a *management buy-out*. 2. *Gen Mgt* the purchase of somebody else's entire stock ownership in a firm. It is more formally known as an acquisition (see *merger*). 3. *HR* an option to transfer benefits of an occupational pension scheme on leaving a company

buy stop order *Fin* an order to buy stock when its price reaches a specified level

Buzan, Tony (*b.* 1942) *Gen Mgt* British writer. Originator of the *Mind Map*™, a technique he explained in *Use Your Head* (1974).

buzz group *Gen Mgt* a small discussion group formed for a specific task such as generating ideas, solving problems, or reaching a common viewpoint on a topic within a specific period of time. The use

---

Conscience is an imitation within ourselves of the government without us. Alexander Bain

of buzz groups was first associated with J.D. Phillips and is sometimes known as the Phillips 66 technique. Large groups may be divided into buzz groups after an initial presentation in order to cover different aspects of a topic or maximise participation. Each group appoints a spokesperson to report the results of the discussion to the larger group. Buzz groups are a form of *brainstorming*.

buzzword-compliant *E-com* familiar with the latest Internet jargon (*slang*)

BV *abbr Fin* the Dutch term for a limited liability company

b-web *E-com* a business web, a group of complementary businesses that come together over the Internet. While each company retains its autonomous identity, the businesses work in unison to generate more income than they could do individually. Characteristics of b-webs include *extranets*, *viral marketing*, online marketplaces, and affiliate schemes. The term was originally used by Don Tapscott, David Ticoll, and Alex Lowry in an article published by *eCompany Now* magazine.

by-bidder *Fin* somebody who bids at an auction solely to raise the price for the seller

Byham, William *Gen Mgt* US consultant and writer. Co-author of *Zapp! The Lightning of Empowerment* (1987), a modern fable in an industrial setting that popularised the benefits that *empowerment* can bring to the workplace.

bylaws *Fin* the rules that govern the operation of an enterprise. In the United Kingdom, they are known as the *articles of association*.

bypass trust *Fin* a trust that leaves money in a will in trust to people other than the prime beneficiary in order to gain tax advantage

by-product *Fin* output of some value that is produced incidentally in manufacturing something else. *See also* ***joint products***

byte *E-com* a unit of computer memory equal to that needed to store a single character, now commonly a group of eight adjacent *bits*

When I saw something that needed doing, I did it. *Nellie Cashman*

CA *abbr Fin* chartered accountant

cache *E-com* a small memory bank inside a computer that stores all the images and text from every website visited. This speeds up the download time when an Internet user revisits a site.

CAD *abbr Ops* computer-aided design

Cadbury, Sir George Adrian Hayhurst (*b.* 1929) *Gen Mgt* British business executive. Former chairman of Cadbury Schweppes and, in the 1990s, chairman of the Committee on the Financial Aspects of *Corporate Governance*.

Cadbury, Sir Nicholas Dominic (*b.* 1940) *Gen Mgt* British industrialist. Chair of the Wellcome Trust, and past chair of Cadbury Schweppes. Sir Dominic Cadbury is celebrated for his oft-quoted dictum 'There is no such thing as a career path; it is crazy-paving and you have to lay it yourself'.

Cadbury Report *Fin* the report of the Cadbury Committee (conducted in December 1992) on the Financial Aspects of Corporate Governance. It was established to consider the following issues in relation to financial reporting and accountability, and to make recommendations on good practice: the responsibilities of executive and non-executive directors for reviewing and reporting performance to shareholders and other financially interested parties; and the frequency, clarity and form in which information should be provided; the case for audit committees of the board, including their composition and role; the principal responsibilities of the auditors and the extent and value of the audit; the links between shareholders, boards and auditors; and any other relevant matters. The report established a Code of Best Practice, and has been influential in the United Kingdom and overseas. *See also Corporate Governance Combined Code*

CAD/CAM *Gen Mgt* the integration of data and technologies from *computer-aided design* and *computer-aided manufacturing* into the entire design-to-manufacture cycle. Data from a combined CAD/CAM database can be used for the control of a totally automated computer-integrated manufacturing system.

CAE *abbr Ops* computer-aided engineering

call *Fin* an option to buy stock. *Also known as call option*

callable *Fin* a financial instrument with a call provision in its indenture

call centre *Gen Mgt* a department or business wholly focused on telephone enquiries. Call centres usually provide a centralised point of contact for an organisation and support *telephone selling*, *after-sales service*, telephone helplines, or information services either for a parent organisation or on a contract basis for other businesses.

called-up share capital *Fin* the amount which a company has required shareholders to pay on shares issued

calling line identification *Gen Mgt see computer telephony integration*

call money *Fin* money that brokers use for their own purchases or to help their customers buy on margin

call off *Fin* a system whereby inventory is held at the customer's premises, to be invoiced only on use

call option *Fin see call*

call payment *Fin* an amount that a company demands in partial payment for stock such as a rights issue that is not paid for at one time

call provision *Fin* a clause in an indenture that lets the issuer of a bond redeem it before the date of its maturity

CAM *abbr Ops* computer-aided manufacturing

campaign *Mkting* a programme of advertising and marketing activities with a specific objective

camp on the line *Gen Mgt* to wait on hold for a long time on the telephone (*slang*)

can (*US*) *HR* to dismiss somebody from employment (*slang*)

Canadian Institute of Chartered Accountants *Fin* in Canada, the principal professional accountancy body that is responsible for setting accounting standards. *Abbr* **CICA**

cap *Fin* an upper limit such as on a rate of interest for a loan

CAPA *abbr Fin* Confederation of Asian and Pacific Accountants: an umbrella organisation for a number of Asia-Pacific accountancy bodies

capacity *Ops* the measure of the capability of a workstation or a plant to produce output. Capacity measures can focus on a variety of factors, which typically include: quantity, for example, the number of items produced over a given period; and scope, for example, the range of items produced by type or size.

capacity planning *Ops* the process of measuring the amount of work that can be completed within a given time and determining the necessary physical and human resources needed to accomplish it. Capacity planning uses *capacity utilisation* to ensure that the maximum amount of product is made and sold. The planning process involves a regulation process that identifies deviations from the plan, allowing corrective action to be taken. A *capacity requirements planning* program can aid in the process of capacity planning.

capacity ratios *Fin* measures of performance in the use of capacity.
⎡EXAMPLE⎤ The more commonly used capacity levels are: full capacity—output (expressed in standard hours) that could

be achieved if sales orders, supplies and workforce were available for all installed workplaces; practical capacity—full capacity less an allowance for known unavoidable volume losses; budgeted capacity—standard hours planned for the period, taking into account budgeted sales, supplies, workforce availability, and efficiency expected; and normal capacity.

On the following given data, the related ratios are set out below:

Full capacity standard hours	100
Practical capacity standard hours	95
Budgeted capacity (budgeted input hours, 90 at 90 per cent efficiency)	81
Actual input hours	85
Standard hours produced	68

Idle capacity ratio:
(Practical capacity – budgeted capacity) × 100/Practical capacity = (95 – 81) × 100/95 = 15%

This figure indicates the budgeted shortfall in capacity as a proportion of practical capacity.

capacity requirements planning *Gen Mgt, Ops* a computerised tracking process that translates production requirements into practical implications for manufacturing resources. Capacity requirements planning is part of manufacturing resource planning and is carried out after a manufacturing resource planning program has been run. This produces an **infinite capacity plan**, as it does not take account of the capacity constraints of each workstation. Where the process is extended to cover capacity requirements, a **finite capacity plan** is produced. This enables *loading* at each workstation to be smoothed and determines the need for additional resources.

capacity usage variance *Fin* the difference in gain or loss in a given period compared to budgeted expectations, caused because the hours worked were longer or shorter than planned

capacity utilisation 1. *Econ* the output of an economy, firm, or plant divided by its output when working at full capacity **2.**

Gen Mgt, Ops a measure of the plant and equipment of a company or industry that is actually being used to produce goods or services. Capacity utilisation usually is the measure of output over a specific period, for example, the average output for a month, or at a given point in time, for example, on a given date. It can be expressed as a ratio, where utilisation = actual output/design capacity. This measure is used in both *capacity planning* and *capacity requirements planning* processes.

Caparo case *Fin* in England, a court decision taken by the House of Lords in 1990 that auditors owe a duty of care to present (and not prospective) shareholders as a body but not as individuals

capital *Fin* money that can be invested by an individual or organisation in order to make a profit

capital account *Fin* the sum of a company's capital at a particular time

capital allowances *Fin* in the United Kingdom and Ireland, an allowance against income or corporation tax available to businesses or sole traders who have purchased plant and machinery for business use. The rates are set annually and vary according to the type of fixed asset purchased, for example, whether it is machinery or buildings. This system effectively removes subjectivity from the calculation of depreciation for tax purposes.

capital appreciation *Fin* the increase in a company's or individual's wealth

capital appreciation fund *Fin* a unit trust that aims to increase the value of its holdings without regard to the provision of income to its owners

capital asset *Fin* an asset that is difficult to sell quickly, for example, land

capital asset pricing model *Econ* a model of the market used to assess the cost of capital for a company based on the rate of return on its assets.
EXAMPLE The capital asset pricing model (CAPM) holds that the expected return of

a security or a portfolio equals the rate on a risk-free security plus a risk premium. If this expected return does not meet or beat a theoretical required return, the investment should not be undertaken. The formula used to create CAPM is:

Risk-free rate + (Market return – Risk-free rate) x Beta value = Expected return

The risk-free rate is the quoted rate on an asset that has virtually no risk. The market return is the percentage return expected of the overall market, typically a published index such as Standard & Poor's. The beta value is a figure that measures the volatility of a security or portfolio of securities, compared with the market as a whole. A beta of 1, for example, indicates that a security's price will move with the market. A beta greater than 1 indicates higher volatility, while a beta less than 1 indicates less volatility.

Say, for instance, that the current risk-free rate is 4%, and the S&P 500 index is expected to return 11% next year. An investment club is interested in determining next year's return for XYZ Software Ltd, a prospective investment. The club has determined that the company's beta value is 1.8. The overall stock market always has a beta of 1, so XYZ Software's beta of 1.8 signals that it is a more risky investment than the overall market represents. This added risk means that the club should expect a higher rate of return than the 11% for the S&P 500. The CAPM calculation, then, would be:

4% + (11% – 4%) x 1.8 = 16.6% Expected Return

What the results tell the club is that given the risk, XYZ Software Ltd has a required rate of return of 16.6%, or the minimum return that an investment in XYZ should generate. If the investment club does not think that XYZ will produce that kind of return, it should probably consider investing in a different company.
Abbr **CAPM**

capital budget *Fin* a subsection of a company's master budget that deals with expected capital expenditure within a defined period. *Also known as* **capital**

expenditure budget, capital investment budget

capital budgeting *Fin* the selection, appraisal, and monitoring of a business's fixed assets

capital commitment *Fin* the estimated amount of capital expenditure that is contracted for but not yet provided for and authorised by the directors of a company but not yet contracted for

capital consumption *Fin* in a given period, the total depreciation of a national economy's fixed assets based on replacement costs

capital controls *Econ* regulations placed by a government on the amount of capital residents may hold

capital cost allowance *Fin* a tax advantage in Canada for the depreciation in value of capital assets

capital costs *Fin* expenses on the purchase of fixed assets

capital deepening *Econ* more capital-intensive production that results when a country's *capital stock* increases but the numbers employed fall or remain constant

capital employed *Fin* the funds used by an entity for its operations. This can be expressed in various ways depending upon the purpose of the computation. For example, for operations evaluation, capital employed may be defined as the total value of non-current assets plus working capital, whereas for investor evaluation, owners' capital plus reserves may be used.

capital expenditure *Fin* an outlay of money, especially on fixed assets. *Also known as capital investment*

capital expenditure budget *Fin see capital budget*

capital flight *Fin* the transfer of large sums of money between countries to seek higher rates of return or to escape a political or economic disturbance

capital formation *Econ* addition to the stock of a country's *real capital* by investment in fixed assets

capital funding planning *Fin* the process of selecting suitable funds to finance long-term assets and working capital

capital gain *Fin* the financial gain made upon the disposal of an asset. The gain is the difference between the cost of its acquisition and net proceeds upon its sale.

capital gains distribution *Fin* a sum of money that, for example, a unit trust pays to its owners in proportion to the owners' share of the organisation's capital gains for the year

capital gains reserve *Fin* a tax advantage in Canada for money not yet received in payment for something that has been sold

capital gains tax *Fin* a tax on the difference between the gross acquisition cost and the net proceeds when an asset is sold. In the United Kingdom, this tax also applies when assets are given or exchanged, although each individual has an annual capital gains tax allowance that exempts gains within that tax year below a stated level. In addition, certain assets may be exempt, for example, a person's principal private residence and transfers of assets between spouses, and the tax may not be levied on the absolute gain. An adjustment is made for inflation and the length of time that the asset has been held. There are also concessions on the sale of a business at retirement. *Abbr* **CGT**

capital gearing *Fin* the amount of fixed-cost debt that a company has for each of its ordinary shares

capital goods *Econ* stocks of physical or financial assets that are capable of generating income

capital inflow *Econ* the amount of capital that flows into an economy from services rendered abroad

capital instruments *Fin* the means that an organisation uses to raise finance, for example, the issue of shares or debentures

capital-intensive *Fin* using a greater proportion of capital as opposed to labour

capital investment *Fin see* **capital expenditure**

capital investment appraisal *Fin* the application of a set of methodologies (generally based on the discounting of projected cash flows) whose purpose is to give guidance to managers with respect to decisions as to how best to commit long-term investment funds. *See also* **discounted cash flow**

capital investment budget *Fin see* **capital budget**

capitalisation *Fin* **1.** the amount of money invested in a company or the worth of the bonds and stocks of a company **2.** the conversion of a company's reserves into capital through a scrip issue

capitalisation issue *Fin* a proportional issue of free shares to existing shareholders. *US term* **stock split**

capitalisation rate *Fin* the rate at which a company's *reserves* are converted into capital by way of a *capitalisation issue*

capitalisation ratio *Fin* the proportion of a company's value represented by debt, stock, assets, and other items.

EXAMPLE By comparing debt to total capitalisation, these ratios provide a glimpse of a company's long-term stability and ability to withstand losses and business downturns.

A company's capitalisation ratio can be expressed in two ways:

= Long-Term Debt / Long-Term Debt + Owners' Equity

and

= Total Debt / Total Debt + Preferred + Common Equity

For example, a company whose long-term debt totals £5,000 and whose owners hold equity worth £3,000 would have a capitalisation ratio of:

5,000 / (5,000 + 3,000) = 5,000 /8,000 = 0.625 capitalisation ratio

Both expressions of the ratio are also referred to as 'component percentages', since they compare a firm's debt with either its total capital (debt plus equity) or its equity capital. They readily indicate how reliant a firm is on debt financing.

Capitalisation ratios need to be evaluated over time, and compared with other data and standards. Care should be taken when comparing companies in different industries or sectors. The same figures that appear to be low in one industry can be very high in another.

capitalise *Fin* **1.** to finance the vehicles, plant, etc. of a business. **2.** to include money spent on the purchase of an asset as an element in a balance sheet

capitalism *Econ* an economic and social system in which individuals can maximise profits because they own the means of production

capitalist *Fin* an investor of capital in a business

capital lease *(US)* *Gen Mgt* = **finance lease**

capital levy *Fin* a tax on fixed assets or property

capital loss *Fin* a loss made through selling an asset for less than its cost

capital maintenance concept *Fin* a concept used to determine the definition of profit, that provide the basis for different systems of inflation accounting

capital market *Fin* a financial market dealing with securities that have a life of more than one year

capital project *Ops see* **capital project management**

capital project management *Gen Mgt* control of a *project* that involves expenditure of an organisation's monetary resources for the purpose of creating *capacity* for *production*. Capital project management often involves the organisation of major construction or engineering work. **Capital projects** are usually large scale, complex, need to be completed quickly, and involve capital investment. Different techniques have evolved for capital project management from those

---

In the long run, failure was the only thing that worked predictably. Joseph Heller

used for normal *project management*, including methods for managing the complexity of such projects, and for analysing return on investment afterwards.

capital property *Fin* under Canadian tax law, assets that can depreciate in value or be sold for a capital gain or loss

capital ratio *Fin* a company's income expressed as a fraction of its tangible assets

capital rationing *Fin* the restriction of new investment by a company

capital redemption reserve *Fin* an account required to prevent a reduction in capital, where a company purchases or redeems its own shares out of distributable profits

capital reserves *Fin* a former name for *undistributable reserves*

capital resource planning *Fin* the process of evaluating and selecting long-term assets to meet strategies

capital stock *Fin* the stock authorised by a company's charter, representing no ownership rights

capital structure *Fin* the proportions of a company's assets and liabilities of various sorts, especially long-term debt

capital sum *Fin* a lump sum of money that an insurer pays, for example, on the death of the insured person

capital surplus *Fin* the value of all of the stock in a company that exceeds the par value of the stock

capital transactions *Fin* transactions affecting non-current items such as fixed assets, long-term debt, or share capital, rather than revenue transactions

capital transfer tax *Fin* in the United Kingdom, a tax on the transfer of assets that was replaced in 1986 by inheritance tax

capital turnover *Fin* the value of annual sales as a multiple of the value of the company's stock

capital widening *Econ* less capital-intensive production that results when both a country's *capital stock* and the numbers employed increase

CAPM *abbr* **1.** *Fin* capital asset pricing model **2.** *Ops* computer-aided production management

captive finance company *Fin* an organisation that provides credit and is owned or controlled by a commercial or manufacturing company, for example, a retailer that owns its store card operation or a car manufacturer that owns a company for financing the vehicles it produces

captive insurance company *Fin* an insurance company that has been established by a parent company to underwrite all its insurance risks and those of its subsidiaries. The benefit is that the premiums paid do not leave the organisation. Many captive insurance companies are established offshore for tax purposes.

capture *E-com* the submission of a credit card transaction for processing and settlement. Capture initiates the process of moving funds from the *issuer* to the *acquirer*.

carbon copy *E-com see cc*

cardholder *E-com* an individual or company that has an active credit card account with an *issuer* with which transactions can be initiated

card-issuing bank *E-com see issuer*

card-not-present merchant account *E-com* an account that permits e-merchants to process credit card transactions without the purchaser being physically present for the transaction

career anchor *HR* a guiding force that influences people's career choices, based on self-perception of their own skills, *motivation*, and values. The term was coined by **Edgar Schein** in *Career Anchors: Discovering Your Real Values*, published in 1985. He believed that people develop one underlying anchor, perhaps subconsciously, that they are unwilling to give up when faced with

---

Loyalty saves the wear and tear of making daily decisions as to what is best to do.
Thomas J. Watson, Sr

different pressures. Schein distinguishes several career anchor groups such as technical/functional competence, managerial *competence*, *creativity*, security or stability, and autonomy.

career break *HR* a planned interruption to working life, usually for a predetermined period of time. A career break is usually designed either to aid *career development* or to enable somebody to balance work and family life. It may take the form of parental leave, or a *sabbatical* for study, research, or exploring alternative activities. A career break may be sanctioned by an employer or taken without the support of an employer.

career change *HR* a switch in profession or in type of job, often to a different employer. Career change may be planned as part of the *CPD* or *career development* processes, or it may be forced on an employee by *redundancy*, ill-health, or a change in personal circumstance.

career development *HR* progression through a sequence of jobs, involving continually more advanced or diverse activities and resulting in wider or improved skills, greater responsibility and prestige, and higher income. Formerly, career development was seen as the responsibility of the employer, and many organisations had formal career development programmes that marked an employee's advancement through the levels of management. It is now more usually held to be the responsibility of the employees, sometimes as part of the *CPD* process.

career ladder *HR* a sequence of posts from most junior to most senior within an organisation or department. A career ladder provides a structured path for an employee to climb up through an organisation. It is most typical of *bureaucracies*, as *flat organisation* structures tend not to be hierarchical to the same extent.

career-limiting move *HR see* **CLM**

career path *HR* a planned, logical progression of jobs within one or more professions throughout working life. A career path can be planned with greater assurance in market conditions of stability and little change. In times of great change and uncertainty, some people, such as *Dominic Cadbury*, have argued that there is no longer such a thing as a planned career path and instead place greater emphasis on the importance of *CPD* in order to maintain *employability*.

career pattern *HR* the sequence of jobs undertaken by somebody during his or her working life. A career pattern can be structured in advance as part of *career development* planning, and may allow for *career breaks* or *career changes*. Career patterns can also be discerned more generally as trends in employee development within particular sectors of the *labour force*.

careline *Mkting* a telephone service allowing customers to obtain information, advice, or assistance from retailers

caring economy *Econ* an economy based on amicable and helpful relationships between businesses and people

Carnegie, Dale Breckinridge (1888–1955) *Gen Mgt* US writer and trainer. Best known for his advice on self-improvement, which focused on *interpersonal communication* and effective *communication skills*, including public speaking. Carnegie's best-seller, *How to Win Friends and Influence People* (1936), included guidance on never criticising, complaining about, or condemning another person, giving sincere appreciation to others, and stimulating in others a specific desire in order to motivate them.

carriage inwards *Fin* delivery expenses incurred through the purchase of goods

carriage outwards *Fin* delivery expenses incurred through the sale of goods

carrier *Gen Mgt* a telecommunications company that provides network infrastructure services and charges customers for carrying their communications over the network. Carriers do not necessarily

---

The better people think they are, the better they will be. Positive self-image creates success.
Liisa Joronen

own their own network, but may rent time on a number of networks.

carrier's note *Fin see* **delivery note**

carrying amount *Fin see* **book value**

carrying cost *Fin* expenses associated with holding stock for a given period, for example, from the time of delivery to the time of despatch. These will include storage and insurance.

carrying value *Fin see* **book value**

cartel *Fin* an alliance of business companies formed to control production, competition, and prices

cartogram *Stats* a diagrammatic map on which statistical information is represented by shading and symbols

cash *Fin* money in the form of banknotes and coins that are legal tender

cash account *Fin* a brokerage account that permits no buying on margin

cash accounting *Fin* **1.** an accounting method in which receipts and expenses are recorded in the accounting books in the period when they actually occur. *See also* **accrual concept 2.** in the United Kingdom, a system for Value Added Tax that enables the tax payer to account for tax paid and received during a given period, thus allowing automatic relief for bad debts

cash advance *Fin* a loan on a credit card account

cash and carry *Gen Mgt see* **wholesaler**

cash at bank *Fin* the total amount of money held at the bank by an individual or company

cash available to invest *Fin* the amount, including cash on account and balances due soon for outstanding transactions, that a client has available for investment with a broker

cashback *Mkting* a sales promotion technique offering customers a cash refund after they buy a product

cash basis *Fin* the bookkeeping practice of accounting for money only when it is actually received or spent

cash bonus *Fin* an unscheduled dividend that a company declares because of unexpected income

cashbook *Fin* a book in which all cash payments and receipts are recorded. In a double-entry bookkeeping system, the balance at the end of a given period is included in the trial balance and then transferred to the balance sheet itself.

cash budget *Fin* a detailed budget of estimated cash inflows and outflows incorporating both revenue and capital items

cash contract *Fin* a contract for actual delivery of a commodity

cash conversion cycle *Fin* the time between the acquisition of a raw material and the receipt of payment for the finished product. *Also known as* **cash cycle**

cash cow 1. *Fin* a subsidiary enterprise that performs well and consistently makes a substantial profit (*slang*) **2.** *Gen Mgt see* **Boston Box 3.** *Mkting* a product that sells well and makes a substantial profit without requiring much advertising or investment (*slang*)

cash crop *Econ* a crop, for example, tobacco, that can be sold for cash, usually by a developing country

cash cycle *Fin see* **cash conversion cycle**

cash deficiency agreement *Fin* a commitment to supply whatever additional cash is needed to complete the financing of a project

cash discount *Fin* a discount offered to a customer who pays for goods or services with cash, or who pays an invoice within a particular period

cash dividend *Fin* a share of a company's current earnings or accumulated profits distributed to shareholders

cash equivalents *Fin* short-term investments that can be converted into cash immediately and that are subject to only a limited risk. There is usually a limit on their duration, for example, three months.

cash float *Fin* notes and coins held by a retailer for the purpose of supplying customers with change

cash flow *Fin* the movement of money through an organisation that is generated by its own operations as opposed to borrowing. It is the money that a business actually receives from sales (the cash inflow) and the money that it pays out (the cash outflow).

cash-flow coverage ratio *Fin* the ratio of income to cash obligations

cash-flow life *HR* a lifestyle characterised by working for individual project fees rather than a regular salary

cash flow per common share *Fin* the amount of cash that a company has for each of its ordinary shares

cash-flow risk *Fin* the risk that a company's available cash will not be sufficient to meet its financial obligations

cash-flow statement *Fin* a record of a company's cash inflows and cash outflows over a specific period of time, typically a year.

EXAMPLE It reports funds on hand at the beginning of the period, funds received, funds spent, and funds remaining at the end of the period. Cash flows are divided into three categories: cash from operations; cash-investment activities; and cash-financing activities. Companies with holdings in foreign currencies use a fourth classification: effects of changes in currency rates on cash.

A standard direct cash-flow statement looks like this:

CRD Ltd
Statement of Cash Flows
For year ended 31 December 20__

CASH FLOWS FROM OPERATIONS

	£
Operating Profit	82,000
Adjustments to net earnings	
Depreciation	17,000
Accounts receivable	(20,000)
Accounts payable	12,000
Inventory	(8,000)
Other adjustments to earnings	4,000
Net cash flow from operations	**87,000**

CASH FLOWS FROM INVESTMENT ACTIVITIES

Purchases of marketable securities	(58,000)
Receipts from sales of marketable securities	45,000
Loans made to borrowers	(16,000)
Collections on loans	11,000
Purchases of plant and land and property assets	(150,000)
Receipts from sales of plant and land and property assets	47,000
Net cash flow from investment activities:	**(−121,000)**

CASH FLOWS FROM FINANCING ACTIVITIES

Proceeds from short-term borrowings	51,000
Payments to settle short-term debts	(61,000)
Proceeds from issuing bonds payable	100,000
Proceeds from issuing capital stock	80,000
Dividends paid	(64,000)
Net cash flow from financing activities	**106,000**
Net change in cash during period	**72,000**
Cash and cash equivalents, beginning of year	27,000
Cash and cash equivalents, end of year	99,000

cash-generating unit *Fin* the smallest identifiable group of assets that generates cash inflows and outflows that can be measured

cashless pay *HR* the payment of a weekly or monthly wage through the electronic transfer of funds directly into the bank account of an *employee*

cashless society *Econ* a society in which all bills and debits are paid by electronic

---

Take care to sell your horse before he dies. The art of life is passing losses on.   **Robert Frost**

money media, for example, bank and credit cards, direct debits, and online payments

cash loan company (*S Africa*) *Fin* a microlending business that provides short-term loans without collateral, usually at high interest rates

cash management models *Fin* sophisticated cash-flow forecasting models which assist management in determining how to balance the cash needs of an organisation. Cash management models might help in areas such as optimising cash balances, in the management of customer, supplier, investor, and company investment needs, in the decision as to invest or buy back shares, or in the decision as to the optimum method of financing working capital.

cash offer *Fin* an offer to buy a company for cash rather than for stock

cash payments journal *Fin* a chronological record of all the payments that have been made from a company's bank account

cash ratio *Fin* the ratio of a company's liquid assets such as cash and securities divided by total liabilities. *Also known as liquidity ratio*

cash receipts journal *Fin* a chronological record of all the receipts that have been paid into a company's bank account

cash sale *Fin* a sale in which payment is made immediately in cash rather than put on credit

cash settlement *Fin* **1.** an immediate payment on an options contract without waiting for expiry of the normal, usually five-day, settlement period **2.** the completion of a transaction by paying for securities

cash surrender value *Fin* the amount of money that an insurance company will pay to terminate a policy at a particular time if the policy does not continue until its normal expiry date

casual worker *HR* somebody who provides labour or services under an irregular or informal working arrangement. A casual worker is usually considered as an independent contractor rather than an **employee**. Consequently, there is no obligation on the part of an employer to provide work, and there is no obligation on the part of the casual worker to accept all offers of work made by an employer.

category management *Mkting* the process of manufacturers and retailers working together to maximise profits and enhance customer value in any given product category. Category management has developed from **brand management** and the techniques of efficient consumer response, and is most prevalent in the fast-moving consumer goods sector. It is founded on the assumption that consumer purchase decisions are made from a range of products within a category and not merely by **brand** and has gained in prominence, as it is believed to meet customer needs better than standard brand management. *Abbr* **CM**

causality *Stats* the relation of events to the effects they produce

cause and effect diagram *Gen Mgt see* **fishbone chart**

CBD *abbr Gen Mgt* central business district: the area of a city where most company offices are located

cc *abbr E-com* carbon copy: a function included on most e-mail programs that enables Internet users to send a copy of the same message to as many people as they choose. All they need to do is place the e-mail addresses of intended recipients in the cc address line. Recipients see all other names. To conceal names, the **bcc** address line can be used.

CC *abbr* (*S Africa*) *Fin* close corporation

CCA *abbr Fin* current-cost accounting

CCAB *abbr Fin* Consultative Committee of Accountancy Bodies

ccc *abbr Fin* cwmni cyfyngedig cyhoeddus: the Welsh term for a public limited company

---

Give me fruitful error any time, full of seeds, bursting with its own corrections.
Vilfredo Pareto

ceiling effect *Stats* the occurrence of clusters of scores near the upper limit of the data in a statistical study

cellular manufacturing *Ops see* **group technology**

cellular organisation *Ops* a form of organisation consisting of a collection of self-managing firms or cells held together by mutual interest. A cellular organisation is built on the principles of self-organisation, member ownership, and entrepreneurship. Each cell within the organisation shares common features and purposes with its sister cells but is also able to function independently. The idea is an extension of the principles of **group technology**, or cellular manufacturing.

cellular production *Ops see* **group technology**

census *Stats* a study in which every member of a population is observed

central bank *Econ* the bank of a country that controls its credit system and its money supply

central business district *Gen Mgt see* **CBD**

centralisation *Gen Mgt* the gathering together, at a corporate headquarters, of specialist functions such as finance, personnel, and information technology. Centralisation is usually undertaken in order to effect economies of scale and to standardise operating procedures throughout the organisation. Centralised management can become cumbersome and inefficient and may produce communication problems. Some organisations have shifted towards **decentralisation** to try to avoid this.

centralised purchasing *Ops* the control by a central department of all the purchasing undertaken within an organisation. In a large organisation centralised purchasing is often located within the headquarters. Centralisation has the advantages of reducing duplication of effort, pooling volume purchases for discounts, enabling more effective inventory control, consolidating transport loads to achieve lower costs, increasing skills development in purchasing personnel, and enhancing relationships with **suppliers**.

Central Provident Fund *HR* in Singapore, a retirement benefit scheme. All employees and employers make compulsory contributions each month. *Abbr* **CPF**

Centrelink *Gen Mgt* an Australian government authority responsible for providing access to government services, including social security allowances and employment schemes. Established in 1997, it maintains a network of around 1,000 outlets.

CEO *abbr Gen Mgt* chief executive officer

CEO churning *Gen Mgt* the rapid rate at which chief executive officers are often removed from their posts (*slang*)

certainty equivalent method *Fin* an approach to dealing with risk in a capital budgeting context. It involves expressing risky future cash flows in terms of the certain cash flow which would be considered, by the decision-maker, as their equivalent.

certificate *Fin* a document representing partial ownership of a company that states the number of shares that the document is worth and the names of the company and the owner of the shares

certificate authority *E-com* an independent organisation that verifies the identity of a purchaser or merchant and issues a **digital certificate** attesting to this for use in e-commerce transactions

certificate of deposit *Fin* a negotiable instrument which provides evidence of a fixed-term deposit with a bank. Maturity is normally within 90 days, but can be longer.

certificate of incorporation *Fin* in the United Kingdom, a written statement by the Registrar of Companies confirming that a new company has fulfilled the necessary legal requirements for incorporation and is now legally constituted

certificate to commence business *Fin* in the United Kingdom, a written statement issued by the Registrar of Companies confirming that a public limited company has fulfilled the necessary legal requirements regarding its authorised minimum share capital

certified accountant *Fin* an accountant trained in industry, the public service, or in the offices of practising accountants, who is a member of the Association of Chartered Certified Accountants. Although they are not chartered accountants, they fulfil much the same role and they are qualified to audit company records.

certified public accountant (*US*) *Fin* an accountant trained in industry, the public service, or in the offices of practising accountants, who is a member of the American Institute of Certified Public Accountants. Although they are not chartered accountants, they fulfil much the same role and they are qualified to audit company records.

cessation *Fin* the discontinuation of a business for tax purposes or its trading on the stock market

CFO *abbr Gen Mgt* chief financial officer

CFR *abbr E-com* cost and freight

CGI Joe *HR* a computer programmer who lacks social skills and charisma. The term is modelled on 'GI Joe', a word for a US soldier that dates from the second world war; its first part is an abbreviation of 'computer generated imagery'. (*slang*)

CGT *abbr Fin* capital gains tax

chaebol *Gen Mgt see* **keiretsu**

chain of command *HR* the line of authority in a hierarchical organisation through which instructions pass. The chain of command usually runs from the most senior personnel, through all reporting links in an organisation's or department's structure, to a targeted person or to front-line employees. *Line management*

relies on the chain of command in order for instructions to pass throughout an organisation.

chainsaw consultant *HR* an outside expert brought into a company to reduce staff levels (*slang*)

chair *Gen Mgt* the most senior executive in an organisation. The chair of an organisation is responsible for running the **AGM**, and meetings of the **board of directors**. He or she may be a figurehead, appointed for prestige or power, and may have no role in the day-to-day running of the organisation. Sometimes the roles of chair and **chief executive** are combined, and the chair then has more control over daily operations; sometimes the chair is a retired chief executive. In the United States, the person who performs this function is often called a **president**. Historically, the term **chairman** was more common. The terms **chairwoman** or **chairperson** are later developments, although chair is now the most generally acceptable. Chairman, however, remains in common use, especially in the corporate sector.

chairman *Gen Mgt see* **chair**

chairman's report *or* **chairman's statement** *Fin* a statement included in the annual report of most large companies in which the chair of the board of directors gives an often favourable overview of the company's performance and prospects

chairperson *Gen Mgt see* **chair**

chairwoman *Gen Mgt see* **chair**

Champy, James (*b.* 1942) *Gen Mgt* US consultant. *See also* **Hammer, Michael**

Chandler, Alfred (*b.* 1918) *Gen Mgt* US academic. Pioneer of business history who established a framework and rationale for the subject and suggested that the main function of an organisation is to implement *strategy*. In *Strategy and Structure* (1962), he argued that the optimum use of resources stemmed not merely from the way they were organised but,

---

Managing intellectual assets has become the single most important task of business.
Thomas Stewart

more importantly, from the organisation's strategic goals. He concluded that organisational structures are driven by the changing demands and pressures of the marketplace, and that market-driven organisations favour a loosely coupled divisional structure.

change agent *Gen Mgt see* ***change management***

change management *Gen Mgt* the co-ordination of a structured period of transition from situation A to situation B in order to achieve lasting change within an organisation. Change management can be of varying scope, from ***continuous improvement***, which involves small on-going changes to existing processes, to radical and substantial change involving organisational strategy. Change management can be reactive or proactive. It can be instigated in reaction to something in an organisation's external environment, for example, in the realms of economics, politics, legislation, or competition, or in reaction to something within the processes, structures, people, and events of the organisation's internal environment. It may also be instigated as a proactive measure, for example, in anticipation of unfavourable economic conditions in the future. Change management usually follows five steps: recognition of a trigger indicating that change is needed; clarification of the end point, or 'where we want to be'; planning how to achieve the change; accomplishment of the transition; and maintenance to ensure the change is lasting. Effective change management involves alterations on a personal level, for example, a shift in attitudes or work routines, and thus personnel management skills such as ***motivation*** are vital to successful change. Other important influences on the success of change management include leadership style, communication, and a unified positive attitude to the change among the workforce. ***Business process reengineering*** is one type of change management, involving the redesign of processes within an organisation to raise performance. **Change agents** are those people within an organisation who are leaders and champions of the change process. With the accelerating pace of change in the business environment in the 1990s and 2000s, change has become accepted as a fact of business life and is the subject of books on management.

changeover time *Fin* the period required to change a workstation from a state of readiness for one operation to a state of readiness for another

channel *Mkting* a method of selling and distributing products to customers, directly or through intermediaries. Channels include direct sales, retail outlets, the Internet, and wholesalers.

channel communications *Mkting* communications aimed at organisations that sell and distribute products to customers, for example, retailers, sales teams, or wholesalers

channel management *Mkting* the organisation of the ways in which companies reach and satisfy their customers. Channel management involves more than just distribution and has been described as management of how and where a product is used and of how the customer and the product interact. Channel management covers processes for identifying key customers, communicating with them, and continuing to create value after the first contact.

channel strategy *Mkting* a management technique for determining the most effective method of selling and distributing products to customers

channel stuffing *Fin* the artificial boosting of sales at the end of a financial year by offering distributors and dealers incentives to buy a greater quantity of goods than they actually need (*slang*)

channel support *Mkting* marketing or financial support aimed at improving the performance of organisations that sell and distribute products to customers, for example, retailers, sales teams, or wholesalers

---

A committee is an animal with four back legs.   *John Le Carré*

chaos 1. *Gen Mgt* a situation of unpredictability and rapid change. **Chaos theory** emerged in the 1970s as a mathematical concept that defied the theory of cause and effect to assert that behaviour is essentially random. Such writers as *Tom Peters*, who wrote *Thriving on Chaos* in 1987, have applied the theory to management, arguing that attempts to plan and control management processes are fundamentally doomed to failure and that, instead, managers should embrace change and flexibility in order to cope with an environment that is altering at an ever-increasing rate. **2.** *Stats* a situation in which a deterministic model displays behaviour that appears to be random

chaos theory *Gen Mgt see* **chaos**

CHAPS *abbr Fin* Clearing House Automated Payment System: a method for the rapid electronic transfer of funds between participating banks on behalf of large commercial customers, where transfers tend to be of significant value

Chapter 11 *Fin* the US Bankruptcy Reform Act (1978) that entitles enterprises experiencing financial difficulties to apply for protection from creditors and thus have an opportunity to avoid bankruptcy

charge *Fin* a legal interest in land or property created in favour of a creditor to ensure that the amount owing is paid off

chargeable assets *Fin* in the United Kingdom, assets that are subject to *capital gains tax*. Exempt assets include an individual's principal private residence, investments held within a PEP or ISA, and gilts and individual chattels worth no more than a certain sum.

chargeable gain *Fin* in the United Kingdom, a profit from the sale of an asset that is subject to *capital gains tax*

chargeable transfer *Fin* in the United Kingdom, gifts that are liable to inheritance tax. Under UK legislation, individuals may gift assets to a certain value during their lifetime without incurring any liability to inheritance tax. These are

regular transfers out of income that do not affect the donor's standard of living. Additionally, individuals may transfer up to £3,000 a year out of capital. If this exemption is not used in one year, or is only partially used, then the unused allowance may be carried forward to the next year providing the full exemption is then used. Each person may also make small annual gifts of up to £250 per donee. Additionally a parent may give up to £5,000 on the occasion of an offspring's marriage, while a grandparent or more remote ancestor may give up to £2,500, and any other person up to £1,000. Other outright gifts during a lifetime to an individual, and certain types of trust, are known as **potentially exempt transfers**: there is no inheritance tax to be paid on these at the time of the gift, but a liability arises if the donor dies within seven years, with that liability decreasing the longer the donor survives. If the donor dies within seven years of the gift, then potentially exempt transfers become chargeable transfers for inheritance tax purposes.

charge account *Fin* a facility with a retailer that enables the customer to buy goods or services on credit rather than pay in cash. The customer may be required to settle the account within a month to avoid incurring interest on the credit. *Also known as* **credit account**

charge and discharge accounting *Fin* formerly, a bookkeeping system in which a person charges himself or herself with receipts and credits himself or herself with payments. This system was used extensively in medieval times before the advent of double-entry bookkeeping.

charismatic authority *Gen Mgt* a style of **leadership** based on the leader's exceptional personal qualities. Charismatic authority is one of *Max Weber*'s three types of legitimate **authority**. A charismatic leader is set apart from others by special qualities that inspire employees to follow and obey of their own free will. This is similar to the **great man theory** of leadership.

I learned then what a bunch of gangsters the banks are. They really are gangsters.
        Alan Sugar

charitable contribution *Fin* a donation by a company to a charity

charity accounts *Fin* the accounting records of a charitable institution, that include a statement of financial activities rather than a profit and loss account. In the United Kingdom, the accounts should conform to the requirements stipulated in the Charities Act (1993).

chartered accountant *Fin* in the United Kingdom, a qualified professional accountant who is a member of an Institute of Chartered Accountants. Chartered accountants are qualified to audit company accounts and some hold management positions in companies. *Abbr* **CA**

Chartered Association of Certified Accountants *Fin* former name for the Association of Chartered Certified Accountants

chartered company *or* **chartered entity** *Fin* in the United Kingdom, an organisation formed by the grant of a royal charter. The charter authorises the entity to operate and states the powers specifically granted.

Chartered Institute of Management Accountants *Fin see* **CIMA**

Chartered Institute of Public Finance and Accountancy *Fin see* **CIPFA**

Chartered Institute of Taxation *Fin* in the United Kingdom, an organisation for professionals in the field of taxation, formerly the Institute of Taxation

chartist *Fin* an analyst who studies past stock market trends, the movement of share prices, and changes in the accounting ratios of individual companies. The chartist's philosophy is that history repeats itself: using charts and graphs, he or she uses past trends and repetitive patterns to forecast the future. Although the chartist approach is considered narrower than that of a traditional analyst, it nevertheless has a good following.

chart of accounts *Fin* a comprehensive and systematically arranged list of the named and numbered accounts applic-

able to an enterprise. Originally devised in Germany, it provides a standard list of account codes for assets, liabilities, capital, revenue, and expenses. It is still used in Germany on a voluntary basis and was adopted as part of the French general accounting plan after the second world war.

chase demand plan *Ops* a *production control* plan that attempts to match *capacity* to the varying levels of forecast demand. Chase demand plans require *flexible working* practices and place varying demands on equipment requirements. Pure chase demand plans are difficult to achieve and are most commonly found in operations where output cannot be stored or where the organisation is seeking to eliminate stores of finished goods.

chat system *E-com* a system that enables Internet users to engage in text-based communication in real time. Messages posted via a chat system will be seen by every member of the participating group. It is a useful means for an organisation to take the pulse of consumers to find out what they are thinking, and to generate unique content.

Online chat can be particularly effective when there is a specific event occurring that is of interest to people, or when an expert can be made available to talk about a subject or product. To be productive, online chat needs to be well moderated, and is really only suited to small groups of people (2 to 20) at any one time.

cheap money *Fin* low interest rates, used as a government strategy to stimulate an economy either at the initial signs of, or during, a recession

check *(US) Fin* = *cheque*

checking account *(US) Fin* = *current account*

cheque *Fin* an order in writing requiring the banker to pay on demand a certain sum in money to a specified person or bearer. Although a cheque can theoretically be written on anything—in a P.G.

Wodehouse story, one was written on the side of a cow—banks issue preprinted, customised forms for completion by an account holder who inserts the date, the name of the person to be paid (the payee), the amount in both words and figures, and his or her signature. The customer is the drawer. *US term* **check**

cherry picking *Gen Mgt* the selection of what is perceived to be the best or most valuable from a series of ideas or options

CHESS *Gen Mgt* Clearing House Electronic Subregister System, a centralised electronic share transfer and settlement system operated by the Australian Stock Exchange. It issues shareholders with regular holding statements.

chief executive *Gen Mgt* the person with overall responsibility for ensuring that the daily operations of an organisation run efficiently and for carrying out strategic plans. The chief executive of an organisation normally sits on the **board of directors**. In a limited company, the chief executive is usually known as a *managing director*.

chief executive officer *Gen Mgt* the highest ranking executive officer within a company or corporation, who has responsibility for overall management of its day-to-day affairs under the supervision of the board of directors. *Abbr* **CEO**

chief financial officer *Gen Mgt* the officer in an organisation responsible for handling funds, signing cheques, the keeping of financial records, and financial planning for the company. *Abbr* **CFO**

chief information officer *Gen Mgt* the officer in an organisation responsible for its internal information systems and sometimes for its e-business infrastructure. *Abbr* **CIO**

chief operating officer *Gen Mgt* the officer in a corporation responsible for its day-to-day management and usually reporting to the chief executive officer. *Abbr* **COO**

chief technology officer *or* **chief technical officer** *Gen Mgt* the officer in an organisation responsible for research and development and possibly for new product plans. *Abbr* **CTO**

childcare provision *HR* a *personnel policy* to supply or to help towards the cost of care for the children of employees during working hours. The aim of childcare provision is to enable primary carers to return to work despite childcare responsibilities. It may apply to children of all ages and can be implemented in a single scheme or as a combination of options, for example, by setting up a workplace nursery or giving childcare vouchers or allowances. To comply with *equal opportunities* legislation, childcare provision has to be made available to both male and female employees.

Chinese wall *Gen Mgt* the procedures enforced within a securities firm to prevent the exchange of confidential information between the firm's departments so as to avoid the illegal use of inside information

chit
call in chits *Gen Mgt* to ask favours from people indebted to you (*slang*)

churn 1. *Fin* to encourage an investor to change stock frequently because the broker is paid every time there is a change in the investor's portfolio (*slang*) **2.** *Gen Mgt* to suffer a high labour turnover rate, especially in areas such as call centres or at chief executive level in large companies **3.** *Gen Mgt* to purchase a quick succession of products or services without displaying loyalty to any of them, often as a result of competitive marketing strategies that continually undercut rival prices, thus encouraging customers to switch brands constantly in order to take advantage of the cheapest or most attractive offers

churn rate 1. *Fin* a measure of the frequency and volume of trading of stocks and bonds in a brokerage account **2.** *Gen Mgt* the rate at which new customers try a product or service and then stop using it

chute
right out of the chute (*US*) *HR* extremely inexperienced (*slang*)

CICA *abbr Fin* Canadian Institute of Chartered Accountants

CIF *abbr E-com* cost, insurance, and freight

cigar
close, but no cigar *Gen Mgt* almost correct, but not quite. The term refers to the fact that cigar-smoking is seen by many businesspeople as a symbol of the celebration of a success. (*slang*)

CIMA *Fin* Chartered Institute of Management Accountants: an organisation that is internationally recognised as offering a financial qualification for business, focusing on strategic business management. Founded in 1919 as the Institute of Cost and Works Accountants, it has offices worldwide, supporting over 128,000 members and students in 156 countries.

CIO *abbr Gen Mgt* chief information officer

CIPFA *abbr Fin* Chartered Institute of Public Finance and Accountancy: in the United Kingdom, one of the leading professional accountancy bodies and the only one that specialises in the public services, for example, local government, public service bodies, and national audit agencies, as well as major accountancy firms. It is responsible for the education and training of professional accountants and for their regulation through the setting and monitoring of professional standards. CIPFA also provides a range of advisory, information, and consultancy services to public service organisations. As such, it is the leading independent commentator on managing accounting for public money.

circle the drain *Gen Mgt* to be on the brink of complete failure (*slang*)

circuit breaker *Fin* a rule created by the major US stock exchanges and the *Securities and Exchange Commission* by which trading is halted during times of extreme price fluctuations (*slang*)

circular file *Gen Mgt* a wastepaper basket in an office (*slang*)

circular flow of income *Econ* a model of a country's economy showing the flow of resources when consumers' wages and salaries are used to buy goods and so generate income for manufacturing firms

circularisation of debtors *Fin* the sending of letters by a company's auditors to debtors in order to verify the existence and extent of the company's assets

circular merger *Gen Mgt see* **merger**

circulation *Mkting* the number of copies sold or distributed of a single issue of a newspaper or magazine

City Code on Takeovers and Mergers *Fin* in the United Kingdom, a code issued on behalf of the Panel on Takeovers and Mergers that is designed principally to ensure fair and equal treatment of all shareholders in relation to takeovers. The Code also provides an orderly framework within which takeovers are conducted. It is not concerned with the financial or commercial advantages or disadvantages of a takeover nor with those issues, such as competition policy, which are the responsibility of government. The Code represents the collective opinion of those professionally involved in the field of takeovers on how fairness to shareholders can be achieved in practice.

claims adjuster (*US*) *Fin* = **loss adjuster**

class action *Fin* a civil law action taken by a group of individuals who have a common grievance against an individual, organisation, or legal entity

class of assets *Fin* the grouping of similar assets into categories. This is done because under International Accounting Standards Committee rules, tangible assets and intangible assets cannot be revalued on an individual basis, only for a class of assets.

classical economics *Econ* a theory focusing on the functioning of a market economy and providing a rudimentary explanation of consumer and producer

---

Run with your head the first two-thirds of a race and with your heart the final one third.
                                                                                                                            Jack Daniels

behaviour in particular markets. The theory postulates that, over time, the economy would tend to operate at full employment because increases in supply would create corresponding increases in demand.

classical system of corporation tax *Fin* a system in which companies and their owners are liable for corporation tax as separate entities. A company's taxed income is therefore paid out to shareholders who are in turn taxed again. This system operates in the United States and the Netherlands. It was replaced in the United Kingdom in 1973 by an *imputation system*.

classification *Fin* the arrangement of items in logical groups having regard to their nature (subjective classification) or purpose (objective classification). *See also* **code**

classified advertising *Mkting* advertising placed in newspapers or magazines under specific categories, for example, motoring or property

classified stock (*US*) *Fin* a company's common stock divided into classes such as Class A and Class B

class interval *Stats* any of the intervals of the frequency distribution in a set of statistical observations

clean float *Econ* a floating exchange rate that is allowed to vary without any intervention from the country's monetary authorities

clean opinion *or* **clean report** *Fin* an auditor's report that is not qualified

clean surplus concept *Fin* the idea that a company's income statement should show the totality of gains and losses, without any of them being taken directly to equity

clearing bank *Fin* a bank that deals with other banks through a clearing house

clearing house 1. *E-com see* **acquirer 2.** *Fin* an institution that settles accounts between banks

Clearing House Automated Payment System *Fin see* **CHAPS**

clearing system *Fin* the system of settling accounts among banks

clear title *Fin see* **good title**

clerical work improvement programme *Gen Mgt* a *clerical work measurement* technique that applies *standard time* data to clerical and administrative jobs, the aim of which is to ensure higher productivity and greater efficiency

clerical work measurement *Gen Mgt* an umbrella term for a collection of methods for measuring administrative and clerical work activities. Clerical work measurement is a variation on conventional *work measurement* practices. The main clerical work measurement techniques include *clerical work improvement programmes* and *group capacity assessment*.

CLI *abbr Gen Mgt* calling line identification

clickable corporation *E-com* a company that operates on the Internet

click rate *E-com see* **click-through rate**

clicks-and-mortar *or* **clicks-and-bricks** *E-com* combining a traditional bricks-and-mortar organisation with the click technology of the Internet. A clicks-and-mortar organisation has both a virtual and a physical presence. Examples include retailers with physical shops on the high street and also websites where their goods can be bought online.

clickstream *E-com* the virtual trail that a user leaves behind while surfing the Internet. A clickstream is a record of a user's activity on the Internet, including every web page visited, how long each page is visited for, and the order in which the pages are visited. Both *ISPs* and individual websites are able to track an Internet user's clickstream.

click-through *E-com* the selection of an ad by clicking on the banner or other on-screen device to take the user to the advertiser's website. The number of times users click on an ad can be counted, the total number of click-throughs being a measure of the success of the ad. *Also known as* **ad click**, **ad transfer**

click-through rate *E-com* the percentage of ad views that result in a click-through, a measure of the success of the ad in enticing users to the advertiser's website. *Also known as* **ad click rate**, **click rate**

click wrap agreement *or* **click wrap licence** *E-com* a contract presented entirely over the Internet, the purchaser indicating assent to be bound by the terms of the contract by clicking on an 'I agree' button. The term stems from 'shrink wrap' agreements, licences that become enforceable when the user removes designated packaging containing a copy of the agreement. *Also known as* **point and click agreement**

client 1. *Mkting* a person or organisation that employs the services of a professional person or organisation **2.** *E-com see* **server**

client base *Mkting* the regular *clients* of an organisation or professional person

clientele effect *Fin* the preference of an investor or group of investors for buying a particular type of security

clinical trial *Stats* a statistical study of human subjects to determine the effectiveness of a medical treatment

Clintonomics *Econ* the policy of former US President Clinton's Council of Economic Advisors to intervene in the economy to correct market failures and redistribute income

CLM *abbr HR* career-limiting move: an action that could endanger your career prospects, for example, criticising your boss publicly (*slang*)

CLOB International *Fin* in Singapore, a mechanism for buying and selling foreign shares, especially Malaysian shares

clock card *Fin* A document on which is recorded the starting and finishing time of

an employee, e.g. by insertion into a time-recording device, for ascertaining total actual attendance time.

Where an employee also clocks on and off different jobs within total attendance time, such cards are referred to as job cards.

clock in 1. *Gen Mgt* to register arrival at work without actually inserting a card into a time clock (*slang*) **2.** *HR* to register your arrival for work by inserting a card into a machine to record the time. Clocking in is a method of officially monitoring employees' *time keeping*.

close company *or* **closed company** *Gen Mgt* a company in which five or fewer people control more than half the voting shares, or in which such control is exercised by any number of people who are also directors

close corporation *or* **closed corporation 1.** (*US*) *Gen Mgt* a public corporation in which all of the voting stock is held by a few shareholders, for example, management or family members. Although it is a public company, shares would not normally be available for trading because of a lack of liquidity. **2.** (*S Africa*) *Fin* a business registered in terms of the Close Corporations Act of 1984, consisting of not more than 10 members who share its ownership and management. *Abbr* **CC**

closed-door policy *Gen Mgt see* **open-door policy**

closed economy *Econ* an economic system in which little or no external trade takes place

closed-end credit *Gen Mgt* a loan, plus any interest and finance charges, that is to be repaid in full by a specified future date. Loans that have property or motor vehicles as collateral are usually closed-end. *See also* **open-ended credit**

closed-end fund *or* **closed-end investment company** *Fin* a unit trust that has a fixed number of shares. *See also* **open-ended fund**

Work keeps us from three great evils: boredom, vice, and poverty. *Voltaire*

closed-end mortgage *Fin* a mortgage in which no prepayment is allowed. *See also* **open-ended mortgage**. *Also known as* **closed mortgage**

closed-loop production system *Ops* an environmentally friendly production system in which any industrial output is capable of being recycled to create another product

closed loop system *Fin* a management control system which includes a provision for corrective action, taken on either a feedforward or a feedback basis

closed mortgage *Fin see* **closed-end mortgage**

closed shop *HR* an agreement requiring members of a particular group of employees to be or to become members of a specified *trade union*. In the United Kingdom, the effect of trade-union and employment-law reforms have made closed shop agreements legally unenforceable.

closely-held corporation *Fin* a company whose shares are publicly traded but held by very few people

closely-held shares *Fin* shares that are publicly traded but held by very few people

Closer Economic Relations agreement *Fin see* **Australia and New Zealand Closer Economic Relations Trade Agreement**

closing balance *Fin* **1.** the amount in credit or debit in a bank account at the end of a business day **2.** the difference between credits and debits in a ledger at the end of one accounting period that is carried forward to the next

closing bell (*US*) *Fin* the end of a trading session at a stock or commodities exchange

closing entries *Fin* in a double-entry bookkeeping system, entries made at the very end of an accounting period to balance the expense and revenue ledgers

closing price *Fin* the price of the last transaction for a particular security or commodity at the end of a trading session

closing quote *Fin* the last bid and offer prices recorded at the close of a trading session

closing rate *Fin* the exchange rate of two or more currencies at the close of business of a balance sheet date, for example at the end of the financial year

closing-rate method *Fin* a technique for translating the figures from a set of financial statements into a different currency using the *closing rate*. This method is often used for the accounts of a foreign subsidiary of a parent company.

closing sale *Fin* a sale that reduces the risk that the seller has through holding a greater number of shares or a longer term contract

closing stock *Fin* a business's remaining stock at the end of an accounting period. It includes finished products, raw materials, or work in progress and is deducted from the period's costs in the balance sheets.

club culture *Gen Mgt* a *corporate culture* in which all lines of communication lead formally or informally to the leader. Club culture was identified by *Charles Handy*.

cluster analysis *Gen Mgt* a statistical method used to analyse complex data and identify groupings that share common features. Cluster analysis is a form of *multivariate analysis* that attempts to explain variability in a set of data. It involves finding unifying elements that enable identification of groups or clusters displaying common characteristics. It could be used, for example, to analyse results of *attitude research* and delineate groups of respondents that share certain attitudes.

clustered data *Stats* data in which sampling units in a study are grouped into clusters sharing a common feature, or longitudinal data in which clusters are defined by repeated measures on the unit

---

Man is born perfect. It is the capitalist system which corrupts him. **Arthur Scargill**

cluster sampling *Ops see **random sampling***

Clutterbuck, David (*b*. 1947) *Gen Mgt* British academic. Best known for his work on **mentoring**, and his research, with Walter Goldsmith, on consistently high-performing companies. Their findings were published in *The Winning Streak* (1984), which was viewed as the British equivalent of *Tom Peters*'s and *Robert Waterman*'s *In Search of Excellence* (1982).

CM *abbr Gen Mgt* category management

CNCC *abbr Fin* Compagnie Nationale des Commissaires aux Comptes

coaching *HR* the development of somebody's skills and knowledge through one-to-one **training**. Coaching is usually conducted by a more senior and experienced colleague. It involves planned training activities that have measurable outcomes and is designed to facilitate learning by providing guidance and support as well as tutoring. ***Executive coaching*** is a form of coaching used with senior managers.

COAG *abbr Gen Mgt* Council of Australian Governments

COB *abbr Fin* Commission des Opérations de Bourse

co-browsing *E-com* a facility that enables two or more Web users to synchronise their ***browsers***, so that they can see the same web pages at the same time.

Frequently employed by customer support services, co-browsing means that a customer service representative, using **live chat** or the telephone, can take a customer through a process, changing the customer's web page as they change their own. It is a particularly valuable feature if complex processes and information have to be delivered. *Also known as **page pushing***

cobweb site *E-com* an Internet site that has not been updated for a long time (*slang*)

code *Fin* a system of symbols designed to be applied to a classified set of items to give a brief, accurate reference, facilitating entry, collation and analysis. For example, in costing systems, composite symbols are commonly used. In the composite symbol 211.392 the first three digits might indicate the nature of the expenditure (subjective classification), and the last three digits might indicate the cost centre or cost unit to be charged (objective classification).

codec *E-com* either a hardware or a software component, used in ***videoconferencing***, that compresses and decompresses the audio and video signals. Hardware codecs are generally faster.

code of conduct *Gen Mgt* a statement and description of required behaviours, responsibilities, and actions expected of employees of an organisation or of members of a professional body. A code of conduct usually focuses on ethical and socially responsible issues and applies to individuals, providing guidance on how to act in cases of doubt or confusion.

code of practice *Gen Mgt* a policy statement and description of preferred methods for organisational ***procedures***.

Codes of practice may govern procedures for industrial relations, health and safety, and, more recently, customer service and professional development. An agreed code of practice enables activities to be carried out to a required organisational standard and provides a basis for dispute resolution.

coefficient of variation *Stats* a measure of the spread of a set of statistical data, calculated as the mean or standard deviation of the data multiplied by 100

co-financing *Fin* the joint provision of money for a project by two or more parties

coherence *Stats* a measure of the strength of association between two time series

cohesion fund *Gen Mgt* the main financial instrument for reducing economic and social disparities within the European Union by providing financial help for projects in the fields of the environment and transport infrastructure

---

Corporate courage is usually no greater than personal courage. *Edward Teller*

cohort *Stats* a group of individuals in a statistical study that have a common characteristic

cohort study *Stats* a study in which a group of individuals such as children with the same birth date are observed over several years

coin analysis *Fin* the quantities and denominations of banknotes and coins required to pay employees on a payroll

coincidence *Stats* the occurrence of events that are related but have no apparent common cause

cold calling *Mkting* the practice of making unsolicited calls to customers or consumers in an attempt to sell products or services. Cold calling is disliked, particularly by individual consumers, and is an inefficient way of selling as the take-up rate is very low.

cold transfer *Gen Mgt* an incoming phone call that is transferred by an operator without giving any notice or explanation to the caller or to the recipient of the call (*slang*)

collaborative working *HR* a method of working in which people at different locations or from different organisations work together electronically using video-conferencing, e-mail, networks, and other communication tools

collar *Fin* a contractually imposed lower limit on a financial instrument

collateral *Fin* property or goods used as security against a loan and forfeited to the lender if the borrower defaults

collateral trust certificate *Fin* a bond for which shares in another company, usually a subsidiary, are used as collateral

collection ratio *Fin* the average number of days it takes a firm to convert its accounts receivable into cash.

EXAMPLE Ideally, this period should be decreasing or constant. A low figure means the company collects its outstanding receivables quickly. Collection ratios are usually reviewed quarterly or yearly.

Calculating the collection ratio requires three figures: total accounts receivable, total credit sales for the period analysed, and the number of days in the period (annual, 365; six months, 182; quarter, 91). The formula is:

Accounts receivable / total credit sales for the period × number of days in the period

For example: if total receivables are £4,500,000, total credit sales in a quarter are £9,000,000, and number of days is 91, then:

$$4,500,000 / 9,000,000 × 91 = 45.5$$

Thus, it takes an average 45.5 days to collect receivables.

Properly evaluating a collection ratio requires a standard for comparison. A traditional rule of thumb is that it should not exceed a third to a half of selling terms. For instance, if terms are 30 days, an acceptable collection ratio would be 40 to 45 days.

Companies use collection ratio information with an *accounts receivable ageing* report. This lists four categories of receivables: 0–30 days, 30–60 days, 60–90 days, and over 90 days. The report also shows the percentage of total accounts receivable that each group represents, allowing for an analysis of delinquencies and potential bad debts. *Also known as days' sales outstanding*

collective agreement *HR* a contract between a *trade union* and an employer, resulting from *collective bargaining* and covering *conditions of employment* and procedural arrangements for resolving disputes. In the United Kingdom, a collective agreement is not legally binding unless it is in writing and specifically states the parties' intention to be bound. An agreement can become legally binding by being incorporated into an employee's personal *contract of employment*. Agreements may be concluded at organisation or industry level.

collective bargaining *HR* negotiations about *conditions of employment* between an employer, a group of employers or their representatives, and employees' representatives such as *trade unions* with a view to reaching a *collective agreement*

Three failures denote uncommon strength. A weakling has not enough grit to fail thrice.
                                                                    Minna Antrim

collocation hosting *E-com* a *hosting option* which involves a customer placing their own servers with a hosting vendor. The customer manages everything that happens on their servers: content, software, and the hardware itself. The hosting provider supplies an agreed speed of access to the Internet and amount of *data transfer*, and usually some minimum service, such as ensuring that the customer's server is up and running, and rebooting it if necessary.

colour supplement *Mkting* a magazine printed in colour and distributed with a newspaper

combination bond *Fin* a government bond for which the collateral is both revenue from the financed project and the government's credit

combined financial statement *Fin* a written record covering the assets, liabilities, net worth, and operating statement of two or more related or affiliated companies

COMEX *abbr Fin* commodity exchange

comfort letter *Fin* **1.** in the United States, a statement from an accounting firm provided to a company preparing for a public offering, that confirms that the unaudited financial information in the prospectus follows *Generally Accepted Accounting Principles* **2.** a letter from the parent company of a subsidiary that is applying for a loan, stating the intention that the subsidiary should remain in business

command and control approach *Gen Mgt* a style of leadership that uses standards, *procedures*, and output statistics to regulate the organisation. A command and control approach to leadership is authoritative in nature and uses a *top-down approach*, which fits well in bureaucratic organisations in which privilege and power are vested in *senior management*. It is founded on, and emphasises a distinction between, executives on the one hand and workers on the other. It stems from the principles of *Frederick*

Winslow Taylor, and the applications of *Henry Ford* and *Alfred Sloan, Jr*. As more empowered, *flat organisations* have come to the fore, command and control leaders have been increasingly criticised for stifling creativity and limiting flexibility.

command economy *Econ* an economy in which all economic activity is regulated by the government, as in the former Soviet Union or China

commerce *Fin* the large-scale buying and selling of goods and services, usually applied to trading between different countries

commerce integration *Fin* the blending of Internet-based commerce capabilities with the *legacy systems* of a traditional business to create a seamless transparent process

commerce server *E-com* **1.** a computer in a network that maintains all transactional and backend data for an e-commerce website **2.** a networked computer that contains the programs required to process transactions via the Internet, including dynamic inventory databases, shopping cart software, and online payment systems

commerce service provider *E-com* an organisation or company that provides a service to a company to facilitate some aspect of electronic commerce, for example, by functioning as an Internet *payment gateway*. *Abbr* **CSP**

commercial¹ *Fin* relating to the buying and selling of goods and services

commercial² *Mkting* an advertising message that is broadcast on television or radio

commercial bank *Fin* a bank that primarily provides financial services to businesses. *See also* *merchant bank*

commercial exposure potential (*US*) *Mkting* the estimated number of possible recipients of a commercial message

commercial hedger *Fin* a company that holds options in the commodities it produces

commercialisation *Fin* the application of business principles to something in order to run it as a business

commercial law *Gen Mgt* the body of law that deals with the rules and institutions of commercial transactions, including banking, commerce, contracts, copyrights, insolvency, insurance, patents, trademarks, shipping, storage, transportation, and warehousing

commercial loan *Fin* a short-term renewable loan or line of credit used to finance the seasonal or cyclical working capital needs of a company

commercial paper *Fin* uncollateralised loans obtained by companies, usually on a short-term basis. *Also known as **mercantile paper***

commercial report *Fin* an investigative report made by an organisation such as a credit bureau that specialises in obtaining information regarding a person or organisation applying for something such as credit or employment

commercial substance *Fin* the economic reality that underlies a transaction or arrangement, regardless of its legal or technical denomination. For example, a company may sell an office block and then immediately lease it back: the commercial substance may be that it has not been sold.

commercial time *Mkting* an interval of time, usually measured in multiples of 15 seconds, during a radio or television broadcast available for purchase by an advertiser to broadcast its commercial message

commercial version *Gen Mgt* a version of a software program that is released for sale to customers. Earlier versions, called test versions or beta versions, are used to develop and test the software.

commercial year *Fin* an artificial year treated as having 12 months of 30 days

each, used for calculating such things as monthly sales data and inventory levels

commission *HR* a payment made to an intermediary, often calculated as a percentage of the value of goods or services provided. Commission is most often paid to sales staff, brokers, or agents.

Commission des Opérations de Bourse *Fin* the body, established by the French government in 1968, that is responsible for supervising France's stock exchanges. *Abbr* **COB**

Commissioners of the Inland Revenue *Fin* in the United Kingdom, officials responsible for hearing appeals by taxpayers against their tax assessment

commitment accounting *Fin* a method of accounting which recognises expenditure as soon as it is contracted

commitment document *Fin* a contract, change order, purchase order, or letter of intent pertaining to the supply of goods and services that commits an organisation to legal, financial, and other obligations

commitment fee *Fin* a fee that a lender charges to guarantee a rate of interest on a loan a borrower is soon to make. *Also known as **establishment fee***

commitment letter (*US*) *Fin* an official notice from a lender to a borrower that the borrower's application has been approved and confirming the terms and conditions of the loan

commitments basis *Fin* the method of recording the expenditure of a public sector organisation at the time when it commits itself to it rather than when it actually pays for it

commitments for capital expenditure *Fin* the amount a company has committed to spend on fixed assets in the future. In the United Kingdom, companies are legally obliged to disclose this amount, and any additional commitments, in their *annual report*.

committed costs *Fin* costs arising from prior decisions, which cannot, in the short run, be changed. Committed cost incurrence often stems from strategic decisions concerning capacity, with resulting expenditure on plant and facilities. Initial control of committed costs at the decision point is through investment appraisal techniques. *See also commitment accounting*

committee *Gen Mgt* a group of people appointed and authorised to study, investigate, or make recommendations on a particular matter

Committee on Accounting Procedure *Fin* in the United States, a committee of the American Institute of Certified Public Accountants that was responsible between 1939 and 1959 for issuing accounting principles, some of which are still part of the Generally Accepted Accounting Principles

commodities exchange *Fin* a market in which raw materials are bought and sold in large quantities as *actuals* or *futures*

commodity *Econ* a good or service, for example, cotton, wool, or a laptop computer, resulting from the process of *production*

commodity-backed bond *Fin* a bond tied to the price of an underlying commodity, for example, gold or silver, often used as a hedge against inflation

commodity contract *Fin* a legal document for the delivery or receipt of a commodity

commodity exchange *Fin* an exchange where futures are traded, for example, the commodity exchange for metals in the United States. *Abbr* **COMEX**

commodity future *Fin* a contract to buy or sell a commodity at a predetermined price and on a particular delivery date

commodity paper *Fin* loans for which commodities are collateral

commodity pool *Fin* a group of people who join together to trade in options

commodity pricing *Fin* pricing a product or service on the basis that it is undifferentiated from all competitive offerings, and cannot therefore command any price premium above the base market price

commodity-product spread *Fin* co-ordinated trades in both a commodity and a product made from it

common cost *Fin* cost relating to more than one product or service

common market *Econ* an economic association, typically between nations, with the goal of removing or reducing trade barriers

common seal *Fin* the impression of a company's official signature on paper or wax. Certain documents, such as share certificates, have to bear this seal. *Also known as company seal*

common-size financial statements *Fin* statements in which all the elements are expressed as percentages of the total. Such statements are often used for making performance comparisons between companies.

common stock *Fin* a stock that pays a dividend after dividends for preferred stock have been paid

common stock ratio *Fin* a measure of the interest each stockholder has in the company's capital

Commonwealth of Australia *Gen Mgt* the full, official name of the country of Australia

Commonwealth of Australia Gazette *Gen Mgt* a journal that reports the actions and decisions of the Australian federal government. It has been published since 1901.

Commonwealth Scientific and Industrial Research Organisation *abbr* (*ANZ*) *Gen Mgt* CSIRO

commorientes *Fin* the legal term for two or more people who die at the same time. For the purposes of inheritance law, in the event of two dying at the same time, it is assumed that the older person died first.

communication *Gen Mgt* the exchange of messages conveying information, ideas, attitudes, emotions, opinions, or instructions between individuals or groups with the aim of creating, understanding, or co-ordinating activities. Communication is essential to the effective operation of an organisation. It may be conducted informally through a *grapevine* or formally by means of letters, reports, briefings, and *meetings*. Communication may be verbal or *non-verbal communication* and include spoken, written, and visual elements.

communications *Gen Mgt* **1.** systems or technologies used for the communication of messages, such as postal and telephone networks, or for communicating within an organisation **2.** messages exchanged in the process of *communication*

communications channel *Gen Mgt* a medium through which a message is passed in the process of *communication*. Communications channels include the spoken, written, and printed word, and electronic or computer-based media such as radio and television, telephones, videoconferencing, and electronic mail. The most effective channel for a specific message depends on the nature of the message and the audience to be reached, as well as the context in which the message is to be transmitted.

communications envelope *E-com see electronic envelope*

communication skills *HR* skills that enable people to communicate effectively with one another. Effective communication involves the choice of the best *communications channel* for a specific purpose, the technical knowledge to use the channel appropriately, the presentation of information in an appropriate manner for the target audience, and the ability to understand messages and responses received from others. The ability to establish and develop mutual understanding, trust, and co-operation is also important. More specifically, communication skills include the ability to speak in public, make presentations, write

letters and reports, chair committees and meetings, and conduct negotiations.

communications management *Mkting* the management, measurement, and control activities undertaken to ensure the effectiveness of communications

communications strategy *Mkting* a management technique for determining the most effective method of communicating with the marketplace

communication technology *Gen Mgt* electronic systems used for communication between individuals or groups. Communication technology facilitates communication between individuals or groups who are not physically present at the same location. Systems such as telephones, telex, fax, radio, television, and video are included, as well as more recent computer-based technologies, including *electronic data interchange* and *e-mail*.

Communism *Econ* a classless society where private ownership of goods is abolished and the means of production belong to the community

community *E-com* a group of Internet users with a shared interest or concept who interact with each other in newsgroups, mailing-list discussion groups, and other online interactive forums

community initiative *Gen Mgt see community involvement*

community involvement *Gen Mgt* programmes through which organisations aim to make a positive contribution to the local community by identifying problems and initiating practical action in order to address them in partnership with local people. Community involvement programmes developed through the growing emphasis on the social responsibility of business in the 1960s and 1970s. Such **community initiatives** often seek to promote economic and social regeneration in urban or rural areas and include activities such as the *secondment* of employees with appropriate skills, educational and training initiatives, *sponsorship* of arts and sports programmes, and *corporate giving* programmes.

Riches are a good handmaid, but the worst mistress. Francis Bacon

Compagnie Nationale des Commissaires aux Comptes *Fin* in France, an organisation that regulates external audit. *Abbr* **CNCC**

companion bond *Fin* a class of a collateralised mortgage obligation that is paid off first when interest rates fall leading to the underlying mortgages being prepaid. Conversely, the principal on these bonds will be repaid more slowly when interest rates rise and fewer mortgages are prepaid.

company *Gen Mgt* an association of people formed into a legal entity for the purpose of doing business. The most common form of company in the United Kingdom is the *registered company*. This is established by registering Articles and a Memorandum of Association with the *Registrar of Companies* at Companies House in accordance with *company law*. The most common forms of registered company are the *public limited company* and the *private company*.

company law *Gen Mgt* the body of legislation that relates to the formation, status, conduct, and *corporate governance* of companies as legal entities

company limited by guarantee *Fin* a type of organisation normally formed for non-profit purposes in which each member of the company agrees to be liable for a specific sum in the event of liquidation

company limited by shares *Fin* a type of organisation in which each member of the company is liable only for the fully paid value of the shares they own. This is the most common form of company in the United Kingdom.

company pension scheme *HR see occupational pension scheme*

company policy *Gen Mgt* a statement of desired standards of behaviour or procedure applicable across an organisation. Company policy defines ways of acting for staff in areas where there appears to be latitude in deciding how best to operate. This may concern areas such as time off for special circumstances, drug or alcohol abuse, *workplace bullying*, personal use of *Internet* facilities, or business travel. Company policy may also apply to customers, for example, policy on *complaints*, *customer retention*, or *disclosure of information*. Sometimes a company policy may develop into a *code of practice*.

company report *Gen Mgt* a document giving details of the activities and performance of a company. Companies are legally required to produce particular reports and submit them to the competent authorities in the country of their registration. These include *annual reports* and financial reports. Other reports may cover specific aspects of an organisation's activities, for example, environmental or social impact.

company seal *Fin see* **common seal**

company secretary *HR* a senior employee in an organisation with director status and administrative and legal authority. The appointment of a company secretary is a legal requirement for all limited companies. A company secretary can also be a **board secretary** with appropriate qualifications. In the United Kingdom, many company secretaries are members of the Institute of Chartered Secretaries and Administrators.

comparative advantage *Gen Mgt* an instance of higher, more efficient production in a particular area. A country that produces far more cars than another, for example, is said to have the comparative advantage in car production. *David Ricardo* originally argued that specialisation in activities in which individuals or groups have a comparative advantage will result in gains in trade.

comparative advertising *Mkting* a form of advertising that gives carefully selected details of competitor products for comparison with a company's own product, usually to the detriment of competitors. Comparative advertising is frequently used to advertise cars, where the availability of features such as a sun roof, air conditioning, advanced braking

---

Some are born great, some achieve greatness, and some hire public relations officers.
Daniel J. Boorstin

systems, fuel efficiency, safety features, and warranty terms in similarly priced cars are given.

comparative balance sheet *Fin* one of two or more financial statements prepared on different dates that lend themselves to a comparative analysis of the financial condition of an organisation

comparative credit analysis *Fin* an analysis of the risk associated with lending to different companies

comparative management *Gen Mgt* the simultaneous study of management or business practice in two or more different cultures, countries, companies, or departments

compassionate leave *HR* exceptional leave that may be granted to an employee on the death or serious illness of a close relative

compensating balance *Fin* **1.** the amount of money a bank requires a customer to maintain in a non-interest-bearing account, in exchange for which the bank provides free services **2.** the amount of money a bank requires a customer to maintain in an account in return for holding credit available, thereby increasing the true rate of interest on the loan

compensation *HR* **1.** *pay* given in recompense for work performed **2.** money paid by an employer on the order of an employment tribunal to an employee who has been unfairly dismissed. In the case of *unfair dismissal*, compensation comprises a basic award calculated by reference to length of *continuous service* and a compensatory award representing the employee's financial losses incurred as a result of the *dismissal*, including loss of future earnings, benefits, and pension. Additional compensation may be made if the employer fails to comply with an order to reinstate the employee. If the employee refuses an offer of reinstatement, or if the employee's conduct has contributed to the dismissal, the tribunal may reduce the amount of compensation awarded.

compensation package (*US*) *HR* a bundle of rewards including *pay*, financial incentives, and fringe benefits offered to, or negotiated by, an employee

competence *Gen Mgt, HR* an acquired personal skill that is demonstrated in an employee's ability to provide a consistently adequate or high level of performance in a specific job function. Competence should be distinguished from *competency*, although in general usage the terms are used interchangeably. Early attempts to define the qualities of effective managers were based on lists of the personality traits and skills of the ideal manager. This is an input model approach, focusing on the skills that are needed to do the job. These skills are competencies and reflect potential ability to do something. With the advent of scientific management, people turned their attention more to the behaviour of effective managers and to the outcomes of successful management. This approach is an output model, in which a manager's effectiveness is defined in terms of actual achievement. This achievement manifests itself in competences, which demonstrate that somebody has learned to do something well. There tends to be a focus in the United Kingdom on competence, whereas in the United States, the concept of competency is more popular. Competences are used in the workplace in a variety of ways. Training is often competence-based, and the UK *National Vocational Qualification* system is based on competence standards. Competences also are used in reward management, for example, in competence-based pay. The *assessment of competence* is a necessary process for underpinning these initiatives by determining what competences an employee shows. At an organisational level, the idea of *core competence* is gaining popularity.

competency *Gen Mgt, HR* an innate personal skill or ability. *See also competence*

competition *Gen Mgt* rivalry between companies to achieve greater *market share*. Competition between companies for customers will lead to product **innovation** and improvement, and ultimately lower prices. The opposite of market competition is either a **monopoly** or a **controlled economy**, where production is governed by quotas. A company that is leading the market is said to have achieved **competitive advantage**.

competitive advantage *Gen Mgt* a factor giving an advantage to a nation, company, group, or individual in competitive terms. Used by **Michael Porter** for the title of his classic text on international corporate strategy, *The Competitive Advantage of Nations* (1990), the concept of competitive advantage derives from the ideas on **comparative advantage** of the 19th-century economist **David Ricardo**.

competitive analysis *Gen Mgt* analysis carried out for marketing purposes that can include industry, customer, and **competitor analysis**. A thorough competitive analysis done within a strategic framework can provide in-depth evaluation of the capabilities of key competitors.

competitive equilibrium price *Econ* the price at which the number of buyers willing to buy a good equals the number of sellers prepared to sell it

competitive forces *Gen Mgt* the external business and economic factors that compel an organisation to improve its competitiveness

competitive intelligence *Gen Mgt* data gathered to improve an organisation's competitive capacity. Competitive intelligence may include, for example, information about competitors' plans, activities, or products, and may sometimes be gained through **industrial espionage**. Such information can have a significant impact on a company's own plans: it could limit the effectiveness of a new product launch, or identify growing threats to important accounts, for example. Unless organisations monitor competitor activity and take appropriate action, their business faces risk.

competitiveness index *Gen Mgt* an international ranking of states using eco-

nomic and other information to list countries in order of their competitive performance. A competitiveness index can show which countries have overall or industry-sector **competitive advantage**.

competitive pricing *Fin* setting a price by reference to the prices of competitive products

competitive saw *Fin* illustration of the principle that every investment in a product, while initially improving the reported performance in relation to competitors, eventually degrades and has to be succeeded by further investment(s) to maintain the competitive position

competitor analysis *or* **competitor profiling** *Gen Mgt* the gathering and analysis of information about competitors, especially in a corporate context, for **competitive intelligence** purposes

complaint *Gen Mgt* an expression of dissatisfaction with a product or service, either orally or in writing, from an internal or external customer. A customer may have a genuine cause for complaint, although some complaints may be made as a result of a misunderstanding or an unreasonable expectation of a product or service. How a complaint is handled will affect the overall level of **customer satisfaction** and may affect long-term customer loyalty. It is important for providers to have clear procedures for dealing rapidly with any complaints, to come to a fair conclusion, and to explain the reasons for what may be perceived by the customer as a negative response. *Also known as* **customer complaint**

complaints management *Mkting* a management technique for assessing, analysing, and responding to customer complaints

complementary goods *Mkting* goods sold separately, but dependent on each other for sales. Examples of complementary goods include toothbrushes and toothpaste or computers and computer desks.

complementor *Gen Mgt* a company that supplies a product that complements a product supplied by another company, for example, computers and software

complex adaptive system *Gen Mgt* a system that overrides conventional human controls because those controls will subdue inevitable change and development within that system. Complex adaptive systems are a product of the application of chaos theory (see *chaos*) and *complexity theory* to the world of organisations. According to writers such as *Richard Pascale*, organisations that are subject to too much control are at risk of failure. The *bureaucracy* has been cited as an example of extreme control and the *top-down approach* to management. However, if a bureaucracy is left to adapt naturally, it could become capable of self-organisation and of creating new methods of operating.

complexity theory *Gen Mgt* the theory that random events, if left to happen without interference, will settle into a complicated pattern rather than a simple one. Complexity theory is a development of chaos theory (see *chaos*). In a business context, it suggests that events within organisations and in the wider economic and social spheres cannot be predicted by simple models but will develop in a seemingly random and complex manner.

compliance audit *Fin* an audit of specific activities in order to determine whether performance is in conformity with a predetermined contractual, regulatory, or statutory requirement

compliance documentation *Fin* documents that a share-issuing company publishes in line with regulations on share issues

compliance officer *Fin* an employee of a financial organisation who ensures that regulations governing its business are observed

compounding *Fin* the calculation, payment, or receipt of *compound interest*

compound interest *Fin* interest calculated on the sum of the original borrowed amount and the accrued interest. *See also simple interest*

comprehensive auditing *Fin see value for money audit*

compressed workweek (*US*) *HR* a standard number of working hours squeezed into fewer than five days. Common models of the compressed working week include four ten-hour days or three twelve-hour days each week. An alternative variation is to lengthen the normal working day to a lesser extent, for example, by 45 minutes, to allow an extra day off every two or three weeks. The minimum modification is to work a slightly longer day for four days in return for a shorter Friday. A compressed workweek is often introduced as an employee benefit to provide an extended weekend through shorter Friday working.

compulsory acquisition *Fin* the purchase, by right, of the last 10% of shares in an issue by a bidder at the offer price

computer-aided design *Ops* the use of a computer to assist with the design of a product. Computer graphics, modelling, and simulation are used to represent a product on screen, so that designers can produce more accurate drawings than is possible on paper alone and to perform calculations easily, thereby optimising designs for production. *Abbr* **CAD**. *Also known as computer-assisted design*

computer-aided diagnosis *Stats* the use of a computer program that presents a patient with a series of diagnostic questions designed to produce a diagnosis of a health problem

computer-aided engineering *Ops* the application of computers to the generation of the engineering specifications of a product. Computer-aided engineering fits into the production process between *computer-aided design* and *computer-aided manufacturing*. It is similar to *CAD/CAM* software, but with a focus on the engineering processes required for converting a design to a manufacturable product. The software package can include aspects of design, analysis, process planning, numerical control, mould and tool design, and *quality control*. *Abbr* **CAE**

People can be themselves only in small comprehensible groups.   *E.F. Schumacher*

computer-aided manufacturing *Ops* a system in which the manufacture and assembly of a product are directed by a computer. Computer-aided manufacturing can be integrated with **computer-aided design** to create a **CAD/CAM** system. *Abbr* **CAM**. *Also known as* **computer-assisted manufacturing**

computer-aided production management *Ops* a system that enables all functions within an organisation that are associated with production management to be directed by computer. *MRP II* is a well-known form of computer-aided production management. *Abbr* **CAPM**

computer-assisted design *Ops see* **computer-aided design**

computer-assisted interview *Stats* an interview in which the interviewee keys in answers to questions displayed on screen by a computer program

computer-assisted manufacturing *Ops see* **computer-aided manufacturing**

computer-based training *HR* training carried out via a stand-alone or networked computer. Programs are usually interactive, so that students can select from multiple-choice options or key in their own answers. A popular medium for computer-based training is CD-ROM, although there is a growing trend towards **online training**, where computer-based training is delivered over the Internet or through company intranets. Computer-based training is a form of *e-learning*.

computer telephony integration *Gen Mgt* the combining of computer and telephone technology to allow a computer to dial telephone numbers, route calls, and send and receive messages. One product of computer telephony integration is the process of **calling line identification**, or CLI. CLI identifies the telephone number a customer is calling from, searches the customer database to identify the caller, and pops up the customer account on the receiver's computer screen, using the facility known as **screen popping**, before the call is answered. *Abbr* **CTI**

computer worm *E-com* a computer *virus* that does not try to damage the files it infects. Its objective is instead to replicate itself as quickly and as often as possible. Computer worms are a major drain on the Internet because they clog up *bandwidth*.

concentration services *Fin* the placing of money from various accounts into a single account

concept board *Mkting* a board used for presenting creative advertising ideas

concept search *E-com* an online search for documents related conceptually to a word, rather than specifically containing the word itself

concept testing *Mkting* research carried out to test the effectiveness of a creative advertising idea

concession *Gen Mgt* **1.** a compromise in opinion or action by a party to a dispute **2.** a reduction in price for a particular group of people **3.** the right of a retail outlet to set up and sell goods within another establishment **4.** an agreement to ignore the failure of a product or service to conform to its specification, with a possible resultant deterioration in the quality of the product or service

conciliation *HR* action taken by an independent negotiator to bring disputing sides together with the aim of restoring trust or goodwill and reaching an agreement or bringing about a reconciliation

concurrent engineering *Ops* a team-based co-operative approach to product design and development, in which all parties are involved in *new product development* work in parallel. Concurrent engineering reduces or removes the time-lag between the different stages of a product's development, and earlier entry into a market is therefore possible. Product quality is improved, development and product costs are minimised, and competitiveness is increased. *Also known as parallel engineering, simultaneous engineering*

Commercialism is doing well that which should not be done at all. *Gore Vidal*

conditional distribution *Stats* the probability distribution of a random variable while the values of one or more random variables are fixed

conditions of employment *Gen Mgt, HR* terms agreed between an employer and employee that are legally enforceable through a *contract of employment*. Conditions of employment include conditions that may be unique to the individual, for example, *notice periods*, remuneration, fringe benefits, and *hours of work*, as well as those that form organisation-wide policies, for example, discipline and *grievance procedures*, and those dictated by legislation.

conference *Gen Mgt* a type of *meeting* held between members of often disparate organisations to discuss matters of mutual interest. Conferences are held for a variety of reasons, including resolving problems, taking decisions, developing co-operation, and publicising ideas, products, and services. They may take place within an organisation but often draw people together regionally, nationally, or internationally, and involve a large number of speakers and delegates. Many conferences are organised for commercial profit.

conference call *Gen Mgt* a telephone call that connects three or more lines so that people in different locations can communicate and exchange information by voice. Conference calls reduce the cost of *meetings* by eliminating travel time and expenditure. Public switched telephone networks or dedicated private networks and a centrally located device called a bridge are used to connect the participants. Microphones and loudspeakers may also be used to make group-to-group communication possible. Conference calls are a type of *teleconferencing*.

confidence indicator *Fin* a number that gives an indication of how well a market or an economy will fare

confidence interval *Stats* the range of values of sample observations in a statistical study that contain the true parameter value within a given probability

confidentiality agreement *Gen Mgt* an agreement whereby an organisation that has access to information about the affairs of another organisation makes an undertaking to treat the information as private and confidential. A potential buyer of a company who requires further information in the process of due diligence may be asked to sign a confidentiality agreement stating that the information will only be used for the purpose of deciding whether to go ahead with the deal and will only be disclosed to employees involved in the negotiations. Such agreements are also used where information is shared in the context of a partnership or *benchmarking* programme.

conflict management *Gen Mgt, HR* the identification and control of conflict within an organisation. There are three main philosophies of conflict management: all conflict is bad and potentially destructive; conflict is inevitable and managers should attempt to harness it positively; conflict is essential to the survival of an organisation and should be encouraged.

conflict of interests *Gen Mgt* a situation in which a person or institution is caught between opposing concerns, loyalties, or objectives that prejudice impartiality. A conflict of interests may be between self-advantage and the benefit of an organisation for which somebody works, or it could arise when somebody is connected with two or more companies that are competing. The correct course of action in such cases is for the person concerned to declare any interests, to make known the way in which those interests conflict, and to abstain from participating in the *decision-making* process involving those interests. A conflict of interests may also arise when an institution acts for parties on both sides of a transaction and could derive an advantage from a particular outcome.

confusion matrix *Gen Mgt see discriminant analysis*

conglomerate *Fin* an entity comprising a number of dissimilar businesses

conglomerate company *Gen Mgt* an organisation that owns a diverse range of companies in different industries. Conglomerates are usually *holding companies* with subsidiaries in wide-ranging business areas, often built up through mergers and takeovers and operating on an international scale.

conglomerate diversification *Gen Mgt* the *diversification* of a *conglomerate company* through the setting up of *subsidiary companies* with activities in various areas

conjoint analysis *Gen Mgt* a research method aimed at discovering the most attractive combination of attributes, including price, package style, and size, for a product or service. In conjoint analysis, respondents express their preferences by filling in a questionnaire and ranking a number of contrasting combinations of attributes from the most to the least preferred. This enables values to be assigned to the range of features that customers consider when making a decision to purchase. *Also known as* **trade-off analysis**

connectivity *Gen Mgt* the ability of electronic products to connect with others, or of individuals, companies, and countries to be connected with one another electronically

connexity *Gen Mgt* the condition of being closely and intricately connected by worldwide communications networks

consequential loss policy *Fin see* **business interruption insurance**

consignment note *Fin see* **delivery note**

consol *Fin* irredeemable UK government stocks carrying fixed coupons. Sometimes used as a general term for an undated or irredeemable bond.

consolidated accounts *Fin see* **consolidated financial statement**

consolidated balance sheet *Fin* a listing of the most significant details of a company's finances

consolidated debt *Fin* the use of a large loan to eliminate smaller ones

consolidated financial statement *Fin* a listing of the most significant details of the finances of a company and of all its subsidiaries. *Also known as* **consolidated accounts**

consolidated fund *Fin* a fund of public money, especially from taxes, used by the government to make interest payments on the national debt and other regular payments

consolidated invoice *Fin* an invoice that covers all items shipped by one seller to one buyer during a particular period

consolidated loan *Fin* a large loan, the proceeds of which are used to eliminate smaller ones

consolidated tape *Fin* a ticker tape that lists all transactions of the New York and other US stock exchanges

consolidated tax return *Fin* a tax return that covers several companies, typically a parent company and all of its subsidiaries

consolidation *Fin* **1.** the uniting of two or more businesses into one company **2.** the combination of several lower-priced shares into one higher-priced one

consortium *Gen Mgt* a group of independent organisations that join forces to achieve a particular goal, for example, to bid for a project or to carry out co-operative purchasing. A consortium goes on to complete the project if its bid is successful and is often dissolved on completion. This form of temporary alliance allows diverse skills, capabilities, and knowledge to be brought together.

Constable, John (*b.* 1936) *Gen Mgt* British educator and consultant. Best known for the report *The Making of British Managers* (1987), with *Roger McCormick*, which led to major changes in the structure of *management development* in the United Kingdom. The publication of the report coincided with the equally influential *The Making of Managers: A Report on Management Education, Training, and Development in the USA, West Germany, France, Japan, and the UK* (1987) by **Charles Handy** and others.

constitutional strike (*US*) *HR* a form of *industrial action* that takes place after all dispute procedures or other provisions for the avoidance of strikes agreed between trade-union and employer representatives have been exhausted. A *no-strike agreement* effectively precludes constitutional strikes because it generally provides for automatic *arbitration*.

constraint *Fin* an activity, resource or policy that limits the ability to achieve objectives. Constraints are commonly used in mathematical programming to describe a restriction which forms part of the boundary for the range of solutions to a problem, and which define the area within which the solution must lie.

constructive dismissal *HR* a form of *unfair dismissal* that occurs when an employee leaves a job and his or her claim of *breach of contract* or overbearing conduct by the employer is proven

consultant *Gen Mgt* an expert in a specialised field brought in to provide independent professional advice to an organisation on some aspect of its activities. A consultant may advise on the overall management of an organisation or on a specific project such as the introduction of a new computer system. Consultants are usually retained by a client for a set period of time during which they will investigate the matter in hand and produce a report detailing their recommendations. Consultants may set up in business independently or be employed by a large consulting firm. Specific types of consultants include *management consultants* and *internal consultants*.

consultative committee *HR* a meeting of representatives of management and staff, convened for the purposes of joint consultation

consultative management *Gen Mgt* a style of management that takes employees' views into account for decision-making purposes

consumer *Mkting* somebody who uses a product or service. A consumer may not be the purchaser of a product or service and should be distinguished from a *customer*, who is the person or organisation that purchased the product or service. *Also known as* **end consumer**

consumer advertising *Mkting* advertising aimed at individuals and the domestic and family market as opposed to *industrial advertising*, which is aimed at businesses

consumer behaviour *Mkting see* **consumer demand**

consumer demand *Mkting* the patterns of **consumer behaviour** that affect their buying decisions. Consumer demand is influenced in various ways. Psychologists and marketers have identified three important factors affecting buying decisions: needs, which are things we must have, such as food; wants, which are nice to have but not essential, such as a new car; and motives, such as keeping up appearances. These factors form part of a profile that includes motivations, personality, perceptions, cognition, attitudes, and values. Other factors that influence demand include gender, age, social grouping, education, location, income, culture, and the seasons. Consumers can therefore be divided into discrete segments, each of which has a particular pattern of buying behaviour. Products and services can then be targeted at specific segments of the market.

consumer goods marketing *Mkting* the promotion of products to members of the public. Consumer goods marketing is aimed at individuals rather than organisations and promotes products directly to the end user rather than to intermediaries. Marketing strategies will be different from those used in *industrial goods marketing*.

consumerism *Mkting* the influence of the general public, as end users of products and services, on the way companies manufacture and sell their goods. Consumers exert considerable power over companies as organisations become more customer-focused. Demand is rising for products that are high quality, ethically produced, well priced, and safe, and consumerism pressurises companies to operate and produce goods and services in accordance with the public's wishes. In fact, the aims of consumerism are not at odds with those of marketing (see *marketing management*), as both have the end goal of pleasing the consumer. In practice, however, marketing does not always succeed, and there is still a need for legislation to back up the right of consumers to demand products that are of good quality and for consumer protection bodies that influence the commercial world on consumers' behalf. A particular form of consumer pressure, motivated by environmental concerns, is **green consumerism**, which campaigns for environmentally friendly goods, services, and means of production.

consumer market research *Mkting* *market research* that focuses on gathering and analysing data on individual or domestic consumers, as opposed to industrial or business customers. *Also known as* *consumer research*

consumer panel *Mkting* a carefully selected group of people whose purchasing habits are regularly monitored. A consumer panel usually consists of a large cross-section of the population so as to provide meaningful data. There are two types of panel: **diary panels**, where members fill in a regular detailed diary of purchases, and, less commonly, **home audit panels**, where visits are made to the homes of members to check purchases, packaging, and used cartons. These panels run over a period of time to gain a broad overview of purchasing habits. A *focus group* is similar to a consumer panel, but is usually used to determine customers' views of a specific product or range of products. Members of a group meet together under the guidance of a facilitator to discuss their opinions on a face-to-face basis.

consumer price index *Econ* an index of the prices of goods and services that consumers purchase, used to measure the cost of living or the rate of inflation in an economy. *Abbr* **CPI**

consumer profile *Mkting* a detailed analysis of a group of like *consumers*, covering influences on their purchasing habits such as age, gender, education, occupation, income, and personal and psychological characteristics. Consumer profiles are built up from extensive *market research* and are used for market segmentation purposes.

consumer protection *Mkting* the safeguarding of *consumer* interests in terms of quality, price, and safety, usually within a statutory framework. In the United Kingdom, the Sale of Goods Acts and related legislation require that goods sold must be of a merchantable quality. The growing purchasing power of consumers and the rise in *consumerism* from the late 1950s onwards led to increased demands for protection against unsafe goods and services and unscrupulous trading practices. As a result, the Office of Fair Trading was set up in 1973 with the main aim of promoting and safeguarding the economic interests of consumers at a national level. Regulators have been set up for all the utility companies—telecommunications, gas, electricity, water, railways—and local authorities have their own Trading Standards Offices. The National Consumer Council was set up in 1975 to represent the views of consumers to local and central government, and a number of smaller consumer councils represent consumers on a sectoral basis, for example, the Gas Consumer Council. Citizens' Advice Bureaux provide legal advice on a very wide range of consumer and other issues.

consumer research *Mkting* see *consumer market research*

Comin' in on a wing and a prayer.

Harold Adamson

consumer services marketing *Mkting* the marketing of services to domestic consumers. Consumer services marketing may promote such services as banking, insurance, travel and tourism, leisure, telecommunications, and services provided by local authorities. Strategies to market these services to business constitute *industrial services marketing*.

consumer spending *Mkting* the total value of household and personal expenditure measured at macro and micro levels. At the macro level, consumer confidence can be measured by the overall levels of consumer spending as published in, for example, *Social Trends* (Stationery Office), the *Family Expenditure Survey*, and other official publications, and from a demonstration that earnings have increased at a faster rate than prices, which indicates that spending power, or disposable income, has increased. At a micro level, there are innumerable market reports on the value of actual and predicted spend on a vast range of consumer goods, including food, pharmaceuticals, clothing, cars, and holidays. *Consumer demand* is a related concept.

consumer-to-consumer commerce *E-com* e-business transactions conducted between two individuals

consumption *Econ* the quantity of resources that consumers use to satisfy their current needs and wants, measured by the sum of the current expenditure of the government and individual consumers

contact card *E-com* a *smart card* in which the microprocessor chip is visible and can make physical contact with the reading device

contactless card *E-com* a *smart card* in which the microprocessor chip is not visible and is accessed by the reading device by radio signals rather than by physical contact. An increasingly common use of this technology is in such applications as toll collection where the card is accessed as the motorist displays it to the reading device in passing.

contact list *HR* a list of people created for the purpose of networking, job searching, and marketing and selling products and services.

Someone wanting to expand and develop their contact list should seek to do so both inside and outside the organisation they work for. Joining professional associations and volunteering for committees are good ways of doing this. Building relationships can take time, and it's better to do this before going to someone for help. It's also important that the relationships are reciprocal; someone building a contact list should think about what they can offer to their contacts, as well as what their contacts can do for them.

A contact list should cover three basic types of network: the personal (friends, family, church, local community), the professional (current and former colleagues, supervisors, teachers, customers, consultants, members of professional organisations), and the work life network (executive recruiters, college placement officers, career counsellors). A good system is needed for keeping track of these contacts, their details (including personal information), and any correspondence with them. Keeping in regular contact with them is vital, and finding ways to thank them for their help will ensure good future relations.

content *E-com* the textual, graphical, and multimedia material that constitutes a web page or website

content management *E-com* the means and methods of managing the textual and graphical content of a website. For large sites with thousands of pages and many interchangeable words and images, it pays to invest in a content management application system that facilitates the creation and organisation of web content. Some content management systems also offer caching (where a server stores frequently requested information) and analysis of site traffic.

Recent years have seen a vast growth in the quantity of content produced by organisations, particularly in digital form.

People don't choose their careers; they are engulfed by them.   *John Dos Passos*

In 2001, it was estimated that there were over 550 billion documents on Internet, intranet, and extranet websites—making professional content management vital. Without it, it becomes almost impossible for a user to find the information they are looking for.

However, excellent content management is expensive, and organisations need to establish a solid business case in order to justify it. The initial point for consideration is that content is not a low-level commodity that merely needs to be stored—it is a critical resource, and its value lies in it being read. So an understanding of who will read it is essential. Decisions need to be taken over what languages the material needs to be published in, and in what media (Web or e-mail, for example). The form of the content—text, audio, video—is also important, as is the sensitivity of the material and the consequent security required.

Simply storing content is data management, but content management should have publication as its main focus, with the intention of informing or entertaining readers. There is a big difference in approach between the two.

contestable market *Econ* a market in which there are no barriers to entry, as in *perfect competition*

context *E-com* information about a product made available on an Internet site that is seen as adding value for the consumer, for example, book reviews on a book site

contingency allowance *Gen Mgt see standard time*

contingency management *Gen Mgt* the capacity for flexibility in varying responses and attitudes to meet the needs of different situations. Contingency management may be practised by both individuals and organisations. Within the latter, it may be formalised through a *contingency plan* linked to *risk* or *crisis management* strategies, or be derived from the results of *scenario planning*.

contingency plan *Gen Mgt* a plan, drawn up in advance, to ensure a positive and rapid response to a changing situation. A contingency plan often results from *scenario planning* and may form part of an organisation's *disaster management* strategy.

contingency table *Stats* a table in which observations on several categorical variables are cross-classified

contingency tax *Econ* a one-off tax levied by a government to deal with a particular economic problem, for example, too high a level of imports coming into the country

contingency theory *Fin* the hypothesis that there can be no universally applicable best practice in the design of organisational units or of control systems such as management accounting systems. The efficient design and functioning of such systems is dependent on an awareness by the system designer of the specific environmental factors which influence their operation, such as the organisational structure, technology base, and market situation.

continuing professional development *HR see CPD*

continuous budget *Fin see rolling budget*

continuous disclosure *Fin* in Canada, the practice of ensuring that complete, timely, accurate, and balanced information about a public company is made available to shareholders

continuous improvement *Gen Mgt, Ops* the seeking of small improvements in processes and products, with the aim of increasing quality and reducing waste. Continuous improvement is one of the tools that underpin the philosophies of *total quality management* and *lean production*. Through constant study and revision of processes, a better product can result at reduced cost. *Kaizen* has become a foundation for many continuous improvement strategies, and for many employees it is synonymous with continuous improvement.

When two men always agree, one of them is unnecessary.   *William Wrigley*

continuous operation costing *or* **continuous process costing** *Fin* the costing method applicable where goods or services result from a sequence of continuous or repetitive operations or processes. Costs are averaged over the units produced during the period, being initially charged to the operation or process.

continuous service *HR* a period of employment with one *employer*, which begins with the day on which the *employee* starts work and ends with the date of *resignation* or *dismissal*. All service, regardless of hours worked, counts towards calculating continuous service. The length of continuous service may affect the length of *notice period* and is taken into account when calculating redundancy pay.

continuous shiftwork *HR* a pattern of work designed to provide cover seven days a week, 24 hours a day, comprising three eight-hour or two twelve-hour *shifts*, or a mix of the two. Continuous shiftwork may be necessary to make full use of expensive capital equipment or to provide round-the-clock customer service. It may be confined to one group of employees, such as computer or security staff, while other parts of the organisation use different shift patterns.

contour plot *Stats* a graphical representation of data in which three variables are plotted on a topographical map

contra *Fin* a bookkeeping term meaning against, or on the opposite side. It is used where debits are matched with related credits, in the same or a different account.

contract *Gen Mgt* a legally binding agreement between two or more parties. A contract is made as a result of an offer by one party and acceptance on the part of the other. It normally involves an undertaking made by one party in consideration of an undertaking made by the other party or parties. Contracts are generally written but may be oral. Contract law may lay down additional conditions for the creation of valid contracts in some cases. Types of contract include contracts for the supply of goods or services and *contracts of employment*.

contract broker *Fin* a broker who fills an order placed by somebody else

contract cost *Fin* aggregated costs of a single contract; usually applies to major long-term contracts rather than short-term jobs

contract costing *Fin* a form of specific order costing in which costs are attributed to individual contracts

contract distribution *Gen Mgt* the *outsourcing* of a company's distribution requirement to a third party under contract. Contract distribution can help a company drive down costs, reduce stockholdings, and achieve increased flexibility of delivery.

contract hire *Gen Mgt* an arrangement whereby an organisation enters into a *contract* for the use of assets owned by another organisation, as an alternative to purchasing the assets itself. Contract hire agreements normally cover a period shorter that the useful economic life of the assets concerned and often include arrangements for maintenance and replacement. Organisations frequently use contract hire arrangements for the provision of company cars or office equipment.

contracting *Gen Mgt* the process of making an agreement governed by a *contract* for the provision of goods or services to an organisation

contracting out 1. *HR* the withdrawal of employees by an employer from the State Earnings-Related Pension Scheme and their enrolment in an occupational pension scheme that meets specified standards **2.** *HR* the withdrawal by an employee from the State Earnings-Related Pension Scheme and the purchase by the employee of an appropriate *personal pension* **3.** *Gen Mgt* see *outsourcing*

contract manufacturing *Ops* the *outsourcing* of a requirement to manufacture

The new economy favours intangible things—ideas, information, and relationships.
Kevin Kelly

a particular product or component to a third-party company. Contract manufacturing enables companies to reduce the level of investment in their own capabilities to manufacture, while retaining a product produced to a high quality, at a reasonable price, and delivered to a flexible schedule.

contract month *Fin* the month in which an option expires and goods covered by it must be delivered. *Also known as **delivery month***

contract note *Fin* a document with the complete description of a stock transaction

contract of employment *Gen Mgt, HR* a legally enforceable agreement, either oral or written, between an employer and employee that defines terms and *conditions of employment* to which both parties must adhere. Express terms of the contract are agreed between the two parties and include the organisation's normal terms and conditions in addition to those that relate specifically to the individual. These terms can only be changed by employee agreement, if the contract itself allows for variation, or by terminating the contract. Terms are also implied in the contract by custom and practice or by common law.

contract purchasing *Ops* a mechanism for buying leased goods. In contract purchasing, a purchaser agrees to buy goods or equipment to be paid for in a series of instalments, each comprising a proportion of the capital and an interest element. After a final payment, legal ownership passes to the user. This mechanism is sometimes used in the United Kingdom to finance the purchase of company cars so that the organisation can get the full writing-down allowance.

contractual obligation *HR* the legal duty to take a stated course of action, as imposed by a commercial *contract* or a *contract of employment*

contributed content website *E-com* a website which allows visitors to contribute content, such as information about their identity, or postings on message boards. A good example is Amazon.com, which encourages users to publish reviews of the books they have read.

contributed surplus *Fin* the portion of shareholders' equity that comes from sources other than earnings, for example, from the initial sale of stock above its par value

contribution *Fin* sales value less variable cost of sales. Contribution may be expressed as total contribution, contribution per unit, or as a percentage of sales.

contribution centre *Fin* a profit centre in which marginal or direct costs are matched against revenue

contribution margin *Fin* a way of showing how much individual products or services contribute to net profit.

EXAMPLE Its calculation is straightforward:

Sales price – variable cost = contribution margin

Or, for providers of services:

Total revenue – total variable cost = contribution margin

For example, if the sales price of a good is £500 and variable cost is £350, the contribution margin is £150, or 30% of sales. This means that 30 pence of every sales pound remain to contribute to fixed costs and to profit, after the costs directly related to the sales are subtracted.

Contribution margin is especially useful to a company comparing different products or services. For example:

	Product A £	Product B £	Product C £
Sales	260	220	140
Variable costs	178	148	65
Contribution margin	82	72	75
Contribution margin (%)	31.5	32.7	53.6

One must have some sort of occupation nowadays. If I hadn't my debts I shouldn't have anything to think about.
Oscar Wilde

Obviously, Product C has the highest contribution percentage, even though Product A generates more total profit. The analysis suggests that the company might do well to aim to achieve a sales mix with a higher proportion of Product C. It further suggests that prices for Products A and B may be too low, or that their cost structures need attention. Notably, none of this information appears on a standard income statement.

Contribution margin can be tracked over a long period of time, using data from several years of income statements. It can also be invaluable in calculating volume discounts for preferred customers, and break-even sales or volume levels.

contribution per unit of limiting factor ratio *Fin* a ratio used in marginal costing to measure the contribution to fixed overhead and profit generated by the use of each unit of limiting factor. It is calculated by dividing the product or service contribution by the product or service usage of units of limiting factor. The ratio is used to rank alternative uses of the limiting factor.

contributions holiday *Fin* a period during which a company stops making contributions to its pension plan because the plan is sufficiently well funded

contribution to sales ratio *Fin* a ratio used in product profit planning and as a means of ranking alternative products. It is calculated as follows:

Revenue minus all variable costs × 100 / Revenue

control *Gen Mgt* the effective monitoring, regulation, and direction of operations and budgets by senior managers. Control is often considered to be the primary task of management and has traditionally been strongly linked to accounting, *stock control*, *production* or *operations management*, and *quality control*. It is usually linked to *management control systems* such as performance measurement and *performance indicators*, procedures, and inspections.

control account *Fin* a ledger account which collects the sum of the postings into the individual accounts which it controls. The balance on the control account should equal the sum of the balances on the individual accounts, which are maintained as subsidiary records.

controllability concept *Fin* the principle that management accounting identifies the elements or activities which management can or cannot influence, and seeks to assess risk and sensitivity factors. This facilitates the proper monitoring, analysis, comparison, and interpretation of information which can be used constructively in the control, evaluation, and corrective functions of management.

controllable cost *Fin* a cost which can be influenced by its budget holder

controlled circulation *Mkting* the number of copies of a newspaper or magazine distributed, usually free of charge, to an approved target audience

controlled disbursement *Fin* the presentation of cheques only once each day

controlled economy *Gen Mgt see competition*

control limits *Fin* quantities or values outside which managerial action is triggered. *See also* **management by exception**

conversion *Fin* **1.** a trade of one convertible financial instrument for another, for example, a bond for shares **2.** a trade of shares of one unit trust for shares of another in the same family

conversion price *Fin* the price per share at which the holder of convertible bonds, or debentures, or preference shares, can convert them into ordinary shares.

EXAMPLE Depending on specific terms, the conversion price may be set when the convertible asset is issued. If the conversion price is set, it will appear in the indenture, a legal agreement between the issuer of a convertible asset and the holder, that states specific terms. If the conversion price does not appear in the agreement, a conversion ratio is used to calculate the conversion price.

A conversion ratio of 25:1, for example, means that 25 shares of stock can be obtained in exchange for each £1,000 convertible asset held. In turn, the conversion price can be determined simply by dividing £1,000 by 25:

£1,000 / 25 = £40 per share

Comparison of a stock's conversion price to its prevailing market price can help decide the best course of action. If the shares of the company in question are trading at £52 per share, converting makes sense, because it increases the value of £1,000 convertible to £1,300 (£52 × 25 shares). But if the shares are trading at £32 per share, then conversion value is only £800 (£32 × 25) and it is clearly better to defer conversion.

conversion rate *Mkting* the percentage of potential customers who actually make a purchase

conversion ratio *Fin* an expression of the quantity of one security that can be obtained for another, for example, shares for a convertible bond.

EXAMPLE The conversion ratio may be established when the convertible is issued. If that is the case, the ratio will appear in the indenture, the binding agreement that details the convertible's terms.

If the conversion ratio is not set, it can be calculated quickly: divide the par value of the convertible security (typically £1,000) by its conversion price.

£1,000 / £40 per share = 25

In this example, the conversion ratio is 25:1, which means that every bond held with a £1,000 par value can be exchanged for 25 ordinary shares.

Knowing the conversion ratio enables an investor to decide whether convertibles (or group of them) are more valuable than the ordinary shares they represent. If the stock is currently trading at 30, the conversion value is £750, or £250 less than the par value of the convertible. It would therefore be unwise to convert.

A convertible's indenture can sometimes contain a provision stating that the conversion ratio will change over the years.

Conversion ratio also describes the number of ordinary shares of one type to be issued for each outstanding ordinary share of a different type when a merger takes place.

conversion value *Fin* the value a security would have if converted into shares

convertible ARM *Fin* an adjustable-rate mortgage that the borrower can convert into a fixed-rate mortgage under specified terms

convertible bond *Fin* a bond that the owner can convert into another asset, especially ordinary shares

convertible loan stock *Fin* a loan which gives the holder the right to convert to other securities, normally ordinary shares, at a predetermined price/rate and time

convertible preference shares *Fin* shares that give the holder the right to exchange them at a fixed price for another security, usually ordinary shares.

EXAMPLE Preference shares and other convertible securities offer investors a hedge: fixed-interest income without sacrificing the chance to participate in a company's capital appreciation.

When a company does well, investors can convert their holdings into ordinary shares that are more valuable. When a company is less successful, they can still receive interest and principal payments, and also recover their investment and preserve their capital if a more favourable investment appears.

Conversion ratios and prices are key facts to know about preference shares. This information is found on the indenture statement that accompanies all issues. Occasionally the indenture will state that the conversion ratio will change over time. For example, the conversion price might be £50 for the first five years, £55 for the next five years, and so forth. Stock splits can affect conversion considerations.

Tap the energy of the anarchist and he will be the one to push your company ahead.
Anita Roddick

In theory, convertible preference shares (and convertible exchangeable preference shares) are usually perpetual in time. However, issuers tend to force conversion or induce voluntary conversion for convertible preference shares within ten years. Steadily increasing ordinary share dividends is one inducement tactic used. As a result, the conversion feature for preference shares often resembles that of debt securities. Call protection for the investor is usually about three years, and a 30- to 60-day call notice is typical.

About 50% of convertible equity issues also have a 'soft call provision'. If the ordinary share price reaches a specified ratio, the issuer is permitted to force conversion before the end of the normal protection period.

convertible security *Fin* a convertible bond, warrant, or preference share

convertible share *Fin* non-equity share such as a preference share, carrying rights to convert into equity shares on predetermined terms

convertible term insurance *Fin* term insurance that the policyholder can convert to fixed life assurance under particular conditions

COO *abbr Gen Mgt* chief operating officer

cookie *E-com* a file written to a computer's hard disk by an Internet application to store small amounts of information that can be accessed to identify users and customise interactions with them. Cookies contain such data as registration or logon information, user preferences, shopping basket items, and credit-card numbers and expiry dates. The name is derived from UNIX objects called 'magic cookies'.

cooling-off period *HR* an agreed pause in a dispute, especially a labour dispute, to allow the tempers of the negotiating parties to cool before the resumption of negotiations

Cooper, Cary (*b*. 1940) *Gen Mgt* US-born academic. Based at the School of Management, University of Manchester Institute of Science & Technology, United Kingdom, Cooper focuses on *occupational psychology*, particularly **stress** management issues. His biggest-selling book is *Living with Stress* (1988, co-author).

co-operative *Mkting* a business that is jointly owned by the people who operate it, with all profits shared equally

co-operative advertising *Mkting* a joint advertising campaign between groups with a shared objective, for example, retailer groups, or manufacturer and retailer

co-operative movement *Gen Mgt* a movement that aims to share profits and benefits from jointly owned commercial enterprises among members. The movement was begun in Rochdale, Lancashire in 1844 by 28 weavers and developed to include manufacturing and wholesale businesses as well as insurance and financial services. The Co-op in the United Kingdom and the *Mondragon co-operative* in Spain are two of the best known examples.

co-opetition *Gen Mgt* co-operation between competing companies (*slang*)

copyright *Mkting* the legal protection for creative ideas, trademarks, and other brand-related material

copy testing *Mkting* research carried out to test the effectiveness of creative advertising copy

copywriter *Mkting* somebody who devises the wording of an advertisement or promotional material. A copywriter may be employed by an advertising agency or, in scientific or technical areas, directly by a manufacturing or distribution company. Many copywriters also work *freelance*.

core business *Gen Mgt* the central, and usually the original, focus of an organisation's activities that differentiates it from others and makes a vital contribution to its success. The concept of core business became prominent in the 1980s when *diversification* by large companies failed to generate the anticipated degree of commercial success. In 1982, *Tom Peters*'s and *Robert Waterman*'s book *In Search of Excellence* suggested that organisations should *stick to the knitting* and avoid diversifying into areas beyond their field of expertise. An organisation's core business should be defined by the *core competences* of the organisation.

core capability *Gen Mgt see core competence*

core competence *Gen Mgt, HR* a key ability or strength that an organisation has acquired that differentiates it from others, gives it *competitive advantage*, and contributes to its long-term success. The concept of core competence is most closely associated with the work of *Gary Hamel* and *C.K. Prahalad*, notably in their book *Competing for the Future* (1994). They describe core competences as bundles of skills and technologies resulting from *organisational learning*. These provide access to markets, contribute to customer value, and are difficult for competitors to imitate. Core competence is a resource-based approach to *corporate strategy*. The terms core competence and **core capability** are often used interchangeably, but some writers make varying distinctions between the two concepts.

core values 1. *Gen Mgt* the guiding principles of an organisation, espoused by senior management, and accepted by employees, often reflected in the *mission statement* of the organisation. Core values often influence the culture of an organisation and are normally long-standing beliefs. As **shared values**, they are included in the *McKinsey 7-S framework*, and are reported in *Richard Pascale*'s and *Anthony Athos*'s *The Art of Japanese Management* in their analysis of the rise of *Konosuke Matsushita*. **2.** *HR* a small set of key concepts and ideals that guide a person's life and help him or her to make important decisions

corpocracy *Gen Mgt* excessive or unwieldy corporate management resulting from the merger of several companies (*slang*)

corporate action *Fin* a measure that a company takes that has an effect on the number of shares outstanding or the rights that apply to shares

corporate amnesia *Gen Mgt* loss of organisational history and memory. Corporate amnesia occurs when senior or long-standing members of staff leave and their personal knowledge, built up from years of experience in the company, goes with them. This is occurring more frequently with the rise in *downsizing* and *delayering*, and the phenomenon goes hand in hand with the *anorexic organisation*. Amnesia can be a significant disadvantage to an organisation, causing it to forget the lessons it has learned and to waste time and effort in doing things again.

corporate appraisal *Fin* a critical assessment of strengths and weaknesses, opportunities and threats (**SWOT analysis**) in relation to the internal and environmental factors affecting an entity in order to establish its condition prior to the preparation of the long-term plan

corporate bond *Fin* a long-term bond with fixed interest issued by a corporation

corporate brand *Gen Mgt* the coherent outward expression projected by an organisation. A corporate brand is a product of an organisation's *corporate strategy*, mission, image, and activities. Corporate brands distinguish organisations from their competitors, orient the organisation in the minds of customers and employees, and create a perception of what an organisation stands for. There is much debate about the precise nature of corporate brands, and about their depth. Corporate branding has been seen as a superficial quick fix to restore a company's tarnished image or revitalise an ailing company. It requires board level co-ordination, however, and rather than being arbitrarily imposed on an

---

Always establish a paper trail to make sure others can't take credit for what you do.
Dennis Stevenson

organisation, it is actually a product of the sum of its activities. Changing a corporate brand, or re-branding a company, can only be accomplished by changing strategy and activity within the company.

corporate climate *Gen Mgt* the environment created by the managerial style and attitudes that pervade an organisation. Corporate climate is strongly linked to *corporate culture* in creating the general feeling and atmosphere of an organisation. The climate within an organisation can affect aspects such as *productivity*, *creativity*, and *customer focus*, and each organisation needs to create a climate that will facilitate organisational success.

corporate communication *Gen Mgt* the activities undertaken by an organisation to communicate both internally with employees and externally with existing and prospective customers and the wider public. Corporate communication is sometimes used to refer principally to external communication and sometimes to internal communication, but strictly speaking covers both. The term implies an emphasis on promoting a sense of *corporate identity* and presenting a consistent and coherent *corporate image*.

corporate concierge *(US) Gen Mgt* an employee whose job involves doing personal tasks such as booking hotels or collecting shopping on behalf of other employees who have little time for these tasks *(slang)*

corporate culture *Gen Mgt* the combined beliefs, values, ethics, procedures, and atmosphere of an organisation. The culture of an organisation is often expressed as 'the way we do things around here' and consists of largely unspoken values, norms, and behaviours that become the natural way of doing things. An organisation's culture may be more apparent to an external observer than an internal practitioner. The first person to attempt a definition of corporate culture was *Edgar Schein*, who said that it consisted of rules, procedures, and processes that governed how things were done, as well as the philosophy that guides the attitude of senior management towards staff and customers. The difficulty in identifying the traits of culture and changing them is borne out by the fact that culture is not merely climate, power, and politics, but all those things and more. There can be several subcultures within an organisation, for example, defined by hierarchy—shopfloor or executive—or by function—sales, design, or production. Changing or renewing corporate culture in order to achieve the organisation's strategy is considered one of the major tasks of organisation *leadership*, as it is recognised that such a change is hard to achieve without the will of the leader. *Also known as organisational culture*

corporate evolution *Gen Mgt* the way in which organisations are transformed through the use of information technology

corporate giving *Gen Mgt* monetary or in-kind donations by organisations as part of the process of *community involvement*

corporate governance *Gen Mgt* the managerial and directorial control of an incorporated organisation, which, when well-practised, can reduce the risk of fraud, improve company performance and leadership, and demonstrate *social responsibility*. The structure of the legislation surrounding corporate governance varies from country to country. In the United Kingdom, the importance of good corporate governance was brought to public attention after a series of corporate collapses and scandals in the 1980s and 1990s. The effectiveness of the *board of directors* of the organisations involved was questioned, and the importance of independent, impartial *non-executive directors* was highlighted. To address the issues raised, the 'Committee on the Financial Aspects of Corporate Governance' was set up, chaired by *Sir Adrian Cadbury*. Following the publication of this committee's report in 1992, a code of best practice was established. Although it is voluntary, all listed companies are expected to comply. Since the Cadbury report, a number of other committees have established best practice in specific areas such as directors' pay. These culminated in the Hampel committee, which established a 'Combined Code' incorporating the Cadbury guidelines, 'Principles of Good Governance', and a 'Code of Best Practice'.

Corporate Governance Combined Code *Fin* the successor to the Cadbury Code, established by the Hampel Committee. The code consists of a set of principles of corporate governance and detailed code provisions embracing the work of the Cadbury, Greenbury, and Hampel Committees. Section 1 of the code contains the principles and provisions applicable to UK listed companies, while section 2 contains the principles and provisions applicable to institutional shareholders in their relationships with companies.

corporate hospitality *Gen Mgt* entertainment provided by an organisation. Corporate hospitality was originally designed to help salespeople build relationships with customers, but it is now increasingly used as a staff incentive and in employee *team building* and training exercises.

corporate identity *Gen Mgt* the distinctive characteristics or personality of an organisation, including *corporate culture*, values, and philosophy as perceived by those within the organisation and presented to those outside. Corporate identity is expressed through the name, symbols, and logos used by the organisation, and the design of communication materials, and is a factor influencing the *corporate image* of an organisation. The creation of a strong corporate identity also involves consistency in the organisation's actions, behaviour, products, and brands, and often reflects the *mission statement* of an organisation. A positive corporate identity can promote a sense of purpose and belonging within the organisation and encourage *employee commitment* and involvement.

corporate image *Gen Mgt* the perceptions and impressions of an organisation by the public as a result of interaction with the organisation and the way the organisation presents itself. Organisations have traditionally focused on the design of communication and advertising materials, using logos, symbols, text, and colour to create a favourable impression on target groups, but a range of additional activities contribute to a positive corporate image. These include *PR* programmes such as *community involvement*, *sponsorship*, and environmental projects, participation in quality improvement schemes, and good practice in industrial relations.

corporate planning *Gen Mgt* the process of drawing up detailed action plans to achieve an organisation's aims and objectives, taking into account the resources of the organisation and the environment within which it operates. Corporate planning represents a formal, structured approach to achieving objectives and to implementing the *corporate strategy* of an organisation. It has traditionally been seen as the responsibility of senior management. The use of the term became predominant during the 1960s but has now been largely superseded by the concept of *strategic management*.

corporate portal *Gen Mgt* a single gateway to information and software applications held within an organisation that also allows links to information outside the organisation. A corporate portal is a development of *intranet* technology. Ideally, it should allow users to access groupware, e-mail, and desktop applications, and to customise both the way information is presented and the way it is used. It should also provide dynamic access to data held within an *MIS*, *decision support system*, or other corporate database, and enable *virtual team* working across an organisation. Like many purely technological solutions, a corporate portal still relies on good *internal communication* and a *corporate culture* that embraces openness and information sharing.

corporate restructuring *Gen Mgt* a fundamental change in direction and strategy for an organisation that affects the way in which the organisation is structured. Corporate restructuring may involve increasing or decreasing the layers of personnel between the top and the bottom of an organisation, or re-assigning roles and responsibilities. Invariably, corporate restructuring has come to mean reorganising after a period of unsatisfactory performance and poor results, and is often manifested in the *divestment* or closure of parts of the business and the *outplacement*, or shedding, of personnel. In this case, corporate restructuring is used as a euphemism for *delayering*, *rationalisation*, *downsizing*, or *rightsizing*.

corporate social accounting *Fin* the reporting of the social and environmental impact of an entity's activities upon those who are directly associated with the entity (employees, customers, suppliers, etc.) or those who are in any way affected by the activities of the entity, as well as an assessment of the cost of compliance with relevant regulations in this area

corporate strategy *Gen Mgt* the direction an organisation takes with the aim of achieving business success in the long term. A number of models such as *Michael Porter*'s Five Forces model and *Gary Hamel*'s and *C.K. Prahalad*'s model of *core competencies* have been used to develop corporate strategy. More recent approaches have focused on the need for companies to adapt to and anticipate changes in the business environment. The formulation of corporate strategy involves establishing the purpose and scope of the organisation's activities and the nature of the business it is in, taking the environment in which it operates, its position in the marketplace, and the competition it faces into consideration. *Corporate planning* and *business plans* are used to implement corporate strategy.

corporate university *HR* a centralised training and education facility within an organisation, offering *training* and development only to employees of that organisation. Traditionally, corporate universities only offered internal qualifications and were used as a means of channelling *employee development* towards meeting corporate goals, sharing corporate information or knowledge, and disseminating *corporate culture*. More recently, some corporate universities have established links with academic institutions in order to offer formal qualifications.

corporate veil *Gen Mgt* immunity granted to shareholders to protect them from legal action in the event of the failure of a business

corporate venturing *Gen Mgt* the undertaking of an investment initiative by a commercial organisation to gain experience of a new technology or an unfamiliar market

corporate vision *Gen Mgt* the overall goal of an organisation that all business activities and processes should contribute towards achieving. Ideally, the workforce should be committed to, and driven by, the vision, because it is they who make it happen. As the vision nears achievement, a new corporate vision or an evolution of the existing one should be established. Corporate vision is usually summed up in a formal *vision statement*.

corporation *(US) Fin* = *limited liability company*

corporation tax *Fin* tax chargeable on companies resident in the United Kingdom or trading in the United Kingdom through a branch or agency as well as on certain unincorporated associations

correlation *Stats* the interdependence between pairs of variables in data

correlation coefficient *Stats* an index of the linear relationship between two variables in data

cosmeceuticals *Gen Mgt* pharmaceuticals such as anti-ageing creams that have a cosmetic rather than a health-related purpose (*slang*)

cost[1] *Fin* the amount of expenditure (actual or notional) incurred on, or attributable to, a specified thing or activity

cost[2] *Fin* to ascertain the cost of a specified thing or activity

cost accounting *Gen Mgt* the maintaining and checking of detailed records of the costs involved in manufacturing a product or providing a service in order to provide the information required for *costing* purposes. Cost accounting tries to identify the costs of outputs. This information is useful for pricing, budgeting, control of manufacturing or service processes, and planning materials and labour.

cost and freight *E-com* indicates that a quoted price includes the costs of the merchandise and the transportation but not the cost of insurance. *Abbr* **CFR**

cost audit *Fin* the verification of cost records and accounts, and a check on adherence to prescribed cost accounting procedures and their continuing relevance

cost behaviour *Fin* the variability of input costs with activity undertaken. A number of cost behaviour patterns are possible, ranging from **variable costs**, whose cost level varies directly with the level of activity, to **fixed costs**, where changes in output have no effect upon the cost level.

cost-benefit analysis *Gen Mgt* a technique for comparing the tangible and intangible costs of a project with the resulting benefits. Cost-benefit analysis assigns monetary value to the costs and benefits (social, environmental, and monetary) associated with a project for the purpose of evaluating and selecting investment project opportunities.

cost centre *Gen Mgt* a department, function, section, or individual whose cost, overall or in part, is an accepted overhead of a business in return for services provided to other parts of the organisation. A cost centre is usually an *indirect cost* of an organisation's products or services.

cost classification *Fin* the arrangement of elements of cost into logical groups with respect to their nature (fixed, variable, value adding etc.), function (production, selling etc.), or use in the business of the entity

cost (at cost) concept *Fin* the practice of valuing assets with reference to their acquisition cost

cost control *Fin* the process which ensures that actual costs do not exceed acceptable limits

cost-cutting *Gen Mgt* the reduction of the amount of money spent on the operations of an organisation or on the provision of products and services. Cost-cutting measures such as budget reductions, salary freezes, and staff redundancies may be taken by an organisation at a time of *recession* or financial difficulty or in situations where inefficiency has been identified. Alternative approaches to cost-cutting include modifying organisational structures and redesigning organisational processes for greater efficiency. Excessive cost-cutting may affect *productivity* and quality or the organisation's ability to add value.

cost driver *Gen Mgt* a factor that determines the cost of an activity. Cost drivers are analysed as part of *activity-based costing* and can be used in *continuous improvement* programmes. They are usually assessed together as multiple drivers rather than singly. There are two main types of cost driver: the first is a **resource driver**, which refers to the contribution of the quantity of resources used to the cost of an activity; the second is an **activity driver**, which refers to the costs incurred by the activities required to complete a particular task or project.

cost-effective *Gen Mgt* offering the maximum benefit for a given level of expenditure. When limited resources are available to meet specific objectives, the cost-effective solution is the best that can be achieved for that level of expenditure and the one that provides good value for money. The term is also used to refer to a level of expenditure that is perceived to be commercially viable.

cost-effectiveness analysis *Gen Mgt* a method for measuring the benefits and effectiveness of a particular item of expenditure. Cost-effectiveness analysis requires an examination of expenditure to determine whether the money spent could have been used more effectively or whether the resulting benefits could have been attained through less financial outlay.

cost estimation *Fin* the determination of cost behaviour. This can be achieved by engineering methods, analysis of the accounts, use of statistics, or the pooling of expert views.

cost function *Econ* a mathematical function relating a firm's or an industry's total cost to its output and factor costs

costing *Fin* the process of determining the costs of products, services, or activities

cost, insurance, and freight *E-com* indicates that a quoted price includes the costs of the merchandise, transportation, and insurance. *Abbr* **CIF**

cost management *Fin* the application of management accounting concepts, methods of data collection, analysis, and presentation, in order to provide the information required to enable costs to be planned, monitored, and controlled

cost of appraisal *Fin* costs incurred in order to ensure that outputs produced meet required quality standards

cost of capital *Fin* the minimum acceptable return on an investment, generally computed as a hurdle rate for use in investment appraisal exercises. The computation of the optimal cost of capital can be complex, and many ways of determining this opportunity cost have been suggested.

cost of conformance *Fin* the cost of achieving specified quality standards. *See also* **cost of appraisal**, **cost of prevention**

cost of entry *Mkting* the cost of introducing a new product to the market. Cost of entry calculations include the cost of all research, development, production, testing, marketing, advertising, and distribution of a product.

cost of external failure *Fin* the cost arising from inadequate quality discovered after the transfer of ownership from supplier to purchaser

cost of internal failure *Fin* the costs arising from inadequate quality which are identified before the transfer of ownership from supplier to purchaser

cost of non-conformance *Fin* the cost of failure to deliver the required standard of quality. *See also* **cost of external failure**, **cost of internal failure**

cost of prevention *Fin* the costs incurred prior to or during production in order to prevent substandard or defective products or services from being produced

cost of quality *Fin* the difference between the actual cost of producing, selling, and supporting products or services and the equivalent costs if there were no failures during production or usage. *See also* **cost of conformance**, **cost of non-conformance**

cost of sales *Fin* the sum of variable cost (see **cost behaviour**) of sales plus factory overhead attributable to the sales

cost per action *E-com see* **CPA**

cost per click-through *E-com* a pricing model for online advertising, where the seller gets paid whenever a visitor clicks on an ad

cost-plus pricing *Mkting* a standard *mark-up* added to the cost of a product or service to establish a selling price. Many companies simply add a percentage of production costs to arrive at a selling price. The degree of mark-up depends on the level of anticipated sales. Low-volume luxury goods may have a high mark-up;

Big things and little things are my job. Middle level management can be delegated.
Konosuke Matsushita

high-volume goods may have a relatively lower mark-up.

cost pool *Fin* the point of focus for the costs relating to a particular activity in an activity-based costing system

cost reduction *Fin* the reduction in unit cost of goods or services without impairing suitability for the use intended

cost table *Fin* a database containing all the costs associated with the production of a product, broken down to include the costs of functions and/or components and sub-assemblies. Cost tables also incorporate the cost changes which would result from a number of possible changes in the input mix.

cost unit *Fin* a unit of product or service in relation to which costs are ascertained

cost-volume-profit analysis *Fin* the study of the effects on future profit of changes in fixed cost, variable cost, sales price, quantity and mix

Council of Australian Governments *Gen Mgt* a body consisting of the heads of the Australian federal, state, and territory governments that meets to discuss matters of national importance. *Abbr* **COAG**

Council of Trade Unions (*ANZ*) *Gen Mgt* see **CTU**

counselling *HR* the provision of help by a trained person to permit somebody to clarify concerns, come to terms with feelings, and take responsibility for and begin to resolve difficulties. Counselling is a technique inherent to the *mentoring* process.

counterfactual *Gen Mgt* untrue (*slang*)

counterfeit *Gen Mgt* to produce forged or imitation goods or money intended to deceive or defraud. Counterfeited goods of inferior quality are often sold at substantially lower prices than genuine products and may bear the *brand* or *trade name* of the company. Counterfeiting violates *trademark* and *intellectual property* rights and may damage the reputation of producers of authentic goods. National

and international legislation provides some recourse to companies against counterfeiters, but strategies such as consumer warnings and labelling methods are also used to minimise the impact of counterfeiting. Efforts to eliminate counterfeiting are co-ordinated by the International Anti-Counterfeiting Coalition.

counterparty (*US*) *Fin* a person with whom somebody is entering into a contract

counterpurchase *Econ see* **countertrade**

countertrade *Econ* a range of reciprocal trading practices. This umbrella term encompasses the direct exchange of goods for goods (or *barter*) where no cash changes hands to more complex variations; **counterpurchase**, which involves a traditional export transaction plus the commitment of the exporter to buy additional goods or services from that country; and *buy-back*, in which the supplier of plant or equipment is paid from the future proceeds resulting from the use of the plant. Countertrade conditions vary widely from country to country and can be costly and administratively cumbersome.

country club management *Gen Mgt see* **Managerial Grid**™

country risk *Fin* the risk associated with undertaking transactions with, or holding assets in, a particular country. Sources of risk might be political, economic, or regulatory instability affecting overseas taxation, repatriation of profits, nationalisation, currency instability, etc.

coupon *Fin* **1.** a piece of paper that a bondholder presents to request payment **2.** the rate of interest on a bond **3.** an interest payment made to a bondholder
clip coupons to collect periodic interest on a bond (*slang*)

covariance *Stats* the value that is predicted from the product of the deviations of two variables from each of their means

covariate *Stats* a variable that is not crucial in an investigation but may affect the crucial variables from which a model is being built

coverage *Mkting* the percentage of a target audience reached by different media

Coverdale training *HR* a system of training that concentrates on improving *teamwork* and methods of getting a job done. Coverdale training is concerned with management behaviour, including setting *objectives*, briefing subordinates, and tackling a job. Groups of people are put into *scenarios* reproducing everyday situations and encouraged to experiment and build up successful working practices.

covered option *Fin* an option whose owner has the shares for the option

covered warrant *Fin* a futures contract for shares in a company

covering letter *HR* a letter sent to a potential employer together with a curriculum vitae (CV). It is used when a jobseeker knows the exact position he or she is applying for, and the name of the person to whom the CV is being sent.

A covering letter is important because it is the first thing the recruiting manager will read, and is key to their forming first impressions of the jobseeker. It must, therefore, be well-presented, well-informed, concise, professional, and yet enthusiastic.

cover note *Fin* a document that an insurance company issues to a customer to serve as a temporary insurance certificate until the issue of the policy itself

Covey, Stephen (*b*. 1932) *Gen Mgt* US writer and consultant. Offers a holistic approach to life and work, based on Mormon principles, the self-drive philosophy of *Dale Carnegie*, and the self-help advice of Samuel Smiles. His message is enshrined in *The Seven Habits of Highly Effective People* (1989), which calls for a re-think of many fundamental assumptions and attitudes.

CPA *abbr* **1.** *E-com* cost per action: a pricing model for online advertising based on the number of times an Internet user clicks on a banner ad that is linked to a particular website **2.** *Fin* customer profitability analysis

CPD *abbr HR* continuing professional development: on-going training and education throughout a career to improve the skills and knowledge used to perform a job or succession of jobs. CPD should be a planned, structured process, involving the assessment of development needs and the tailoring of training to meet those needs. CPD is founded on the belief that the development of professionals should not finish after initial qualification, especially in a fast-changing business environment in which skills are likely to obsolesce quickly. CPD requires commitment and resources from the employee, the employer, and supportive agencies such as professional bodies. Advocates of CPD argue that it can enhance *employability* and *career development* by keeping skills up to date and broadening a person's skill base. *Dominic Cadbury* has said that CPD should be centred on the individual, who must take responsibility for the continuing assessment and satisfaction of his or her own development needs. Much can be found in support of the principle of CPD in the concepts of *David Kolb*'s *experiential learning* cycle, *Peter Honey*'s and *Alan Mumford*'s learning types, the *personal development* cycle, and *lifelong learning*.

CPF *abbr HR* Central Provident Fund

CPI *abbr Econ* consumer price index

CPIX (*ANZ*) *Econ* the *consumer price index* excluding interest costs, on the basis that these are a direct outcome of monetary policy

CPM *abbr E-com* cost per thousand impressions: a pricing model for online advertising. The M represents the Roman numeral for 1,000.

crash 1. *Fin* a precipitous drop in value, especially of the stocks traded in a market **2.** *E-com* a hardware failure or program error that stops a computer working. If data has not been backed up it can be lost

---

I don't think that ambition is a bad word if you work hard yourself. **Lynn Forrester**

as a result of a crash. **3.** *Econ* a sudden and catastrophic downturn in an economy. The crash in the United States in 1929 is one of the most famous.

creative accounting *Fin* the use of accounting methods to hide aspects of a company's financial dealings in order to make the company appear more or less successful than it is in reality (*slang*)

creative consultancy *Mkting* an organisation that plans and creates advertising on behalf of a client

creative director *Mkting* an employee of an advertising agency who is responsible for planning and managing the creative work of a campaign

creative strategy *Mkting* a technique for determining the most effective creative approach to reach a target audience

creative thinking *Gen Mgt see* **creativity**

creativity *Gen Mgt* the generation of new ideas by approaching problems or existing practices in innovative or imaginative ways. Psychologists have disagreed on the nature of creativity. Until about 1980, research concentrated on identifying the personality traits of creative people, but more recently psychologists have focused on the mental processes involved. Creativity involves re-examining assumptions and reinterpreting facts, ideas, and past experience. A growing interest in creativity as a source of *competitive advantage* has developed in recent years, and creativity is considered important, not just for the development of new products and services, but also for its role in organisational *decision-making* and *problem-solving*. Many organisations actively seek a *corporate culture* that encourages creativity. There are a number of techniques used to foster **creative thinking**, including *brainstorming* and *lateral thinking*. Creativity is linked to *innovation*, the process of taking a new idea and turning it into a market offering.

credit *Fin* the trust that people have in somebody's ability to repay a loan, or a loan itself

credit account *Fin see* **charge account**

credit available *Fin* the amount of money that somebody can borrow at a given time

credit balance *Fin* the amount of money that somebody owes on a credit account

credit bureau *Fin* a company that assesses the creditworthiness of people for businesses or banks in the United States. *See also* **mercantile agency**

credit capacity *Fin* the amount of money that somebody can borrow and be expected to repay

credit card *E-com, Fin* a card issued by a bank or financial institution and accepted by a merchant in payment for a transaction for which the cardholder must subsequently reimburse the issuer

credit ceiling *Fin* the largest amount that a lender will permit somebody to borrow, for example, on a credit card

credit committee *Fin* a committee that evaluates a potential borrower's creditworthiness

credit company *Fin* a company that extends credit to people

credit co-operative *Fin* an organisation of people who join together to gain advantage in borrowing

credit creation *Fin* the collective ability of lenders to make money available to borrowers

credit crunch *Fin* a situation in which money for borrowing is unavailable

credit deposit *E-com* the value of the credit-card purchases deposited in a merchant's bank account after the acquirer's fees are deducted

credit derivative *Fin* a financial instrument that transfers a lender's risk to a third party

credit entity *Fin* a borrower or lender

credit entry *Fin* an item on the asset side of a financial statement

credit exposure *Fin* the risk to a lender of a borrower defaulting

credit-granter *Fin* a person or organisation that lends money

credit history *Fin* a potential borrower's record of debt repayment

crediting rate *Fin* the interest rate paid on an insurance policy that is an investment

credit limit *Fin* the highest amount that a lender will allow somebody to borrow, for example, on a credit card

credit line *Fin see* **line of credit**

credit note *Fin* a document stating that a shop owes somebody an amount of money and entitling the person to goods to the specified value

creditor *Fin* a person or organisation that is owed money

creditor days *Fin* the number of days on average that a company requires to pay its creditors.

EXAMPLE To determine creditor days, divide the cumulative amount of unpaid suppliers' bills (also called trade creditors) by sales, then multiply by 365. For example, if suppliers' bills total £800,000 and sales are £9,000,000, the calculation is:

(800,000 / 9,000,000) × 365 = 32.44 days

The company takes 32.44 days on average to pay its bills.

Creditor days is an indication of a company's creditworthiness in the eyes of its suppliers and creditors, since it shows how long they are willing to wait for payment. Within reason, the higher the number the better, because all companies want to conserve cash. At the same time, a company that is especially slow to pay its bills (100 or more days, for example) may be a company having trouble generating cash, or one trying to finance its operations with its suppliers' funds.

See also **debtor days**

creditor days ratio *Fin* a measure of the number of days on average that a company requires to pay its creditors.

EXAMPLE To determine creditor days, divide the cumulative amount of unpaid suppliers' bills (also called trade creditors) by sales, then multiply by 365. For example, if suppliers' bills total £800,000 and sales are £9,000,000, the calculation is:

(800,000 / 9,000,000) x 365 = 32.44 days

This means the company takes 32.44 days on average to pay its bills.

creditor nation *Econ* a country that has a balance of payments surplus

creditors' committee *Fin* a group that directs the efforts of creditors to receive partial repayment from a bankrupt person or organisation. *Also known as* **creditors' steering committee**

creditors' meeting *Fin* a meeting of those to whom a bankrupt person or organisation owes money

creditors' settlement *Fin* an agreement on partial repayment to those to whom a bankrupt person or organisation owes money

creditors' steering committee *Fin see* **creditors' committee**

credit rating *or* **credit ranking** *Fin* **1.** an assessment of somebody's creditworthiness **2.** the process of assessing somebody's creditworthiness

credit rating agency (*US*) *Fin* = **credit-reference agency**

credit rationing *Fin* the process of making credit less easily available or subject to high interest rates

credit-reference agency *Fin* a company that assesses the creditworthiness of people on behalf of businesses or banks. *US term* **credit rating agency**

credit report *Fin* information about an individual or entity relevant to a decision to grant credit

credit risk *Fin* **1.** the chance that a borrower will default on a loan **2.** a borrower who may default on a loan **3.** the possibility that a loss may occur from the failure of another party to perform according to the terms of a contract

credit sale *Fin* a sale for which the buyer need not pay immediately

credit scoring *Fin* a calculation done in the process of credit rating

credit side *Fin* the part of a financial statement that lists assets

credit squeeze *Fin* a situation in which credit is not easily available or is subject to high interest rates

credit standing *Fin* the reputation that somebody has with regard to meeting financial obligations

credit system *Fin* a set of rules and organisations involved in making loans

credit union *Fin* a co-operative savings association that lends money to members at low rates of interest

creditworthy *Fin* regarded as being reliable in terms of meeting financial obligations

creeping takeover *Fin* a takeover achieved by the gradual acquisition of small amounts of stock over an extended period of time (*slang*)

creeping tender offer *Fin* an acquisition of many shares in a company by purchase, especially to avoid US restrictions on tender offers

CREST *Fin* the paperless system used for settling stock transactions electronically in the United Kingdom

crisis management *Mkting* actions taken by an organisation in response to unexpected events or situations with potentially negative effects that threaten resources and people or the success and continued operation of the organisation. Crisis management includes the development of plans to reduce the risk of a crisis occurring and to deal with any crises that do arise, and the implementation of these plans so as to minimise the impact of crises and assist the organisation to

recover from them. Crisis situations may occur as a result of external factors such as the development of a new product by a competitor or changes in legislation, or internal factors such as a product failure or faulty *decision-making*, and often involve the need to make quick decisions on the basis of uncertain or incomplete information. *See also* **risk management**, **disaster management**

critical mass *Gen Mgt* the point at which an organisation or **project** has gained sufficient momentum or **market share** to be either self-sustaining or worth the input of extra investment or resources

critical-path method *Gen Mgt, Ops* a **network analysis** planning technique used especially in **project management** to identify the activities within a project that are critical for its success. In critical-path method, individual activities within a project and their duration are recorded in a diagram or flow chart. A critical path is plotted through the diagram, showing the sequence in which activities must be completed in order to complete the project in the shortest amount of time, incurring the least cost.

critical-ratio analysis *Gen Mgt* a technique used in inventory control to calculate comparative priorities for the reordering of stock. Critical-ratio analysis requires the division of remaining stock items by the likely daily demand for them. This figure is then divided by the time taken to process an order, to derive the critical ratio. The smaller the ratio, the greater the reorder priority. A ratio of less than 1 indicates an imminent shortage. Critical ratios are also used in conjunction with **MRP II** systems to determine the sequence in which orders should be processed. In this case, a ratio of less than 1 indicates that the order is behind schedule.

critical region *Stats* the range of values of a test statistic that lead a researcher to reject the null hypothesis

critical restructuring *Gen Mgt* major economic or social changes that fundamentally reshape traditional patterns of organisation

critical success factors *Gen Mgt* the aspects of a business that are identified as vital for successful targets to be reached and maintained. Critical success factors are normally identified within such areas as production processes, employee and organisation skills, functions, techniques, and technologies. The identification and strengthening of such factors may be similar to identifying *core competences*, and is considered an essential element in achieving and maintaining *competitive advantage*.

critical value *Stats* the value with which a researcher compares a statistic from sample data in order to determine whether or not the null hypothesis should be rejected

CRM *abbr Mkting* customer relationship management

crony capitalism *Econ* a form of capitalism in which business contracts are awarded to the family and friends of the government in power rather than by open-market tender

Crosby, Philip (1926–2001) *Gen Mgt* US business executive and consultant *Quality* guru who introduced and popularised catchphrases such as 'zero defects', 'get it right first time', and 'quality is free'. Crosby summarised his approach towards quality improvement as the Fourteen Steps, set down in *Quality is Free* (1979).

cross *Fin* a transaction in securities in which one broker acts for both parties

cross-border trade *Econ* trade between two countries that have a common frontier

cross-hedging *Fin* a form of hedging using an option on a different but related commodity, especially a currency

cross listing *Fin* the practice of offering the same item for sale in more than one place

crossposting *E-com* the act of posting the same Internet messages into several different news or discussion groups at the same time

cross-rate *Econ* the rate of exchange between two currencies expressed in terms of the rate of exchange between them and a third currency, for example, sterling and the peso in relation to the dollar

cross-sectional study *Stats* a statistical study in which a range of information is collected at the same time, for example, in a single telephone call

cross-sell *Mkting* to sell existing customers different products from the company's range

crowding out *Fin* the effect on markets of credit produced by extraordinarily large borrowing by a national government

crude annual death rate *Stats* the total number of deaths in a population in one year divided by the total population at the midpoint of the year

cryptography *E-com* a powerful means of restricting access to part or all of a website, whereby only a user with an assigned 'key' can request and read the information

crystallisation *Fin* the process whereby a floating charge relating to company assets becomes fixed to the assets to which it relates

CSIRO *abbr* (*ANZ*) *Gen Mgt* Commonwealth Scientific and Industrial Research Organisation: an Australian federal government body in charge of scientific research, established in 1949

CSP *abbr E-com* commerce service provider

CTI *abbr Gen Mgt* computer telephony integration

CTO *abbr Gen Mgt* chief technical officer

CTU *abbr Gen Mgt* Council of Trade Unions: New Zealand's national trade union organisation. It has 19 affiliated unions and represents approximately 200,000 workers.

Join the union, girls, and together say Equal Pay for Equal Work.   **Susan B. Anthony**

cube farm (*US*) *Gen Mgt* an office that is divided into cubicles (*slang*)

cue *Gen Mgt* a factor that differentiates a high-value product from an ordinary commodity

CUL *abbr Gen Mgt* see you later (*slang*)

cultural creative *HR* somebody who values personal and spiritual development, enjoys change, likes learning about new cultures, and typically desires to live a simpler way of life

cultural synergy *Gen Mgt* the harmonisation of the direction and operation of separate organisations into a whole. Whether cultural synergy can be achieved lies in the degree to which there is congruence of vision, mission, values, strategy, and operational processes in the different organisations. The lack of cultural and *strategic fit* is the main cause of failure of *mergers*, sometimes because of the major partner imposing its own *corporate culture*, rather than developing a shared culture. Cultural integration, therefore, needs to be carefully analysed, planned, and implemented.

culture shock *Gen Mgt* the effects on an employee or organisation when faced with new, unfamiliar, or rapidly changing circumstances. Symptoms of culture shock include uncertainty, *stress*, confusion, disorientation, or simply not knowing how to act in the circumstances. Culture shock can occur in a number of scenarios, for example, when *expatriates* come across new cultures and customs in a foreign country, when new staff are thrown into the deep end of a busy department, when two organisations merge with poor strategic, operational, or *cultural synergy*, or when public sector organisations adopt private sector practices. The degree of shock can be reduced through careful analysis, planning, training, and consequent preparedness.

cum *Fin* with

cum rights *Fin* an indication that the buyer of the shares is entitled to participate in a forthcoming rights issue

cumulative method *Fin* a system in which items are added together

cumulative preference shares *Fin* shares which entitle the holders to a fixed rate of dividend, and the right to have any arrears of dividend paid out of future profits with priority over any distribution of profits to the holders of ordinary share capital

cumulative preferred stock *Fin* preferred stock for which dividends accrue even if they are not paid when due

currency *Fin* the money in circulation in a particular country

currency future *Fin* an option on currency

currency hedging *Fin* a method of reducing *exchange rate risk* by diversifying currency holdings and adjusting them according to changes in exchange rates

currency note *Fin* a bank note

currency risk *Fin* **1.** the risk that a currency used for a transaction may lose value **2.** the possibility of a loss or gain due to future changes in exchange rates

currency unit *Econ* each of the notes and coins that are the medium of exchange in a country

current account *Fin* a bank account in which deposits can be withdrawn at any time, but do not usually earn interest, except in the case of some online accounts. It is the most common type of bank account. *US term* **checking account**

current account equilibrium *Econ* a country's economic circumstances when its expenditure equals its income from trade and invisible earnings

current account mortgage *Fin* a long-term loan, usually for the purchase of a property, in which the borrower pays interest on the sum loaned in monthly instalments and repays the principal (see *mortgage*) in one lump sum at the end of the term. When calculating the interest payments, the lender takes into account the balance in the borrower's current and/or savings accounts. It is the borrower's responsibility to make provisions to accumulate the required capital during the period of the mortgage, usually by contributing to tax efficient investment plans such as Individual Savings Accounts or by relying on an anticipated inheritance. *See also* **mortgage**

current assets *Fin* cash or assets that are readily convertible to cash

current assets financing *Fin* the use of current assets as collateral for a loan

current cash balance *Fin* the amount, which excludes balances due soon for outstanding transactions, that a client has available for investment with a broker

current-cost accounting *Fin* accounting based on the cost of items at the time of the financial statement

current earnings *Fin* the annual earnings most recently reported by a company

current liabilities *Fin* business liabilities that are to be cleared within the financial year

current principal factor *Fin* the portion of the initial amount of a loan that remains to be paid

current purchasing power accounting *Fin* a method of accounting in which the values of non-monetary items in the historical cost accounts are adjusted, using a general price index, so that the resulting profit allows for the maintenance of the purchasing power of the shareholders' interest in the organisation

current ratio *Fin* a ratio of *current assets* to *current liabilities*, used to measure a company's liquidity and its ability to meet its short-term debt obligations. *Also known as* **working capital ratio**

EXAMPLE The current ratio formula is simply:

Current assets /Current liabilities = Current ratio

Current assets are the ones that a company can turn into cash within 12 months during the ordinary course of business.

Current liabilities are bills due to be paid within the coming 12 months.

For example, if a company's current assets are £300,000 and its current liabilities are £200,000, its current ratio would be:

$$300,000 / 200,000 = 1.5$$

As a rule of thumb, the 1.5 figure means that a company should be able to get hold of £1.50 for every £1.00 it owes.

The higher the ratio, the more liquid the company. Prospective lenders expect a positive current ratio, often of at least 1.5. However, too high a ratio is cause for alarm too, because it indicates declining receivables and/or inventory—which may mean declining liquidity.

current stock value *Fin* the value of all stock in a portfolio, including stock in transactions that have not yet been settled

current value *Fin* a ratio indicating the amount by which *current assets* exceed *current liabilities*

current yield *Fin* the interest being paid on a bond divided by its current market price, expressed as a percentage

curriculum vitae *HR see* **CV**

cushion bond *Fin* a bond that pays a high rate of interest but sells at a low premium because of the risk of its being called soon

customer *Mkting* a purchaser of a product or service. A customer is a person or organisation that purchases or obtains goods or services from other organisations such as manufacturers, retailers, wholesalers, or service providers. A customer is not necessarily the same person as the *consumer*, as a product or service can be paid for by one party, the customer, and used by another, the *consumer*.

customer capital *Gen Mgt* the value of an organisation's relationships with its customers, which involves factors such as market share, customer retention rates, and profitability of customers

customer care *Mkting see* **customer relations**

Whoever wants to accomplish great things must devote a lot of profound thought to details.
Paul Valéry (attrib.)

customer-centric model *Gen Mgt* a business model organised around the needs of the customer

customer complaint *Gen Mgt see* ***complaint***

customer expectation *Gen Mgt* the needs, wants, and preconceived ideas of a customer about a product or service. Customer expectation will be influenced by a customer's perception of the product or service and can be created by previous experience, advertising, hearsay, awareness of competitors, and ***brand image***. The level of ***customer service*** is also a factor, and a customer might expect to encounter efficiency, helpfulness, reliability, confidence in the staff, and a personal interest in his or her custom. If customer expectations are met, then ***customer satisfaction*** results. *Also known as* ***buyer expectation***

customer flow *Mkting* the number and pattern of customers coming into a shop or passing through a railway or bus station, airport, or other large service, retail, or leisure area. Customer flow can be monitored by observation, time lapse or normal closed circuit television, or, less satisfactorily, by analysis of purchase data. This provides useful information about the number of customers, flow patterns, bottlenecks, areas not visited, and other aspects of consumer behaviour.

customer focus *Mkting* an organisational orientation towards satisfying the needs of potential and actual ***customers***. Customer focus is considered to be one of the keys to business success. Achieving customer focus involves ensuring that the whole organisation, and not just front-line service staff, puts its customers first. All activities, from the planning of a new product to its production, marketing, and after-sales care, should be built around the customer. Every department and every employee should share the same customer-focused vision. This can be aided by practising good ***customer relationship management*** and maintaining a ***customer relations*** programme.

customer profitability *Mkting* the degree to which a ***customer*** or segment of customers contributes towards organisation profits. Customer profitability has been shown to be produced primarily by a small proportion of customers, perhaps 10% to 20%, who generate up to 80% of a company's profits. Up to 40% of customers may generate only moderate profits, and the other 40% may be loss-making. Such data enables companies to focus efforts on the most profitable segments.

customer profitability analysis *Fin* analysis of the revenue streams and service costs associated with specific customers or customer groups. *Abbr* **CPA**

customer recovery *Mkting* activities intended to win back customers who no longer buy from an organisation

customer relations *Mkting* the approach of an organisation to winning and retaining customers. The most critical activity of any organisation wishing to stay in business is its approach to dealing with its customers. Putting customers at the centre of all activities is seen by many as an integral part of quality, pricing, and product differentiation. On one level, customer relations means keeping customers fully informed, turning complaints into opportunities, and genuinely listening to customers. On another level, being a customer-focused organisation means ensuring that all activities relating to trading—for example, planning, design, production, marketing, and after-sales of a product or service—are built around the customer, and that every department and individual employee understands and shares the same vision. Only then can a company deliver continuous ***customer satisfaction*** and experience good customer relations. *Also known as* ***customer care***

customer relationship management *Mkting* the cultivation of meaningful relationships with actual or potential purchasers of goods or services. Customer relationship management aims to increase an organisation's sales by promoting customer satisfaction, and can be achieved using tools such as relationship marketing.

CRM is particularly important in the sphere of e-commerce, as there is no personal interaction between the vendor and the customer. A website therefore has to work hard to develop the relationship with customers and demonstrate that their business is valued. A CRM system generally includes some or all of the following components: customer information systems, *personalisation* systems, *content management* systems, *call centre* automation, *data warehousing*, *data mining*, sales force automation, and campaign management systems. All these elements combine to provide the essentials of CRM: understanding customer needs; anticipating their information requirements; answering their questions promptly and comprehensively; delivering exactly what they order; making deliveries on time; and suggesting new products that they will be genuinely interested in. *Abbr* **CRM**

customer retention *Mkting* the maintenance of the custom of people who have purchased a company's goods or services once and the gaining of repeat purchases. Customer retention occurs when a customer is loyal to a company, *brand*, or to a specific product or service, expressing long-term commitment and refusing to purchase from competitors. A company can adopt a number of strategies to retain its customers. Of critical importance to such strategies are the wider concepts of *customer service*, *customer relations*, and relationship marketing. Companies can build loyalty and retention through the use of a number of techniques, including *database marketing*, the issue of loyalty cards, redeemable against a range of goods or services, preferential *discounts*, free gifts, special promotions, newsletters or magazines, members' clubs, or customised products in limited editions. It has been argued that customer retention is linked to employee loyalty, since loyal employees build up long-term relationships with customers.

customer satisfaction *Mkting* the degree to which customer expectations of a product or service are met or exceeded. Corporate and individual customers may have widely differing reasons for purchasing a product or service and therefore any measurement of satisfaction will need to be able to measure such differences. The quality of *after-sales service* can also be a crucial factor in influencing any purchasing decision. More and more companies are striving, not just for customer satisfaction, but for customer delight, that extra bit of added value that may lead to increased customer loyalty. Any extra added value, however, will need to be carefully costed.

customer service *Mkting* the way in which an organisation deals with its *customers*. Customer service is most evident in sales and *after-sales service*, but should infuse all the processes in the *value chain*. Good customer service is the result of adopting *customer focus*. Poor customer service can be a product of poor *customer relations*.

customisation *Gen Mgt* the process of modifying products or services to meet the requirements of individual customers

customised service *Gen Mgt* a service tailored to the requirements of an individual customer

cut-off *Fin* a date and procedure for isolating the flow of cash and goods, stocktaking and the related documentation, to ensure that all aspects of a transaction are dealt with in the same financial period

cutthroat *Mkting* aggressively ruthless, especially in dealing with competitors

cutting-edge *Gen Mgt* at the forefront of new technologies or markets

CV *HR* a document that provides a summary of somebody's career history, skills, and experience. A curriculum vitae is usually prepared to aid in a job application. A job advertisement may ask for a curriculum vitae or instead may require a candidate to complete an *application form*.

The trouble with a free market economy is that it requires so many policemen to make it work.
Dean Acheson

Every CV should include: the job-seeker's name and contact details; a clear and concise description of his or her career objective; some kind of outline of work experience; and a list of education and qualifications. It is important to customise a curriculum vitae to the type of job or career being applied for.

There are four basic types of curriculum vitae: the chronological, the functional, the targeted, and the capabilities curriculum vitae. A chronological curriculum vitae is useful for people who stay in the same field and do not make major career changes. They should start with and focus on the most recent positions held. A functional curriculum vitae is the preferred choice for those seeking their first professional job, or those making a major career change. It is based around 3–5 paragraphs, each emphasizing and illustrating a particular, important skill or accomplishment. A targeted curriculum vitae is useful for jobseekers who are very clear about their job direction and need to make an impressive case for a specific job. Like a functional curriculum vitae, it should be based around several capabilities and accomplishments that are relevant to the job target, focusing on action and results. A capabilities curriculum vitae is used for people applying for a specific job within their current organisation. It should focus on 5–8 skills and accomplishments achieved with the company. *US term* **résumé**

cyberbole *E-com* hype about the Internet and the online world (*slang*)

cybercrud *E-com* confusing and useless computer jargon (*slang*)

cyber mall *E-com* a website shared by two or more commercial organisations, usually with some similarity in appearance, function, product, or service. *Also known as* **e-commerce mall**, **electronic mall**, **online shopping mall**

cybermarketing *E-com* the use of Internet-based promotions of any kind. This may involve targeted e-mail, bulletin boards, websites, or sites from which the customer can download files.

cybersales *E-com, Fin* sales made electronically through computers and information systems

cyberslacker *Gen Mgt* somebody who spends time surfing the Internet for personal purposes during office hours (*slang*)

cyberspace *E-com* the online world and its communication networks

cycle plot *Stats* a graphical representation of the behaviour of seasonal time series

cycle time *Ops* the period required to complete an operation on one unit of a **batch**. *See also* **lead time**

cyclical stock *Fin* a stock whose value rises and falls periodically, for example, according to the seasons of the year or economic cycles

cyclical unemployment *Econ* unemployment, usually temporary, caused by a lack of **aggregate demand**, for example, during a downswing in the business cycle

cyclic variation *Stats* the repeatable systematic variation of a variable over time

---

He that would govern others, first should be the master of himself.   Philip Massinger

D

daily price limit *Fin* the amount by which the price of an option can rise or fall within one trading day

daisy chaining *Fin* an illegal financial practice whereby traders create artificial transactions in order to make a particular security appear more active than it is in reality (*slang*)

dancing baloney *E-com* animated visual computer effects that serve little practical purpose but look impressive (*slang*)

dancing frog *E-com* a problem or image on somebody's computer screen that disappears when shown to somebody else (*slang*)

Darwin Trade Development Zone *Gen Mgt* a free trade zone in the city of Darwin in the Northern Territory of Australia. Companies operating within the zone, which is intended to facilitate trade with Asia, are exempt from certain state taxes and customs duties.

data *Stats* the measurements and observations collected during a statistical investigation

database *Gen Mgt* a structured collection of related information held in any form, especially on a computer. The creation of a database assists organisations in keeping records and facilitates the retrieval of specific facts or different categories of information as and when required. Databases of various kinds may form part of an organisation's *MIS*.

database management system *Stats* a dedicated computer program designed to manipulate a collection of information

database marketing *Mkting* the collection and analysis of information about customers and their buying habits, lifestyles, and other such data. Database marketing is used to build profiles of individual customers, who are then targeted with customised mailings, special offers, and other incentives to encourage spending. Database marketing is a form of relationship marketing.

data capture *Mkting* the acquisition of information through advertisement coupons, inquiry forms, or other response mechanisms

data cleansing *Mkting* the process of ensuring that data is up to date and free of duplication or error

data dredging *Stats* the process of making comparisons and drawing conclusions from data that was not part of the original brief for a study

data editing *Stats* the removal of keying or format errors from data

Data Encryption Standard *E-com* see *DES*

dataholic *Gen Mgt* somebody who is obsessed with obtaining information, especially on the Internet (*slang*)

data mining 1. *E-com* the process of using sophisticated software to identify commercially useful statistical patterns or relationships in online databases **2.** *Mkting* the extraction of information from a *data warehouse* to assist managerial *decision-making*. The information obtained in this way helps organisations gain a better understanding of their customers and can be used to improve customer support and marketing activities.

data protection *Mkting* the safeguards that govern the storage and use of personal data held on computer systems and in paper-based filing systems. The growing use of computers to store information about individuals has led to the enactment of legislation in many countries designed to protect the privacy of individuals and prevent the disclosure of information to unauthorised persons. In the United Kingdom, the Data Protection Act 1998 requires organisations that hold personal data in any form to register with a central authority and maintain

---

In the past the man was first. In the future the system will be first.   F.W. Taylor

standards of confidentiality and security. The legislation also stipulates what use may be made of the information and how it may be processed.

data reduction *Stats* the process of summarising large data sets into histograms or frequency distributions so that calculations such as means can be made

data screening *Stats* the process of assessing a set of observations to detect significant deviations such as *outliers*

data set *Stats* all of the measurements or observations collected in a statistical investigation

data smoothing algorithm *Stats* a procedure for removing meaningless data from a sequence of observations so that a pattern can be detected

data transfer *E-com* the amount of data downloaded from a website. This information can be useful, particularly for measuring the number of visitors to a website.

data warehouse *Gen Mgt* a collection of subject-orientated data collected over a period of time and stored on a computer to provide information in support of managerial *decision-making*. A data warehouse contains a large volume of information selected from different sources, including operational systems and organisational databases, and brought together in a standard format to facilitate retrieval and analysis. Like *EIS*s, data warehouses can be used to support *decision-making*, but the ways in which they can be searched are not predetermined. Organisations often use data warehouses for marketing purposes, for example, the analysis of customer information, or for market segmentation. *Data mining* techniques are used to access the information in a data warehouse.

DAX *abbr Fin* Deutscher Aktienindex: the principal German stock exchange, based in Frankfurt

day in the sun *Gen Mgt* the period of time during which a product is successful in the marketplace

day order *Fin* for dollar trading only, an order that is valid only during one trading day

day release *HR* the discharge of an employee from normal work to take part in education or training. Day release is normally for one day each week, fortnight, or month, and it enables an employee to study for further education or *vocational qualifications* on a part time basis.

days' sales outstanding *Fin see collection ratio*

day trader *Fin* somebody who makes trades with very close dates of maturity

day trading *Fin* the making of trades that have very close dates of maturity

DCM *abbr* (*S Africa*) *Fin* Development Capital Market

dead cat bounce *Fin* a short-term increase in the value of a stock following a precipitous drop in value (*slang*)

dead tree edition *E-com* the print version of a publication that is also available in electronic form (*slang*)

dead wood *HR* employees who are no longer considered to be useful to a company (*slang*)

deal
cut somebody a deal *Gen Mgt* to agree on terms for a business arrangement with somebody (*slang*)

dealership *Mkting* a retail outlet distributing, selling, and servicing products such as cars or construction plant on behalf of a manufacturer

death by committee *Gen Mgt* the prevention of serious consideration of a proposal by assigning a committee to look at it

Death Valley curve (*US*) *Gen Mgt* a point in the development of a new business when losses begin to erode the company's equity base, so that it becomes difficult to raise new equity (*slang*)

debenture *Fin* **1.** an unsecured bond backed only by the issuer's credit standing **2.** a bond, usually repayable at a fixed date

debit card *Fin* a card issued by a bank or financial institution and accepted by a merchant in payment for a transaction. Unlike the procedure with a **credit card**, purchases are deducted from the cardholder's account, as with a cheque, when the transaction takes place.

debit note *Fin* a document prepared by a purchaser notifying the seller that the account is being reduced by a stated amount, for example, because of an allowance, return of goods, or cancellation

de Bono, **Edward** (*b.* 1933) *Gen Mgt* Maltese-born academic and consultant. Creator of the concept of **lateral thinking**, which was introduced in *Lateral Thinking: a Textbook of Creativity* (1970).

debt *Fin* an amount of money owed to a person or organisation

debt capacity *Fin* the extent to which an entity can support and/or obtain loan finance

debt collection agency *Fin* a business that secures the repayment of debts for third parties on a commission or fee basis

debt counselling *Fin* a service offering advice and support to individuals who are financially stretched

debt/equity ratio *Fin* the ratio of what a company owes to the value of all of its outstanding shares

debt forgiveness *Fin* the writing off of all or part of a nation's debt by a lender

debt instrument *Fin* any document used or issued for raising money, for example, a bill of exchange, bond, or promissory note

debtnocrat *Fin* a senior bank official who specialises in lending extremely large sums, for example, to developing nations (*slang*)

debtor *Fin* a person or organisation that owes money

debtor days *Fin* the number of days on average that it takes a company to receive payment for what it sells.

EXAMPLE To determine debtor days, divide the cumulative amount of accounts receivable by sales, then multiply by 365. For example, if accounts receivable total £600,000 and sales are £9,000,000, the calculation is:

$$(600{,}000 / 9{,}000{,}000) \times 365 = 24.33 \text{ days}$$

The company takes 24.33 days on average to collect its debts.

Debtor days is an indication of a company's efficiency in collecting monies owed. Obviously, the lower the number the better. An especially high number is a telltale sign of inefficiency or worse. *See also* **creditor days**

debt rescheduling *Gen Mgt* the renegotiation of debt repayments. Debt rescheduling is necessary when a company can no longer meet its debt payments. It can involve deferring debt payments, deferring payment of interest, or negotiating a new loan. It is usually undertaken as part of **turnaround management** to avoid **business failure**. Debt rescheduling is also undertaken in less developed countries that encounter national debt difficulties. Such arrangements are usually overseen by the International Monetary Fund.

debt/service ratio *Econ* the ratio of a country's or company's borrowing to its equity or **venture capital**

debugging *Stats* the identification and removal of errors in a computer program or system

decentralisation *Gen Mgt* the dispersal of decision-making control. Decentralisation involves moving power, authority, and decision-making control within an organisation or from a central headquarters or from high managerial levels to subsidiaries, branches, divisions, or departments. As an organisational concept, decentralisation implies **delegation** of both power and responsibility by top management in order to promote flexibility through faster decision-making and

---

The vaster the power gained, the vaster the appetite for more. Ursula K. Le Guin

improved response times. Decentralisation is, therefore, strongly related to the concept of **empowerment**, though the latter is perhaps more focused on direct working front-line staff.

decision lozenge *Gen Mgt see flow chart*

decision-maker *Gen Mgt* somebody with the responsibility and authority to make decisions within an organisation, especially those that determine future direction and strategy. *Decision theory* is used to assist decision-makers in the process of *decision-making*.

decision-making *Gen Mgt* the process of choosing between alternative courses of action. Decision-making may take place at an individual or organisational level. The process may involve establishing objectives, gathering relevant information, identifying alternatives, setting criteria for the decision, and selecting the best option. The nature of the decision-making process within an organisation is influenced by its culture and structure, and a number of theoretical models have been developed. One well-known method for individual decision-making was developed by *Charles Kepner* and *Benjamin Tregoe* in their book *The New Rational Manager* (1981). *Decision theory* can be used to assist in the process of decision-making. Specific techniques used in decision-making include *heuristics* and *decision trees*. Computer systems designed to assist managerial decision-making are known as *decision support systems*.

decision-making unit *Mkting* a group of people who directly or indirectly influence the purchase of a product or service

decision support system *Fin* a computer system whose purpose is to aid managers to make unstructured decisions, where the nature of the problem requiring resolution may be unclear. *Abbr* **DSS**

decision theory *or* **decision analysis** *Gen Mgt* a body of knowledge that attempts to describe, analyse, and model the process of *decision-making* and the factors influencing it. Decision theory encompasses both formal mathematical and statistical approaches to solving decision problems, using quantitative techniques such as probability and *game theory*, and more informal behavioural approaches. It is used to inform and assist decision-making in organisations.

decision tree *Fin* a pictorial method of showing a sequence of interrelated decisions and their expected outcomes. Decision trees can incorporate both the probabilities and values of expected outcomes, and are used in decision-making.

declaration date *Fin* in the United States, the date when the directors of a company meet to announce the proposed dividend per share that they recommend be paid

declaration of dividend *Fin* a formal announcement by a company's directors of the proposed dividend per share that they recommend be paid. It is subsequently put to a shareholders' vote at the company's annual general meeting.

declaration of solvency *Fin* in the United Kingdom, a document, lodged with the Registrar of Companies, that lists the assets and liabilities of a company seeking voluntary liquidation to show that the company is capable of repaying its debts within 12 months

declining balance method *Fin see accelerated depreciation*

decompilation *Ops see reverse engineering*

deconstruction *Gen Mgt* the breaking up of traditional business structures to meet the requirements of the modern economy

de-diversify *Gen Mgt* to sell off parts of a company or group that are not considered directly relevant to a corporation's main area of interest

deductible *Fin* the part of a commercial insurance claim that has to be met by the policyholder rather than the insurance

---

A woman is like a teabag—only in hot water do you realise how strong she is. Nancy Reagan

company. A deductible of £500 means that the company pays all but £500 of the claim for loss or damage. *See also* ***excess***

deduction at source *Fin* a UK term for the collection of taxes from an organisation or individual paying an income rather than from the recipient, for example, from an employer paying wages, a bank paying interest, or a company paying dividends

deed *Fin* a legal document, most commonly one that details the transfer or sale of a property

deed of assignment *Fin* a legal document detailing the transfer of property from a debtor to a creditor

deed of covenant *Fin* a legal document in which a person or organisation promises to pay a third party a sum of money on an annual basis. In certain countries this arrangement may have tax advantages. For example, in the United Kingdom, it is often used for making regular payments to a charity.

deed of partnership *Fin* a legal document formalising the agreement and financial arrangements between the parties that make up a partnership

deed of variation *Fin* in the United Kingdom, an arrangement that allows the will of a deceased person to be amended, provided certain conditions are met and the amendment is signed by all the original beneficiaries

deep discount bond *Fin* a bond that is issued at a discount of at least 15%, or 0.5% for each year of a bond's term, on its par value

deep-in-the-money call option *Fin* a call option that has become very profitable and is likely to remain so

deep-in-the-money put option *Fin* a put option that has become very profitable and is likely to remain so

deep market *Fin* a commodity, currency, or stock market where such is the volume of trade that a considerable number of transactions will not influence the market price

de facto standard *Gen Mgt* a standard set in a given market by a highly successful product or service

default notice *Fin* a formal document issued by a lender to a borrower who is in default. *US term* **notice of default**

defended takeover bid *Fin* a bid for a company takeover in which the directors of the target company oppose the action of the bidder

defensive stock *Fin* stock that prospers predictably regardless of external circumstances such as an economic slowdown, for example, the stock of a company that markets a product everyone must have

deferred coupon *Fin* a coupon that pays no interest at first, but pays relatively high interest after a specified date

deferred credit *or* **deferred income** *Fin* revenue received but not yet reported as income in the profit and loss account, for example, payment for goods to be delivered or services provided at a later date, or government grants received for the purchase of assets. The deferred credit is treated as a credit balance on the balance sheet while waiting to be treated as income. *See also* ***accrual concept***

deferred month *Fin* a month relatively late in the term of an option

deferred ordinary share *Fin* **1.** a share, usually held by founding members of a company, often with a higher dividend that is only paid after other shareholders have received their dividends and, in some cases, only when a certain level of profit has been achieved **2.** a share that pays no dividend for a certain number of years after its issue date but that then ranks with the company's ordinary shares

deferred shares *Fin* a special class of shares ranking for dividend after preference and ordinary shares

deficit *Fin see* ***budget deficit***

deficit financing *Fin* the borrowing of money because expenditures will exceed receipts

deficit spending *Fin* government spending financed through borrowing rather than taxation

deflation *Econ* a reduction in the general level of prices sustained over several months, usually accompanied by declining employment and output

deflationary fiscal policy *Econ* a government policy that raises taxes and reduces public expenditure in order to reduce the level of *aggregate demand* in the economy

deflationary gap *Econ* a gap between *GDP* and the potential output of the economy

de Geus, Arie (*b.* 1930) *Gen Mgt* Dutch business executive, adviser, and consultant. Former strategist for Royal Dutch Shell who, in *The Living Company* (1997), identified the characteristics of long-lived companies: financial conservatism, sensitivity to their environment, cohesiveness, and tolerance of unconventional thinking.

degree mill *HR* an establishment that offers to award a qualification for little or no work, often on payment of a large sum of money. Degree mills mostly operate on the edge of the law, often being unaccredited or unregistered as educational institutions. Most degree mills fail to offer any worthwhile education, and those that do lack the appropriate accreditation that makes their qualifications acceptable by employers, with the result that they award *bogus degree* certificates.

delayed settlement processing *E-com* a procedure for storing authorised transaction settlements online until after the merchant has shipped the goods to the purchaser

delayering *Gen Mgt* the removal of supposedly unproductive layers of middle management to make organisations more efficient and customer-responsive. The term came into vogue during the 1980s.

When taken to extremes, delayering can lead to an *anorexic organisation*.

del credere agent *Fin* an agent who agrees to sell goods on commission and pay the principal even if the buyer defaults on payment. To cover the risk of default, the commission is marginally higher than that of a general agent.

delegation *HR* the process of entrusting somebody else with the appropriate responsibility and authority for the accomplishment of a particular activity. Delegation involves briefing somebody else to carry out a task for which the delegator holds individual responsibility, but which need not be executed by him or her. It does not involve the delegate doing something he or she is already paid to do as part of his or her job. There are various degrees of delegation: for example, a manager may delegate responsibility, but not necessarily full authority, and continue to supervise the activity. Delegation should be a positive activity, for example, as an aid to *employee development*, rather than a negative one, for example, passing on an unpopular task. It should be accompanied by support and encouragement from the delegator to the delegatee. An extension of delegation is *empowerment*, in which complete authority for a task is passed to somebody else, who takes full responsibility for its objectives, execution, and results.

delist (*US*) *Fin* to remove a company from the list of companies whose stocks are traded on an exchange

delivery month *Fin see* **contract month**

delivery note *Fin* a document containing details of the quantity and specifications of accompanying goods. A signed copy of the delivery note often acts as proof of delivery. An **advice note** contains similar information, but is sent to inform a third party of delivery. *Also known as* **carrier's note**, **consignment note**, **despatch note**

Dell, Michael (*b.* 1965) *Gen Mgt* US business executive. Founder of Dell Computer Corporation and youngest CEO to run a

Fortune 500 company, whose business achieved success through building to order, *direct selling*, minimising *inventory*, and using *Internet* technology.

Delphi technique *Gen Mgt* a qualitative *forecasting* method in which a panel of experts respond individually to a questionnaire or series of questionnaires, before reaching a consensus. The Delphi technique requires individual submission of, and response to, the questionnaire on the topic under investigation, in order to avoid the effect of a dominant personality influencing a group discussion. A summary of the written replies is then distributed so that responses can be revised in the light of the views expressed. This cycle is repeated until the co-ordinator of the group is satisfied that the best possible consensus has been reached. The Delphi technique was developed at the Rand Corporation during the late 1940s and 1950s and owes its name to the Greek oracle at Delphi, which was believed to make predictions about the future.

demand forecasting *Gen Mgt* the activity of estimating the quantity of a product or service that consumers will purchase. Demand forecasting involves techniques including both informal methods, such as educated guesses, and quantitative methods, such as the use of historical sales data or current data from test markets. Demand forecasting may be used in making pricing decisions, in assessing future capacity requirements, or in making decisions on whether to enter a new market.

demarcation dispute *HR* an industrial *dispute* between *trade unions*, or between members of the same union, regarding the allocation of work between different types of workers. Demarcation disputes are much less prevalent than in the past because of *multiskilling* agreements between employers and unions and the greater use of *teamwork*.

demassifying *Gen Mgt* the process of changing a mass medium to a medium that is customised to meet the requirements of individual consumers

Deming, W. Edwards (1900–93) *Gen Mgt* US academic and statistician. A leading champion of the *quality* movement and the most influential catalyst for the economic resurgence of post-war Japan, Deming's approach is summarised in his 14 points, which form the central thesis to his book *Out of the Crisis* (1986).

Deming Prize *Gen Mgt* an annual award to a company that has achieved significant performance improvement through the successful application of company-wide *quality control*. The Deming Prize was set up in recognition of the work carried out by *W. Edwards Deming* in post-war Japan to improve manufacturing quality by reducing the potential for error. The Deming Prize has been awarded annually since 1951 by the Union of Japanese Scientists and Engineers. Contenders have to be able to demonstrate that, by applying the disciplines outlined by the assessment components, the productivity, growth, and financial performance of the organisation have been improved. Entrants require a substantial resource in order to be able to submit their entry, which can take years to prepare. The focus of the Deming Prize reflects a rigour for the identification and elimination of defects through teamwork. The prize was also the first to apply the process of self-assessment, which has been adopted by other models such as the *Malcolm Baldrige National Quality Award* and the *EFQM Excellence Model*.

democracy *Gen Mgt* a form of government in which people govern themselves, usually by electing representatives from their own number who are charged with governing in the best interests of the people. Democracy enables participation by the electorate in *decision-making* and thus encourages *empowerment*. In an organisational context, it is known as *industrial democracy*.

demographics *Stats* the characteristics of the size and structure of a human population, such as its distribution and age range

denial of service attack *E-com* an attack on a computer system by a **hacker** or **virus** that does not seek to break into the system, but rather to crash a website by deluging it with phoney traffic. Such attacks are difficult to defend against, but **firewall**s can be designed to block repeated traffic from a particular source.

department *Gen Mgt* a section of an organisation, usually centred on a specialised function, under the responsibility of a head of department or team leader

departmental accounts *Fin* revenue and expenditure statements for departments of an entity. These usually take the form of a trading and profit and loss account for each department, or operating accounts for service departments.

departmental budget *Fin see functional budget*

departmentalisation *Gen Mgt* the division of an organisation into sections. Departmentalisation is usually based on operating function, and organisations will commonly have departments such as finance, personnel, or marketing. Such organisational structure is typical of a **bureaucracy**. It may be used in **centralisation**, when a particular activity is undertaken by one department in one location on behalf of the whole organisation, but may equally be a feature of a **decentralised** organisation, in which departments are used as individual operating units responsible for their own management.

deposit account *Gen Mgt see savings account*

deposit protection *Fin* insurance that depositors have against loss

deposit slip *Fin* a US term for the slip of paper that accompanies money or cheques being paid into a bank account

depreciation *Gen Mgt* an allocation of the cost of an asset over a period of time for accounting and tax purposes. Depreciation is charged against earnings, on the basis that the use of capital assets is a legitimate cost of doing business. Depreciation is also a non-cash expense that is added into net income to determine cash-flow in a given accounting period.

EXAMPLE To qualify for depreciation, assets must be items used in the business that wear out, become obsolete, or lose value over time from natural causes or circumstances, and they must have a useful life beyond a single tax year. Examples include vehicles, machines, equipment, furnishings, and buildings, plus major additions or improvements to such assets. Some intangible assets also can be included under certain conditions. Land, personal assets, stock, leased or rented property, and a company's employees cannot be depreciated.

Straight-line depreciation is the most straightforward method. It assumes that the net cost of an asset should be written off in equal amounts over its life. The formula is:

$$\text{(Original cost - scrap value) / Useful life (years)}$$

For example, if a vehicle cost £30,000 and can be expected to serve the business for seven years, its original cost would be divided by its useful life:

$$(30,000 - 2,000) / 7 = 4,000 \text{ per year}$$

The £4,000 becomes a depreciation expense that is reported on the company's year-end income statement under 'operation expenses'.

In theory, an asset should be depreciated over the actual number of years that it will be used, according to its actual drop in value each year. At the end of each year, all the depreciation claimed to date is subtracted from its cost in order to arrive at its 'book value', which would equal its market value. At the end of its useful business life, any un-depreciated portion would represent the salvage value for which it could be sold or scrapped.

For tax purposes, some accountants prefer to use *accelerated depreciation* to record larger amounts of depreciation in the asset's early years in order to reduce tax bills as soon as possible. In contrast to the straight-line method, the **declining balance method** assumes that the asset depreciates more in its earlier years of use. The table below compares the depreciation amounts that would be available, under these two methods, for a £1,000 asset that is expected to be used for five years and then sold for £100 as scrap.

The depreciation method to be used for a particular asset is fixed at the time that the asset is first placed in service. Whatever rules or tables are in effect for that year must be followed as long as the asset is owned.

Depreciation laws and regulations change frequently over the years as a result of government policy changes, so a company owning property over a long period may have to use several different depreciation methods.

depression *Econ* a high level of unemployment during a downturn in the business cycle, sustained for months or years

deprival value *Fin* a basis for asset valuation based on the maximum amount which an organisation would be willing to pay rather than forgo the asset. *Also known as* **value to the business**, **value to the owner**

deregulation *Gen Mgt* the process of removing government regulations from an industry

derivative *Fin* a security, such as an option, the price of which has a strong correlation with an underlying financial instrument

Derivative Trading Facility *Fin* a computer system and associated network operated by the Australian Stock Exchange to facilitate the purchase and sale of exchange-traded options. *Abbr* **DTF**

DES *abbr E-com* Data Encryption Standard: the most widely used standard for encrypting sensitive business information

design audit *Mkting* an examination of the branding, style, and design of an organisation's marketing material. A design agency may carry out a design audit free of charge in the hope that an organisation will accept their recommendations and place design of material with them.

design consultancy *Mkting* an organisation that plans and carries out design work for clients, including packaging, corporate identity, products, and publication graphics

design for manufacturability, **design for assembly**, *or* **design for production** *Gen Mgt* the process of designing a product for best-fit with the manufacturing system of an organisation in order to reduce the problems of bringing a product to market. Design for manufacturability is

Straight-line Method

Year	Annual Depreciation	Year-end Book Value
1	£900 × 20% = £180	£1,000 – £180 = £820
2	£900 × 20% = £180	£820 – £180 = £640
3	£900 × 20% = £180	£640 – £180 = £460
4	£900 × 20% = £180	£460 – £180 = £280
5	£900 × 20% = £180	£280 – £180 = £100

Declining-balance Method

Year	Annual Depreciation	Year-end Book Value
1	£1,000 × 40% = £400	£1,000 – £400 = £600
2	£600 × 40% = £240	£600 – £240 = £360
3	£360 × 40% = £144	£360 – £144 = £216
4	£216 × 40% = £86.40	£216 – £86.40 = £129.60
5	£129.60 × 40% = £51.84	£129.60 – £51.84 = £77.76

There is nothing so easy but that it becomes difficult when you do it reluctantly.   **Terence**

a team approach to manufacturing that pairs those responsible for the design of a product with those who build it. The manufacturing issues that need to be taken into account in the design process may include using the minimum number of parts, selecting appropriate materials, ease of assembly, and minimising the number of machine set-ups. Design for manufacturability is one of the elements of *concurrent engineering* and is sometimes used as a synonym for it. *Also known as engineering for excellence, manufacturing for excellence, producibility engineering*

design protection *Mkting see copyright*

deskfast *Gen Mgt* breakfast eaten in the office at a desk (*slang*)

de-skilling *HR* the removal of the need for skill or judgment in the performance of a task, often because of new technologies. While it can be argued that de-skilling has adversely affected some *manual workers* in traditional manufacturing industries, the technologies used in modern production systems require a wider range and higher level of skill among the workforce as a whole.

desk jockey *Gen Mgt* somebody who works at a desk (*slang*)

desk research *Mkting* research carried out using documents, telephone interviews, or the Internet

despatch note *Fin see delivery note*

Deutscher Aktienindex *Fin see DAX*

devaluation *Econ* a reduction in the official fixed rate at which one currency exchanges for another under a fixed-rate regime, usually to correct a balance of payments deficit

developing country *Econ* a country, often a producer of primary goods such as cotton or rubber, that cannot generate investment income to stimulate growth and possesses a national income that is vulnerable to change in commodity prices

development capital *Gen Mgt* finance for the expansion of an established business

Development Capital Market (*S Africa*) *Fin* a sector on the JSE Securities Exchange for listing smaller developing companies. Criteria for listing in the Development Capital Market sector are less stringent than for the main board listing. *Abbr* **DCM**

development cycle *Mkting see new product development*

Diagonal Street (*S Africa*) *Fin* an informal term for the financial centre of Johannesburg or, by extension, South Africa

dial and smile (*US*) *Mkting* to cold call potential customers of a product or service (*slang*)

dicing and slicing *Mkting* the analysis of raw data to extract information under different categories (*slang*)

differential cost *Fin* the difference in total cost between alternatives, calculated to assist decision-making. *Also known as incremental cost*

differential pricing *Mkting* a method of pricing that offers the same product at different prices, for example, in different markets, countries, or retail outlets

differentiation *Mkting see product differentiation*

digerati *E-com* people who have or claim to have a sophisticated understanding of Internet or computer technology (*slang*)

digital cash *E-com* an anonymous form of *digital money* that can be linked directly to a bank account or exchanged for physical money. As with physical cash, there is no way to obtain information about the buyer from it, and it can be transferred by the seller to pay for subsequent purchases. *Also known as e-cash, electronic cash*

digital certificate *E-com* an electronic document issued by a recognised authority that validates a purchaser. It is used much as a driving licence or passport is used for identification in a traditional business transaction.

His imagination resembled the wings of an ostrich. It enabled him to run, though not to soar.
Thomas Babington Macaulay

digital coins *E-com* a form of electronic payment authorised for instant transactions that facilitates the purchase of items priced in small denominations of *digital cash*. Digital coins are transferred from customer to merchant for a transaction such as the purchase of a newspaper using a *smart card* for payment.

digital coupon *E-com* a voucher or similar form that exists electronically, for example, on a website, and can be used to reduce the price of goods or services

digital Darwinism *E-com* the idea that the development of Internet companies is governed by rules similar to Darwin's theory of evolution, and that those that adapt best to their environment will be the most successful

digital economy *Econ* an economy in which the main productive functions are in electronic commerce, for example, trade on the Internet

digital goods *E-com* merchandise that is sold and delivered electronically, for example, over the Internet

digital hygienist *Gen Mgt* somebody within a company who is responsible for checking employees' e-mails and surfing habits for non-work-related activity (*slang*)

digital money *E-com* a series of numbers with an intrinsic value in some physical currency. Online digital money requires electronic interaction with a bank to conduct a transaction; offline digital money does not. Anonymous digital money is synonymous with *digital cash*. Identified digital money carries with it information revealing the identities of those involved in the transaction. *Also known as* **e-money**, **electronic money**

digital nervous system *Gen Mgt* an information system that allows an organisation to respond to external events through the accumulation, management, and transfer of knowledge

digital strategy *Gen Mgt* a business strategy that is based on the use of information technology

digital wallet *E-com* software on the hard drive of an online shopper from which the purchaser can pay for the transaction electronically. The wallet can hold in encrypted form such items as credit card information, digital cash or coins, a digital certificate to identify the user, and standardised shipping information. *Also known as* **electronic wallet**

digithead (*US*) *Gen Mgt* somebody who is very knowledgeable about technology and mathematics but has poor social skills (*slang*)

digitisable *E-com* capable of being converted to digital form for distribution via the Internet or other networks

dilberted (*US*) *HR* badly treated by your boss. The term derives from the same fictional character who gave his name to the *Dilbert principle*. (*slang*)

Dilbert principle (*US*) *HR* the principle that the most inefficient employees are moved to the place where they can do the least damage. Dilbert is the main character in a comic strip and cartoon series by Scott Adams that satirises office and corporate life.

dilution *Fin* a reduction in the earnings and voting power per share caused by an increase or potential increase in the number of shares in issue. For the purpose of calculating diluted earnings per share, the net profit attributable to ordinary shareholders and the weighted average number of shares outstanding should be adjusted for the effects of all dilutive potential ordinary shares.

DINKY *abbr Gen Mgt* Dual Income, No Kids (*slang*)

direct action marketing *Mkting see direct response marketing*

direct channel *Mkting* a method of selling and distributing products direct to customers. Direct channels include direct sales, sales force, mail order, and the Internet.

The shock of unemployment becomes a pathology in its own right. **Robert Farrar Capon**

direct connection *E-com* a permanent connection between a computer system and the Internet

direct cost *Gen Mgt, Ops* a variable cost directly attributable to production. Items that are classed as direct costs include materials used, labour deployed, and marketing budget. Amounts spent will vary with output. *See also indirect cost*

direct debit *Fin* a direct claim on an individual or organisation by a creditor, and paid by the individual's or organisation's bank. Variations in period claims are admissible.

direct labour *HR* personnel directly involved in the manufacturing of products or the provision of services. Direct labour includes blue-collar workers.

direct labour cost percentage rate *Fin* an *overhead absorption rate* based on direct labour cost

direct labour hour rate *Fin* an *overhead absorption rate* based on direct labour hours

direct mail *Mkting* the sending by post, fax, or e-mail of *advertising* communications addressed to specific prospective customers. Direct mail is one tool that can be used as part of a marketing strategy. The use of direct mail is often administered by third-party companies that own databases containing not only names and addresses, but also social, economic, and lifestyle information. It is sometimes seen as an invasion of personal privacy, and there is some public resentment of this form of advertising. This is particularly true of e-mailed direct mail, known derogatively as *spam*. By enabling advertisers to target a specific type of potential customer, however, direct mail can be more cost-efficient than other *advertising media*. It is frequently used as part of a relationship marketing strategy.

direct mail preference scheme *Mkting* an arrangement that allows individuals and organisations to refuse direct mail by having participating organisations remove them from their mailing lists

direct marketing *Mkting see direct response marketing*

directorate *Gen Mgt* the governing or controlling body of an organisation responsible for the organisation's *corporate strategy* and accountable to its *stakeholders* for business results. A directorate may also be known as a *board of directors* or council, or at an inner level, the executive or management committee.

director's dealing *Fin* the purchase or sale of a company's stock by one of its directors

direct product profitability *Fin* used primarily within the retail sector, DPP involves the attribution of costs other than the purchase price (for example, distribution, warehousing, retailing) to each product line. Thus a net profit, as opposed to a gross profit, can be identified for each product. The cost attribution process uses a variety of measures (for example, warehousing space or transport time) to reflect the resource consumption of individual products.

direct response marketing *or* **direct response advertising** *Mkting* the use of direct forms of *advertising* to elicit enquiries or sales from potential customers directly to producers or service providers. Direct response marketing aims to bypass intermediaries such as retailers or wholesalers. Forms of communication used include *direct mail*, home shopping channels, and television and press advertisements. *Also known as direct action marketing, direct marketing*

direct selling *Mkting* the selling of products or services directly to customers without the use of intermediaries such as wholesalers, retailers, or brokers. Direct selling offers many advantages to the customer, including lower prices and shopping from home. Potential disadvantages include lack of *after-sales service*, an inability to inspect products prior to purchase, lack of specialist advice, and difficulties in returning or exchanging goods. Methods of direct selling include mail-order catalogues and door-to-door and telephone sales, and direct selling has increased with the growth of the Internet, which enables producers to make direct contact with potential customers.

direct tax *Fin* a tax on income or capital that is paid directly rather than added to the price of goods or services

dirty float *Econ* a floating exchange rate that cannot float freely because a country's central bank intervenes on foreign exchange markets to alter its level

dirty price *Fin* the price of a debt instrument that includes the amount of accrued interest that has not yet been paid

disaggregation *Gen Mgt* the breaking apart of an alliance of companies to review their strengths and contributions as a basis for rebuilding an effective business web

disaster management *Gen Mgt* the actions taken by an organisation in response to unexpected events that are adversely affecting people or resources and threatening the continued operation of the organisation. Disaster management includes the development of **disaster recovery plans**, for minimising the risk of disasters and for handling them when they do occur, and the implementation of such plans. Disaster management usually refers to the management of natural catastrophes such as fire, flooding, or earthquakes. Related techniques include *crisis management*, *contingency management*, and *risk management*.

disaster recovery plan *Gen Mgt see disaster management*

disbursing agent *Fin see paying agent*

disciplinary procedure *HR see discipline*

discipline *HR* standards of required behaviour or performance. Good practice requires an organisation to establish a **disciplinary procedure** in order to ensure just decisions. A disciplinary procedure should consist of a formal system of documented warnings and hearings, with rights of representation and appeal at each stage.

disclosure of information *Gen Mgt* the release of information that may be considered confidential to a third party or parties. The disclosure of information in the public interest may be prohibited, permitted, or required, by legislation in a variety of contexts. For example: *data protection* legislation restricts the disclosure of personal data held by organisations; *company law* requires the publication of certain financial and company data; and *whistleblowing* legislation entitles employees to divulge information relating to unethical or illegal conduct in the workplace. Restrictive covenants and *confidentiality agreements* also regulate the information that may be disclosed to third parties.

discount *Fin, Gen Mgt* a reduction in the price of goods or services in relation to the standard price. A discount is a selling technique that is used, for example, to encourage customers to buy in large quantities or to make payments in cash. It can also be used to improve sales of a slow-moving line. The greater the purchasing power of the buyer, the greater the discounts that can be negotiated. Some companies inflate original list prices to give the impression that discounts offer value for money; conversely too many genuine discounts may harm profitability.

discount broker *Fin* a broker who charges relatively low fees because he or she provides restricted services

discounted bond *Fin* a bond that is sold for less than its face value because its yield is not as high as that of other bonds

discounted cash flow *Fin* the discounting of the projected net cash flows of a capital project to ascertain its present value. The methods commonly used are: yield, or internal rate of return (IRR), in which the calculation determines the return in the form of a percentage; net present value (NPV), in which the discount rate is chosen and the present value is expressed as a sum of money; and discounted payback, in which the discount rate is chosen and the payback is the number of years required to repay the original investment. *See also* **capital investment appraisal**

discounted dividend model *Fin* a method of calculating a stock's value by reducing future dividends to the present value. *Also known as* **dividend discount model**

discount loan *Fin* a loan that amounts to less than its face value because payment of interest has been subtracted

discount rate *E-com* a percentage fee that an e-commerce merchant pays to an account provider or independent sales organisation for settling an electronic transaction

discount security *Fin* a security that is sold for less than its face value in lieu of bearing interest

discrete variable *Stats* a variable in a statistical study that has only a whole-number value, such as the number of deaths in a population

discretionary account *Fin* a securities account in which the broker has the authority to make decisions about buying and selling without the customer's prior permission

discretionary cost *Fin* a cost whose amount within a time period is determined by, and is easily altered by, a decision taken by the appropriate budget holder. Marketing, research, and training are generally regarded as discretionary costs. Control of discretionary costs is through the budgeting process.

discretionary order *Fin* a security transaction in which a broker controls the details, such as the time of execution

discriminant analysis *Gen Mgt* a statistical technique designed to predict the groups or categories into which individual cases will fall on the basis of a number of independent variables. Discriminant analysis attempts to identify which vari-

ables or combinations of variables accurately discriminate between groups or categories by means of a scatter diagram or classification table called a **confusion matrix**. Discriminant analysis has applications in finance, for example, credit risk analysis, or in the prediction of company failure, and in the field of marketing, for market segmentation purposes.

discriminating monopoly *Econ* a company able to charge different prices for its output in different markets because it has power to influence prices for its goods

discrimination *HR* unfavourable treatment in employment based on prejudice. Major forms of outlawed discrimination include sex discrimination, *racial discrimination*, disability discrimination, and, in some countries, *age discrimination*. Discrimination may also be practised through *indirect discrimination*.

discussion board *E-com* an area on a website that allows people to contribute opinions, ideas, and announcements. It is particularly suitable for casual, one-off interactions because little commitment is required from participants. They can generally review a discussion topic without subscribing, although they do have to subscribe if they want to contribute something themselves.

It is not essential for the website owner to moderate discussion boards, although it is important to watch out for the emergence of 'off-topic' subjects—contributions that are unnecessarily negative or perhaps libellous—and copyright infringement.

A prime example of the success of the discussion board approach is how Amazon.com uses it to allow its consumers to publish book reviews.

discussion list *E-com* an arrangement for sending e-mail messages to a number of people that also allows recipients to respond and everyone else on the list to see these responses. A discussion list is similar to a distribution list except that it is based on a two-way model. Discussion lists can be moderated or unmoderated.

When you are marketing a drinks brand, it can take over your life. Andrew Allan

In a moderated list, all mail is screened by an intermediary, typically the individual or organisation that set up the list. Unmoderated lists involve no editorial process, so any subscriber can contribute anything he or she wants to the e-mail discussion. Unlike newsgroups, discussion lists do not provide a consolidated record of responses.

disequilibrium price *Econ* the price of a good set at a level at which demand and supply are not in balance

dishonour *Fin* to refuse payment of a cheque because the account for which it is written holds insufficient money. *Also known as* **bounce**

disinflation *Econ* the elimination or reduction of inflation or inflationary pressures in an economy by fiscal or monetary policies

disintermediation *E-com* the elimination of intermediaries, for example, the wholesalers found in traditional retail channels, in favour of direct selling to the consumer. *See also* **reintermediation**

dismissal *HR* the termination of an **employee's** employment by his or her **employer**. Dismissal may take place with or without notice, when a fixed-term contract expires and is not renewed, or when an employee leaves claiming **constructive dismissal**. The employer must show that the main reason for dismissal was for one of five fair reasons: incapability, misconduct, **redundancy**, legal restrictions, or some other substantial reason. In addition, the employer must have followed a reasonable procedure before deciding on dismissal. If any of these conditions is not met, the employee may be entitled to claim **unfair dismissal**.

dispersion *Stats* the amount by which a set of observations deviates from its mean

display advertising *Mkting* newspaper or magazine advertisements that use eye-catching typography and graphic images

disposable income *Fin* income that is left for spending after tax and other deductions

dispute *HR* a disagreement. An **industrial dispute** is a disagreement between an **employer** and an employees' representative, usually a **trade union**, over pay and conditions and can result in **industrial action**. A **commercial dispute** is a disagreement between two businesses, usually over a contract. There are three main types of dispute resolution: litigation, **arbitration**, and alternative dispute resolution.

dispute benefit *HR see* **strike pay**

distance learning *Gen Mgt* a course of study that involves minimal or no attendance at an academic institution, but relies instead on personal study, using books, audio-visual materials, and computer-based materials. Tutorial support may be available via the telephone or Internet, and attendance at weekend or summer schools may be required. The best-known provider of such courses in the United Kingdom is the Open University. Distance learning is similar to **open learning**.

distance sampling *Stats* a method of sampling in ecological statistics used to determine the number of animals that feed or plants that grow in a particular habitat

distribution centre *Ops* a warehouse or storage facility where the emphasis is on processing and moving goods on to wholesalers, retailers, or consumers rather than on storage

distribution channel *Ops* the route by which a product or service is moved from a producer or supplier to customers. A distribution channel usually consists of a chain of intermediaries, including **wholesalers**, **retailers**, and distributors, that is designed to transport goods from the point of production to the point of consumption in the most efficient way.

distribution cost *Fin* the cost of warehousing saleable products and delivering them to customers

---

Very few people in the world can be relied upon to work without praise or recognition.
Varindra Tarzie Vittachi

distribution list *E-com* a list of e-mail addresses given one collective title. Internet users can send a message to all the addresses on the list simultaneously by referring to the list title.

distribution management *Ops* the management of the efficient transfer of goods from the place of manufacture to the point of sale or consumption. Distribution management encompasses such activities as *warehousing*, *materials handling*, packaging, *stock control*, order processing, and transportation.

distribution resource planning *Ops* a computerised system that integrates distribution with manufacturing by identifying requirements for finished goods and producing schedules for *inventory* and its movement within the distribution process. Distribution resource planning systems receive data on sales forecasts, customer order and delivery requirements, available inventory, *logistics*, and manufacturing and purchasing *lead times*. This data is analysed to produce a time-phased schedule of resource requirements that is matched against existing supply sources and production schedules to identify the actions that must be taken to synchronise supply and demand. The effective integration of material requirements planning and distribution resource planning systems leads to the more effective and timely delivery of finished goods to the customer, and to reduced inventory levels and lower material costs. *Abbr* **DRP**

distributive network *E-com* a system or infrastructure that enables products and services to move around. Offline distributive networks include roads, telephone companies, electrical power grids, and the postal service. In the new economy, distributive networks include online banks and Web-enabled mobile telephones.

distributor *Mkting* an organisation that distributes products to retailers on behalf of a manufacturer

distributor support *Mkting* marketing or financial support by manufacturers aimed at improving the performance of organisations that distribute their products

diversification *Gen Mgt* a strategy to increase the variety of business, service, or product types within an organisation. Diversification can be a growth strategy, taking advantage of market opportunities, or it may be aimed at reducing risk by spreading interests over different areas. It can be achieved through *acquisition* or through internal research and development, and it can involve managing two, a few, or many different areas of interest. Diversification can also be a *corporate strategy* of investment in acquisitions within a broad portfolio range by a large *holding company*. One distinct type is **horizontal diversification**, which involves expansion into a similar product area, for example, a domestic furniture manufacturer producing office furniture. Another is **vertical diversification**, in which a company moves into a different level of the *supply chain*, for example, a manufacturing company becoming a retailer. A well-known example of diversification is the move of Bic, the ballpoint pen manufacturer, into the production of disposable razors.

diversified investment company *Fin* a unit trust with a variety of types of investments

diversity *Gen Mgt* difference between people, for example, in race, age, gender, disability, geographic origin, family status, education, or personality, that can affect workplace relationships and achievement. Diversity management aims to value these differences and encourage each person to fulfil his or her potential in terms of organisational objectives. The approach goes beyond *equal opportunities*, which stresses the rights of particular disadvantaged groups rather than those of the individual.

diverted hours *Fin* the available hours of nominally direct workers who are diverted to indirect activities, for example, cleaning machines, and are therefore charged as indirect labour. This contrasts

---

Always be smart enough to hire people brighter than yourself. Caroline Marland

with the hours worked by indirect workers, whose entire time is charged as indirect.

divestment *Gen Mgt* the sale or closure of one or several businesses, or parts of a business. Divestment often takes place as part of a *rationalisation* effort to cut costs or to enable an organisation to concentrate on core business or competences, and may take the form of a *management buy-out*.

dividend *Fin* an amount payable to shareholders from profits or other distributable reserves. Dividends are normally paid in cash, but *scrip dividends*, paid by the issue of additional shares, are permissible. Listed companies normally pay two dividends per year, an interim dividend, based on interim profits reported during the accounting period, and a final dividend, based on the final audited accounts and approved at the *Annual General Meeting*.

dividend clawback *Fin* an agreement that dividends will be reinvested as part of the financing of a project

dividend cover *Fin* the number of times a company's dividends to ordinary shareholders could be paid out of its net after-tax profits. This measures the likelihood of dividend payments being sustained, and is a useful indication of sustained profitability.

EXAMPLE If the figure is 3, for example, a firm's profits are three times the level of the dividend paid to shareholders.

Dividend cover is calculated by dividing earnings per share by the dividend per share:

Earnings per share / dividend per share =
dividend cover

If a company has earnings per share of £8, and it pays out a dividend of 2.1, dividend cover is:

8 / 2.1 = 3.80

An alternative formula divides a company's net profit by the total amount allocated for dividends. So a company that earns £10 million in net profit and allocates £1 million for dividends has a dividend cover of 10, while a company that earns £25 million and pays out £10 million in dividends has a dividend cover of 2.5:

10,000,000 / 1,000,000 = 10 and 25,000,000 / 10,000,000 = 2.5

A dividend cover ratio of 2 or higher is usually adequate, and indicates that the dividend is affordable. A dividend cover ratio below 1.5 is risky, and a ratio below 1 indicates a company is paying the current year's dividend with retained earnings from a previous year: a practice that cannot continue indefinitely. On the other hand, a high dividend cover figure may disappoint an investor looking for income, since the figure suggests directors could have declared a larger dividend.
See also payout ratio

dividend discount model *Fin see discounted dividend model*

dividend growth model *Fin* a financial model which can be used to value companies based on assumptions about their current and future dividend payments

dividend limitation *Fin* a provision in a bond limiting the dividends that may be paid

dividend payout ratio *Fin* a ratio which shows the proportion of earnings which are distributed to the ordinary shareholders by way of dividends. It is calculated as follows:

Ordinary dividends for the year / Earnings
attributable to the ordinary shareholders

dividend per share *Fin* total amounts declared as dividends per share. The dividend per share is actually paid in respect of a financial year. Special rules apply if equity shares are issued during the year.

dividend reinvestment plan *Fin* a plan that provides for the reinvestment of dividends in the shares of the company paying the dividends. *Abbr* **DRIP**

dividend rights *Fin* rights to receive dividends

dividends-received deduction *Fin* a tax advantage on dividends that a company receives from a company it owns

dividend yield *Fin* dividends expressed as a percentage of a share's price

division of labour *Ops* the allocation of each task in a process to a different worker. Division of labour is a concept originated by **Adam Smith** in order to increase output. It enables workers to become highly skilled at one job, but they may lack transferable skills and find their work monotonous. To a certain extent, division of labour has been superseded by *multiskilling*.

document *E-com* an electronic file containing text, graphics, multimedia, or hyperlinks

documentary credit *Fin* an arrangement, used in the finance of international transactions, whereby a bank undertakes to make a payment to a third party on behalf of a customer

dog *Gen Mgt see Boston Box*
that dog won't hunt *Gen Mgt* that idea will not work (*slang*)

dog and pony show (*US*) *Gen Mgt* a national tour by the top staff of a company aimed at persuading investors to invest in the company (*slang*)

dog-eat-dog *Mkting* ruthless, especially in the marketplace (*slang*)

dogfood *E-com* temporary software used by an organisation for testing purposes

dogs of the Dow (*US*) *Fin* the stocks in the Dow Jones Industrial Average that pay the smallest dividends as a percentage of their prices (*slang*)

dole bludger (*ANZ*) *Gen Mgt* somebody who lives off social security payments and makes no attempt to find work (*slang*)

dollar cost averaging (*US*) *Fin* = *pound cost averaging*

dollar roll (*US*) *Fin* an agreement to sell a stock and buy it later for a specified price

dollars-and-cents (*US*) *Fin* considering money as the determining factor

domain name *E-com* the officially registered address of a website. Domain names typically contain two or more parts separated from each other by a dot, for example, www.yahoo.com. The domain name suffix (following the final dot) is intended to indicate either the nature or location of the website, for example, com for a commercial website and co.uk for a British website.

domicilium citandi et executandi (*S Africa*) *Fin* the address where a summons or other official notice should be served when or if necessary, which must be supplied by somebody applying for credit or entering into a contract

donut (*US*) *Mkting* the middle section of a commercial where the product information is usually placed (*slang*)

dot bam *E-com* a real-world business with a strong Web presence. The 'bam' stands for 'bricks and mortar'.

dot-bomb *or* **dot.bomb** *E-com* an e-commerce enterprise that has gone out of business (*slang*)

dot-com *or* **dot.com** *E-com* an e-commerce enterprise. It markets its products through the Internet, rather than through traditional channels.

dotted-line relationships *HR* the links, as shown on an organisational chart, that exist between managers and staff whom they oversee indirectly rather than on a day-to-day basis (*slang*)

double-blind *Stats* relating to an experiment, usually a medical one, in which neither the experimenter nor the subject knows whether the treatment being administered is genuine or a control procedure

double dipping (*US*) *Gen Mgt* the practice of receiving income from a government pension as well as social security payments

double indemnity *Fin* a provision in an insurance policy that guarantees payment of double its face value on the accidental death of the holder

---

To succeed at reengineering, you have to be a missionary, a motivator, and a leg breaker.
Michael Hammer

double opt-in *E-com* a type of *subscription process* for users wanting to sign up to receive specific information or services via a website. The double opt-in approach is emerging as the industry standard for subscription management, as it protects the user from being maliciously subscribed to a service by a third party.

The user requests a subscription, via e-mail or web form. The vendor's system replies with a verification message, requesting an affirmative reply to the message. Only when an affirmative reply is received from the user is the subscription completed.

double taxation *Fin* the taxing of something twice, usually the combination of corporation tax and tax on the dividends that shareholders earn

double taxation agreement *Fin* an agreement between two countries intended to avoid a situation in which income is subject to taxation in both

doubtful debts provision *Fin* an amount charged against profit and deducted from debtors to allow for the estimated non-recovery of a proportion of the debts. *See also* **bad debt**

doughnut principle *Gen Mgt* a concept that likens an organisation to an **inverted doughnut** with a centre of dough—the core activities—surrounded by a hole—a flexible area containing the organisation's partners. The doughnut principle was originated by **Charles Handy** in *The Empty Raincoat* (1994). He saw organisations as having an essential core of jobs and people, surrounded by a space filled with flexible workers and flexible supply contracts. He maintained that organisations often neglect the core, developing the surrounding hole instead. The doughnut analogy is a way of helping a balance to be achieved between what has to be done and what could be done, by analysing the dough and the hole of a particular organisation. The principle has also been applied to personal life.

Dow Jones Averages *Fin* an index of the prices of selected stocks on the New York Stock Exchange compiled by Dow Jones & Company, Inc

downshifting *Gen Mgt* the concept of giving up all or part of your work commitment and income in exchange for improved quality of life. The term was coined by **Charles Handy**. Downshifting has increased in popularity because of rising *stress* in the workplace caused partly by the *downsizing* trend of the late 20th century, and may be contrasted with the concept of the *organisation man*. Downshifting is integral to the idea of *portfolio working*, in which individuals opt out of a formal employee relationship to sell their services at a pace and at a price to suit themselves.

Most people consider downshifting because of family demands, or because they have been asked to do something by their organisation that goes strongly against their values, pushing them to question why they are working so hard for that organisation. Others downshift as they approach retirement, in order to smooth the transition. People who downshift need to be very sure that that is what they really want and know why they want it, as it can be hard to reverse the decision.

Someone wanting to take the risk of downshifting should make a thorough assessment of his or her short-term and long-term financial situation by way of preparation. They will need to have a good bed of savings to rely on in the first year. It may be necessary to consider moving to a smaller, cheaper place. Deciding what to keep of the old life and what to let go is another important part of the preparation. Some downshifters will want to completely leave their old work life behind them, starting a new job in a slower-paced organisation, or setting up on their own. Others will want to stay with their organisation but perhaps move to a less demanding job. Once these things have been considered and decided upon, it is time for the downshifter to make an action plan with a schedule which includes regular re-assessment periods.

downsizing *HR* the reduction of the size of a business, especially by making staff redundant. Downsizing may be part of a **rationalisation** process, or **corporate restructuring**, with the removal of hierarchies or the closure of departments or functions either after a period of unsatisfactory results or as a consequence of strategic review. The terms **upsizing** and **resizing** are applied when an organisation increases the number of staff employed.

downstream *Ops* later in the production process

downstream progress *Gen Mgt* movement by a company towards achieving its objectives that is easy because it involves riding a wave or trend and benefiting from favourable conditions. *See also* **upstream progress**

downtime *Ops* a period of time during which a machine is not available for use because of maintenance or breakdown

Dow Theory *Fin* the theory that stock market prices can be forecast on the basis of the movements of selected industrial and transport stocks

Doz, Yves (*b*. 1947) *Gen Mgt* French academic. Collaborator with **C.K. Prahalad** and **Gary Hamel** in researching **strategic models** to tackle the complexities and **globalisation** of markets. His *Alliance Advantage* (1998, co-author), focuses on **strategic partnering**.

draft *Fin* a written order to pay a particular sum from one account to another, or to a person. *See also* **sight draft**, **time draft**

drawee *Fin* the individual or institution to whom a bill of exchange or cheque is addressed

drawing account *Fin* an account that permits the tracking of withdrawals

dress-down day *HR* a day on which employees are allowed to wear informal clothes to work

drilling down *Mkting* a technique for managing data by arranging it in hierarchies that provide increasing levels of detail

DRIP *Fin see* **dividend reinvestment plan**

drip method *Mkting* a marketing method that involves calling potential customers at regular intervals until they agree to make a purchase (*slang*)

drive time *Mkting* the time of the day when most people are likely to be in their cars, usually early in the morning or late in the afternoon, considered to be the optimum time to broadcast a radio commercial (*slang*)

drop lock *Fin* the automatic conversion of a debt instrument with a floating rate to one with a fixed rate when interest rates fall to an agreed percentage

drownloading *E-com* the act of simultaneously downloading so many files that a computer crashes (*slang*)

DRP *Ops see* **distribution resource planning**

Drucker, Peter (*b*. 1909) *Gen Mgt* US academic. Recognised as the father of management thinking. His earlier works studied management practice, while later he tackled the complexities and the management implications of the post-industrial world. *The Practice of Management* (1954), best known perhaps for the introduction of **management by objectives**, remains a classic. He also anticipated other management themes such as the importance of marketing (see **marketing management**) and the rise of the **knowledge worker**.

DSO *abbr Fin* days' sales outstanding. *See* **collection ratio**

DTF *abbr* (*ANZ*) *Fin* Derivative Trading Facility

dual currency bond *Fin* a bond that pays interest in a currency other than the one used to buy it

dual economy *Econ* an economy in which the manufacturing and service sectors are growing at different rates

dual pricing *Fin* a form of transfer pricing in which the two parties to a common transaction use different prices

---

I have direct knowledge. I don't have to call someone to ask a question.   Nancy Peretsman

dual trading *Fin* the practice of acting as agent both for a broker's firm and its customers

duck

get your ducks in a row *or* **line up your ducks** *Gen Mgt* (*slang*) **1.** to get everything properly organised **2.** (*US*) to get all concerned parties to agree to a plan of action

due-on-sale clause *Fin* a provision requiring a homeowner to pay off a mortgage upon sale of the property

dumbsizing *HR* the process of reducing the size of a company to such an extent that it is no longer profitable or efficient (*slang*)

DUMP *Gen Mgt* Destitute Unemployed Mature Professional (*slang*)

dumping *Econ* the selling of a commodity on a foreign market at a price below its *marginal cost*, either to dispose of a temporary surplus or to achieve a monopoly by eliminating competition

Dunlap, Albert (*b.* 1937) *Gen Mgt* US business executive. He is noted for his *turnaround management* capabilities, based on *downsizing* and *cost-cutting*, which earned him the nickname 'Chainsaw Al' and which are described in his book *Mean Business* (1996).

duopoly *Econ* a market in which only two sellers of a good exist. If one decides to alter the price, the other will respond and influence the market's response to the first decision.

Dutch auction *Fin* an auction in which the lot for sale is offered at an initial price which, if there are no takers, is then reduced until there is a bid

duvet day *Gen Mgt* a day sanctioned by an employing organisation as a day when an employee may call in and say that they will not attend work that day because they do not feel like it. A duvet day does not form part of an employee's *leave* entitlement, but will be recorded as a sanctioned absence. Duvet days are more popular in the United States than in the United Kingdom, and those organisations that allow them do not usually make them part of written policy, limit them to two or three per year, and sometimes only offer them to key employees.

Dynamic HTML *E-com* a relatively limited animation tool for creating website graphics which, if properly designed, can be viewed by most *browsers*. Its major advantage is that it does not require a *plug-in* to view. *Abbr* **DHTML**

dynamic pricing *Gen Mgt* pricing that changes in line with patterns of demand

dynamic programming *Gen Mgt* a mathematical technique used in *management science* to solve complex problems in the fields of production planning and inventory control. Dynamic programming divides the problem into subproblems or decision stages that can be addressed sequentially, normally by working backwards from the last stage. Applications of the technique include maintenance and replacement of equipment, resource allocation, and process design and control. The term comes from the work of Richard Bellman published in the late 1950s and early 1960s.

One man can be a crucial ingredient on a team, but one man cannot make a team.
Kareem Abdul-Jabbar

E2E *E-com see* **exchange** *(sense 1)*

EAI *E-com see* **enterprise application integration**

e-alliance *E-com* a partnership forged between organisations in order to achieve business objectives, for enterprises conducted over the Web. There has been a surge in such alliances since the Internet took off in the mid-1990s, and studies show that the most successful have been those involving traditional offline businesses and online entities—the **clicks-and-mortar** strategy—such as that between Amazon.com and Toys 'R' Us. Toys 'R' Us had the physical infrastructure and brand, while Amazon.com had the online infrastructure and experience of making e-commerce work.

E&O *abbr Fin* errors and omissions

EAP *(US) HR see* **employee assistance programme**

ear candy *HR* pleasant but meaningless noise or talk (*slang*)

early adopter *Gen Mgt* an individual or organisation that is among the first to make use of a new technology

early retirement *HR* **retirement** from work before the statutory retirement age or before the normal retirement age set by an employer. Early retirement may be taken because of ill health or at the request of the employee or employer. An employer may offer opportunities for early retirement on advantageous financial terms as a way of reducing staff numbers without **redundancies**. *Also known as* **premature retirement**

earned income *Fin* money generated by an individual's or an organisation's labour, for example, wages, salaries, fees, royalties, and business profits. *See also* **unearned income**

earnings 1. *Fin* income or profit from a business, quoted gross or net of tax, which

may be retained and distributed in part to the shareholders **2.** *HR* a sum of money gained from paid employment, usually quoted before tax, including any extra rewards such as **fringe benefits**, allowances, or incentives. *Also known as* **pay**

earnings before interest and taxes *Ops abbr* **EBIT**. *See* **operating income**

earnings before interest, tax, depreciation, and amortisation *Fin see* **EBITDA**

earnings per share *Fin* a financial ratio that measures the portion of a company's profit allocated to each outstanding ordinary share. It is the most basic measure of the value of a share, and also is the basis for calculating several other important investment ratios.

EXAMPLE EPS is calculated by subtracting the total value of any preference shares from net income (earnings) for the period in question, then dividing the resulting figure by the number of shares outstanding during that period.

Net income – Dividends on any preference shares / Average number of shares outstanding

Companies usually use a weighted average number of shares outstanding over the reporting period, but shares outstanding can either be 'primary' or 'fully diluted'. Primary EPS is calculated using the number of shares that are currently held by investors in the market and able to be traded. Diluted EPS is the result of a complex calculation that determines how many shares would be outstanding if all exercisable warrants and options were converted into shares at the end of a quarter.

Suppose, for example, that a company has granted a large number of share options to employees. If these options are capable of being exercised in the near future, that could significantly alter the number of shares in issue and thus the EPS–even though the net income is

---

The payoff for failure is almost as much as for succeeding.   *Anonymous*

the same. Often in such cases, the company might quote the EPS on the existing shares and the fully diluted version.
Abbr **EPS**

earnings report *(US) Fin = published accounts*

earnings retained *Fin see* **retained profits**

earnings surprise *Fin* a report by a company that its earnings vary considerably from expectations

earnings yield *Fin* money earned by a company during a year, expressed as a percentage of the price of one of its shares

earn-out arrangement *Fin* a procedure whereby owner/managers selling an organisation receive a portion of their consideration linked to the financial performance of the business during a specified period after the sale. The arrangement gives a measure of security to the new owners, who pass some of the financial risk associated with the purchase of a new enterprise to the sellers.

EASDAQ *abbr Fin* European Association of Securities Dealers Automated Quotations: a stock exchange for technology and growth companies based in Europe and modelled on *NASDAQ* in the United States

eased *Fin* used in stock market reports to describe a market that has experienced a slight fall in prices

easy money *Fin see* **cheap money**

EBIT *abbr Ops* earnings before interest and taxes

EBITDA *abbr Fin* earnings before interest, tax, depreciation, and amortisation: The earnings generated by a business's fundamental operating performance, frequently used in accounting ratios for comparison with other companies. Interest on borrowings, tax payable on those profits, depreciation, and amortisation are excluded on the basis that they can distort the underlying performance.

EXAMPLE It is calculated as follows:

Revenue – Expenses (excluding tax and interest, depreciation, etc.) = EBITDA

It is important to note that EBITDA ignores many factors that impact true cash-flow, such as working capital, debt payments, and other fixed expenses. Even so, it may be useful in terms of evaluating firms in the same industry with widely different capital structures, tax rates, and depreciation policies.

EBQ *abbr Ops* economic batch quantity: the optimum batch size for the manufacture of an item or component, at the lowest cost. The batch size is a trade-off between unit costs that increase with batch size and those that decrease. The point of lowest combined or total cost indicates the most economic batch size for production. *Also known as* **economic lot quantity**. *See* **economic order quantity**

EBRD *abbr Fin* European Bank for Reconstruction and Development: the bank, which was established in 1991, developed programmes to tackle a range of issues. These included: the creation and strengthening of infrastructure; privatisation; the reform of the financial sector, including the development of capital markets and the privatisation of commercial banks; the development of productive competitive private sectors of small and medium-sized enterprises in industry, agriculture, and services; the restructuring of industrial sectors to put them on a competitive basis; and encouraging foreign investment and cleaning up the environment. The EBRD had 41 original members: the European Commission, the European Investment Bank, all the EEC countries, and all the countries of Eastern Europe except Albania, which finally became a member in October 1991, followed by all the republics of the former USSR in March 1992.

e-business *E-com* **1.** the conduct of business on the Internet, including the electronic purchasing and selling of goods and services, servicing customers, and communications with business partners. *Also known as* **electronic business 2.** a company that conducts business on the Internet

---

There is no merit in sowing dissension among subordinates; any beginner can do it.
Henri Fayol

e-cash *E-com see* **digital cash**

ECB *abbr Fin* European Central Bank: the financial institution that replaced the European Monetary Institute (EMI) in 1998 and which is responsible for carrying out EU monetary policy and administering the euro

ECGD *abbr Mkting* Export Credit Guarantee Department

ECML *abbr E-com* electronic commerce modelling language

ecoconsumer *Gen Mgt* a customer who will only select from, or subscribe to, goods that meet environmentally sound considerations

ecolabel *Gen Mgt* a label used to characterise products that satisfy particular total *environmental management* considerations with regard to their production, usage, or disposal

ecological priority *Gen Mgt* the priority for organisations and governments to put as much emphasis on environmental protection as economic performance

ecological statistics *Stats* statistical studies in the field of ecology using such techniques as *distance sampling*

ECO-Management Audit Scheme *Gen Mgt see* **environmental management**. *Abbr* **EMAS**

e-commerce *E-com* the exchange of goods, information products, or services via an electronic medium such as the Internet. Originally limited to buying and selling, it has evolved to include such functions as customer service, marketing, and advertising. *Also known as* **electronic commerce, web commerce**

e-commerce mall *E-com see* **cyber mall**

e-commerce processes *E-com* the flow of information through planning, design, manufacture, sales, order processing, distribution, and quality in an e-business

e-company *E-com* an e-commerce enterprise (*slang*)

econometric model *Econ* a way of representing the relationship between economic variables as an equation or set of equations with statistically precise parameters linking the variables

econometrics *Econ* the setting up of mathematical models to describe relationships in an economy, for example, between wage rates and levels of employment

Economic and Monetary Union *Fin see* **EMU**

economic assumption *Econ* an assumption built into an economic model, for example, that output will grow at 2.5% in the next tax year

economic batch quantity *Ops see* **EBQ**

Economic Development Board *Fin* an organisation established in 1961 that aims to promote investment in Singapore by providing various services and assistance schemes to foreign and local companies. *Abbr* **EDB**

economic goods *Econ* services or physical objects that can command a price in the market

economic growth *Econ* an increase in the national income of a country created by the long-term productive potential of its economy

economic indicator *Econ* a statistic that may be important for a country's long-term economic health, for example, rising prices or falling exports

economic life *Econ* the conditions of trade and manufacture in a country that contribute to its prosperity or poverty

economic lot quantity *Ops see* **EBQ**

economic miracle *Econ* the rapid growth after 1945 in countries such as Germany and Japan, where in ten years economies shattered by the Second World War were regenerated

economic order quantity *Ops* a reorder method that attempts to estimate the best order quantity by balancing the conflicting costs of holding stock and of placing replenishment orders. For large orders, the unit cost may be lower, but storage costs will be higher, because the average storage time will increase. For small orders, the cost of order processing and unit cost may be higher, but storage costs will be lower, because the average storage time is less. *Abbr* **EOQ**

economic paradigm *Econ* a basic unchanging economic principle

Economic Planning and Advisory Council *Fin* a committee of business people and politicians appointed to advise the Australian government on economic issues.

economic pressure *Econ* a condition in a country's economy in which economic indicators are unfavourable

economics *Econ* the study of the consumption, distribution, and production of wealth in a society

economic surplus *Econ* the difference between an economy's output and the costs incurred, for example, wages, raw material costs, and depreciation

economic theory of the firm *Gen Mgt* the theory that states the only duty that a company has to those external to it is financial. The economic theory of the firm holds that shareholders should be the prime beneficiaries of an organisation's activities. The theory is associated with *top-down leadership*, and *cost-cutting* through *rationalisation* and *downsizing*. With immediate share price dominating management activities, economic theory has been criticised as being too short term, as opposed to the longer-term thinking behind *stakeholder theory*.

economic value added *Fin* a way of judging financial performance by measuring the amount by which the earnings of a project, an operation, or a company exceed or fall short of the total amount of capital that was originally invested by its owners.

EXAMPLE EVA is conceptually simple: from net operating profit, subtract an appropriate charge for the opportunity cost of all capital invested in an enterprise—the amount that could have been invested elsewhere. It is calculated using this formula:

Net operating profit less applicable taxes – Cost of capital = EVA

If a company is considering building a new plant, and its total weighted cost over ten years is £80 million, while the expected annual incremental return on the new operation is £10 million, or £100 million over ten years, then the plant's EVA would be positive, in this case £20 million:

£100 million – £80 million = £20 million

An alternative but more complex formula for EVA is:

(% Return on invested capital – % Cost of capital) × original capital invested = EVA

An objective of EVA is to determine which business units best utilise their assets to generate returns and maximise shareholder value; it can be used to assess a company, a business unit, a single plant, office, or even an assembly line. This same technique is equally helpful in evaluating new business opportunities.

economic welfare *Econ* the level of prosperity in an economy, as measured by employment and wage levels

economies of scale *Fin* reductions in unit average costs caused by increasing the scale of production

economies of scope *Fin* reductions in unit average costs caused by the simultaneous production of a number of related products, permitting benefits such as the sharing of joint costs over a larger volume than would otherwise be possible

economist *Econ* somebody who studies the consumption, distribution, and production of wealth in a society

economy *Econ* the distribution of wealth in a society and the means by which that wealth is produced and consumed

economy efficiency principle *Econ* the principle that if an economy is efficient, no one can be made better off without somebody else being made worse off

---

To stay ahead, you must have your next idea waiting in the wings.   **Rosabeth Moss Kanter**

ecopreneur *Gen Mgt* an entrepreneur who is concerned with environmental issues

EDB *abbr Fin* Economic Development Board

EDC *abbr E-com* electronic data capture

EDI *abbr E-com* electronic data interchange

EDI envelope *E-com see electronic envelope*

EDIFACT *E-com see UN/EDIFACT*

EDI for Administration, Commerce, and Trade *E-com see UN/EDIFACT*

educational leave *HR special leave* granted to assist those undertaking a course of study

Edwardes, Sir Michael (*b.* 1930) *Gen Mgt* South African-born business executive. Chairman of British Leyland from 1977 to 1982, he was appointed to rescue the company from financial difficulties and industrial disruption. His re-assertion of the manager's right to manage led to the coining of the term *macho management*. He recorded his experiences in *Back from the Brink* (1983).

e-economy *Econ* an economy that is characterised by extensive use of the Internet and information technology

effect *Stats* the change in a response that is created by a change in one or more of the explanatory *variables* in a statistical study

effective annual rate *Fin* the average interest rate paid on a deposit for a period of a year. It is the total interest received over 12 months expressed as a percentage of the principal at the beginning of the period.

effective capacity *Ops* the volume that a workstation or process can produce in a given period under normal operating conditions. Effective capacity can be influenced by the age and condition of the machine, the skills, training, and flexibil-

ity of the workforce, and the availability of *raw materials*.

effective date *Fin* the date when an action, such as an issuance of new stock, is effective

effectiveness *Fin* the utilisation of resources such that the output of the activity achieves the desired result

effective price *Fin* the price of a share adjusted to take into account the effects of a rights issue. *See also rights issue*

effective sample size *Stats* the remaining size of a sample after irrelevant or excluded factors have been removed

effective spread *Fin* the difference between the price of a newly issued share and what the underwriter pays, adjusted for the effect of the announcement of the offering

effective strike price *Fin* the price of an option at a specified time, adjusted for fluctuation since the initial offering

effective tax rate *Fin* the average tax rate applicable to a given transaction, whether it is income from work undertaken, the sale of an asset, or a gift, taking into account personal allowances and scales of tax. It is the amount of money generated by the transaction divided by the additional tax payable because of it.

effective yield *Fin see gross yield to redemption*

efficiency *Gen Mgt* the achievement of goals in an economical way. Efficiency involves seeking a good balance between economy in terms of resources such as time, money, space, or materials, and the achievement of an organisation's aims and objectives. A distinction is often made between technical and economic efficiency. **Technical efficiency** means producing maximum output with a minimum input, while economic efficiency means the production and distribution of goods at the lowest possible cost. In management, a further distinction is often made between efficiency and effectiveness, with the latter denoting performance in terms of achieving objectives.

Chaos often breeds life, when order breeds habit. *Henry Brooks Adams*

Achieving efficient performance is one of the key drivers behind *scientific management*.

efficiency ratio *Fin* a way of measuring the proportion of operating revenues spent on overhead expenses.

EXAMPLE Often identified with banking and financial sectors, the efficiency ratio indicates a management's ability to keep overhead costs low. In banking, an acceptable efficiency ratio was once in the low 60s. Now the goal is 50, while better-performing banks boast ratios in the mid 40s. Low ratings usually indicate a higher return on equity and earnings.

This measurement is also used by mature industries, such as steel manufacture, chemicals, or car production, that must focus on tight cost controls to boost profitability because growth prospects are modest.

The efficiency ratio is defined as operating overhead expenses divided by turnover. If operating expenses are £100,000, and turnover is £230,000, then:

100,000 / 230,000 = 0.43 efficiency ratio

However, not everyone calculates the ratio in the same way. Some institutions include all non-interest expenses, while others exclude certain charges and intangible asset amortisation.

A different method measures efficiency simply by tracking three other measures: accounts payable to sales, days' sales outstanding, and stock turnover. This indicates how fast a company is able to move its merchandise. A general guide is that if the first two of these measures are low and the third is high, efficiency is probably high; the reverse is likewise true.

To find the stock turnover ratio, divide total sales by total stock. If net sales are £300,000, and stock is £140,000, then:

300,000 / 140,000 = 2.14 stock turnover ratio

To find the accounts payable to sales ratio, divide a company's accounts payable by its annual net sales. A high ratio suggests that a company is using its suppliers' funds as a source of cheap financing because it is not operating efficiently enough to generate its own funds. If accounts payable are £42,000, and total sales are £300,000, then:

42,000 / 300,000 = 0.14 × 100 =
14% accounts payable to sales ratio

efficient capital market *Gen Mgt* a market in which share prices reflect all the information available to the market about future economic trends and company profitability

efficient markets hypothesis *Fin* the hypothesis that the stock market responds immediately to all available information, with the effect that an individual investor cannot, in the long run, expect to obtain greater than average returns from a diversified portfolio of shares. There are three forms: the weak form, in which security prices instantaneously reflect all information on past price and volume changes in the market; the semi-strong form, in which security prices reflect all publicly available information; and the strong form, in which security prices reflect instantaneously all information available to investors, whether publicly available or otherwise.

EFQM Excellence Model *or* **EFQM European Excellence Award** *Gen Mgt* a framework that can be used to assess a company's achievement of business *excellence*. The European Foundation for Quality Management (EFQM) was founded in the late 1980s by leading companies in Western Europe that saw a need for the implementation of a *quality award* in Europe. EFQM launched the **European Quality Award** in 1991. In the United Kingdom, the British Quality Foundation promoted the model, now often referred to as the **Business Excellence Model**. The model was revised in 1999 and renamed the EFQM European Excellence Model. The model focuses on all the key elements that sustain business success, and incorporates nine criteria that cover all aspects of business.

EFT *abbr Fin* electronic funds transfer

EGM *abbr Gen Mgt* extraordinary general meeting

I got my start by giving myself a start.   *C.J. Walker*

egosurfing *Gen Mgt* the practice of surfing the Internet in search of references to yourself (*slang*)

EIB *abbr Fin* European Investment Bank: a financial institution whose main task is to further regional development within the EU by financing capital projects, modernising or converting undertakings, and developing new activities

86 *Gen Mgt* to discard something such as a proposal or a document (*slang*)

eighty-twenty rule *Gen Mgt* the principle that explores the natural balance between the causes and effects of business activities, and holds that all business activities display an 80%/20% split. Developed by **Vilfredo Pareto**, the eighty-twenty rule can be used to concentrate management control and identify problem areas. Examples of the eighty-twenty rule in practice might include: 20% of the workforce accounting for 80% of the salary bill; 80% of a company's profits coming from 20% of its products; 80% of the stock value being tied up in 20% of the inventory. The rule can be represented graphically in the form of a Pareto chart, which is a bar chart identifying the relationships between causes and effects of activities. *Also known as* **Pareto analysis**, **Pareto's principle**. *See also* **Pareto's Law**

EIS *abbr Gen Mgt* **1.** Environmental Impact Statement **2.** Environmental Impact Study **3.** executive information system: a computer system designed to collect, store, process, and provide access to information appropriate to the needs of senior management. Executive information systems combine internal organisational information with data from external sources. The emphasis of executive information systems is on supporting strategic *decision-making* by presenting information in accessible formats and enabling users to get an overview of trends, often through the use of advanced graphical capabilities. Decision-making at managerial levels is supported by *decision support systems*.

Eisner, Michael (*b.* 1942) *Gen Mgt* US business executive. CEO and chairman of Disney who *turned around* the company, by encouraging *creativity* while maintaining financial control and discipline. His autobiography *Work in Progress* (1998) explains his *leadership* philosophy.

either-way market *Fin* a currency market with identical prices for buying and selling, especially for the euro

e-lance *Gen Mgt* a type of *freelance* work that makes use of the *Internet*. It enables a freelancer to take up work opportunities anywhere in the world.

elasticity *Fin* the measure of the sensitivity of one variable to another.

EXAMPLE In practical terms, elasticity indicates the degree to which consumers respond to changes in price. It is obviously important for companies to consider such relationships when contemplating changes in price, demand, and supply.

Demand elasticity measures how much the quantity demanded by a customer changes when the price of a product or service is increased or lowered. This measurement helps companies to find out whether demand will remain constant despite price changes. Supply elasticity measures the impact on supply when a price is changed.

The general formula for elasticity is:

Elasticity = % change in x / % change in y

In theory, x and y can be any variable. However, the most common application measures price and demand. If the price of a product is increased from £20 to £25, or 25%, and demand in turn falls from 6,000 to 3,000, elasticity would be calculated as:

–50% / 25% = –2

A value greater than 1 means that demand is strongly sensitive to price, while a value of less than 1 means that demand is not price-sensitive.

eldercare (*US*) *HR* an organisation's approach towards care for employees' elderly relatives in the form of an *employee assistance programme*

e-learning *HR* the facilitation of learning through the *Internet* or an *intranet*.

Without work, all life goes rotten, but when work is soulless, life stifles and dies.

Albert Camus

E-learning is a development from *computer-based training* and consists of self-contained learning materials and resources that can be used at the pace and convenience of the learner. An e-learning package normally incorporates some form of test that can demonstrate how much an e-learner has assimilated from a course, as well as some form of monitoring to enable managers to check the use of the system of e-learning. Successful e-learning depends largely on the self-motivation of individuals to study effectively. Because it is Internet-based, it has the potential to respond to a company's rapidly changing needs and offer new learning opportunities relevant to a company's new position very quickly. *Also known as* **electronic learning**

elected officers *HR* officials such as directors or union representatives chosen by a vote of the members or shareholders of an organisation, who hold a *decision-making* position on a committee or board

electronic business *E-com see e-business*

electronic cash *E-com see digital cash*

electronic catalogue *E-com* a listing of available products that can be viewed in an electronic format, for example, on a website, and can include information such as illustrations, prices, and product descriptions

electronic cheque *E-com* a payment system in which fund transfers are made electronically from the buyer's current account to the seller's bank account. *US term* **electronic check**

electronic commerce *E-com see e-commerce*

electronic commerce modelling language *E-com* a standardisation of field names to streamline the process by which e-merchants electronically collect information from consumers about order shipping, billing, and payment. *Abbr* **ECML**

electronic data capture *E-com* the use of a point-of-sale terminal or other data-processing equipment to validate and submit credit or debit card transactions. *Abbr* **EDC**

electronic data interchange *E-com* a standard for exchanging business documents such as invoices and purchase orders in a standard form between computers through the use of electronic networks such as the Internet. *Abbr* **EDI**

electronic envelope *E-com* the header and trailer information that precedes and follows the data in an electronic transmission to provide routing information and security. *Also known as* **communications envelope, EDI envelope, envelope**

electronic funds transfer *Fin* the system used by banking organisations for the movement of funds between accounts and for the provision of services to the customer. *Abbr* **EFT**

electronic funds transfer at point of sale *Fin* the payment for goods or services by a bank customer using a card that is swiped through an electronic reader on the till, thereby transferring the cash from the customer's account to the retailer's or service provider's account.

electronic learning *HR see e-learning*

electronic mail *E-com see e-mail*

electronic mall *E-com see cyber mall*

electronic money *E-com see digital money*

electronic office *Gen Mgt see paperless office*

electronic payment system *E-com* a means of making payments over an electronic network such as the Internet

electronic procurement *E-com see e-procurement*

electronic retailer *E-com see e-retailer*

electronic shopping *E-com* the process of selecting, ordering, and paying for goods or services over an electronic network such as the Internet. *Also known as* **online shopping**

electronic software distribution *E-com* a form of electronic shopping in which computer programs can be purchased and downloaded directly from the Internet

electronic store *E-com* a website that is specifically designed to provide product information and handle transactions, including accepting payments

electronic trading *Fin* the buying and selling of investment instruments using computers

electronic wallet *E-com see* **digital wallet**

elements of cost *Fin* the constituent parts of costs according to the factors upon which expenditure is incurred, namely, material, labour, and expenses

elephant *Gen Mgt* a large corporate institution (*slang*)

elevator pitch (*US*) *E-com* the practice of pitching dot-com business plans to investors in a short space of time

eligible paper *Fin* **1.** in the United Kingdom, bills of exchange or securities accepted by the Bank of England as security for loans to discount houses **2.** in the United States, first class paper (such as a bill of exchange or a cheque) acceptable for rediscounting by the Federal Reserve System. *See also* **lender of last resort**

eligible reserves *Fin* in the United States, the sum of the cash held by a bank plus the money it holds at its local Federal Reserve Bank

Eligible Service Period *Gen Mgt* the amount of time an employee works for one employer or contributes to a particular superannuation scheme. *Abbr* **ESP**

Eligible Termination Payment *Fin* a sum paid to an employee when he or she leaves a company, that can be transferred to a concessionally taxed investment account, such as an Approved Deposit Fund. *Abbr* **ETP**

Elvis year *Gen Mgt* the year in which the popularity of a product, service, or individual is at its peak (*slang*)

e-mail *E-com* electronic mail, a message sent across the Internet, or a system for transferring messages between computers, mobile phones, or other communications attached to the Internet

e-mail address *E-com* somebody's electronic address on the Internet or an intranet. An e-mail address is commonly formed by joining the user name and the mail server name, separating the two by an @ symbol.

e-mail mailing list *E-com* a marketing technique particularly suited to discussing complex topics over a period of time. Members can be drawn from anywhere in the world, and come together to share information and experience on a particular theme or subject area. It works as follows: a **moderator** compiles a list of e-mail addresses for possible members, and mails them with the theme for discussion. People then join up, via e-mail or **Web form**. The moderator invites contributions, which are duly published by e-mail; subscribers then react to the initial publication with their opinions and feedback. A selection of these reactions is published in the next e-mail sent out—and so on. If successful, a feedback and opinion loop is created, with new topics being introduced as older topics have received sufficient discussion.

e-mail signature *E-com* the text at the bottom of an e-mail that contains information about the sender.

In general, the signature should be no longer than five lines, but it can be used in marketing to place a short, two-line ad. E-mail signature promotion was used very effectively when Andersen Consulting changed its name to Accenture. Every time one of its 60,000 employees sent an e-mail, there was a short e-mail signature ad notifying the recipient of the change of name.

e-mail system *E-com* the collective e-mail software that allows somebody to create, send, receive, and store e-mail messages

---

Procrastination is the thief of time. *Edward Young*

e-marketplace *E-com* an Internet-based environment that brings together business-to-business buyers and sellers so that they can trade more efficiently online.

The key benefits for users of an e-marketplace are reduced purchasing costs, greater flexibility, saved time, better information, and better collaboration. However, the drawbacks include costs in changing procurement processes, cost of applications, set-up, and integration with internal systems, and transaction/subscription fees.

There are three distinct types of e-marketplace: independent, in which public environments seek simply to attract buyers and sellers to trade together; consortium-based, in which sites are set up on an industry-wide basis, typically when a number of key buyers in a particular industry get together; and private, in which e-marketplaces are established by a particular organisation to manage its purchasing alone.

EMAS *abbr Gen Mgt* ECO-Management Audit Scheme

embezzlement *Fin* the illegal practice of using money entrusted to an individual's care by a third party for personal benefit

emerging market *Fin* a country that is becoming industrialised

Emery, Frederick Edmund (1928–97) *Gen Mgt* Australian psychologist and sociologist. Contributor to the development of theories of *industrial democracy* in collaboration with *Einar Thorsrud* at the Tavistock Institute of Human Relations.

e-money *E-com see digital money*

emotag *E-com* a tag such as <smile> or <growl> used in an e-mail instead of an emoticon (*slang*)

emoticon *E-com* a symbol commonly used in e-mail and newsgroup messages to denote a particular emotion by representing a face on its side. For example,:-) indicates happiness by representing a smiley face. The word is a combination of 'emotion' with 'icon'.

emotional capital *Gen Mgt* the intangible organisational asset created by employees' cumulative emotional experiences, which give them the ability to successfully communicate and form interpersonal relationships. Emotional capital is increasingly being seen as an important factor in company performance. Low emotional capital can result in conflict between staff, poor *teamwork*, and poor *customer relations*. By contrast, high emotional capital is evidence of *emotional intelligence* and an ability to think and feel in a positive way that results in good *interpersonal communication* and self-motivation. Related concepts are *intellectual capital* and *social capital*.

emotional intelligence *HR* the ability to perceive and understand personal feelings and those of others. Emotional intelligence means recognising emotions and acting on them in a reflective and rational manner. It involves self-awareness, empathy, and self-restraint. In the workplace, this ability can greatly enhance *interpersonal communication* and people skills. Emotional intelligence was first broadly discussed by *Daniel Goleman*.

employability *HR* the potential for obtaining and keeping fulfilling work through the development of skills that are transferable from one employer to another. Employability is affected by market demand for a particular set of skills and by personal circumstances. Employees may take responsibility for developing their own employability through learning and training, or as part of the *psychological contract*, employers may assist their employees in enhancing their employability. An important factor in employability is the concept of *lifelong learning*.

employee *HR* someone taken on by an employer under a *contract of employment* to carry out work on a regular basis at the employer's behest. An employee works either at the employer's premises or at a place otherwise agreed, is paid regularly, and enjoys *fringe benefits* and *employment protection*.

If you see a bandwagon, it's too late. *James Goldsmith*

employee assistance programme (*US*) *HR* a structured and integrated support service that identifies and resolves the concerns of employees that may affect performance. Employee assistance programmes can range from support for staff during periods of intensive change, *counselling* to tackle the problem of *stress*, return-to-work, and *eldercare* initiatives, to defined organisational policies on substance abuse and bullying. Employee assistance programmes are set up by employers who recognise that providing professional support for their staff makes good business sense. Some organisations find it cost-effective to *outsource* the programme depending on the nature of the problem and on the size of the organisation. *Abbr* **EAP**

employee association *HR* a professional or social body of employees who work for the same organisation

employee attitude survey *HR* a systematic investigation of the views and opinions of those employed by an organisation on issues relating to the work of that organisation or their role within it. Employee attitude surveys may be conducted by means of questionnaires or interviews. They may be undertaken occasionally or at regular intervals and may be used to make a general assessment of employee morale or focus on a specific issue such as the introduction of a new policy. Aims may be to identify or gain an understanding of problems so that action to resolve them can be taken, to encourage employee involvement and commitment, or to assist in planning, implementing, and evaluating new initiatives.

employee commitment *HR* the psychological bond of an employee to an organisation, the strength of which depends on the degree of *employee involvement*, employee loyalty, and belief in the values of the organisation. Employee commitment was badly damaged in the late 20th century during corporate re-organisations and *downsizing*, which undermined job security and

resulted in fewer *promotion* opportunities. This led to the re-negotiation of the *psychological contract* and the need to develop strategies for increasing commitment. These included *flexible working* and *work-life balance* policies, *teamwork*, *training* and development, *employee participation*, and *empowerment*.

employee development *HR* the enhancement of the skills, knowledge, and experience of employees with the purpose of improving performance. Employee development, unlike *personal development*, is usually co-ordinated by the employing organisation. It can use a range of *training* methods, and is usually conducted on a planned basis, perhaps as a result of a *performance appraisal*.

employee discount *HR* a reduction in the price of company goods or services offered to employees as one of their *fringe benefits*

employee handbook *HR* a reference document containing information on what an employee should know about his or her organisation or employment. Employee handbooks typically include information on terms and *conditions of employment*, organisational policies and procedures, and *fringe benefits*.

employee involvement *HR* a range of management practices centred on *empowerment* and trust that are designed to increase *employee commitment* to organisational objectives and performance improvement. The term employee involvement is often used interchangeably with *employee participation*, but employee involvement practices tend to take place at individual or workgroup level, rather than at higher *decision-making* levels.

employee ownership *HR* the possession of shares in a company, in whole or in part, by the workers. There are various forms of employee ownership that give employees a greater or lesser stake in the business. These include: *employee share schemes*, employee *buy-outs*, co-operatives, and employee trusts. Ownership does not necessarily lead to greater *employee participation* in *decision-making*, although the evidence suggests that where employees are involved in this, the company is more successful.

employee participation *HR* the involvement of workers in *decision-making*. Employee participation can take either a representational or direct form. Representation takes place through bodies such as consultative committees or *works councils*. This type of direct participation can be achieved through communication methods such as newsletters, *employee attitude surveys*, *team briefing*, and *open-book management*, or through involvement initiatives such as self-managed teams, *suggestion schemes*, and *quality circles*.

employee referral programme *HR* a policy, popular in the United States, for encouraging employees, usually through cash incentives, to nominate potential job candidates as part of the recruiting process. Employee referral programmes have been developed in an attempt to address the recruitment difficulties experienced by organisations in times of full employment. Although they can be very successful, there is a danger that if a referral programme is relied on too heavily, only limited sectors of the potential labour force will be available for recruitment, which might lead to a reduction in the *diversity* of the workforce.

employee share ownership plan *HR* a scheme sponsored by a company by which a trust holds shares in the company on behalf of *employees* and distributes those shares to employees. In the United States, shares can only be sold when an employee leaves the organisation, and are thus thought of as a form of pension provision. In the United Kingdom, shares can be disposed of at any time. There are two types of employee share ownership plan in the United Kingdom: the case-law employee share ownership plan, which can benefit all or some employees but may not qualify for tax benefits; and the

employee share ownership trust. *Abbr* **ESOP**

employee share scheme *HR* a plan to give, or encourage employees to buy, a stake in the company that employs them by awarding free or discounted shares. Employee share schemes may be available to some or all employees, and schemes approved by the Inland Revenue enjoy tax advantages. Types of scheme include *employee share ownership plans*, *share options*, *save as you earn*, and employee share ownership trusts. Among the potential benefits are improved *employee commitment* and productivity, but the success of a scheme may depend on linking it to employee performance and the performance of the share price.

employee stock fund *Fin* in the United States, a fund from which money is taken to buy shares of a company's stock for its employees

employer *HR* a person or organisation that pays people to carry out specified activities. An employer usually contracts an *employee* to fill a permanent or temporary position to carry out work on a regularly paid basis within the relevant legal framework of the country of residence. In the United Kingdom, employers are required to contribute towards employees' National Insurance Contributions, deduct their income tax, provide paid *leave*, and ensure compliance with regulations relevant to the work concerned and to health and safety requirements.

employers' association *HR* a body that regulates relations between employers and employees, represents members' views on public policy issues affecting their business to national and international policy makers, and supplies support and advice. An employers' association represents companies within one or many sectors at regional, national, or international level and is usually a non-profit, non-party-political organisation, funded by subscriptions paid by its members.

An advertising agency is 85 percent confusion and 15 percent commission.   Fred Allen

Employment Court *HR* a higher court in New Zealand responsible for arbitrating in industrial relations disputes. It hears cases relating to disputes between employers and employees or unions as well as appeals referred to the court by *employment tribunals*.

employment equity *(S Africa) HR* the policy of giving preference in employment opportunities to qualified people from sectors of society that were previously discriminated against, for example, black people, women, and people with disabilities

employment law *HR* the collection of statutes, common law rules, and decisions in court or employment tribunal cases that govern the rights and duties of employers and employees. The *contract of employment* forms the cornerstone of employment law, which also embraces *discrimination*, *unfair dismissal*, and *redundancy* rights, *collective bargaining*, health and safety, union membership, and *industrial action*.

employment pass *(S Africa) Gen Mgt* a visa issued to a foreign national who is a professional earning in excess of R1,500 per month

employment protection *HR* the legal framework for establishing and defending the rights of employees. Employment protection in the United Kingdom was greatly extended by the Employment Protection Act 1975 and the Employment Protection (Consolidation) Act 1978. Since then, UK legislation and case law has continued to develop. The Employment Rights Act 1996 consolidated most of the existing law on individual employment rights.

employment tribunal *HR* a government body responsible for hearing and adjudicating in disputes between employees and employers

empowerment *Gen Mgt* the redistribution of *power* and *decision-making* responsibilities, usually to *employees*, where such *authority* was previously a

management prerogative. Empowerment is based on the recognition that employee abilities are frequently underused, and that, given the chance, most employees can contribute more. Empowered workplaces are characterised by managers who focus on energising, supporting, and *coaching* their staff in a blame-free environment of trust.

empty suit *Gen Mgt* a corporate executive who dresses very smartly and follows all procedures exactly without actually contributing anything of significance to the company (*slang*)

EMS *abbr* **1.** *Fin* European Monetary System: the first stage of economic and monetary union of the EU, which came into force in March 1979, giving stable, but adjustable, exchange rates **2.** *Gen Mgt* environmental management system

EMU *abbr Fin* Economic and Monetary Union, or European Monetary Union: the timetable for EMU was outlined in the Maastricht Treaty in 1991. The criteria were that national debt must not exceed 60% of GDP; budget deficit should be 3% or less of GDP; inflation should be no more than 1.5% above the average rate of the three best-performing economies of the EU in the previous 12 months; and applicants must have been members of the *ERM* for two years without having realigned or devalued their currency.

encryption *E-com* a means of encoding information, especially financial data, so that it can be transmitted over the Internet without being read by unauthorised parties.

Within an Internet security system, a secure server uses encryption when transferring or receiving data from the Web. Credit card information, for example, which could be targeted by a *hacker*, is encrypted by the server, turning it into special code that will then be decrypted only when it is safely within the server environment. Once the information has been acted on, it is either deleted or stored in encrypted form.

encryption key *E-com* a sequence of characters known to both or all parties to a

---

I would constructively rebel by changing the rules but, once agreed, I would observe them.
Howard Davies

communication, used to initiate the *encryption* process

end-around (*US, Canada*) *Gen Mgt* an approach to a problem that does not attack it directly but rather tries to avoid it

end consumer *Mkting see* **consumer**

endogenous variable *Stats* the dependent variable in an econometric study

endorsement *Gen Mgt* the public approval of a product by a person or organisation. The endorsement can be used to promote the product to other organisations that may be more cautious in their approach to adopting new products.

endowment assurance *Fin* life cover that pays a specific sum of money on a specified date, or earlier in the event of the policyholder's death. Part of the premium paid is for the life cover element, while the remainder is invested in property and stocks and shares (either a 'with-profits' or 'without-profits' policy) or, in the case of a unit-linked policy, is used to purchase units in a life fund. The sum the policyholder receives at the end of the term depends on the size of the premiums and the performance of the investments. *See also* **term assurance**

endowment fund *Fin* a unit trust that supports a non-profit institution

endowment mortgage *Fin* a long-term loan, usually for the purchase of a property, in which the borrower makes two monthly payments, one to the lender to cover the interest on the loan, and the other as a premium paid into an endowment assurance policy. At the end of the loan's term, the proceeds from the endowment policy are used to repay the principal. *See also* **mortgage**

endowment policy *Fin* an insurance policy that pays a set amount to the policyholder when the policy matures, or to a beneficiary if the policyholder dies before it matures

endpoint *Stats* a point at which a definable event in a study takes place, for example, the recovery of a patient in a medical study

energy audit *Gen Mgt* a review, inspection, and evaluation of sources and uses of energy within an organisation to ensure efficiency and lack of waste

energy conservation *Gen Mgt* the minimisation of fuel consumption. Energy conservation, through the monitoring and control of the amounts of electricity, gas, and other fuels used in the workplace, can help reduce costs and damage to the environment. An energy management scheme provides a systematic method of assessing, evaluating, and improving an organisation's energy usage. This forms part of an organisation's approach to *environmental management*.

engineered cost *Fin* a cost which varies in proportion to a measure of activity. Direct materials and royalty payments are engineered costs. Control is through flexible budgeting or standard costing.

engineering for excellence *Ops see* **design for manufacturability**

English disease *Gen Mgt* the supposed predilection of British workers to opt for *strike* action. In the United Kingdom in the 1960s and 1970s, strikes were commonly used by workers for *dispute* resolution. Government legislation in the 1980s, however, made striking more difficult for workers.

enterprise *Gen Mgt* a venture characterised by *innovation*, *creativity*, dynamism, and risk. An enterprise can consist of one project, or may refer to an entire organisation. It usually requires several of the following attributes: flexibility, initiative, *problem-solving* ability, independence, and imagination. Enterprises flourish in the environment of *delayered*, non-hierarchical organisations but can be stifled by *bureaucracy*. Enterprises are often created by *entrepreneurs*.

enterprise application integration *E-com* the unrestricted sharing of data and business processes via integrated and compatible software programs. As businesses expand and recognise the need for their information and applications to be shared between systems, they are investing in enterprise application integration in order to streamline processes and keep all the elements of their organisations, for example, human resources and inventory control, connected. *Abbr* **EAI**

enterprise culture *Gen Mgt* an organisational or social environment that encourages and makes possible initiative and *innovation*. An organisation with an enterprise culture is usually more competitive and more profitable than a *bureaucracy*. Such an organisation is believed to be more rewarding and stimulating to work in. A society with an enterprise culture facilitates individuality and requires people to take responsibility for their own welfare. Conservative governments in the United Kingdom during the 1980s and 1990s promoted an enterprise culture by introducing market principles into all areas of economic and social life. These included policies of deregulation of financial services, *privatisation* of utilities and national monopolies, and commercialisation of the public sector.

enterprise portal *E-com* a website that assembles a wide range of content and services for employees of a particular organisation, with the aim of bringing together all the key information they need to do a better job. The key difference between an enterprise portal and an *intranet* is that an enterprise portal contains not just internal content, but also external content that may be useful—such as specialised news feeds, or access to industry research reports. Ensuring that content is relevant, current, and frequently refreshed is essential for such sites to succeed, and enterprise portals are thus expensive to maintain.

enterprise resource planning *Gen Mgt* see **ERP**

enterprise zone *Gen Mgt* an area in which the government offers financial incentives to new business activities

entertainment expenses *HR* costs, reimbursable by the *employer*, that are incurred by an *employee* in hosting social events for clients or suppliers in order to obtain or maintain their custom or goodwill

entitlement *Gen Mgt* the expectation that an organisation or individual will make large profits regardless of their contribution to the economy

entitlement offer *Fin* an offer that cannot be transferred to anyone else

entity *Fin* an economic unit that has a separate, distinct identity, for example, an industrial or commercial company, charity, local authority, government agency, or fund

entrapment *Fin* restrictions placed on an organisation due to the limitations of its existing resource base and management competencies, which prevent it from responding to changes in its environment

entreprenerd *Gen Mgt* an entrepreneur with computing skills, especially one who starts up an Internet business (*slang*)

entrepreneur *Gen Mgt* somebody who sets up a business or *enterprise*. An entrepreneur typically demonstrates effective application of a number of enterprising attributes such as creativity, initiative, risk-taking, problem-solving ability, and autonomy, and will often risk his or her own capital to set up a business. *See also* **intrapreneur**

entropy *Stats* a measure of the rate of transfer of the information that a system such as a computer program or factory machine receives or outputs

entry barrier *Mkting* a perceived or real obstacle preventing a competitor from entering a market

envelope *E-com see* **electronic envelope**

environment *E-com* the different computers, *browsers*, or *bandwidth* access points from which a user may access a website. Web pages may download at very different speeds according to the environment, so when building a website, it is important to test its performance within as many different environments as possible.

environmental analysis *Gen Mgt see* *environmental scanning*

environmental audit *Gen Mgt* the regular systematic gathering of information to monitor the effectiveness of environmental policies. An environmental audit now often forms part of an organisation's *environmental management* systems, and is concerned with checking conformity with legislative requirements and environmental standards such as ISO 14001 (see *ISO 14000*), as well as with company policy. The audit may also cover potential improvements in environmental performance and systems.

Environmental Impact Statement *Gen Mgt* a report on the results of an Environmental Impact Study. *Abbr* **EIS**

Environmental Impact Study *Gen Mgt* an analysis of the potential effects of a building development or a similar project on the natural environment. *Abbr* **EIS**

environmental management *Gen Mgt* a systematic approach to minimising the damage created by an organisation to the environment in which it operates. Environmental management has become an issue in organisations because consumers now expect them to be environmentally aware, if not environmentally friendly. Senior managers and directors are increasingly being held liable for their organisations' environmental performance, and the onus is on them to adopt a *corporate strategy* that balances economic growth with environmental protection.

Environmental management involves reducing pollution, waste, and the consumption of natural resources by implementing an environmental action plan. This plan brings together the key elements of environmental management, including an organisation's *environmental policy* statement, an *environ-*

mental audit, *environmental management system*, and standards such as the EC **ECO-Management Audit Scheme** and *ISO 14000*.

environmental management system *Gen Mgt* a procedure to manage and control an organisation's impact on the environment. An environmental management system is part of an organisation's *environmental management* practice. It includes creation of an *environmental policy*, which sets objectives and targets a programme of implementation, effectiveness monitoring, problem correction, and system review. An environmental management system should also identify key resources and holders of responsibility for determining and implementing environmental policy. Systems for environmental management have been formalised in the *ISO 14000* quality standards. *Abbr* **EMS**

environmental policy *Gen Mgt* a statement of organisational intentions regarding the safeguarding of the environment. Clause 4.2 of the ISO 14001 (see *ISO 14000*) series of environmental management standards, which many organisations now either apply in full or make use of for guidance on environmental management, focuses on environmental policy and states the necessary themes and commitments for an environmental policy that conforms to ISO 14001 requirements.

environmental scanning *Gen Mgt* the monitoring of changes in the external environment in which an organisation operates in order to identify threats and opportunities for the future and maintain *competitive advantage*. The process of environmental scanning includes gathering information on an organisation's task environment of competitors, markets, customers, and suppliers, carrying out a *PEST analysis* of social, economic, technological, and political factors that may affect the organisation, and analysing the implications of this research. Environmental scanning may be undertaken systematically by a dedicated department or unit within an organisation or more informally by project groups and may be used in the planning and development of *corporate strategy*. *Also known as environmental analysis*

environmental statistics *Stats* statistical studies concerning environmental matters such as pollution

EOQ *abbr Fin* economic order quantity

epidemiology *Stats* the statistical study of the incidence of a particular disease in a given population

e-procurement *E-com* the business-to-business sale and purchase of goods and services over an electronic network such as the Internet. *Also known as electronic procurement*

EPS *abbr Gen Mgt* earnings per share

equal opportunities *HR* the granting of equal rights, privileges, and status regardless of gender, age, race, religion, disability, or sexual orientation. Equality in employment is regulated by law in most Western countries. An organisational equal opportunities policy aims to go further than the regulatory framework demands. Such a policy should focus on preventing discriminatory or harassing behaviour in the workplace and achieving equal access to training, job, and promotion opportunities. *Positive discrimination*, which is referred to as affirmative action in the United States, is a controversial approach to encouraging the advancement of minorities. *Diversity* management builds on and goes beyond equal opportunities by looking at the rights of individuals rather than groups.

equal pay *HR* the principle and practice of paying men and women in the same organisation at the same rate for like work, or work that is rated as of equal value. Work is assessed either through an organisation's *job evaluation* scheme or by the judgment of an independent expert appointed by an industrial tribunal. Although many countries have legislation on equal pay, a gap still exists between men's pay and women's pay and is attrib-

uted to sexual discrimination in job evaluation and payment systems.

equal treatment *HR* a principle of the *EU* that requires member states to ensure that there is no *discrimination* with regard to employment, vocational training, and working conditions. The principle of equal treatment is applied through Europe-wide directives and national legislation of the member states.

equilibrium price *Econ* the price that regulates supply and demand. Suppliers increase prices when demand is high and reduce prices when demand is low.

equilibrium quantity *Econ* the quantity that regulates supply and demand. Suppliers increase quantity when demand is high and reduce quantity when demand is low.

equilibrium rate of interest *Econ* the rate at which the expected interest rate in a market equals the actual rate prevailing

equipment trust certificate *Fin* a bond sold for a 20% down payment and collateralised by the equipment purchased with its proceeds

equity *Fin* the issued ordinary share capital plus reserves, statutory and otherwise, which represent the investment in a company by the ordinary shareholders

equity claim *Fin* a claim on earnings that remain after debts are satisfied

equity contribution agreement *Fin* an agreement to provide equity under specified circumstances

equity dilution *Fin* the reduction in the percentage of a company represented by each share for an existing shareholder who has not increased his or her holding in the issue of new ordinary shares

equity dividend cover *Fin* an accounting ratio, calculated by dividing the distributable profits during a given period by the actual dividend paid in that period, that indicates the likelihood of the dividend being maintained in future years. *See also capital reserves*

The Law is a sort of hocus-pocus science that smiles in yer face while it picks yer pocket.
Charles Macklin

equity floor *Fin* an agreement to pay whenever some indicator of a stock market's value falls below a specified limit

equity multiplier (*US*) *Fin* a measure of a company's worth, expressed as a multiple of each dollar of its stock's price

equity share capital *Fin* a company's issued share capital less capital which carries preferential rights. Equity share capital normally comprises ordinary shares.

equivalent annual cash flow *Fin* the value of an annuity required to provide an investor with the same return as some other form of investment

equivalent bond yield *Fin see bond equivalent yield*

equivalent taxable yield *Fin* the value of a taxable investment required to provide an investor with the same return as some other form of investment

equivalent units *Fin* notional whole units representing uncompleted work. Used to apportion costs between work in progress and completed output, and in performance assessment.

e-retailer *E-com* a business that uses an electronic network such as the Internet to sell its goods or services. *Also known as electronic retailer, e-tailer*

erf (*S Africa*) *Fin* a plot of rural or urban land, usually no larger than a smallholding

ergonomics *Gen Mgt, HR* the study of workplace design and the physical and psychological impact it has on workers. Ergonomics is about the fit between people, their work activities, equipment, work systems, and environment to ensure that workplaces are safe, comfortable, efficient, and that *productivity* is not compromised. Ergonomics may examine the design and layout of buildings, machines, and equipment, as well as aspects such as lighting, temperature, ventilation, noise, colour, and texture. Ergonomic principles also apply to working methods such as systems and *pro-*

cedures, and the allocation and scheduling of work.

ERM *abbr Fin* Exchange Rate Mechanism: a system to maintain exchange rate stability used in the past by member states of the European Community

ERP *abbr Gen Mgt* enterprise resource planning: a software system that coordinates every important aspect of an organisation's production into one seamless process so that maximum efficiency can be achieved

ERR *abbr Fin* expected rate of return

error account *Fin* an account for the temporary placement of funds involved in a financial transaction known to have been executed in error

errors and omissions *Fin* mistakes from incorrect record-keeping or accounting. *Abbr* **E&O**

ESC *abbr Fin* European Social Charter: a charter adopted by the European Council of the EU in 1989. The 12 rights it contains are: freedom of movement, employment, and remuneration; social protection; improvement of living and working conditions; freedom of association and collective bargaining; worker information; consultation and participation; vocational training; equal treatment of men and women; health and safety protection in the workplace; pension rights; integration of those with disabilities; protection of young people.

e-shock *E-com* the forward momentum of electronic commerce, considered as irresistible

ESOP *abbr HR* employee share ownership plan

ESP *abbr Gen Mgt* Eligible Service Period

establishment fee *Fin see commitment fee*

estate *Fin* **1.** a substantial area of land that normally includes a large house such as a stately home **2.** a deceased person's net assets

---

Talent is formed in quiet, character in the stream of human life.

Johann Wolfgang von Goethe

estimate *Gen Mgt* **1.** an approximate calculation of an uncertain value. An estimate may be a reasonable guess based on knowledge and experience or it may be calculated using more sophisticated techniques designed to forecast projected costs, profits, losses, or value. **2.** an approximate price quoted for work to be undertaken by an organisation

estimation *Stats* the provision of a numerical value for a parameter of a population that has been sampled

e-tailer *E-com see e-retailer*

e-tailing *E-com* the practice of doing business over an electronic network such as the Internet

ethical investment *Fin* investment only in companies whose policies meet the ethical criteria of the investor. *Also known as **socially-conscious investing***

ethnic monitoring *HR* the recording and evaluation of the racial origins of employees or customers with the aim of ensuring that all parts of the population are represented. When ethnic monitoring is carried out as a part of the ***recruitment*** process, candidates are asked to indicate their ethnic origin on an anonymous basis. Information thus supplied is removed from the application as soon as it is received by the prospective employer.

ETP *abbr Fin* Eligible Termination Payment

EU *abbr Fin* European Union: a social, economic, and political organisation of European countries whose aim is integration for all member nations. So called since November 1993 under the Maastricht Treaty, before which it was known as the European Community (EC), and before that as the European Economic Community.

EUREX *abbr Fin* Eureka Research Expert System: EUREX was established by Eureka (European Research and Co-ordination Agency) in 1985 on a French initiative for non-military industrial research in advanced technologies in Europe

euro *Fin* the currency of 12 member nations of the European Union. The euro was introduced in 1999, when the first 11 countries to adopt it joined together in an Economic and Monetary Union and fixed their currencies' exchange rate to the euro. Notes and coins were brought into general circulation in January 2002, although banks and other financial institutions had before that time carried out transactions in euros.

Eurobank *Fin* a US bank that handles transactions in foreign currencies

Eurobond *Fin* a bond specified in the currency of one country and sold to investors from another country. *Also known as **global bond***

Euro-commercial paper *Fin* short-term uncollateralised loans obtained by companies in foreign countries

Eurocredit *Fin* intermediate-term notes used by banks to lend money to governments and companies

Eurocurrency *Fin* money deposited in one country but denominated in the currency of another country

Eurodeposit *Fin* a short-term deposit of Eurocurrency

Eurodollar *Fin* a US dollar deposited in a European bank or other bank outside the United States

Euroequity issue *Fin* a note issued by banks in several countries

Euroland *Fin* the area of Europe comprising those countries that have adopted the euro

Euro-note *Fin* a note in the Eurocurrency market

European Association of Securities Dealers Automated Quotations *Fin see EASDAQ*

European Bank for Reconstruction and Development *Fin see EBRD*

European Central Bank *Fin see ECB*

A banker is a man who lends another man the money of a third man. *Guy de Rothschild*

European Economic Community or **European Community** Fin see EU

European Investment Bank Fin see EIB

European Monetary System Fin see EMS

European Monetary Union Fin see EMU

European option Fin an option that the buyer can exercise only on the day that it expires. See also **American option**

European Quality Award Gen Mgt see EFQM Excellence Model

European Social Charter Fin see ESC

European Union Fin see EU

Euroyen bond Fin a Eurobond denominated in yen

EVA abbr Fin economic value added

evaluation of training HR a continuous cycle consisting of defining training objectives, carrying out **training needs analysis**, delivering training, assessing reactions to training, and measuring the bottom-line effects of training

event marketing Mkting the promotion and marketing of a specific event such as a conference, seminar, exhibition, or trade fair. Event marketing may encompass **corporate hospitality** activities, business or charity functions, or sporting occasions. The planning, marketing, and managing of the function on the day are sometimes entirely **outsourced** to companies specialising in event management.

evergreen loan Fin a series of loans providing a continuing stream of capital for a project

ex Fin 'without', as in **ex dividend**, where security purchases do not include rights to the next dividend payment, and **ex-rights**, where rights attaching to share ownership, such as a scrip issue, are not transferred to a new purchaser

ex-all Fin having no right in any transaction that is pending with respect to shares, such as a split, or the issue of dividends

ex ante Fin before the event. An **ex ante** budget, or standard, is set before a period of activity commences, and is based on the best information available at **that time** on expected levels of cost, performance, etc.

excellence Gen Mgt, Ops a state of organisational performance achieved through the successful integration of a variety of operational and strategic elements that enables an organisation to become one of the best in its field. Excellence is initially evident when an organisation rises above its competitors, and it is usually measured by the ability to sustain a leading or significant market share. The strategic and operational elements contributing to excellence include the organisation's approach to **total quality management**, **quality assurance**, **quality awards** and **quality standards**, core competency, **benchmarking**, **customer service**, the **balanced scorecard**, and **leadership**. Taken altogether, these components should produce an organisational approach to the generation, development, and delivery of products and services that is better, cheaper, and smarter than that of the competition. Attempts at becoming an excellent organisation have spawned terms such as **best practice**, **best-in-class**, and **world class manufacturing** and are usually associated with a holistic approach to **competitive advantage**.

exception reporting Gen Mgt the passing on of information only when it breaches or transcends agreed norms. Exception reporting is intended to reduce **information overload** by minimising the circulation of repetitive or old information. Under this system, only information that is new and out of the ordinary will be transmitted. See also **management by exception**

excess Fin 1. the part of an insurance claim that has to be met by the policyholder rather than the insurance company. An excess of £50 means that the company pays all but £50 of the claim for loss or damage. See also **deductible 2.** in a financial institution, the amount by which assets exceed liabilities

excess profits tax *Fin* a tax levied by a government on a company that makes extraordinarily large profits in times of unusual circumstances, for example, during a war. An excess profits tax was imposed in both the United States and the United Kingdom during the Second World War.

excess reserves *Fin* reserves held by a financial institution that are higher than those required by the regulatory authorities. As such reserves may indicate that demand for loans is low, banks often sell their excess reserves to other institutions.

exchange[1] **1.** *E-com* the main type of business-to-business marketplace. The **B2B exchange** enables suppliers, buyers, and intermediaries to come together and offer products to each other according to a set of criteria. **B2B web exchanges** provide constant price adjustments in line with fluctuations of supply and demand. In **E2E** or 'exchange-to-exchange' e-commerce, buyers and sellers conduct transactions not only within exchanges but also between them. **2.** *Fin* the conversion of one type of security for another, for example, the exchange of a bond for shares

exchange[2] *Fin* **1.** to trade one currency for another **2.** to barter

exchange controls *Econ* the regulations by which a country's banking system controls its residents' or resident companies' dealings in foreign currencies and gold

exchange equalisation account *Econ* the Bank of England account that sells and buys sterling for gold and foreign currencies to smooth out fluctuations in the exchange rate of the pound

exchange offer *Fin* an offer to trade one security for another

exchange rate *Fin* the rate at which one country's currency can be exchanged for that of another country

Exchange Rate Mechanism *Fin* see **ERM**

exchange rate parities *Fin* relationships between the values of various currencies

exchange rate risk *Fin* the risk of suffering loss on converting another currency to the currency of a company's own country.

EXAMPLE Exchange rate risks can be arranged into three primary categories. Economic exposure: operating costs will rise due to changes in rates and make a product uncompetitive in the world market. Little can be done to reduce this routine business risk that every enterprise must endure. Translation exposure: the impact of currency exchange rates will reduce a company's earnings and weaken its balance sheet. To reduce translation exposure, experienced corporate fund managers use a range of techniques known as *currency hedging*. Transaction exposure: there will be an unfavourable move in a specific currency between the time when a contract is agreed and the time it is completed, or between the time when a lending or borrowing is initiated and the time the funds are repaid. Transaction exposure can be eased by *factoring*: transferring title to foreign accounts receivable to a third-party factoring house.

Although there is no definitive way of forecasting exchange rates, largely because the world's economies and financial markets are evolving so rapidly, the relationships between exchange rates, interest rates, and inflation rates can serve as leading indicators of changes in risk. These relationships are as follows. Purchasing Power Parity theory (PPP): while it can be expressed differently, the most common expression links the changes in exchange rates to those in relative price indices in two countries:

Rate of change of exchange rate = Difference in inflation rates

International Fisher Effect (IFE): this holds that an interest-rate differential will exist only if the exchange rate is expected to change in such a way that the advantage of the higher interest rate is offset by the loss on the foreign exchange transactions. Practically speaking, the IFE

Unhappiness is best defined as the difference between our talents and our expectations.
Edward de Bono

implies that while an investor in a low-interest country can convert funds into the currency of a high-interest country and earn a higher rate, the gain (the interest-rate differential) will be offset by the expected loss due to foreign exchange rate changes. The relationship is stated as:

Expected rate of change of the exchange rate = Interest-rate differential

Unbiased Forward Rate Theory: this holds that the forward exchange rate is the best unbiased estimate of the expected future spot exchange rate.

Expected exchange rate = Forward exchange rate

exchange rate spread *Fin* the difference between the price at which a broker or other intermediary buys and sells foreign currency

exchequer *Fin* in the United Kingdom, the government's account at the Bank of England into which all revenues from taxes and other sources are paid

excise duty *Fin* a tax on goods such as alcohol or tobacco produced and sold within a particular country

exclusive economic zone *Econ* a zone in a country in which particular economic conditions apply. The Special Economic Zone (SEZ) in China, where trade is conducted free of state control, is an example.

execution only *Fin* used to describe a stock market transaction undertaken by an intermediary who acts on behalf of a client without providing advice

executive *Gen Mgt* an employee in a position of senior responsibility in an organisation. An executive is involved in planning, strategy, policy making, and *line management*. The term executive can also be used as an alternative to *manager*, *consultant*, *executive officer*, or **agent**.

executive chairman *Gen Mgt see* **chair**

executive coaching *HR* regular one-to-one *coaching* for leaders, designed as part of a *management development* programme to provide knowledge and skills in a particular area. Executive coaching involves giving *feedback* to a leader and

assisting in the creation of a development plan, often using *360 degree appraisal*. It can include in-depth development coaching conducted by colleagues, superiors, or specialist trainers, lasting perhaps six to twelve months.

executive director *Gen Mgt* a senior employee of an organisation, usually with line responsibility for a particular function and usually, but not always, a member of the *board of directors*

executive information system *Gen Mgt see* **EIS**

executive officer *Gen Mgt see* **executive**

executive pension plan *Fin* in the United Kingdom, a pension scheme for senior executives of a company. The company's contributions are a tax-deductible expense but are subject to a cap. The plan does not prevent the executive being a member of the company's group pension scheme although the executive's total contributions must not exceed a certain percentage of his or her salary.

executive search *HR* the identification of suitable external candidates for senior positions on behalf of an organisation by recruitment agents or consultants, often using *headhunting* techniques. Executive search consultants work from personal recommendation and lists of their own contacts, and monitor rising stars or key personnel in particular organisations or professions. The number of potential candidates is usually limited because of the speciality or seniority of the post, so that the search takes place within upper salary ranges. Executive search consultants rarely advertise because the publicity may be unfruitful or detrimental to the organisation for which they are working, and they do not find posts for individual job-hunters.

executive share option scheme *Fin* a UK term for an arrangement whereby certain directors and employees are given the opportunity to purchase shares in the company at a fixed price at a future date.

Petrol is much more likely than wheat to be a cause of international conflict. **Simone Weil**

In certain jurisdictions, such schemes can be tax efficient if certain local tax authority conditions are met. *See also employee share ownership plan*

executor *Fin* the person appointed under a will to ensure the deceased's estate is distributed according to the terms of the will

exempt gift *Fin* a gift that is not subject to US gift tax

exempt investment fund *Fin* in the United Kingdom, a collective investment, usually a unit trust, for investors who have certain tax privileges, for example, charities or contributors to pension plans

exemption *Fin* an amount per family member that an individual can subtract when reporting income to be taxed

exempt purchaser *Fin* an institutional investor who may buy newly issued securities without filing a prospectus with a securities commission

exempt securities *Fin* securities that are not subject to a provision of law such as margin or registration requirements

exempt supplies *Fin* in the United Kingdom, items or services on which VAT is not levied, for example, the purchase of, or rent on, property and financial services

exercise notice *Fin* an option-holder's notification to the option's writer of his or her desire to exercise the option

exercise of warrants *Fin* the use of a warrant to purchase stock

exercise price *Fin* the price at which an option to purchase or to sell shares or other items, **call option** or **put option**, may be exercised

exercise value *Fin* the amount of profit that can be realised by cashing in an option

ex gratia *Fin* as an act of favour, without obligation

ex-gratia payment *HR* a one-off extra payment in addition to normal *pay*, made

out of gratitude or courtesy, or in recognition of a special contribution

exhibition *Mkting* an event organised to bring together buyers and sellers at a single venue

Eximbank *abbr Fin* Export-Import Bank: a US bank founded in 1934 that provides loans direct to foreign importers of US goods and services

existential culture *Gen Mgt* a form of *corporate culture* in which the organisation exists to serve the individual, rather than individuals being servants of the organisation. Existential culture was identified by *Charles Handy*. It typically consists of a group of professionals who work together, but have no leader.

exit interview *HR* a meeting between an employee and a management representative on the employee's departure from an organisation. An exit interview is conducted in order to ascertain why an employee is leaving, either because of pull factors, such as better pay and conditions, or push factors, such as poor training or management. Another purpose of the exit interview is to capture information relating to the departing employee's knowledge and experience.

exit PE ratio *Fin* the price-earnings ratio when a company changes hands

exogenous variable *Stats* any variable in an econometric study that has an impact on it from outside

expatriate *HR* somebody who has left his or her home country to live or work abroad, either for a long period of time or permanently

expectancy theory *HR* a view that people will be motivated to behave in particular ways if they believe that doing so will bring them rewards they both seek and value. Expectancy theory was first applied in the context of the workplace by *Victor Vroom* in the 1960s. He defined the concepts of valence and expectancy to explain how people decide to act. Valence refers to somebody's perception of the value of the reward or outcome that might be obtained if he or she performs a task successfully.

expected rate of return *Fin* the projected percentage return on an investment, based on the weighted probability of all possible rates of return. *Abbr* **ERR**

EXAMPLE It is calculated by the following formula:

$$E[r]=\Sigma sP(s)rs$$

where E[r] is the expected return, P(s) is the probability that the rate rs occurs, and rs is the return at s level.

The following example illustrates the principle which the formula expresses.

The current price of ABC Ltd stock is trading at £10. At the end of the year, ABC shares are projected to be traded:

25% higher if economic growth exceeds expectations—a probability of 30%

12% higher if economic growth equals expectations—a probability of 50%

5% lower if economic growth falls short of expectations—a probability of 20%

To find the expected rate of return, simply multiply the percentages by their respective probabilities and add the results:

(30% × 25%) + (50% × 12%) + (25% × –5%) =
7.5 + 6 + –1.25 = 12.25% ERR

A second example:

if economic growth remains robust (a 20% probability), investments will return 25%;

if economic growth ebbs, but still performs adequately (a 40% probability), investments will return 15%;

if economic growth slows significantly (a 30% probability), investments will return 5%;

if the economy declines outright (a 10% probability), investments will return 0%.

Therefore:

(20% × 25%) + (40% × 15%) + (30% × 5%) +
(10% × 0%) = 5% + 6% + 1.5% + 0% =
12.5% ERR.

*See also **capital asset pricing model***

expected value *Fin* the financial forecast of the outcome of a course of action multiplied by the probability of achieving that outcome. The probability is expressed as a value ranging from 0 to 1.

expenditure switching *Econ* government action to improve the attractiveness of home-produced goods at the expense of imports or to make domestic spending switch from imports to home-produced goods

expense *Fin* **1.** a cost incurred in buying goods or services **2.** a charge against a company's profit

expense account *HR* an amount of money that an employee or group of employees can draw on to reclaim personal *expenses* incurred in carrying out activities for an organisation

expenses *HR* personal costs incurred by an employee in carrying out activities for an organisation that are reimbursed by the employer

experience curve *Gen Mgt see **learning curve***

experience economy *Gen Mgt* an economy in which products are differentiated through the quality of the 'consumer experience' or level of added value (*slang*)

experiential learning *HR* a model that views learning as a cyclical process in four stages: concrete experience, reflective observation, abstract conceptualisation, and active experimentation. Experiential learning relates to participants' activities and reactions to a training event, in contrast to passive learning. Proposed by *David Kolb* in 1971, the model was later expanded by other practitioners including *Peter Honey* and *Alan Mumford*. Experiential learning differs from *action learning* in that it can apply to an individual working alone while action learning is seen essentially as a group activity.

experimental design *Stats* the planning of the procedures to be used in an *experimental study*

experimental study *Stats* a statistical investigation in which the researcher can influence events in the study

expert system *Gen Mgt* a computer program that emulates the reasoning and *decision-making* of a human expert in a particular field. The main components of an expert system are the knowledge base,

---

Nobody who has wealth to distribute ever omits himself. Leon Trotsky

which consists of facts and rules about appropriate courses of action based on the knowledge and experience of human experts; the inference engine, which simulates the inductive reasoning of a human expert; and the user interface, which enables users to interact with the system. Expert systems may be used by non-experts to solve well-defined problems when human expertise is unavailable or expensive, or by experts seeking to find solutions to complex questions. They are used for a wide variety of tasks including medical diagnostics and financial decision-making, and are an application of *artificial intelligence*.

explicit knowledge *Gen Mgt see knowledge*

exploding bonus *HR* a bonus offered to recent graduates that encourages them to sign for a job as quickly as possible as it reduces in value with every day of delay (*slang*)

exponential smoothing *Gen Mgt* a statistical technique used in quantitative *forecasting*, particularly in the areas of inventory control and *sales forecasting*, that adjusts data to give a clearer view of trends in the long term. In exponential smoothing, values are calculated using a formula that takes all previous values into account but assigns greatest weight to the most recent data.

exponential trend *Stats* a statistical trend that is revealed in a *time series*

export agent *Gen Mgt* an intermediary who acts on behalf of a company to open up or develop a market in a foreign country. Export agents are often paid a commission on all sales and may have exclusive rights in a particular geographical area. A good agent will know or get to know local market conditions and will have other valuable information that can be used to mutual benefit.

Export Credit Guarantee Department *Mkting* a UK government department that provides financial and insurance assistance for exporters. The Export Credit Guarantee Department works to benefit organisations exporting UK goods and services and sets up insurance for UK companies investing overseas. *Abbr* **ECGD**

Export-Import Bank *Fin see Eximbank*

exporting *Mkting* the process of selling goods to other countries. Exporting provides access to non-domestic markets and can be co-ordinated by an **export manager**. As with all business activities, careful *market research* needs to be undertaken. This can be carried out by the company itself or through an experienced *export agent*. Many companies produce goods almost entirely for export. Services also can be exported, but require different delivery mechanisms through subsidiary offices or local *franchise*, or *licensing agreements*.

export-led growth *Econ* growth in which a country's main source of income is from its export trade

export manager *Mkting see exporting*

ex post *Fin* after the event. An ex post budget, or standard, is set after the end of a period of activity, when it can represent the optimum achievable level of performance in the conditions which were experienced. Thus the budget can be flexed, and standards can reflect factors such as unanticipated changes in technology and in price levels. This approach may be used in conjunction with sophisticated cost and revenue modelling to determine how far both the plan and the achieved results differed from the performance that would have been expected in the circumstances which were experienced.

exposure *E-com see ad view*

ex-rights *Fin* for sale without rights, for example, voting or conversion rights. The term can be applied to transactions such as the purchase of new shares.

ex-rights date *Fin* the date when a stock first trades ex-rights

extendable bond *Fin* a bond whose maturity can be delayed by either the issuer or the holder

---

Experience is a good teacher, but she sends in terrific bills. *Minna Antrim*

extendable note *Fin* a note whose maturity can be delayed by either the issuer or the holder

extended fund facility *Econ* a credit facility of the *IMF* that allows a country up to eight years to repay money it has borrowed from the Fund

external account *Fin* in the United Kingdom, a bank account at a UK branch held by a customer who is an overseas resident

external audit *Fin* an audit of a company done by people who are external to, and independent of, the organisation. *See also* **internal audit**

external communication *Gen Mgt* the exchange of information and messages between an organisation and other organisations, groups, or individuals outside the formal structure of the organisation. The aims of external communication are to facilitate co-operation with groups such as suppliers, investors, and shareholders, and to present a favourable image of an organisation and its products or services to potential and actual customers and to society at large. A variety of channels may be used for external communication including face-to-face meetings, print or broadcast media, and electronic communication technologies such as the Internet. External communication includes the fields of *PR*, media relations, *advertising*, and *marketing management*.

external debt *Econ* the part of a country's debt that is owed to creditors who are not residents of the country

external finance *Fin* money that a company obtains from investors, for example, by loans or by issuing stock

external funds *Fin* money that a business obtains from a third party rather than from its own resources

external growth *Fin* business growth as a result of a merger, a takeover, or through a partnership with another organisation

extranet *E-com* a closed network of websites and e-mail systems that is open to people outside as well as inside an organisation. An extranet enables third-party access to internal applications or information—usually subject to some kind of signed agreement. This is useful for organisations that need to share internal systems and information with potential partners. As with *intranets*, extranets provide all the benefits of Internet technology (browsers, web servers, HTML, etc.) with the added benefit of security, being confined to an isolated network.

Because this is a work environment and partners enter it to access information as quickly as possible, extranet design generally focuses on minimal graphics and maximum content. Security being a key issue, it is generally password-protected in order to maintain confidentiality. Content management is also essential, as the extranet is only as useful as the information it contains. Many extranets fall down because the content is not updated and managed properly.

extraordinary general meeting *Gen Mgt* any general meeting of an organisation other than the *AGM*. Directors can usually call an extraordinary general meeting at their discretion, as can company members who either hold not less than 10% of the paid-up voting shares, or who represent not less than 10% of the voting rights. Directors are obliged to call an EGM if there is a substantial loss of capital. Fourteen days' written notice must be given, or 21 days' written notice if a special resolution is to be proposed. Only special business can be transacted at the meeting, the general nature of which must be specified in the convening notice. *Abbr* **EGM**

extraordinary resolution *Fin* in the United Kingdom, an exceptional issue that is put to the vote at a company's general meeting, for example, a change to the company's articles of association. *Also known as* **special resolution**

extrapolate *Stats* to estimate from a data set values that lie beyond the range of the data collected

extreme value *Stats* either of the smallest or largest variate values in a sample of observations from a statistical study

eyeballing *Stats* the process of informally inspecting statistical data by simply looking at it to assess results (*slang*)

eyeballs *E-com* a measure of the number of visits made to a website (*slang*)

eyebrow management *Gen Mgt* a management style whereby a manager or top executive can change a course of action simply by implying his or her disapproval (*slang*)

eye candy *Gen Mgt* visually attractive material (*slang*)

eye service *HR* the practice of working only when a supervisor is present and able to see you (*slang*)

e-zine *E-com* a regular publication on a particular topic distributed in digital form, mainly via the Web but also by e-mail

---

Industrial relations are like sexual relations. It's better between consenting parties.
Vic Feather

F2F *abbr Gen Mgt* face-to-face (*slang*)

face time *HR* time spent in face-to-face communication as opposed to time spent communicating electronically (*slang*)

facilitation *HR* the process of helping groups, or individuals, to learn, find a solution, or reach a consensus, without imposing or dictating an outcome. Facilitation aims to *empower* individuals or groups to learn for themselves or find their own answers to problems without control or manipulation. Facilitators need good *communication skills*, including listening, questioning, and reflecting. Facilitation is used in a range of contexts including *training*, *experiential learning*, conflict resolution, and *negotiation*.

facilities management *Gen Mgt* **1.** the management of an organisation's property **2.** the provision of equipment or services to an organisation by an agent or company

facility-sustaining activities *Fin* activities undertaken to support the organisation as a whole, which cannot be logically linked to individual units of output. Accounting is a facility-sustaining activity. *See also* **hierarchy of activities**

facing matter *Mkting* advertisements printed opposite editorial material in newspapers or magazines

factor *Stats* a variable investigated in a statistical study

factor analysis *Stats* the examination of the covariances, correlations, or relationships between the variables observed in a statistical study

factored goods *Fin* goods purchased for resale

factor four *Ops* a concept of environmentally-friendly production based on increasing the productivity of resources by a factor of four to reduce waste

factoring *Fin* the sale of debts to a third party (the factor) at a discount, in return for prompt cash. A factoring service may be with recourse, in which case the supplier takes the risk of the debt not being paid, or without recourse when the factor takes the risk. *See also* **invoice discounting**

factor market *Econ* a market in which factors of production are bought and sold, for example, the capital market or the labour market

factory *Gen Mgt* a building or set of buildings housing workers and equipment for the sole purpose of manufacturing goods, often on a large scale

factory gate price *Ops* the actual cost of manufacturing goods before any *mark-up* is added to give profit. The factory gate price includes direct costs such as labour, *raw materials*, and energy, and indirect costs such as interest on loans, plant maintenance, or rent.

failure *Gen Mgt see* **business failure**

failure mode effects analysis *Gen Mgt see* **FMEA**

fallen angel *Fin* a stock that was once very desirable but has now dropped in value (*slang*)

family business *Gen Mgt* a *small* or *medium-sized business*, run by a family owner, often with the help of other family members, and passed on within the family. If a family business grows, it may be run as an unregistered partnership or, more commonly, registered as a limited company, although in both cases the partners or the directors will be appointed from within the family to retain family control. In the case of larger, *public limited* family businesses, family members are usually majority shareholders and retain control of the *board of directors*, although non-family directors and shareholders will have an influence on the way the company is run. The most common cause of *business failure* in family-owned businesses is poor *succession planning*.

family-friendly policy *HR* a range of working practices designed to enable employees to achieve a satisfactory *work-life balance*. A family-friendly policy is often introduced by an organisation to facilitate the reintroduction of women with children into the workplace. *Equal opportunities* legislation and corporate good practice, however, require that such a policy is open to all employees. Typically, a family-friendly policy will allow for a range of *flexible working* practices and may go further by providing childcare or care for employees' elderly relatives, or paid time off for participation in community activities as part of a *community involvement* programme. Although the introduction of a family-friendly policy may initially be expensive, benefits to the organisation, including improved employee retention and higher *motivation* and *job satisfaction* levels, are believed to offset these costs.

Fannie Mae *(US) Fin see FNMA*

FAO *abbr Gen Mgt* the Food and Agriculture Organisation of the United Nations: the FAO's priority objectives include encouraging sustainable agriculture and rural development and ensuring the availability of adequate food supplies

FAQ *abbr E-com* frequently asked question: FAQ pages are often included on websites to provide first-time visitors with answers to the most likely questions they may have. FAQ pages are also used in newsgroups and software applications.

far month *Fin* the latest month for which there is a futures contract for a particular commodity. *See also nearby month*

FASB *abbr Fin (US)* Financial Accounting Standards Board: a body responsible for establishing the standards of financial reporting and accounting for US companies in the private sector. The Securities and Exchange Commission (SEC) performs a comparable role for public companies.

FASTER *Fin* Fully Automated Screen Trading and Electronic Registration, a computer-based clearing, settlement, registration, and information system operated by the New Zealand Stock Exchange

fast track *Gen Mgt* a rapid route to success or advancement. The fast track involves competition and a race to get ahead, and is associated with high ambition and great activity. An employee can be on a fast track, for example, to *promotion*, but an activity also can be said to take the fast track, for example, to rapid *product development*. The *horizontal fast track* is a variation on the idea of the fast track in which advancement is not upwards but sideways.

fat
trim the fat *Gen Mgt* to lay off unnecessary staff in an organisation during a time of economic difficulty *(slang)*

faxback *Mkting* a method of distributing information in which customers dial a dedicated fax machine that automatically sends information back to the customer's fax machine

Fayol, Henri Louis (1841–1925) *Gen Mgt* French engineer and industrialist. First European to define *management* as a process, consisting, he argued, of five activities—planning, organising, co-ordinating, commanding, and controlling—with further detail contained in 14 general principles. Fayol's ideas were published in *Administration Industrielle et Générale* (1916), and were practised by others, notably *Alfred Sloan, Jr*.

FCM *abbr Fin* futures commission merchant

FCOL *abbr Gen Mgt* for crying out loud *(slang)*

FDI *abbr Fin* foreign direct investment

feasibility study *Gen Mgt* an investigation into a proposed plan or project to determine whether and how it can be successfully and profitably carried out.

Frequently used in **project management**, a feasibility study may examine alternative methods of reaching objectives or be used to define or redefine the proposed project. The information gathered must be sufficient to make a decision on whether to go ahead with the project or to enable an investor to decide whether to commit finances to it. This will normally require analysis of technical, financial, and market issues, including an estimate of resources required in terms of materials, time, personnel, and finance, and the expected return on investment.

feasible region *Fin* the area contained within all of the constraint lines shown on a graphical depiction of a linear programming problem. All feasible combinations of output are contained within, or located on, the boundaries of the feasible region.

Federal Funds *Fin* deposits held in reserve by the US Federal Reserve System

federal organisation *Gen Mgt* a form of **organisation structure**, identified by **Charles Handy**, in which subsidiaries federate to gain benefits of scale. In a federal organisation, the leader provides coordination and vision, and initiatives are generated from the component subsidiary organisations. Federal organisation is one of the many ways in which organisations **restructure** in order to deal with the dilemmas of power and control. According to Handy, federal organisation offers an enabling framework for autonomy to release corporate energy for people to do things in their own way, provided that it is in the common interest, and for people to be well informed so as to be able to interpret that common interest. Handy cites Royal Dutch Shell, Unilever, and ABB as exemplars of federalism.

Federal Reserve Bank *Fin* a bank that is a member of the US Federal Reserve System

Federal Reserve Board (*US*) *Fin* a body of seven governors appointed by Congress on the nomination of the President, that supervises the US Federal Reserve System. Appointees serve for 14 years. *Abbr* **FRB**

Federal Reserve note *Fin* a note issued by the US Federal Reserve System to increase the availability of money temporarily

Federal Reserve System *Fin* the central banking system of the United States, founded in 1913 by an Act of Congress. The board of governors, made up of seven members, is based in Washington DC and 12 Reserve Banks are located in major cities across the United States.

Fed pass *Fin* the US Federal Reserve's addition of reserves to the Federal Reserve System to increase credit availability

Fedwire *Fin* the US Federal Reserve System's electronic system for transferring funds

feedback *Gen Mgt* the communication of responses and reactions to proposals and changes, or of the findings of **performance appraisals** with the aim of enabling improvements to be made. Feedback can be either positive or negative. In the context of performance evaluation, or **performance appraisal**, positive feedback should be delivered to reinforce good performance, whereas negative feedback should be intended to correct or improve poor performance. Feedback that is delivered inappropriately can be very demotivating, so good communication skills are a prerequisite.

feedback control *Fin* the measurement of differences between planned outputs and actual outputs achieved, and the modification of subsequent action and/or plans to achieve future required results

feedforward control *Fin* the forecasting of differences between actual and planned outcomes, and the implementation of action, before the event, to avoid such differences

feeding frenzy *Fin* a period of frantic buyer activity in a market (*slang*)

feet
get your feet wet *Gen Mgt* to begin a new project or activity (*slang*)

Starting companies is very hard and time-consuming. You want to keep those to a minimum.
Jay S. Walker

fee work *Gen Mgt* work on a project carried out by independent workers or contractors, rather than employees of an organisation

Feigenbaum, Armand Vallin (*b.* 1920) *Gen Mgt* US manager and author. Originator of the concept of total **quality control**, the forerunner of **total quality management**. In *Quality Control* (1951), Feigenbaum argued that quality should be a company-wide process.

Ferguson, Sir Alex (*b.* 1941) *Gen Mgt* British football manager. Considered to be one of the most successful club managers of all time, whose management methods, particularly in the area of **motivation**, are studied by other business leaders. His approach is set out in *Managing My Life: My Autobiography* (1999).

FID *abbr* (*ANZ*) *Fin* Financial Institutions Duty

field plot *Stats* a statistical study, usually in agriculture, of the results of an operation such as planting GM crops

field research *Mkting* the collection of data directly from contact with customers and potential customers through surveys, interviews, and other forms of **market research**

field staff *HR* sales staff who cover a specific geographical region and who travel regularly to meet customers. The term field staff may also be applied to professional and technical staff who operate mainly on site, such as conservationists and archaeologists.

field trial *Mkting* a limited pilot test of a product under real conditions. A field trial is undertaken to test the physical or engineering properties of a product in order to identify and iron out any technical shortcomings prior to marketing. Customers may be involved in some trials, for example, in testing a new washing powder. Field trials should not be confused with **test marketing**, which is used to determine the likely market for, and

likely consumer response to, a new product or service.

field work *Mkting* practical work, study, or research carried out in the real world away from the desk. In a marketing context, field work forms primary **market research** and involves obtaining customers' views and opinions on a face-to-face basis or through postal questionnaires or telephone surveys.

FIFO *abbr Ops* first in first out: a method of stock control where the stock of a given product first placed in store is used before more recently produced or acquired goods or materials

FIF Tax *abbr* (*ANZ*) *Fin* Foreign Investment Funds Tax

file server *E-com* a computer that stores and makes software programs and data available to other computers on a network

file transfer protocol *E-com see FTP*

filter *Gen Mgt* a process for analysing large amounts of incoming information to identify any material that might be of interest to an organisation

Filthy Five *Gen Mgt* a list of companies with a poor environmental record, compiled annually by *Mother Jones Magazine* in the United States

final average monthly salary (*US*) *Fin* = *pensionable earnings*

finance *Fin* the money needed by an individual or company to pay for something, for example, a project or stocks

finance bill *Fin* an act passed by a legislature to provide money for public spending

finance company *Fin* a business that lends money to people or companies against collateral, especially to make purchases by hire purchase

finance house *Fin* a financial institution

finance lease *Fin* a lease that is treated as though the lessee had borrowed money and bought the leased assets.
  If a lease agreement does not meet any

A wise man will make more opportunities than he finds. *Francis Bacon*

of the criteria below, the lessee treats it as an *operating lease* for accounting purposes. If, however, the agreement meets one of the criteria below, it is treated as a finance lease.

1. The lease agreement transfers ownership of the assets to the lessee during the term of the lease.

2. The lessee can purchase the assets leased at a bargain price (also called a bargain purchase option), such as £1, at the end of the lease term.

3. The lease term is at least 75% of the economic life of the leased asset.

4. The present value of the minimum lease payments is 90% or more of the asset's value.

Finance leases are reported by the lessee as if the assets being leased were acquired and the monthly rental payments as if they were payments of principal and interest on a debt obligation. Specifically, the lessee capitalises the lease by recognising an asset and a liability at the lower of the present value of the minimum lease payments or the value of the assets under lease. As the monthly rental payments are made, the corresponding liability decreases. At the same time, the leased asset is depreciated in a manner that is consistent with other owned assets having the same use and economic life.

US term **capital lease**. *See also* **operating lease**

financial *Fin* relating to finance

financial accounting *Fin* the classification and recording of the monetary transactions of an entity in accordance with established concepts, principles, accounting standards, and legal requirements, and their presentation, by means of profit and loss accounts, balance sheets, and cash flow statements, during and at the end of an accounting period

Financial Accounting Standards Board (*US*) *Fin see* **FASB**

financial adviser *Fin* somebody whose job is to give advice about investments

financial analyst *Fin see* **investment analyst**

financial control *Fin* the control of divisional performance by setting a range of financial targets and the monitoring of actual performance towards these targets

financial distress *Fin* the condition of being in severe difficulties over money, especially being close to bankruptcy

financial economies of scale *Fin* financial advantages gained by being able to do things on a large scale

financial engineering *Fin* the conversion of one form of financial instrument into another, such as the swap of a fixed-rate instrument for a floating-rate one

financial incentive scheme *Gen Mgt see* **incentive scheme**

Financial Institutions Duty (*ANZ*) *Fin* a tax on monies paid into financial institutions imposed by all state governments in Australia except for Queensland. Financial institutions usually pass the tax on to customers. *Abbr* **FID**

financial instrument *Fin* a document that has a cash face value or represents a financial transaction

financial leverage *Fin* the use of debt finance to increase the return on equity by deploying borrowed funds in such a way that the return generated is greater than the cost of servicing the debt. If the reverse is true, and the return on deployed funds is less than the cost of servicing the debt, the effect of financial leverage is to reduce the return on equity. *Also known as* **gearing**

financial liability *Fin* any liability that is a contractual obligation to either deliver cash or another financial asset to another entity or to exchange financial instruments with another entity under conditions that are potentially unfavourable

financial management *Fin* the management of all the processes associated with the efficient acquisition and deployment of both short- and long-term financial resources

Financial Ombudsman *Fin* the person responsible for investigating and resolving complaints involving money from members of the public against a company, institution, or other organisation

financial planning *Fin* planning the acquisition of funds to finance planned activities

Financial Planning Association of Australia *Fin* a national organisation representing companies and individuals working in the Australian financial planning industry. Established in 1992, the association is responsible for monitoring standards among its members. *Abbr* **FPA**

Financial Reporting Review Panel *Fin* a UK review panel established to examine contentious departures, by large companies, from accounting standards

Financial Reporting Standards Board (*ANZ*) *Fin* a peak body that is responsible for setting and monitoring accounting standards in New Zealand. *Abbr* **FRSB**

financial risk *Fin* the possibility of loss in an investment or speculation

financial statements *Fin* summaries of accounts to provide information for interested parties. The most common financial statements are: trading and profit and loss account; profit and loss appropriation account; balance sheet; cash-flow statement; report of the auditors; statement of total recognised gains and losses; and reconciliation of movements in shareholders' funds.

financier *Fin* somebody who provides financing

financing gap *Econ* the gap in funding for institutions such as the *IMF* caused by cancelling the debts of poorer countries such as those in West Africa

find time *Mkting* the time it takes a consumer to locate a company's product among other products on the shelf (*slang*)

finished goods *Ops* completed goods that are available for sale to customers

finite capacity plan *Ops see capacity requirements planning*

finite loading *Ops* the scheduling or *loading* of jobs onto a workstation so that the number of jobs matches the *effective capacity* of that station over a given time period. Finite loading is often used in a computerised operation of *loading*. *See also infinite loading*

finite population *Stats* a statistical population that has a limited size

FIRB *abbr* (*ANZ*) *Fin* Foreign Investment Review Board

firewall *E-com* a combination of hardware, software, and procedures that controls access to an intranet. Firewalls help to control the information that passes between an intranet and the Internet. A firewall can be simple or complex depending on how an organisation decides to control its Internet traffic. It may, for example, be set up to limit Internet access to e-mail only, so that no other types of information can pass between the intranet and the Internet.

firm *Gen Mgt* a *partnership* business. A firm is strictly the name for a business run by partners, but it is often used more generally as a synonym for a *company*, or *organisation*, usually in the *private sector*.

first in first out *Ops see* **FIFO**

first-line management *HR see supervisory management*

first mover *Mkting* the company that first introduces a new type of product or service to a market. Those organisations that follow a first mover to market are known as **followers** or **laggards**—terms that also describe companies that are not the recognised leaders in a sector.

first mover advantage *Gen Mgt* the benefit produced by being the first to enter a market with a new product or service. First mover advantages include becoming a market leader (see *market share*) in a new area establishing a new leading *brand*; being able to charge a premium until competitor products appear; enhanced reputation, design, and

---

Confusion is a word we have invented for an order which is not understood.   **Henry Miller**

copyright protection; and possibly setting an industry standard to which other competitors may have to aspire. Disadvantages include: cheaper, and possibly better, **follower** products; the possibility of having to reduce prices or continuously having to add value to stay ahead; first mover development costs; a possible shift in consumer tastes away from the product; obsolescence; and a follower product being accepted as the industry standard.

first-round financing *Fin* the first infusion of capital into a project

fiscal *Fin* relating to financial matters, especially in respect of governmental collection, use, and regulation of money through taxation

fiscal balance *Econ* a taxation policy that keeps a country's employment and taxation levels in balance

fiscal drag *Fin* the effect that inflation has on taxation in that it raises the amount of tax collected as earnings rise without increasing tax rates

fiscal policy *Econ* the central government's policy on lowering or raising taxation or increasing or decreasing public expenditure in order to stimulate or depress *aggregate demand*

fishbone chart *Gen Mgt* a diagram resembling the skeleton of a fish that is used to identify and categorise the possible causes of problems. Within a fishbone chart, the topic or problem to be discussed is placed in a box at the right-hand side that corresponds to the fish's head, and the major elements to be investigated are shown as branches at an angle to the horizontal spine. Questions are asked to identify possible causes of problems in each area and the results are added to the diagram as additional layers of branches. This ensures that all aspects of the problem are considered systematically. The fishbone chart is also known as a **cause and effect diagram** or an **Ishikawa diagram** after the originator, Professor *Kaoru Ishikawa* of Tokyo

University, and is frequently used in *brainstorming* and *problem-solving*.

5-S concept *Ops* a technique that evolved in Japan to establish and maintain a quality culture environment within an organisation. The 5-S concept has been associated with *total productive maintenance* and *industrial housekeeping* in both manufacturing and services. It is seen as being fundamental to quality and productivity. The 5-Ss relate to Japanese words that have been variously translated into English. The words are: Seiri, for sort; Seiton, for simplify or straighten; Seiso, for shine or sweep; Seiketsu, for standardise; and Shitsuke, for sustain or self-discipline. The application of these ideas can reduce waste, and increase efficiency, productivity, and quality.

fixed asset *Fin* a long-term asset of a business such as a machine or building that will not usually be traded

fixed budget *Fin* a budget which is normally set prior to the start of an accounting period, and which is not changed in response to subsequent changes in activity or costs/revenues. Fixed budgets are generally used for planning purposes.

fixed charge *Fin* a form of protection given to secured creditors relating to specific assets of a company. The charge grants the holder the right of enforcement against the identified asset (in the event of default on repayment) so that the creditor may realise the asset to meet the debt owed. Fixed charges rank first in order of priority in receivership or liquidation.

fixed cost *Fin see cost behaviour*

fixed exchange rate system *Fin* a system of currency exchange in which there is no change of rate

fixed-interest loan *Fin* a loan whose rate of interest does not change

fixed interval re-order system *Ops see periodic inventory review system*

fixed rate *Gen Mgt* an interest rate for loans that does not change with fluctuating conditions in the market

---

You can build a lasting competitive edge through the excellence of your organisation structure.
Percy Barnevik

fixed-rate loan *Fin* a loan with an interest rate that is set at the beginning of the term and remains the same throughout

flagpole
let's run it up a flagpole and see who salutes *Gen Mgt* let's try this idea and see what level of support or popularity it commands (*slang*)

flame *E-com* a hostile or aggressive message sent via e-mail or posted into an online newsgroup. Typically, flame messages are sent in response to **spam** or unsolicited commercial e-mail. If a flame message is responded to in a similarly hostile manner, it can lead to a **flame war**.

flat organisation *Gen Mgt, HR* a slimmed-down **organisation structure**, with fewer levels between top and bottom than a traditional **bureaucracy**, that is supposedly more responsive and better able to cope with fast-moving change. A flat organisation can be the result of **delayering**. *Also known as* **horizontal organisation**

flat yield curve *Fin* a **yield curve** with the same interest rates for long-term bonds as for short-term bonds

flexecutive *HR* a multiskilled executive able to switch jobs or tasks easily (*slang*)

flexed budget *Fin see* **budget cost allowance**

flexible benefit *HR see* **fringe benefits**

flexible budget *Fin* a budget which, by recognising different **cost behaviour** patterns, is designed to change as volume of activity changes

flexible exchange rate system *Fin* a system of currency exchange in which rates change from time to time

flexible manufacturing system *Ops* an integrated, computer-controlled production system which is capable of producing any of a range of parts, and of switching quickly and economically between them. *Abbr* **FMS**

flexible working *HR* a generic term for employment practices that differ from the traditional norm in terms of the hours worked, the length of contract, or the place of work. Flexible working practices can be divided into three categories: those that give flexibility in the management of time through **flexible working hours** schemes such as **flexitime** or **shiftwork**; those that allow employers to cater for peaks or troughs in demand through numerical flexibility, for example, by employing temporary staff; and those that give flexibility regarding the place of work, for example, teleworking.

flexible working hours *HR* flexibility in the management of working time. Flexible working hours are achieved through systems such as **annual hours**, **part-time work**, **flexitime**, or job sharing that are arranged to meet organisational requirements or to help employees reconcile the demands of work and personal circumstances.

flexilagger *HR* a company or organisation considered to put too little emphasis on flexibility in its employment practices (*slang*)

flexileader *HR* a company or organisation considered to put a great deal of emphasis on flexibility in its employment practices (*slang*)

flexitime *HR* a system of **flexible working hours** based on a set number of hours to be worked per week. Employees are able to determine their precise hours of work, provided business demands are met and attendance at work during core periods is achieved. A debit or credit of hours can be carried forward into the next accounting period.

flight risk *HR* an employee who may be planning to leave a company in the near future (*slang*)

flip *Gen Mgt* a start-up company that aims to build market share quickly and generate short-term personal wealth for its founders through flotation or sell-off

float¹ *Fin* to sell shares or bonds, for example, to finance a project

---

Too many people are on boards because they want to have nice-looking visiting cards.

Utz Fecht

float² *Fin* the period between the presentation of a cheque as payment and the actual payment to the payee or the financial advantage provided by this period to the drawer of a cheque

floating charge *Fin* a form of protection given to secured creditors which relates to assets of the company which are changing in nature. Often current assets like stock or debtors are the subject of this type of charge. In the event of default on repayment, the chargeholder may take steps to enforce the charge so that it crystallises and becomes attached to the current assets to which it relates. Floating charges rank after certain other prior claims in receivership or liquidation.

floating debt *Fin* a short-term borrowing that is repeatedly refinanced

floating rate *Fin* an interest rate that is not fixed and which changes according to fluctuations in the market

floor *Fin* a lower limit on an interest rate, price, or the value of an asset

floor effect *Stats* the occurrence of clusters of scores near the lower limit of the data in a statistical study

flotation *Fin* the financing of a company by selling shares in it or a new debt issue, or the offering of shares and bonds for sale on the stock exchange

flow chart *or* **flow diagram** *Gen Mgt* a graphical representation of the stages in a process or system, or of the steps required to solve a problem. A flow chart is commonly used to represent the sequence of functions in a computer program or to model the movement of materials, money, or people in a complex process. Two primary symbols used in flow charts are the **process box**, indicating a process or action taking place, and the **decision lozenge**, indicating the need for a decision.

flow line production *or* **flow lines** *Ops* see *flow production*

flow on *Gen Mgt* a pay increase awarded to one group of workers as a result of a pay rise awarded to another group working in the same field

flow production *Ops* a production method in which successive operations are carried out on a product in such a way that it moves through the factory in a single direction. Flow production is most widely used in **mass production** on production lines. More recently, it has been linked with **batch production**. Under flow production, stock is often kept to the minimum necessary to ensure continued activity. Stoppages and interruptions to the flow indicate a fault, and corrective action can be taken. **Assembly line** production is an extreme version of flow production. *Also known as* **flow line production**

flow theory *Gen Mgt* a theory of the way in which people become engaged with, or disengaged from, change. Flow theory suggests that people harmonise in change situations, and open, honest, trusting relationships emerge. The theory recognises the unpredictability and rigidity of human nature when faced with change. *See also* **change management**

fluff it and fly it *Mkting* to make a product look good and then sell it (*slang*)

FMEA *abbr Gen Mgt* failure mode effects analysis: a technique for analysing the causes, risks, and effects of potential systems or component failures that is used as a basis for prevention and contingency planning. FMEA was developed by engineers primarily to prevent defects in electrical and mechanical systems. All possible failures and their potential effects are listed and ranked according to severity of impact and probability of occurrence so that prevention efforts can be focused on the most critical issues.

FMS *abbr Ops* flexible manufacturing system

FNMA *abbr* (*US*) *Fin* Federal National Mortgage Association: the largest source of housing finance in the United States, the FNMA trades in mortgages guaranteed by the Federal Housing Finance

Board. Created in 1938, the FNMA is a shareholder-owned private company and its stock is traded on the New York Stock Exchange. It has two principal regulators; the Department for Housing and Urban Development (HUD) aims to make sure that liquidity in the residential mortgage finance market is increased, while the Office of Federal Housing Enterprise Oversight (OFHEO) monitors soundness of accounting practice and financial safety.

focus group *Mkting* a carefully selected representative range of consumers or employees used for the purposes of providing feedback on consumer preferences and responses to a selected range of products or marketing issues. A focus group usually operates with a *facilitator* to guide discussion. Although primarily used for marketing purposes, focus groups are also being more widely used to obtain employee feedback on a wide range of employment and other issues within an organisation.

followback survey *Stats* a further survey of a statistical population carried out a period of years after an original survey

follower *Mkting see first mover*

Fong Kong (*S Africa*) *Gen Mgt* a product with a fake designer label, especially sports shoes (*slang*)

Food and Agriculture Organisation *Gen Mgt see FAO*

footer *E-com* an information section at the bottom of a web page, usually containing a copy of the essential links, contact information, and links to copyright and privacy policy information

footfall *Mkting* a measure of the number of people who walk past a shop (*slang*)

Forbes 500 *Fin* a list of the 500 largest public companies in the United States, ranked according to various criteria by *Forbes* magazine

force field analysis *Gen Mgt* a technique for promoting change by identifying positive and negative factors and by

working to lessen the negative forces while developing the positive ones. Force field analysis was developed by **Kurt Lewin** as an aid to **decision-making**, **problem-solving**, and conflict prevention.

Ford, Henry (1863–1947) *Gen Mgt* US industrialist. Founder of the Ford Motor Company, who organised the **assembly line** along the scientific management principles of **Frederick Winslow Taylor** and recorded his philosophy in *My Life and Work* (1922)

After spending time as a machinist's apprentice, a watch repairer, and a mechanic, Ford built his first car in 1896. He quickly became convinced of the vehicle's commercial potential and started his own company in 1903. His first car was the Model A. After a year in business he was selling 600 a month.

In 1907 Ford professed that his aim was to build a motor car for the masses. In 1908 his Model T was born. Through innovative use of new mass-production techniques, 15 million Model Ts were produced between 1908 and 1927.

At that time, Ford's factory at Highland Park, Michigan, was the biggest in the world. Over 14,000 people worked on the 57-acre site. He was quick to establish international operations as well. Ford's first overseas sales branch was opened in France in 1908 and, in 1911, Ford began making cars in the United Kingdom.

In 1919 Henry Ford resigned as the company's president, letting his son, Edsel, take over. By then the Ford company was making a car a minute and Ford's market share was in excess of 57%.

forecast *Fin* a prediction of future events and their quantification for planning purposes

forecasting *Gen Mgt* the prediction of outcomes, trends, or expected future behaviour of a business, industry sector, or the economy through the use of statistics. Forecasting is an **operational research** technique used as a basis for management planning and decision-making. Common types of forecasting include trend analysis, **regression analysis**,

Delphi technique, time series analysis, *correlation*, *exponential smoothing*, and input–output analysis.

foreclosure *Gen Mgt see* **repossession**

foreign bill *Fin* a bill of exchange that is not payable in the country where it is issued

foreign currency *Econ* the currency or interest-bearing bonds of a foreign country

foreign currency translation *Fin* the restatement of the foreign currency accounts of overseas subsidiaries and associated companies into the domestic currency of the country in which the group is incorporated, for the purpose of producing consolidated group accounts

foreign debt *Fin* hard-currency debt owed to a foreign country in payment for goods and services

foreign direct investment *Fin* the establishment of new overseas facilities or the expansion of existing overseas facilities, by an investor. FDI may be inward (domestic investment by overseas companies) or outward (overseas investment by domestic companies). *Abbr* **FDI**

foreign dividend *Fin* in the United Kingdom, a dividend paid by another country, possibly subject to special rules under UK tax codes

foreign equity market *Fin* the market in one country for equities of companies in other countries

foreign exchange *Fin* the currencies of other countries, or dealings in these

foreign exchange option *Fin* a contract which, for a fee, guarantees a worst-case exchange rate for the future purchase of one currency for another. Unlike a *forward transaction*, the option does not obligate the buyer to deliver a currency on the settlement date unless the buyer chooses to. These options protect against unfavourable currency movements while allowing retention of the ability to participate in favourable movements.

foreign income dividend *Fin* a dividend paid from earnings in other countries

Foreign Investment Funds Tax (*ANZ*) *Fin* a tax imposed by the Australian government on unrealised gains made by Australian residents from offshore investments. It was introduced in 1992 to prevent overseas earnings being taxed at low rates and never brought to Australia. *Abbr* **FIF Tax**

Foreign Investment Review Board (*ANZ*) *Fin* a nonstatutory body that regulates and advises the federal government on foreign investment in Australia. It was set up in 1976. *Abbr* **FIRB**

foreign reserve *Fin* the currency of other countries held by an organisation, especially a country's central bank

foreign subsidiary company *Gen Mgt see* **subsidiary company**

foreign tax credit *Fin* a tax advantage for taxes that are paid to or in another country

forensic accounting *Fin* the use of accounting records and documents in order to determine the legality or otherwise of past activities

forfaiting *Fin* the purchase of financial instruments such as bills of exchange or letters of credit on a non-recourse basis by a forfaiter, who deducts interest (in the form of a discount) at an agreed rate for the period covered by the notes. The forfaiter assumes the responsibility for claiming the debt from the importer (buyer) who initially accepted the financial instrument drawn by the seller of the goods. Traditionally, forfaiting is fixed-rate, medium-term (one- to five-year) finance.

formica parachute *HR* unemployment insurance (*slang*)

Fortune 500 *Fin* a list of the 500 largest industrial companies in the United States, compiled annually by *Fortune* magazine

forum *E-com* a newsgroup, mailing-list discussion group, chat room, or other

---

One man that has a mind and knows it can always beat ten men who haven't and don't.
                                        George Bernard Shaw

online area that enables Internet users to read, post, and respond to messages

forward contract *Fin* a private futures contract for delivery of a commodity

forward cover *Fin* the purchase for cash of the quantity of a commodity needed to fulfil a futures contract

forward integration *Ops* a means of guaranteeing *distribution channels* for products and services by building relationships with, or taking control of, *distributors*. Forward integration can free the supplier from the threat or influence of major buyers and can also provide a barrier to market entry by potential rivals. *Backward integration* can provide similar guarantees on the supply side. Forward integration is a feature of Japanese *keiretsu*.

forward interest rate *Fin* an interest rate specified for a loan to be made at a future date

forward-looking study *Stats* a survey of a statistical population carried out for a period such as a year after an original survey

forward pricing *Fin* the establishment of the price of a share in a unit trust based on the next asset valuation

forward rate *Fin* an estimate of what an interest rate will be at a specified future time

forward scheduling *Ops* a method for determining the start times for the various operations involved in a particular *job*. Forward scheduling is most often used when the operations department sets the delivery date for a job, rather than the sales or marketing departments. Jobs are scheduled for the various operations as the workstations are expected to become available. The customer can then be informed of the projected delivery date. *See also backward scheduling*

forward transaction *Fin* an agreement to buy one currency and sell another on a date some time beyond two business days.

This allows an exchange rate on a given day to be locked in for a future payment or receipt, thereby eliminating exchange rate risk.

founders' shares *Fin see deferred shares*

fourth level of service *Gen Mgt* a very high rating in a system of measuring the added value in a product or service

fourth market *Fin* trading carried out directly without brokers, usually by large institutions

FPA *abbr Fin* Financial Planning Association of Australia

fractional currency *Fin* the paper money that is in denominations smaller than one unit of a standard national currency

frames *E-com* a feature of *HTML* that allows different web pages to be displayed in one window simultaneously. Frames enable websites to keep a standard navigation bar on the screen regardless of the web page a visitor decides to access. However, there are a number of problems with frames. For instance, pages can be more difficult to print and bookmark because browsers can often only recognise one frame at a time.

franchise *Mkting* an agreement enabling a third party to sell or provide products or services owned by a manufacturer or supplier. A franchise is granted by the manufacturer, or **franchisor**, to a **franchisee**, who then retails the product. The franchise is regulated by a **franchise contract**, or **franchise agreement**, that specifies the terms and conditions of the franchise. These may include an obligation for the franchisor to provide national advertising or training for sales staff in return for the meeting of agreed sales targets by the franchisee. The franchisee normally retains a percentage of sales income. In other cases, a franchise may involve the *licensing* of a franchisee to manufacture a product to the franchisor's specification, and the sale of this product

---

Doubt is a necessary precondition to meaningful action. Fear is the great mover in the end.
Donald Barthelme

to retailers. Franchises can also be organised by issue of a *master franchise*.

franchise agreement *Mkting see franchise*

franchise chain *Mkting* a number of retail outlets operating the same *franchise*. A franchise chain may vary in size from a few to many thousands of outlets and in coverage from a small local area to worldwide.

franchise contract *Mkting see franchise*

franchisee *Mkting see franchise*

franchisor *Mkting see franchise*

franked investment income *Fin* the total of dividends received plus their associated tax credit

franked payments *Fin* the total of dividends paid plus their associated tax credit

fraud *Gen Mgt* the use of dishonesty, deception, or false representation in order to gain a material advantage or to injure the interests of others. Types of fraud include false accounting, theft, third party or investment fraud, employee collusion, and computer fraud.

FRB *abbr* (*US*) *Fin* Federal Reserve Board

free agent (*US*) *HR* a worker who operates on a *freelance* or *e-lance* basis, offering skills and expertise to companies anywhere in the world. A free agent works independently and may follow a pattern of *portfolio working*.

freebie *Mkting* a product or service that is given away, often as a business promotion

free cash flow *Fin* cash flow from operations after deducting interest, tax, dividends, and ongoing capital expenditure, but excluding capital expenditure associated with strategic acquisitions and/or disposals

free coinage *Fin* a government's minting of coins from precious metals provided by citizens

free enterprise *Econ* the trade carried on in a free-market economy, where

resources are allocated on the basis of supply and demand

free gold *Fin* gold held by a government but not pledged as a reserve for the government's currency

freelance *Gen Mgt* working on the basis of being self-employed, and possibly working for several employers at the same time, perhaps on a temporary basis. Freelance workers have been described by *Charles Handy* as ideally suited to *portfolio working*.

Freelancers must be good at *multitasking*; they require the skills of a manager, bookkeeper, and a promoter. People thinking about becoming freelance, should conduct plenty of research, not only into the industry in which they will be offering their services, but also into their own motivation for freelancing and their character-suitability. Before leaving their day job, they should put together a business plan plotting the first year's goals and activity, perhaps considering the possibility of starting their freelance business on a part-time basis, so that they can initially rely on their current income.

An important part of this first year will be in marketing and promoting the business. Freelancers should develop a target list of companies they wish to work for, learning all they can about each company before approaching them with marketing and proposals. Good customer service could be the thing to make or break their career. Being liked is as valuable as being prompt and doing a professional job, and will encourage future business. It is, though, inevitable that a set of clients will change as time goes by. To protect themselves against this, freelancers should try to plan six months ahead, and create diversity in their client base.

free market *Econ* a market in which supply and demand are unregulated, except by the country's competition policy, and rights in physical and intellectual property are upheld

freephone *Mkting* a telephone service in which the cost of calls to an organisation is borne by the organisation rather than the caller

freepost *Mkting* a postal service in which the cost of postage to an organisation is borne by the organisation rather than the sender

free stock *Fin* stock on hand or on order which has not been scheduled for use

freeware *E-com* free software programs

free worker *HR* somebody who frequently moves from one job or project to another, transferring skills and ideas. The term free worker was coined by the Industrial Society in the United Kingdom in 2000. Free workers have knowledge or skills that organisations value. They do not subscribe to the idea of a job for life or long-term loyalty to any one organisation but instead work on short-term *personal contracts*. They depend largely on networking to find new assignments. They may be *freelance* or *e-lance* workers and may follow a pattern of *portfolio working*.

freeze-out *Gen Mgt* the exclusion of minority *shareholders* in a company that has been taken over. A freeze-out provision may exist in a *takeover* agreement, which permits the acquiring organisation to buy the non-controlling shares held by small shareholders. A fair price is usually set, and the freeze-out may take place at a specified time, perhaps two to five years after the takeover. A freeze-out can still take place, even if provision for it is not made in a corporate charter, by applying pressure to minority shareholders to sell their shares to the acquiring company.

freight *Ops* goods loaded for onward transport, most often by sea or by air

freight forwarder *Ops* an organisation that collects shipments from a number of businesses and consolidates them into larger shipments for economies of scale. A freight forwarder often also deals with route selection, price negotiation, and documentation of distribution, and can act as a distribution agent for a business. By consolidating loads, a freight forwarder can negotiate cheaper rates of transporta-

tion than the individual businesses and can pre-book space to ensure a more rapid delivery schedule.

frequency analysis *Mkting* a technique for comparing the number of opportunities to reach the same target audience in different media

frequency distribution *Stats* the process of dividing a sample of observations in a statistical study into classes and listing the number of observations in each class

frequency polygon *Stats* a diagrammatic representation showing the values in a *frequency distribution*

frequently asked question *E-com see* FAQ

frictional unemployment *Econ* a situation in which people are temporarily out of the labour market. They could be seeking a new job, incurring search delays as they apply, attending interviews, and relocating.

friction-free market *Gen Mgt* a market in which there is little differentiation between competing products, so that the customer has exceptional choice

fringe benefits *HR* rewards given or offered to employees in addition to their wages or salaries and included in the *contract of employment*. Fringe benefits range from share options, company cars, expense accounts, cheap loans, medical insurance, and other types of *incentive scheme* to discounts on company products, subsidised meals, and membership of social and health clubs. Many of these benefits are liable for tax. A **cafeteria benefits** scheme permits employees to select from a variety of such benefits, although usually some are deemed to be core and not exchangeable for others. Minor benefits, sometimes appropriated rather than given, are known as **perks**.

front end *Gen Mgt* the part of an organisation that deals with customers on a face-to-face basis

front-end loading *Fin* the practice of taking the commission and administrative expenses from the early payments made to an investment or insurance plan. *See also* **back-end loading**

FRSB *abbr* (*ANZ*) *Fin* Financial Reporting Standards Board

FTP *abbr E-com* file transfer protocol: a set of communication rules that allow data or files to be transferred between computers over a network

FTSE index *Fin* established in 1984, the Financial Times–Stock Exchange 100 share index is based on the share prices of the 100 largest public companies in the United Kingdom

fulfilment *Mkting* the process of responding to customer inquiries, orders, or sales promotion offers

fulfilment house *Mkting* an organisation that specialises in responding to inquiries, orders, or sales promotion offers on behalf of a client

full bank *Fin* a local or foreign bank permitted to engage in the full range of domestic and international services

full coupon bond *Fin* a bond whose interest rate is competitive in the current market

full-text index *E-com* an index consisting of every single word of every document catalogued

full-time *HR* standard hours of *attendance* in an organisation, on the basis of a permanent *contract of employment*, for example, 9am–5pm, five days a week

full-time job *HR* a position of paid employment that occupies all somebody's normal working hours

Fully Automated Screen Trading and Electronic Registration (*ANZ*) *Gen Mgt* see *FASTER*

fully connected world *Gen Mgt* a world in which most people and organisations are linked by networks such as the Internet

fully diluted earnings per (common) share *Fin* earnings on a share that take

into account commitments to issue more shares, for example, as a result of convertibles, share options, or warrants

fully distributed issue *Fin* an issue of shares sold entirely to investors rather than held by dealers

functional analysis *Fin* an analysis of the relationships between product functions, their perceived value to the customer, and their cost of provision

functional budget *Fin* a budget of income and/or expenditure applicable to a particular function. A function may refer to a department or a process. Functional budgets frequently include the following: production cost budget (based on a forecast of production and plant utilisation); marketing cost budget; sales budget; personnel budget; purchasing budget; and research and development budget. *Also known as* **departmental budget**

functional relationship *Stats* the relationship between the variables in a study, in which there is no bias or any other distorting factor

fund accounting *Fin* the preparation of financial statements for an entity which is a fund. Such statements are usually on a cash basis and are most commonly found in the public sector.

fundamental analysis *Fin* analysis of external and internal influences on the operations of a company with a view to assisting in investment decisions. Information accessed might include fiscal/monetary policy, financial statements, industry trends, competitor analysis etc. *See also* **technical analysis**

funded debt *Fin* long-term debt or debt that has a maturity date in excess of one year. Funded debt is usually issued in the public markets or in the form of a private placement to qualified institutional investors.

funding risk *Fin* the risk that an entity will encounter difficulty in realising assets or otherwise raising funds to meet commitments associated with financial instruments

fund manager *Fin* somebody who manages the investments of a unit trust or large financial institution

fund of funds (*S Africa*) *Fin* a registered unit trust that invests in a range of underlying unit trusts and in which subscribers own units in the fund of funds, not in the underlying unit trusts

fungible *Fin* interchangeable and indistinguishable for business purposes from other items of the same type

funny money *Fin* an unusual type of financial instrument created by a company

future *Fin* a contract to deliver a commodity at a future date. *Also known as futures contract*

future option *Fin* a contract in which somebody agrees to buy or sell a commodity, currency, or security at an agreed price for delivery in the future. *Also known as futures option*

futures commission merchant *Fin* somebody who acts as a broker for futures contracts. *Abbr* **FCM**

futures contract *Fin see future*

futures exchange *Fin* an exchange on which futures contracts are traded

futures market *Fin* a market for buying and selling securities, commodities, or currencies that tend to fluctuate in price over a period of time. The market's aim is to reduce the risk of uncertainty about future prices.

futures option *Fin see future option*

futures research *Gen Mgt* the identification of possible future *scenarios* with the aim of anticipating and perhaps influencing what the future holds. Futures research is important to the process of *issues management*. It normally identifies several possible scenarios for any particular set of circumstances, and enables an informed decision to be made.

future value *Fin* the value that a sum of money will have in the future, taking into account the effects of inflation, interest rates, or currency values.

EXAMPLE Future value calculations require three figures: the sum in question, the percentage by which it will increase or decrease, and the period of time. In this example, these figures are £1,000, 11%, and two years.

At an interest rate of 11%, the sum of £1,000 will grow to £1,232 in two years:

£1,000 × 1.11 = £1,110 (first year) × 1.11 = £1,232 (second year, rounded to whole pounds)

Note that the interest earned in the first year generates additional interest in the second year, a practice known as compounding. When large sums are in question, the effect of compounding can be significant.

At an inflation rate of 11%, by comparison, the sum of £1,000 will shrink to £812 in two years:

£1,000 / 1.11 = £901 (first year) / 1.11 = £812 (second year, rounded to whole pounds)

In order to avoid errors, it is important to express the percentage as 1.11 and multiply and divide by that figure, instead of using 11%; and to calculate each year, quarter, or month separately. *See also present value*

futurise *Gen Mgt* to ensure that an organisation is taking full advantage of the latest technologies

futuristic planning *Fin* planning for that period which extends beyond the planning horizon in the form of future expected conditions which may exist in respect of the entity, products/services, and environment, but which cannot usefully be expressed in quantified terms. An example would be working out the actions needed in a future with no motor cars.

fuzzword *Gen Mgt* a piece of jargon that is obscure or difficult to understand (*slang*)

FWIW *abbr Gen Mgt* for what it's worth (*slang*)

FYI *abbr Gen Mgt* for your information (*slang*)

G7 *Fin* the group of seven major industrial nations established in 1985 to discuss the world economy, consisting of the United States, Canada, the United Kingdom, France, Germany, Italy, and Japan

G8 *Fin* the group of eight major industrial nations consisting of the *G7* plus Russia

GAB *abbr Fin* General Arrangements to Borrow: a fund financed by the Group of Ten that is used when the IMF's own resources are insufficient, for example, when there is a need for large loans to one or more industrialised countries

GAAP *abbr Fin* Generally Accepted Accounting Principles

gain sharing *HR* a group-based *bonus scheme* to share profits from improvements in production efficiency between employees and the company. There are many variants of gain sharing, the *Rucker* and *Scanlon plans* being the best known.

game theory *Gen Mgt* a mathematical technique used in *operational research* to analyse and predict the outcomes of games of strategy and conflicts of interest. Game theory is used to represent conflicts and problems involved in formulating marketing and organisational strategy, with the aim of identifying and implementing optimal strategies. It involves assessing likely strategies to be adopted by players in a given situation under a particular set of rules. It was initially developed by John Von Neumann, who later developed the theory further with Oskar Morgenstern to apply it to economics.

Gantt, Henry Laurence (1861–1919) *Gen Mgt* US mechanical engineer and consultant. Originated the *Gantt chart*, which was popularised by Wallace Clark in *The Gantt Chart: a Working Tool of Management* (1952).

Gantt chart *Gen Mgt* a graphic tool widely used in *project management* for planning and scheduling work, setting out tasks and the time periods within which they should be completed. The Gantt chart looks like a lateral bar chart and was initially developed by *Henry Gantt* during the 1900s. It is still used both in its traditional form and in the evolved form of programme evaluation and review technique.

gap analysis *Mkting* a marketing technique used to identify gaps in market or product coverage. In gap analysis, consumer information or requirements are tabulated and matched to product categories in order to identify product or service opportunities or gaps in product planning.

garage *Fin* **1.** a UK term meaning to transfer assets or liabilities from one financial centre to another to take advantage of a tax benefit. **2.** the annex to the main floor of the New York Stock Exchange (*slang*)

garbatrage (*US*) *Fin* stocks that rise because of a takeover but are not connected to the target company (*slang*)

garden leave *Gen Mgt* a clause in a *contract of employment* that allows the employer to send an employee home on full pay, but not require him or her to work, during the employee's contractual *notice period*. Garden leave thereby prevents the employee from working in competition with the employer until the notice period has expired, by which time any confidential information the employee holds is likely to have become commercially out of date and links with customers will have been broken. Such a clause may be unenforceable if judged by the courts to be in restraint of trade.

gatekeeper *Gen Mgt* somebody within an organisation who controls the flow of information and therefore influences policy

Gates, Bill (*b.* 1955) *Gen Mgt* US entrepreneur. Founder of the Microsoft™

Corporation, which led the information technology revolution and still dominates the world software market through the Windows™ operating system and the Web browser Internet Explorer. Microsoft has made Gates one of the richest men in the world, although anti-trust proceedings have forced him to step down as CEO. His book *Business@the Speed of Thought* (1999) focuses on the impact of technology on business.

gateway *E-com* a point where two or more computer networks meet and can exchange data

gateway page *E-com* a web page customised to each search engine with specific meta-tags and keywords. These pages are intended to appeal to search engine robots and are not always visible to customers who visit the website.

GATT *Fin* General Agreement on Tariffs and Trade: a treaty signed in Geneva in 1947 that aimed to foster multilateral trade and settle trading disputes between adherent countries. Initially signed by 23 nations, it started to reduce trade tariffs and, as it was accepted by more and more countries, tackled other barriers to trade. It was replaced on 1 January 1995 by the World Trade Organization.

gazelle *Gen Mgt* a fast-growing and volatile new company (*slang*)

gazump *Fin* in the period between agreeing verbally to sell to one buyer but before the agreement becomes legally binding, to accept a higher offer from another buyer. Gazumping is normally associated with the property market, although it can occur in any market where the prices are rising rapidly.

gazunder *Fin* in the period between agreeing verbally to buy at one price but before the agreement is legally binding, to offer a lower price. Gazundering is normally associated with the property market, although it can occur in any market where the prices are falling rapidly.

GBE (*ANZ*) *Gen Mgt see* **Government Business Enterprise**

GDP *abbr Econ* gross domestic product: the total flow of services and goods produced by an economy over a quarter or a year, measured by the aggregate value of services and goods at market prices

GDP per capita *Econ GDP* divided by the country's population so as to achieve a figure per head of population

GEAR *abbr* (*S Africa*) *Fin* Growth, Employment, And Redistribution: the macro-economic reform programme of the South African government, intended to foster economic growth, create employment, and redistribute income and opportunities in favour of the poor

geared investment trust *Fin* an investment trust that borrows money in order to increase its portfolio. When the market is rising, shares in a geared investment trust rise faster than those in an ungeared trust, but they fall faster when the market is falling.

gearing *Fin see* **financial leverage**

gearing ratios *Fin* ratios that indicate the level of risk taken by a company as a result of its capital structure. A number of different ratios may be calculated, for example, debt ratio (total debt divided by total assets), debt-to-equity or leverage ratio (total debt divided by total equity), or interest cover (earnings before interest and tax divided by interest paid). *US term* **leverage ratios**

geisha bond *Fin see* **shogun bond**

Geneen, Harold (1910–97) *Gen Mgt* British-born business executive. CEO of International Telephone and Telegraph (ITT) in the 1960s and 1970s, who turned a moderately successful US company into a massive, international conglomerate. Geneen built a business machine that was almost without parallel in terms of its systematic efficiency. He explained his approach in *Managing* (1985). ITT was broken up following anti-trust proceedings during the 1980s and **taken over** in 1997.

Whatever I am engaged in I must push inordinately. *Andrew Carnegie*

General Agreement on Tariffs and Trade *Fin see* **GATT**

General Arrangements to Borrow *Fin see* **GAB**

General Commissioners *Fin* a body of unpaid individuals appointed by the Lord Chancellor in England, Wales, and Northern Ireland, and the Secretary of State for Scotland in Scotland, to hear appeals on tax matters

general ledger *Fin* a book that lists all of the financial transactions of a company

Generally Accepted Accounting Principles *Fin* a summary of best practice in respect of the form and content of financial statements, the form and content of auditor's reports, and best practice and acceptable alternatives in respect of accounting policies and disclosures adopted for the preparation of financial information. GAAP does not have any statutory or regulatory authority in the United Kingdom, unlike in a number of other countries where the term is in use, such as the United States, Canada, and New Zealand. *Abbr* **GAAP**

general manager *Gen Mgt, HR* a *manager* whose work encompasses all areas of an organisation. A general manager is traditionally non-specialist, has a working knowledge of all aspects of an organisation's activities, and oversees all operating functions. In large companies and the public sector, specialist managers with expert knowledge may control departments, while a general manager provides unifying *leadership* from the top.

Generation X *Gen Mgt, HR* the generation of people born between 1963 and 1981 who entered the workplace from the 1980s onwards, bringing new attitudes to working life that run contrary to traditional corporate expectations. The term was popularised by the writing of Douglas Coupland and also by *Bruce Tulgan* in *Managing Generation X* (1995). Those who belong to Generation X are said to be not solely motivated by money, but they look to a *work-life balance*, favour *flexible working*, embrace the concept of *employability*, and value opportunities for learning, self-advancement, and new challenges. Human resource management practices are increasingly being adapted to accommodate the favoured new ways of working.

generic strategy *Gen Mgt* a strategy for marketing products or services. Generic strategy is a term introduced by *Michael Porter*. He suggested there are three generic strategies for marketing products or services: cost leadership, differentiation, and focus. The first implies supplying products in a more cost-effective way than competitors; the second refers to adding value to products or services; and the third focuses on a specific product market segment with the aim of establishing a *monopoly*.

gensaki *Fin* the Japanese term for a bond sale incorporating a repurchase agreement at a later date

geographical information systems *Mkting* technology used to integrate maps and data to provide multidimensional marketing information. *Abbr* **GIS**

Ghoshal, Sumantra (*b.* 1946) *Gen Mgt* Indian-born academic. Author of work that has shifted its focus from international *strategy* to the importance of people and *creativity*. Ghoshal put forward a new model of transnational enterprise to cope with the complexities of *competition* and the growing global marketplace. He also suggested the **three Ps** of Purpose, Process, and People to replace the old model of Strategy, Structure, and Systems and proposed a new moral contract. He first came to prominence with *Managing Across Borders* (1989), coauthored with *Christopher Bartlett*.

ghost rider *Gen Mgt* somebody who claims to have been in a vehicle that was involved in an accident in order to claim compensation (*slang*)

GIF *Abbr E-com* Graphics Interchange Format: a type of file used to compress and store images for transfer via the Internet. The major advantage of GIF files is that you do not need a *plug-in* to view them, so almost any *browser* can display them. GIF is ideal for small, simple icons and basic images. More complex images, including photographs, can be compressed using *JPEG* files.

gift-leaseback *Fin* the practice of giving somebody a property and then leasing it back, usually for tax advantage or charitable purposes

gift with reservation *Fin* a gift with some benefit retained for the donor, for example, the legal transfer of a dwelling when the donor continues in residence

gig *Gen Mgt* an individual project or assignment, typical of a working pattern made up of a series of one-off projects rather than a career with a single employer

gigabyte *Gen Mgt* a measure of the memory capacity of a computer. One gigabyte equals 1024 megabytes.

Gilbreth, Frank (1868–1924) *Gen Mgt* US consulting engineer. Formed a husband-and-wife team with *Lillian Gilbreth* and pioneered the principles of *motion study*, which embraced *work simplification*, and took a strong interest in *occupational psychology*. Their work, which straddled the *scientific management* and *human relations* schools of management, is recorded in *Writings of the Gilbreths* (1953), edited by William R. Spriegel and Clark E. Myers.

Gilbreth, Lillian (1878–1972) *Gen Mgt* US consulting engineer. *See Gilbreth, Frank*

gilt *Fin see gilt-edged security*

gilt-edged security *Fin* **1.** a security issued by the UK government that pays a fixed rate of interest on a regular basis for a specific period of time until the redemption date when the principal is returned. Their name, for example, Exchequer 10½% 2005 (abbreviated to Ex 10½% '05) or Treasury 11¾% 2003–07 (abbreviated to Tr 11¾% '03–'07) indicates the rate and redemption date. Thought to have originated in the 17th century to help fund the war with France, today they form a large part of the National Debt. *Also known as gilt*. *See also index-linked gilt* **2.** a US term used to describe a security issued by a blue-chip company, which is therefore considered very secure

gilt repos *Fin* the market in agreed sales and repurchase of gilt-edged securities, launched in 1996 by the Bank of England to make gilts more attractive to overseas investors

gilt strip *Fin* a zero-coupon bond created by unbundling the interest payments from a gilt-edged security so that it produces a single cash payment at maturity

gilt unit trust *Fin* in the United Kingdom, a unit trust where the underlying investments are gilt-edged securities

Ginnie Mae *(US) Fin see GNMA*

giro *Fin* **1.** a European term for the transfer of money from one bank account to another. *Also known as bank giro* **2.** a benefit paid by the state *(slang)*

GIS *abbr Mkting* geographical information systems

Glacier studies *Gen Mgt* research experiments conducted at the Glacier Metal Company in London from 1948 to 1965 to investigate the development of group relations, the effects of *change*, and employee roles and responsibilities. The Glacier studies were conducted by the Tavistock Institute of Human Relations with the research being headed by *Elliot Jaques* and *Frederick Emery*. Findings from the initial study came from a methodology called 'working-through', which examined possible social and personal factors at play in any potential dispute. From this arose an early form of *works council* where employees could participate in setting policy for their department. It was also discovered that employees felt the need to have their role and status defined in a way acceptable to both themselves and their colleagues. This research into job roles led Jaques to come up with the notion of the *time span of discretion*, according to which all jobs, no matter how strictly defined, have some level of content that requires judgment and therefore discretion by the jobholder. Jaques then examined this phenomenon in bureaucratic organisations. In defining a *bureaucracy* as a hierarchical system in which employees are accountable to their bosses for the work they do, he took a different stance from *Max Weber*. Much like the *Hawthorne experiments*, the Glacier studies had far-reaching implications for the way organisations were managed. The initial findings were written up by Jaques in *The Changing Culture of a Factory* (1951). In 1965, Jaques published the *Glacier Project Papers* with *Wilfred Brown*, the managing director of Glacier.

glad-hand *Gen Mgt* to shake hands with and greet people at a business party or meeting (*slang*)

glamour stock (*US*) *Fin* a fashionable security with an investment following

glass ceiling *Gen Mgt* the level in an organisation beyond which women are supposedly unable to gain *promotion*. A glass ceiling often exists at *senior management* level and is perceived as an invisible barrier to career progression for women. *Equal opportunities* policies and legislation aim to break such ceilings to make equal career advancement opportunities available to both men and women.

Glass-Steagall Act *Fin* a US law that enforces the separation of the banking and brokerage industries

glaze *Gen Mgt* to doze or sleep with your eyes open during a business meeting (*slang*)

global bank *Fin* a bank that is active in the international markets and that has a presence in several continents

global bond *Fin see* **Eurobond**

global bond issue *Fin* an issue of bonds that incorporates a settlement mechanism allowing for the transfer of titles between markets

global brand *Mkting* the brand name of a product that has worldwide recognition. A global brand has the advantage of economies of scale in terms of production, recognition, and packaging. While the product or brand itself remains the same, the marketing must take into account the local market conditions and the resulting marketing campaign must be tailored accordingly. Care must also be taken to ensure that there is nothing offensive in terms of the name or packaging in the various cultures and languages. A problem with global branding is that if problems are experienced in one country, there could be worldwide repercussions for the brand. *Also known as* **global product**

global co-ordinator *Fin* the lead manager of a global offering who is responsible for overseeing the entire issue and is usually supported by regional and national co-ordinators

global custody *Fin* a financial service, usually only available to institutional investors, that includes the safekeeping of securities certificates issued in markets across the world, the collection of dividends, dealing with tax, valuation of the investments, foreign exchange, and the settlement of transactions

global hedge *Fin see* **macrohedge**

globalisation *Gen Mgt* the creation of international strategies by organisations for overseas expansion and operation on a worldwide level. The process of globalisation has been precipitated by a number of factors including rapid technology developments that make global communications possible, political developments such as the fall of communism, and transport developments that make travelling faster and more frequent. These produce greater development opportunities for companies with the opening up of additional markets, allow greater customer harmonisation as a result of the increase in shared cultural values, and provide a superior competitive position with lower operating costs in other

---

My life has been a series of discoveries, of revelations, and continues to be so.

John Makepeace

countries and access to new raw materials, resources, and investment opportunities.

global marketing *Mkting* a marketing strategy used mainly by multinational companies to sell goods or services internationally. Global marketing requires that there is harmonisation between the marketing policies for different countries and that the *marketing mix* for the different countries can be adapted to the local market conditions. Global marketing is sometimes used to refer to overseas expansion efforts through *licensing, franchises,* and *joint ventures.*

global offering *Fin* the offering of securities in several markets simultaneously, for example, in Europe, the Far East, and North America

global pricing contract *Ops* a contract between a customer and a supplier whereby the supplier agrees to charge the customer the same price for the delivery of parts or services anywhere in the world. As *globalisation* increases, more customers are likely to press their suppliers for global pricing contracts. Through such contracts suppliers can benefit by gaining access to new markets and growing their business, achieving economies of scale, developing strong relationships with customers, and thereby gaining a *competitive advantage* that is difficult for competitors to break. There are risks involved, too, for example, being in the middle of a conflict between a customer's head office and its local business units, or being tied to one customer when there are more attractive customers to serve.

global product *Mkting see* **global brand**

glocalisation *Gen Mgt* the process of tailoring products or services to different local markets around the world. Glocalisation is a combination of globalisation and localisation. Improved communication and advancements in technology have made worldwide markets accessible to even small companies but, rather than being homogenous, the global market is in fact made up of many different localities.

Success in a globalised environment is more likely if products are not globalised or *mass marketed*, but glocalised and customised for individual local communities that have different needs and different cultural approaches.

glue *Gen Mgt* something such as information that unifies organisations, supply chains, and other commercial groups

GmbH *abbr Gen Mgt* Gesellschaft mit beschränkter Haftung: the German term for a private limited company

GNMA *abbr Fin* Government National Mortgage Association: a US-owned corporation that issues mortgage-backed bonds

gnomes of Zurich *Fin* a derogatory term for Swiss bankers and currency dealers (who have a reputation for secrecy), often used when unknown currency speculators cause havoc in the currency markets (*slang*)

GNP *abbr Econ* gross national product: GDP plus domestic residents' income from investment abroad less income earned in the domestic market accruing to foreigners abroad

GNP per capita *Econ* GNP divided by the country's population so as to achieve a figure per head of population

goal *Gen Mgt see* **objective**

goal congruence *Fin* in a control system, the state which leads individuals or groups to take actions which are in their self-interest and also in the best interest of the entity. Goal incongruence exists when the interests of individuals or of groups associated with an entity are not in harmony.

gofer *Gen Mgt* US term **gopher**

go-go fund *Fin* a unit trust that trades heavily and predominantly in high-return, high-risk investments

going concern concept *Fin* the assumption that an entity will continue in operational existence for the foreseeable future. The assumption that a particular

---

Great men can't be ruled. *Ayn Rand*

entity is a going concern can now be operationally tested by statistical models for firms operating in well-defined business areas. *See also* **Z score**

going short *Fin* selling an asset one does not own with the intention of acquiring it at a later date at a lower price for delivery to the purchaser. *See also* **bear**

gold bond *Fin* a bond for which gold is collateral, often issued by mining companies

goldbricker *or* **gold brick** (*US*) *HR* a lazy employee who attempts to get away with doing the least possible amount of work (*slang*)

gold card *Fin* a gold-coloured credit card, generally issued to customers with above average incomes, that may include additional benefits, for example, an overdraft at an advantageous interest rate, and may have an annual fee

gold certificate *Fin* a document that shows ownership of gold

golden goodbye *HR see* **golden handshake**

golden handcuffs *HR* a package of *fringe benefits* designed to tie an employee to an organisation, and prevent another organisation from successfully **headhunting** them. A golden handcuffs payment may be paid out only if an employee remains with an organisation for a specified period of time. (*slang*)

golden handshake *HR* a sum of money given to a senior executive on his or her involuntary departure from an employing organisation as a form of *severance pay*. A golden handshake can be offered when an executive is required to leave before the expiration of his or her contract, for example, because of a *merger* or *corporate restructuring*. It is intended as compensation for loss of office. It can be a very large sum of money, but often it is not related to the perceived performance of the executive concerned. (*slang*) *Also known as* **golden goodbye**

golden hello *HR* a welcome package for a new *employee* that may include a *bonus* and share options. A golden hello is designed as an incentive to attract employees. Some of the contents of the welcome package may be contingent on the performance of the employee.

golden parachute *HR* a clause inserted in the *contract of employment* of a senior employee that details a financial package payable if the employee is dismissed. A golden parachute provides an executive with a measure of financial security and may be payable if the employee leaves the organisation following a *takeover* or *merger*, or is dismissed as a result of poor performance. *Also known as* **golden umbrella**

golden rolodex (*US*) *Gen Mgt* the small group of experts who are most frequently quoted in news stories or asked to appear on television to give an opinion. 'Rolodex' is a trademark for a desktop card index. (*slang*)

golden share *Fin* a controlling shareholding retained by a government in a company that has been privatised after having been in public ownership

golden umbrella *HR see* **golden parachute**

gold fix *Fin* the daily setting of the gold price in London and Zurich

Goldratt, Eliyahu (*b.* 1948) *Gen Mgt* Israeli author and educator. Disseminator of theories, through the medium of novels, on optimising *production* methods and *project management*. Goldratt explained the technique of *optimised production technology* in *The Goal* (1993, co-authored), and his theory later broadened into the *Theory of Constraints*. His third book applies the concept of the theory of constraints to *project management*.

gold reserve *Fin* gold coins or bullion held by a central bank to support a paper currency and provide security for borrowing

---

gold standard *Fin* a system in which a currency unit is defined in terms of its value in gold

Goleman, Daniel (*b.* 1946) *Gen Mgt* US psychologist and journalist. Developer of the concept of *emotional intelligence*, who is credited with making it generally accessible, initially through the book of the same name (1995). He was influenced by *Richard Boyatzis*.

good for the day *Fin* used to describe instructions to a broker that are valid only for the day given

good for this week/month *Fin* used to describe instructions to a broker that are valid only for the duration of the week/month given. *Abbr* **GTW/GTM**

Goods and Services Tax 1. *Fin* a 3% tax payable on all purchase transactions. *Abbr* **GST 2.** *Gen Mgt* a government-imposed consumption tax, currently of 10%, added to the retail cost of goods and services in Australia **3.** *Gen Mgt* a former Canadian tax on goods and services. It was a value-added tax and was replaced by the *harmonised sales tax*. *Abbr* **GST**

goods received note *Fin* a record of goods at the point of receipt

good 'til cancel *Fin* relating to an order to buy or sell a security that is effective until an investor cancels it, up to a maximum of 60 days

good title *Fin* the legally unquestionable title to property. *Also known as* **clear title**

goodwill *Fin* an intangible asset of a company that includes factors such as reputation, contacts, and expertise, for which a buyer of the company may have to pay a premium.

EXAMPLE Goodwill becomes an intangible asset when a company has been acquired by another. It then appears on a balance sheet in the amount by which the price paid by the acquiring company exceeds the net tangible assets of the acquired company. In other words:

   Purchase price – net assets = goodwill

If, for example, an airline is bought for £12 billion and its net assets are valued at £9 billion, £3 billion of the purchase would be allocated to goodwill on the balance sheet.

The treatment of goodwill in accounts is determined by FRS10, 'Goodwill and Intangible Assets', issued by the Accounting Standards Board of the Institute of Chartered Accountants in England and Wales.

gopher *Gen Mgt* an employee who carries out menial duties for a manager or another employee (*slang*)

go plural *Gen Mgt* to engage in a form of *downshifting* by leaving full-time employment in order to undertake *part-time work* or *portfolio working* (*slang*)

go private *Fin* to revert from being a public limited company quoted on a stock exchange to a private company without a stock market listing

go public *Gen Mgt* to float the shares of a *company* on a stock exchange, thereby changing the company status to that of a *public limited company*

go-slow *HR* a protest in which employees demonstrate their dissatisfaction by carrying out their work slowly. A go-slow is a form of *industrial action* designed to inconvenience an employer without the more serious effects of an all-out *strike*.

Government Business Enterprise (*ANZ*) *Gen Mgt* an Australian business that is fully or partly owned by the state. *Abbr* **GBE**

government gazette (*ANZ*) *Gen Mgt* a journal published by the Australian federal government or a state or territory government that reports all actions and decisions made by that body

Government National Mortgage Association (*US*) *Fin see* **GNMA**

government securities/stock *Fin* securities or stock issued by a government, for example, US Treasury bonds or UK gilt-edged securities

---

gradual retirement *HR see* **phased retirement**

graduated payments mortgage (*US*) *Fin* a low start mortgage. *Abbr* **GPM**

granny bond *Fin see* **index-linked savings certificate**

grant of probate *Fin* in the United Kingdom, a document issued by the Probate Court that pronounces the validity of a will and upholds the appointment of the executor(s)

grantor *Fin* a person who sells an option

grapevine *Gen Mgt* an informal communication network within an organisation that conveys information through unofficial channels independent of management control. Information travels much more quickly through the grapevine than through formal channels and may become distorted. A grapevine may reinterpret official corporate messages or spread gossip and rumour in the absence of effective organisation channels. It can, however, also complement official communication, provide feedback, and strengthen social relationships within the organisation.

graph *Gen Mgt* a diagram depicting the relationship between dependent and independent variables through the use of lines, curves, or figures on horizontal and vertical axes. Time is the most common independent variable, showing how the dependent variable has altered over a defined period.

graphical user interface *E-com* an easy-to-use interface or operating system that allows a user to give a computer instructions by using icons, menus, and windows. *Abbr* **GUI**

Graphics Interchange Format *E-com see* **GIF**

graphology *HR* the study of handwriting styles in an attempt to identify personality traits and to predict how somebody may react in particular situations. Graphology is sometimes used as part of the *recruitment* process. Because it cannot be substantiated, it is not recommended as a formal test and tends to be used informally.

grass ceiling *Gen Mgt* the set of social and cultural factors that discourage or prevent women from using golf to conduct business (*slang*)

graveyard market *Fin* **1.** a UK term for a market for shares that are infrequently traded either through lack of interest or because they are of little or no value **2.** a bear market where investors who dispose of their holdings are faced with large losses, as potential investors prefer to stay liquid until the market shows signs of improving

greater fool theory *Fin* the investing strategy that assumes it is wise to buy a stock that is not worth its current price. The assumption is that somebody will buy it from you later for an even greater price.

great man theory *Gen Mgt* the idea that *leaders* possess innately superior qualities that distinguish them from other people, including the ability to capture the imagination and loyalty of the masses

green ban (*ANZ*) *HR* a ban imposed by unions on work that is perceived to pose a threat to the natural environment or an area of historical significance

greenfield site *Gen Mgt* a location for a new development, such as a factory, office, or warehouse, that has not been built on before

greenmail *Fin, Gen Mgt* the purchase of enough of a company's shares to threaten it with takeover, so that the company is forced to buy back the shares at a higher price to avoid the takeover (*slang*)

green marketing *Mkting* marketing that highlights an organisation's environmentally friendly policies or achievements

green pound *Econ* the fixed European Currency Unit (ECU) in which prices of agricultural goods in the European Union are set

---

If you want truly to understand something, try to change it.   *Kurt Lewin (attrib.)*

green shoe or **greenshoe option** *Fin* an option, offered by the company raising the capital, for the issue of further shares to cover a shortfall in the event of over-allocation. It gets its name from the Green Shoe Manufacturing Company which was the first to include the feature in a public offering. (*slang*)

green taxes *Fin* taxes levied to discourage behaviour that will be harmful to the environment

greenwash *Gen Mgt* information produced by an organisation to present an environmentally responsible public image (*slang*)

greybar-land *Gen Mgt* a state of vagueness induced by staring at the grey bar that appears on a computer screen when the computer is processing something (*slang*)

grey knight *Gen Mgt see* **knight**

grey market *Mkting* **1.** a *market* in which goods are sold that have been manufactured abroad and imported. A grey market product is one that has been imported legally, in contrast to one on the *black market*, which is illegal. Such markets arise when there is a supply shortage, usually for exclusive goods, and offer goods for sale at lower prices than the equivalent goods manufactured in the home country. **2.** the market segment occupied by older members of a population **3.** the unofficial trading of securities that have not yet been formally issued

grey marketing *Mkting* marketing aimed at older age groups

grey matter *Gen Mgt* older and more experienced business experts who are hired by young companies to give an impression of seriousness and reliability (*slang*)

grey wave *Fin* used to describe a company that is thought likely to have good prospects in the distant future. It gets its name from the fact that investors are likely to have grey hair before they see their expectations fulfilled (slang).

grievance procedure *HR* a process for settling or redressing employee complaints. A grievance procedure is part of an organisation's *personnel policy* and sets out how an employee with a work-related grievance can bring up the issue and how it may be addressed and resolved. Such a procedure should focus on settling the matter as soon as possible, so as to promote employee satisfaction and prevent the issue escalating into a *dispute*.

gross *Fin* total, before consideration of taxes

gross domestic fixed capital formation *Econ* investment in the fixed asset in an economy, including depreciation

gross domestic product *Econ see* **GDP**

gross interest *Fin* interest earned on a deposit or security before the deduction of tax. *See also* **net interest**

gross lease *Fin* a lease that does not require the lessee to pay for things the owner usually pays for. *See also* **net lease**

gross margin *Fin* **1.** the differential between the interest rate paid by a borrower and the cost of the funds to the lender **2.** the differential between the manufacturing cost of a unit of output and the price at which it is sold

gross misconduct *HR* behaviour in the workplace that may lead to a warning or to dismissal in extreme cases. Most contracts of employment provide guidelines on the type of behaviour that constitutes gross misconduct.

gross national product *Econ see* **GNP**

gross negligence *Gen Mgt see* **negligence**

gross profit *Gen Mgt* sales revenue less the cost of goods sold. *See also* **net profit**

gross profit margin *Gen Mgt see* **profit margin**

gross profit percentage *Fin* a ratio used to gain an insight into the relationship between production/purchasing costs and sales revenues. It is calculated as follows:

**(Sales – cost of sales) × 100 /
Sales for the period**

gross receipts *Fin* the total revenue received by a business

gross redemption yield *Fin see* **gross yield to redemption**

gross yield *Fin* the share of income return derived from securities before the deduction of tax

gross yield to redemption *Fin* the total return to an investor if a fixed interest security is held to maturity, in other words, the aggregate of gross interest received and the capital gain or loss at redemption, annualised. *Also known as* **gross redemption yield**. *US term* **yield to maturity**

group *Fin* a parent company and all its subsidiaries

group capacity assessment *Gen Mgt* the application of **work measurement** techniques such as **activity sampling** and **standard time** data to clerical, administrative, and indirect staff to measure group effort and establish optimum performance levels. Group capacity assessment is used to plan and control payroll costs for groups of clerical and administrative workers.

group certificate *(ANZ) HR* a document provided by an employer that records an employee's income, income tax payments, and superannuation contributions during the previous financial year

group discussion *Mkting* a research technique in which groups of people discuss attitudes to a product or organisation

group dynamics *HR* the interaction and interpersonal relationships between members of a group and the ways in which groups form, function, and dissolve. Group dynamics is an important aspect of successful **teamwork** and is a factor influencing the outcome of any form of group activity, including **training** courses. Issues of power, influence, and interpersonal conflict all affect dynamics

and group performance. One means of helping people to create positive group dynamics is **sensitivity training**.

group incentive scheme *HR* a reward system giving **bonuses** to workers in a team. A group incentive scheme is designed to promote effective **teamwork**, as the bonus is dependent on the performance and output of the team as a whole.

group interview *HR see* **group selection**

group investment *Fin* an investment made by more than one person

group life assurance *Fin* a life assurance policy that covers a number of people, for example, members of an association or club, or a group of employees at a company

Group of Seven *Fin* the seven leading industrial nations: Canada, France, Germany, Italy, Japan, the United States, and the United Kingdom

Group of Ten *Fin* the group of ten countries who contribute to the General Arrangements to Borrow fund: Belgium, Canada, France, Germany, Italy, Japan, the Netherlands, Sweden, the United States, and the United Kingdom. Switzerland joined in 1984. *Also known as* **Paris Club**. *See also* **GAB**

group selection *HR* a method of **recruitment** in which candidates are assessed in groups rather than individually. Group selection can take place in an **assessment centre**. It should not be confused with a **panel interview**, which involves one candidate but several interviewers. *Also known as* **group interview**

group technology *Ops* the practice of gathering operations and resources for the manufacture of specific components or products into groups or cells with the aim of simplifying manufacturing operations. Group technology is an attempt to take advantage of the benefits of both **batch production** and **flow production**. Similar tasks or products are identified and are grouped into families. This requires a robust coding or classification scheme. The manufacturing resources, including workers, for each family are then grouped together into cells. The sense of ownership encouraged by such organisation has resulted in benefits including improved quality, *productivity*, and *motivation* of employees, as well as reductions in work in progress, inventory, and materials movement. *Also known as cellular manufacturing, cellular production*

groupthink *Gen Mgt* a phenomenon that occurs during *decision-making* or *problem-solving* when a team's desire to reach an agreement overrides its ability to appraise the problem properly. It is similar to the *Abilene paradox* in that it is based on people's desire to conform and please others.

group tool *Gen Mgt* an electronic tool such as videoconferencing, networking, or electronic mail that allows people in different locations to collaborate on a project

groupware *Gen Mgt* software that enables a group whose members are based in different locations to work together and share information. Groupware enables collective working by providing communal diaries, address books, work planners, bulletin boards, newsletters, and so on, in electronic format on a closed network. This network may take the form of an *intranet*. Groupware can be used to facilitate collaborative *project management* or to co-ordinate any kind of work involving input from more than one person, and is particularly useful to those working in a *virtual team*.

Grove, Andrew (*b.* 1936) *Gen Mgt* US business executive. Chairman of Intel Corporation, which became the world's largest semiconductor manufacturer. He coined the term *strategic inflection point*, which he discusses in *Only the Paranoid Survive* (1996).

Growth, Employment, And Redistribution *Fin see GEAR*

growth and income fund *Fin* a unit trust that tries to maximise growth of capital while paying significant dividends

growth capital *Fin* funding that allows a company to accelerate its growth. For new start-up companies, growth capital is the second stage of funding after *seed capital*.

growth company *Econ* a company whose contribution to the economy is growing because it is increasing its workforce or earning increased foreign exchange for its exported goods

growth curve *Stats* a line plotted on a graph that shows statistically an increase over a period of time

growth equity *Fin* an equity that is thought to have good investment prospects

growth fund *Fin* a unit trust that tries to maximise growth of capital without regard to dividends

growth industry *Fin* an industry that has the potential to expand at a faster rate than other industries

growth rate *Econ* the rate of an economy's growth as measured by its technical progress, the growth of its labour, and the increase in its *capital stock*

growth share 1. *Fin* a share that offers investors the prospect of longer-term earnings, rather than a quick return **2.** *Gen Mgt* a share that has been rising greatly in value, relative to its industry or to the market as a whole

growth stock *Fin* stock that offers investors the prospect of longer-term earnings, rather than a quick return

grupo *Gen Mgt* a group of companies in Mexico, based on a parent company or central family. Grupos may be involved in a cross-section of industries, much like a *conglomerate company*. Some grupos are integrated financially, legally, and administratively, while others have a looser structure with stockholding interests and interrelated directorates.

GST *abbr Fin* Goods and Services Tax

Wages are the measure of dignity that society puts on a job. Johnnie Tillmon

guan xi *Gen Mgt* a Mandarin term for 'connections', used to describe the level of personal trust required between business partners

guarantee *Fin* a promise made by a third party, or guarantor, that he or she will be liable if one of the parties to a contract fails to fulfil their contractual obligations. A guarantee may be acceptable to a bank as security for borrowing provided the guarantor has sufficient financial means to cover his or her potential liability.

guaranteed bond *Fin* in the United States, a bond on which the principal and interest are guaranteed by a company other than the one who issues them, or a stock in which the dividends are similarly guaranteed. *See also* **guaranteed stocks**

guaranteed employment *HR* an arrangement to protect employees in the event of a shortage of work. Guaranteed employment requires the payment of a minimum wage for a maximum number of workless days or hours. In some cases, a worker may qualify for a legal right to a guaranteed payment. An employer cannot lay off workers without a term in the individual *contract of employment*. The right to do so usually lies in a *collective agreement* incorporated into the contract of employment. *Also known as* **guaranteed wage**, **guaranteed week**

guaranteed fund *Fin* a fixed term investment where a third party promises to repay the investors' principal in full should the investment fall below the initial sum invested

guaranteed income bond *Fin* a bond issued by a UK life assurance company designed to provide an investor with a fixed rate of income for a specified period of time. Changes to the regulations now only permit those policies with an independent third party guarantee to receive this denomination.

guaranteed investment certificate *Fin* an investment instrument issued by an insurance company that guarantees interest but not the principal originally invested

guaranteed stocks *Fin* in the United Kingdom, bonds issued by nationalised industries that incorporate an explicit guarantee from the government. *See also* **guaranteed bond**

guaranteed wage *HR see* **guaranteed employment**

guaranteed week *HR see* **guaranteed employment**

guarantor *Fin* a person or organisation that guarantees repayment of a loan if the borrower defaults or is unable to pay

guard book *Mkting* a book or folder for storing copies of published advertisements

guerilla marketing *Mkting* a marketing technique, the aim of which is to damage the market share of competitors

GUI *abbr Gen Mgt* graphical user interface

Gulick, Luther (1892–1993) *Gen Mgt* US academic. Member of President Roosevelt's Committee on Administrative Management (1936–38), who, following the earlier work of *Henri Fayol*, coined the acronym *POSDCORB* to describe the functions of management.

gun jumping (*US*) *Fin* insider trading

GW *abbr E-com* payment gateway

gweeping *Gen Mgt* the activity of spending many hours at a time surfing the Internet (*slang*)

hacker *E-com* somebody who gains unauthorised access to computer systems, usually to corrupt or steal stored data

haggle *Fin* to negotiate a price with a buyer or seller by the gradual raising of offers and lowering of asking prices until a mutually agreeable price is reached

half-normal plot *Stats* a plot of statistical data used to check for the presence of *outliers* in the data

Hamel, Gary (*b*. 1954) *Gen Mgt* US academic. With **C.K. Prahalad**, introduced the concept of *core competences* and argued for an innovative approach to *corporate-strategy* creation, based on emotion as well as analysis. They co-authored *Competing for the Future* (1994), which set out their revolutionary but well-respected view of strategy.

Hamel believes that too many managers operate essentially on a hand-to-mouth basis, not devoting sufficient time to thinking about and planning for the future. He argues that developing strategy ('strategising' in his terminology) should be an ongoing, radical, and inclusive process that habitually challenges existing assumptions, involves as many people as possible, and looks for its inspiration as often outside the organisation as within it.

Hammer, Michael (*b*. 1948) *Gen Mgt* US academic and consultant. Advocate of re-engineering, a concept he explained in the book *Reengineering the Corporation* (1993), co-authored with *James Champy*.

hammering the market *Fin* used to describe a situation where there is intense selling (*slang*)

Hampel, Sir Ronald Claus (*b*. 1932) *Gen Mgt* British business executive. Former chairman of ICI and chairman of the Committee on *Corporate Governance* (1995–98).

hand-hold *HR* to reassure a nervous client or colleague (*slang*)

hand off (*US*) (*Canada*) *Gen Mgt* to transfer responsibility for a project

hand signals *Fin* the signs used by traders on the trading floors at exchanges for futures and options to overcome the problem of noise

hands-off *Gen Mgt* without continuing management attention

hands-on *Gen Mgt* favouring first-hand personal involvement in a task

Handy, Charles (*b*. 1932) *Gen Mgt* Irish-born academic, writer, and social commentator. Known for his work on *organisation structures*, the future of work, and the implications of change for people. Since his landmark book *Understanding Organizations* (1976), he has originated concepts such as the *shamrock organisation*, the *federal organisation*, the *doughnut principle*, and *portfolio working*.

After graduating from Oxford, Handy worked for Shell until 1972, when he left to teach at the London Business School. He also spent time at MIT where he came into contact with many of the leading lights in the human relations school of thinking, including *Ed Schein*.

hang-out loan *Fin* the amount of a loan that is still outstanding after the termination of the loan

Hang Seng index *Fin* an index of the prices of selected shares on the Hong Kong Stock Exchange

happy camper *Gen Mgt* somebody who has no grievances against his or her employer (*slang*)

hara-kiri swap *Fin* an interest rate swap made without a profit margin

hard commodities *Fin* metals and other solid raw materials. *See also commodity, soft commodities*

hard currency *Econ* a currency that is traded in a foreign exchange market and for which demand is persistently high in comparison to its supply. *See also* **soft currency**

hard disk *E-com* a thin rigid magnetised disk inside a computer, used for storing data and programs

hard landing *Econ* a sustained period of growth that ends with the economy moving rapidly into recession and business stagnation

hard sell *Mkting* a heavily persuasive and highly pressured approach used to sell a product or service. In a hard sell situation, salespeople may use incentives such as a limited special offer or a discount to encourage people to buy, or to sign an agreement to buy on the spot.

hard systems *Gen Mgt see* **systems method**

hardware *E-com* the physical components of a computer system such as the processor, keyboard, and monitor. **Software** is the name given to operating systems and applications.

harmonisation *Gen Mgt* **1.** the resolution of inequalities in the **pay** and **conditions of employment** between different categories of workers **2.** the alignment of the systems of pay and benefits of two companies on **merger**, acquisition, or takeover **3.** the convergence of social regulation in the European Union

harmonised sales tax *Fin* a Canadian tax on goods and services. It is a value-added tax that replaced the Goods and Services Tax. *Abbr* **HST**

Harrigan, Kathryn Mary Rudie (*b.* 1951) *Gen Mgt* US academic. Known for her work on mature and declining industries, and on **strategic alliances**.

harvesting strategy *Fin* a reduction in or cessation of marketing for a product prior to it being withdrawn from sale resulting in an increase in profits on the back of previous marketing and advertising campaigns

Harvey-Jones, Sir John (*b.* 1924) *Gen Mgt* British business executive. Chairman of ICI (1982–87), who recorded his reflections on leadership in *Making It Happen* (1987). After his retirement, he advised ailing British companies in a television series, 'Troubleshooter'.

hate site *Gen Mgt see* **anti-site**

Hawthorne effect *Gen Mgt see* **Hawthorne experiments**

Hawthorne experiments *Gen Mgt* a series of studies undertaken at the Hawthorne plant of Western Electric in the United States from which **Elton Mayo** concluded that an approach emphasising **employee participation** can improve **productivity**. The Hawthorne experiments began in 1924 as a study conducted by the National Research Council into the relationship between workplace lighting and employee efficiency, and was then extended to include **wage incentives** and **rest periods**. It was found that whatever variations were applied upwards or downwards, output rose, and this was termed the **Hawthorne effect**. The increased productivity was attributed to several causes, including small group size, earnings, the novelty of being part of an experiment, and the increased attention given to the employees being studied. The style of the supervisor, which was relaxed and friendly, in contrast to the then standard practice, was found to be particularly important. In a second group of employees, however, it was observed that, as the experiments progressed, output was restricted, and that whatever the incentive, the group showed a resistance to it. In 1929 and 1930, Elton Mayo visited Hawthorne. He linked supervisory style and levels of morale with productivity. High productivity resulted from an engaged supervisory style that encouraged participation. Low productivity resulted when a supervisor remained remote and retained a traditional supervisory role. The Hawthorne experiments established the importance of management style and interpersonal skills to organisational success.

You must somehow steer between the Scylla of humility and the Charybdis of foolhardiness.
    Stan Rapp

Hayes, Robert (*b*. 1936) *Gen Mgt* US academic. Harvard professor who came to prominence following the publication in 1981 of his co-authored *Harvard Business Review* article, 'Managing Our Way to Economic Decline'. Hayes argued that US manufacturing companies were at a competitive disadvantage as a result of a too heavy reliance on detached, precisely structured analysis. A more positive future was foreseen by Hayes in the co-written *Restoring Our Competitive Edge* (1984), which examines the structural changes required of manufacturing in order to succeed and provides some guidance on how management practices need to change.

hazardous substance *Gen Mgt* a substance that creates a potential danger to people in the workplace. Employers have a duty to assess the risks from hazardous substances to personnel and customers, and to ensure that no one is endangered. Substances classed as hazards could be raw materials used in production, fumes, or other byproducts resulting from workplace activities. They may also be substances linked to seemingly innocuous activities, for example, cleaning fluids and toner for photocopiers. *Health and safety* policies must cover this area, and *risk assessments* must be carried out to ascertain the potential dangers.

head and shoulders *Fin* used to describe a graph plotting a company's share price that resembles the silhouette of a person's head and shoulders. Chartists see this as an early indication of a market fall.

headcount *HR* the total number of *employees* in an organisation

headhunting *HR* the practice of approaching people already working for one company with an offer of a job at another. Headhunting is usually carried out by a recruiter—either an employee within a company or an employment agency—who keeps an eye on the performance of targeted personnel. The recruiter then matches high-performing

personnel with job vacancies, contacting individuals directly, without the knowledge of the employer, with a job offer. Headhunters most often perform *executive searches*, but they may also work at lower levels with the intention of picking out those with management potential. Headhunting is often seen as poaching, and it can create employee-retention problems, since a company's best staff can be tempted to leave by better job offers.

headline rate of inflation *Econ* a measure of inflation that takes account of home owners' mortgage costs

heads of agreement *Gen Mgt* the most important elements of a commercial agreement

health and safety *Gen Mgt, HR* the area of policy and legislation covering employee well-being. Health and safety within an organisation is often co-ordinated by a particular person, but it is the responsibility of all employees. Maintaining a safe working environment and safe working practices and ensuring that employees' health is not detrimentally affected by their work is a statutory duty of organisations. In the United Kingdom, it is co-ordinated by the Health and Safety Executive.

health screening *HR* the checking of employees' health to ensure they are fit for work. Health screening can take the form of **pre-employment screening**, which takes place after a new employee has been appointed, but before employment commences. It also is a feature of *occupational health* schemes and involves the monitoring of employee health at work. This is particularly important if the work involves hazardous substances or strenuous physical conditions. Health screening can also be used, for example, to detect substance abuse or to carry out eyesight tests for users of VDUs.

heatseeker *E-com* somebody who always buys the latest version of a software product as soon as it comes on the market (*slang*)

Transformational change requires enormous energy.   *Robert H. Miles*

heavy hitter *Gen Mgt* an executive or company that performs extremely well (*slang*)

heavy site *E-com see* **sticky site** (*slang*)

hedge *Fin* a transaction to reduce or eliminate an exposure to risk

hedge fund *Fin* a unit trust that takes considerable risks, including heavy investment in unconventional instruments, in the hope of generating great profits

hedging against inflation *Fin* investing in order to avoid the impact of inflation, thus protecting the purchasing power of capital. Historically, equities have generally outperformed returns from savings accounts in the long term and beaten the Retail Price Index. They are thus considered as one of the best hedges against inflation, although it is important to bear in mind that no stock market investment is without risk.

held order *Fin* an order that a dealer does not process immediately, often because of its great size

Helgeson, Sally (*b.* 1948) *Gen Mgt* US consultant and author. Researcher on the effects of changing technology, demographics, and the knowledge economy on organisations and **leadership**. Her book *The Female Advantage* (1990) considers women's **management styles**.

helicopter view *Gen Mgt* an overview of a problem (*slang*)

helpline *Mkting* a telephone service operated by a company that offers customers product information, advice, or technical support

Henderson, Bruce (1915–92) *Gen Mgt* Australian engineer and consultant. Founder of the Boston Consulting Group (1963), a firm that has specialised in **corporate strategy** and conceived the **experience curve** and the **Boston Box**.

herding cats *Gen Mgt* a very difficult, or impossible, activity. The phrase is taken from the title of Warren Bennis's book, *Managing People is Like Herding Cats.* (*slang*)

Herzberg, Frederick (*b.* 1923) *Gen Mgt* US psychologist and academic. Took a particular interest in **motivation** and put forward the 'hygiene-motivation theory' of **job satisfaction**. Herzberg was a co-author of *The Motivation to Work* (1959) and the author of 'One More Time: How Do You Motivate Employees?' (1968), one of the most requested reprints of all time from *Harvard Business Review*. Through his work for the US Public Health Service, Herzberg became an influential figure in the human relations school of the 1950s.

heuristics *Gen Mgt* a method for **problem-solving** or **decision-making** that arrives at solutions through exploratory means such as experimentation, trial and error, or evaluation

HHOK *abbr Gen Mgt* ha ha only kidding (*slang*)

hidden tax *Fin* a tax that is not immediately apparent. For example, while a consumer may be aware of a tax on retail purchases, a tax imposed at the wholesale level, which consequently increases the cost of items to the retailer, will not be apparent.

hierarchy of activities *Fin* classification of activities according to the level within the organisation to which they relate, for example, product level activities, batch level activities, product sustaining activities, or facility sustaining activities

high concept *Gen Mgt* a compelling idea expressed clearly and economically

highdome (*US*) *Gen Mgt* a scientist. This term stems from the stereotype of scientists, who are often depicted as having high foreheads that are supposed to be a sign of intelligence. (*slang*)

high-end *Gen Mgt* relating to the most expensive, most advanced, or most powerful in a range of things, for example, computers

higher-rate tax *Fin* in the United Kingdom, the highest of the three bands of

---

income tax. Most countries have bands of income tax with different rates applicable to income within each band.

high-flier *or* **high-flyer** *Fin* a heavily traded stock that increases in value quickly over a short period

high/low method *Fin* a method of estimating cost behaviour by comparing the total costs associated with two different levels of output. The difference in costs is assumed to be caused by variable costs increasing, allowing the unit variable cost to be calculated. From this, since total cost is known, the fixed cost can be derived.

high-premium convertible debenture *Fin* a convertible bond sold at a high premium that offers a competitive rate of interest and has a long term

high-pressure *Mkting* a selling technique in which the sales representative attempts to persuade a buyer very forcefully and persistently

high-risk company *Gen Mgt* a company that is exposed to high levels of business risk

high street *Gen Mgt* a main street considered as an important retail area

high yielder *Fin* a security that has a higher than average yield and is consequently often a higher risk investment

hip shooter *Gen Mgt* an executive who follows his or her immediate instinct when responding to a question or problem rather than considering it rationally (*slang*)

hired gun (*slang*) **1.** *Gen Mgt* an adviser, lawyer, or accountant brought into a company during a takeover battle **2.**(*US*) *HR* somebody who works for whoever will contract for his or her services for as long as he or she is needed for a particular project

hire purchase *Fin* a method of paying for a product or service in which the buyer pays by a series of instalments over a period of time. *US term* **instalment plan**. *Abbr* **HP**

historical cost *Fin* the original acquisition cost of an asset, unadjusted for subsequent price level or value changes

historical cost accounting *Fin* a system of accounting in which all values are based on the historical costs incurred. This is the basis prescribed in the Companies Act for published accounts.

historical pricing *Fin* basing current prices on prior period prices, perhaps uplifted by a factor such as inflation

historical summary *Fin* in the United Kingdom, an optional synopsis of a company's results over a period of time, often five or ten years, featured in the annual accounts

historic pricing *Fin* the establishment of the price of a share in a unit trust on the basis of the most recent values of its holdings

hit *E-com* a measure of the number of files or images that are sent to a browser from a website in response to a single request.

The measure is one of the most abused statistics on the Internet, as hits do not provide an accurate picture of website visitor activity. Every web page is made up of a number of components—graphics, text, programming elements—and many have anything from 10 to 20 components. Each component is counted as a hit. Therefore, the total number of hits is generally very high and bears little or no relation to the number of people visiting.

hit squad *Gen Mgt* a company's acquisitions team (*slang*)

hockey stick *Fin* a performance curve typical of businesses in their early stages that descends then rises sharply in a straight line, creating a shape similar to that of a hockey stick (*slang*)

Hofstede, Geert (*b.* 1928) *Gen Mgt* Dutch academic and business executive. Identified four work-related dimensions of national culture, thus providing a framework for understanding cultural differences within business. His work, first

---

Don't worry about people stealing an idea. If it's original, you will have to ram it down their throats.
Howard Aiken

published in *Culture's Consequences* (1980), has been extended by *Fons Trompenaars*.

After spending time working in factories as a foreman and plant manager, Hofstede became chief psychologist on the international staff of IBM, and then joined IMEDE, the Swiss business school, in 1971. He has also worked at the European Institute for Advanced Studies in Management in Brussels and at the University of Limburg in Maastricht, where he is now emeritus professor of organisational anthropology and international management.

holdback *E-com* funds from a merchant's credit card transactions held in reserve for a predetermined time by the merchant account provider to cover possible disputed charges. *Also known as* **reserve account**

holder *Fin* the person who is in possession of a bill of exchange or promissory note

holding company *Gen Mgt* a parent organisation that owns and controls other companies. In the United Kingdom, a holding company has to own over half of the nominal share capital in companies that are deemed to be its subsidiaries. A holding company may have no other business than the holding of shares of other companies.

holding cost *Fin* the cost of retaining an asset, generally stock. Holding cost includes the cost of financing the asset in addition to the cost of physical storage.

holiday *HR* a day of work on which an employee is not required to be at work but is paid by the employer. The number of days of holiday is agreed in the *contract of employment* and may be dependent on the employee's length of service. *US term* **vacation**

home loan *Fin* a mortgage

homepage *E-com* the first and/or main page on a website

home run 1. *Fin, Gen Mgt* a very great achievement **2.** *Fin, Gen Mgt* an investment that produces a high rate of return in a short time **3.** *Gen Mgt* the journey home at the end of the working day (*slang*)

home shopping *Mkting* the ordering of goods from home by telephone, Internet, mail order, or direct-response television

homeworker *HR* somebody who carries out paid work in his or her home for one or more businesses, but who is not *self-employed*. The method of working can be a permanent or occasional arrangement, or may involve a split of work between an employer's premises and home. *See also* **teleworker**

homogenisation *Gen Mgt* the removal of characteristic differences between separate markets and cultures. Globalisation is frequently blamed for homogenisation.

Honey, Peter *Gen Mgt* British psychologist and consultant. With *Alan Mumford*, he identified four types of *learning style* and devised an instrument to determine somebody's predominant style in their book, *The Manual of Learning Styles* (1982).

honorarium *HR* a token sum given in recognition of the recipient's performance of specific, non-onerous duties. An honorarium may take the form of an annual retainer.

HOPEFUL *abbr Gen Mgt* Hard-up Older Person Expecting Full Useful Life (*slang*)

HOQ *abbr Ops* house of quality

horizontal diversification *Gen Mgt see* **diversification**

horizontal fast track *Gen Mgt* a variation of *fast track* developed by *Charles Handy* in which talented people are moved around from task to task to test and develop their capability in different working situations

horizontal integration *Gen Mgt* the merging of functions or organisations that operate on a similar level. Horizontal integration involves the union of

Most people sell their souls and live with a good conscience on the proceeds.
Logan Pearsall Smith

companies producing the same kinds of goods or operating at the same stage of the *supply chain*. It may also describe the merging of departments within an organisation that carry out similar tasks. *See also vertical integration*

horizontal keiretsu *Gen Mgt see keiretsu*

horizontal merger *Gen Mgt see merger*

horizontal organisation *Gen Mgt see flat organisation*

horizontal spread *Fin* a purchase of two options that are identical except for their dates of maturity

horse-trading *Fin* hard bargaining that results in one party giving the other a concession

hostile bid *Fin* a takeover bid that is opposed by the target company. *See also greenmail, knight*

hostile takeover *Gen Mgt see takeover*

hosting *E-com* the process of putting a website on the Internet so that people can visit it.

There are two basic options: internal or external hosting. Internal hosting is often the option when dealing with an intranet, because most of the access to the intranet will be from within the organisation. For most public websites, it makes sense to use a third-party hosting company. Such companies have mastered the complexities of website hosting and can offer excellent service. Issues that need to be considered when deciding whether to outsource include: whether you need a *domain name*; how many visitors you expect each month; how much space and what access speeds are needed; whether you require *e-commerce* or special programming facilities; whether you need to deal with *e-mail*; what support is offered, and price and payment options. *See also hosting options*

hosting options *E-com* the different kinds of *hosting*, usually offered by third-party hosting companies. There are several options: *non-virtual hosting*, *virtual*

hosting, *collocation hosting*, and *managed hosting*.

hot button *Mkting* a sales or marketing offer that particularly appeals to a buyer (*slang*)

hot card *Fin* a credit card that has been stolen

hot-desking *Gen Mgt* a flexible working practice enabling employees to occupy any vacant workspace instead of sitting at a permanent personalised desk. Organisations using a hot-desking system may have a set of standardised workspaces equipped with *information and communications technologies*, and employees may sit at a different desk each day. Alternatively, the majority of employees may have their own desks, but some employees, such as consultants or part-time workers, may sit at any desk that happens to be free that day. Most conventional offices are only full for a fraction of the time they are open because of sickness, holidays, or *teleworking* and this results in empty desks and wasted resources. Hot-desking enables expensive office space to be fully utilised and forms part of the concept of the *virtual office*. Although employees practising hot-desking may have limited storage space in the form of a filing cabinet or locker, most of their work and information will be stored electronically.

hotelling *Gen Mgt* the practice of occupying a desk or workspace in another employer's premises. Hotelling is normally carried out by employees such as consultants or sales people, who spend more time with customers than at their employers' offices and rely on their clients to provide desk space. Hotelling has developed through improved *information and communications technologies* and is an extension of the *virtual office*.

hot file *Fin* a list of stolen credit cards

hot issue *Fin* a new security that is expected to trade at a significant premium to its issue price. *See also hot stock*

hot money *Fin* **1.** money that has been obtained by dishonest means. *See also*

Everyone likes innovation until it affects himself, and then it's bad. Walter Wriston

***money laundering* 2.** money that is moved at short notice from one financial centre to another to secure the best possible return

hot stock *Fin* a share, usually a new issue, that rises quickly on the stock market. *See also **hot issue***

hours of work **1.** *Gen Mgt* the actual hours worked by an employee, often well in excess of those stated in the ***contract of employment*** and sometimes without the payment of ***overtime*** **2.** *HR* the hours agreed between an employer and employee for which the employee is paid

house journal *Gen Mgt see **newsletter***

house of quality *Ops* a ***decision-making*** and planning tool that brings customers and engineers together in the product design process. House of quality is one of the four houses or phases of ***quality function deployment***. House of quality provides a structure for the design and development cycle. The name is derived from the use of matrices that explore the relationship between customer needs and design attributes. The matrices used in the analysis fit together to form a house-like structure. *Abbr* **HOQ**. *Also known as **quality table***

HP *abbr Fin* hire purchase

HR *abbr HR* human resources

HREOC *abbr (ANZ) HR* Human Rights and Equal Opportunities Commission

HRIS *abbr HR* human resource information system

HRM *HR* **human resource management**, a model of ***personnel management*** that focuses on the individual rather than taking a collective approach. Responsibility for human resource management is often devolved to ***line management***. It is characterised by an emphasis on strategic integration, ***employee commitment***, workforce flexibility, and quality of goods and services.

HR service centre *HR* a ***centralised*** office that handles routine administration

and answers enquiries from managers and staff throughout an organisation on ***human resources*-related** matters

HST *abbr Fin* harmonised sales tax

HTH *abbr Gen Mgt* hope this helps (*slang*)

HTML *abbr E-com* hypertext markup language: a computer code used to build and develop web pages. It is used to format the text of a document and indicate ***hyperlinks*** to other web pages and describes the layout of the web page.

HTTP *abbr E-com* hypertext transport (or transfer) protocol: the communications mechanism used to exchange information on the Internet

hub and spoke *Gen Mgt* any arrangement of component parts resembling a wheel, with a central hub and a series of spokes radiating outwards. The metaphor of the hub and spoke arrangement can be applied to any area. Examples include ***organisation structure***, computer network design, work processes, service delivery methods, and transport systems.

humanagement *Gen Mgt* a style of management that emphasises the ***empowerment*** of people

human asset accounting *HR see **human capital accounting***

human capital *HR* the ***employees*** of an organisation. The term builds on the concept of capital as an asset of an organisation, implying recognition of the importance and monetary worth of the skills and experience of its employees. It is measured through ***human capital accounting***.

human capital accounting *HR* an attempt to place a financial figure on the knowledge and skills of an organisation's ***employees*** or ***human capital***. *Also known as **human asset accounting**, **human resource accounting***

human factors engineering *Gen Mgt* the analysis of human needs and abilities in the design of workplace activities, facilities, and systems in order to optimise employee performance. Human factors engineering uses **ergonomics** in the design of the workplace and aims to offer a better choice of computer software by striving to obtain a fit between human operators and the equipment or technology that they are using. In this way, human factors engineering tries to reduce risk by raising safety levels, and to produce cost savings by improving performance.

human relations *HR* an interdisciplinary study of social relations in the workplace that embraces sociology, social anthropology, and social psychology. The human relations movement presents a counterpoint to the scientific management view that focuses on maximising the productivity and income of individual manual workers and on the separation of mental and physical work between management and workers. In contrast, supporters of the human relations movement believe that workers want to feel part of a team with socially supportive relationships and to grow and develop. *Motivation*, communication, *employee participation*, and *leadership* are significant issues.

human resource accounting *HR see human capital accounting*

human resource information system *HR* a data *MIS*, usually computerised, that facilitates strategic and operational *decision-making* for human resource management (see *HRM*). *Abbr* **HRIS**

human resource management *HR see HRM*

human resource planning *HR* the development of strategies for matching the size and skills of the workforce to organisational needs. Human resource planning assists organisations to recruit, retain, and optimise the deployment of the personnel needed to meet business objectives and to respond to changes in the external environment. The process involves carrying out a *skills analysis* of the existing workforce, carrying out *manpower forecasting*, and taking action to ensure that supply meets demand. This

may include the development of training and retraining strategies. *Also known as manpower planning*

human resources *HR* **1.** the discipline of managing people in an organisation. *Abbr* **HR 2.** the employees of an organisation

Human Rights and Equal Opportunities Commission (*ANZ*) *HR* an Australian federal government body that administers legislation relating to human rights, anti-discrimination, privacy, and social justice. It was set up in 1986, replacing the Human Rights Commission. *Abbr* **HREOC**

Humble, John William (*b.* 1925) *Gen Mgt* British consultant. Popularised *Peter Drucker's* concept of *management by objectives*, which he explained in *Improving Business Results* (1967).

hunch marketing *Mkting* marketing based on instinct rather than research (*slang*)

hurdle rate *Fin* a rate of return which a capital investment proposal must achieve if it is to be accepted. Set by reference to the cost of the capital, the hurdle rate may be increased above the basic cost of capital to allow for different levels of risk.

hurry sickness *Gen Mgt* a state of anxiety caused by the feeling of not having enough time in the day to achieve everything that is required (*slang*)

hybrid *Fin* a combination of financial instruments, for example, a bond with warrants attached, or a range of cash and derivative instruments designed to mirror the performance of a financial market

hybrid financial instrument *Fin* a financial instrument such as a convertible bond that has characteristics of multiple types of instruments, often convertible from one to another

hygiene factors *Gen Mgt see job satisfaction*

hymn sheet
sing from the same hymn sheet *HR* to be in agreement about something with another person or group of people (*slang*)

I like the way we work really hard behind the scenes to make it look easy up front.

Barbara Cassani

hyperinflation *Econ* very rapid growth in the rate of inflation so that money loses value and physical goods replace currency as a medium of exchange. This happened in Latin America in the early 1990s, for example.

hyperlink *E-com* an image or piece of text that enables the user, by clicking on it, to move directly to other web pages. Hyperlinks are most commonly found on web pages, and can be used to connect web pages within the same site, as well as to link to other websites. Hyperlinks can be added to web pages by using simple **HTML** commands. They can also be used in e-mail messages, for example, to include the address of a company's website. *Also known as **hypertext link***

hyperpartnering *E-com* a form of commerce in which companies use Internet technology to form partnerships and execute transactions at high speed and low cost in order to take advantage of business opportunities as soon as they appear

hypertext link *E-com see **hyperlink***

hypertext markup language *E-com see* **HTML**

hypertext transport protocol *or* **hypertext transfer protocol** *E-com see* **HTTP**

hyper time *E-com* the apparent fast pace and decentralised nature of Internet time

hypothecate *Fin* to use a property as collateral for a loan

hypothesis testing *Stats* the process of testing sample data from a statistical study to determine whether it is consistent with what is known about the sample population

---

To accuse is so easy that it is infamous to do so where proof is impossible.   Zoë Akins

Iacocca, Lee (*b.* 1924) *Gen Mgt* US business executive. President of the Ford Motor Company and subsequently Chairman and Chief Executive of the Chrysler Corporation. His experiences are described in *Iacocca: an Autobiography* (1985).

IANAL *abbr Gen Mgt* I am not a lawyer (*slang*)

IAP *abbr E-com* Internet access provider

IAS *abbr* (*ANZ*) *Fin* Instalment Activity Statement

IASC *abbr Fin* International Accounting Standards Committee: an organisation based in London that works towards achieving global agreement on accounting standards

IBOR *abbr Fin* Inter Bank Offered Rate: the rate of interest at which banks lend to each other on the interbank market

IBRC *abbr Fin* Insurance Brokers Registration Council: in the United Kingdom, a statutory body established under the Insurance Brokers Registration Act of 1977 that was deregulated following the establishment of the Financial Services Authority and the General Insurance Services Council. Its complaints and administration functions passed to the Institute of Insurance Brokers.

IBRD *abbr Fin* International Bank for Reconstruction and Development: a United Nations organisation that provides funds, policy guidance, and technical assistance to facilitate economic development in its poorer member countries

ICA *abbr* (*ANZ*) *Gen Mgt* Insurance Council of Australia

Icarus factor *Gen Mgt* the tendency of managers or executives to embark on overambitious projects which then fail. In Greek mythology, Icarus made himself wings of wax and feathers to attempt to escape from Crete, but flew too near the sun and drowned in the sea after the wax melted. (*slang*)

ICC *abbr Fin* International Chamber of Commerce: an organisation that represents business interests to governments, aiming to improve trading conditions and foster private enterprise

iceing *Gen Mgt* dismissal from employment. The first part of the word is derived from 'involuntary career event'. (*slang*)

ICSA *abbr Fin* Institute of Chartered Secretaries and Administrators: in the United Kingdom, an organisation that aims to promote the efficient administration of commerce, industry, and public affairs. Founded in 1891 and granted a Royal Charter in 1902, it represents the interests of its members to government, publishes journals and other materials, promotes the standing of its members, and provides educational support and qualifying schemes.

ICT *abbr Gen Mgt* information and communications technologies

IDA *abbr* **1.** *Fin* International Development Association: an agency administered by the IBRD to provide assistance on concessional terms to the poorest developing countries. Its resources consist of subscriptions and general replenishments from its more industrialised and developed members, special contributions, and transfers from the net earnings of the IBRD. **2.** *Gen Mgt* Infocomm Development Authority

idea
let's put some ideas on the ground and see if any of them walk *Gen Mgt* let's try some of these ideas and see whether any of them is successful (*slang*)

idea hamster *Gen Mgt* somebody who appears to have an endless supply of new ideas (*slang*)

Identrus *E-com* a consortium of financial institutions engaged in developing a

---

standard for a network over which business-to-business e-commerce can be conducted securely

idle time *Gen Mgt* time spent waiting to continue working on a task while there is a delay (*slang*)

IEA *abbr Fin* International Energy Authority: an autonomous agency within the OECD whose objectives include improving global energy co-operation, developing alternative energy sources, and promoting relations between oil-producing and oil-consuming countries

IFC *abbr Fin* International Finance Corporation: a United Nations organisation promoting private sector investment in developing countries to reduce poverty and improve the quality of people's lives. It finances private sector projects that are profit-oriented and environmentally and socially sound, and helps to foster development. IFC has a staff of 2,000 professionals around the world who seek profitable and creative solutions to complex business issues.

IIB *abbr Fin* Institute of Insurance Brokers: in the United Kingdom, the professional body for insurance brokers and the caretaker for the deregulated Insurance Brokers Registration Council's complaints scheme

ILG *abbr Fin* index-linked gilt

illegal parking *Fin* a stock market practice that involves a broker or company purchasing securities in another company's name though they are guaranteed by the real investor (*slang*)

illiquid *Fin* **1.** used to describe a person or business that lacks cash or assets such as securities that can readily be converted into cash **2.** used to refer to an asset that cannot be easily converted into cash

IMA *abbr* (ANZ) *Fin* Investment Management Agreement

image advertising *Mkting* a form of advertising that attempts to create a positive attitude to a product, brand, or company

imaginisation *Gen Mgt* an approach to *creativity* originated by **Gareth Morgan** in 1993. Imaginisation is concerned with improving our ability to see and understand situations in new ways, with finding new ways of organising, with creating shared understanding and personal *empowerment*, and with developing a capability for continuing self-organisation.

IMAP *abbr E-com* Internet Message Access Protocol: a protocol that enables e-mails to be received from any computer

IMF *abbr Fin* International Monetary Fund: the organisation that industrialised nations have established to reduce trade barriers and stabilise currencies, especially those of less industrialised nations

IMHO *abbr Gen Mgt* in my humble opinion (*slang*)

immediate holding company *Fin* a company with one or more subsidiaries but which is itself a subsidiary of another company (the holding company)

IMNSHO *abbr Gen Mgt* in my not so humble opinion (*slang*)

IMO *abbr Gen Mgt* in my opinion (*slang*)

impact day *Fin* the day when the terms of a new issue of shares are announced

impaired capital *Fin* a company's capital that is worth less than the par value of its stock

impairment of capital *Fin* the extent to which the value of a company is less than the par value of its stock

imperfect competition *Fin* a situation that exists in a market when there are strong barriers to the entry of new competitors

impersonal account *Fin* any account other than a personal account, being classified as either a real account, in which property is recorded, or a nominal account, in which income, expenses, and capital are recorded. *See also* **account**, *personal account*

Man is an imagining being.

implicit knowledge *Gen Mgt see* **knowledge**

import *Mkting* a product or service brought into another country from its country of origin either for sale or for use in manufacturing

import duty *Fin* a tax on goods imported into a country. Although it may simply be a measure for raising revenue, it can also be used to protect domestic manufacturers from overseas competition.

import penetration *Econ* a situation in which one country's imports dominate the market share of those from other industrialised countries. This is the case, for example, with high-tech imports to the United States from Japan.

imposed budget *Fin* a budget allowance which is set without permitting the ultimate budget holder to have the opportunity to participate in the budgeting process. *Also known as* **top-down budget**

impression *E-com* a measure of the number of times an online advertisement is viewed. One impression is equal to one *click-through*.

imprest account *Fin* a UK term for a record of the transactions of a type of petty cash system. An employee is given an advance of money, an imprest, for incidental expenses and when most of it has been spent, he or she presents receipts for the expenses to the accounts department and is then reimbursed with cash to the total value of the receipts.

imprest system *Fin* a method of controlling cash or stock: when the cash or stock has been reduced by disbursements or issues, it is restored to its original level

improvement curve *Gen Mgt see* **learning curve**

imputation system *Fin* a system in which recipients of dividends gain tax advantage for taxes paid by the company that paid the dividends

in box (*US*) *Gen Mgt, HR* = *in tray*

inc *abbr* (*US*) *Gen Mgt* incorporated

incentive programme *Mkting* an award or reward scheme designed to improve salesforce or retail performance

incentive scheme *HR* a programme set up to give benefits to employees to reward them for improved commitment and performance and as a means of motivation. An incentive scheme is designed to supplement *basic pay* and *fringe benefits*. A **financial incentive scheme** may offer share options or a cash bonus, whereas a **non-financial incentive scheme** offers benefits such as additional paid holidays. Awards from incentive schemes may be made on an individual or team basis.

incentive stock option *Fin* in the United States, an employee stock option plan that gives each qualifying employee the right to purchase a specific number of the corporation's shares at a set price during a specific time period. Tax is only payable when the shares are sold.

incestuous share dealing *Fin* transactions by companies within a group in the shares of the other companies within that group. The legality of such transactions depends on the objective of the deals.

inchoate instrument *Fin* a negotiable instrument that is incomplete because, for example, the date or amount is missing. The person to whom it is delivered has the prima facie authority to complete it in any way he or she considers fit.

incidence of tax *Fin* used to indicate where the final burden of a tax lies. For example, although a retailer pays any sales tax to the tax collecting authority, the tax itself is ultimately paid by the customer.

income *Fin* **1.** money received by a company or individual **2.** money received from savings or investments, for example, interest on a deposit account or dividends from shares. This is also known as unearned income. **3.** money generated by a business

income and expenditure account *Fin* a financial statement for non-profit entities such as clubs, associations, and charities. It shows the surplus or deficit, being the excess of income over expenditure or vice versa, for a period, and is drawn up on the same accruals basis as a profit and loss account.

income bond *Fin* a bond that a company repays only from its profits

income distribution *Fin* **1.** the UK term for the payment to investors of the income generated by a collective investment, less management charges, tax, and expenses. It is distributed in proportion to the number of units or shares held by each investor. *US term* **income dividend 2.** the distribution of income across a particular group, such as a company, region, or country. It shows the various wage levels and gives the percentage of individuals earning at each level.

income dividend (*US*) *Fin* = *income distribution*

income-linked gilt *Fin* a bond issued by the United Kingdom whose principal and interest track the retail price index

income redistribution *Econ* a government policy to redirect income to a targeted sector of a country's population, for example, by lowering the rate of tax paid by low-income earners

income shares/stock *Fin* **1.** ordinary shares sought because of their relatively high yield as opposed to their potential to produce capital growth **2.** fixed interest securities acquired for their relatively high yield as opposed to their potential to produce capital growth **3.** certain funds, for example, investment trusts, that issue split level funds where holders of the income element receive all the income (less expenses, charges, and tax), while holders of the capital element receive only the capital gains (less expenses, charges, and tax)

income smoothing *Fin* a UK term for a form of creative accounting that involves the manipulation of a company's financial statements to show steady annual profits rather than large fluctuations

incomes policy *Econ* a government policy that seeks to restrain increases in wages or prices by regulating the permitted level of increase

income statement *Fin see trading, profit and loss account*

income stream *Fin* the income received by a company from a particular product or activity

income tax *Fin* a tax levied directly on the income of a person and paid to the government

income tax return *Fin* a form used for reporting income and computing the tax due on it

income unit *Fin* a unit in a unit trust that makes regular payments to its unit holders

in-company training *HR* programmes of *employee development* that are delivered within an organisation by external training providers. In-company training allows programmes to be tailored to a company's specific needs. It is the opposite of **public training programmes**, which have a set syllabus and are open to employees of any organisation.

incomplete records *Fin* an accounting system which is not double-entry bookkeeping. Various degrees of incompleteness can occur, for example, **single-entry bookkeeping**, in which usually only a cash book is maintained.

incorporation *Fin* the legal process of creating a corporation or company. All incorporated entities have a legal status distinct from that of their owners and most have limited liability.

incremental analysis *Fin* analysis of the changes in costs and revenues caused by a change in activity. Normally the technique is used where a significant volume change occurs, causing changes to both variable and fixed costs, and possibly to selling prices. Incremental or differential costs and revenues are compared to determine the financial effect of the activity change.

A happy atmosphere is something that customers pick up on.   *Tom Farmer*

incremental budgeting *Fin* a method of setting budgets in which the prior period budget is used as a base for the current budget, which is set by adjusting the prior period budget to take account of any anticipated changes

incremental cost *Fin see differential cost*

incrementalism *Gen Mgt* a collective term for the many initiatives of the 1980s and 1990s that took a small-step approach to improving quality and productivity and reducing costs. Incrementalism encompasses initiatives such as *total quality management*, *continuous improvement*, and *benchmarking*. Although incrementalism originally provided a source of *competitive advantage*, it is generally recognised today that a more radical approach is required.

indaba (*S Africa*) *Gen Mgt* a meeting or conference

indemnity *Fin* an agreement by one party to make good the losses suffered by another. *See also indemnity insurance, letter of indemnity*

indemnity insurance *Fin* an insurance contract in which the insurer agrees to cover the cost of losses suffered by the insured party. Most insurance contracts take this form except personal accident and life assurance policies where fixed sums are paid as compensation, rather than reimbursement, for a loss that cannot be quantified in monetary terms.

independent service organisation *E-com see ISO*

index *Fin* **1.** a standard that represents the value of stocks in a market, particularly a figure such as the Hang Seng, FTSE 100, or Nikkei average **2.** an amount calculated to represent the relative value of a group of things

indexation *Fin* the linking of a rate to a standard index of prices, interest rates, share prices, or similar items

index fund *Fin* a unit trust composed of companies listed in an important stock market index in order to match the market's overall performance. *See also managed fund. Also known as index-tracker, tracker fund*

index futures *Fin* a futures contract trading in one of the major stock market indices such as the FTSE 100. *See also Dow Jones Averages, FTSE index*

index-linked bond *Fin* a security where the income is linked to an index, such as a financial index. *See also index-linked gilt, index-linked savings certificate*

index-linked gilt *Fin* an inflation-proof UK government bond, first introduced for institutional investors in 1981 and then made available to the general public in 1982. It is inflation-proof in two ways: the dividend is raised every six months in line with the Retail Price Index and the original capital is repaid in real terms at redemption, when the indexing of the repayment is undertaken. The nominal value of the stock, however, does not increase with inflation. Like other gilts, ILGs are traded on the market. Price changes are principally dependent on investors' changing perceptions of inflation and real yields. *Abbr* **ILG**

index-linked savings certificate *Fin* a National Savings Certificate issued by the UK National Savings organisation with a return linked to the rate of inflation. *Also known as granny bond*

index number *Econ* a weighted average of a number of observations of an economic attribute such as retail prices expressed as a percentage of a similar weighted average calculated at an earlier period

index-tracker *Fin see index fund*

indicated dividend *Fin* the forecast total of all dividends in a year if the amount of each dividend remains as it is

indicated yield *Fin* the yield that an indicated dividend represents

indication price *Fin* an approximation of the price of a security as opposed to its firm price

indicative price *Fin* the price shown on a screen-based system for trading securities such as the UK Stock Exchange Automated Quotations system. The price is not firm, as the size of the bargain will determine the final price at which market makers will actually deal.

indirect channel *Mkting* the selling and distribution of products to customers through intermediaries such as wholesalers, distributors, agents, dealers, or retailers

indirect cost *Gen Mgt* a fixed or overhead cost that cannot be attributed directly to the production of a particular item and is incurred even when there is no output. Indirect costs may include the *cost centre* functions of finance and accounting, information technology, administration, and personnel. *See also direct cost*

indirect discrimination *HR* apparently *equal treatment* that in fact *discriminates* because the employment requirement can only be met by a proportion of those in the relevant group and cannot be justified on non-discriminatory grounds

indirect labour *HR* personnel not directly engaged in the manufacturing of products or the provision of services. Indirect labour includes *white-collar workers* and office and support staff.

individual retirement account *(US) Fin see IRA*

Individual Savings Account *Fin see ISA*

induction *HR* a process through which a new employee is integrated into an organisation, learning about its *corporate culture*, policies, and *procedures*, and the specific practicalities of his or her job. An induction programme should not consist of a one-day introduction, but should be planned and paced over a few days or weeks. In the United States there is a growing use of *boot camps*, which aim to assimilate a new employee rapidly into the culture of the employing organisation. *US term* **orientation**

industrial action *HR* concerted action taken by employees to pressurise an employer to accede to a demand, usually work-related, but sometimes of a political or social nature. Examples of industrial action include *strikes*, overtime bans, *go-slows*, and extended tea breaks.

industrial advertising *Mkting* the advertising of technical products and services to the industrial or business sectors

industrial co-operative *Gen Mgt* a group of individuals who together produce goods or provide services and share any profits that are made. Industrial co-operatives are an extension of the *co-operative movement* that developed during the 1800s.

industrial court *(ANZ) HR* a state body in Australia responsible for arbitrating in industrial disputes and setting wage awards

industrial democracy *HR* a way of running an organisation that involves employees in strategy and *decision-making*. Industrial democracy involves *employee participation* in management, which empowers employees and aids *motivation*. It can be facilitated by such set-ups as *works councils* and consultation committees. In an industrial democracy, workers should not only share in inputs to the running of the organisation but also in its outputs, for example, by taking part in a profit-sharing scheme.

industrial dispute *Gen Mgt see dispute*

industrial engineering *Gen Mgt* an applied science discipline concerned with the prediction, planning, evaluation, and improvement of company effectiveness. The purpose of industrial engineering is to maximise efficiency, quality, and production through the best use of personnel, materials, facilities, and equipment.

industrial espionage *Gen Mgt* the practice of spying on a business competitor in order to obtain their trade or commercial secrets. Information sought through industrial espionage will often refer to new products, designs, formulas, manufacturing processes, marketing surveys, research, or future plans. The aim of industrial espionage is either to injure the business prospects or market share of the target company, or to use the secrets discovered for another organisation's commercial benefit.

industrial goods *Ops* goods produced for industry, which include processed or *raw materials*, goods used to produce other goods, machinery, components, and equipment

industrial goods marketing *Mkting* the *industrial marketing* of products. Industrial goods marketing is different from the marketing of consumer goods in that it is directed at organisations, businesses, and other institutions, rather than at the individual end-user of a product. It may require different marketing strategies from those used in *consumer goods marketing* to be effective.

industrial housekeeping *Gen Mgt* the process of ensuring that the workplace is kept clean and tidy. Industrial housekeeping forms part of the general responsibility of managers. It includes the provision of adequate workspace, adequate storage arrangements, both around the workstation and within the unit, and the development of effective administration and procedures to ensure a culture of tidiness and cleanliness within the workforce. A lack of concern with housekeeping can result in an increase in accidents and machine failure and in a reduction in the overall efficiency of the unit. The introduction of the Japanese 5-S concept into Western companies has renewed a general management interest in industrial housekeeping.

industrialisation *Gen Mgt* the change from a society based on agriculture to one based on manufacturing. Industrialisation is the process undergone in much of the developed world during the Industrial Revolution. Features of the process include *automation*, scientific development, the introduction of factories, the *division of labour*, the replacement of barter with a money-based economy, a more mobile workforce, and the growth of urban centres. The phase of development following industrialisation is the *post-industrial society*.

industrial marketing *Mkting* the marketing of goods or services to companies, as opposed to individual consumers. Industrial marketing involves a number of key differences from selling to consumers. These include a smaller customer base with higher-value or larger-unit purchases, more technically complex or specially tailored products, professionally qualified purchasers, closer buyer-seller relationships, and possible group-purchasing decision-making. *Also known as B2B marketing*

industrial market research *Mkting market research* into the **marketing** of services and goods to industry, businesses, and other institutions. Industrial market research is used as an aid to *decision-making* and concerns the manufacture, selling, and distribution of products with the aim of reducing costs and increasing profits. It considers factors such as the available labour force, location of the firm, export market potential, and use of resources.

industrial production *Econ* the output of a country's productive industries. Until the 1960s, this was commonly iron and steel or coal, but since then lighter engineering in motor car or robotics manufacture has taken over.

industrial psychology *HR see occupational psychology*

Industrial Relations Commission *Gen Mgt see Australian Industrial Relations Commission*

Industrial Relations Court of Australia *HR* an Australian superior court responsible for enforcing industrial awards, hearing and ruling on claims for unfair dismissal, and ruling on points of industrial law. *Abbr* **IRCA**

industrial revenue bond *Fin* a bond that a private company uses to finance construction

industrial-sector cycle *Econ* a business cycle that reflects patterns of an old economy rather than the new electronic economy

industrial services marketing *Mkting* the *industrial marketing* of services. Industrial services marketing may promote services such as maintenance contracts, insurance, training, transportation, office cleaning, and advertising to industry, businesses, and other institutions. Many services offered to industry are also offered to the consumer, but promoting them to consumers requires a range of strategies derived from *consumer services marketing*.

industry rules *Gen Mgt* the unwritten conventions that are considered to govern the interactions of organisations within an industry

inertia selling *Mkting* a method of selling that involves the sending of unsolicited goods on a sale or return policy. Inertia selling relies on the passive reaction of a potential purchaser to choose to pay for the goods received rather than undertake the effort to send them back. The receiver of the goods is not bound by law to pay for them but must keep them in good condition until they are collected or returned. Regarded by some as unethical, inertia selling is the principle by which many postal book, record, and video clubs operate.

inference *Stats* a conclusion drawn by a researcher about a statistical population after observing individuals in the population

infinite capacity plan *Ops see capacity requirements planning*

infinite loading *Ops* the scheduling or loading of jobs onto a workstation as if it had a limitless capacity to handle them. *See also finite loading*

inflation *Fin* a general increase in the price level over time. *See also hyperinflation*

inflation accounting *Fin* the adjustment of a company's accounts to reflect the effect of inflation and provide a more realistic view of the company's position

inflationary *Econ* characterised by excess demand or high costs creating an excessive increase in the country's money supply

inflationary gap *Econ* a gap that exists when an economy's resources are utilised and *aggregate demand* is more than the full-employment level of output. Prices will rise to remove the excess demand.

inflationary spiral *Econ* the vicious circle in which, in inflationary conditions, excess demand causes producers to raise prices and workers to demand wage rises to sustain their living standards

inflation-proof security (*US*) *Fin* a security that is indexed to inflation

inflation rate *Econ* the rate at which general price levels increase over a period of time

inflation tax *Econ* an incomes policy that taxes companies that grant pay rises above a particular level

Infocomm Development Authority *Gen Mgt* a statutory board responsible for developing the information and communications sector in Singapore. It was formed in 1999 as a result of the merger of the Telecommunications Authority of Singapore and the National Computer Board. *Abbr* **IDA**

infoholic *Gen Mgt* somebody who is obsessed with obtaining information, especially on the Internet (*slang*)

infomatics *Gen Mgt* the process of automation using information systems

infomediary *E-com* a website that provides and aggregates relevant customer or industry information for other companies

infomercial *Mkting* a television or cinema commercial that includes helpful information about a product as well as advertising content

info rate *Fin* a money market rate quoted by dealers for information only

informal economy *Econ* the economy that runs in parallel to the formal economy but outside the reach of the tax system, most transactions being paid for in cash or goods

information and communications technologies *Gen Mgt* computer and telecommunications technologies considered collectively. Information and communications technology convergence has given rise to technologies such as the *Internet*, *videoconferencing*, *groupware*, *intranets*, and third-generation mobile phones. Information and communications technologies enable organisations to be more flexible in the way they are structured and in the way they work, and this has given rise to both the *virtual organisation* and the *virtual office*. *Abbr* **ICT**

information architecture *E-com* the means and methods of designing metadata, navigation, search, and content layout for a website

information management *Gen Mgt* the acquisition, recording, organising, storage, dissemination, and retrieval of information. Good information management has been described as getting the right information to the right person in the right format at the right time.

information overload *E-com* the problem caused by the excessive quantity of web and e-mail-based information and the Internet's inability to discriminate between useful and useless material. In 1997, the problem of information overload was identified in an influential report from the MCA (Marketing and Communication Agency). The report concluded that 'information overload is not simply the problem of too much information. It is the problem of too much *irrelevant* information caused by the heavy reliance on one medium (the Internet) to distribute information'.

information space *E-com* the abstract concept of all the knowledge, expertise, and information accessible on the Web

infotainment *Gen Mgt* television programmes that deal with serious issues or current affairs in an entertaining way

infrastructure *Gen Mgt* the basic elements that together support something, for example, the network and systems that support computing or the public services and facilities that support business activity

in-house newsletter *Gen Mgt see newsletter*

initial offer *Fin* the first offer that a company makes to buy the shares of another company

initial public offering *Fin* the first instance of making particular shares available for sale to the public. *Abbr* **IPO**

initial yield *Gen Mgt* the estimated yield at the launch of an investment fund

injunction *Fin* a court order forbidding an individual or organisation from doing something

inland bill *Fin* a UK term for a bill of exchange that is payable and drawn in the same country

Inland Revenue *Fin see Board of Inland Revenue*

Inland Revenue Department *(ANZ) Fin* the New Zealand government body responsible for the administration of the national taxation system. *Abbr* **IRD**

innovation *Gen Mgt* the creation, development, and implementation of a new product, process, or service, with the aim of improving efficiency, effectiveness, or *competitive advantage*. Innovation may apply to products, services, manufacturing processes, managerial processes, or the design of an organisation. It is most often viewed at a product or process level, where product innovation satisfies a customer's needs, and process innovation improves efficiency and effectiveness. Innovation is linked with *creativity* and the creation of new ideas, and involves taking those new ideas and turning them into reality through invention, research, and *new product development*.

input tax *Fin see VAT*

input tax credit *(ANZ) Fin* an amount paid as *Goods and Services Tax* on supplies purchased for business purposes, which can be offset against Goods and Services Tax collected

insert *Mkting* a loose piece of advertising material, for example, a card or brochure, placed inside a newspaper or magazine

insertion rate *Mkting* the cost of a single appearance of an advertisement

inside information *Fin* information that is of advantage to investors but is only available to people who have personal contact with a company

inside quote *Fin* a range of prices for a security, from the highest offer to buy to the lowest offer to sell

insider *Gen Mgt* somebody who has access to information that is privileged and unavailable to most members of the public

insider trading *or* **insider dealing** *Fin* profitable, usually illegal, trading in securities carried out using privileged information

insolvency *Fin, Gen Mgt* the inability to pay debts when they become due. Insolvency will apply even if total assets exceed total liabilities, if those assets cannot be readily converted into cash to meet debts as they mature. Even then, insolvency may not necessarily mean *business failure*. *Bankruptcy* may be avoided through *debt rescheduling* or *turnaround management*.

insourcing *Gen Mgt* the use of in-house personnel or an internal department to meet an organisation's need for specific services. Insourcing is seen as a reaction to the growing popularity of *outsourcing* that has not always met expectations. An insourcing strategy is chosen where it appears that a better service can be provided from internal resources than from an external supplier. In some cases,

organisations opt for a combination of outsourcing and insourcing in which external service providers work in co-operation with in-house personnel.

inspector of taxes *Fin* in the United Kingdom, an official who reports to the Board of Inland Revenue and is responsible for issuing tax returns and assessments, agreeing tax liabilities, and conducting appeals on matters of tax

instalment *Fin* one of two or more payments or repayments for the purchase of an initial public offering

Instalment Activity Statement *(ANZ) Fin* a standard form used in Australia to report *Pay-As-You-Go* instalment payments on investment income. *Abbr* **IAS**

instalment credit *Fin* the UK term for a loan that is repaid with fixed regular instalments, and with a rate of interest fixed for the duration of the loan. *US term instalment loan*

instalment loan *(US) Fin* = *instalment credit*

instalment plan *(US) Fin* = *hire purchase*

instalment purchase *Fin* a financing arrangement in which the buyer pays by a series of instalments over a period of time

instant messaging *E-com see live chat*

Institute of Chartered Accountants *Fin* in the United Kingdom and the Republic of Ireland, one of three professional accountancy bodies that provide qualification by examinations, ensure high standards of education and training, and supervise professional conduct

Institute of Chartered Secretaries and Administrators *Fin see ICSA*

Institute of Financial Services *Fin* the trading name of the Chartered Institute of Bankers

Institute of Insurance Brokers *Fin see IIB*

institutional investor *Fin* an institution that makes investments

---

Education is when you read the fine print; experience is what you get when you don't.
Pete Seeger

institutional survey *Stats* a statistical investigation in which an institution such as a company is the unit of analysis

instrument 1. *Fin* a generic term for either securities or derivatives. *See also financial instrument, negotiable instrument* **2.** *Fin* an official or legal document **3.** *Fin* a means to an end, for example, a government's expenditure and taxation in its quest for reducing unemployment **4.** *HR see psychometric test*

insurable risk *Fin see risk*

insurance 1. *Fin* in financial markets, hedging or any other strategy that reduces risk while permitting participation in potential gains **2.** *Gen Mgt* an arrangement in which individuals or companies pay another company to guarantee them compensation if they suffer loss resulting from risks such as fire, theft, or accidental damage

insurance agent *Fin* in the United States, an individual who sells the insurance policies of a particular company

Insurance and Superannuation Commission (*ANZ*) *Gen Mgt* an Australian federal government body responsible for regulating the superannuation and insurance industries. *Abbr* **ISC**

insurance broker *Fin* a person or company that acts as an intermediary between companies providing insurance and individuals or companies who need insurance

Insurance Brokers Registration Council *Fin see* **IBRC**

Insurance Council of Australia *Gen Mgt* an independent body representing the interests of businesses involved in the insurance industry. It was set up in 1975 and currently represents around 110 companies. *Abbr* **ICA**

insurance intermediary *Fin* an individual or firm that provides advice on insurance or assurance and can arrange policies. *See also* **IIB, IBRC**

insurance policy *Gen Mgt* a document that sets out the terms and conditions for providing insurance cover against specified risks

insurance premium tax *Fin* a tax on household, motor vehicle, travel, and other general insurance

insured *Fin* covered by a contract of insurance

insured account (*US*) *Fin* an account with a bank or savings institution that belongs to a federal or private insurance organisation

insurer *Fin* the underwriter of an insurance risk

intangible asset *Fin* an asset such as *intellectual property* or *goodwill* that is not physical

integrated accounts *Fin* a set of accounting records which provides both financial and cost accounts using a common input of data for all accounting purposes

integrated implementation model *Gen Mgt see* **new product development**

Integrated Services Digital Network *E-com see* **ISDN**

intellectual assets *Gen Mgt* the knowledge, experience, and skills of its staff that an organisation can make use of

intellectual capital *Fin* knowledge which can be used to create value. Intellectual capital includes: human resources, the collective skills, experience, and knowledge of employees; intellectual assets, knowledge which is defined and codified such as a drawing, computer program, or collection of data; and intellectual property, intellectual assets which can be legally protected, such as patents and copyrights.

intellectual property *Gen Mgt* the ownership of rights to ideas, designs, and inventions, including *copyrights*, *patents*, and *trademarks*. Intellectual property is protected by law in most countries, and the World Intellectual Property Organisation is responsible for harmonising the law across different countries and promoting the protection of intellectual property rights.

intelligence test *HR see **aptitude test***

intelligent e-mail *E-com* an automated e-mail system that is automatically able to analyse incoming messages without the need for criteria pre-set by each user

interactive *E-com* relating to a facility of an online service or software program that allows the user to enter data or issue commands

interactive planning *Gen Mgt* a process that promotes participation in both the design of a desirable future and the developments that enable this future to be achieved rather than waiting for it to happen. Interactive planning is associated with *Russell Ackoff*, and was outlined in *Creating the Corporate Future* (1981).

Inter Bank Offered Rate *Fin see IBOR*

interchange *E-com* a transaction between the acquiring bank and the issuing bank

interchangeable bond *Fin* a bond whose owner can change it at will between bearer and book-entry form

interchange fee *E-com* the charge on a transaction between the acquiring bank and the issuing bank, paid by the acquirer to the issuer

intercommodity spread *Fin* a combination of purchase and sale of options for related commodities with the same delivery date

intercompany pricing *Gen Mgt* the setting of prices by companies within a group to sell products or services to each other, rather than to external customers

interdependency concept *Fin* the principle that management accounting, in recognition of the increasing complexity of business, must access both external and internal information sources from interactive functions such as marketing, production, personnel, procurement, and finance. This assists in ensuring that the information is adequately balanced.

interest *Fin* the rate that a lender charges for the use of money that is a loan

interest arbitrage *Fin* transactions in two or more financial centres in order to make an immediate profit by exploiting differences in interest rates. *See also **arbitrage***

interest assumption *Fin* the expected rate of return on a portfolio

interest charged *Fin* the cost of borrowing money, expressed as an absolute amount, or as a percentage interest rate. *See also **annual percentage rate**, **nominal interest rate**, **real interest rate***

interest cover *Fin* The amount of earnings available to make interest payments after all operating and non-operating income and expenses—except interest and income taxes—have been accounted for.

EXAMPLE Interest cover is regarded as a measure of a company's creditworthiness because it shows how much income there is to cover interest payments on outstanding debt.

It is expressed as a ratio, comparing the funds available to pay interest—earnings before interest and taxes, or EBIT—with the interest expense. The basic formula is:

EBIT / interest expense = interest coverage ratio

If interest expense for a year is £9 million, and the company's EBIT is £45 million, the interest coverage would be:

45 million / 9 million = 5:1

The higher the number, the stronger a company is likely to be. A ratio of less than 1 indicates that a company is having problems generating enough cash flow to pay its interest expenses, and that either a modest decline in operating profits or a sudden rise in borrowing costs could eliminate profitability entirely. Ideally, interest coverage should at least exceed 1.5; in some sectors, 2.0 or higher is desirable.

Variations of this basic formula also exist. For example, there is:

Operating cash flow + interest + taxes / interest = Cash-flow interest coverage ratio

This ratio indicates the firm's ability to

use its cash flow to satisfy its fixed financing obligations. Finally, there is the fixed-charge coverage ratio, which compares EBIT with fixed charges:

EBIT + lease expenses / interest + lease expense = Fixed-charge coverage ratio

'Fixed charges' can be interpreted in many ways, however. It could mean, for example, the funds that a company is obliged to set aside to retire debt, or dividends on preferred stock.

interest-elastic investment *Fin* an investment with a rate of return that varies with interest rates

interest-inelastic investment *Fin* an investment with a rate of return that does not vary with interest rates

interest in possession trust *Fin* a trust that gives one or more beneficiaries an immediate right to receive any income generated by the trust's assets. It can be used for property, enabling the beneficiary either to enjoy the rent generated by the property or to reside there, or as a life policy, a common arrangement for Inheritance Tax planning.

interest-only mortgage *Fin* a long-term loan, usually for the purchase of a property, in which the borrower only pays interest to the lender during the term of the mortgage, with the principal (see *mortgage*) being repaid at the end of the term. It is thus the borrower's responsibility to make provisions to accumulate the required capital during the period of the mortgage, usually by contributing to tax efficient investment plans such as Individual Savings Accounts or by relying on an anticipated inheritance. *See also* ***mortgage***

interest rate *Fin* the amount of interest charged for borrowing a sum of money over a specified period of time

interest rate cap *Fin* an upper limit on a rate of interest, for example, in an adjustable-rate mortgage

interest rate effect *Econ* the mechanism by which interest rates adjust so that investment is equal to savings in an economy

interest rate exposure *Fin* the risk of a loss associated with movements in the level of interest rates. *See also* ***bond***

interest rate floor *Fin* a lower limit on a rate of interest, for example, in an adjustable-rate mortgage

interest rate future *Fin see* ***future***

interest rate guarantee *Fin* **1.** an interest rate cap, collar, or cap and collar **2.** a tailored indemnity protecting the purchaser against future changes in interest rates

interest rate option *Fin see* ***option***

interest rate parity theory *Fin* a method of predicting foreign exchange rates based on the hypothesis that the difference between the interest rates in two countries should offset the difference between the spot rates and the forward foreign exchange rates over the same period

interest rate swap *Fin* an exchange of two debt instruments with different rates of interest, made to tailor cash flows to the participants' different requirements

interest sensitive *Fin* used to describe assets, generally purchased with credit, that are in demand when interest rates fall but considered less attractive when interest rates rise

interest yield *Fin* the annual rate of interest earned on a security, excluding the effect of any increase in price to maturity

interface *Gen Mgt* **1.** the point of contact between two or more things, for example, between a computer and user, or customer and seller **2.** a face-to-face meeting (*slang*)

interfirm comparison *Fin* systematic and detailed comparison of the performance of different companies generally operating in a common industry. Companies participating in such a scheme normally provide standardised, and therefore comparable, information to the scheme administrator, who then distributes to participating members only the information supplied by participants. Normally the information distributed is in the form of ratios, or in a format which prevents the identity of individual scheme members from coming to light.

interfirm co-operation *Gen Mgt* a formal or informal agreement between organisations to collaborate in achieving common or new aims more efficiently or effectively. Interfirm co-operation usually takes the form of a *joint venture*, *strategic alliance*, or *strategic partnering* arrangement.

interim certificate *Fin* a document certifying partial ownership of stock that is not totally paid for at one time

interim dividend *Fin* a dividend whose value is determined on the basis of a period of time of less than a full fiscal year

interim financial statement *Fin* a financial statement that covers a period other than a full financial year. Although UK companies are not legally obliged to publish interim financial statements, those listed on the London Stock Exchange are obliged to publish a half-yearly report of their activities and a profit and loss account which may either be sent to shareholders or published in a national newspaper. In the United States, the practice is to issue quarterly financial statements.

interim financing *Fin* financing by means of bridging loans

interim management *Gen Mgt* the temporary employment of an experienced manager by an organisation seeking to fill a temporary vacancy or co-ordinate a particular project. Interim managers are generally used to bring in skills not already present in an organisation. Sometimes they are employed when an organisation is facing *business failure*, but increasingly they are used as a strategic resource as and when required. **Interim managers** work on a *freelance* or *portfolio working* basis.

Interim managers differ from both temporary staff and consultants. In general, they are considerably senior to most other temporary workers, and fulfil assignments—often long term—that drive the future of the employing company. They also provide hands-on, day-to-day expertise, in contrast to the prescriptive, advisory support that management consultants deliver.

interim manager *Gen Mgt see interim management*

interim statement *Fin* a financial statement relating to a period of time of less than a full fiscal year

interlocking accounts *Fin* a system in which cost accounts are kept distinct from the financial accounts, the two sets of accounts being kept continuously in agreement by the use of control accounts or reconciled by other means. *Also known as non-integrated accounts*

intermarket spread *Fin* a combination of purchase and sale of options for the same commodity with the same delivery date on different markets

intermediary *Fin* somebody who makes investments for others

intermediate goods *Ops* goods bought for use in the production of other products

intern (*US*) *HR* a trainee working in a junior position in a company

internal audit *Fin* an audit of a company undertaken by its employees. *See also external audit*

internal check *Fin* the procedures designed to provide assurance that everything which should be recorded has been recorded; errors or irregularities are identified; assets and liabilities exist and are correctly recorded

internal communication *Gen Mgt* communication between employees or departments across all levels or divisions of an organisation. Internal communication is a form of *corporate communication* and can be formal or informal, upward, downward, or horizontal. It can take various forms such as *team briefing*, *interviewing*, employee or *works councils*, *meetings*, *memos*, an *intranet*, *newsletters*, *suggestion schemes*, the *grapevine*, and reports.

internal consultant *Gen Mgt* an employee who uses knowledge and expertise to offer advice or business solutions to another department or business unit within an organisation. **Internal consulting** is one aspect of work carried out by a *management services* department.

internal consulting *Gen Mgt see internal consultant*

internal cost analysis *Gen Mgt* an examination of an organisation's value-creating activities to determine sources of profitability and to identify the relative costs of different processes. Internal cost analysis is a tool for analysing the *value chain*. Principal steps include identifying those processes that create value for the organisation, calculating the cost of each value-creating process against the overall cost of the product or service, identifying the cost components for each process, establishing the links between the processes, and working out the opportunities for achieving relative cost advantage.

internal differentiation analysis *Gen Mgt* an examination of processes in the *value chain* to determine which of them create differentiation of the product or service in the customer's eyes, and thus enhance its value. Internal differentiation analysis enables an organisation to focus on improving the identified processes to maximise *competitive advantage*. Steps involve identification of value-creating activities, evaluation of strategies that can enhance value for the customer, and assessment of which differentiation strategies are the most sustainable.

internal growth *Fin* organic growth created within a business, for example, by inventing new products and so increasing its market share, producing products that are more reliable, offering a more efficient service than its competitors, or

being more aggressive in its marketing. *See also* **external growth**

internal marketing *Mkting* the application of the principles of marketing within an organisation. Internal marketing involves the creation of an internal market by dividing departments into *business units*, with control over their own operations and expenditure, with attendant impacts on *corporate culture*, politics, and power. Internal marketing also involves treating employees as internal customers with the aim of increasing employees' motivation and *customer focus*.

internal rate of return *Fin* the annual percentage return achieved by a project, in which the sum of the discounted cash inflows over the life of the project is equal to the sum of the discounted cash outflows. *Abbr* **IRR**

internal recruitment *HR recruitment* carried out within the existing workforce. Internal recruitment gives employees opportunities for *promotion* and to develop new skills.

Internal Revenue Code (*US*) *Fin* the complex series of federal tax laws

Internal Revenue Service *Fin see IRS*

internal versus external sourcing *Gen Mgt see purchasing versus production*

International Accounting Standards Board *Fin* an independent and privately funded accounting standards setter based in London. The Board, whose members come from nine countries and a range of backgrounds, is committed to developing a single set of high quality, understandable, and enforceable global standards that require transparent and comparable information in general purpose financial statements. It also works with national accounting standard setters to achieve convergence in accounting standards around the world. *Abbr* **IASB**

International Accounting Standards Committee *Fin see IASC*

I've learned one thing in politics. You don't take a decision until you have to.

Margaret Thatcher

International Bank for Reconstruction and Development *Fin see* **IBRD**

International Chamber of Commerce *Fin see* **ICC**

International Development Association *Fin see* **IDA**

International Energy Authority *Fin see* **IEA**

International Finance Corporation *Fin see* **IFC**

international fund *Fin* a unit trust that invests in securities both inside and outside a country

International Fund for Agricultural Development *Fin* a specialised United Nations agency with a mandate to combat hunger and rural poverty in developing countries. Established as an international financial institution in 1977 following the 1974 World Food Conference, it has financed projects in over 100 countries and independent territories, to which it has committed US$7.7 billion in grants and loans. It has three sources of finance (contributions from members, loan repayments, and investment income) and an annual commitment level of approximately US$450 million.

international management *Gen Mgt* **1.** the maintenance and development of an organisation's *production* or market interests across national borders with either local or *expatriate* staff **2.** the process of running a *multinational business*, made up of formerly independent organisations **3.** the body of skills, knowledge, and understanding, required to manage cross-cultural operations

International Monetary Fund *Fin see* **IMF**

International Organization of Securities Commissions *Fin* an organisation of securities commissions from around the world, based in Madrid. Its objectives are to promote high standards of regulation, exchange information, and establish standards for and effective surveillance of international securities transactions. *Abbr* **IOSCO**

International Securities Market Association *Fin* the self-regulatory organisation and trade association for the international securities market. Its primary role is to oversee the fast-changing marketplace through the issuing of rules and recommendations relating to trading and settlement practices. Established in 1969, the organisation has over 600 members from 51 countries. *Abbr* **ISMA**

International Standards Organisation *Gen Mgt see* **ISO**

International Union of Credit and Investment Insurers *Fin* an organisation that works for international acceptance of sound principles of export credit and foreign investment insurance. Founded in 1934, the London-based Union has 51 members in 42 countries who play a role of central importance in world trade, both as regards exports and foreign direct investments. *Also known as* **Berne Union**

Internesia *E-com* the tendency to find interesting websites on the Internet and then forget how to locate them again (*slang*)

Internet *E-com* the global network of computers accessed with the aid of a modem. The Internet includes websites, e-mail, newsgroups, and other forums. It is a public network, though many of the computers connected to it are also part of *intranets*. It uses the **Internet Protocol** (IP) as a communication standard.

Internet access provider *E-com* a company or organisation that provides its customers with an entry point to the Internet via a dial-up connection, cable modem, or wireless application. *Abbr* **IAP**

Internet commerce *E-com* the part of *e-commerce* that consists of commercial transactions conducted over the Internet

Internet marketing *E-com* marketing of products or services over the Web.
  Although similar in many ways to traditional marketing, Internet marketing is best suited to several particular purposes. It is ideal for marketing: products and

services that require a lot of information to sell, such as travel and books; products and services that people feel strongly about, such as music and films (much of the success of *The Blair Witch Project* was credited to fans getting together on the Internet and promoting it through enthusiastic reviews and dialogue); products and services that are bought by the Internet demographic.

In terms of advertising, online advertisements do not have the same impact as television or glossy media, as consumers are generally unwilling to download them. However, due to extensive *personalisation* capabilities, Internet marketing has a unique ability to reach niche markets and target just the right consumer with just the right product.

Internet marketing is thus best used as an adjunct to a traditional offline marketing strategy. Offline marketing is used to raise consumer awareness and arouse interest; Internet marketing educates and answers questions by having comprehensive information on offer.

Internet merchant *E-com* a businessman or businesswoman who sells a product or service over the Internet

Internet Message Access Protocol *E-com see* **IMAP**

Internet payment system *E-com* any mechanism for fund transfer from customer to merchant or business to business via the Internet. There are many payment options available, including credit card payment, credit transfer, electronic cheques, direct debit, smart cards, prepaid schemes, loyalty scheme points-based approaches, person-to-person payments, and mobile phone schemes.

Getting the online payment system right is critical to the success of e-commerce. Currently, the most common form of online consumer payment is by credit card (90% in the United States; 70% in Europe). The most common business-to-business payments, however, are still offline—probably because such transactions often involve large sums of money.

Good online payment systems share

key characteristics: ease of use; robustness and reliability; proper authentication (to combat fraud); efficient integration with the vendor's own internal systems; security and assurance procedures which check that the seller gets the money and the buyer gets the goods.

Internet Protocol *E-com see* **Internet**

Internet security *E-com* the means used to protect websites and other electronic files from attack by *hackers* and *viruses*. The Internet is, by definition, a network; networks are open, and are thus open to attack. A poor Internet security policy can result in a substantial loss of productivity and a drop in consumer confidence.

The essential elements of Internet security are: constant vigilance—one day's 'perfect' Internet security system will be out of date the next; a combination of software and human expertise—security software can only do so much, it must be combined with human experience; and internal as well as external security—many security breaches come from within an organisation.

Internet service provider *E-com see* **ISP**

interoperability *Gen Mgt* the ability of products from different manufacturers to be used in conjunction with each other

interpersonal communication *HR* all aspects of personal interaction, contact, and communication between individuals or members of a group. Effective interpersonal communication depends on a range of **interpersonal skills** including listening, asserting, influencing, persuading, empathising, sensitivity, and diplomacy. Important aspects of communication between people include *body language* and other forms of *non-verbal communication*.

interpersonal skills *HR see* **interpersonal communication**

interquartile range *Stats* the difference between the first and third quartiles of a statistical sample, used to measure the spread of variables in the data

interstate commerce *Fin* commerce that involves more than one US state and is therefore subject to regulation by Congress. *See also* **intrastate commerce**

interstitial *E-com* a Web advertisement that appears on its own page. This can either be sandwiched between content pages on a website, in a similar way to that used in traditional magazine advertising, or appear on its own before the actual web page loads. The latter gets visitors' attention, but can be very frustrating.

intervention *Econ* government action to manipulate market forces for political or economic purposes

interviewer bias *Stats* distortion in the results of a statistical survey caused by actions of the interviewer such as cues given to the interviewee

interviewing *HR* the practice of asking questions of another person in order to gain information and make an assessment. Interviewing is a selection tool used in recruitment to assess somebody's suitability for a job. A **structured interview** relies on asking the same job-related questions of all candidates and systematically evaluating their responses. There are two principal models: the **behavioural interview**, which aims to find out how applicants have behaved in the past in similar situations; and the **situational interview**, in which they are asked hypothetical questions to determine how they might act in the future. Interviewing is a technique also used in *counselling*, *performance appraisal*, and as part of a disciplinary procedure. *See also* **discipline**

intranet *E-com* a corporate network of computers utilising Internet tools and technology for the purpose of communication and information sharing. Intranets have been introduced by many organisations as an aid to *internal communication*. Where an intranet is extended beyond the employees of an organisation, perhaps to suppliers, customer, or distributors, it is called an *extranet*.

At their best, intranets can combine internal and external information resources in a one-stop information shop, and become the intellectual capital library of an organisation, capturing staff knowledge, facilitating teamwork and collaboration, and providing an excellent induction vehicle for new employees. However, if not managed properly, intranets can easily evolve in a haphazard way with no clear objectives, and simply become information dumps. Consequently, staff do not use them and their potential is lost.

intrapreneur *Gen Mgt* an *employee* who uses the approach of an *entrepreneur* within an organisational setting. An intrapreneur must have freedom of action to explore and implement ideas, although the outcome of such work will be owned by the organisation rather than the intrapreneur, and it is the organisation that will take the associated risk. Managers of organisations in which intrapreneurs are allowed to operate subscribe to the view that *innovation* can be achieved by encouraging *creative* and exploratory activity in semi-autonomous units.

intrastate commerce *Fin* commerce that occurs within a single state of the United States. *See also* **interstate commerce**

in tray *Gen Mgt, HR* a receptacle for documents and other items requiring the attention of an individual. An in tray is normally placed on the desk or in the office of the person responsible for dealing with the contents. *US term* **in box**

in-tray learning *HR* a training exercise in which the trainee plays the role of a manager dealing with the contents of an *in tray* within a set period of time. In-tray training is a form of *simulation* used to develop the *decision-making*, prioritising, and *time management* skills of managers and supervisors in the context of the normal working day.

intrinsic value *Fin* the extent to which an option is in the money

introducing broker *Fin* a broker who cannot accept payment from customers

intuitive management *Gen Mgt* a *management style* that relies on gut feeling or a sixth sense, rather than on analytical or objective reasoning. Intuitive management exploits the holistic, imaginative, spiritual skills of the right side of the brain, whereas the conventional school of management favours left side of the brain skills, which are logical, rational, linear, and mathematical in nature. Intuitive management is closely linked to a style of *decision-making* that encourages *creativity* and *innovation*. Because this style of decision-making has no rational basis, however, it can be difficult to justify decisions that turn out to be wrong.

inventory 1. (*US*) *Fin* the total of an organisation's commercial assets **2.** *Gen Mgt* the stock of finished goods, raw materials, and work in progress held by a company

inventory record *Ops* a record of the *inventory* held by an organisation. An inventory record forms an important part of material requirements planning systems. Such records usually make use of some form of part numbering or classification system, and include a description of the part, the quantity held, and the location of all the holdings. A **transaction file** keeps track of inventory use and replenishment.

inventory turnover *Fin* an accounting ratio of the number of times *inventory* is replaced during a given period. The ratio is calculated by dividing net sales by average inventory over a given period. Values are expressed as times per period, most often a year, and a higher figure indicates a more efficient manufacturing operation. Its formula is:

Cost of goods sold / Inventory

For example, if COGS is £2 million, and inventory at the end of the period is £500,000, then:

2,000,000 / 500,000 = 4.

Also known as **stock turns**

inverse floating rate note *Fin* a note whose interest rate varies inversely with a *benchmark interest rate*

inverted doughnut *Gen Mgt see* **doughnut principle**

inverted market *Fin* a situation in which near-term futures cost more than long-term futures for the same commodity

inverted yield curve *Fin* a yield curve with lower interest rates for long-term bonds than for short-term bonds. *See also* **yield curve**

investment *Fin* any application of funds which is intended to provide a return by way of interest, dividend, or capital appreciation

investment analyst *Fin* an employee of a stock-exchange company who researches other companies and identifies investment opportunities for clients. *Also known as* **financial analyst**

investment bank *Fin* **1.** a bank that specialises in providing funds to corporate borrowers for start-up or expansion **2.** (*US*) = **merchant bank**

investment bill *Fin* a bill of exchange that is an investment

investment bond *Fin* in the United Kingdom, a product where the investment is paid as a single premium into a life assurance policy with an underlying asset-backed fund. The bondholder receives a regular income until the end of the bond's term when the investment—the current value of the fund—is returned to the bondholder.

investment borrowing *Econ* funds borrowed to encourage a country's economic growth or to support the development of particular industries or regions by adding to physical or human capital

investment centre *Fin* a profit centre with additional responsibilities for capital investment, and possibly for financing, whose performance is measured by its return on investment

investment club *Fin* a group of people who join together to make investments in securities

---

Management in a global environment is increasingly affected by cultural differences.

Fons Trompenaars

investment committee (*US*) *Fin* a group of employees of an investment bank who evaluate investment proposals

investment company (*US*) *Fin* a company that pools for investment the money of several investors by means of unit trusts

investment dealer (*Canada*) *Fin* a securities broker

investment fund *Fin* a savings scheme that invests its clients' funds in corporate start-up or expansion projects

Investment Management Agreement (*ANZ*) *Fin* a contract between an investor and an investment manager required under SIS legislation. *Abbr* **IMA**

investment manager *Fin see* **fund manager**

investment portfolio *Fin see* **portfolio**

investment properties *Fin* either commercial buildings (for example, shops, factories, or offices) or residential dwellings (for example, houses or apartments) that are purchased by businesses or individuals for renting to third parties

investment revaluation reserve *Fin* in the United Kingdom, the capital reserve where changes in the value of a business's investment properties when they are revalued are disclosed

investment tax credit (*US*) *Fin* a tax advantage for investment, available until 1986 in the United States

investment trust *Fin* an association of investors that invests in securities

investomer *Fin* a customer of a business who is also an investor (*slang*)

investor *Fin* a person or organisation that invests money in something, especially in shares of publicly owned corporations

investor relations research *Mkting* research carried out on behalf of an organisation in order to gain an understanding of how financial markets regard the organisation, its shares, and its sector

Investors in People *HR* a national programme in the United Kingdom for *employee development*. Investors in People is a UK government initiative in which organisations that meet the required standards are awarded the status of 'Investor in People'. The goal of the programme is to encourage organisations in all sectors to develop their staff in order to better achieve organisational objectives. Criteria are based on established best practice, and an organisation is assessed for evidence that it is actively developing the skills of its employees.

invisible asset *Fin see* **intangible asset**

invisible exports *Econ* the profits, dividends, interest, and royalties received from selling a country's services abroad

invisible imports *Econ* the profits, dividends, interest, and royalties paid to foreign service companies based in a country

invisibles *Econ* items such as financial and leisure services, as opposed to physical goods, that are traded by a country

invisible trade *Econ* trade in items such as financial and other services that are listed in the current account of the balance of payments

invitation to tender *Gen Mgt* a formal statement of requirements sent to shortlisted suppliers, inviting the submission of a formal proposal for completing a particular piece of work. An invitation to tender should provide background information on the organisation and identify the key areas that suppliers need to address such as functionality and operating requirements. A timetable for the tendering process should also be included.

invoice *Fin* a document prepared by a supplier showing the description, quantities, prices, and values of goods delivered or services rendered. To the supplier this is a sales invoice; to the purchaser the same document is a purchase invoice.

---

invoice date *Fin* the date on which an invoice is issued. The invoice date may be different from the delivery date.

invoice discounting *Fin* the selling of invoices at a discount for collection by the buyer

invoicing *Fin* the process of issuing invoices

involuntary liquidation preference *Fin* a payment that a company must make to holders of its preference shares if it is forced to sell its assets when facing bankruptcy

inward investment *Fin* investment by a government or company in its own country or region, often to stimulate employment or develop a business infrastructure

IOSCO *abbr Fin* International Organization of Securities Commissions

IOU *Fin* a rendition in letters of 'I owe you' that can be used as legal evidence of a debt, although it is most commonly used by an individual as a reminder that small change has been taken, for example, from a float

IOW *abbr Gen Mgt* in other words (*slang*)

IP *E-com see* **Internet**

IP address *E-com* Internet protocol address, an identifier for a computer or other Internet-enabled device on the Internet and other **TCP/IP** networks. The format of an IP address is a numeric address written as four groups of numbers separated by dots. For example, 1.542.20.350 could be an IP address.

IPO *abbr Fin* initial public offering

IRA *abbr* (*US*) *Fin* individual retirement account: a pension plan, designed for individuals without a company pension scheme, that allows annual sums, subject to limits dependent upon employment income, to be set aside from earnings tax-free. Individuals with a company pension may invest in an IRA, but only from their net income. IRAs, including the Education IRA, designed as a way of saving for children's education, may invest in

almost any financial security except property.

IRCA *HR see* **Industrial Relations Court of Australia**

IRD (*ANZ*) *Fin see* **Inland Revenue Department**

IRD number (*ANZ*) *Fin* a numeric code assigned to all members of the New Zealand workforce for the purpose of paying income tax

IRL *abbr Gen Mgt* in real life (*slang*)

IRR *abbr Fin* internal rate of return

irrevocable letter of credit *Fin see* **letter of credit**

irritainment *Gen Mgt* television programmes or other forms of entertainment that are irritating but nevertheless compulsive viewing (*slang*)

IRS *abbr Fin* Internal Revenue Service: in the United States, the branch of the federal government charged with collecting the majority of federal taxes

ISA *abbr Fin* Individual Savings Account: a portfolio created according to rules that exempt its proceeds, including dividends and capital gains, from taxes. It was launched in 1999 with the intention that it would be available for at least ten years. Individuals may invest up to £7,000 each year, £3,000 of which may be invested in a savings account and £1,000 in life assurance. Either the remaining £3,000, or the entire £7,000, may be invested in the stock market. A 'maxi' ISA is an investment of up to the maximum amount, whether divided or entirely in the stock market, that has been purchased from one provider only. A 'mini' ISA is one of the three individual components which may be purchased from different providers. Investors may therefore have up to three 'minis', but only one 'maxi'.

ISC (*ANZ*) *Gen Mgt see* **Insurance and Superannuation Commission**

ISDN *abbr E-com* Integrated Services Digital Network: a digital telephone network supporting advanced communications

---

Capital must be propelled by self-interest; it cannot be enticed by benevolence.

Walter Bagehot

services and used for high-speed data transmission

Ishikawa, Kaoru (1915–89) *Gen Mgt* Japanese academic. Originator of *fishbone charts* and champion of other *quality control* tools such as *Pareto charts*, as explained in *Guide to Quality Control* (1976).

Ishikawa diagram *Gen Mgt see fishbone chart*

ISMA *abbr Fin* International Securities Market Association

ISO *abbr* **1.** *E-com* independent service organisation: a company that processes online credit card transactions for small businesses, usually in exchange for a fee or percentage of sales **2.** *Gen Mgt* International Standards Organisation: an organisation responsible for determining and managing common standards for products and for business and manufacturing processes

ISO 14000 *Gen Mgt* a series of internationally recognised *quality standards* providing a framework that organisations can use to regulate the environmental impact of their activities. ISO 14000 is a management system standard rather than a performance standard and can be applied to organisations of all shapes and sizes, wherever they may be located. The standard does not identify specific goals but presents a framework for carrying out environmental management. **ISO 14001** is the part of the standard that specifies the requirements that organisations must meet if they are to obtain certification. ISO 14001 gives a framework for identifying operations, processes, and products that impact on the environment, for evaluating these impacts, for setting objectives and targets for reducing any negative impacts that have been identified, and for implementing activities to achieve targets. ISO 14000 provides a certified standard that can be seen as a reflection of an organisation's ethical achievements. It pays no attention, however, to cultural or human dimensions and disregards the fact that organisations

will need to perceive bottom-line cost benefits if they are to implement the standard.

ISO 14001 *Gen Mgt see ISO 14000*

ISO 9000 *Fin* a quality system standard which requires complying organisations to operate in accordance with a structure of written policies and procedures that are designed to ensure the consistent delivery of a product or service to meet customer requirements

ISP *abbr E-com* Internet service provider: a company or organisation that not only provides an entry point to the Internet, like an *Internet access provider*, but also additional services such as website hosting and web-page development

issuance costs *Fin* the underwriting, legal, and administrative fees required to issue a debt. These fees are significant when issuing debt in the public markets, such as bonds. However, other types of debt, such as private placements or bank loans, are cheaper to issue because they require less underwriting, legal, and administrative support.

issue *Fin* a set of stocks or bonds that a company offers for sale at one time

issue by tender *Fin see sale by tender*

Issue Department *Fin* the department of the Bank of England that is responsible for issuing currency

issued share capital *Fin* the type, class, number, and amount of the shares held by shareholders

issued shares *Fin* those shares that comprise a company's authorised capital that has been distributed to investors. They may be either fully paid or partly paid shares.

issue price *Fin* the price at which securities are first offered for sale

issuer *E-com* a financial institution that issues payment cards such as credit or debit cards, pays out to the merchant's account, and bills the customer or debits the customer's account. The issuer guarantees payment for authorised transactions using the payment card. *Also known as* *card-issuing bank*, *issuing bank*

issuer bid *Fin* an offer made by an issuer for its own securities when it is disappointed by the offers of others

issues management *Gen Mgt* the anticipation and assessment of key trends and themes of the next decade, and the relation of these to the organisation. Issues management is informed by *futures research* in order to formulate strategic plans and actions.

issuing bank *E-com see* *issuer*

issuing house *Fin* in the United Kingdom, a financial institution that specialises in the flotation of private companies. *See also* *investment bank*, *merchant bank*

itchy finger syndrome *E-com* the Internet user's need for interactivity. Sites can combat this by adding interactive elements such as *hyperlinks* and online *forums*.

item non-response *Stats* a refusal to respond to a question in a statistical survey or a response that cannot be fitted into the given response design

Japanese management *Gen Mgt, HR* a *management style* with particular emphasis on employees and manufacturing techniques, to which the Japanese economic miracle that began in the 1960s is attributed. Japanese management practices have been studied in the rest of the world in the hope that the economic success they brought to Japan can be recreated elsewhere. These practices emphasise forming collaborations, particularly in times of uncertainty, human resources, closer superior-subordinate relationships, and consensus as a means of facilitating implementation. *Richard Pascale* and *Anthony Athos* suggested that the Japanese *competitive advantage* stemmed from skills, staff, and superordinate goals, the softer features identified by the *McKinsey 7-S framework*. Other dominant characteristics include people-centred management, loyalty to employees, *just-in-time*, *kaizen*, *continuous improvement*, *quality control*, *total quality management*, and the ideas of *W. Edwards Deming*. *William Ouchi* expounded *Theory J* and *Theory Z*, which demonstrated the differences between US and Japanese styles of management. With the downturn in the Japanese economy in the 1990s, management practices were reappraised, and there emerged a focus on radical change as opposed to incremental improvement. Customers were offered less variety, there was a shift towards simplicity, and an alternative to consensus-based decision-making was adopted, with individuals making decisions based on high-tech information systems.

Japanese payment option *E-com* a series of extensions to the *SET* protocol to facilitate handling features unique to the Japanese market. *Abbr* **JPO**

Jaques, Elliot (*b*. 1917) *Gen Mgt* Canadian psychologist and writer. Best known for his participation in the *Glacier studies*, and for originating the *time span of discretion* theory.

Java *E-com* a programming language developed in the mid-1990s to enhance the visual appearance and interactive elements of web documents. Java is automatically translated using a Java-compatible web browser. For example, an Internet user can connect to a Java *applet* on the Web, download it, and run it, all at the click of a mouse.

jelly
like nailing jelly to a tree *Gen Mgt* used for describing a task that is considered impossible, especially when the difficulty arises from poor or sloppy specifications (*slang*)

JEPI *abbr E-com* joint electronic payment initiative

jikan *Fin* in Japan, the priority rule relating to transactions on the Tokyo Stock Exchange whereby the earlier of two buy or sell orders received at the same price prevails

JIT *abbr Ops* just-in-time

job 1. *HR* a position of employment **2.** *Ops* a batch of work that undergoes a specific action through a workstation or workshop

jobber's turn *Fin* formerly, a term used on the London Stock Exchange for a *spread*

jobbing *Ops see* **job production**

jobbing backwards *Fin* a UK term for the analysis of an investment transaction with a view to learning from mistakes rather than apportioning blame

job card *Fin see* **clock card**

job classification *HR* the listing of jobs in groups according to areas of similarity. The term job classification normally applies to a broad classification of work such as the schemes produced by the

---

It can take just as much effort to run a small company as a much larger one.
Barbara Thomas

Office for National Statistics in the United Kingdom or the International Labour Office in Geneva. At an organisational level, job classification is more usually referred to as **job grading** and is used for *job evaluation* purposes.

job costing *Fin* a form of specific order costing in which costs are attributed to individual jobs

job cost sheet *Fin* a detailed record of the amount, and cost, of the labour, material, and overhead charged to a specific job

job design *HR* the process of putting together various elements to form a job, bearing in mind organisational and individual worker requirements, as well as considerations of health, safety, and *ergonomics*. The *scientific management* approach of *Frederick Winslow Taylor* viewed job design as purely mechanistic, but the later *human relations* movement rediscovered the importance of workers' relationship to their work and stressed the importance of *job satisfaction*.

job enlargement *HR* the addition of extra similar tasks to a job. In job enlargement, the job itself remains essentially unchanged, the employee rarely needs to acquire new skills to carry out the additional task, and the motivational benefits of job enrichment are not experienced. Job enlargement is sometimes viewed by employees as a requirement to carry out more work for the same amount of pay.

job evaluation *HR* a technique that aims to provide a systematic, rational, and consistent approach to defining the relative worth of jobs within an organisation. Job evaluation is a system for analysing and comparing different jobs and placing them in a ranking order according to the overall demands of each one. It is not concerned with the volume of work, or with the person doing it, or with determining pay. It is used in order to provide the basis for an equitable and defensible pay structure, particularly in determining *equal pay* for equal value. Job evaluation schemes can be divided into two main

categories: non-analytical and analytical. In non-analytical schemes a job is compared with others as a whole, but such schemes have a limited use, because they are unlikely to succeed as a defence against an equal value claim. In an analytical scheme, a job is split up into a number of different aspects and each factor is measured separately. The main types of analytical schemes are factor comparison, point-factor rating, competency-based schemes, and the *profile method*.

job family *HR* a category of jobs in a similar area. Examples of job families might be engineering, agriculture, health, and sport and leisure. Job families are also found within an organisation, for example, clerical, sales, information technology, and so on. Such families are sometimes used when determining *pay scales* or for statistical analysis of the *workforce*.

job grading *HR see job classification*

job lock *Gen Mgt* the inability to leave a job because of a fear of losing the benefits associated with it (*slang*)

job lot *Fin* a UK term for a miscellaneous assortment of items, including securities, that are offered as a single deal

job process system *Ops see job production*

job production *Ops* the manufacture of different products in unit quantities or in very small numbers. In job production, a complete task may be handled by one worker and is often carried out in a *job shop*. A company may operate under a **job process system**, producing small batches of sometimes unique products and so becoming a job shop in itself. Job production is characterised by a functional grouping of equipment and staff and by the considerable variation in the time it takes to complete a given job. *Also known as jobbing*

job rotation *HR* the movement of employees through a range of jobs in order to increase interest and *motivation*.

Never confuse movement with action.   *Ernest Hemingway*

Job rotation can improve **multiskilling** but involves the need for greater **training**.

job satisfaction *HR* the sense of fulfilment and pride felt by people who enjoy their work and do it well. Various factors influence job satisfaction, and our understanding of the significance of these stems in part from **Frederick Herzberg**. He called elements such as remuneration, working relationships, status, and job security '**hygiene factors**' because they concern the context in which somebody works. Hygiene factors do not in themselves promote job satisfaction, but serve primarily to prevent job dissatisfaction. **Motivators** contribute to job satisfaction and include achievement, recognition, the work itself, responsibility, advancement, and growth. An absence of job satisfaction can lead to poor **motivation**, **stress**, **absenteeism**, and high labour turnover.

job-share *HR* a form of employment in which two or more people occupy a single job. Each person works on a part-time basis and is paid pro-rata for the number of hours they work in the job.

job shop *Ops* a manufacturing facility designed to work on a **job production** basis, producing small quantities of what are often specialised or expensive items. A job shop can be a special facility within a factory, or a whole company can be run as a job shop. Job shops often have the ability to produce a wide variety of products.

job vacuum *Gen Mgt* an employee who voluntarily takes on extra duties (*slang*)

Johari window *HR* a **communication** model that facilitates analysis of both how someone gives and receives information and the dynamics of **interpersonal communication**. The Johari window was developed by Joseph Luft and Henry Ingram. It is normally represented in the form of a grid divided into four sections, each of which represents a type of communication exchange. First, there is the open self: you have awareness of the impact you have on the other and the impact they have on you, so that the risk of interpersonal conflict is minimised. The second sector covers the hidden self: you have awareness of your impact on others, but not of their impact on you. This leads to defensive behaviour in which you seek to hide what you want and increases the possibility of interpersonal conflict. In the third sector, or blind self, you have awareness of what the other wants, but you lack self-awareness of the impact of your communication or actions. Finally, there is the undiscovered self: you lack self-awareness and are either unaware of or cannot understand the other. Although the Johari window can be used in a number of situations, it is most frequently used as a tool for **training** or **coaching** purposes, in order to provide feedback on communication skills.

Johnson, Spencer *Gen Mgt* US writer and consultant. Collaborated with **Kenneth Blanchard** on the concept of one-minute management, but is also known for *Who Moved My Cheese?* (1998), a parable on **change management**.

joined-up *Gen Mgt* relating to an idea or initiative that involves both the community and government in an effort to improve the quality of life for everyone (*slang*)

joint account *Fin* an account, for example one held at a bank or by a broker, that two or more people own in common and have access to

joint and several liability *Fin* a legal liability that applies to a group of individuals as a whole and each member individually, so that if one member does not meet his or her liability, the shortfall is the shared responsibility of the others. Most guarantees given by two or more individuals to secure borrowing are joint and several. It is a typical feature of most partnership agreements.

joint cost *Fin* the cost of a process which results in more than one main product

joint electronic payment initiative *E-com* a proposed industry standard protocol

---

for electronic payment in e-commerce transactions. *Abbr* **JEPI**

joint float *Econ* a situation in which a group of currencies maintains a fixed relationship relative to each other but moves jointly relative to another currency

joint life annuity *Fin* an annuity that continues until both parties have died. They are attractive to married couples as they ensure that the survivor has an income for the rest of his or her life.

joint ownership *Gen Mgt* ownership by more than one party, each with equal rights in the item owned. Joint ownership is often applied to property or other assets.

Joint Photographics Experts Group *E-com see* **JPEG**

joint products *Fin* two or more products produced by the same process and separated in processing, each having a sufficiently high saleable value to merit recognition as a main product. *See also by-product*

joint return *Fin* a tax return filed jointly by a husband and a wife

joint stock bank *Fin* a term that was formerly used for a commercial bank (one that is a partnership), rather than a High Street bank (one that is a public limited company)

joint venture *Fin* a project undertaken by two or more persons/entities joining together with a view to profit, often in connection with a single operation

journal *Fin* a record of original entry, into which transactions are normally transferred from source documents. The journal may be subdivided into: sales journal/day book for credit sales; purchases journal/day book for credit purchases; cash book for cash receipts and payments; and the journal proper for transactions which could not appropriately be recorded in any of the other journals.

JPEG *E-com* Joint Photographics Experts Group: a file format used to compress and store photographic images for transfer over the Internet. *See also* **GIF**

JPO *abbr E-com* Japanese payment option

JSE *abbr Fin* Johannesburg Stock Exchange: the former unofficial name of the JSE Securities Exchange

judgment creditor *Fin* in a legal action, the individual or business who has brought the action and to whom the court orders the judgment debtor to pay the money owed. In the event of the judgment debtor not conforming to the court order, the judgment creditor must return to the court to request that the judgment be enforced.

judgment debtor *Fin* in a legal action, the individual or business ordered to pay the judgment creditor the money owed

jumbo mortgage (*US*) *Fin* a mortgage that is too large to qualify for favourable treatment by a US government agency

junior debt *Fin* a debt that has no claim on a debtor's assets, or less claim than another debt. *See also* **senior debt**. *Also known as* **subordinated debt**

junior mortgage *Fin* a mortgage whose holder has less claim on a debtor's assets than the holder of another mortgage. *See also* **senior mortgage**

junk bond *Fin* a bond with high return and high risk

Juran, Joseph Moses (*b*. 1904) *Gen Mgt* Romanian-born engineer and consultant. Introduced ideas on *total quality management* to Japan and later, like **W. Edwards Deming**, to the West. Juran's methods, first published in *Quality Control Handbook* (1951), centre on building a customer-focused organisation through planning, control and improvement, and good people management.

Juran trained as an electrical engineer, worked for Western Electric in the 1920s, becoming quality manager at their Chicago plant, and later went to work for AT&T. In 1953, he made his first visit to Japan, where he spent two months observing Japanese practices and training managers and engineers in what he called managing for quality. For the next quarter of a century, Juran continued to give seminars on the subject of quality throughout the world. In 1979 he founded the Juran Institute to spread and facilitate the implementation of quality-management programmes worldwide.

just-in-time *Ops* a system whose objective is to produce or to procure products or components as they are required by a customer or for use, rather than for stock. A just-in-time system is a *pull system*, which responds to demand, in contrast to a *push system*, in which stocks act as buffers between the different elements of the system, such as purchasing, production, and sales. *Abbr* **JIT**

just-in-time production *Fin* a production system which is driven by demand for finished products, whereby each component on a production line is produced only when needed for the next stage

just-in-time purchasing *Fin* a purchasing system in which material purchases are contracted so that the receipt and usage of material coincide to the maximum extent possible

K *abbr Fin* a thousand

kaizen *Gen Mgt, Ops* the Japanese term for the **continuous improvement** of current processes. Kaizen is derived from the words 'kai', meaning 'change', and 'zen', meaning 'good' or 'for the better'. It is a philosophy that can be applied to any area of life, but its application has been most famously developed at the Toyota Motor Company, and it underlies the philosophy of **total quality management**. Under kaizen, continuous improvement can mean waste elimination, innovation, or working to new standards. The kaizen process makes use of a range of techniques, including small-group **problem-solving**, **suggestion schemes**, statistical techniques, **brainstorming**, and **work study**. Although kaizen forms only part of a strategy of continuous improvement, for many employees it is the element that most closely affects them and is therefore synonymous with continuous improvement.

kaizen budget *Fin* a budget into which is incorporated the expectation of continuous performance improvement throughout the budget period

kakaku yusen *Fin* in Japan, the price priority system operated on the Tokyo Stock Exchange whereby a lower price takes precedence over a higher price for a sell order, and vice versa for a buy order. *See also* **jikan**

kanban *Ops* a Japanese production management technique that uses cards attached to components to monitor and control workflow in a factory. The kanban system was first developed by the car manufacturer Toyota.

kanbrain *Gen Mgt* relating to the technology that is used in the transmission of knowledge (*slang*)

kangaroo *Fin* an Australian share traded on the London Stock Exchange (*slang*)

Kansas City Board of Trade *Fin* a commodities exchange, established in 1856, that specialises in futures and options contracts for red winter wheat, the Value Line® Index, natural gas, and the ISDEX® Internet Stock Index

Kanter, Rosabeth Moss (*b.* 1943) *Gen Mgt* US academic. Known for her interest in new **organisation structures**, with a focus on harnessing **change**, encouraging **innovation**, and increasing **empowerment** among employees. Her research has also embraced **globalisation**. Among her many books is *The Change Masters* (1988).

Kaplan, Robert *Gen Mgt* US academic. Co-developer, with **David Norton**, of the **balanced scorecard**, which looks at intangible assets such as **customer satisfaction** alongside traditional financial measures. This concept, introduced in a *Harvard Business Review* article of 1992 with the saying 'What you measure is what you get', was explained in *The Balanced Scorecard* (1996).

KBG *Gen Mgt, Ops see* **keiretsu**

Keidanren *Fin* the Japanese abbreviation for the Japan Federation of Economic Organizations. Established in 1946, it aims to work towards a resolution of the major problems facing the Japanese and international business communities and to contribute to the sound development of their economies. The equivalent of the Confederation of British Industry, its members include over 1,000 of Japan's leading corporations (including over 50 foreign companies) and over 100 industry-wide groups representing such major sectors as manufacturing, trade, distribution, finance, and energy.

keiretsu *or* **keiretsu business group** *Gen Mgt, Ops* a Japanese loose **conglomerate company** that promotes interdependencies between firms with interlocking interests in each other and is characterised by close internal control, policy co-ordination, and cohesiveness. Keiretsu business groups are alliances between firms that share close buyer-supplier relationships. The issue of interlocking shares by group affiliated companies to member companies of the group keeps ownership in friendly hands, helps prevent foreign *takeovers*, and aids a company's long-term survival and growth. There are two sorts of keiretsu operation: **horizontal keiretsu**, in which member firms are involved in different industries, and **vertical keiretsu**, in which member firms in one industry form themselves into a hierarchy with a lead company. Vertical KBGs consist largely of manufacturing companies and their subcontractors. Some keiretsu are 350 years old, but most developed from the pre-war *zaibatsu*. The Korean equivalent of the keiretsu is the **chaebol**, and a Mexican equivalent is the *grupo*. *Abbr* **KBG**

Keough Plan *Fin* a pension subject to tax advantage in the United States for somebody who is self-employed or has an interest in a small company. *See also stakeholder pension*

Kepner, Charles Higgins (*b.* 1922) *Gen Mgt* US manager and consultant. Originator with *Benjamin Tregoe* of a methodological approach to *decision-making* based on information gathering, organisation, and analysis, which was first explained in *The Rational Manager* (1965).

kerb market *Fin* a stock market that exists outside the stock exchange. The term originates from markets held in the street.

Kets de Vries, Manfred Florian Robert (*b.* 1942) *Gen Mgt* Dutch psychoanalyst and academic. His principal academic interests focus on the interface between psychoanalysis/dynamic psychiatry and *management*, *leadership*, *entrepreneurship*, and *family business*.

key account management *Mkting* the management of the customer relationships that are most important to a company. Key accounts are those held by customers who produce most *profit* for a company or have the potential to do so, or those who are of strategic importance. Development of these *customer relations* and *customer retention* is important to business success. Particular emphasis is placed on analysing which accounts are key to a company at any one time, determining the needs of these particular customers, and implementing procedures to ensure that they receive premium *customer service* and to increase *customer satisfaction*.

keyboard plaque *Gen Mgt* the build-up of dirt that becomes ingrained in computer keyboards (*slang*)

key factor *Fin see limiting factor*

key-man insurance *Gen Mgt see key-person insurance*

Keynesian economics *Econ* the economic teachings and doctrines associated with John Maynard Keynes

key-person insurance *Gen Mgt* an insurance policy taken out to cover the costs of replacing a key *employee*. Key-person insurance comes into play in the case of an employee's medium- to long-term illness or death. *Also known as key-man insurance*

keyword *E-com* a word used by a search engine to help locate and register a website. Companies need to think very carefully about the keywords they place in their *meta-tags* and in web pages in order to attract relevant search-engine traffic.

keyword search *E-com* a search for documents containing one or more words that are specified by a search-engine user

kiasu *Gen Mgt* a Hokkien word, used to describe the 'must win, never lose' mentality of Singaporeans

kickback *Fin* a sum of money paid illegally in order to gain concessions or favours (*slang*)

kicker *Fin* an addition to a standard security that makes it more attractive, for example, options and warrants (*slang*) *See*

---

*also **bells and whistles** (sense 2), **sweetener** (sense 3)*

killer app *E-com* a computer application that is extremely effective or commercially successful

killerbee *Fin* somebody, especially a banker, who helps a company avoid being taken over

killfile *E-com* a list on an Internet newsreader of undesirable authors or threads that can be filtered out by the user (*slang*)

killing *Fin* a considerable profit on a transaction (*slang*)

Kim, W. Chan *Gen Mgt* Korean-born academic. INSEAD professor, Fellow of the World Economic Forum, writer on the knowledge economy and collaborator with *Renée Mauborgne* on research into *corporate strategy* and *value innovation*.

kimono
open the kimono *Gen Mgt* to inspect something that has not been open for examination before, especially a company's accounts (*slang*)

KISS *abbr Gen Mgt* keep it simple stupid (*slang*)

kiss up to sb (*US*) *Gen Mgt* to attempt to ingratiate yourself with somebody who is in a position of power (*slang*)

kite *Fin* a fraudulent financial transaction, for example, a bad cheque that is dated to take advantage of the time interval required for clearing
fly a kite 1. *Fin* to use a fraudulent financial document such as a bad cheque **2.** *Gen Mgt* to make a suggestion in order to test people's opinion of it

kite-flying *Fin* in the United States, a preliminary or pathfinder prospectus (*slang*)

kiwibond *Fin* a eurobond denominated in New Zealand dollars

knight *Fin* a term borrowed from chess strategy to describe a company involved in the politics of a *takeover* bid. There are three main types of knight. A **white**

knight is a company that is friendly to the board of the company to be acquired. If the white knight gains control, it may retain the existing *board of directors*. A **black knight** is a former white knight that has disagreed with the board of the company to be acquired and has set up its own hostile bid. A **grey knight** is a white knight that does not have the confidence of the company to be acquired.

Knight, Phil (*b*. 1938) *Gen Mgt* US entrepreneur. Founder of Nike Inc, whose worldwide success is based on strong *brand building*, aggressive marketing, and the *outsourcing* of production to Asia.

knock-for-knock *Fin* used to describe a practice between insurance companies whereby each will pay for the repairs to the vehicle it insures in the event of an accident

knocking copy *Gen Mgt* advertising copy that consists of criticism of a competitor's product or company

knock-out option *Fin* an option to which a condition relating to the underlying security or commodity's present price is attached so that it effectively expires when it goes out of the money

knowledge *Gen Mgt* information acquired by the interpretation of experience. Knowledge is built up from interaction with the world and organised and stored in each individual's mind. It is also stored on an organisational level within the minds of employees and in paper and electronic records. Two forms of knowledge can be distinguished: **tacit knowledge** or **implicit knowledge**, which is held in a person's mind and is instinctively known without being formulated into words; and **explicit knowledge**, which has been communicated to others and is contained in written documents and procedures. Organisations are increasingly recognising the value of knowledge, and many employees are now recognised as *knowledge workers*. A major writer in this area is *Ikujiro Nonaka*, co-author of *The Knowledge-creating Company* (1995), who asserted that

---

Of course being called the acceptable face of capitalism would be equally insulting.
Tiny Rowland

knowledge is the greatest core capability (see *core competence*) that an organisation can have.

knowledge-based system *E-com* a specialised search facility on a website that enables a user to type in a question, rather than using keywords, or choosing from a list of frequently asked questions *FAQ*s. The response may involve the user being asked a series of questions in order to narrow down the area of interest. The Ask Jeeves website, www.askjeeves.com, is an example of this approach.

knowledge capital *Gen Mgt* knowledge that a company possesses and can put to profitable use

knowledge management *Gen Mgt* **1.** the process of acquiring, storing, distributing and using information within a company. The information is generally held on a powerful database and distributed via a communications network. **2.** the co-ordination and exploitation of an organisation's *knowledge* resources, in order to create benefit and *competitive advantage*

knowledge worker *Gen Mgt* an *employee* who deals in information, ideas, and expertise. Knowledge workers are products of the so-called information age, in which the emphasis is on *creativity* and *innovation* rather than on maintaining the status quo. According to *Peter Drucker*, in the new economy every employee is becoming a knowledge worker.

Kolb, David (*b*. 1939) *Gen Mgt* US academic. Originator of the concept of *experiential learning*, a model describing how adults learn, which he explained in the book of the same name (1984).

Kotler, Philip (*b*. 1931) *Gen Mgt* US academic. Acknowledged as an expert in **marketing** theory, which he has made a major business function and academic discipline, and which he explained in *Marketing Management* (first published 1980).

Krugerrand *Fin* a South African coin consisting of one ounce of gold, first minted in 1967, bearing the portrait of Paul Kruger on the obverse

---

laboratory training *Gen Mgt see* **sensitivity training**

labor union *(US) Gen Mgt, HR* = **trade union**

labour dispute *HR* **1.** a disagreement or conflict between an **employer** and **employees** or between the **employers' association** and **trade union 2.** *see* **strike**

labour force *HR* people of working age who are available for paid employment, including the unemployed looking for work, but excluding categories such as full-time students, carers, and the long-term sick and disabled

labour force survey *Stats* a survey carried out every quarter in the United Kingdom, covering such topics as unemployment and hours of work

labour-intensive *Fin* involving large numbers of workers or high labour costs

labour market *HR* a market that brings together employers and people who are looking for employment

labour shortage *HR* **1.** a lack of workers or potential workers to fill the jobs available **2.** a lack of suitably qualified and skilled workers to fill particular vacancies. This is more correctly described as a *skills shortage*.

labour tourist *HR* somebody who lives in one country but works in another (*slang*)

Lady Macbeth strategy *Gen Mgt* a change of approach on the part of a presumed **white knight**, in which it becomes a black knight. A Lady Macbeth strategy is usually associated with **take-over** battles and has connotations of treachery.

laggard *Mkting see* **first mover**

lagging indicator *(US) Econ* a measurable economic factor, for example, corporate profits or unemployment, that

changes after the economy has already moved to a new trend, which it can confirm but not predict

LAN *E-com see* **network**

land bank *Fin* the land that a builder or developer has that is available for development

land banking *(US) Fin* the practice of buying land that is not needed immediately, but with the expectation of using it in the future

land tax *Fin* a form of wealth tax imposed in Australia on the value of residential land. The level and conditions of the tax vary from state to state.

lapping *(US) Fin* = **teeming and lading**

lapse *Fin* the termination of an option without trade in the underlying security or commodity

lapse rights *Fin* rights, such as those to a specified premium, owned by the person who allows an offer to lapse

large-sized business *Gen Mgt* an organisation that has grown beyond the limits of a *medium-sized business* and has 500 or more employees. It is usually from the ranks of large-sized businesses that *multinational businesses* arise.

last-in first-out *HR see* **LIFO**

last survivor policy *Fin* an assurance policy covering the lives of two or more people. The sum assured is not paid out until all the policyholders are deceased. *See also* **joint life annuity**

latent market *Mkting* a group of people who have been identified as potential consumers of a product that does not yet exist

lateral thinking *Gen Mgt* a creative method of problem-solving that ignores traditional logic and approaches problems from unorthodox perspectives. Lateral

---

The man who views the world at fifty the same as he did at twenty has wasted thirty years of his life.
Muhammad Ali

thinking was developed by **Edward de Bono**, who distinguished two forms of thinking: vertical thinking, which is based on logic; and lateral thinking, which disregards apparently rational trains of thought and branches out at tangents. Lateral thinking involves the examination of a problem and its possible solutions from all angles. Seemingly intractable problems often can be solved in this manner, and it is a technique used in **brainstorming**, or to help generate **creativity** and **innovation** within organisations.

launch *Mkting* the process of introducing a new product to the market

laundering *Fin* the process of making money obtained illegally appear legitimate by passing it through banks or businesses

law of diminishing returns *Gen Mgt* a rule stating that as one factor of production is increased, while others remain constant, the extra output generated by the additional input will eventually fall. The law of diminishing returns therefore means that extra workers, extra capital, extra machinery, or extra land may not necessarily raise output as much as expected. For example, increasing the supply of raw materials to a production line may allow additional output to be produced by using any spare capacity workers have. Once this capacity is fully used, however, continually increasing the amount of raw material without a corresponding increase in the number of workers will not result in an increase of output.

law of supply and demand *Gen Mgt see* **supply and demand**

lay-by (*ANZ*) *Gen Mgt* the reservation of an article for purchase by the payment of an initial deposit followed by regular interest-free instalments, on completion of which the article is claimed by the buyer

lay off *HR* **1.** to dismiss workers permanently **2.** to suspend workers temporarily because of lack of work

layoff (*US*) *Gen Mgt* = **redundancy**

layout by function *Ops see* **process layout**

LBO *abbr Fin* leveraged buyout

LCH *abbr Fin* London Clearing House

LCM *abbr Fin* lower of cost or market

LDC *abbr Econ* less developed country

lead *Fin* in an insurance policy from Lloyd's, the first named underwriting syndicate

leader **1.** *Gen Mgt, HR* a business executive who possesses exceptional leadership qualities as well as management skills **2.** *Mkting* the most successful product or company in a marketplace

leadership *Gen Mgt, HR* the capacity to establish direction and to influence and align others towards a common aim, motivating and committing them to action and making them responsible for their performance. Leadership theory is one of the most discussed areas of management, and many different approaches are taken to the topic. Some notions of leadership are related to types of **authority** delineated by **Max Weber**. It is often suggested that leaders possess innate personal qualities that distinguish them from others: **great man theory** and **trait theory** express this idea. Other theories, such as **Behaviourist Theories of Leadership**, suggest that leadership is defined by action and behaviour, rather than by personality. A related idea is that leadership style is not fixed but should be adapted to different situations, and this is explored in **contingency theory** and situational theory. A further branch of research that examines relationships between leaders and followers is found in **transactional**, **transformational**, **attribution**, and **power and influence theories of leadership**. Perhaps the most simple model of leadership is **action-centred leadership**, which focuses on what an effective leader actually does. These many approaches and differences of opinion illustrate the complexity of the leadership role and the intangibility of the essence of good leadership.

The nature of business is swindling. **August Bebel**

leading economic indicator *Econ* a factor such as private-sector wages that is used as a reference for public-sector wage claims

leading-edge *Gen Mgt* situated at the forefront of *innovation*. A leading-edge company is ahead of others in such areas as inventing or implementing new technologies, and in entering new markets.

lead manager *Fin* the financial institution with overall responsibility for a new issue including its co-ordination, distribution, and related administration

lead partner *Gen Mgt* the organisation that takes the lead role in an alliance

leads and lags *Fin* in businesses that deal in foreign currencies, the practice of speeding up the receipt of payments (leads) if a currency is going to weaken, and slowing down the payment of costs (lags) if a currency is thought to be about to strengthen, in order to maximise gains and reduce losses

lead time *Ops* 1. in inventory control, the time between placing an order and its arrival on site. Lead time differs from delivery time in that it also includes the time required to place an order and the time it takes to inspect the goods and receive them into the appropriate store. Inventory levels can afford to be lower and orders smaller when purchasing lead times are short. 2. in *new product development* and manufacturing, the time required to develop a product from concept to market delivery. Lead time increases as a result of the poor sequencing of dependent activities, the lack of availability of resources, poor quality in the component parts, and poor plant layout. The technique of *concurrent engineering* focuses on the entire concept-to-customer process with the aim of reducing lead time. Companies can gain a *competitive advantage* by achieving a lead-time reduction and so getting products to market faster. *Also known as cycle time*

lead underwriter *(US) Fin* = *lead manager*

leaky reply *E-com* an e-mail response that is accidentally sent to the wrong recipient and causes embarrassment to the sender (*slang*)

lean enterprise *Ops* an organisational model that strategically applies the key ideas behind *lean production*. The concept of the lean enterprise was proposed by J.P. Womack and D.T. Jones in their 1994 *Harvard Business Review* article 'From lean production to the lean enterprise'. They view the lean enterprise as a group of separate individuals, functions, or organisations that operate as one entity. The aim is to apply lean techniques that create individual breakthroughs in companies and to link these up and down the *supply chain* to form a continuous value stream to raise the whole chain to a higher level.

lean manufacturing *Ops see lean production*

lean operation *Ops see lean production*

lean production *Ops* a methodology aimed at reducing waste in the form of overproduction, excessive *lead time*, or product defects in order to make a business more effective and more competitive. Lean production originates in the production systems established by Toyota in Japan in the 1950s. In the early 1980s there was a significant increase in the application of lean production in Western companies. Lean production is characterised by **lean operations** with low *inventories*, *quality management* through prevention of errors, small batch runs, *just-in-time* production, high commitment human resource policies, team-based working, and close relations with suppliers. The term lean production was popularised by researchers on the International Motor Vehicle Program of the Massachusetts Institute of Technology in their book *The Machine that Changed the World*. Concepts that can help an organisation move towards lean production include *continuous improvement* and

---

Draw your salary before spending it.   *George Ade*

world class manufacturing. *Also known as* *lean manufacturing*

LEAPS *Fin* long-term equity anticipation securities, options that expire between one and three years in the future

learning by doing *Gen Mgt* the acquisition of knowledge or skills through direct experience of carrying out a task. Learning by doing often happens under supervision, as part of a training or *induction* process, and is closely associated with the practical experience picked up by '**sitting with Nellie**'. It is an outcome of the research into learning of *David Kolb* and *Reg Revans*. A more formalised approach to learning by doing is *experiential learning*.

learning curve *Gen Mgt* **1.** a graphic representation of the acquisition of knowledge or experience over time. A steep learning curve reflects a substantial amount of learning in a short time, and a shallow curve reflects a slower learning process. The curve eventually levels out to a plateau, during which time the knowledge gained is being consolidated. **2.** the proportional decrease in effort when production is doubled. The learning curve has its origin in *productivity* research in the aeroplane industry of the 1930s, when *T.P. Wright* discovered that in assembling an aircraft, the time and effort decreased by 20% each time the cumulative number of planes produced doubled. *Bruce Henderson* of the Boston Consulting Group formulated the learning curve as a strategic planning device in the 1960s by plotting product costs against cumulative volume.

learning organisation *Gen Mgt* an organisational model characterised by a *flat* structure and *customer-focused* teams, that engenders the collective ability to develop shared visions by capturing and exploiting employees' willingness, commitment, and curiosity. The concept of the learning organisation was proposed by *Chris Argyris* and *Donald Schön* as part of their work on *organisational learning*, but was brought back to public attention in the 1990s by *Peter Senge*. For Senge, a learning organisation is one with the capacity to shift away from views inherent in a traditional hierarchical organisation, towards the ability of all employees to challenge prevailing thinking and gain a balanced perspective. Senge believes the five major elements of a learning organisation are mental models, personal mastery, *systems thinking*, shared vision, and team learning. Because of the requirement for an open, risk-tolerant culture, which is the opposite of the *corporate culture* of most organisations today, the learning organisation remains, for many, an unattainable ideal.

learning relationship *Gen Mgt* a relationship between a supplier and a customer in which the supplier modifies or customises a product as it learns more about the customer's requirements

learning style *Gen Mgt* the way in which somebody approaches the acquisition of knowledge and skills. Learning styles have been divided into four main types by *Peter Honey* and *Alan Mumford*, in their *Manual of Learning Styles* (1982). The types of learner are: the activist, who likes to get involved in new experiences and enjoys the challenges of change; the theorist, who likes to question assumptions and methodologies and learns best when there is time to explore links between ideas and situations; the pragmatist, who prefers practicality and learns best when there is a link between the subject matter and the job in hand and when he or she can try out what he or she has learned; and the reflector, who likes to take his or her time and think things through, and who learns best from activities where he or she can observe and carry out research. One person can demonstrate more than one learning style, and the category or categories that best describe somebody can be determined through use of a learning styles questionnaire.

leaseback *Fin see* *sale and leaseback*

leave *HR* work time when an employee is paid, but is not required to be at work.

Leave takes several forms and includes *holiday* entitlement. The number of days of holiday is agreed in the *contract of employment* and may be dependent on the employee's length of service. It may also take the form of *sick leave*, *compassionate leave*, *garden leave*, *educational leave*, or *maternity* or *paternity leave*.

Leavitt, Harold (*b.* 1922) *Gen Mgt* US psychologist and academic. Researcher with an interest in *organisation behaviour* and psychology, and originator of *Leavitt's Diamond* and author of *Managerial Psychology* (1958).

Leavitt's Diamond *Gen Mgt* a model for analysing management change, developed by *Harold Leavitt*. Leavitt's Diamond is based on the idea that it is rare for any change to occur in isolation. Leavitt sees technology, tasks, people, and the organisational structure in which they function as four interdependent variables, visualised as the four points of a diamond. Change at any one point of the diamond will impact on some or all of the others. Thus, a changed task will necessarily affect the people involved in it, the structure in which they work, and the technology that they use. Failure to manage these interdependencies at critical times of change can create problems. *See also change management*

ledger *Fin* a collection of accounts, maintained by transfers from the books of original entry. The ledger may be subdivided as follows: the sales ledger/debtors ledger contains the personal accounts of all customers; the purchases ledger/creditors ledger contains all the personal accounts of suppliers; the private ledger contains accounts relating to the proprietor's interest in the business such as capital and drawings; the general ledger/nominal ledger contains all other accounts relating to assets, expenses, revenue, and liabilities.

legacy system *E-com* an existing computer system that provides a strategic function for a specific part of a business. Inventory management systems, for example, are legacy systems.

legal loophole *Gen Mgt* an area in the law that is insufficiently explicit or comprehensive and allows the law to be circumvented

legal tender *Fin* banknotes and coins that have to be accepted within a given jurisdiction when offered as payment of a debt. *See also limited legal tender*

legs *Gen Mgt* a longer-than-usual life for an advertising campaign, film, book, or other short-lived product (*slang*)

lekgotla (*S Africa*) *Gen Mgt see bosberaad*

lemon (*slang*) **1.** *Fin* an investment that is performing poorly **2.** *Gen Mgt* a product, especially a car, that is defective in some way

lender of last resort *Fin* a central bank that lends money to banks that cannot borrow elsewhere

length of service *HR* the period in which a person has been continually employed within an organisation, without breaks in the *contract of employment*. Length of service may determine entitlement to employment rights or *fringe benefits*, for example, the amount of annual leave allocated.

less developed country *Econ* a country whose economic development is held back by the lack of natural resources to produce goods demanded on world markets. *Abbr* **LDC**

lessee *Fin* the person who has the use of a leased asset

lessor *Fin* the person who provides the asset being leased

letter of agreement *Gen Mgt* a document that constitutes a simple form of contract

letter of allotment *Fin* a document that says how many shares have been allotted to a shareholder

letter of comfort *Fin* a letter from a holding company addressed to a bank where one of its subsidiaries wishes to borrow money. The purpose of the letter is to support the subsidiary's application to borrow funds and offer reassurance—although not a guarantee—to the bank that the subsidiary will remain in business for the foreseeable future, often with an undertaking to advise the bank if the subsidiary is likely to be sold. *US term **letter of moral intent***

letter of credit *Fin* a letter issued by a bank that can be presented to another bank to authorise the issue of credit or money

letter of indemnity *Fin* a statement that a share certificate has been lost, destroyed, or stolen and that the shareholder will indemnify the company for any loss that might result from its reappearance after the company has issued a replacement to the shareholder

letter of intent *Fin* a document in which an individual or organisation indicates an intention to do something, for example, buy a business, grant somebody a loan, or participate in a project. The intention may or may not depend on certain conditions being met and the document is not legally binding. *See also **letter of comfort***

letter of licence *Fin* a letter from a creditor to a debtor who is having problems repaying money owed, giving the debtor a certain period of time to raise the money and an undertaking not to bring legal proceedings to recover the debt during that period

letter of moral intent (*US*) *Fin* = *letter of comfort*

letter of renunciation *Fin* a form used to transfer an allotment

level playing field *Gen Mgt* a situation in which all competitors are in a position of equal strength or weakness (*slang*)

level production *Gen Mgt* see *production smoothing*

level term assurance *Fin* a life assurance policy in which an agreed lump sum is paid if the policyholder dies before a certain date. A joint form of this life cover is often popular with couples who have children.

leverage *Fin* a method of corporate funding in which a higher proportion of funds is raised through borrowing than share issue

leveraged bid *Fin* a takeover bid financed by borrowed money, rather than by an issue of shares

leveraged buyout *Fin* a takeover using borrowed money, with the purchased company's assets as collateral. *Abbr* **LBO**

leveraged required return *Fin* the rate of return from an investment of borrowed money needed to make the investment worthwhile

leverage ratios (*US*) *Fin* = *gearing ratios*

Levitt, Theodore (*b.* 1925) *Gen Mgt* German-born academic. Harvard professor, who wrote the landmark article 'Marketing myopia', *Harvard Business Review* (July/August 1960). In this article, which has sold over 500,000 reprints and genuinely changed basic perceptions of business practice, Levitt argued that the central preoccupation of corporations should be with satisfying their customers, rather than simply producing goods. According to Levitt, production-led thinking inevitably led to narrow perspectives, the ultimate result of which would be that customers would be overlooked.

Lewin, Kurt (1890–1947) *Gen Mgt* German-born social psychologist. Known for studies of *leadership* styles and group *decision-making*, developer of *force field analysis* with a linked *change management* model, pioneer of *action research* and the T-Group (*see sensitivity training*) approach.

Lewin was a professor of philosophy and psychology at Berlin University until 1932 when he fled from the Nazis to the United States. He was professor of child psychology at the Child Welfare Research Station in Iowa until 1944. After leaving Iowa, Lewin worked at MIT, with *Douglas*

McGregor among others, founding a research centre for group dynamics.

liability *Fin* a debt that has no claim on a debtor's assets, or less claim than another debt

liability insurance *Fin* insurance against legal liability that the insured might incur, for example, from causing an accident

liability management *Fin* any exercise carried out by a business with the aim of controlling the effect of liabilities on its profitability. This will typically involve controlling the amount of risk undertaken, and ensuring that there is sufficient liquidity and that the best terms are obtained for any funding needs.

LIBID *abbr Fin* London Inter Bank Bid Rate

LIBOR *abbr Fin* London Inter Bank Offered Rate

licence *Gen Mgt* a contractual arrangement, or a document representing this, in which one organisation gives another the rights to produce, sell, or use something in return for payment

licensing *Mkting* the transfer of rights to manufacture or market a particular product to another individual or organisation through a legal arrangement or contract. Licensing usually requires that a fee, commission, or royalty is paid to the licensor. *See also franchise*

licensing agreement *Mkting* an agreement permitting a company to market or produce a product or service owned by another company. A licensing agreement grants a licence in return for a fee or royalty payment. Items licensed for use can include patents, trademarks, techniques, designs, and expertise. This kind of agreement is one way for a company to penetrate overseas markets in that it provides a middle path between direct export and investment overseas.

life annuity *Fin* an annuity that pays a fixed amount per month until the holder's death

life assurance *Fin* insurance that pays a specified sum to the insured person's beneficiaries after the person's death. *US* term **life insurance**. *Also known as* **life cover**

life assured *Fin* the person or persons covered by a life assurance policy. The *life office* pays out on the death of the policyholder.

lifeboat (*S Africa*) *Fin* a low-interest emergency loan made by a central bank to rescue a commercial bank in danger of becoming insolvent

life cover *Fin see life assurance*

life cycle *Gen Mgt* the sales pattern of a product or service over a period of time. Typically, a life cycle falls into four stages: introduction, growth, maturity, and decline.

life-cycle costing *Fin* the maintenance of physical asset cost records over the entire life of an asset, so that decisions concerning the acquisition, use, or disposal of the assets can be made in a way that achieves the optimum asset usage at the lowest possible cost to the entity. The term may be applied to the profiling of cost over a product's life, including the pre-production stage (**terotechnology**), and to both company and industry life cycles.

life-cycle savings motive *Econ* the reasons that a household or individual has for saving or spending in the course of life. These can include spending when starting a family or saving when near retirement.

life expectancy *Stats* the number of years that somebody of a given age is expected to live

life insurance (*US*) *Fin* = **life assurance**

lifelong learning *Gen Mgt* the continual acquisition of knowledge and skills throughout somebody's life. Lifelong learning occurs in preparation for, and in response to, the different roles, situations, and environments that somebody will encounter in the course of a lifetime. It is

---

Over the past 25 years, economic forecasters have missed four of the past five recessions.
Anonymous

supported by formal and informal education systems, both within and outside the workplace, through which somebody can both learn and receive guidance and encouragement. The adoption of lifelong learning is seen as a key element in *CPD*, and as an important tool in maintaining *employability*.

life office *Fin* a company that provides life assurance

life policy *Fin* a life assurance contract

lifestyle business *Fin* a typically small business run by individuals who have a keen interest in the product or service offered, for example, handmade greetings cards or jewellery, antique dealing or restoring. Such businesses tend to operate during hours that suit the owners, and generally provide them with a comfortable living.

life table *Stats* a table that shows the probabilities of death, survival, and remaining years of life for people of given ages

lifetime customer value *Mkting* a measure or forecast of a customer's total expenditure on an organisation's products over a period of time

lifetime transfer *Fin* see *chargeable transfer*

lifetime value *Gen Mgt* a measure of the total value to a supplier of a customer's business over the duration of their transactions.

In a consumer business, customer lifetime value is calculated by analysing the behaviour of a group of customers who have the same recruitment date. The revenue and cost for this group of customers is recorded, by campaign or season, and the overall contribution for that period can then be worked out. Industry experience has shown that the benefits to a business of increasing lifetime value can be enormous. A 5% increase in customer retention can create a 125% increase in profits; a 10% increase in retailer retention can translate to a 20% increase in sales; and extending customer life cycles by three years can treble profits per customer.

LIFFE *abbr Fin* London International Financial Futures and Options Exchange

LIFO *abbr HR* last in first out: a technique used when selecting employees for *redundancy*, where the most recent recruits are the first to be made redundant. The LIFO technique has the benefits of reducing redundancy costs and of being seen as fair by some employees. Its disadvantages, however, are increasingly being recognised. It can result in a serious imbalance in the age profile of the workforce and can remove recently acquired skills. It may also be discriminatory, as men are more likely to have built up periods of *continuous service* than women.

lift

let's put it in a lift and see what floor it stops at *Gen Mgt* let's try this idea and see what happens (*slang*)

lightning strike *HR* a *strike* that occurs at very short notice. It may be of short duration and may not be sanctioned by a *trade union*.

light pages *E-com* web pages that are under 50KB in size, enabling them to download quickly

Likert, Rensis (1903–81) *Gen Mgt* US psychologist and academic. Known for situational leadership research and in particular for establishing four systems of management to interpret the way managers behave towards others. In *New Patterns of Management* (1961), Likert described these systems as exploitive/authoritative, benevolent/authoritative, consultative, and participative. He later suggested a system 5 in which the authority of hierarchy disappears.

LIMEAN *abbr Fin* London Inter Bank Mean Rate

limit *Fin* an amount above or below which a broker is not to conclude the purchase or sale of a security for the client who specifies it

---

By definition, risk-takers often fail. So do morons. In practice it's difficult to sort them out.
Scott Adams

limit down *Fin* the most that the price of an option may fall in one day on a particular market

Limited *Fin* used to indicate that a UK company is a limited company when placed at the end of the company's name

limited by guarantee *Fin see public limited company*

limited company *Gen Mgt, HR see private company, public limited company*

limited legal tender *Fin* in some jurisdictions, low denomination notes and all coins that may only be submitted up to a certain sum as legal tender in any one transaction

limited liability *Fin* the restriction of an owner's loss in a business to the amount of capital he or she has invested in it

limited liability company *Fin* a company in which a number of people provide finance in return for shares. The principle of limited liability limits the maximum loss a shareholder can make if the company fails. *US term* **corporation**

limited market *Fin* a market in which dealings for a specific security are difficult to transact, for example, because it has only limited appeal to investors or, in the case of shares, because institutions or family members are unlikely to sell them

limiting factor *Fin* anything which limits the activity of an entity. An entity seeks to optimise the benefit it obtains from the limiting factor. Examples are a shortage of supply of a resource, or a restriction on sales demand at a particular price. *Also known as* **key factor**

limit up *Fin* the most that the price of an option may rise in one day on a particular market

linear programming *Fin* the use of a series of linear equations to construct a mathematical model. The objective is to obtain an optimal solution to a complex operational problem, which may involve the production of a number of products in an environment in which there are many constraints.

line item budget *Fin* the traditional form of budget layout showing, line by line, the costs of a cost object analysed by their nature (salaries, occupancy, maintenance, etc.)

line management *Gen Mgt, HR* a hierarchical **chain of command** from executive to front-line level. Line management is the oldest and least complex management structure, in which top management have total and direct authority and employees report to only one **supervisor**. Managers in this type of **organisation structure** have direct responsibility for giving orders to their subordinates. Line management structures are usually organised along functional lines, although they increasingly undertake cross-functional duties such as **employee development** or strategic direction. The lowest managerial level in an organisation following a line management structure is **supervisory management**.

line manager *HR* an employee's immediate superior, who oversees and has responsibility for the employee's work. A line manager at the lowest level of a large organisation is a **supervisor**, but a manager at any level with direct responsibility for employees' work can be described as a line manager.

line of credit *Fin* an agreed finance facility that allows a company or individual to borrow money. *Also known as* **credit line**

line organisation *Gen Mgt* an **organisation structure** based on **line management**

link *E-com* a pointer to another record, embedded in a document. One or more documents can be connected by inserting links. On the Internet, a link is a reference either to another website or to another document.

linking *E-com* connecting two websites or documents by inserting **links**.

Linking is one of the simplest, yet most effective, Internet marketing devices available. It is like embedded word of mouth: if another website links to yours, it

---

There's no such thing as bad publicity except your own obituary.   *Brendan Behan*

is essentially recommending you to its own visitors. Likewise, it is important to be certain that any other websites that you place links to within your own site are likely to be of interest to your own visitors.

link rot *E-com* the process by which links to websites become obsolete as the websites to which they refer change address or cease to function (*slang*)

liquid asset ratio *Fin* the ratio of liquid assets to total assets

liquid assets *Fin* financial assets that can be quickly converted to cash

liquidated damages *Fin* an amount of money somebody pays for breaching a contract

liquidation *Fin* a process in which a company ceases to be a legal entity, usually because it is insolvent. The company's assets are then sold by a *liquidator* to discharge debts.

liquidation value *Fin* the amount of money that a quick sale of all of a company's assets would yield

liquidator *Fin* the person appointed by a company, its creditors, or its shareholders to sell the assets of an insolvent company. The proceeds of the sale are used to discharge debts to creditors, with any surplus distributed to shareholders.

liquidity *Fin* the ability to convert an asset to cash quickly at its market value

liquidity agreement *Fin* an agreement to allow conversion of an asset into cash

liquidity preference *Econ* a choice made by people to hold their wealth in the form of liquid cash rather than bonds or stocks

liquidity ratio *Fin see* **cash ratio**

liquidity trap *Fin* a central bank's inability to lower interest rates once investors believe rates can go no lower

liquid market *Fin* a market in which an ample number of shares is being traded

list broker *Fin, Gen Mgt* a person or organisation that makes the arrangements for one company to use another company's direct mail list

listed company *Fin* a company whose shares trade on an exchange

listed security *Fin* a security listed on an exchange

listing requirements *Fin* the conditions that have to be met before a security can be traded on a recognised stock exchange. Although exact requirements vary from one exchange to another, the two main ones are that the issuing company's assets should exceed a minimum amount and that the required information about its finances and business should have been published.

list price *Ops* the price of goods or services published by a supplier. The list price of an item may be discounted to regular customers or for bulk purchases.

list renting *Gen Mgt* an arrangement in which a company that owns a direct mail list lets another company use it for a fee

litigation *Gen Mgt* the process of bringing a lawsuit against an individual or organisation

Little Board *Fin* the American Stock Exchange (*slang*). *See also* **Big Board**

live chat *E-com* a facility that enables two or more Web users to communicate with each other in real time, using text.
   Live chat is frequently employed in customer support services. This is because one of its main benefits is that a customer does not need to disconnect from the Internet in order to telephone a support line: live chat means they can receive text-based support without having to disconnect. *Also called* **instant messaging**

livery *Mkting* a mark of corporate identity used on a company vehicle

living wage *HR* a level of *pay* that provides just enough income for normal day-to-day subsistence

LME *abbr Fin* London Metal Exchange

load *Fin* an initial charge in some investment funds. *See also* **load fund**

load fund *Fin* a unit trust that charges a fee for the purchase or sale of shares. *See also* **no-load fund**

loading 1. (*ANZ*) *HR* a payment made to workers over and above the basic wage in recognition of special skills or unfavourable conditions, for example, for overtime or shiftwork **2.** *Ops* the assignment of tasks or jobs to a workstation. The loading of jobs is worked out through the use of *master production scheduling*. Workstations may be loaded to *finite* or *infinite loading* levels.

loan *Fin* borrowing either by a business or a consumer where the amount borrowed is repaid according to an agreed schedule at an agreed interest rate, typically by regular instalments over a set period of years. However, the principal may be repayable in one instalment. *See also* **balloon loan**, **fixed-rate loan**, **interest-only mortgage**, **variable interest rate**

loanable funds theory *Fin* the theory that interest rates are determined solely by supply and demand

loanback *Fin* the ability of a holder of a pension fund to borrow money from it

loan capital *Fin* debentures and other long-term loans to a business

loan constant ratio *Fin* the total of annual payments due on a loan as a fraction of the amount of the principal

Loan Council (*ANZ*) *Fin* an Australian federal body made up of treasurers from the states and the Commonwealth of Australia that monitors borrowing by state governments

loan loss reserves *Fin* the money a bank holds to cover losses through defaults on loans that it makes

loan production cycle *Fin* the period that begins with an application for a loan and ends with the lending of money

loan schedule *Fin* a list of the payments due on a loan and the balance outstanding after each has been made

loan shark *Fin* somebody who lends money at excessively, and often illegally, high rates of interest

loan stock *Fin* bonds and debentures

loan to value ratio *Fin* the ratio of the amount of a loan to the value of the collateral for it

loan value *Fin* the amount that a lender is willing to lend a borrower

lobby *Gen Mgt* a pressure group that seeks to influence government or legislators on behalf of a particular cause or interest

localisation *E-com* the translation of a website into the language or idiom of the target user.
    Studies have shown that if a vendor is serious about selling to foreign marketplaces, localising their website is essential: without it, sales will be minimal and returns very high because of misunderstanding by people who are purchasing in a foreign language.

lock-out *HR* a form of industrial action taken by an employer during a dispute in which employees are prevented from entering the business premises

logistics *Ops* the management of the movement, storage, and processing of materials and information in the *supply chain*. Logistics encompasses the acquisition of raw materials and components, manufacturing or processing, and the distribution of finished products to the end user. Each organisation focuses on a different aspect of logistics, depending on its area of interest. For example, one might apply logistics to find a way of linking *physical distribution management* with earlier events in the supply chain, another to plan its acquisition and storage, while a third might use logistics as a support operation.

logistics management *Ops* the management of the distribution of products to the market

---

Familiarity is the culmination of successful brand building.   *Robert Heller*

logo *Gen Mgt* a graphic device or symbol used by an organisation as part of its corporate identity. A logo is used to facilitate instant recognition of an organisation and to reinforce *brand* expectations and public image.

log of claims *(ANZ)* *HR* a document listing the demands made by employees on an employer or vice versa, often submitted during industrial negotiations

LOL *abbr Gen Mgt* laugh out loud *(slang)*

London Bullion Market *Fin* the world's largest market for gold where silver is also traded. It is a wholesale market, where the minimum trades are generally 1,000 ounces for gold and 50,000 ounces for silver. Members typically trade with each other and their clients on a principal-to-principal basis so that all risks, including those of credit, are between the two parties to the transaction.

London Chamber of Commerce and Industry *Fin* in the United Kingdom, the largest chamber of commerce that aims 'to help London businesses succeed by promoting their interests and expanding their opportunities as members of a worldwide business network'. *See also* **ICC**

London Clearing House *Fin* an organisation that acts on behalf of its members as a central counterparty for contracts traded on the London International Financial Futures and Options Exchange, the International Petroleum Exchange, and the London Metal Exchange. When the LCH has registered a trade, it becomes the buyer to every member who sells and the seller to every member who buys, ensuring good financial performance. To protect it against the risks assumed as central counterparty, the LCH establishes margin requirements. *See also* **margining**. *Abbr* **LCH**

London Commodity Exchange *Fin see* **London International Financial Futures and Options Exchange**

London Inter Bank Bid Rate *Fin* on the UK money markets, the rate at which banks will bid to take deposits in eurocurrency from each other. The deposits are for terms from overnight up to five years. *Abbr* **LIBID**

London Inter Bank Mean Rate *Fin* the average of the London Inter Bank Offered Rate and the London Inter Bank Bid Rate, occasionally used as a reference rate. *Abbr* **LIMEAN**

London Inter Bank Offered Rate *Fin* on the UK money markets, the rate at which banks will offer to make deposits in eurocurrency from each other, often used as a reference rate. The deposits are for terms from overnight up to five years. *Abbr* **LIBOR**

London International Financial Futures and Options Exchange *Fin* an exchange for trading financial futures and options. Established in 1982, it offered contracts on interest rates denominated in most of the world's major currencies until 1992, when it merged with the London Traded Options Market, adding equity options to its product range. In 1996 it merged with the London Commodity Exchange, adding a range of soft commodity and agricultural commodity contracts to its financial portfolio. From November 1998, trading was gradually migrated from the floor of the exchange to screen-based trading. *Abbr* **LIFFE**

London Metal Exchange *Fin* one of the world's largest non-ferrous metal exchanges that deals in aluminium, tin, and nickel. The primary roles of the exchange are hedging, providing official international reference prices, and appropriate storage facilities. Its origins can be traced back to 1571, though in its present form it dates from 1877. *Abbr* **LME**

London Traded Options Market *Fin see* **London International Financial Futures and Options Exchange**

long *Fin* having more shares than are promised for sale

No man can produce great things who is not thoroughly sincere in dealing with himself.
James Russell Lowell

long-dated bond *Fin* a bond issued by the United Kingdom with a maturity at least 15 years in the future

long-dated gilt *Fin see gilt-edged security*

longitudinal study *Stats* a statistical study that produces data gathered over a period of time

long position *Fin* a situation in which dealers hold securities, commodities, or contracts, expecting prices to rise

long-service award *HR* a gift to recognise the *length of service* of an employee within an organisation. A long-service award may be cash or may take the form of something an employee will value. The tradition of a clock or watch for 25 or 40 years of service is being replaced by awards recognising shorter durations of employment and the greater mobility of employees.

long-service leave (*ANZ*) *HR* a period of paid leave awarded by some employers to staff who have completed several years of service

long-term *Gen Mgt* involving a long period of time, for example, years rather than weeks or months

long-term bond *Fin* a bond that has at least 10 years before its redemption date, or, in some markets, a bond with more than seven years until its redemption date

long-term debt *Fin* loans that are due after at least one year

long-term equity anticipation securities *Fin see LEAPS*

long-term financing *Fin* forms of funding such as loans or stock issue that do not have to be repaid immediately

long-term lease *Fin* a lease of at least ten years

long-term liabilities *Fin* forms of debt such as loans that do not have to be repaid immediately

lookback option *Fin* an option whose price the buyer chooses from all of the prices that have existed during the option's life

loop
in the loop *Gen Mgt* up to date with what is happening currently (*slang*)

loss *Fin* a financial position in which costs exceed income

loss adjuster *Fin, Gen Mgt* a professional person acting on behalf of an insurance company to assess the value of an insurance claim. *Also known as* **claims adjuster**

loss assessor *Fin* in the United Kingdom, a person appointed by a insurance policyholder to assist with his or her claim. *See also* **loss adjuster**

loss control *Gen Mgt see total loss control*

lossmaker *Gen Mgt* a product or company that fails to make a profit or break even

lost time record *Fin* a record of the time a machine or employee is not producing, usually stating reasons and responsibilities. Lost time can include waiting time and maintenance.

lot *Fin* **1.** the minimum quantity of a commodity that may be purchased on an exchange, for example, 1,000 ounces of gold on the London Bullion Market **2.** an item or a collection of related items being offered for sale at an auction **3.** (*US*) a group of shares held or traded together, usually in units of 100 **4.** (*US*) a piece of land that can be sold

lottery *Fin* the random method of selecting successful applicants, occasionally used when a new issue is oversubscribed

lowball *Gen Mgt* to begin a sales negotiation by quoting low prices, and then raise them once a buyer appears interested (*slang*)

lower level domain *E-com* the main part of a domain name. For most e-business sites this is usually the company or brand name.

lower of cost or market *Fin* a method used by manufacturing and supply firms when accounting for their homogeneous stocks that involves valuing them either at their original cost or the current market price, whichever is lower. *Abbr* **LCM**

low-hanging fruit (*slang*) **1.** *Gen Mgt* something that is easy to obtain. Low-hanging fruit is highly visible, easily obtained, and provides good short-term opportunities for profit. Such fruit must be taken advantage of quickly, because it is accessible to anyone and there might be considerable competition. Picking low-hanging fruit may involve, for example, taking over a company or choosing the easiest tasks to do first, in order to achieve a quick result. **2.** *Mkting* people who are easy marketing targets because they are already thinking about buying a product or signing up for a service

low start mortgage *Fin* a long-term loan, usually for the purchase of a property, in which the borrower only pays the interest on the loan for the first few years, usually three. After that, the repayments increase to cover the interest and part of the original loan, as in a *repayment mortgage*. Low start mortgages are popular with first-time buyers as the lower initial costs may free up funds for furnishings or home improvements. *See also* **mortgage**

loyalty bonus *Fin* in the United Kingdom in the 1980s, a number of extra shares, calculated as a proportion of the shares originally subscribed, given to original subscribers of privatisation issues providing the shares were held continually for a given period of time

loyalty scheme *Mkting* a sales promotion technique to encourage customers to continue buying a product or using an organisation's services. It works by rewarding customers who spend more and/or stay longer with an organisation. Examples include a shopper card that gives discounts on purchases over a period of time.

There are several other loyalty scheme approaches: points systems—which give points to customers based on what they purchase; premium customer programmes—where customers who spend certain amounts of money and are repeat purchasers gain special status and receive benefits such as discounts, exclusive offers, and gifts; buyers' clubs—where a certain number of customers can club together to buy a particular product, at a special volume discount.

If implementing a loyalty scheme, it is important to remember that it must be there for the long term, and the level of incentive must be right. Offering too much will hurt your profits; offering too little will not attract members. Customers also need to be able to check up on their status easily—to see, for example, how many points they have currently accumulated.

Ltd *Fin see* **limited liability company**

lump sum *Fin* **1.** used to describe a loan that is repayable with one instalment at the end of its term. *See also* **balloon loan**, **interest-only mortgage 2.** an amount of money received in one payment, for example, the sum payable to the beneficiary of a life assurance policy on the death of the policyholder

lurk *E-com* to visit an Internet newsgroup without taking part. People wishing to promote their company's products or services within a newsgroup lurk to see whether the group accepts commercial messages or whether there are any questions they could answer. Lurking is important because inappropriate messages are likely to receive a hostile response from newsgroup members and may even be considered as **spam**. Lurking in relevant newsgroups can also be an effective means of online market research.

luxury tax *Fin* a tax on goods or services that are considered non-essential

---

The almighty dollar, that great object of universal devotion throughout our land.
Washington Irving

M1 *Econ* the narrowest definition of the amount of money in the economy, including notes and coins in public circulation and sterling sight deposits held in the private sector

Ma and Pa shop *Gen Mgt* a small family-run business (*slang*)

Machiavelli, Niccolò (1469–1527) *Gen Mgt* Italian politician. Machiavelli's *The Prince* (1532) is one of the earliest works on political theory, embracing the concepts of *power*, *authority*, and *leadership*. In *Management and Machiavelli* (1967), Antony Jay sought to show the relevance of Machiavelli's philosophy to modern society.

Machiavelli was born in Florence, and served as an official in the Florentine government. His work brought him into contact with some of Europe's most influential ministers and government representatives. His chief diplomatic triumph occurred when Florence obtained the surrender of Pisa. But in 1512 when the Medicis returned to power, his career came to an abrupt end. He was accused of being involved in a plot against the government. For this he was imprisoned, tortured, and finally exiled.

He retired to a farm outside Florence and began a successful writing career, producing plays and a history of Florence as well as the books on politics for which he is now chiefly remembered.

machine code *E-com* a set of instructions to a computer in the form of a binary code

machine hour rate *Fin* an *overhead absorption rate* based on machine hours

macho management *Gen Mgt* an authoritarian management style that asserts a manager's right to manage. Macho management is a term coined by *Michael Edwardes*, and it was adopted by the media in the 1980s. Macho managers tend to take a tough approach to improving *productivity* and efficiency, and are unsympathetic to *trade unions*.

macroeconomics *Econ* the branch of economics that studies national income and the economic systems of national economies

macroeconomy *Econ* those broad sectors of a country's economic activity, for example, the financial or industrial sector, that are aggregated to form its economic system as a whole

macrohedge *Fin* a hedge that pertains to an entire portfolio. *See also* **microhedge**. *Also known as* **global hedge**

Macromedia Flash™ *E-com* a trademark for a type of web animation software. Its small file sizes and easy *scaleability* make Flash one of the more flexible animation packages, and it uses *streaming* technology so that animations can be viewed more quickly. Flash also allows sound to be added to an animation effectively.

mail form *E-com* a web page that requires the user to input data, for example, name, address, or order or shipping information, that is transmitted to an e-merchant via e-mail

mailing house *Mkting* an organisation that specialises in planning, creating, and implementing direct mail campaigns for clients

mailing list *Mkting* the names and addresses of a particular group of people compiled for marketing purposes. A mailing list may be compiled internally or bought or rented from an outside agency, and can be used for advertising, fundraising, news releases, or for *direct mail* or a *mailshot*. A mailing list is usually compiled for a selected group using one or more criteria, such as men between the ages of 15 and 20.

mail order *Mkting* a form of retailing in which consumers order products from a catalogue for delivery to their home

---

When women ask for equality, men take them to be demanding domination.

Elizabeth Janeway

mail-out *Gen Mgt* a single instance of using direct mail

mail server *E-com* a remote computer enabling people and organisations to send and receive e-mail

mailshot *Mkting* the speculative targeting of a particular or specified group of people by mail. A mailshot normally contains *advertising*, fundraising requests, or *press releases*.

mailsort *Mkting* a sorting service offered to organisations by the Post Office, intended to reduce the cost and time spent on direct mail

mainframe *E-com* a powerful computer capable of supporting hundreds of thousands of users simultaneously

mainstream corporation tax *Fin* formerly the balance of corporation tax due after deducting ACT. *See also* **Advance Corporation Tax**

maintenance *Ops* the process of keeping physical assets in working order to ensure their availability and to reduce the chance of failure. An effective maintenance programme can enhance safety, increase reliability, reduce quality errors, lower operating costs, and increase the lifespan of assets. There are different maintenance approaches, including *reactive maintenance*, *predictive maintenance*, and *preventive maintenance*. Two strategies that have more recently become prominent are *reliability-centred maintenance* and *total productive maintenance*.

maintenance bond *Fin* a bond that provides a guarantee against defects for some time after a contract has been fulfilled

majority shareholder *Fin* a shareholder with a controlling interest in a company. *See also* **minority interest**

make or buy *Gen Mgt* see *purchasing versus production*

make-to-order *Ops* the production of goods or components to meet an existing order. Make-to-order products are made to the customer's specification, and are often processed in small batches.

Malcolm Baldrige National Quality Award *Gen Mgt* an award, given to US companies, recognising achievements in quality and business performance. The Malcolm Baldrige National Quality Award was launched by the US government in 1987 to encourage US companies to publicise successful quality and improvement strategies, to adopt *total quality management*, and to encourage competitiveness. In assessing companies for the Award, examiners allocate points in seven major areas: 1. Leadership, 2. Information and analysis, 3. Strategic planning, 4. Human resource development, 5. Process management, 6. Customer focus and satisfaction, 7. Business results. The Award also involves evaluation of companies according to three main factors: 1. What is the organisation's approach to achieving its goals: how does it attempt to achieve top-class performance? 2. How is this approach put into practice in the organisation, what resources are being brought to bear, and how widespread is this action throughout the organisation? 3. What evidence is there to demonstrate that improvements are really taking place?

managed currency fund *Fin* a unit trust that makes considered investments in currencies

managed economy *Fin* an economy directed by a government rather than the free market

managed float *Econ* the position when the exchange rate of a country's currency is influenced by government action in the foreign exchange market

managed fund *Fin* a unit trust that makes considered investments. *See also* **index fund**

managed hosting *E-com* a *hosting option* in which the hosting provider is principally responsible for a client's servers. This responsibility can range from the vendor supplying and managing the hardware only, to supplying the

---

Without organisations, there would be chaos and decay.   *Theodore Levitt*

software as well. This type of vendor is called an **ASP** (application service provider).

managed rate *Fin* the rate of interest charged by a financial institution for borrowing, that is not prescribed as a margin over base rate, but is set from time to time by the institution

management *Gen Mgt, HR* the use of professional skills for identifying and achieving organisational objectives through the deployment of appropriate resources. Management involves identifying what needs to be done, and organising and supporting others to perform the necessary tasks. A manager has complex and ever-changing responsibilities, the focus of which shifts to reflect the issues, trends, and preoccupations of the time. At the beginning of the 20th century, the emphasis was both on supporting the organisation's administration and managing *productivity* through increased efficiency. Organisations following *Henri Fayol*'s and *Max Weber*'s models built the functional divisions of personnel management, production management, marketing management, operations management, and financial management. At the beginning of the 21st century, those original drivers are still much in evidence, although the emphasis has moved to the key areas of *competence* within the National Occupational Standards for Management, particularly people management. Although management is a profession in its own right, its skill-set often applies to professionals of other disciplines.

management accountant *Fin* a person who contributes to management's decision-making processes by, for example, collecting and processing data, relating to a business's costs, sales, and the profitability of individual activities

management accounting *Fin* the preparation and use of financial information to support management decisions

management audit *Gen Mgt see operational audit*

management buy-in *Gen Mgt* the purchase of an existing business by an individual manager or management group outside that business. In the United Kingdom, the unique company 3i is often involved in supporting management buy-ins. 3i has also promoted a hybrid form of management buy-in and *management buy-out*, given the acronym **BIMBO**, which involves an incoming chief executive sharing his or her investment with the company's existing management team. *Abbr* **MBI**

management buy-out *Gen Mgt* the purchase of an existing business by an individual manager or management group from within that business. *Abbr* **MBO**

management by exception *Gen Mgt* a system of management in which only deviations from the plan or the norm are to be reported to the manager, ensuring management attention is only given when necessary

management by objectives *or* **management by results** *Gen Mgt* a method of managing an organisation by setting a series of *objectives* that contribute towards the achievement of its goals. *Abbr* **MBO**

management by walking around *Gen Mgt* a hands-on style of management based on regularly walking around to speak to, question, and listen to employees, and to learn more about work processes

management company *Gen Mgt* a company that takes over responsibility from internal staff for managing facilities such as computer systems, telecommunications, or maintenance. The process is known as *outsourcing*.

management consultancy *Gen Mgt* **1.** the activity of advising on management techniques and practices. Management consultancy usually involves the identification of a problem, or the analysis of a specific area of one organisation, and the reporting of any resulting findings. The consultancy process can sometimes be extended to help put into effect the recommendations made. **2.** a firm of *management consultants*

management consultant *Gen Mgt* a person professionally engaged in advising on, and providing, a detached, external view about a company's management techniques and practices. A management consultant may be self-employed, a partner, or employed within a *management consultancy*. Consultants can be called in for many reasons, but are employed particularly for projects involving business improvement, *change management*, information technology, and long-term planning.

management control *Fin* all of the processes used by managers to ensure that organisational goals are achieved and procedures adhered to, and that the organisation responds appropriately to changes in its environment

management control systems *Gen Mgt* measures, procedures, *performance indicators*, and other instruments used to systematically check and regulate operations. Management control systems are set up to maintain management *control* on a routine basis, and can include *budgets* and budgetary controls, credit control, working procedures, inventory control, production processes, and quality measures or controls.

management development *HR* the process of creating, and enhancing, the *competences* of *managers* and potential managers. Management development is usually thought of as a planned process, focusing on a long-term development programme to increase managerial effectiveness, but it also incorporates informal and unplanned elements such as learning from day-to-day experience. Management development programmes within an organisation aim to identify and recruit potential managers, and develop their knowledge and skills to meet organisational needs. They also equip managers for more senior posts. Management

development activities include short courses, *management education* programmes, *management training*, *coaching*, and *mentoring*.

management education *HR* formal instruction in the principles and techniques of *management*, and in related subjects, leading to a qualification. Management education aims to develop management knowledge, understanding, and *competence* through classroom or distance-based methods. Management education is a main component of *management development*, and differs from *management training* in that the latter may exploit any one of a variety of formal or informal methods, tends to be focused on a specific skill, and does not result directly in a formal qualification.

management guru *Gen Mgt* an informal term for a *management theorist*

management information system *Gen Mgt see MIS*

management science *Gen Mgt* the application of scientific methods and principles to management *decision-making* and *problem-solving*. Management science encompasses the use of quantitative, mathematical, and statistical techniques. The term can be used to denote scientific management, which has origins in the work of *Frederick Winslow Taylor*, *Henry Gantt*, and *Frank* and *Lillian Gilbreth*. Management science lies at the opposite end of the spectrum to the *human relations* school.

management services *Gen Mgt* a department or team of internally employed technical and professional specialists offering services or advice to management. Management services can cover areas such as work study, legal, computer, information, economic intelligence, and similar specialist support services.

management standards *Gen Mgt* published guidelines to best practice, outlining the knowledge, understanding, and personal *competences* that managers need to develop and demonstrate if they

---

We cannot work for others without working for ourselves.   *Jean-Jacques Rousseau*

are to be effective. Management standards form the core criteria on which management *National Vocational Qualifications* in the United Kingdom are based. They are split into seven key areas: manage activities; manage people; manage resources; manage information; manage energy; manage quality; and manage projects.

management style *Gen Mgt* the general manner, outlook, attitude, and behaviour of a manager in his or her dealings with subordinates. Organisations may have, or seek to have, distinctive management styles, and sometimes train employees to try to ensure that a preferred style, fitting in with the desired *corporate culture*, is always used. Management styles can vary widely between extremes of control and consultation. The latter are generally thought to encourage degrees of *employee participation* in management with consequently improved *employee commitment*, *employee involvement*, and *empowerment*. More participatory styles are also usually related to more open organisational cultures and flatter organisational structures. One well-known instrument for distinguishing individual management styles is *Robert Blake*'s and *Jane Mouton*'s *Managerial Grid*™.

management succession *Gen Mgt see succession planning*

management team *Gen Mgt see senior management*

management theorist *Gen Mgt* somebody who puts forward original ideas and theories about management. The work of a management theorist is usually presented through books or articles, and often has its base in practical or academic research, and consultancy or practical work experience.

management threshold *Gen Mgt* an outmoded term for a level of seniority in an organisation which somebody cannot surmount. The management threshold is reached by an *employee* who has risen to a certain level in an organisation and seems unable to rise any further. It can

lead to plateauing, where an employee is unable to gain *promotion* and stays in the same role for many years. Failure to surmount the management threshold can be caused by lack of opportunities for advancement, lack of ambition, or lack of skills or ability.

management trainee *HR* an employee who holds a junior management position while undergoing formal training in management techniques

management training *HR* planned activities for *management development*. Management training methods include public or *in-company training* courses and *on-the-job training* designed to improve managerial *competences*. Management training tends to be practical and to focus on specific management techniques. Unlike *management education*, it does not result in a formal qualification.

manager *Gen Mgt* a person who identifies and achieves organisational objectives through the deployment of appropriate resources. A manager can have responsibilities in one or more of five key areas: managing activities; managing resources; managing information; managing people; and managing him- or herself at the same time as working within the context of the organisational, political, and economic business environments. There are managers in all disciplines and activities, although some may not bear the title of manager. Some specialise in areas such as personnel, marketing, production, finance, or project management, while others are *general managers*, applying *management* skills across all business areas. Very few jobs are entirely managerial, and very few exist without any management responsibilities. It is the capability to harness resources that largely distinguishes a manager from a non-manager.

Managerial Grid™ *Gen Mgt* a tool to measure and understand managerial behaviour which places concern for task and concern for people on two matrices against which a manager's style can be plotted. The Managerial Grid™ grades each matrix 1 to 9, and identifies five different managerial behaviour patterns: 1-1, or impoverished management, in which a minimum of concern for either people or task is displayed; 9-1, or **authority-compliance management**, in which a preoccupation with task is displayed; 5-5, or **middle of the road management**, in which a balance between task and people is striven for; 1-9, **country club management**, which is concerned with human relations to the detriment of output; and 9-9, **team management**, the ideal, in which production and human requirements are integrated in a team approach to achieving results.

managerialism *Gen Mgt* emphasis on efficient management, and the use of systems, planning, and management practice. Managerialism is often used in a critical sense, especially from the perspective of the public sector, to imply over-enthusiasm for efficiency, or private sector management techniques and systems, possibly at the expense of service or quality considerations. The term is also used to describe confrontational attitudes, or actions displayed by management towards trade unions.

managing director *Gen Mgt* a director of a company who has overall responsibility for its day-to-day operations. *Abbr* **MD**

M&A *abbr Fin* mergers and acquisitions

mandarin *Gen Mgt* a high-ranking and influential adviser, especially in government circles

mandatory quote period *Fin* a period of time during which prices of securities must be displayed in a market

manpower forecasting *Gen Mgt* the prediction of future levels of demand for, and supply of, workers and skills at organisational, regional, or national level. A range of techniques are used in manpower forecasting, including the statistical analysis of current trends and the use of mathematical models. At national level, these include the analysis of census statistics; at organisational level, projections of future requirements may be made from sales and production figures. Manpower forecasting forms part of the *manpower planning* process.

manpower planning *Gen Mgt* the development of strategies to match the supply of workers to the availability of jobs at organisational, regional, or national level. Manpower planning involves reviewing current manpower resources, forecasting future requirements and availability, and taking steps to ensure that the supply of people and skills meets demand. At a national level, this may be carried out by government or industry bodies, and at an organisational level, by human resource managers. A more current term for manpower planning at organisational level is *human resource planning*.

manual worker *HR* an employee who carries out physical work, especially in a factory or outdoors. *Also known as blue-collar worker*

manufacture *Ops* the large-scale production of goods from raw materials or constituent parts

manufacturer *Ops* a person or organisation involved in *production*

manufacturer's agent *Ops* a person or organisation with authority to act for a *manufacturer* in obtaining a *contract* with a third party

manufacturing *Gen Mgt see production*

manufacturing cost *Ops* the expenditure incurred in carrying out the *production* processes of an organisation. The manufacturing cost includes *direct costs*, for example, labour, materials, and expenses, and indirect costs, for example, *subcontracting* and overheads.

manufacturing for excellence *Gen Mgt see design for manufacturability*

manufacturing information system *Ops* an *MIS* designed specifically for use in a *production* environment

manufacturing management *Gen Mgt* see *production management*

manufacturing resource planning *Ops* see *MRP II*

manufacturing system *Ops* a method of organising *production*. Manufacturing systems include assembly and *batch production*, *flexible manufacturing systems*, *lean production*, *group technology*, *job production*, *kanban*, and *mass production*.

manufacturing to order *Ops* a production management technique in which goods are produced to meet firm orders, rather than being produced for stock

MAPS *abbr E-com* Mail Abuse Prevention System: the leading US organisation campaigning against unsolicited commercial e-mail messages, or *spam*

Marché des Options Négotiables de Paris *Fin* in France, the traded options market. *Abbr* **MONEP**

Marché International de France *Fin* in France, the international futures and options exchange

Margerison, Charles (*b*. 1940) *Gen Mgt* British business researcher and writer. *See McCann, Dick*

margin 1. *Fin, Gen Mgt* the difference between the cost and the selling price of a product or service **2.** (*ANZ*) *HR* a payment made to workers over and above the basic wage in recognition of special skills

margin account *Fin* an account with a broker who lends money for investments

marginal analysis *Econ* the study of how small changes in an economic variable will affect an economy

marginal cost *Econ* the amount by which the costs of a firm will be increased if its output is increased by one more unit, or if one more customer is served.

EXAMPLE If the price charged is greater than the marginal cost, then the revenue gain will be greater than the added cost. That, in turn, will increase profit, so the expansion in production or service makes economic sense and should proceed. The reverse is also true: if the price charged is less than the marginal cost, expansion should not go ahead.

The formula for marginal cost is:

Change in cost /change in quantity

If it costs a company £260,000 to produce 3,000 items, and £325,000 to produce 3,800 items, the change in cost would be:

£325,000 – £260,000 = £65,000

The change in quantity would be:

3,800 – 3,000 = 800

When the formula to calculate marginal cost is applied, the result is:

£65,000 /800 = £81.25

If the price of the item in question were £99.95, expansion should proceed.

Relying on marginal cost is not fail-safe, however; putting more products on a market can drive down prices and thus cut margins. Moreover, committing idle capacity to long-term production may tie up resources that could be directed to a new and more profitable opportunity. An important related principle is contribution: the cash gained (or lost) from selling an additional unit.

marginal costing *Fin* the accounting system in which variable costs are charged to cost units and fixed costs of the period are written off in full against the aggregate contribution. Its special value is in recognising cost behaviour, and hence assisting in decision-making. *Also known as variable costing*

marginal costs and benefits *Econ* the amount by which an individual or household will lose or benefit from a small change in a variable, for example, food consumption or income received

marginalisation *Gen Mgt* the process by which countries lose importance and status because they are unable to participate in mainstream activities such as industrialisation or the Internet economy

marginal lender *Fin* a lender who will make a loan only at or above a particular rate of interest

marginal private cost *Econ* the cost to an individual of a small change in the price of a variable, for example, petrol

marginal revenue *Gen Mgt* the revenue generated by additional units of production

marginal tax rate *Fin* the rate of tax payable on a person's income after business expenses have been deducted

margining *Fin* the system by which the London Clearing House (LCH) controls the risk associated with a London International Financial Futures and Options Exchange clearing member's position on a daily basis. To achieve this, clearing members deposit cash or collateral with the LCH in the form of initial and variation margins. The initial margin is the deposit required on all open positions (long or short) to cover short-term price movements and is returned to members by the LCH when the position is closed. The variation margin is the members' profits or losses, calculated daily from the marked-to-market-close value of their position (whereby contracts are revalued daily for the calculation of variation margin), and credited to or debited from their accounts.

margin of error *Ops* an allowance made for the possibility of miscalculation

margin of safety *Ops* the difference between the level of activity at which an organisation breaks even and the level of activity greater than this point. For example, a margin of safety of £200,000 is achieved when the breakeven point is £600,000 and sales reach £800,000. This measure can be expressed as a proportion of sales value, as a number of units sold, or as a percentage of *capacity*.

margin of safety ratio *Fin* a ratio which indicates the percentage by which forecast turnover exceeds or falls short of that required to break even. It is calculated as follows:

(Forecast turnover – breakeven turnover) × 100 /Forecast turnover

mark-down *Fin* a reduction in the selling price of damaged or slow-selling goods

marked cheque *Fin* a certified cheque (*slang*)

marked price *Gen Mgt* the original displayed price of a product in a shop. In a sale, customers may be offered a saving on the marked price.

market 1. *Fin* the rate at which financial commodities or securities are being sold **2.** *Gen Mgt* a grouping of people or organisations unified by a common need **3.** *Gen Mgt* a gathering of sellers and purchasers to exchange commodities

marketable *Mkting* possessing the potential to be commercially viable. To determine whether a new product or service is marketable, an assessment needs to be carried out to see if it is likely to make a profit. The assessment is often based on detailed *market research* analysing the potential market, and the projected financial returns and any other benefits for the company.

market analysis *Mkting* the study of a market to identify and quantify business opportunities

market area *Mkting* the geographical location of a market

market based pricing *Fin* setting a price based on the value of the product in the perception of the customer. *Also known as perceived value pricing*

market bubble *Fin* a stock market phenomenon in which values in a particular sector become inflated for a short period. If the bubble bursts, share prices in that sector collapse.

market coverage *Gen Mgt* the degree to which a product or service meets the needs of a market

market development *Mkting* marketing activities designed to increase the overall size of a market through education and awareness

market driven *Mkting* using market knowledge to determine the *corporate strategy* of an organisation. A market driven organisation has a *customer focus*, together with awareness of competitors, and an understanding of the *market*.

market economy *Econ* an economy in which a *free market* in goods and services operates

marketeer *Mkting* a small company that competes in the same market as larger companies. Examples of marketeers are restaurants, travel agents, computer software providers, garages, and insurance brokers.

marketer *Mkting* somebody who is responsible for developing and implementing marketing prices

marketface *Gen Mgt* the interface between suppliers and customers

market-facing enterprise *Gen Mgt* an organisation that aligns itself with its markets and customers

market-focused organisation *Mkting* an organisation whose strategies are determined by market requirements rather than organisational demands

market fragmentation *Mkting* a situation in which the buyers or sellers in a market consist of a large number of small organisations

market gap *Mkting* an opportunity in a market where no supplier provides a product or service that buyers need

market if touched *Fin* an order to trade a security if it reaches a specified price. *Abbr* **MIT**

marketing *Mkting see* *marketing management*
4 Ps of marketing *Gen Mgt see* *marketing mix*

marketing audit *Mkting* an analysis of either the external marketing environment or a company's internal marketing aims, objectives, operations, and efficiency. An external marketing audit covers issues such as economic, political, infrastructure, technological, and consumer perspectives; *market size* and *structure*; and competitors, suppliers, and distributors. An internal marketing audit

covers aspects such as the company's *mission statement*, aims, and objectives; its structure, corporate culture, systems, operations, and processes; *product development* and pricing; profitability and efficiency; *advertising*; and deployment of the *salesforce*.

marketing consultancy *Mkting* an organisation that plans and develops marketing strategies and programmes on behalf of clients

marketing cost *Fin* the cost of researching potential markets and promoting a product or service

marketing information system *Mkting* an information system concerned with the collection, storage, and analysis of information and data for marketing *decision-making* purposes. Information for use in marketing information systems is gathered from customers, competitors and their products, and from the market itself.

marketing management *Mkting* one of the main management disciplines, encompassing all the strategic planning, operations, activities, and processes involved in achieving organisational objectives by delivering value to customers. Marketing management focuses on satisfying customer requirements by identifying needs and wants, and developing products and services to meet them. In seeking to satisfy customer requirements, **marketing** aims to build long-term relationships with customers and with other interested parties and to provide value to them. This begins with *market research*, which analyses needs and wants in society, and continues with attracting customers and the cultivation of mutually beneficial exchange processes with them. Tools used in this process are diverse and include market segmentation, *brand management*, *PR*, *logistics*, *direct response marketing*, *sales promotion*, and *advertising*.

marketing manager *Mkting* an employee of a client organisation who is responsible for planning and controlling its marketing activities and budgets

marketing mix *Mkting* the range of integrated decisions taken by a marketing manager to ensure successful marketing. These decisions are taken in four key areas known as the **4 Ps of marketing**—product, price, place, and promotion—and cover issues such as the type of product to be marketed, brand name, pricing, advertising, publicity, geographical coverage, retailing, and distribution.

marketing myopia *Mkting* the name given to the theory that challenged the assumption that organisations should be production-oriented by suggesting that to be successful, the wants of customers must be their central consideration. First promoted by *Theodore Levitt* in 'Marketing myopia', published in the *Harvard Business Review* during 1960, the theory has gained such widespread acceptance that it now appears commonplace.

marketing plan *Mkting* overall marketing objectives and the strategies and programmes of action designed to achieve those objectives

marketing planning *Mkting* the process of producing a *marketing plan*. Marketing planning requires a careful examination of all strategic issues, including the business environment, the markets themselves, competitors, the corporate *mission statement*, and organisational capabilities. The resulting marketing plan should be communicated to appropriate staff through an oral briefing to ensure it is fully understood.

market intelligence *Mkting* a collection of internal and external data on a given market. Market intelligence focuses particularly on competitors, customers, consumer spending, market trends, and suppliers.

market leader *Mkting see market share*

market logic *Fin* the prevailing forces or attitudes that determine a company's success or failure on the stock market

market maker *Fin* **1.** somebody who works in a stock exchange to facilitate trade in one particular company **2.** a broker or bank that maintains a market for a security that does not trade on any exchange

market order *Fin* an order to trade a security at the best price the broker can obtain

market penetration *HR* a measure of the percentage or potential percentage of the market that a product or company is able to capture, expressed in terms of total sales or turnover. Market penetration is often used to measure the level of success a new product or service has achieved.

market penetration pricing *Mkting* the policy of pricing a product or service very competitively, and sometimes at a loss to the producer, in order to increase its *market share*

market position *Mkting* the place held by a product or service in a *market*, usually determined by its percentage of total sales. An ideal market position is often pre-defined for a product or service. Analysis of potential customers and competing products can be used with product differentiation techniques to formulate a product to fill the desired market position.

market potential *Mkting* a forecast of the size of a market in terms of revenue, numbers of buyers, or other factors

market power *Mkting* the dominance of a market either by customers, who create a buyer's market, or by a particular company, which creates a seller's market. Individuals or companies retain control of the market by fixing the pricing and number of products available.

market price *Econ* in economics, the theoretical price at which supply equals demand

market research *Mkting* research carried out to assess the size and nature of a market

market risk *Fin* risk that cannot be diversified away, also known as systematic risk. **Non-systematic** or **unsystematic**

risk applies to a single investment or class of investments, and can be reduced or eliminated by diversification.

market risk premium *Fin* the extra return required from a share to compensate for its risk compared with the average risk of the market

market sector *Mkting* a subdivision of a *market*. Market sectors are usually determined by market segmentation, which divides a market into different categories. Car buyers, for example, could be put into sectors such as car fleet buyers, private buyers, buyers under 20 years old, and so on. The smaller the sector, the more its members will have in common.

market segment *Mkting* a part of a market that has distinctive characteristics. Sellers may decide to compete in the whole market or only in segments that are attractive to them or where they have an advantage.

market sentiment *Fin* the mood of those participating in exchange dealings that can range from absolute euphoria to downright gloom and despondency and tends to reflect recent company results, economic indicators, and comments by politicians, analysts, or opinion formers. Optimism increases demand and therefore prices, while pessimism has the opposite effect.

market share *Mkting* the proportion of the total market value of a product or group of products or services that a company, service, or product holds. Market share is shown as a percentage of the total value or output of a market, usually expressed in sterling or US dollars, by weight (tons or tonnes), or as individual units, depending on the commodity. The product, service, or company with a dominant market share is referred to as the **market leader**.

market site *E-com* a website shared by multiple e-commerce vendors, each having a different speciality, to conduct business over the Internet

market size *Fin* the largest number of shares that a market will handle in one trade of a particular security

market structure *Mkting* the make-up of a particular *market*. Market structure can be described with reference to different characteristics of a market, including its size and value, the number of providers and their *market share*, consumer and business purchasing behaviour, and growth forecasts. The description may also include a demographic and regional breakdown of providers and customers and an analysis of pricing structures, likely technological impacts, and domestic and overseas sales.

market targeting *Mkting* the selection of a particular market segment towards which all marketing effort is directed. Market targeting enables the characteristics of the chosen segment to be taken into account when formulating a product or service and its advertising.

market valuation *Fin* **1.** the value of a portfolio at market prices **2.** the opinion of an expert professional as to the current worth of a piece of land or property

market value *Fin* the price that buyers are willing to pay for a good or service

market value added *Fin* the difference between a company's market value (derived from the share price), and its economic book value (the amount of capital that shareholders have committed to the firm throughout its existence, including any retained earnings)

marking down *Fin* the reduction by market makers in the price at which they are prepared to deal in a security, for example, because of an adverse report by an analyst, or the announcement or anticipated announcement of a profit warning by a company

mark-up *Gen Mgt* the difference between the cost of a product or service and its selling price. Mark-up is often calculated as a percentage of the production and overhead costs, and represents the profit made on the product or service.

Capitalism without bankruptcy is like Christianity without hell. *Frank Borman*

Marxism *Econ* a view of social development found in the writings of Karl Marx, stating that a country's culture is determined by how its goods and services are produced

marzipan *HR* belonging to the level of management immediately below the top executives (*slang*)

Maslow, Abraham (1908–70) *Gen Mgt* US psychologist and behavioural scientist. Known for his work on *motivation*, principally the hierarchy of needs, which was set out in his book *Motivation and Personality* (1954). Maslow's concepts were originally offered as general explanations of human behaviour but are now seen as a significant contribution to workplace motivation theory. He is often mentioned in connection with his contemporaries *Douglas McGregor* and *Frederick Herzberg*, all part of the *human relations* movement in management.

massaging *Fin* the adjustment of financial figures to create the impression of better performance (*slang*)

mass customisation *Ops* a process that allows a standard, mass-produced item, for example, a bicycle, to be individually tailored to specific customer requirements

mass market *Mkting* a market that covers substantial numbers of the population. A mass market may consist of a whole population or just a segment of that population. *Mass customisation* of products has allowed a greater number of single products to satisfy a mass market.

mass medium *Mkting* an advertising medium such as television or national newspapers which reaches a very large audience

mass meeting *HR* the assembling of most or all of the members of a *trade union* in order to reach a decision on workforce policy. Mass meetings were frequently called during the 1960s and 1970s to determine whether or not *industrial action* would take place. In the

United Kingdom, the most memorable examples occurred at British Leyland.

mass production *Ops* large-scale manufacturing, often designed to meet the demand for a particular product. Mass production methods were developed by *Henry Ford*, founder of the Ford Motor Company. Mass production involves using a moving production or assembly line on which the product moves while operators remain at their stations carrying out their work on each passing product. Mass production is now challenged by methods including *just-in-time* and *lean production*.

master budget *Fin* the budget into which all subsidiary budgets are consolidated, normally comprising budgeted profit and loss account, budgeted balance sheet, and budgeted cash flow statement. These documents, and the supporting subsidiary budgets, are used to plan and control activities for the following year.

master franchise *Mkting* a licence issued by the owner of a product or service to another party or master franchisee allowing them to issue further *franchise* licences. A master franchise can benefit the original franchisor, as the master franchisee effectively develops the *franchise chain* on their behalf. A master franchise usually grants further licences within a defined geographical area, and several master franchises may cover a country.

master limited partnership *Fin* a partnership of a type that combines tax advantages and advantages of liquidity

Master of Business Administration *Gen Mgt see* **MBA**

master production scheduling *Ops* a technique used in material requirements planning systems to develop a detailed plan for product manufacturing. The master production schedule, compiled by a master scheduler, takes account of the requirements of various departments, including sales (delivery dates), finance (inventory minimisation), and manufacturing (minimisation of set-up times), and it schedules production and the purchasing of materials within the capacity of and resources available to the production system.

masthead *E-com* the area at the top of a web page, usually containing the logo of the organisation, often with a **search** box and a set of essential links to important areas of the website

matador bond *Fin* a foreign bond in the Spanish domestic market (*slang*)

matched bargain *Fin* the linked sale and repurchase of the same security. *See also **bed and breakfast deal***

material cost *Ops* the cost of the raw materials that go into a product. The material cost of a product excludes any *indirect costs*, for example, overheads or wages, associated with producing the item.

material facts *Fin* **1.** information that has to be disclosed in a prospectus. *See also **listing requirements** **2.** in an insurance contract, information that the insured has to reveal at the time that the policy is taken out, for example, that a house is located on the edge of a crumbling cliff. Failure to reveal material facts can result in the contract being declared void.

material news *Fin* price sensitive developments in a company, for example, proposed acquisitions, mergers, profit warnings, and the resignation of directors, that most stock exchanges require a company to announce immediately prior to the exchange. *US term **material information***

material requirements planning (MRP I) *Fin* a system that converts a production schedule into a listing of the materials and components required to meet that schedule, so that adequate stock levels are maintained and items are available when needed

materials handling *Ops* the techniques employed to move, transport, store, and distribute materials, with or without the aid of mechanical equipment

materials management *Ops* an approach for planning, organising, and controlling all those activities principally concerned with the flow of materials into an organisation. The scope of materials management varies greatly from company to company and may include material planning and control, **production planning**, **purchasing**, inventory control and stores, in-plant materials movement, and **waste management**.

materials requisition *Fin* a document which authorises the issue from a store of a specified quantity of materials. *Also known as **stores requisition***

materials returned note *Fin* a record of the return to stores of unused material

materials testing *Ops* the process of analysing the physical and chemical characteristics of materials against a specification

materials transfer note *Fin* a record of the transfer of material between stores, cost centres, or cost units

maternity leave *HR* time off work because of pregnancy and childbirth. All female *employees*, regardless of *length of service* and *hours of work*, are legally entitled to statutory maternity leave and to statutory *maternity pay*. Many *employers* offer improved maternity arrangements but these vary from organisation to organisation and often depend on length of service.

maternity pay *HR* earnings paid by an *employer* to *employees* who take *maternity leave*, or leave employment because of pregnancy, and who satisfy certain qualifying conditions

matrix *Gen Mgt* a chart showing data set out squarely, and symmetrically, in columns and rows with the potential to show both vertical and horizontal relationships. A matrix is often used as form of *organisation chart* to show reporting relationships for a *matrix organisation*, or within a *matrix management* context.

matrix management *Gen Mgt* management based on two or more reporting systems linked to the vertical organisation hierarchy, and to horizontal relationships based on geographic, product, or project requirements

matrix organisation *Gen Mgt* organisation by both vertical administrative functions and horizontal tasks, areas, processes, or projects. Matrix organisation originated in the 1960s and 1970s, particularly within the US aerospace industry, when *organisation charts* showing how the management of a given *project* would relate to *senior management* were often required to win government contracts. A two-dimensional *matrix* chart best illustrates the dual horizontal, and vertical, reporting relationships. Matrix organisation is closely linked to *matrix management*.

matrix structure *Gen Mgt* a form of *organisation structure* based on horizontal and vertical relationships. The matrix structure is linked closely to *matrix management*, and is related to *project management*. It emerged on an improvised rather than a planned basis as a way of showing how people work with or report to others in their organisation, project, geographic region, process, or team.

Matsushita, Konosuke (1894–1989) *Gen Mgt* Japanese entrepreneur, business executive, and philanthropist. Founder of Matsushita Electric, and owner of the Panasonic brand, noted for his humanistic approach to business, which was described by John Kotter in *Matsushita Leadership* (1997).

mature economy *Fin* an economy that is no longer developing or growing rapidly

maturity *Gen Mgt* the stage at which a financial instrument, such as a bond, is due for repayment

maturity date *Fin* the date when an *option* expires

maturity yield *Fin see* **yield**

Mauborgne, Renée *Gen Mgt* French academic. INSEAD professor, Fellow of the World Economic Forum, and collaborator of **W. Chan Kim** on research into *corporate strategy* and *value innovation*.

maximax criterion *Fin* an approach to decision-making under uncertainty in which an 'optimistic' view of the possible outcome is adopted. The favoured strategy is therefore to implement the course of action which leads to the highest possible profit, irrespective of (a) the probability of that profit actually being achieved, and (b) the outcome if it is not successful. A risk-taker may make decisions on this basis.

maximin criterion *Fin* an approach to decision-making under uncertainty in which a 'pessimistic' view of the possible outcome is adopted. The favoured strategy is therefore to implement the course of action whose worst possible outcome generates the highest profit. This basis for decision-making characterises risk-averse decision-makers.

maximum stock level *Fin* a stock level, set for control purposes, which actual stockholding should never exceed. It is calculated as follows:

((reorder level + EOQ) – (minimum rate of usage × minimum lead time))

Mayo, Elton (1880–1949) *Gen Mgt* Australian psychologist and academic. Responsible for finding, through the *Hawthorne experiments*, that *job satisfaction* increases through employee participation in decision-making, rather than through short-term incentives. The results of the Hawthorne studies were published in Mayo's *The Human Problems of an Industrial Civilization* (1933), and were further publicised by one of his collaborators, *Fritz Jules Roethlisberger*. Mayo is recognised as the founder of the *human relations* school of management.

In the early part of his career, Mayo studied in London and Edinburgh and taught at Queensland University. He arrived in the United States in 1923 and worked at the University of Pennsylvania before moving to Harvard. It was while he was at Harvard that Mayo became involved in the Hawthorne Studies.

The market has no morality.   *Michael Heseltine*

MBA *abbr Gen Mgt* Master of Business Administration: a post-graduate qualification awarded after a period of study of topics relating to the strategic management of businesses. A Master of Business Administration course can be followed at a *business school* or university, and covers areas such as finance, personnel, and resource management, as well as the wider business environment and skills such as information technology use. The course is mostly taken by people with experience of managerial work, and is offered by universities worldwide. Part-time or distance learning MBAs are available, so that students can study while still working. There is an increasing number of MBA graduates, as an MBA is seen as a passport to a better job and higher salary. For many positions at a higher level within organisations, an MBA is now a prerequisite.

MBI *abbr Gen Mgt* management buy-in

MBIA *abbr Fin* Municipal Bond Insurance Association: a group of insurance companies that insure high-rated municipal bonds

MBO *abbr Gen Mgt* **1.** management buy-out **2.** management by objectives

McCann, Dick (*b.* 1943) *Gen Mgt* Australian business researcher and writer. Developer, with *Charles Margerison*, of the *Team Management Wheel*™, and the team management index/questionnaire, as originally reported in *How to Lead a Winning Team* (1985). Their work on team roles and work preferences compares with that of Carl Jung and *R. Meredith Belbin*.

McClelland, David Clarence (1917–98) *Gen Mgt* US academic. Initiator of research into the use of *competences* to predict effective job performance, later developed by *Richard Boyatzis*. He was author of 'Testing for competence rather than for intelligence', *American Psychologist* (1973).

McCormick, Roger *Gen Mgt* UK business executive

McGregor, Douglas (1906–64) *Gen Mgt* US social psychologist and academic. Developer of *Theory X* and *Theory Y*, which describe two views of people at work and two opposing *management styles*. McGregor's writings on *motivation* and *leadership*, first published in *The Human Side of Enterprise* (1960), have been very influential. *William Ouchi* later developed the idea of *Theory Z*.

The son of a clergyman, McGregor graduated from the City College of Detroit (now Wayne University) in 1932. He then went on to Harvard to study for a PhD. After working at Harvard, MIT, and Antioch College in Ohio, McGregor returned to MIT in 1954 as a professor of management. At MIT he attracted some of the stars of the emerging generation of thinkers to work with him, including *Warren Bennis* and *Ed Schein*.

McKinsey 7-S framework *Gen Mgt* a model for identifying and exploiting an organisation's *human resources* in order to create *competitive advantage*. The McKinsey 7-S framework was developed by McKinsey consultants, including *Tom Peters* and *Robert Waterman*, with the academic partnership of *Richard Pascale* and *Anthony Athos* in the early 1980s. It sought to present an emphasis on human resources, rather than the traditional mass production tangibles of capital, infrastructure, and equipment. The 7-Ss are: Structure, Strategy, Skills, Staff, Style, Systems, and Shared values (see *core values*).

m-commerce *E-com* electronic transactions between buyers and sellers using mobile communications devices such as mobile phones, personal digital assistants (PDAs), or laptop computers

MD *Gen Mgt see* **managing director**

mean *Stats* a central value or location for a continuous variable in a statistical study

mean reversion *Fin* the tendency of a variable such as price to return towards its average value after approaching an extreme position

---

The man who is activated by love of power is more apt to inflict pain than to permit pleasure.
Bertrand Russell

measurement error *Stats* an error in the recording, calculating, or reading of a numerical value in a statistical study

mechanical handling *Ops* the use of machines for moving and positioning materials in a warehouse or factory

mechanisation *Gen Mgt see automation*

medallion *E-com* the microprocessor chip in a *smart card*

media independent *Mkting* an organisation that specialises in planning and buying advertising for clients or advertising agencies

median *Stats* the value that divides a set of ranked observations into two parts of equal size

media plan *Mkting* an assessment and outline of the various *advertising media* to be used for a campaign

media planner *Mkting* an employee of an advertising agency or media independent who chooses the media, timing, and frequency of advertising

media schedule *Mkting* a document that sets out the choice of media, timing, and frequency for advertising

mediation *HR* intervention by a third party in a dispute in order to try to reach agreement between the disputing parties. Where a commitment or award is imposed on either party the process is known as *arbitration*. *Also known as conciliation*

Medicare 1. *Fin* a US health insurance programme in which the government pays part of the cost of medical care and hospital treatment for people over 65 **2.** *(ANZ) Gen Mgt* the Australian public health insurance system. It was created in 1983 and is funded by a levy on income.

medium of exchange *Fin* anything that is used to pay for goods. Nowadays, this always take the form of money (banknotes and coins), but in ancient societies, it included anything from cattle to shells.

medium-sized business *Gen Mgt* an organisation with between 100 and 500 employees. *See also small business, large-sized business*

medium-term bond *Fin* a bond that has at least five but no more than 10 years before its redemption date. *See also long-term bond*

meeting *Gen Mgt* a gathering of two or more people for a particular purpose. Meetings are convened for a variety of purposes, including planning, *decision-making*, *problem-solving*, communication, and the exchange of information. They may be informal, for example, a few people getting together to discuss ideas, or they may be formal, following strict procedures. Formal meetings are conducted by a chairperson (*see chair*) according to an *agenda* set in advance, and the proceedings are recorded in *minutes*. Some meetings, such as company board meetings and *AGMs*, are a legal requirement, and take place on a regular basis.

megacity *Gen Mgt* a very large city in which media and political power is concentrated because of its key role in global information networks

megacorporation *or* **megacorp** *(US) Gen Mgt* an informal term for an extremely large and powerful business organisation

megatrend *Gen Mgt* a general shift in thinking or approach affecting countries, industries, and organisations. The term was made popular by *John Naisbitt* in his bestseller *Megatrends* (1982).

MEGO *abbr Gen Mgt* my eyes glaze over: an often sarcastic exclamation of wonder at the complexity of what a person has just said (*slang*)

meltdown *Fin* an incidence of substantial losses on the stock market. Black Monday (19 October 1987) was described as Meltdown Monday in the press the following day.

member bank *Fin* a bank that is a member of the US Federal Reserve System

---

Large, centralised organisations foster alienation like stagnant ponds breed algae.
Ricardo Semler

member firm *Fin* a firm of brokers or market makers that are members of the London Stock Exchange

member of a company *Fin* in the United Kingdom, a shareholder whose name is recorded in the register of members

members' voluntary liquidation *Fin* in the United Kingdom, a special resolution passed by the members of a solvent company for the winding-up of the organisation. Prior to the resolution the directors of the company must make a declaration of solvency. Should the appointed liquidator have grounds for believing that the company is not solvent, the winding-up will be treated as compulsory liquidation. *See also* **voluntary liquidation**

memo *Gen Mgt* a documented note that acts as a reminder and is used for conveying and recording information. The memo has to some extent been displaced by e-mail, although it is still sometimes used for important communications.

memorandum of association *Gen Mgt* an official company document, registered with the **Registrar of Companies**. A memorandum of association sets out company name, status, address of the registered office, objectives of the company, statement of **limited liability**, amount of guarantee, and the amount of authorised share capital. The **articles of association** is a related document.

memory *E-com* the facility that enables a computer to store data and programs

mentoring *HR* a form of **employee development** whereby a trusted and respected person—the mentor—uses their experience to offer guidance, encouragement, career advice, and support to another person—the mentee. The aim of mentoring is to facilitate the mentee's learning and development and to enable them to discover more about their potential. Mentoring can occur informally or it can be arranged by means of an organisational scheme.

Mentor/mentee relationships can take any form that suits the individuals involved, but in practice there are a few rules that apply to most such arrangements—the most important of which is that anything discussed remains confidential. The relationship also needs to be based on trust and candid communication. A mentor does not have to belong to the same organisation as the mentee, but can come from any sphere of the mentee's life—trade association, college, local committee, for example—just as long as he or she is not the mentee's direct supervisor or working in the same department. Mentoring does not have to be paid for; in fact it is usually seen as an honour by the mentor...many accomplished individuals consider it good professional citizenship to participate in the process of helping those coming up after them. It can also frequently be beneficial to volunteer to be a mentor, as many organisations consider mentoring a valuable hallmark of leadership material.

mercantile *Econ* relating to trading or commercial activity

mercantile agency *Fin* a company that evaluates the creditworthiness of potential corporate borrowers. *See also* **credit bureau**

mercantile paper *Fin see* **commercial paper**

mercantilism *Econ* the body of economic thought developed between the 1650s and 1750s, based on the belief that a country's wealth depended on the strength of its foreign trade

merchandising *Mkting* **1.** the process of increasing the market share of a product in retail outlets using display, stocking, and sales promotion techniques **2.** the promotion of goods associated with a particular **brand**, film, or celebrity. Merchandising based on a specific film, for example, may significantly add to its total revenues through appropriate **licensing** opportunities. Merchandising may include clothing, toys, food products, or music and often extends well beyond the **core business** of the producer of the original product.

The modern history of economic theory is a tale of evasions of reality.   *Thomas Balogh*

merchant account *E-com* an account established by an e-merchant at a financial institution or **merchant bank** to receive the proceeds of credit card transactions

merchant bank 1. *E-com* a financial institution at which an e-merchant has opened a **merchant account** into which the proceeds of credit card transactions are credited after the institution has subtracted its fee **2.** *Fin* a bank that does not accept deposits but only provides services to those who offer securities to investors and also to those investors. *US term* **investment bank**

merger *Gen Mgt* the union of two or more organisations under single ownership, through the direct **acquisition** by one organisation of the net assets or liabilities of the other. A merger can be the result of a friendly **takeover**, which results in the combining of companies on an equal footing. After a merger, the legal existence of the acquired organisation is terminated. There is no standard definition of a merger, as each union is different, depending on what is expected from the merger, and on the negotiations, strategy, stock and assets, human resources, and shareholders of the players. Four broad types of mergers are recognised. A **horizontal merger** involves firms from the same industry, while a **vertical merger** involves firms from the same supply chain. A **circular merger** involves firms with different products but similar distribution channels. A **conglomerate company** is produced by the union of firms with few or no similarities in production or marketing but that come together to create a larger economic base and greater profit potential. *Also known as* **acquisition, one-to-one merger**. *See also* **consolidation, joint venture, partnership**

mergers and acquistions *Fin* a blanket term covering the main ways in which organisations change hands. *Abbr* **M&A**

merit rating *or* **merit pay** *HR* a payment system in which the personal qualities of an employee are rated according to organisational requirements, and a pay increase or bonus is made against the results of this rating. Merit rating has been in use since the 1950s. Unlike new **performance-related pay** systems, which focus rewards on the output of an employee, merit rating examines an employee's input to the organisation—for example, their attendance, adaptability, or aptitude—as well as the quality or quantity of work produced. In merit rating schemes, these factors may be weighted to reflect their relative importance and the resultant points score determines whether the employee earns a bonus or pay increase.

metadata *E-com* essential information on a document or web page, such as publication date, author, keywords, title, and summary. This information is used by search engines to find relevant websites when a user requests a search.

When designing metadata, there are several rules which it is useful to keep in mind. Always remember the type of person who will be looking for the content—how would he or she like the content classified? Only collect metadata that is genuinely useful—someone has to fill in all the metadata, and if you ask for too much, it will slow down the publishing process and make it more expensive. Make sure that all essential information is collected—if copyright information is needed, make certain that copyright is part of the metadata list. Check that people are not abusing metadata—some will put popular keywords in their metadata just to increase the chance of their documents coming up in a search, whether relevant or not. Remember that metadata should be strongly linked with advanced search—the metadata form the parameters for refining an advanced search. *See also* **meta-tag**

meta-tag *E-com* any of the keyword and description commands used in a web page code that are used to help search engines index the website

Metcalfe's law *E-com* the proposition that networks dramatically increase in

---

value with each additional user. Metcalfe's law was formulated by Robert Metcalfe, founder of 3Com, and has been instrumental in developing the concept of *viral marketing*.

methods-time measurement *Gen Mgt* a system of *standard times* for movements made by people in the performance of work tasks. Methods-time measurement was developed in the 1940s and is the most widely used of *predetermined motion-time systems* of *work measurement* designed to increase efficiency and consistency in work operations. Work operations are broken down into a set of basic motions such as reach, grasp, position, and release and standard times for each motion are calculated by analysing films of industrial operations. Simplified versions of the system called MTM2 and MTM3, approved in 1965 and 1970 respectively, use combinations of the basic motions, such as get and put. *Abbr* **MTM**

method study *Gen Mgt* the systematic recording, examination, and analysis of existing and proposed ways of carrying out work tasks in order to discover the most efficient and economical methods of performing them. The basic procedure followed in method study is as follows: select the area to be studied; record the data; examine the data; develop alternative approaches; install the new method; maintain the new method. Method study forms part of *work study* and is normally carried out prior to *work measurement*. The technique was initially developed to evaluate manufacturing processes but has been used more widely to evaluate alternative courses of action. It is based on research into *motion study* carried out by *Frank* and *Lillian Gilbreth* during the 1920s and 1930s.

Mickey Mouse *Gen Mgt* so simple as to appear silly or trivial (*slang*)

microbusiness *Gen Mgt* a very *small business* with fewer than ten employees

microcash *E-com* a form of electronic money with no denominations, permit-

ting sub-denomination transactions of a fraction of a penny or cent

microeconomic incentive *Econ* a tax benefit or subsidy given to a business to achieve a particular objective such as increased sales overseas

microeconomics *Econ* the branch of economics that studies the contribution of groups of consumers or firms, or of individual consumers, to a country's economy

microeconomy *Econ* those narrow sectors of a country's economic activity that influence the behaviour of the economy as a whole, for example, consumer choices

microhedge *Fin* a hedge that relates to a single asset or liability. *See also* **macrohedge**

micromanagement *Gen Mgt* **1.** managing the finer details of a project or enterprise, for example, examining the operational minutiae of a task **2.** a style of management where a manager becomes over-involved in the details of the work of subordinates, resulting in the manager making every decision in an organisation, no matter how trivial. Micromanagement is a euphemism for meddling, and has the opposite effect to *empowerment*. Micromanagement can retard the progress of *organisational development* as it robs employees of their self-respect.

micromarketing *Mkting* marketing to individuals or very small groups. Micromarketing contrasts with mass marketing and targets the specific interests and needs of individuals by offering customised products or services. It is similar to *niche marketing*, but rather than targeting one large niche, a micromarketing company targets a large number of very small niches.

micromerchant *E-com* a provider of goods or services on the Internet in exchange for electronic money

micropayment *E-com, Fin* a payment protocol for small amounts of electronic money, ranging from a fraction of a cent or penny to no more than ten US dollars or euros

middleman *Gen Mgt* an intermediary in a transaction. With direct sales models, manufacturers cut out the middleman by dealing directly with end customers.

middle management *HR* the position held by managers who are considered neither senior nor junior in an organisation. Middle managers were subject to *delayering* and *downsizing* in the 1980s as organisations sought to reduce costs by removing the layer of managers between those who had direct interface with customers and senior decision-makers.

middle price *Fin* a price, halfway between the bid price and the offer price, that is generally quoted in the press and on information screens

mid-range *Stats* the mean of the largest and smallest values in a statistical sample

migrate *Gen Mgt* to transfer data and applications from an existing computer system to a new one

millennium bug *Gen Mgt* the inability of some computer systems to recognise the year 2000 as a date. The millennium bug arose from the computer programming practice of using two digits to represent a year. It was thought that this could cause great problems when digital clocks turned from 1999 to 2000, because computers would read 00 and cease to function. The millennium bug was thought to affect any business system that used electronically generated date information. Speculation on what would happen sparked fears of global disaster. Much work was carried out in the late 1990s in order to correct the problem and systems that did not have the bug were referred to as **Y2K-compliant**, Y2K being shorthand for Year 2000. In the event, the anticipated disaster did not occur.

millionerd *E-com* somebody who has become a millionaire through working in a high-tech business (*slang*)

MIME *abbr E-com* multipurpose Internet mail extension: a standard Internet protocol enabling users to send binary files as e-mail attachments

Mind Map™ *Gen Mgt* a graphical tool that can be used to visualise and clarify thoughts or ideas. In a Mind Map, the central image or idea is drawn in the middle of a piece of paper with major branches radiating from it to denote related themes. Second and third levels of thought are connected by thinner branches. Mind Maps can include the use of colour or pictures. Developed by *Tony Buzan*, the Mind Mapping technique can be used to introduce order and rationality to thought processes, and develop the creative, artistic, logical, and mathematical elements of the brain.

mindshare *Mkting* the process of fostering favourable attitudes towards a product or organisation

minimax regret criterion *Fin* an approach to decision-making under uncertainty in which the opportunity cost (regret) associated with each possible course of action is measured, and the decision-maker selects the activity which minimises the maximum regret, or loss. Regret is measured as the difference between the best and worst possible payoff for each option.

minimum lending rate (*US*) *Fin* an interest rate charged by a central bank, which serves as a floor for loans in a country

minimum quote size *Fin* the smallest number of shares that a market must handle in one trade of a particular security

minimum salary *HR* the lowest amount of money that an employee is guaranteed to earn. A minimum salary is *basic pay*, which may be increased if an employee qualifies for a *bonus* by performing well. *Payment by results*, *performance-related pay*, and sales *commission* are paid on top of a minimum salary.

minimum stock level *Fin* a stock level, set for control purposes, below which

Retail has been described as selling things which don't come back to customers who do.
Tom Farmer

stockholding should not fall without being highlighted. It is calculated as follows:

(reorder level – (average rate of usage × average lead time))

minimum subscription *Fin* the smallest number of shares or securities that may be applied for in a new issue

minimum wage *HR* an hourly rate of pay, usually set by government, to which all *employees* are legally entitled

minority interest *Fin* the nominal value of shares held in a subsidiary undertaking by members other than the parent company or its nominees plus the appropriate portion of the accumulated reserves, including share premium account

minority ownership *Fin* ownership of less than 50% of a company's ordinary shares, which is not enough to control the company

Mintzberg, Henry (*b*. 1939) *Gen Mgt* Canadian academic. Known for his views on *strategic management* and *strategic planning*, and for analysing managerial work. In *The Nature of Managerial Work* (1973), he showed that the work done by managers was substantially different from the way it was described in business theory.

Mintzberg graduated in mechanical engineering from McGill University in 1961 and later obtained a PhD in management from MIT. He is currently professor of management at McGill University, Montreal, and professor of organisation at INSEAD in Fontainebleau, France.

minutes *Gen Mgt* an official written record of the proceedings of a *meeting*. Minutes normally record points for action, and indicate who is responsible for implementing decisions. Good practice requires that the minutes of a meeting be circulated well in advance of the next meeting, and that those attending that meeting read the minutes in advance. Registered companies are required to keep minutes of meetings and make them available at their registered offices for inspection by company members and shareholders.

mirror *E-com* a copy of a website held on a different server and therefore available at a different location. Mirror sites can be used to accelerate download times by alleviating website congestion. Sites offering software downloads are the most common form of mirror site.

MIS *abbr Ops* management information system: a computer-based system for collecting, storing, processing, and providing access to information used in the management of an organisation. Management information systems evolved from early electronic data processing systems. They support managerial *decision-making* by providing regular structured reports on organisational operations. Management information systems may support the functional areas of an organisation such as finance, marketing, or production. *Decision support systems* and *EISs* are types of MIS developed for more specific purposes.

mismanagement *Gen Mgt* functional or ethical dereliction of duty due to ignorance, negligence, incompetence, avoidance, or criminality

missing value *Stats* an observation that is absent from a set of statistical data, for example, because a member of a population to be sampled was not at home when the researcher called

mission statement *Gen Mgt* a short memorable statement of the reasons for the existence of an organisation. *See also vision statement*

MIT *abbr Fin* market if touched

Mittelstand *Gen Mgt* a German term which incorporates the meaning of *small and medium-sized enterprises*

mixed economy *Econ* an economy in which both public and private enterprises participate in the production and supply of goods and services

MMC *abbr Fin* Monopolies and Mergers Commission

When money is at stake, never be the first to mention sums.　　　*Ahmed Zaki Yamani*

mobile office *Gen Mgt* the practice of working on the move. Mobile office equipment would typically include a mobile phone, laptop computer, and a modem to link the computer to the Internet or a company's main office.

mobile worker *HR* an employee who does not have one fixed place of work. Mobile workers are linked to a central base by telephone and sometimes by computer technology. A *teleworker* is a form of mobile worker.

mode *Stats* the most frequently occurring value in a set of ranked observations

model building *Stats* the process of providing an adequate fit to the data in a set of observations in a statistical study

modem *E-com* a device that transforms computer data into signals that can be sent over telephone lines. The modem enables computers to transmit and receive data. The speed at which it can send and receive data is measured in BPS (bits per second).

moderator *E-com* somebody in charge of a newsgroup, mailing list discussion group, or similar forum

modernisation *Gen Mgt* investing in new equipment or upgrading existing equipment to bring resources up to date or improve efficiency

modified ACRS *Fin* a system used in the United States for computing the depreciation of some assets acquired after 1985 in a way that reduces taxes. The ACRS applies to older assets. *See also accelerated cost recovery system*

modified book value *Fin see adjusted book value*

modified cash basis *Fin* the bookkeeping practice of accounting for short-term assets on a cash basis and for long-term assets on an accrual basis

Moller, Claus (*b.* 1942) *Gen Mgt* Danish consultant. Founder of Time Manager International™ (1975), advocate of the theory that effective *customer service* is achieved through employees' personal development, he is the originator of the concepts 'Time Manager' and 'Putting People First'.

mom-and-pop operation (*US*) (*& Canada*) *Gen Mgt = Ma and Pa shop* (*slang*)

moment of conception *Gen Mgt* the point at which a new organisation takes shape in the mind of its founder

Monday-morning quarterback (*US*) (*& Canada*) *Gen Mgt* somebody who criticises a decision only when it is too late to change it (*slang*)

Mondex *E-com* an electronic cash system that uses a smart card for both traditional shopping and e-commerce transactions

Mondragon co-operative *Gen Mgt* a large, worker-ownership movement based in the town of Mondragon, in the Basque region of northwest Spain. The Mondragon co-operative movement started in 1956, and was founded on the teachings of *José Maria Arizmendietta*. It consists of worker-owned businesses, supported by a savings bank that raises money for the co-operative enterprises. Mondragon is not part of the traditional *co-operative movement*, and is instead based on ten principles: equality of opportunity; the democratic election of managers; sovereignty of labour; a requirement for capital to be used by labour rather than labour used by capital; participative management; low pay differentials; co-operation with other co-operative movements; social change; solidarity with those working for peace, justice, and development; and education.

MONEP *abbr Fin* Marché des Options Négotiables de Paris

monetarism *Econ* an economic theory that states that inflation is caused by increases in a country's money supply

monetary *Fin* relating to or involving money, cash, or assets

monetary assets *Fin* a generic term for accounts receivable, cash, and bank balances: assets that are realisable at the amount stated in the accounts. Other assets, for example, facilities and machinery, inventories, and marketable securities will not necessarily realise the sum stated in a business's balance sheet.

monetary base *Econ* the stock of a country's coins, notes, and bank deposits with the central bank

monetary base control *Econ* government measures to restrict the amount of stocks of *liquid assets* in an economy

monetary policy *Econ, Fin* government economic policy concerning a country's rate of interest, its exchange rate, and the amount of money in the economy

monetary reserve *Fin* the foreign currency and precious metals that a country holds, usually in a central bank

monetary system *Econ* the set of government regulations concerning a country's monetary reserves and its holdings of notes and coins

monetary unit *Fin* the standard unit of a country's currency

monetise *Econ* to establish a currency as a country's legal tender

money *Econ* a medium of exchange that is accepted throughout a country as payment for services and goods and as a means of settling debts

money at call and short notice *Fin* **1.** in the United Kingdom, advances made by banks to other financial institutions, or corporate and personal customers, that are repayable either upon demand (call) or within 14 days (short notice) **2.** in the United Kingdom, balances in an account that are either available upon demand (call) or within 14 days (short notice)

money broker *Fin* an intermediary who works on the money market

moneyer *Fin* somebody who is authorised to coin money

money illusion *Econ* the tendency of consumers to react to prices in monetary

terms rather than taking account of factors such as inflation

money laundering *Fin* the process of making money obtained illegally appear legitimate by passing it through banks or businesses

moneylender *Fin* a person who lends money for interest

money market *Fin* the short-term wholesale market for securities maturing in one year, such as certificates of deposit, treasury bills, and commercial paper

money market account *Fin* an account with a financial institution that requires a high minimum deposit and pays a rate of interest related to the wholesale money market rates and so is generally higher than retail rates. Most institutions offer a range of term accounts, with either a fixed rate or variable rate, and notice accounts, with a range of notice periods at variable rates.

money market fund *Fin* a unit trust that invests in short-term debt securities

money market instruments *Fin* short-term (usually under 12 months) assets and securities, such as certificates of deposit, and commercial paper and treasury bills, that are traded on money markets

money national income *Econ* GDP measured using money value, not adjusted for the effect of inflation

money of account *Fin* a monetary unit that is used in keeping accounts but is not necessarily an actual currency unit

money order *Fin* a written order to pay somebody a sum of money, issued by a bank or post office

money purchase pension scheme *Fin* in the United Kingdom, a pension plan where the fund that is built up is used to purchase an annuity. The retirement income that the beneficiary receives therefore depends on his or her contributions, the performance of the investments those contributions are used to buy, the

---

I try to avoid experience if I can. Most experience is bad.   **E.L. Doctorow**

annuity rates, and the type of annuity purchased at retirement.

money-purchase plan *Fin* in the United States, a pension plan (a defined benefit plan) in which the participant contributes part and the firm contributes at the same or a different rate

money substitute *Econ* the use of goods as a medium of exchange because of the degree of devaluation of a country's currency

money supply *Econ* the stock of *liquid assets* in a country's economy that can be given in exchange for services or goods

money wages *Econ* wages that are expressed in terms of money units and are not adjusted for changes in price. *US term* **nominal wages**

Monopolies and Mergers Commission *Fin* in the United Kingdom, a commission that was replaced by the Competition Commission in April 1999. *Abbr* **MMC**

monopoly *Gen Mgt* a *market* in which there is only one producer or one seller. A company establishes a monopoly by entering a new market or eliminating all competitors from an existing market. A company that holds a monopoly has control of a market and the ability to fix prices. For this reason, governments usually try to avoid monopoly situations and in the United Kingdom the Competition Commission exists to regulate this area. Some monopolies, however, such as government-owned utilities, are seen as beneficial to *consumers*.

Monte Carlo method *Gen Mgt* a statistical technique used in business *decision-making* that involves a number of uncertain variables, such as capital investment and resource allocation. The name of the Monte Carlo method derives from the use of random numbers as generated by a roulette wheel. The numbers are used in repeated simulations, often performed by spreadsheet programs on computers, to calculate a range of possible outcomes. The technique was developed by mathematicians in the early 1960s for use in nuclear physics and *operational research* but has since been used more widely.

moonlighting *HR* undertaking a second job, often for cash and in the evenings, in addition to a full-time permanent job

Moore's law *E-com* the proposition that every 18 months computer chip density (and hence computer power) will double while costs remain constant, creating ever more powerful computers without raising their price. Moore's law was formulated by Intel founder Gordon Moore in the 1960s. IBM and Intel research published in 1997 corroborates it.

moral hazard *Fin* the risk that the existence of a contract will cause behavioural changes in one or both parties to the contract, as where asset insurance causes less care to be taken over the safeguarding of the assets

morality in business *Gen Mgt see* **business ethics**

moratorium *Fin* a period of delay, for example, additional time agreed by a creditor and a debtor for recovery of a debt

more bang for your buck (*US*) *Fin* a better return on your investment (*slang*)

Morgan, Gareth (*b.* 1943) *Gen Mgt* Canadian academic. Originator of the term *imaginisation*, which he described in the book of the same name (1993).

Morita, Akio (1921–99) *Gen Mgt* Japanese business executive. Co-founder and chairman of the electronics company Sony, whose global success has been based on product innovation, most famously the Walkman. The phrase 'Think global, act local' has been attributed to Morita. His experiences are recorded in his autobiography *Made in Japan* (1986).

mortgage *Fin* **1.** a financial lending arrangement whereby an individual borrows money from a bank, or another lending institution, in order to buy property or land. The original amount borrowed, the **principal**, is then repaid with interest to the lender over a fixed number of years.

The higher our income, the more resources we control and the more havoc we wreak.
Paul Carter Harrison

2. a borrowing arrangement whereby the lender is granted a legal right to an asset, usually a property, should the borrower default on the repayments. Mortgages are usually taken out by individuals who wish to secure a long-term loan to buy a home. *See also current account mortgage, endowment mortgage, interest-only mortgage, low start mortgage, repayment mortgage*

mortgage-backed security *Fin* a security for which a mortgage is collateral

mortgage bond (*US*) *Fin* a debt secured by land or property

mortgage broker *Fin* a person or company that acts as an agent between people seeking mortgages and organisations that offer them

mortgagee *Fin* a person or organisation that lends money to a borrower under a mortgage agreement. *See also mortgagor*

mortgage equity analysis *Fin* a computation of the difference between the value of a property and the amount owed on it in the form of mortgages

mortgage insurance *Fin* insurance that provides somebody holding a mortgage with protection against default

mortgage lien *Fin* a claim against a property that is mortgaged

mortgage note *Fin* a note that documents the existence and terms of a mortgage

mortgage pool *Fin* a group of mortgages with similar characteristics packaged together for sale

mortgage portfolio *Fin* a group of mortgages held by a mortgage banker

mortgage rate *Fin* the interest rate charged on a mortgage by a lender

mortgage tax *Fin* a tax on mortgages

mortgagor *Fin* somebody who has taken out a mortgage to borrow money. *See also mortgagee*

Mosaic *E-com* the first web browser made available for Macintosh and Windows. It

was developed by Netscape founder Marc Andreesen.

most distant futures contract *Fin* a futures option with the latest delivery date. *See also nearby futures contract*

MOTAS *abbr Gen Mgt* member of the appropriate sex (*slang*)

motion study *Gen Mgt* the observation of physical movements involved in the performance of work, and investigation of how these can be made more effective and cost efficient. Motion study was originally developed by *Frank* and *Lillian Gilbreth*, and is now often grouped with *time study*, to form *time and motion study*.

motion-time analysis *Gen Mgt see predetermined motion-time system*

motivate (*S Africa*) *Gen Mgt* to argue for a position or request, especially in a proposal

motivation *Gen Mgt* **1.** the creation of stimuli, incentives, and working environments which enable people to perform to the best of their ability in pursuit of organisational success. Motivation is commonly viewed as the magic driver that enables managers to get others to achieve their targets. In the 20th century, there was a shift, at least in theory, away from motivation by dictation and discipline, exemplified by *Frederick Winslow Taylor*'s scientific management, towards motivation by creating an appropriate corporate climate and addressing the needs of individual employees. Although it is widely agreed to be one of the key management tasks, it has frequently been argued that one person cannot motivate others but can only create conditions for others to self-motivate. Many *management theorists* have provided insights into motivation. *Elton Mayo*'s *Hawthorne experiments* identify some root causes of self-motivation, and *Abraham Maslow*'s hierarchy of needs provides insight into personal behaviour patterns. Other influential research has been carried out

---

People ask you for criticism but they only want praise.   *W. Somerset Maugham*

by *Frederick Herzberg*, who looked at *job satisfaction*, and *Douglas McGregor* whose *Theory X* and *Theory Y* suggest management styles that motivate and demotivate employees. **2.** (*S Africa*) a formal written proposal

motivators *HR see job satisfaction*

MOTOS *abbr Gen Mgt* member of the opposite sex (*slang*)

MOTSS *abbr Gen Mgt* member of the same sex (*slang*)

mouse milk *Gen Mgt* to do a disproportionately large amount of work on a project that yields very little return (*slang*)

mouse potato *E-com* a person who spends an excessive amount of time using a computer (*slang*)

mousetrap
build a better mousetrap *Mkting* to create a new or better product (*slang*)

Mouton, Jane (1930–87) *Gen Mgt* US psychologist. *See Blake, Robert*

mover and shaker *Gen Mgt* an influential and dynamic person within an organisation or group of people (*slang*)

move time *Fin* the time taken in moving a product between locations during the production process. *See also cycle time*

MRP II *abbr Ops* manufacturing resource planning: a computer-based manufacturing, inventory planning and control system that broadens the scope of production planning by involving other functional areas that affect production decisions. Manufacturing resource planning evolved from material requirements planning to integrate other functions in the planning process. These functions may include engineering, marketing, purchasing, production scheduling, business planning, and finance.

MSB *abbr Fin* mutual savings bank

MTM *abbr Gen Mgt* methods-time measurement

multi-channel *E-com* using a combination of online and offline communication methods to conduct business

multicurrency *Fin* relating to a loan that gives the borrower a choice of currencies

multi-employer bargaining *HR* the centralisation of *pay* negotiations at industry level, either nationally or regionally, usually conducted by *employers' associations* and *trade unions*. Multi-employer bargaining is a form of *collective bargaining*. Seen as having a moderating influence on pay rises, it hinders flexibility to link pay awards to company or individual employee performance.

multifunctional card *Fin* a plastic card that may be used for two or more purposes, for example, as a cash card, a cheque card, and a debit card

multilevel marketing *Gen Mgt see network marketing*

multimedia *Gen Mgt* a method of presenting information on a computer, CD-ROM, television, or games console. The presentation combines different media such as sound, graphics, video, and text.
    Multimedia has had problems on the Web, due mainly to limited *bandwidth*. Web browsers are not designed to view most multimedia so extra software is required: a *plug-in*.

multimedia document *Gen Mgt* an electronic document that incorporates interactive material from a range of different media such as text, video, sound, graphics, and animation. Such documents can be viewed on a multimedia computer or transmitted via the Internet.

multinational business *or* **multinational company** *Gen Mgt* a company, or corporation, that operates internationally, usually with subsidiaries, offices, or production facilities in more than one country

multiparty auction *E-com* a method of buying and selling on the Internet in which prospective buyers make electronic bids

---

War is capitalism with the gloves off. *Tom Stoppard*

multiple application *Fin* the submission of more than one share application for a new issue which is expected to be oversubscribed. In most jurisdictions, this practice is illegal.

multiple exchange rate *Fin* a two-tier rate of exchange used in certain countries where the most advantageous rate may be for tourists or for businesses proposing to build a factory

multiple regression analysis *Gen Mgt* see *regression analysis*

multiple sourcing *Ops* a *purchasing* policy of using two or more suppliers for products or services. Multiple sourcing prevents reliance on any one supplier, as is the case in *single sourcing*. It encourages competition between suppliers, and ensures access to a wide range of goods or services. Dealing with more than one supplier can improve access to market information but can also entail more administration.

multiple time series *Stats* two or more *time series* that are observed simultaneously

multiskilling *HR, Ops* a process by which employees acquire new skills. Multiskilling is a form of *flexible working* in which employees are available to undertake a number of different jobs. It has led to a reduction in *demarcation disputes* and greater *employability* for employees.

multitasking *Gen Mgt* the practice of performing several different tasks simultaneously (*slang*)

multivariate analysis *Gen Mgt* any of a number of statistical techniques used in *operational research* to examine the characteristics and relationships between multiple variables. Multivariate analysis techniques include *cluster analysis*, *discriminant analysis*, and multiple *regression analysis*.

multivariate data *Stats* data for which each observation involves values for more than one random variable

mum and dad investors (*ANZ*) *Gen Mgt* people who hold or wish to purchase shares but have little experience or knowledge of the stock market (*slang*)

Mumford, Alan *Gen Mgt* British academic. *See* **Honey, Peter**

Mumford, Enid (*b*. 1924) *Gen Mgt* British academic. She adopted the socio-technical approach of the Tavistock Institute of Human Relations, applying it to the design and implementation of information technology. Mumford termed her method ETHICS (Effective Technical and Human Implementation of Computer-based Systems), which is explained in *Effective Systems Design and Requirements Analysis: The ETHICS Approach* (1995).

municipal bond *Fin* in the United States, a security issued by states, local governments, and municipalities to pay for special projects such as motorways

Murphy's Law (*US*) *Gen Mgt* = *Sod's Law*

mushroom job (*US*) *Gen Mgt* a job that is unpleasant (*slang*)

mutual *Fin* used to describe an organisation that is run in the interests of its members and that does not have to pay dividends to its shareholders, so surplus profits can be ploughed back into the business. In the United Kingdom, building societies and friendly societies were formed as mutual organisations, although in recent years many have demutualised, either by becoming public limited companies or by being bought by other financial organisations, resulting in members receiving cash or share windfall payments. In the United States, **mutual associations**, a type of savings and loan association, and state-chartered mutual savings banks are organised in this way.

mutual association (*US*) *Fin see* **mutual**

mutual company *Fin* a company that is owned by its customers who share in the profits

mutual fund (*US*) *Fin* = *unit trust*

---

mutual insurance *Fin* an insurance company that is owned by its policy-holders who share the profits and cover claims with their pooled premiums

mutual savings bank *Fin* in the United States, a state-chartered savings bank run in the interests of its members. It is governed by a local board of trustees, not the legal owners. Some of these banks have recently begun offering accounts and services that are typical of commercial banks. *Abbr* **MSB**

Myers-Briggs type indicator *HR* a *psychometric test* that identifies four basic preferences in people's behaviour. The indicator was created in the 1940s by *Katherine Cook Briggs* and her daughter *Isabel Briggs-Myers*. It is based largely on the Jungian theory of personality types. The four preferences identified are made up of pairs of opposites: extraversion and introversion; sensing and intuition; thinking and feeling; and judgment and perception. The indicator provides a framework allowing people to understand themselves and others more fully, as well as encouraging the appreciation of different styles and perceptions. It is often used in *team building* and in the *recruitment* process.

MYOB *abbr Gen Mgt* mind your own business (*slang*)

mystery shopping *Mkting* the use of employees or agents to visit a store or use a service anonymously and assess its quality. Mystery shopping is used to assess such factors as the quality of customer service, including general and technical efficiency, and friendliness of staff, layout, and appearance of the premises, and quality and range of goods or services on offer. Mystery shoppers fill in a questionnaire based on their impressions and this information is then used to identify possible areas for business or service improvement.

Naisbitt, John (*b*. 1930) *Gen Mgt* US business executive and forecaster. Known for the publication of *Megatrends* (1982) in which he predicted ten main patterns of change that would shape the world.

naked debenture *Fin see debenture*

naked option *Fin* an option in which the underlying asset is not owned by the seller, who risks considerable loss if the price of the asset falls

naked writer *Fin* a writer of an option who does not own the underlying shares

name *Fin* an individual who is a member of Lloyd's of London

Napsterise *E-com* to distribute without charge something that somebody else owns. The term stems from the peer-to-peer business model pioneered by Napster, a software package for electronically distributing copies of copyrighted music without charge or payment of royalties. (*slang*)

narrowcasting *E-com* targeting information to a niche audience. Owing to its ability to personalise information to the requirements of individual users, the Internet is generally viewed as a narrowcast (rather than broadcast) medium.

narrow market *Fin* a market where the trading volume is low. A characteristic of such a market is a wide spread of bid and offer prices.

narrow range securities *Fin see trustee investment*

NASD *abbr Fin* National Association of Securities Dealers

NASDAQ *abbr Fin* National Association of Securities Dealers Automated Quotation system: a screen-based quotation system supporting market-making in US-registered equities. NASDAQ International has operated from London since 1992.

NASDAQ Composite Index *Fin* a specialist US share price index covering shares of high-technology companies

National Association of Investors Corporation (*US*) *Fin* a US organisation that fosters investment clubs

National Association of Securities Dealers *Fin* in the United States, the self-regulatory organisation for securities dealers that develops rules and regulations, conducts regulatory reviews of members' business activities, and designs and operates marketplace services facilities. It is responsible for the regulation of the NASDAQ Stock Market as well as the extensive US over-the-counter securities market. Established in 1938, it operates subject to the Securities Exchange Commission oversight and has a membership that includes virtually every US broker or dealer doing securities business with the public. *Abbr* **NASD**

national bank *Fin* **1.** a bank owned or controlled by the state that acts as a bank for the government and implements its monetary policies **2.** (*US*) a bank that operates under federal charter and is legally required to be a member of the Federal Reserve System

national debt *Econ, Fin* the total borrowing of a country's central government that is unpaid

national demand *Econ* the total demand of consumers in an economy

National Guarantee Fund *Fin* a supply of money held by the Australian Stock Exchange which is used to compensate investors for losses incurred when an exchange member fails to meet its obligations

national income *Econ* the total earnings from a country's production of services and goods in a particular year

national income accounts *Fin* economic statistics that show the state of a nation's economy over a given period of time, usually a year. *See also* **gross domestic product, gross national product**

National Insurance contributions *Fin* in the United Kingdom, payments made by both employers and employees to the government. The contributions, together with other government receipts, are used to finance state pensions and other benefits such as the dole. *Abbr* **NIC**

nationalisation *Gen Mgt* the taking over of privately owned companies by government. Nationalisation has strong political connotations. Recent global political trends have moved away from nationalisation by introducing more competition and liberalisation into markets. *See also privatisation*

National Market System *Fin* in the United States, an inter-exchange network system designed to foster greater competition between domestic stock exchanges. Legislated for in 1975, it was implemented in 1978 with the Intermarket Trading System that electronically links eight markets: American, Boston, Cincinnati, Chicago, New York, Pacific, Philadelphia, and the NASD over-the-counter market. It allows traders at any exchange to seek the best available price on all other exchanges that a particular security is eligible to trade on. *Abbr* **NMS**

National Occupational Health and Safety Commission *(ANZ) Gen Mgt* an Australian statutory body responsible for co-ordinating efforts to prevent injury, disease, and deaths occurring in the workplace. *Abbr* **NOHSC**. *Also known as Worksafe Australia*

National Savings *Fin* in the United Kingdom, a government agency accountable to the Treasury that offers a range of savings products directly to the public or through post offices. The funds raised finance the national debt.

National Savings Bank *Fin* in the United Kingdom, a savings scheme established in 1861 as the Post Office Savings

Bank and now operated by National Savings. *Abbr* **NSB**

National Savings Certificate *Fin* in the United Kingdom, either a fixed-interest or an index-linked certificate issued for two or five year terms by National Savings with returns that are free of income tax. *Abbr* **NSC**

National Vocational Qualification *HR* a qualification awarded following *vocational training*. National vocational qualifications are based on national standards developed by leading bodies from industrial and commercial sectors, defining the skills or *competences* required in particular occupations. Work-based evidence to demonstrate competence is assessed, and a qualification is awarded on the basis of the assessment. There is no formal examination. Five levels of NVQs are awarded, with level 1 equating to GCSE qualifications and level 5 equating to a higher degree. *Abbr* **NVQ**

national wage agreement *HR* a country-wide *collective agreement* reached through *collective bargaining* between *trade unions* and employers, which sets a national rate of *pay* within an industry or for a particular job

natural capitalism *Gen Mgt* an approach to capitalism in which protection of the earth's resources is a strategic priority

NAV *abbr Fin* net asset value

navigate *E-com* to find your way around the Internet, a website, or an *HTML* document.

Research has shown that people navigate in a certain way when reading content in a website, and certain standards and conventions of navigation are emerging for website design. More important than anything else is functionality: visitors want to find the information they are seeking quickly and easily, and are not particularly interested in style.

The most basic design convention, termed 'essential' or 'global' navigation, holds that every web page should have a set of essential navigation tools that are visible when the first screen loads, linking to key areas within the website. Essential navigation should contain links such as Home, About, Products, Customers, and Contact.

It is also important to let visitors know where they are on a website, with each page clearly displaying what part of the overall *classification* it represents. If it is the home page, for example, this should be made clear; or if it is a page dealing with pricing information, the heading at the top of the page should say so.

Users also find it useful to know where they have been on a website—usually done by changing the colour of *hyper-link*s that have been clicked on from blue to purple.

NBV *abbr Fin* net book value

NDA *abbr Gen Mgt* non-disclosure agreement, non-disparagement agreement

NDP *abbr Econ* net domestic product

nearby futures contract *Fin* a futures option with the earliest delivery date. *See also **most distant futures contract***

nearby month *Fin* the earliest month for which there is a futures contract for a particular commodity. *Also known as **spot month**. See also **far month***

near money *Fin* assets that can quickly be turned into cash, for example, some types of bank deposit, short-dated bonds, and certificates of deposit

negative amortisation *Fin* an increase in the principal (see *mortgage*) of a loan due to the inadequacy of payments to cover the interest

negative carry *Fin* interest that is so high that the borrowed money does not return enough profit to cover the cost of borrowing

negative cash flow *Fin* a cash flow with higher outgoings than income

negative equity *Fin* a situation in which a fall in prices leads to a property being worth less than was paid for it

negative gearing *Fin* the practice of borrowing money to invest in property or shares and claiming a tax deduction on the difference between the income and the interest repayments

negative income tax *(US) Econ* payments such as tax credits made to households or individuals to make their income up to a guaranteed minimum level

negative pledge clause *Fin* a provision in a bond that prohibits the issuer from doing something that would give an advantage to holders of other bonds

negative yield curve *Fin* a representation of interest rates that are higher for short-term bonds than they are for long-term bonds

negligence *Gen Mgt* the breach of a duty of care, resulting in harm to one or more people. Negligence occurs when an organisation causes harm or injury through carelessness or inattention to the needs of the groups to which it owes a duty of care. These can include its customers, consumers of its product or service, shareholders, or the local community. Victims of negligence are entitled to claim compensation. Negligence is considered to be **gross negligence** if it is the result of excessively careless behaviour.

negotiable certificate of deposit *Fin* a certificate of deposit with a very high value that can be freely traded

negotiable instrument *Fin* a document of title which can be freely traded, such as a bill of exchange or other certificate of debt

negotiable order of withdrawal *Fin* a cheque drawn on an account that bears interest

negotiable security *Fin* a security that can be freely traded

negotiate *Fin* to transfer financial instruments such as bearer securities, bills of exchange, cheques, and promissory notes, for consideration to another person

---

Costs merely register competing attractions. *Frank H. Knight*

negotiated budget *Fin* a budget in which budget allowances are set largely on the basis of negotiations between budget holders and those to whom they report

negotiated commissions *Fin* commissions that result from bargaining between brokers and their customers, typically large institutions

negotiated issue *Fin see* **negotiated offering**

negotiated market *Fin* a market in which each transaction results from negotiation between a buyer and a seller

negotiated offering *Fin* a public offering, the price of which is determined by negotiations between the issuer and a syndicate of underwriters. *Also known as negotiated issue*

negotiated sale *Fin* a public offering, the price of which is determined by negotiations between the issuer and a single underwriter

negotiation *Gen Mgt* a discussion with the aim of resolving a difference of opinion or dispute, or to settle the terms of an agreement or transaction

Nellie
sitting with Nellie *HR see* **on-the-job training** (*slang*)

nest egg *Fin* assets, usually other than a pension plan or retirement account, that have been set aside by an individual for his or her retirement (*slang*)

nester *Mkting* in advertising or marketing, a consumer who is not influenced by advertising hype but prefers value for money and traditional products (*slang*)

net advantage of refunding *Fin* the amount realised by refunding debt

net advantage to leasing *Fin* the amount by which leasing something is financially better than borrowing money and purchasing it

net advantage to merging *Fin* the amount by which the value of a merged enterprise exceeds the value of the pre-existing companies, minus the cost of the merger

net assets *Fin* the amount by which the value of a company's assets exceeds its liabilities

net asset value *Fin* a sum of the values of all that a unit trust owns at the end of a trading day. *Abbr* **NAV**

NetBill *E-com* a micropayment system developed at Carnegie Mellon University for purchasing digital goods over the Internet. After the goods are delivered in encrypted form to the purchaser's computer, the money is debited from the purchaser's prefunded account and the goods are decrypted for the purchaser's use.

net book value *Fin* the historical cost of an asset less any accumulated depreciation or other provision for diminution in value, for example, reduction to net realisable value, or asset value which has been revalued downwards to reflect market conditions. *Also known as written-down value*

net capital *Fin* the amount by which net assets exceed the value of assets not easily converted to cash

net cash balance *Fin* the amount of cash that is on hand

NetCheque *E-com* a trademark for an electronic payment system developed at the University of Southern California to allow users to write electronic cheques to each other

net current assets *Fin* the amount by which the value of a company's current assets exceeds its current liabilities

net dividend *Fin* the value of a dividend after the recipient has paid tax on it

net domestic product *Econ* the figure produced after factors such as depreciation have been deducted from *GDP*

net errors and omissions *Fin* the net amount of the discrepancies that arise in calculations of balances of payments

net fixed assets *Fin* the value of fixed assets after depreciation

---

I'm all in favour of free expression, provided it's kept strictly under control. **Alan Bennett**

net foreign factor income *Fin* income from outside a country, constituting the amount by which a country's gross national product exceeds its gross domestic product

nethead *E-com* somebody who is obsessed with the Internet (*slang*)

Net imperative *E-com* the idea that Internet business processes must be adopted by organisations for future success

net income *Fin* **1.** an organisation's income less the costs incurred to generate it **2.** gross income less tax **3.** a salary or wage less tax and other statutory deductions, for example, National Insurance contributions

net interest *Fin* gross interest less tax

netiquette *E-com* the etiquette of the Internet. The term is used mainly in the context of e-mail and newsgroup communication.

netizen *E-com* a regular user of the Internet

net lease *Fin* a lease that requires the lessee to pay for things that the owner usually pays for. *See also* **gross lease**

net liquid funds *Fin* an organisation's cash plus its marketable investments less its short-term borrowings, such as overdrafts and loans

net margin *Fin* the percentage of revenues that is profit

net operating income *Fin* the amount by which income exceeds expenses, before considering taxes and interest

net operating margin *Fin* net operating income as a percentage of revenues

net pay *HR see* **take-home pay**

net position *Fin* the difference between an investor's long and short positions in the same security

net present value *Fin* the value of an investment calculated as the sum of its initial cost and the ***present value*** of expected future cash flows. *Abbr* **NPV**

EXAMPLE A positive NPV indicates that the project should be profitable, assuming that the estimated cash flows are reasonably accurate. A negative NPV indicates that the project will probably be unprofitable and therefore should be adjusted, if not abandoned altogether.

NPV enables a management to consider the time-value of money it will invest. This concept holds that the value of money increases with time because it can always earn interest in a savings account. When the time-value-of-money concept is incorporated in the calculation of NPV, the value of a project's future net cash receipts in 'today's money' can be determined. This enables proper comparisons between different projects.

For example, if Global Manufacturing Ltd is considering the acquisition of a new machine, its management will consider all the factors: initial purchase and installation costs; additional revenues generated by sales of the new machine's products, plus the taxes on these new revenues. Having accounted for these factors in its calculations, the cash flows that Global Manufacturing projects will generate from the new machine are:

Year 1:	−100,000 (initial cost of investment)
Year 2:	30,000
Year 3:	40,000
Year 4:	40,000
Year 5:	35,000
Net Total:	145,000

At first glance, it appears that cash flows total 45% more than the £100,000 initial cost, a sound investment indeed. But time-value of money shrinks return on the project considerably, since future pounds are worth less than present pounds in hand. NPV accounts for these differences with the help of present-value tables, which list the ratios that express the present value of expected cash-flow pounds, based on the applicable interest rate and the number of years in question. In the example, Global Manufacturing's

Year	Cash-flow	Table factor (at 9%)	Present value
1	(£100,000) ×	1.000000 =	(£100,000)
2	£30,000 ×	0.917431 =	£27,522.93
3	£40,000 ×	0.841680 =	£33,667.20
4	£40,000 ×	0.772183 =	£30,887.32
5	£35,000 ×	0.708425 =	£24,794.88
NPV =	£16,873.33		

cost of capital is 9%. Using this figure to find the corresponding ratios on the present value table, the £100,000 investment cost and expected annual revenues during the five years in question, the NPV calculation looks as in the table above.

NPV is still positive. So, on this basis at least, the investment should proceed.

net price *Fin* the price paid for goods or services after all relevant discounts have been deducted

net proceeds *Fin* the amount realised from a transaction minus the cost of making it

net profit *Fin* **gross profit** minus costs

net profit margin *Gen Mgt see* **profit margin**

net profit ratio *Fin* the ratio of an organisation's net profit to its total net sales. Comparing the net profit ratios of companies in the same sector shows which are the most efficient.

net realisable value *Fin* the value of an asset if sold, allowing for costs

net residual value *Fin* the anticipated proceeds of an asset at the end of its useful life, less the costs of selling it, for example, transport and commission. It is used when calculating the annual charge for the straight-line method of depreciation. *Abbr* **NRV**

net return *Fin* the amount realised on an investment, taking taxes and transaction costs into account

net salvage value *Fin* the amount expected to result from terminating a project, taking tax consequences into consideration

network[1] *E-com* a group of computers that are able to communicate with each other. There are two types of computer network: **LAN** (a local area network) and **WAN** (a wide area network). LANs are typically used by organisations that have a large number of computers based in one location and connected to a single computer server. They are often used as the basis for private networks such as *intranets*. WANs are slower than LANs because they use telephone cables as well as computer servers. The Internet is the main WAN in existence.

network[2] *HR* to build up and maintain relationships with people whose interests are similar or whose friendship could bring advantages such as job or business opportunities.

It is important to network for the good of the organisation and the professional field in which the networker operates. The networker should know what they hope to accomplish by networking, and what they have to offer other people: it is a two-way process, as the more someone has to offer other people, the more those people will want to do things for them.

In order to network effectively, it is useful to make a list of organisations and events for networking, a *contact list*, and an action plan with a schedule. The organisations and events list helps the networker identify and target places and situations where they are likely to meet with people who may be of assistance to them in their career or with a particular project. The contact list allows the networker to keep track of the people they have met, or want to meet. It is a good idea to prioritise this list according to who is most likely to be helpful. Using these

---

There was worlds of reputation in it, but no money.   Mark Twain

two lists, the networker can then put together a schedule for making or maintaining connections.

network analysis *Gen Mgt, Ops* any of a set of techniques developed to aid the planning, monitoring, and controlling of complex *projects* and project resources. Network analysis is a tool of *project management* that involves breaking down a project into component parts or individual activities and recording them on a network diagram or *flow chart*. The resulting chart shows the interaction and interrelations between activities and can be used to determine project duration, time and resource limitations, and cost estimates. Constituent techniques include the *critical-path method* and the programme evaluation and review technique. *Also known as* **network flow analysis**

network culture *Gen Mgt* forms of culture that are heavily influenced by communication using global networks

network flow analysis *Gen Mgt, Ops see* **network analysis**

network management *Gen Mgt* the coordinated control of computer systems and programs to allow access to and delivery of information to a number of users. Network management enables users to connect by means of cabling within a LAN (see *network*) or via telecommunications lines in a wide area network.

network marketing *Mkting* the selling of goods or services through a network of self-employed agents or representatives. Network marketing usually involves several levels of agents, each level on a different commission rate. Each agent is encouraged to recruit other agents. In genuine network marketing, in contrast to *pyramid selling*, there is an end product or service sold to customers. Another version of network marketing is the loose co-operative relationship between a company, its competitors, collaborators, suppliers, and other organisations affecting the overall marketing function. *Also known as* **multilevel marketing**

network organisation *Gen Mgt* a company or group of companies that has a minimum of formal structures and relies instead on the formation and dissolution of teams to meet specific objectives. A network organisation utilises *information and communications technologies* extensively, and makes use of know-how across and within companies along the *value chain*. *See also* **virtual organisation**

network revolution *Gen Mgt* the fundamental change in business practices triggered by the growth of global networks

network society *Gen Mgt* a society in which patterns of work, communication, and government are characterised by the use of global networks

net worth *Fin* the difference between the assets and liabilities of a person or company

net yield *Fin* the rate of return on an investment after considering all costs and taxes

neural network *Stats* a computer system designed to mimic the neural patterns of the human brain

neurolinguistic programming *Gen Mgt* an approach to recognising, applying, developing, and reproducing behaviour, thought processes, and ways of communicating that contribute to success. Neurolinguistic programming was developed by Richard Bandler and John Grinder through their observations of how therapists achieved excellent results with clients. It is popular in the business environment, where its influencing techniques can help firms implement change initiatives, improve communication and management skills, and develop training techniques. *Abbr* **NLP**

newbie *Gen Mgt* a person who is new to using the Internet (*slang*)

new economy *Econ* firms in the e-commerce sector and in the *digital economy* that often trade online rather than in the bricks and mortar of physical premises in the high street

---

Everybody is always in favour of general economy and particular expenditure.

Anthony Eden

new entrants *Mkting* organisations or products that have recently come into a market or sector

new issue *Fin* **1.** a new security, for example, a bond, debenture, or share, being offered to the public for the first time. *See also float¹, initial public offering* **2.** a rights issue, or any further issue of an existing security

new issues market *Fin* the part of the market in which securities are first offered to investors by the issuers. *See also float¹, initial public offering, primary market*

newly industrialised economy *Econ* a country whose industrialisation has reached a level beyond that of a developing country. Mexico and Malaysia are examples of newly industrialised economies.

new product development *Mkting* the processes involved in getting a new product or service to market. The traditional **product development cycle**, the **stage-gate model**, embraces the conception, generation, analysis, development, testing, marketing, and commercialisation of new products or services. Alternative models of new product development fall into two broad categories: **accelerating time to market models** and **integrated implementation models**. These aim to achieve both flexibility and acceleration of development. All activities such as design, production planning, and test marketing are carried out in parallel rather than going through a sequential linear progression. *Abbr* **NPD**

newsgroup *E-com see bulletin board*

newsletter *Gen Mgt* an informal publication, issued periodically by an organisation or agency to provide information to a particular audience. A newsletter may be issued externally or it may take the form of an **in-house newsletter**, or **house journal**, used to aid the *internal communication* process. It is becoming more common for newsletters to be issued in electronic format.

newsreader *E-com* a program that enables Internet users to send and access newsgroup messages. Newsreader programs are contained within e-mail software available as independent programs.

New York Mercantile Exchange *Fin* the world's largest physical commodity exchange and North America's most important trading exchange for energy and precious metals. It deals in crude oil, petrol, heating oil, natural gas, propane, gold, silver, platinum, palladium, and copper. *Abbr* **NYMEX**

New York Stock Exchange *Fin see* **NYSE**

New Zealand Stock Exchange *Fin* the principal market in New Zealand for trading in securities. It was established in 1981, replacing the Stock Exchange Association of New Zealand and a number of regional trading floors. *Abbr* **NZSE**

New Zealand Trade Development Board *Fin* a government body responsible for promoting New Zealand exports and facilitating foreign investment in New Zealand. *Also known as* **TRADENZ**

next futures contract *Fin* an option for the month after the current month

NIC *abbr Fin* National Insurance contribution

nice guys finish last *Gen Mgt* an axiom used in business to suggest that people should think about themselves first (*slang*)

nice-to-haves *HR* benefits of a job, such as free parking or subsidised meals, that are good to have but not essential (*slang*)

niche market *Mkting* a very specific market segment within a broader segment. A niche market involves specialist goods or services with relatively few or no competitors. Niche consumers often look for exclusiveness or some other differentiating factor such as high status. Alternatively, they may have a specific requirement not satisfied by standard products. Allergy sufferers, for example, may require specially formulated soaps

---

In matters of grave importance, style, not sincerity, is the vital thing. Oscar Wilde

and detergents. Niche markets are often targeted by small companies that produce specialised goods and services. *See also* **micromarketing**

niche player *Fin* **1.** an investment banker specialising in a particular field, for example, management buyouts **2.** a broking house that deals in securities of only one industry. *Also known as* **boutique investment house**

nickel (*US*) *Fin* five basis points (*slang*)

nifty fifty (*US*) *Fin* on Wall Street, the fifty most popular stocks among institutional investors (*slang*)

night shift *HR* a **shift** within a **shiftwork** pattern that takes place during the evening and overnight. Night shifts involve particular health and social issues, and the antisocial hours usually incur a pay premium.

NIH syndrome *Gen Mgt* a problem afflicting large old-fashioned companies which reject ideas that come from outside the company simply because they were 'not invented here' (*slang*)

Nikkei 225 *or* **Nikkei Index** *Fin* the Japanese share price index

nil paid *Fin* with no money yet paid. This term is used in reference to the purchase of newly issued shares, or to the shares themselves, when the shareholder entitled to buy new shares has not yet made a commitment to do so and may sell the rights instead.

NIMBY *abbr Gen Mgt* Not In My Back Yard (*slang*)

NLP *abbr Gen Mgt* neurolinguistic programming

NMS *abbr Fin* National Market System

no-brainer *Fin* a transaction that is so favourable, no intelligence is required when deciding whether to enter into it (*slang*)

node *E-com* any single computer connected to a network

NOHSC *abbr Gen Mgt* National Occupational Health and Safety Commission

noise *Fin* irrelevant or insignificant data which overload a feedback process. The presence of noise can confuse or divert attention from relevant information; efficiency in a system is enhanced as the ratio of information to noise increases.

Nolan, Lord Michael Patrick, Baron of Brasted (*b.* 1928) *Gen Mgt* British lawyer. Chairman of the Committee on Standards in Public Life 1994–97.

no-load fund *Fin* a unit trust that does not charge a fee for the purchase or sale of shares. *See also* **load fund**

nomadic worker *HR see* **mobile worker**

nominal account *Fin* a record of revenues and expenditures, liabilities and assets classified by their nature, for example, sales, rent, rates, electricity, wages, share capital

nominal annual rate *Fin see* **APR**

nominal capital *Fin* the total value of all of a company's stock

nominal cash flow *Fin* cash flow in terms of currency, without adjustment for inflation

nominal exchange rate *Fin* the exchange rate as specified, without adjustment for transaction costs or differences in purchasing power

nominal interest rate *Fin* the interest rate as specified, without adjustment for compounding or inflation

nominal ledger *Fin* a ledger listing revenue, operating expenses, assets, and capital

nominal price *Fin* the price of an item being sold when consideration does not reflect the value

nominal share capital *Fin see* **authorised share capital**

nominal value *Fin* the value of a newly issued share

That action is best which provides the greatest happiness for the greatest numbers.
Francis Hutcheson

nominal wages (*US*) *Econ* = *money wages*

nominee holding *Fin* a shareholding in a company registered in the name of a nominee, instead of that of the owner

nominee name *Fin* a financial institution, or an individual employed by such an institution, that holds a security on behalf of the actual owner. While this may be to hide the owner's identity, for example, in the case of a celebrity, it is also to allow an institution managing any individual's portfolio to carry out transactions without the need for the owner to sign the required paperwork.

non-acceptance *Fin* on the presentation of a bill of exchange, the refusal by the person on whom it is drawn to accept it

Nonaka, Ikujiro (*b.* 1935) *Gen Mgt* Japanese academic. Focuses on the creation of organisational *knowledge*, believing this to be the most meaningful *core competence* for a company, particularly because it leads to *innovation* and *competitive advantage*. His ideas on knowledge management, published in *The Knowledge-creating Company* (1995, co-authored by Hirotaka Takeuchi) draw on *Peter Drucker*'s earlier ideas of the *knowledge worker* and the knowledge society.

non-branded goods *Mkting* generic goods that are not linked to a particular *brand* name, manufacturer, or producer, such as food produce, floor coverings, furniture, computer keyboards, or hand tools. Non-branded goods are often widely available in street markets or by mail order and like *own brands* are often perceived to be of low quality.

non-business days *Fin* those days when banks are not open for all their business activities, for example, in the West, Saturdays, Sundays, and public holidays

non-conformance costs *Gen Mgt see quality costs*

non-conforming loan *Fin* a loan that does not conform to the lender's standards, especially those of a US government agency

non-contributory pension plan (*US*) *Fin* = *non-contributory pension scheme*

non-contributory pension scheme *Fin* a pension scheme to which the employee makes no contribution

non-current assets *Fin see fixed asset*

nondeductible *Fin* not allowed to be deducted, especially as an allowance against income taxes

non-disclosure agreement *HR* a legally enforceable agreement preventing present or past *employees* from disclosing commercially sensitive information belonging to the employer to any other party. A non-disclosure agreement can remain in force for several years after an employee leaves a company. In the event of a dispute, a company may be required to prove that the information in question belongs to the company itself, is not in the public domain, or cannot be obtained elsewhere. *Abbr* **NDA**

non-disparagement agreement *HR* an agreement that prevents present or past *employees* from criticising an employing organisation in public. Non-disparagement agreements are a relatively new type of agreement and have arisen primarily to prevent employees putting comments about their employing organisation onto the Internet. Case law has yet to determine whether such agreements are legally binding. *Abbr* **NDA**

non-executive director *Gen Mgt* a part-time, non-salaried member of the *board of directors*, involved in the planning, strategy, and policy-making of an organisation but not in its day-to-day operations. The appointment of a non-executive director to a board is normally made in order to provide independence and balance to that board, and to ensure that good *corporate governance* is practised. A non-executive director may be selected for the prestige they bring or for their experience, contacts, or specialist knowledge. *Also known as* *part-time director, outside director*

non-financial asset *Fin* an asset that is neither money nor a financial instrument, for example, real or personal property

non-financial incentive scheme *HR see incentive scheme*

non-financial performance measures *Fin* measures of performance based on non-financial information which may originate in and be used by operating departments to monitor and control their activities without any accounting input.

Non-financial performance measures may give a more timely indication of the levels of performance achieved than financial ratios, and they may be less susceptible to distortion by factors such as uncontrollable variations in the effect of market forces on operations.

Examples of non-financial performance measures:

The values expected may vary significantly between industries/sectors.

non-integrated accounts *Fin see interlocking accounts*

non-interest-bearing bond *Fin* a bond that is sold at a discount instead of with a promise to pay interest

non-judicial foreclosure *Fin* a foreclosure on property without recourse to a court

non-linear programming *Fin* a process in which the equations expressing the interactions of variables are not all linear but may, for example, be in proportion to the square of a variable

non-negotiable instrument *Fin* a financial instrument that cannot be signed over to anyone else

Area assessed	*Performance measure*
Service quality	Number of complaints
	Proportion of repeat bookings
	Customer waiting time
	On-time deliveries
Production performance	
	Set-up times
	Number of suppliers
	Days' inventory in hand
	Output per employee
	Material yield percentage
	Schedule adherence
	Proportion of output requiring rework
	Manufacturing lead times
Marketing effectiveness	
	Trend in market share
	Sales volume growth
	Customer visits per salesperson
	Client contact hours per salesperson
	Sales volume forecast v. actual
	Number of customers
	Customer survey response information
Personnel	
	Number of complaints received
	Staff turnover
	Days lost through absenteeism
	Days lost through accidents/sickness
	Training time per employee

non-operational balances *Fin* accounts that banks maintain at the Bank of England without the power of withdrawal

non-optional *Fin* not subject to approval by shareholders

non-participating preference share *Fin* the most common type of preference share that pays a fixed dividend regardless of the profitability of the company. *See also participating preference share*

non-performing asset *Fin* an asset that is not producing income

non-profit organisation *Gen Mgt, HR* an *organisation* that does not have financial profit as a main strategic objective. Non-profit organisations include charities, professional associations, trade unions, and religious, arts, community, research, and campaigning bodies. These organisations are not situated in either the *public* or *private sectors*, but in what has been called the **third sector**. Many have paid staff and working capital but, according to *Peter Drucker*, their fundamental purpose is not to provide a product or service, but to change people. They are led by values rather than financial commitments to shareholders.

non-random sampling *Ops* a *sampling* technique which is used when it cannot be ensured that each item has an equal chance of being selected, or when selection is based on expert knowledge of the population. *See also random sampling*

non-recourse debt *Fin* a debt for which the borrower has no personal responsibility, typically a debt of a limited partnership

non-recoverable *Fin* relating to a debt that will never be paid, for example, because of the borrower's bankruptcy

non-recurring charge *Fin* a charge that is made only once

non-resident *Fin* used to describe an individual who has left his or her native country to work overseas for a period. Non-residency has tax implications, for example, while a UK national is working overseas only their income and realised capital gains generated within the United Kingdom are subject to UK income tax. During a period of non-residency, many expatriates choose to bank offshore.

Non-Resident Withholding Tax *Fin* a duty imposed by the New Zealand government on interest and dividends earned by a non-resident from investments. *Abbr* NRWT

non-store retailing *E-com* the selling of goods and services electronically without setting up a physical store

non-tariff barrier *Econ see NTB*

non-taxable *Fin* not subject to tax

non-verbal communication *Gen Mgt* any form of *communication* that is not expressed in words. Non-verbal communication is estimated to make up 65–90% of all communication, and understanding, interpreting, and using it are essential skills. Forms of non-verbal communication include actions and behaviour such as silence, failure or slowness to respond to a message, and lateness in arriving for a meeting. *Body language* is also an important part of non-verbal communication. Non-verbal elements of communication may reinforce or contradict a verbal message.

non-virtual hosting *E-com* the most basic *hosting option*, which is often provided free, and is advisable only for very small businesses. The client does not have their own domain name; instead, their address would be: www.hostingcompany.com/clientname.

The most serious drawback of this kind of package is the lack of flexibility: the client cannot change their hosting company without changing their web address.

non-voting shares *Fin* ordinary shares that are paid a dividend from the company's profits, but that do not entitle the shareholder to vote at the Annual General Meeting or any other meeting of shareholders. Such shares are unpopular with institutional investors. *Also called* **A shares**

Nordström, Kjell (*b.* 1958) *Gen Mgt* Swedish academic. Known for a focus on *globalisation*, *innovation*, *agility*, and *product differentiation*. Co-author of *Funky Business* (2000), with *Jonas Ridderstråle*.

norm *Stats* a range of statistics that are normal for a population

normal capacity *Fin* a measure of the long-run average level of capacity that may be expected. This is often used in setting the budgeted fixed overhead absorption rate which gives it stability over time, although budgeted fixed overhead volume variances are generally produced as a consequence.

normal distribution *Stats* the probability distribution of a random variable

normal loss *Fin* an expected loss, allowed for in the budget, and normally calculated as a percentage of the good output from a process during a period of time. Normal losses are generally either valued at zero, or at their disposal values.

normal profit *Econ* the minimum level of profit that will attract an entrepreneur to begin a business or remain trading

normal yield curve *Fin* a yield curve with higher interest rates for long-term bonds than for short-term bonds. *See also* *yield curve*

Norton, David (*b.* 1941) *Gen Mgt* US consultant. *See* *Kaplan, Robert*

no-strike agreement *HR* a formal understanding between an *employer* and a *trade union* that the union will not call its members out on *strike*. A no-strike agreement is usually won by the employer in exchange for improved terms and *conditions of employment*, including pay, and sometimes *guaranteed employment*.

notch (*S Africa*) *HR* an increment on a salary scale

notes to the accounts *Fin* explanation of particular items in a set of accounts

notes to the financial statements *Fin* explanation of particular items in a set of financial statements

notice of default (*US*) *Fin* = *default notice*

notice period *HR* the amount of time specified in the terms and *conditions of employment* that an *employee* must work between resigning from an organisation and leaving the employment of that organisation. Part of a notice period may sometimes be waived while in other circumstances employees may be required to take *garden leave*.

notional cost *Fin* a cost used in product evaluation, decision-making, and performance measurement to represent the cost of using resources which have no conventional 'actual cost'. Notional interest, for example, may be charged for the use of internally generated funds.

notional principal amount *Fin* the value used to represent a loan in calculating *interest rate swaps*

not negotiable *Fin* wording appearing on a cheque or bill of exchange that it is deprived of its inherent quality of negotiability. When such a document is transferred from one person to another, the recipient obtains no better title to it than the signatory. *See also* *negotiable instrument*

NPD *abbr Mkting* new product development

NPV *abbr Fin* net present value

NRV *abbr Fin* net residual value

NRWT *abbr Fin* Non-Resident Withholding Tax

NSB *abbr Fin* National Savings Bank

NSC *abbr Fin* National Savings Certificate

NTB *abbr Econ* non-tariff barrier: a country's economic regulation on something such as safety standards that impedes imports, often from developing countries

nuisance parameter *Stats* a parameter in a statistical model that is insignificant in itself but whose unknown value is needed to make inferences about significant variables in a study

numbered account *Fin* a bank account identified by a number to allow the holder to remain anonymous

numerical control *Ops* the use of numerical data to influence the operation of equipment. Numerical control allows the operation of machinery to be automated and usually involves the use of computer systems. Data is generated, stored, manipulated, and retrieved while a process is in operation.

NVQ *abbr HR* National Vocational Qualification

NYMEX *abbr Fin* New York Mercantile Exchange

NYSE *abbr Fin* New York Stock Exchange: the leading stock exchange in New York which is self-regulatory but has to comply with the regulations of the US Securities and Exchange Commission

NZSE *abbr Fin* New Zealand Stock Exchange

NZSE10 Index *Fin* a measure of changes in share prices on the New Zealand Stock Exchange, based on the change in value of the stocks of the 10 largest companies

NZSE30 Selection Index *Fin* a measure of changes in share prices on the New Zealand Stock Exchange, based on the change in value of the stocks of the 30 largest companies. *Abbr* **NZSE30**

NZSE40 *Fin* the principal measure of changes in share prices on the New Zealand Stock Exchange, based on the change in value of the stocks of the 40 largest companies. The makeup of the index is reviewed every three months.

Obeng, Eddie (*b.* 1959) *Gen Mgt* Ghanaian-born academic and consultant. Pioneer of the first virtual business school. Obeng founded the school, named Pentacle, in 1994, to assist managers and organisations facing the pressures and challenges of the global economy, a situation described in his book *New Rules for the New World* (1997).

OBI *abbr E-com* open buying on the Internet

object and task technique (*US*) *Gen Mgt* a method of budgeting that involves assessing a project's objectives, determining the tasks required for their accomplishment, and then estimating the cost of each task

objective *Gen Mgt, HR* an end towards which effort is directed and on which resources are focused, usually to achieve an organisation's *strategy*. There is endless discussion on whether objective, **goal**, **target**, and **aim** are the same. In general usage, the terms are often used interchangeably, so it is important that if an organisation has a particular meaning for one of these terms, it must define it in its documentation. Sometimes an objective is seen as the desired final end result, while a goal is a smaller step on the road to it. Objective setting is given a practical application in *management by objectives*.

obscuranto *Gen Mgt* incomprehensible jargon used by large international organisations such as the European Commission (*slang*)

OBSF *abbr Fin* off-balance-sheet financing

obsolescence *Mkting* the decline of products in a market due to the introduction of better competitor products or rapid technology developments. Obsolescence of products can be a planned process, controlled by introducing deliberate minor cosmetic changes to a product every few years to encourage new purchases. It can also be unplanned, however, and in some sectors the pace of technological change is so rapid that the rate of obsolescence is high. This is the case particularly in consumer and industrial electronics, affecting computers, Internet-related products, telecommunications, and television, audio, and car technology. Obsolescence is part of the product *life cycle*, and if a product cannot be turned around, it may lead to *product abandonment*.

occupational health *HR* the well-being of *employees* at work. An occupational health service is concerned with reacting to and preventing work-related illness and injury, and with maintaining and improving employees' health. Occupational health may involve some or all of these elements: health screening, including pre-employment screening (see *health screening*); monitoring compliance with health and safety legislation; health promotion activities; and initiating and maintaining health-related policies. There may be some overlap with *employee assistance programmes*. An occupational health service aims to reduce *absenteeism* and improve employee morale and performance.

occupational illness *HR* an illness associated with a particular job. Occupational illnesses include lung disease, which can affect miners, *repetitive strain injury*, which can be suffered by keyboard users, and asbestosis, caused by working with asbestos. *Occupational health* policies must take all hazards into account and minimise the potential for these diseases to develop. Government benefits are sometimes available to people who are disadvantaged because of occupational illness.

occupational pension scheme *HR* a pension scheme, run by an organisation for its employees, which has satisfied the conditions allowing the employer to contract out of the state earnings related

---

Nothing is illegal if a hundred businessmen decide to do it.　　　　　*Andrew Young*

pension scheme. Occupational pensions are regarded as deferred pay and form part of the total compensation package. Until recently, most schemes were based on final salary but there has been a shift towards money purchase schemes, particularly amongst smaller companies. Alternatively, employers may choose to contribute to an employee's *personal pension*. *Also known as company pension scheme*

occupational psychology *HR* the branch of psychology concerned with the assessment of the well-being of *employees* within their work environment in order to improve performance and efficiency, *job satisfaction*, and *occupational health*. The eight main areas of occupational psychology include: human-machine interaction; design of working environment; *health and safety*; personnel *recruitment* and assessment; *performance appraisal* and career development; *counselling* and *personal development*; *training*; *motivation*; industrial relations; and organisation change and development. *Also known as industrial psychology*

OCR *abbr Fin* official cash rate

Odiorne, George Stanley *Gen Mgt* US academic. Known for his popularisation in the United States of *Peter Drucker*'s *Management by Objectives*. Odiorne is said to have coined the saying 'If you can't measure it, you can't manage it'.

OECD *abbr Fin* Organisation for Economic Co-operation and Development: a group of 30 member countries, with a shared commitment to democratic government and the market economy, that has active relationships with some 70 other countries via non-governmental organisations. Formed in 1961, its work covers economic and social issues from macroeconomics to trade, education, development, and scientific innovation. Its goals are to promote economic growth and employment in member countries in a climate of stability; to assist the sustainable economic expansion of both member and non-member countries; and to support a balanced and even-handed expansion of world trade.

OEIC *abbr Fin* open-ended investment company

OEM *abbr Ops* original equipment manufacturer

off-balance-sheet financing *Fin* financing obtained by means other than debt and equity instruments, for example, partnerships, joint ventures, and leases. *Abbr* **OBSF**

offer *Fin* the price at which a market maker will sell a security, or a unit trust manager in the United Kingdom will sell units. It is also the net asset value of a mutual fund plus any sales charges in the United States. It is the price investors pay when they buy a security. *Also known as ask, offering price, offer price*

offer by prospectus *Fin* in the United Kingdom, one of the ways available to a lead manager of offering securities to the public. *See also float, initial public offering, new issue, offer for sale*

offer document *Fin* a description of the loan a lender is offering to provide

offer for sale *Fin* an invitation by a party other than the company itself to apply for shares in a company based on information contained in a prospectus

offering memorandum *Fin* a description of an offer to sell securities privately

offering price *Fin see offer price*

offeror *Fin* somebody who makes a bid

offer price *Fin* the price at which somebody offers a share of a stock for sale. *Also known as offering price*

office design *Gen Mgt* the arrangement of work space so that work can be carried out in the most efficient way. Office design incorporates both *ergonomics* and **work flow**, which examine the way in which work is performed in order to optimise layout. Office design is an important factor in *job satisfaction*. It affects the way in which employees work, and many organisations have implemented open-plan offices to encourage **teamwork**. The development of **information and communications technologies** has led to changes in traditional layouts and some offices are designed to facilitate **hot-desking** or **hotelling**. The design of work spaces must conform to health and safety legislation.

office-free *HR* used to refer to employees whose jobs do not require them to work in an office (*slang*)

office junior *HR* an employee with no responsibilities who carries out mundane or routine tasks in an office

office politics *Gen Mgt* interpersonal dynamics within a workplace. Office politics involves the complex network of power and status that exists within any group of people.

officer *Gen Mgt see **executive***

officer of a company *HR* an individual who acts in an official capacity in a company, for example, the company secretary, a director, or a manager

official banks *Fin* banks that have charters from governments

official books of account *Fin* the official financial records of an institution

official cash rate *Fin* the current interest rate as set by a central bank. *Abbr* **OCR**

official development assistance *Fin* money that the Organisation for Economic Co-operation and Development's Development Assistance Committee gives or lends to a developing country

official list *Fin* in the United Kingdom, the list maintained by the Financial Services Authority of all the securities traded on the London Stock Exchange

official receiver *Gen Mgt* an officer of the court who is appointed to wind up the affairs of an organisation that goes bankrupt. In the United Kingdom, an official receiver is appointed by the Department

of Trade and Industry and often acts as a **liquidator**. The job involves realising any assets that remain to repay debts, for example, by selling property. *Abbr* **OR**

off-line transaction processing *E-com* the receipt and storage of order and credit or debit card information through a computer network or point-of-sale terminal for subsequent authorisation and processing

offset *Fin* a transaction that balances all or part of an earlier transaction in the same security

offset clause *Fin* a provision in an insurance policy that permits the balancing of credits against debits so that, for example, a party can reduce or omit payments to another party that owes it money and is bankrupt

offshore bank *Fin* a bank that offers only limited wholesale banking services to non-residents

offshore company *Fin* a company that is registered in a country other than the one in which it conducts most of its business, usually for tax purposes. For example, many captive insurance companies are registered in the Cayman Islands.

offshore finance subsidiary *Fin* a company created in another country to handle financial transactions, giving the owning company certain tax and legal advantages in its home country. *US term* *offshore financial subsidiary*

offshore financial centre *Fin* a country or other political unit that has banking laws intended to attract business from industrialised nations

offshore financial subsidiary (*US*) *Fin* = *offshore finance subsidiary*

offshore holding company *Fin* a company created in another country to own other companies, giving the owning company certain legal advantages in its home country

offshore production *Ops* the manufacture of goods abroad for import to the domestic market

offshore trading company *Fin* a company created in another country to handle commercial transactions, giving the owning company certain legal advantages in its home country

off-the-shelf company *Fin* a company for which all the legal formalities, except the appointment of directors, have been completed so that a purchaser can transform it into a new company with relative ease and low cost

off-topic *Gen Mgt* irrelevant or off the subject (*slang*)

Ohmae, Kenichi (*b.* 1943) *Gen Mgt* Japanese consultant, writer, and politician. Herald of Japanese management techniques in the West, arguing that the success of Japanese companies could be attributed to Japanese strategic thinking based on *creativity* and *innovation*. In *The Mind of the Strategist* (1982), Ohmae identified key differences between the strategies adopted by Japanese managers and their Western counterparts. He later challenged all companies to take account of *globalisation* in their *strategic planning* and to focus on the relationship between business and the nation state. His recent work examines the relationship between old economy and *new economy* companies and identifies the basic forces influencing the new economy.

Ohmae is a graduate of Waseda University and the Tokyo Institute of Technology, and has a PhD in nuclear engineering from the Massachusetts Institute of Technology. He joined McKinsey in 1972, becoming managing director of its Tokyo office.

Ohno, Taiichi (*b.* 1912) *Gen Mgt* Japanese business executive. Responsible for much of the background work and thinking that created the *Toyota production system*, explained in the book of the same name (1988).

ohnosecond *Gen Mgt* the short time required to realise that you have made a serious mistake (*slang*)

oil

the good oil (*ANZ*) *Gen Mgt* accurate and useful information (*slang*)

OINK *Gen Mgt* One Income, No Kids (*slang*)

older worker *HR* generally considered to mean an employee aged 50 or over but in some industries, such as IT, an older worker is somebody over 30. Older workers can be subject to *age discrimination*.

Old Lady of Threadneedle Street *Fin* the Bank of England, which is located in Threadneedle Street in the City of London (*slang*)

old old *Mkting* the oldest age group, consisting of people over the age of 75

oligarchy *Gen Mgt* an organisation in which a small group of managers exercises control. Within an oligarchy, the controlling group often directs the organisation for its own purposes, or for purposes other than the best interests of the organisation.

oligopoly *Econ* a market in which there are only a few, very large, suppliers

ombudsman *Gen Mgt* an official who investigates complaints against public departments, large organisations, or business sectors. *See also* **Financial Ombudsman**

omitted dividend *Fin* a regularly scheduled dividend that a company does not pay

omnibus account *Fin* an account of one broker with another that combines the transactions of multiple investors for the convenience of the brokers

omnibus survey *Mkting* a survey covering a number of topics usually undertaken on behalf of several clients who share the cost of conducting the survey. It is a cost-effective means of researching several subjects at the same time, and is also suitable for measuring attitudes and behaviour towards different types of products and services, or monitoring

---

In good times, people want to advertise; in bad times, they have to.   Bruce Barton

changes in attitude among groups of consumers.

on account *Fin* paid in advance against all or part of money due in the future

on demand *Fin* **1.** used to describe an account from which withdrawals may be made without giving a period of notice **2.** used to describe a loan, usually an overdraft, that the lender can request the borrower to repay immediately **3.** used to describe a bill of exchange that is paid upon presentation

one-stop shopping *Fin* the ability of a single financial institution to offer a full range of financial services

one-to-one marketing *Mkting* a marketing technique using detailed data, personalised communications, and customised products or services to match the requirements of individual customers

one-to-one merger *Gen Mgt see* **merger**

one-year money *Fin* money placed on a money market for a fixed period of one year, with either a fixed or variable rate of interest. It can only be removed during the fixed term upon payment of a penalty.

on-hold advertising *Mkting* telephone advertising aimed at consumers who are being kept on hold while waiting to speak to somebody (*slang*)

online capture *E-com* a payment transaction generated after goods have been shipped, in which funds are transferred from issuer to acquirer to merchant account

online catalogue *E-com* a business-to-business marketplace that collects the catalogue data of every supplier in a particular industry and places it on one web resource. Catalogues are important to companies for marketing purposes because they are one of the main ways to distribute product information to public marketplaces and private exchanges. *Also known as* **procurement portal**

online community *E-com* a means of allowing Web users to engage with one another and with an organisation through use of interactive tools such as e-mail, *discussion boards*, and *chat systems*.

They are a means by which a website owner can take the pulse of consumers to find out what they are thinking, and to generate unique content. As stand-alone businesses, online communities have been found to be weak: they work best when they are supporting the need for an organisation to collect on-going feedback.

online shopping *E-com see* **electronic shopping**

online shopping mall *E-com see* **cyber mall**

online training *HR see* **computer-based training**

on-pack offer *Mkting* a sales promotion technique in which customers are offered a premium on the pack

on-target earnings *HR* the amount earned by a person working on **commission** who has achieved the targets set. *Abbr* **OTE**

on-the-job training *HR* **training** given to employees in the workplace as they perform everyday work activities. On-the-job training is based on the principle of **learning by doing** and includes demonstration and explanation by a more experienced employee, supervisor, or manager; performance of tasks under supervision; and the provision of appropriate **feedback**. On-the-job training is sometimes informally referred to as **sitting with Nellie**. Types of on-the-job training include **coaching**, **delegation**, **job rotation**, **secondment**, and participation in special projects.

OPEC *abbr Fin* Organization of the Petroleum Exporting Countries: an international organisation of 11 developing countries, each one largely reliant on oil revenues as its main source of income, that tries to ensure there is a balance between supply and demand by adjusting the members' oil output. The current members, Algeria, Indonesia, Iran, Iraq, Kuwait, Libya, Nigeria, Qatar, Saudi

---

Good fortune brings success, but it is endeavour that deserves praise.

Marcus Terentius Varro

Arabia, the United Arab Emirates, and Venezuela, meet at least twice a year to decide on output levels and discuss recent and anticipated oil market developments.

open-book management *Gen Mgt* a *management style* in which everything is revealed to employees and there are no secrets. Open-book management involves not only revealing a company's full financial information to its employees but also making transparent all of the workings of the company. Open-book management has been viewed as enabling the *empowerment* and *involvement* of the workforce, increasing employee *motivation* and organisational efficiency.

open buying on the Internet *E-com, Fin* a standard built round a common set of business requirements for electronic communication between buyers and sellers that, when implemented, allows different e-commerce systems to talk to one another. *Abbr* **OBI**. *See also* **open trading protocol**

open cheque *Fin* **1.** a cheque that is not crossed and so may be cashed by the payee at the branch of the bank where it is drawn **2.** (*US*) a signed cheque where the amount payable has not been indicated

open-collar worker *HR* a person who works from home (*slang*)

open communication *Gen Mgt* a communications policy intended to ensure that employees have full information about their organisation

open-door policy *Gen Mgt* a receptive, listening approach to management characterised by a ready, informal availability on the part of the manager towards employees. Open-door management removes the need to make appointments or to show the deference traditionally associated with relationships between superiors and subordinates in hierarchies. The opposite management style is a **closed-door policy**, which is more formal. Open- and closed-door policies can reflect different kinds of *corporate culture*.

open economy *Econ* an economy that places no restrictions on the movement of capital, labour, foreign trade, and payments into and out of the country

open-end credit (*US*) *Fin* = **open-ended credit**

open-ended credit *Fin* a form of credit that does not have an upper limit on the amount that can be borrowed or a time limit before repayment is due

open-ended fund *Fin* a unit trust that has a variable number of shares. *US term* **open-end fund**

open-ended investment company *Fin* a unit trust, as distinguished from an investment trust, or **closed-end fund**. *See also* **open-ended fund**. *US term* **open-end investment company**

open-ended management company *Fin* a company that sells unit trusts. *US term* **open-end management company**

open-ended mortgage *Fin* a mortgage in which prepayment is allowed. *US term* **open-end mortgage**

open-end fund (*US*) *Fin* = **open-ended fund**

open-end investment company (*US*) *Fin* = **open-ended investment company**

open-end management company (*US*) *Fin* = **open-ended management company**

open-end mortgage (*US*) *Fin* = **open-ended mortgage**

opening balance *Fin* the value of a financial quantity at the beginning of a period of time, such as a day or a year

opening balance sheet *Fin* an account showing an organisation's opening balances

opening bell *Fin* the beginning of a day of trading on a market

opening price *Fin* a price for a security at the beginning of a day of trading on a market

---

opening purchase *Fin* a first purchase of a series to be made in options of a particular type for a particular commodity or security

opening stock *Fin* on a balance sheet, the closing stock at the end of one accounting period that is transferred forward and becomes the opening stock in the one that follows. *US term* **beginning inventory**

open interest *Fin* options that have not yet been closed

open learning *HR* a flexible approach to a course of study that allows individuals to learn at a time, place, and pace to suit their needs. A typical open learning programme might offer the student a range of delivery methods, including tutorials, workshops, formal lectures, and the Internet, supported by a variety of learning materials such as textbooks, workbooks, and video, audio, and computer-based materials. *See also* **distance learning**

open loop system *Fin* a management control system which includes no provision for corrective action to be applied to the sequence of activities

open-market operation *Fin* a transaction by a central bank in a public market

open-market value *Fin* the price that an asset or security would realise if it was offered on a market open to all

open standard *Gen Mgt* a standard for computers and related products that allows pieces of equipment from different manufacturers to operate with each other

open system *Fin* an operating system whose developer encourages the development of applications that use it

open systems thinking *Gen Mgt* a learning and **problem-solving** approach that involves describing the behaviour of a system, then exploring possibilities for improving it. Open systems thinking encourages **creativity** and is used by **learning organisations**.

open trading protocol *E-com* a standard designed to support Internet-based retail transactions that allows different systems to communicate with each other for a variety of payment-related activities. The **open buying on the Internet** protocol is a competing standard. *Abbr* **OTP**. *See also* **open buying on the Internet**

operating budget *Fin* a budget of the revenues and expenses expected in a forthcoming accounting period

operating cash flow *Fin* the amount used to represent the money moving through a company as a result of its operations, as distinct from its purely financial transactions

operating costing *Ops* a costing system that is applied to continuous operations in mass production or in the service industries. In the simplest form of operating costing, the costing period is set at a specific length of time, usually a calendar month or four weeks. The costs incurred over the period are related to the number of units produced, and the division of the first by the second gives the average unit cost for the period. *Also known as* **batch costing**

operating cycle *Ops* the cycle of business activity in which cash is used to buy resources which are converted into products or services and then sold for cash

operating income *Ops* revenue minus the cost of goods sold and normal operating expenses. *Also known as* **earnings before interest and taxes**

operating lease *Gen Mgt* a lease that is regarded by accountants as rental rather than as a **finance lease**. The monthly lease payments are simply treated as rental expenses and recognised on the income statement as they are incurred. There is no recognition of a leased asset or liability.

operating leverage *Fin* the ratio of a business's fixed costs to its total costs. As the fixed costs have to be paid regardless of output, the higher the ratio, the higher

---

If a gentleman is frivolous, he will lose the respect of his inferiors.   *Confucius*

the risk of losses in an economic downturn.

operating margin *Fin see profit margin*

operating risk *Fin* the risk of a high operating leverage

operating statement *Fin* a regular report for management of actual costs and revenues, as appropriate. Usually compares actual with budget and shows variances.

operating system *Ops* a program that controls the basic operation of a computer and its communication with devices such as the keyboard, printer, and mouse

operational audit *Gen Mgt* a structured review of the systems and procedures of an organisation in order to evaluate whether they are being carried out efficiently and effectively. An operational audit involves: establishing performance *objectives*, agreeing the standards and criteria for assessment, and evaluating actual performance against targeted performance. *Also known as management audit, operations audit*

operational control *Gen Mgt* the management of daily activities in accordance with strategic and tactical plans

operational gearing *Fin* the relationship of the fixed cost to the total cost of an operating unit. The greater the proportion of total costs that are fixed (high operational gearing), the greater the advantage to the organisation of increasing sales volume. Conversely, should sales volumes drop, a highly geared organisation would find the high proportion of fixed costs to be a major problem, possibly causing a rapid swing from profitability into significant loss-making. *See also leverage*

operational research *Gen Mgt* the application of scientific methods to the solution of managerial and administrative problems, involving complex systems or processes. Operational research aims to find the optimum plan for the control and operation of a system or process. It was originally used during the second world war as a means of solving logistical prob-

lems. It has since developed into a planning, scheduling, and **problem-solving** technique applied across the industrial, commercial, and public sectors.

operation planning *Ops see planning*

operations *Ops see operations management*

operations audit *Gen Mgt see operational audit*

operations management *Ops* the maintenance, control, and improvement of organisational activities that are required to produce goods or services for consumers. Operations management has traditionally been associated with manufacturing activities but can also be applied to the service sector. The measurement and evaluation of operations is usually undertaken through a process of business appraisal. Efficiency and effectiveness may be monitored by the application of *ISO* 9001 quality systems, or *total quality management* techniques.

operations plans *Ops* the fully detailed specifications by which individuals are expected to carry out the predetermined cycles of operations to meet sectoral objectives

operation time *Ops* the period required to carry out an operation on a complete batch exclusive of set-up and breaking-down times

opinion leader *Mkting* a high-profile person or organisation that can significantly influence public opinion. An opinion leader can be a politician, religious, business or community leader, journalist, or educationalist. Show business and sports personalities can exert a great deal of influence on young people's leisure lifestyles and buying habits and are consequently frequently used in *advertising campaigns*.

opinion leader research *Mkting* the investigation of the perceptions of *corporate image* and reputation among the people at the top of a company, industry, or profession

---

The only reason to invest in the market is because you think you know something others don't.
R. Foster Winans

opinion shopping (*US*) *Gen Mgt* the practice of searching for an auditor whose views are in line with those of a company being audited. Opinion shopping can take place when a company is about to be audited and has recently undertaken questionable dealings. Auditors are sought whose interpretation of the law matches the company's own, and who will approve the company's financial statements.

opinion survey *Stats* a survey carried out to determine what members of a population think about a given topic

opportunity cost *Fin, Gen Mgt* an amount of money lost as a result of choosing one investment rather than another

OPT *abbr Ops* optimised production technology

optimal portfolio *Fin* a theoretical set of investments that would be most profitable for an investor

optimal redemption provision *Fin* a provision that specifies when an issuer can call a bond

optimise *Fin* to allocate such things as resources or capital as efficiently as possible

optimised production technology *Ops* a sophisticated *production planning* and *control* system, based on *finite loading* procedures, that concentrates on reducing *bottlenecks* in the system in order to improve efficiency. The key task of OPT is to increase total systems throughput by realising existing capacity in other parts of the system. OPT is a practical application of the **theory of constraints**. *Abbr* **OPT**

optimum capacity *Ops* the level of output at which the minimum cost per unit is incurred

opt-in *E-com* a type of *subscription process* for users of a website wanting to sign up to receive specific information or services. An opt-in approach is where a user actively decides to provide their e-mail address, so the website owner can send

them e-mail. However, the emerging convention is *double opt-in*.

option *Fin* a contract for the right to buy or sell an asset, typically a commodity, under certain terms. *Also known as* **option contract**

option account *Fin* a brokerage account used for trading in options

optionaire *Fin* a millionaire whose wealth consists of share options (*slang*)

option buyer *Fin* an investor who buys an option

option class *Fin* a set of options that are identical with respect to type and underlying asset

option contract *Fin see* **option**

option elasticity *Fin* the relative change in the value of an option as a function of a change in the value of the underlying asset

option income fund *Fin* a unit trust that invests in options

option premium *Fin* the amount per share that a buyer pays for an option

option price *Fin* the price of an option

option pricing model *Fin* a model that is used to determine the fair value of options

options clearing corporation *Fin* the organisation in the United States that is responsible for the listing of options and clearing trades in them

option seller *Fin see* **option writer**

option series *Fin* a collection of options that are identical in terms of what they represent

options market *Fin* the trading in options, or a place where options trading occurs

options on physicals *Fin* options on securities with fixed interest rates

option writer *Fin* a person or institution who sells an option. *Also known as* **option seller**

Technology—the knack of so arranging the world that we need not experience it. **Max Frisch**

OR *abbr Fin* official receiver

order 1. *Fin* an occasion when a broker is told to buy or sell something for an investor's own account **2.** *Ops* a *contract* made between a customer and a supplier for the supply of a range of goods or services in a determined quantity and quality, at an agreed price, and for delivery at or by a specified time

order book *Ops* a record of the outstanding orders that an organisation has received. An order book may be physical, with the specifications and delivery times of orders recorded in it, or the term may be used generally to describe the health of a company. A full order book implies a successful company, while an empty order book can indicate an organisation at risk of *business failure*.

order confirmation *E-com* an e-mail message informing a purchaser that an order has been received

order picking *Ops* selecting and withdrawing goods or components from a store or warehouse to meet production requirements or to satisfy customer orders

order point *Fin* the quantity of an item that is on hand when more units of the item are to be ordered

order processing *Ops* the tracking of *orders* with suppliers and from customers

orders pending *Fin* orders that have not yet resulted in transactions

ordinary interest *Fin* interest calculated on the basis of a year having only 360 days

ordinary shares *Fin* shares that entitle the holder to a dividend from the company's profits after holders of preference shares have been paid

organigram *Gen Mgt see* **organisation chart**

organisation *Gen Mgt* an arrangement of people and resources working in a planned manner towards specified strategic goals. An organisation can be any structured body such as a business, company, or firm in the private or public sector, or in a non-profit association. *See also* **organisation structure**, **organisation theory**

organisational analysis *Gen Mgt* a type of internal business appraisal aimed at identifying areas of inefficiency and opportunities for streamlining and re-organisation

organisational change *Gen Mgt see* **change management**

organisational chart *Gen Mgt see* **organisation chart**

organisational commitment *Gen Mgt* **1.** the commitment of an organisation to given aims and objectives, as demonstrated through its stated aims and policies, and its actions and allocation of resources **2.** the degree of *employee commitment* within an organisational workforce

organisational culture *Gen Mgt see* **corporate culture**

organisational design *Gen Mgt see* **organisation structure**

organisational development *Gen Mgt* a planned approach to far-reaching, organisation-wide change designed to enable an organisation to respond and adapt to changing market conditions and to set a new agenda. Organisational development is frequently linked to *organisation structure*, which can act either as an enabling or restrictive mechanism for change. For organisational development to succeed, any policies or strategies introduced must fit with the *corporate culture*.

organisational federalism *Gen Mgt see* **federal organisation**

organisational learning *Gen Mgt* a culture of change and improvement within an organisation, characterised by employee enthusiasm, energy, and high levels of *creativity* and *innovation*. In their book *Organizational Learning* (1978), **Chris Argyris**, and **Donald Schön** suggest that if a number of employee development activities are in progress within an organisation, a sense of organisational movement and development can be achieved, and that with the right encouragement, support, and reward, this can become self-perpetuating. The concept of organisational learning was further developed by **Peter Senge**, and re-popularised as the *learning organisation*.

organisational planning *Gen Mgt* deciding on, and designing, the most appropriate structure for an organisation. Stages of the organisation planning process include: identifying and grouping activities or processes, setting out lines of authority and areas of responsibility, and possibly illustrating these through a formal organisation chart.

organisation behaviour *Gen Mgt* the study of human and group behaviour within organisational settings. The study of organisation behaviour involves looking at the attitudes, interpersonal relationships, performance, *productivity*, *job satisfaction*, and commitment of employees, as well as levels of *organisational commitment* and industrial relations. Organisation behaviour can be affected by *corporate culture*, *leadership*, and *management style*. Organisation behaviour emerged as a distinct specialism from *organisation theory* in the late 1950s and early 1960s through attempts to integrate different perspectives on human and management problems and develop an understanding of behavioural dynamics within organisations.

organisation chart *Gen Mgt* a graphic illustration of an *organisation's structure*, showing hierarchical authority and relationships between departments and jobs. The horizontal dimension of an organisation chart shows the nature of job function and responsibility and the vertical dimension shows how jobs are co-ordinated in reporting or authority relationships. Some charts include managers' names, others only job titles. Organisation charts are widely used to bring order and clarity to the way the organisation is structured. Despite this, they reflect little

of the way organisations actually work and can appear complex, especially in highly *bureaucratic* organisations. The first recorded organisation chart was produced in the United States by David C. McCallum for the New York and Erie Railroad. *Also known as* **organigram**, **organisational chart**, **org chart**

Organisation for Economic Co-operation and Development *Fin see* **OECD**

organisation hierarchy *Gen Mgt* the vertical layers of ranks of personnel within an organisation, each layer subordinate to the one above it. Organisation hierarchy is often shown in the form of an *organisation chart*. An extended hierarchy is typical of a *bureaucracy*, but during the later 20th and early 21st centuries the layers of hierarchical positions within large organisations have often been reduced as part of *downsizing* exercises. These result in the shallow or non-existent hierarchies of flexible, *flat organisations* within which there is greater employee *empowerment* and autonomy.

organisation man *Gen Mgt* somebody who fully accepts and may be absorbed by organisational objectives and values. *The Organisation Man*, a best-selling novel by **William Whyte**, is the source of the phrase.

organisation structure *Gen Mgt* the form of an organisation that is evident in the way divisions, departments, functions, and people link together and interact. Organisation structure reveals vertical operational responsibilities, and horizontal linkages, and may be represented by an *organisation chart*. The complexity of an organisation's structure is often proportional to its size and its geographic dispersal. The traditional organisation structure for many businesses in the 20th century was the *bureaucracy*, originally defined by **Max Weber**. More recent forms include the *flat*, *network*, *matrix*, and *virtual organisations*. These forms have become more prevalent during the last decades of the

---

The race is over, but the work never is done while the power to work remains.

Oliver Wendell Holmes, Jr

20th century as a result of the trend towards restructuring and downsizing and developments in telecommunications technology. According to **Harold Leavitt**, organisation structure is inextricably linked to the technology and people who carry out the tasks. **Charles Handy** has shown that it is also directly linked to *corporate culture*.

organisation theory *Gen Mgt* the body of research and knowledge concerning organisations. Organisation theory originally focused primarily on the organisation as a unit, as opposed to *organisation behaviour*, which explored individual and group behaviour within the organisation. Organisation behaviour emerged as a separate discipline in the late 1950s and early 1960s but there remains a large amount of overlap between the two. Organisation theory covers a range of areas including *organisation structure* and organisational psychology.

Organization of the Petroleum Exporting Countries *Fin see* OPEC

org chart *Gen Mgt see* **organisation chart**

orientation *(US) HR* = **induction**

original equipment manufacturer 1. *Fin* a company that makes a product that works with a basic and common product, for example, a computer **2.** *Ops* a company that assembles components from other suppliers or subcontractors to produce a complete product such as a car or aircraft. *Abbr* **OEM**

original face value *Fin* the amount of the principal of a mortgage on the day it is created

original issue discount *Fin* the discount offered on the day of sale of a debt instrument

original maturity *Fin* a date on which a debt instrument is due to mature

origination fee *Fin* a fee charged by a lender for providing a mortgage, usually expressed as a percentage of the principal

orthogonal *Stats* statistically independent

OTC market *abbr Fin* over-the-counter market

OTE *abbr HR* on-target earnings

other capital *Fin* capital that is not listed in specific categories

other current assets *Fin* assets that are not cash and are due to mature within a year

other long-term capital *Fin* long-term capital that is not listed in specific categories

other prices *Fin* prices that are not listed in a catalogue

other short-term capital *Fin* short-term capital that is not listed in specific categories

OTOH *abbr Gen Mgt* on the other hand *(slang)*

OTP *abbr E-com* open trading protocol

Ouchi, William *(b.* 1943) *Gen Mgt* Japanese-US academic. Best known for **Theory Z** (1981) which developed the work of **Douglas McGregor**.

out box *(US) Gen Mgt* = **out tray**

outdoor advertising *Mkting* the use of outdoor advertising media in venues such as airports, shopping malls, bus shelters, and railway stations

outdoor training *HR see* **adventure training**

outlier *Stats* a statistical observation that deviates significantly from other members of a sample

out-of-date cheque *Fin* a cheque which has not been presented to the bank on which it is drawn for payment within a reasonable time of its date (six months in the UK) and which may therefore be dishonoured by the bank without any breach of the banker–customer contract

out of the loop *Gen Mgt* excluded from communication within a group. Somebody who is out of the loop may have been deliberately or inadvertently

---

Lack of confidence is not the result of difficulty; the difficulty comes from lack of confidence.
Seneca

excluded from the decision-making process or the information flow around an organisation. That person is likely to feel isolated and will be unable to contribute fully to the organisation. Effective networking may help to prevent this from happening. (*slang*)

outplacement *HR* a programme of resources, information, and advice provided by an employing organisation for employees who are about to be made redundant. Outplacement agencies typically help by drafting *curricula vitae*, offering career guidance, providing practice interviews, and placing redundant employees in new jobs. Outplacement programmes are often put into place well before the redundant employees leave the employer and, in the case of large-scale redundancy programmes, may remain in place for several years.

output *Fin* anything produced by a company, usually physical products

output gap *Econ* the difference between the amount of activity that is sustainable in an economy and the amount of activity actually taking place

output method *Econ* an accounting system that classifies costs according to the *outputs* for which they are incurred, not the inputs they have bought

output tax (*ANZ*) *Fin* the amount of *GST* (goods and services tax) paid to the tax office after the deduction of *input tax credits*

outside director *Gen Mgt* a member of a company's *board of directors* neither currently, or formerly, in the company's employment. An outside director is sometimes described as being synonymous with a *non-executive director*, and as usually being employed by a holding or associated company. In the United States, an outside director is somebody who has no relationships at all to a company. In US public companies, compensation and audit committees are generally made up of outside directors, and use of outside

directors to select board directors is becoming more common.

outsourcing *Gen Mgt* the transfer of the provision of services previously carried out by in-house personnel to an external organisation, usually under a *contract* with agreed standards, costs, and conditions. Areas traditionally outsourced include legal services, transport, catering, and security. An increasing range of activities, including IT services, training, and public relations are now being outsourced. Outsourcing, or **contracting out**, is often introduced with the aim of increasing efficiency and reducing costs, or to enable the organisation to develop greater flexibility or to concentrate on *core business* activities. The term *subcontracting* is sometimes used to refer to outsourcing.

outstanding share *Fin* a share that a company has issued and somebody has bought

outstanding share capital *Fin* the value of all of the stock of a company minus the value of retained shares

out tray *Gen Mgt* a receptacle for documents and other items that have been dealt with. An out tray is normally placed in the office or on the desk of the person responsible for dealing with the contents. Items are placed in the out tray before being filed or delivered to another person. *US term* **out box**

outward bound training *HR see adventure training*

outwork *Fin, Gen Mgt* work carried out for a company away from its premises, for example, by subcontractors or employees working from home

outworker *Fin, Gen Mgt* a sub-contractor or employee carrying out work for a company away from its premises

overall capitalisation rate *Fin* net operating income other than debt service divided by value

overall market capacity *Econ* the amount of a service or good that can be absorbed in a market without affecting the price

overall rate of return *Fin* the yield of a bond held to maturity, expressed as a percentage

overall return *Fin* the aggregate of all the dividends received over an investment's life together with its capital gain or loss at the date of its realisation, calculated either before or after tax. It is one of the ways an investor can look at the performance of an investment.

overbid *Fin* **1.** to bid more than necessary **2.** an amount that is bid that is unnecessarily high

overbought market *Fin* a market where prices have risen beyond levels that can be supported by fundamental analysis. The market for internet companies in 2001 was overbought and subsequently collapsed when it became clear that their trading performance could not support such price levels.

overcapacity *Ops* an excess of capability to produce goods or provide a service over the level of demand

overcapitalised *Fin* used to describe a business that has more capital than can profitably be employed. An overcapitalised company could buy back some of its own shares in the market; if it has significant debt capital it could repurchase its bonds in the market; or it could make a large one-off dividend to shareholders.

overdraft *Fin* the amount by which the money withdrawn from a bank account exceeds the balance in the account

overdraft facility *Fin* a credit arrangement with a bank, allowing a person or company with an account to use borrowed money up to an agreed limit when nothing is left in the account

overdraft line *Fin* an amount in excess of the balance in an account that a bank agrees to pay in honouring cheques on the account

overdraft protection *Fin* the bank service, amounting to a line of credit, that assures that the bank will honour overdrafts, up to a limit and for a fee

overdraw *Fin* to withdraw more money from a bank account than it contains, thereby exceeding an agreed credit limit

overdrawn *Fin* in debt to a bank because the amount withdrawn from an account exceeds its balance

overdue *Fin* an amount still owed after the date due

over-geared *Fin* used to describe a company with debt capital and preference shares that outweigh its ordinary share capital

overhanging *Fin* a large amount of commodities or securities that has not been sold and therefore has a negative effect on prices, for example, the element of a new issue left in the hands of the underwriters

overhead absorption rate *Fin* a means of attributing overhead to a product or service, based for example on direct labour hours, direct labour cost, or machine hours. The choice of overhead absorption base may be made with the objective of obtaining 'accurate' product costs, or of influencing managerial behaviour, for example, overhead applied to labour hours or part numbers appears to make the use of these resources more costly, thus discouraging their use.

overhead cost *Gen Mgt* the indirect recurring costs of running a business

over-insuring *Fin* insuring an asset for a sum in excess of its market or replacement value. However, it is unlikely that an insurance company will pay out more in a claim for loss than the asset is worth or the cost of replacing it.

over-invested *Fin* used to describe a business that invests heavily during an economic boom only to find that when it starts to produce an income, the demand for the product or service has fallen

overnight position *Fin* a trader's position in a security or option at the end of a trading day

---

The least one can say about power is that a vocation for it is suspicious. **Jean Rostand**

overprice *Mkting* to set the price of a product or service too high, with the result that it is unacceptable to the market

overrated *Fin* used to describe something that is valued more highly than it should be

overseas company *Fin* a branch or subsidiary of a business that is incorporated in another country

Overseas Investment Commission *Fin* an independent body reporting to the New Zealand government that regulates foreign investment in New Zealand. It was set up in 1973 and is funded by the Reserve Bank of New Zealand.

overseas taxation *Fin* see *double taxation*, *double taxation agreement*

oversold *Fin* used to describe a market or security that is considered to have fallen too rapidly as a result of excessive selling. *See also* *bear market*

overstocked *Fin* used to describe a business that has more stock than it needs

over the counter (OTC) market *Fin* a market in which trading takes place directly between licensed dealers, rather than through an auction system as used in most organised exchanges

overtime *HR* extra time worked beyond normal *hours of work*. Overtime is a traditional form of *flexible working*, often used by employers to cover periods of peak demand without incurring a permanent increase in costs. Some workers are entitled to a higher rate of *overtime pay* for the extra hours, but salaried workers in particular can be expected to work overtime with no additional reward.

overtime pay *HR* remuneration for *overtime* worked. Overtime pay often comes at a premium rate but in some occupations overtime is paid at a lower rate than the standard rate of pay.

overtrading *Fin* the condition of a business which enters into commitments in excess of its available short-term

resources. This can arise even if the company is trading profitably, and is typically caused by financing strains imposed by a lengthy operating cycle or production cycle.

Owen, Robert (1771–1858) *Gen Mgt* British industrialist, and social reformer. Owner of a factory at New Lanark that he ran on model lines, pioneering improved working and living conditions for his employees. Author of *A New View of Society* (1813).

own brand *Mkting* a product or range of products offered by a retailer under their own name in competition with branded goods. Own brand products, like *nonbranded goods*, are normally cheaper than branded items but are often perceived to be of a lower quality. *Also known as* *own-label*. US term *private label*

owner *Gen Mgt* **1.** a person or organisation that has legal title to products or services **2.** the person who controls a private company

owner-operator *Gen Mgt* see *sole proprietor*

owners' equity *Fin* a business's total assets less its total liabilities. *See also* *capital*, *ordinary shares*

ownership of companies *Gen Mgt* the possession of shares in companies. Company ownership structures can differ widely. Owners of public companies may be institutions, or individuals, or a mixture of both. Directors are often offered company shares as incentives and more participative companies may offer shares to employees through *employee ownership* schemes. Private companies are usually owned by individuals, families, or groups of individual shareholders. Nationalised industries are publicly owned. Co-operatives are wholly owned by employees. A separation between the ownership and control of companies became a widely discussed issue during the 20th century, especially in the United States and the United Kingdom where shareholders have tended to be more passive. Managers were viewed as having come to occupy controlling positions as the scale of industry grew. From the 1980s, this position changed to some extent as *privatisation*, *management buy-outs*, restructuring, and *share incentive schemes* led to greater share ownership among managers and produced less passive shareholders.

own-label *Mkting see* **own brand**

P

P2P *abbr E-com* peer-to-peer: a means of optimising the networking capabilities of the Internet among groups of computers. Effectively it puts every computer on an equal footing, in that each can be both a publisher and consumer of information. The traditional model on the Web is the client-server one: the client is a computer that is able only to receive information; the server, on the other hand, publishes information on a website. Peer-to-peer makes a computer both a server and a client. Perhaps the best-known example of peer-to-peer is Napster, which enabled person A to search for and download music from person B's computer, while person B could search for and download music from person A's computer.

There are several options for the use of peer-to-peer technologies. Information/content: where the content on your computer becomes accessible to everyone else in the peer-to-peer environment, and vice versa. Processing sharing: where computers with spare processing capacity network together in order to combine resources. Using a large number of computers, this can create very significant processing capabilities. Services: a computer user can offer services to other people in the peer-to-peer network. File sharing: if person A downloads a file from a central server (an e-learning course from the Internet, for example), other people can use it from person A's machine instead of having to download it again, significantly reducing strain on *bandwidth*.

The main problem with peer-to-peer is the issue of security, and therefore it is essential to authenticate users. Many peer-to-peer interactions also use *encryption*, which ensures that the communication is secure as it is being passed from computer to computer.

paced line *Ops* a production line that moves at a constant speed. A paced line, such as a car *assembly line*, moves partly finished products past a *workstation* or zone at a constant speed. Work is carried out on the product within each work zone as the line continues to move. The speed of movement of the line is set to match worker proficiency or machine processing speed.

packaging 1. *Fin* the practice of combining securities in a single trade. *See also* *bundling* **2.** *Ops* materials used for containing, protecting, and presenting goods during the delivery process from the producer to the consumer. Packaging has evolved from the basic function of protection to become an important marketing tool for communicating brand values.

Packard, David (1912–96) *Gen Mgt* US entrepreneur and business executive. Co-founder of Hewlett-Packard. Hewlett-Packard was noted for its *corporate culture* and *management style* based on openness, and respect for its employees. See Packard's book *The HP Way* (1995).

Pac Man defence *Fin* avoiding purchase by making an offer to buy the prospective buyer

page counter *E-com* a utility program that registers the number of times a web page is visited, for example, by means of a *click-through*

page impressions *E-com* the number of customers who land on a web page, as in an *ad view*. *Also known as* *page views*

page pushing *E-com see* *co-browsing*

page views *E-com see* *page impressions*

paid cheque *Fin* a cheque which has been honoured by the bank on which it was drawn, and bears evidence of payment on its face

paid circulation *Mkting* the number of copies of a newspaper or magazine that are actually bought

paid-up policy *Fin* **1.** in the United Kingdom, an endowment assurance

---

If civilisation has risen from the Stone Age, it can rise again from the Wastepaper Age.
Jacques Barzun

policy, for which the policyholder has decided not to continue paying premiums, that continues to provide life cover while the cost of the premiums is covered by the underlying fund. If the fund is sufficient to pay the premiums for the remainder of the term, the remaining funds will be paid to the policyholder at maturity. **2.** in the United States, an insurance policy on which all the premiums have been paid

paid-up share *Fin* a share for which shareholders have paid the full contractual amount. *See also call, called-up share capital, paid-up share capital, share capital*

paid-up share capital *Fin* the amount which shareholders are deemed to have paid on the shares issued and called up

painting the tape *Fin* an illegal practice in which traders break large orders into smaller units in order to give the illusion of heavy buying activity. This encourages investors to buy, and the traders then sell as the price of the stock goes up. (*slang*)

palmtop *Gen Mgt* a very small portable computer. Compared to a personal computer or laptop, the functionality of a palmtop is currently limited but it is increasing.

pandas *Fin* a series of Chinese gold and silver bullion/collector coins, each featuring a panda, that were first issued in 1982. Struck with a highly polished surface, the smallest gold coin weighs 0.05 ounces, the largest 12 ounces.

P & L *Fin see profit and loss account*

panel interview *HR* an interview that takes place before two or more interviewers who may be from different parts of the interviewing organisation or external to it.

Organisations tend to use panel interviews as they save time by bringing all the interviewers together rather than shuffling the applicant around from one office to the next. They are also used for their consistency of information: from the applicant and from the organisation.

As with any job interview, it is import-ant beforehand for applicant to find out not only about the position they are applying for, but the organisation to which they are applying. It may also help them to mentally rehearse the panel interview situation. With several interviewers, the applicant may feel bombarded by questions. He or she should aim to answer all the questions, taking one at a time, and if necessary, ask for clarification where a question is not clear.

The interview is an opportunity for the applicant to showcase his or her strengths to several interviewers at once, and so while it is not wise to interrupt the interviewers, he or she should resist the temptation to let them do most of the talking. Making meaningful eye contact with all members of the panel when talking is a good way for the applicant to convey a sense of confidence and calm—the key to success in the panel interview.

Panel on Takeovers and Mergers *Fin* see *City Code on Takeovers and Mergers*

panel study *Stats* a study that surveys a selected group of people over a period of time

panic buying *Fin* an abnormal level of buying caused by fear or rumours of product shortages or by severe price rises

PANSE *Gen Mgt* Politically Active and Not Seeking Employment (*slang*)

pants
drop your pants *Mkting* to lower the price of a product in order to sell it (*slang*)
put some pants on something (*US*) *Gen Mgt* to supply the missing details of a plan or idea (*slang*)

paper *Fin* **1.** a certificate of deposits and other securities **2.** a rights issue or an issue of bonds launched by a company to raise additional capital (*slang*) **3.** all debt issued by a company (*slang*)

paper architecture *Gen Mgt* an ambitious business project that never gets beyond the planning stage, because of lack of funding or because it is not feasible (*slang*)

Bureaucracies indicate a lack of trust and mutual regard and respect. *Shiv Nadar*

paper company *Fin* a company that only exists on paper and has no physical assets

paperless office *Gen Mgt* a workplace in which as much communication and as many procedures as possible have been computerised. The paperless office was predicted in the 1960s. The recent widespread availability of *e-mail*, the *Internet*, and word processing, file transfer, and *intranet* systems means that it is beginning to become achievable for those organisations that wish to pursue it. In a truly paperless office, document storage is on computer rather than in filing cabinets and written communication is not circulated in hard copy but e-mailed. This is largely unattainable, as most people still prefer paper to electronic copy, especially when faced with reading more than one page. Encouraging employees to cut down on paper usage can help achieve *environmental management* targets, and storing information electronically can lead to greater communication efficiency which may result in *competitive advantage*.

paper millionaire *Fin* an individual who owns shares that are worth in excess of a million in currency, but which may fall in value. In 2001, many of the founders of dot-com companies were paper millionaires. *See also* *paper profit*

paper money *Fin* 1. banknotes 2. payments in paper form, for example, cheques

paper profit *Fin* an increase in the value of an investment that the investor has no immediate intention of realising

paper trail *Gen Mgt* all of the documentation of an event, especially a decision (*slang*)

par *Fin* the nominal value of a bond, being the price denominated for the purpose of setting the interest rate (coupon) payable

PAR *abbr Fin* prime assets ratio

paradigm shift *Gen Mgt* a change in an accepted pattern of thought or behaviour

parallel engineering *Ops see* **concurrent engineering**

parallel pricing *Fin* the practice of varying prices in a similar way and at the same time as competitors, which may be done by agreement with them

paralysis by analysis *Gen Mgt* the inability of managers to make decisions as a result of a preoccupation with attending meetings, writing reports, and collecting statistics and analyses. Paralysis of effective *decision-making* in organisations can occur in situations where there is horizontal conflict, disagreement between different hierarchical levels, or unclear objectives.

parameter *Stats* a quantity that is numerically characteristic of a whole model or population

parameter design *Stats* a process aimed at reducing variation in processes or products

parent company *Fin* a company that owns or controls a number of other companies

Pareto, Vilfredo Frederico Damaso (1848–1923) *Gen Mgt* Italian economist, mathematician, and sociologist. Originator of the *eighty-twenty rule*, and of the law of income distribution known as *Pareto's Law*, which he explained in *Cours d'Économie Politique* (1896–97).

Pareto analysis *Gen Mgt see* **eighty-twenty rule**

Pareto chart *Gen Mgt see* **eighty-twenty rule**

Pareto's Law *Econ* a theory of income distribution. Developed by **Vilfredo Pareto**, Pareto's Law states that regardless of political or taxation conditions, income will be distributed in the same way across all countries.

Pareto's principle *Gen Mgt see* **eighty-twenty rule**

pari passu *Fin* ranking equally

No task is a long one but the task on which one dare not start. It becomes a nightmare.
Charles Baudelaire

Paris Club *Fin see Group of Ten*

Paris Inter Bank Offered Rate *Fin* the French equivalent of the London Inter Bank Offered Rate. *Abbr* **PIBOR**

parity *Fin* a situation when the price of a commodity, foreign currency, or security is the same in different markets. *See also arbitrage*

parity bit *E-com* an odd or even digit used to check binary computer data for errors

parity value *Fin see conversion value*

park *Fin* to place owned shares with third parties to disguise their ownership, usually illegally

Parker Follett, Mary (1868–1933) *Gen Mgt* US academic. Applied psychological and social science insights to the study of industrial organisation at a time when the *scientific management* methods of *Frederick Winslow Taylor* were predominant. Recent interest in her work owes much to Pauline Graham's writings, including *Mary Parker Follett: Prophet of Management* (1995). Follett's career was largely spent in social work, though her books appeared regularly—*The New State* (1918) was an influential description of her own brand of dynamic democracy, and *Creative Experience* (1924) was her first business-oriented book. In her later years she was in great demand as a lecturer.

parking *Fin* **1.** the transfer of shares in a company to a nominee name or the name of an associate, often for non-legitimate or illegal reasons (*slang*) **2.** (*US*) putting money into safe investments while deciding where to invest the money

Parkinson, C. Northcote (1909–93) *Gen Mgt* British academic. Known for *Parkinson's Law* (1957).

Parkinson's Law *HR* the facetious assertion that work will expand to fill the time available

Parquet *Fin* the Paris Bourse (*slang*)

partial retirement *HR see phased retirement*

participating bond *Fin* a bond that pays the dividends that stockholders receive as well as interest

participating insurance *Fin* insurance in which policy holders receive a dividend from the insurer's profits

participating preference share *Fin* a type of preference share that entitles the holder to a fixed dividend and, in addition, to the right to participate in any surplus profits after payment of agreed levels of dividends to ordinary shareholders has been made. *See also* **nonparticipating preference share**

participative budgeting *Fin* a budgeting system in which all budget holders are given the opportunity to participate in setting their own budgets. *Also known as bottom-up budgeting*

partly-paid share *Fin* a share for which shareholders have not paid the full contractual amount. *See also* **call**, **share capital**

partnering *Gen Mgt see* **strategic partnering**

partnership *Gen Mgt* a contractual relationship between two or more people who agree to share in the profits and losses of a business. A partnership is not an incorporated company and the individual partners are responsible for decisions and debts. A partnership at the organisational level is known as a *joint venture* or *strategic alliance*.

partnership accounts *Fin* the capital and current accounts of each partner in a partnership, or the accounts recording the partnership's business activities

partnership agreement *Fin* the document that sets up a partnership, detailing the capital contributed by each partner, whether an individual partner's liability is limited, the apportionment of the profit, salaries, and possibly procedures to be followed, for example, in the event of a partner retiring or a new partner joining. In the United Kingdom, when a partnership agreement is silent on any matter, the provisions of the Partnership Act 1890 apply. *Also known as **articles of partnership***

part-time director *Gen Mgt see non-executive director*

part-time work *Gen Mgt* work that occupies fewer hours than *full-time* work. Traditionally, part-time simply meant working fewer hours a day, or fewer days a week, than a full-time employee, but part-time working is now seen as one of several *flexible working hours* alternatives to the 9–5 working day.

party plan *Mkting* a sales technique in which local agents host parties to demonstrate or sell products to customers

Pascale, Richard Tanner (*b.* 1938) *Gen Mgt* US academic and consultant. Co-developer of the *McKinsey 7-S framework* of corporate success, and co-author, with *Anthony Athos*, of *The Art of Japanese Management* (1981). Pascale also originated the concept of organisational *agility*. Pascale and Athos collaborated with *Tom Peters* and *Bob Waterman* on the 7-S model at the management consultancy company McKinsey. Peters and Waterman cited US examples of success in *In Search of Excellence*, but it was Pascale and Athos who explored the model in greater depth, tracing many of its origins to working practice in Japanese organisations.

passbook *Fin* a small booklet issued by banks, building societies, and other financial institutions to record deposits, withdrawals, interest paid, and the balance on savings and deposit accounts. In all but the smaller building societies, it has now largely been replaced by statements.

passing off *Fin* a form of fraud in which a company tries to sell its own product by deceiving buyers into thinking it is another product

passive investment management *Fin* the managing of a unit trust or other investment portfolio by relying on automatic adjustments such as indexation instead of making personal judgments. *See also active fund management*

passive portfolio strategy *Fin* the managing of an investment portfolio by relying on automatic adjustments or tracking an index

password *E-com* a series of characters that enables a user to access a private file, website, computer, or application

patent *Mkting* a type of *copyright* granted as a fixed-term monopoly to an inventor by the state to prevent others copying an invention, or improvement of a product or process.

The granting of a patent requires the publication of full details of the invention or improvement but the use of the patented information is restricted to the patent holder or any organisations licensed by them.

A patent's value is usually the sum of its development costs, or its purchase price if acquired from someone else. It is generally to a company's advantage to spread the patent's value over several years. If this is the case, the critical time period to consider is not the full life of the patent (20 years in the United Kingdom), but its estimated useful life.

For example, in January 2000 a company acquired a patent issued in January 1995 at a cost of £100,000. It concludes that the patent's useful commercial life is 10 years, not the 15 remaining before the patent expires. In turn, patent value would be £100,000, and it would be spread (or *amortised* in accounting terms) over 10 years, or £10,000 each year.

patent attorney *Gen Mgt* a lawyer who specialises in the type of intellectual property called a patent

paternity leave *HR* time off work given to a new father on the birth of his child. Paternity leave is a form of *special leave*, and is granted at an organisation's discretion. It may be paid, or unpaid. Paternity leave forms an important part of an organisation's *family-friendly policies*.

path analysis *Stats* a means of showing the correlation between variables in a statistical study

---

Man is a tool-using animal . . . Without tools he is nothing, with tools he is all.

Thomas Carlyle

path diagram *Stats* a diagram that shows the correlation between variables in a statistical study

pathfinder prospectus *Fin* a preliminary prospectus used in initial public offerings to gauge the reaction of investors

pawnbroker *Fin* a person who lends money against the security of a wide range of chattels, from jewellery to cars. The borrower may recover the goods by repaying the loan and interest by a certain date. Otherwise, the items pawned are sold and any surplus after the deduction of expenses, the loan, and interest is returned to the borrower.

pay *HR* a sum of money given in return for work done or services provided. Pay, in the form of *salary* or *wages*, is generally provided in weekly or monthly fixed amounts, and is usually expressed in terms of the total sum earned per year. It may also be allocated using a *piece-rate system*, where workers are paid for each unit of work they carry out.

payable to order *Fin* on a bill of exchange or cheque, used to indicate that it may be transferred. *See also* **endorsement**

Pay As You Earn *HR* in the United Kingdom, a system for collecting direct taxes that requires employers to deduct taxes from employees' *pay* before payment is made. *Abbr* **PAYE**

pay-as-you-go (*Canada*) *HR* a means of financing a pension system whereby benefits of current retirees are financed by current workers

Pay-As-You-Go (*ANZ*) *Fin* a system used in Australia for paying income tax instalments on business and investment income. PAYG is part of the new tax system introduced by the Australian government on 1 July 2000. *Abbr* **PAYG**

payback *Fin* the time required for the cash inflows from a capital investment project to equal the cash outflows

payback period *Fin* the length of time it will take to earn back the money invested in a project.

EXAMPLE The straight payback period method is the simplest way of determining the investment potential of a major project. Expressed in time, it tells a management how many months or years it will take to recover the original cash cost of the project. It is calculated using the formula:

cost of project / annual cash revenues = payback period

Thus, if a project cost £100,000 and was expected to generate £28,000 annually, the payback period would be:

100,000 / 28,000 = 3.57 years

If the revenues generated by the project are expected to vary from year to year, add the revenues expected for each succeeding year until you arrive at the total cost of the project.

For example, say the revenues expected to be generated by the £100,000 project are:

	Revenue	*Total*
Year 1	£19,000	£19,000
Year 2	£25,000	£44,000
Year 3	£30,000	£74,000
Year 4	£30,000	£104,000
Year 5	£30,000	£134,000

Thus, the project would be fully paid for in Year 4, since it is in that year the total revenue reaches the initial cost of £100,000. The precise payback period would be calculated as:

((100,000 – 74,000) /(1000,000 – 74,000)) × 365 = 316 days + 3 years

The picture becomes complex when the time-value-of-money principle is introduced into the calculations. Some experts insist this is essential to determine the most accurate payback period. Accordingly, the annual revenues have to be discounted by the applicable interest rate, 10% in this example. Doing so produces significantly different results:

	Revenue	*Present value*	*Total*
Year 1	£19,000	£17,271	£17,271
Year 2	£25,000	£20,650	£37,921
Year 3	£30,000	£22,530	£60,451
Year 4	£30,000	£20,490	£80,941
Year 5	£30,000	£18,630	£99,571

Flextime is the essence of respect for and trust in people.   *David Packard*

This method shows that payback would not occur even after five years.

Generally, a payback period of three years or less is desirable; if a project's payback period is less than a year, some contend it should be judged essential.

PAYE *abbr HR* Pay As You Earn

payee *Fin* **1.** the person or organisation to whom a cheque is payable. *See also drawee* **2.** the person to whom a payment has to be made. *See also* **endorsement**

payer *Fin* the person making a payment

PAYG *abbr (ANZ) Fin* Pay-As-You-Go

paying agent *Fin* the institution responsible for making interest payments on a security and repaying capital at redemption. *Also known as* **disbursing agent**

paying banker *Fin* the bank on which a bill of exchange or cheque is drawn

paying-in book *Fin* book of detachable slips that accompany money or cheques being paid into a bank account

payload *Fin* the amount of cargo that a vessel can carry

paymaster *Fin* the person responsible for paying an organisation's employees

payment by results *HR* a system of *pay* that directly links an employee's *compensation* to their work output. The system is based on the view put forward by *Frederick Winslow Taylor* that payment by results will increase workers' productivity by appealing to their materialism. The concept is closely related to *performance-related pay* which rewards employees for behaviour and skills rather than quantifiable productivity measures.

payment gateway *E-com* a company or organisation that provides an interface between a merchant's point-of-sale system, *acquirer* payment systems, and *issuer* payment systems. *Abbr* **GW**

payment in advance *Fin* payment made for goods when they are ordered but before they are delivered. *See also* **prepayment**

payment in due course *Fin* the date on which a bill of exchange becomes payable

payment-in-kind *HR* an alternative form of *pay* given to employees in place of monetary reward but considered to be of equivalent value. A payment in kind may take the form of use of a car, purchase of goods at cost price, or other non-financial exchange that benefits the employee. It forms part of the total pay package rather than being an extra benefit.

payment-in-lieu *HR* payment that is given in place of an entitlement

payment terms *Fin* the stipulation by a business as to when it should be paid for goods or services supplied, for example, cash with order, payment on delivery, or within a particular number of days of the invoice date

payout ratio *Fin* an expression of the total dividends paid to shareholders as a percentage of a company's net profit in a given period of time. This measures the likelihood of dividend payments being sustained, and is a useful indication of sustained profitability. The lower the ratio, the more secure the dividend, and the company's future.

The payout ratio is calculated by dividing annual dividends paid on ordinary shares by earnings per share:

Annual dividend / earnings-per-share = payout ratio

Take the company whose earnings per share is £8 and its dividend payout is 2.1. Its payout ratio would be:

2.1 / 8 = 0.263 or 26.3%

A high payout ratio clearly appeals to conservative investors seeking income. However, when coupled with weak or falling earnings it could suggest an imminent dividend cut, or that the company is short-changing reinvestment to maintain its payout. A payout ratio above 75% is a warning. It suggests the company is failing to reinvest sufficient profits in its business, that the company's earnings are faltering, or that it is trying to attract investors who otherwise would not be interested. *See also* **dividend cover**

Pay Pal *E-com* a web-based service that enables Internet users to send and receive payments electronically. To open a Pay Pal account, users register and provide their credit card details. When they decide to make a transaction via Pay Pal, their card is charged for the transfer.

pay-per-click *E-com* a website that charges a *micropayment* to see digital information, for example, an e-book or e-magazine

pay-per-play *E-com* a website that charges a *micropayment* to play an interactive game over the Internet

pay-per-view 1. *E-com* a website that charges a *micropayment* to see digital information, for example, an e-book or e-magazine **2.** *Fin* a method of collecting revenue from television viewers. The viewer pays a fee for watching an individual programme, typically a sports or entertainment event.

payroll *HR* the organisational function that is responsible for the payment of employees. Payroll also can refer to the list of employees and their *pay* details, or to the total cost of pay to an organisation.

payroll analysis *Fin* an analysis of a payroll for cost accounting purposes, giving, for example, gross pay by department or operation, gross pay by class of labour, gross pay by product, or constituent parts of gross pay, such as direct pay and lost time

pay scale *HR* a framework that groups together jobs of broadly equivalent worth into job grades, based on *job evaluation*, with a *pay* range given to each grade. Although pay scales are still widely used, other pay structures such as *broadbanding* are replacing the traditional approach. Some organisations do not have a formal structure and instead rely on *personal contracts*. *Also known as* **salary scale**, **wage scale**. *See also* **job family**

payslip *HR* a document given to employees when they are paid, providing a statement of *pay* for that period. A payslip includes details of deductions such as *income tax*, national insurance contributions, pension contributions, and trade union dues.

PDA *abbr E-com* personal digital assistant: a handheld mobile device that can access the Internet and act as a personal organiser

PDF *Gen Mgt, Mkting* an electronic document format that allows all elements of a document, including page layout, text, photographs, and colours to be viewed on different computers or systems

PDR *abbr Fin* price-dividend ratio

P/E *abbr Fin* price-earnings ratio

peer-to-peer *E-com see* **P2P**

peg *Fin* **1.** to fix the exchange rate of one currency against that of another or of a basket of other currencies **2.** to fix wages and salaries during a period of inflation to help prevent an inflationary spiral

penalty *Fin* an arbitrary pre-arranged sum that becomes payable if one party breaks a term of a contract or an undertaking. The most common penalty is a high rate of interest on an unauthorised overdraft. *See also* **overdraft**

penalty rate *(ANZ) HR* a higher than normal rate of pay awarded for work performed outside normal working hours

pencil-whip *Gen Mgt* to criticise somebody in writing (*slang*)

penetrated market *Mkting* the existing customers within a market

penetration pricing *Fin* setting prices low, especially for new products, in order to maximise market penetration

penny shares *Fin* very low-priced stock that is a speculative investment

pension *Fin* money received regularly after *retirement*, from a *personal pension* scheme, *occupational pension scheme*, or state pension scheme. *Also known as* **retirement pension**

pensionable earnings *Fin* in an occupational pension scheme with a defined benefit, the earnings on which the pension is based. Generally, overtime payments, benefits in kind, bonuses, and territorial allowances, for example, payments for working in a large city, are not pensionable earnings. *US term* **final average monthly salary**

people churner *HR* a bad boss with a reputation for losing talented staff (*slang*)

PEP *abbr Fin* personal equity plan

P/E ratio *Fin* the price/earnings ratio, calculated by dividing a company's share price by its earnings per share

per capita income *Econ* the average income of each of a particular group of people, for example, citizens of a country

perceived value pricing *Fin see* **market based pricing**

percussive maintenance *Gen Mgt* the practice of hitting or shaking an electronic device in order to make it work (*slang*)

per diem *HR* a rate paid per day, for example, for expenses when an employee is working away from the office

perfect capital market *Econ* a capital market in which the decisions of buyers and sellers have no effect on market price

perfect competition *Econ* a market in which no buyer or seller can influence prices. In practice, perfect markets are characterised by few or no barriers to entry and by many buyers and sellers.

perfect hedge *Fin* a hedge that exactly balances the risk of another investment

performance appraisal *HR* a face-to-face discussion in which one employee's work is discussed, reviewed, and appraised by another, using an agreed and understood framework. Usually, line managers conduct the appraisals of their staff, although peers can appraise each other, and line managers can themselves be appraised by their staff through *360 degree appraisal*. The appraisal process focuses on behaviours and outcomes, and aims to improve *motivation*, growth, and performance of the appraisee. Performance appraisals should be carried out at least once per year. *Also known as* **performance evaluation**

performance bond *Fin* a guarantee given by a bank to a third party stating that it will pay a sum of money if its customer, the account holder, fails to complete a specified contract

performance criteria *Fin* the standards used to evaluate a product, service, or employee

performance evaluation *HR see* **performance appraisal**

performance fund *Fin* an investment fund designed to produce a high return, reflected in the higher risk involved

performance indicator *HR* a key measure designed to assess an aspect of the qualitative or quantitative performance of a company. Performance indicators can relate to operational, strategic, confidence, behavioural, and ethical aspects of a company's operation and can help to pinpoint its strengths and weaknesses. They are periodically monitored to ensure the company's long-term success.

performance management *Gen Mgt* the facilitation of high achievement by employees. Performance management involves enabling people to carry out their work to the best of their ability, meeting and perhaps exceeding targets and standards. Performance management can be co-ordinated by an interrelated framework between manager and employee. Key areas of the framework to be agreed are *objectives*, human resource management (see *HRM*), standards and *performance indicators*, and means of reward. For successful performance management, a culture of collective and individual responsibility for the continuing improvement of business processes needs to be established, and individual skills and contributions need to be encouraged and nurtured. One tool for monitoring performance management is *performance* *appraisal*. For organisations, performance management is usually known as company performance and is monitored through business appraisal.

performance measurement *Fin* the process of assessing the proficiency with which a reporting entity succeeds, by the economic acquisition of resources and their efficient and effective deployment, in achieving its objectives. Performance measures may be based on non-financial as well as on financial information.

performance-related pay *HR* a *compensation* system in which the level of *pay* is dependent on the employee's performance. Performance-related pay can be entirely dependent or only partly dependent on performance. There are usually three stages to a performance-related pay system: determining the criteria by which the employee is assessed, establishing whether the employee has met the criteria, and linking the employee's achievements to the pay structure. Performance measures can incorporate skills, knowledge, and behavioural indicators. The system can be compared to *payment by results*, which is based solely on quantitative productivity measures.

period bill *Fin* a bill of exchange payable on a certain date rather than on demand. *Also known as* **term bill**

period cost *Fin* a cost which relates to a time period rather than to the output of products or services

periodic inventory review system *Ops* a system for placing orders of varying sizes at regular intervals to replenish *inventory* up to a specified or target inventory level. A periodic inventory review system fixes a specific reorder period, but the reorder quantity can vary according to need. The quantity reordered is calculated by subtracting existing inventory and on-order inventory from the target inventory level. *Also known as* *fixed interval re-order system*

periodicity concept *Fin* the requirement to produce financial statements at set time intervals. This requirement is embodied, in the case of UK corporations, in the Companies Acts.

perk *HR see* **fringe benefits**

permalancer *HR* a freelance worker who has worked in one company for so long that he or she is virtually a permanent member of staff (*slang*)

permanent interest-bearing shares *Fin* shares issued by a building society to raise capital because the law prohibits it from raising capital in more conventional ways. *Abbr* **PIBS**

permission marketing *E-com* any form of online direct marketing that involves gaining each recipient's permission. This type of marketing typically involves sending promotional material via e-mail to an opt-in list of subscribers. The term was popularised by business author Seth Godin, who has written a book on the subject, *Permission Marketing* (1999).

Perot (*US*) *Gen Mgt* to leave, fail, or give up something unexpectedly. The term comes from the sudden withdrawal from the US presidential race of candidate Ross Perot in the 1990s. (*slang*)

perpetual bond *Fin* a bond that has no date of maturity

perpetual debenture *Fin* a debenture that pays interest in perpetuity, having no date of maturity

perpetual inventory *Fin* the daily tracking of inventory

perpetuity *Fin* a periodic payment continuing for a limitless period. *See also* *annuity*

per se *Gen Mgt* by itself or in itself

personal account *Fin* a record of amounts receivable from or payable to a person or an entity

personal allowances *Fin* the amount of money that an individual can earn without having to pay income tax. The allowances vary according to age, marital status, and whether the person is a single parent.

personal contract *HR* a *contract of employment* that is negotiated on an employee by employee basis, rather than using a traditional structured system that gives identical contracts to groups of workers

personal development *HR* the acquisition of knowledge, skills, and experience for the purpose of enhancing individual performance and self-perception. Personal development is usually led by the individual, in contrast to *employee development*, which is initiated by an employing organisation. To be effective, it should follow a personal development cycle: establish the purpose or the reason for development; identify the skills or knowledge areas that need developing; look at development opportunities; formulate an action plan; undertake the development; record the outcomes of the development activity; review and evaluate the outputs and benefits. Personal development is an important aspect of *CPD*. *Also known as self-development*

personal digital assistant *Gen Mgt see* **PDA**

Personal Equity Plan *Fin* a scheme sponsored by the UK government to promote investment in company shares, unit trusts, and equity-based investment trusts by offering tax benefits to investors. The arrival of ISAs in 1999 meant that no new personal equity plans could be opened, but existing plans carry on as before. *Abbr* **PEP**

personal financial planning *Fin* short- and long-term financial planning by an individual, either independently or with the assistance of a professional adviser. It will include the use of tax efficient schemes such as Individual Savings Accounts, ensuring adequate provisions are being made for retirement, and examining short- and long-term borrowing requirements such as overdrafts and mortgages.

Personal Identification Number *Fin see* **ATM**. *abbr* **PIN**

Personal Investment Authority *Fin* a self-regulatory organisation responsible for supervising the activities of financial intermediaries selling financial products to individuals. *Abbr* **PIA**

personalisation *E-com* the process by which a website presents customers with selected information on their specific needs. To do this, personal information is collected on the individual user and employed to customise the website for that person. Used properly, personalisation is a powerful tool that allows customers to access the right content more quickly, thus saving them valuable time. Personalisation is particularly useful if a website contains a very large quantity of material, meaning that a visitor is slow in finding the information they seek. It also requires a large number of visitors to the website, because personalisation systems are complex and expensive to install.

Information on the customer is usually collected in one of two ways. Either the individual is asked to fill out a personal profile, perhaps informing the organisation of the type of product and service he or she is interested in, or the organisation uses software that tracks the way a customer uses the website. For example, a customer interested in Product X last week, might receive details of an update for Product X upon their next visit to the website. A popular method by which such tracking is carried out is the use of *cookies*, which reside on an individual's browser and collect information on that person's web behaviour. Because it requires the collection of personal information, personalisation raises key *privacy policy* issues.

personality promotion *Mkting* a method of promoting a product or service by fronting the campaign with a famous person. For example, the footballer David Beckham is employed to promote a variety of products.

personality test *HR see* *psychometric test*

The decision to do that extra bit must be embedded in the company's culture. Tom Farmer

personal pension *HR* a pension taken out by an individual with a private sector insurance company or bank. A personal pension usually takes the form of a scheme in which an individual regularly contributes money to a pension provider who invests it in a pension fund. On retirement, a lump sum is available for the purchase of an annuity that provides weekly or monthly payments. Under the Finance Act (1987), all employees have the right to arrange their own pensions. *Stakeholder pensions* have recently been introduced that are government regulated but are administered by private sector companies.

personnel *HR* **1.** the people employed in an organisation, considered collectively **2.** the department of an organisation that deals with the employment of staff and staffing issues

personnel management *HR* the part of management that is concerned with people and their relationships at work. Personnel management is the responsibility of all those who manage people, as well as a description of the work of specialists. *Personnel managers* advise on, formulate, and implement *personnel policies* such as *recruitment*, *conditions of employment*, *performance appraisal*, *training*, industrial relations, and *health and safety*. There are various models of personnel management, of which human resource management (see *HRM*) is the most recent.

personnel manager *HR* a professional specialist and manager responsible for advising on, formulating, and implementing personnel or human resources strategy and personnel policies. The nature of the personnel manager's job is dependent on the size of the organisation and the extent to which personnel responsibilities are devolved to *line managers*.

personnel planning *HR see human resource planning*

personnel policy *HR* a set of rules that define the manner in which an organisa-tion deals with a *human resources* or *personnel*-related matter. A personnel policy should reflect good practice, be written down, be communicated across the organisation, and should adapt to changing circumstances.

PEST analysis *Gen Mgt* a management technique that enables an analysis of four external factors that may impact on the performance of the organisation. These factors are: Political, Economic, Social, and Technological. PEST analysis is often carried out using *brainstorming* techniques. It offers an environment-to-organisation perspective as opposed to the organisation-to-environment perspective offered by *SWOT analysis*.

PESTLE *Mkting* an acronym that describes the six influences to which a market is subject, namely, political, economic, social, technological, legal, and environmental

Peter, Laurence (1919–90) *Gen Mgt* Canadian academic. Founder of the *Peter Principle*, described in the book of the same name (co-authored with Raymond Hull, 1970).

Peter Principle *HR* a tenet holding that all employees tend to rise to their level of incompetence within an organisation, at which point it is too late to move them down or sideways

Peters, Tom (*b.* 1942) *Gen Mgt* US consultant, writer, and lecturer. Co-developer of the *McKinsey 7-S framework* of corporate success, and co-author, with *Bob Waterman*, of *In Search of Excellence* (1982), which identified eight characteristics of successful companies. Peters moved the discussion of *management* away from the established structure of *bureaucracy* towards a more innovative, intuitive, and people-centred approach in which change is to be embraced, not resisted. *In Search of Excellence* was one of the first books to make management ideas generally accessible and his seminar presentations have earned Peters a reputation as an energetic, entertaining performer.

I am extraordinarily patient, provided I get my own way in the end.   **Margaret Thatcher**

petites et moyennes entreprises *Gen Mgt* French for small and medium-sized businesses. *Abbr* **PME**

petty cash *Fin* a small store of cash used for minor business expenses

PFI *abbr Fin* Private Finance Initiative

phantom bid *Fin* a reported but non-existent attempt to buy a company

phantom income *Fin* income that is subject to tax even though the recipient never actually gets control of it, for example, income from a limited partnership

phased retirement *HR* a gradual reduction in hours of work, typically through working a three- or four-day week in the last six months leading up to *retirement*. Phased retirement is a *personnel policy* introduced by organisations to try to ease the transition between employment and retirement, which for many employees can prove to be a traumatic change. *Also known as* **gradual retirement**

Phillips curve *Stats* a graphical representation of the relationship between unemployment and the rate of inflation

phone lag *Gen Mgt* tiredness caused by having to conduct business on the telephone with people who are based in different time zones (*slang*)

physical asset *Fin* an asset that has a physical embodiment, as opposed to cash or securities

physical distribution management *Ops* the planning, monitoring, and control of the distribution and delivery of manufactured goods

physical market *Fin* a market in futures that involves physical delivery of the commodities involved, instead of simple cash transactions

physical price *Fin* the price of a commodity for immediate delivery

physical retail shopping *Gen Mgt* shopping carried out by visiting high-street shops rather than buying online

physicals *Fin* commodities that can be bought and used, as contrasted with commodities traded on a futures contract

physical stocktaking *Fin* the ascertainment of stocks held (by counting physical objects) for comparison with accounting records. Modern practice is to stocktake different items with different frequencies, classifying items according to the degree of control required. **Periodic stocktaking** is a process whereby all stock items are counted and valued at a set point in time, usually the end of an accounting period. **Continuous stocktaking** is the process of counting and valuing selected items at different times, on a rotating basis.

physical working conditions *HR* the surroundings within which somebody works, taking into account aspects such as temperature, air quality, lighting, safety, cleanliness, and noise

PIA *abbr Fin* Personal Investment Authority

PIBOR *abbr Fin* Paris Inter Bank Offered Rate

PIBS *abbr Fin* permanent interest-bearing shares

pick and shovel work *Gen Mgt* boring and detailed work such as the examination of documents for mistakes (*slang*)

picture *Fin* the price and trading quantity of a particular stock on Wall Street, used for example, in the question to a specialist dealer 'What's the picture on ABC?'. The response would give the bid and offer price and number of shares for which there would be a buyer and seller. (*slang*)

piece-rate system *or* **piece work** *HR* a system of payment through which an employee is paid a pre-determined amount for each unit of output. The rate of *pay*, or piece rate, is usually fixed subjectively, rather than by a more objective technique such as *work study*. Rates are said to be tight when it is difficult for an employee to earn a bonus and loose when bonuses are easily earned. Piece-rate systems, or **piece work**, are a form of *payment by results* or *performance-related pay*.

pie chart *Stats* a chart drawn as a circle divided into proportional sections like portions of a pie

piggyback advertising *Mkting* an offer or promotion that runs in parallel with another campaign and incurs no costs

piggyback loan *Fin* a loan that is raised against the same security as an existing loan

piggyback rights *Fin* the permission to sell existing shares in conjunction with the sale of like shares in a new offering

pig in a python *Gen Mgt* the large increase in the birth rate between 1946 and 1964 (*slang*)

pilot fish *HR* a junior executive who follows close behind a more senior executive (*slang*)

pilot survey *Mkting* a preliminary piece of research carried out before a complete survey to test the effectiveness of the research methodology

PIN *abbr Fin* personal identification number

pin-drop syndrome *HR* stress induced by extreme quietness in a working environment (*slang*)

pink advertising *Mkting* advertising aimed at the gay and lesbian community

pink-collar job *HR* a sexist term for a position normally held by a woman, especially a young one (*slang*)

pink dollar (*US*) *Fin* = *pink pound*

pink form *Fin* in the United Kingdom, a preferential application form at an initial public offering that is reserved for the employees of the company being floated

pink pound *Fin* money spent by gays and lesbians. *US term* **pink dollar**

pink slip
get your pink slip (*US*) *HR* to be dismissed from employment (*slang*)

pink slipper (*US*) *HR* a person who has been dismissed from employment (*slang*)

Pink 'Un *Fin* the Financial Times (*slang*)

piracy *Gen Mgt* illegal copying of a product such as software or music

pit *Fin* the area of an exchange where trading takes place. It was traditionally an octagonal stepped area with terracing so as to give everyone a good view of the proceedings during open outcry.

pit broker *Fin* a broker who transacts business in the pit of a futures or options exchange

pitch *Gen Mgt* an attempt to win business from a customer, especially a *sales presentation*

placement *Fin* see *placing*, *private placing*

placement fee *Fin* a fee that a stockbroker receives for a sale of shares

placing *Fin* a method of raising share capital in which there is no public issue of shares, the shares being issued, rather, in a small number of large 'blocks', to persons or institutions who have previously agreed to purchase the shares at a predetermined price

plain text e-mail *E-com* a basic format option for e-mails, which is simple and cheap to produce. The advantage is that even older e-mail systems will be able to read plain text, whereas they may be unable to receive more heavily designed *HTML* messages.

If conducting an e-mail marketing campaign, the appearance of the e-mail is important. With plain text layout, it is best to keep the line length between 65 and 70 characters (to avoid lines breaking), and to keep paragraphs short—five or six lines at most. Because plain text does not allow the use of bold type or font sizing, capitalising is the only way to add emphasis.

plain vanilla *Fin* a financial instrument in its simplest form (*slang*)

---

plan comptable *Fin* in France, a uniformly structured and detailed bookkeeping system that companies are required to comply with

plank
make somebody walk the plank *HR* to dismiss somebody from employment (*slang*)

planned maintenance *Ops see preventive maintenance*

planned obsolescence *Ops* a policy of designing products to have a limited lifespan so that customers will have to buy replacements

planning *Fin* the establishment of objectives, and the formulation, evaluation, and selection of the policies, strategies, tactics, and action required to achieve them. Planning comprises long-term/strategic planning and short-term operation planning. The latter is usually for a period of up to one year.

planning horizon *Fin* the furthest time ahead for which plans can be quantified. It need not be the planning period. *See also* **planning, futuristic planning**

planning period *Fin* the period for which a plan is prepared and used. It differs according to product or process life cycle. For example, forestry requires a period of many years whereas fashion garments require only a few months.

plant *Ops* the capital assets used to produce goods, typically factories, production lines, and large equipment

plant layout *Ops* the grouping of equipment and operations in a factory for the greatest degree of efficiency. *See also* **process layout, product layout**

plastic *or* **plastic money** *Fin* a payment system using a plastic card (*slang*). *See also* **credit card, debit card, multifunctional card**

plateauing *HR* the process of reaching a phase where performance is stable. Plateauing may be experienced by an employee due to a lack of ambition or ability or a lack of opportunity for *promotion* within the organisational hierarchy. One form of plateau is the **management threshold**.

platform *Gen Mgt* a product used as a basis for building more complex products or delivering services. For example, a communications network is a platform for delivering knowledge or data.

plc *or* **PLC** *abbr Fin see* **public limited company**

plentitude *Econ* a hypothetical condition of an economy in which manufacturing technology has been perfected and scarcity is replaced by an abundance of products

plough back *Fin* to reinvest a company's earnings in the business instead of paying them out as dividends

ploughed back profits *Fin* retained profits

plug and play *HR* relating to a new member of staff who does not require training (*slang*)

plug-in *E-com* a software application that can be added to a web browser to enable added functionality, for example, the receipt of audio or multimedia files

plum *Fin* a successful investment (*slang*)

PME *abbr Gen Mgt* petites et moyennes entreprises

PMTS *abbr Gen Mgt* predetermined motion-time system

poaching *HR* the practice of recruiting people from other companies by offering inducements

point (*US*) *Fin* a unit used for calculation of a value, such as a hundredth of a percentage point for interest rates

point and click agreement *E-com see* **click wrap agreement**

point-factor system *HR see* **points plan**

point of presence *Gen Mgt* an access point to the *Internet*. A point of presence is usually controlled by an Internet service provider. Subscribers can use this to gain access to the Internet, normally by dialling a local number, and thereby saving the cost of a national phone call. A point of presence has a unique **IP address**.

point of purchase *Gen Mgt see point of sale*

point-of-purchase display *Gen Mgt* the physical arrangement of products and marketing material at the place where an item is bought. A point-of-purchase display is designed to encourage sales. It can include posters, showcards, leaflets, and dispensers to attract customers.

point of sale *Gen Mgt* the place at which a product is purchased by the customer. The point of sale can be a retail outlet, a display case, or even a particular shelf. Retailers refer to both point of sale and to **point of purchase**. The distinction is a fine one, but a sale and a purchase do not always take place at the same time. The difference becomes relevant where they are clearly separate, for example, with *mail order* and *Internet* shopping. *Abbr* **POS**

points plan *HR* a method of *job evaluation* that uses a points scale for rating different criteria. *Also known as* **point-factor system**

poison pill *Fin* a measure taken by a company to avoid a hostile takeover, for example, the purchase of a business interest that will make the company unattractive to the potential buyer (*slang*)

policy *Fin* an undated, long-lasting, and often unquantified statement of guidance regarding the way in which an organisation will seek to behave in relation to its stakeholders

policyholder *Fin* a person or business covered by an insurance policy

political economy *Econ* a country's economic organisation

political price *Gen Mgt* the negative impact on a government of a business or economic decision such as raising interest rates

political risk *Gen Mgt* the potential negative impact on a government of a business or economic decision

politics *Gen Mgt* the theory of government, the making of policy, or the power struggles within an organisation

POP *abbr E-com* Post Office protocol: the most common Internet standard for e-mail. Once POP is in use, all new incoming messages are downloaded from the server as soon as the e-mail account is accessed. All POP e-mails are stored on the server until the user removes them.

population *Stats* the entire collection of units such as events or people from which a sample may be observed in a statistical study

population pyramid *Stats* a graphical presentation of data in the form of two histograms with a common base, showing a comparison of a human population in terms of sex and age

pop-under ad *E-com* a Web advertisement that launches in a separate browser window from the rest of a website

portable document format *Gen Mgt, Mkting see* **PDF**

portable pension *Fin* in the United Kingdom, a pension plan that moves with an employee when he or she changes employer. *See also* **personal pension, stakeholder pension**

portal *E-com* a website that provides access and links to other sites and pages on the Web. **Search engines** and directories are the most common portal sites.

Porter, Michael (*b.* 1947) *Gen Mgt* US academic and consultant. Known for his theories such as the **value chain** designed to help businesses examine their competitive capabilities. In *Competitive Strategy* (1980), Porter argued that to gain **competitive advantage**, an organisation needs to perform the activities in the value chain more cheaply or in a better way than its competitors. More recently, in response to thinkers such as **Gary Hamel**, he advised on using the value chain to achieve differentiation from other players in a market.

Porter studied at Harvard, and at the age of 26 he became one of the youngest tenured professors in the school's history. He has served as a counsellor on competitive strategy to many leading US and international companies and plays an active role in economic policy with the US Congress, business groups, and as an advisor to foreign governments.

portfolio *Fin* the range of investments, such as stocks and shares, owned by an individual or an organisation

portfolio career *HR* a career based on a series of varied shorter-term jobs—either concurrently or consecutively—as opposed to one based on a progression up the ranks of a particular profession. The portfolio worker is frequently self-employed, offering his or her services on a *freelance* or consultancy basis to one or more employers at the same time. However, a portfolio approach can also be taken to full-time employment with a single employer, if the employee chooses to expand his or her experience and responsibilities through taking different roles within the organisation.

To critics, the portfolio approach to career development may appear unfocused and directionless. However, it is an excellent opportunity to experience the many different avenues available in modern life. It is important, in general, for the portfolio worker to maintain some overall sense of purpose or strategic direction in the work they undertake, and to view their portfolio career as a unified whole rather than a collection of 'odd jobs'.
See **portfolio working**

portfolio immunisation *Fin* measures taken by traders to protect their share portfolios (*slang*)

portfolio insurance *Fin* options that provide hedges against stock in a portfolio

portfolio investment *Fin* a form of investment that aims for a mixture of income and capital growth

portfolio manager *Fin* a person or company that specialises in managing an investment portfolio on behalf of investors

portfolio working *HR* the working pattern of following several simultaneous career pursuits at any one time. Portfolio working was coined by **Charles Handy** to describe a style of working life which no longer involves working full-time for one employer. *See also* **downshifting**. *Also known as* **portfolio career**

POS *abbr Gen Mgt* point of sale

POSDCORB *abbr Gen Mgt* Planning, Organising, Staffing, Directing, Co-ordinating, Reporting, and Budgeting: coined in 1935 by **Luther Gulick** to describe the functional elements of the work of a **chief executive**. It is based on the functional analysis of management of **Henri Fayol**.

position *Fin* the number of shares of a security that are owned

position audit *Fin* part of the planning process which examines the current state of an entity in respect of the following: resources of tangible and intangible assets and finance; products, brands, and markets; operating systems such as production and distribution; internal organisation; current results; and returns to stockholders

position limit *Fin* the largest amount of a security that any group or individual may own

positive discrimination *HR* preferential treatment, usually through a quota system, to prevent or correct discriminatory employment practices, particularly relating to recruitment and promotion. The term positive discrimination is widely used in the United Kingdom, whereas in the United States **affirmative action** is the preferred term.

positive economics *Econ* the study of economic propositions that are capable of being verified by observing economic events in the real economy

possessor in bad faith *Fin* somebody who occupies land even though they do not believe they have a legal right to do so

possessor in good faith *Fin* somebody who occupies land believing they have a legal right to do so

possessory action *Fin* a lawsuit over the right to own land

post a credit *Fin* to enter a credit item in a ledger

postal survey *Mkting* a research technique in which questionnaires are sent and returned by post

Post Big Bang *Fin* used to describe the trading mechanism on the London Stock Exchange after 26 October 1986. *See also Big Bang*

postdate *Fin* to put a later date on a document or cheque than the date when it is signed, with the effect that it is not valid until the later date

post-industrial society *Gen Mgt* a society in which the resources of labour and capital are replaced by those of knowledge and information as the main sources of wealth creation. The post-industrial society involves a shift in focus from manufacturing industries to service industries and is enabled by technological advances. The idea is associated with sociologist Daniel Bell, who wrote *The Coming of Post-Industrial Society: A Venture in Social Forecasting* (1973).

post-purchase costs *Fin* costs incurred after a capital expenditure decision has been implemented and facilities acquired. These costs may include training, maintenance, and the cost of upgrades.

potential GDP *Econ* a measure of the real value of the services and goods that can be produced when a country's factors of production are fully employed

potentially exempt transfer *Fin see chargeable transfer*

pot trust *Fin* a trust, typically created in a will, for a group of beneficiaries

pound cost averaging *Fin* investing the same amount at regular intervals in a security regardless of its price. *US term dollar cost averaging*

poverty trap *Fin* a situation whereby low income families are penalised by a progressive tax system: an increase in income is either counteracted by a loss of social benefit payments or by an increase in taxation

power *Gen Mgt* the ability to compel others to obey. Power refers to an authority or influence over others which, in an organisational context, may be derived from the holder's rank or status, or from their personality. According to *Max Weber*, power refers to the probability of imposing your own will despite resistance. It is closely linked to, but not the same as, *leadership*, *authority*, and *responsibility*. Organisational power is linked to *organisation structure* and is an inherent part of any hierarchy or *bureaucracy*.

power and influence theory of leadership *Gen Mgt* the idea that *leadership* is based on the form of relationships between people rather than on the abilities of a single person. The power and influence theory of leadership sees a network of interaction between people, shaped by the power and influence emanating from the leader. Leadership and followership are products of the flow of power between individuals.

power centre *Gen Mgt* the part of an organisation that has the strongest influence on policy

power lunch *Gen Mgt see working lunch*

power of attorney *Fin* a legal document granting one person the right to act on behalf of another

power structure *Gen Mgt* the way in which power is distributed among different groups or individuals in an organisation

---

If you are capable of displaying energy, hold office, if not resign.   *Zhou Ren*

pp *Fin* used beside a signature at the end of a letter meaning 'on behalf of'

PPP *abbr Econ* purchasing power parity

PR *abbr Mkting* public relations: the presentation of an organisation and its activities to target audiences with the aim of gaining awareness and understanding, influencing public opinion, generating support, and developing trust and co-operation. Public relations programmes aim to create and maintain a positive *corporate image* and enhance an organisation's reputation. The work of a public relations department includes research into current perceptions of the organisation, the production of publicity material, the organisation of events and *sponsorship* programmes, and the evaluation of responses to these activities. Target audiences include the media, government bodies, customers and suppliers, investors, the wider community, or an organisation's own employees. Public relations practice originated in the United States in the mid-19th century. Public relations forms part of an organisation's overall *external communication* strategy.

Prahalad, C.K. (*b.* 1941) *Gen Mgt* Indian-born academic. Developer with *Gary Hamel* of a new view of competitiveness, *strategy*, and *organisations* in reaction to traditional strategic thinking. Prahalad and Hamel originated the ideas of strategic intent, *core competences*, and strategy as stretch, and published them in *Competing for the Future* (1994).

prairie dogging (*US*) *Gen Mgt* in an office that is divided into cubicles, the sudden appearance of people's heads over the top of the cubicle walls when something interesting or noisy happens (*slang*)

pre-acquisition profits/losses *Fin* the profits or losses of a subsidiary undertaking, attributable to a period prior to its acquisition by a parent company. Such profits are not available for distribution as dividends by the parent company unless the underlying value of the subsidiary undertaking is at least equal to its net carrying value in the books of the parent company.

preauthorised electronic debit *Fin* a scheme in which a payer agrees to let a bank make payments from an account to somebody else's account

prebilling *Fin* the practice of submitting a bill for a product or service before it has actually been delivered

precious metals *Fin* gold, silver, platinum, and palladium

predatory pricing *Fin* the practice of setting prices for products that are designed to win business from competitors or to damage competitors. This may involve dumping, which is selling a product in a foreign market at below cost or below the domestic market price (subject to adjustments for taxation differences, transportation costs, specification differences etc.).

predetermined motion-time system *Gen Mgt* a *work measurement* technique that uses a set of established times for basic human motions to build up *standard times* for jobs and processes at a specific level of performance. The predetermined motion-time system is based on the idea, first conceived by *Frederick Winslow Taylor* and later developed by *Frank* and *Lillian Gilbreth*, that the same length of time is required for basic human motions in whatever context they are performed. These standard times are established using *time study* techniques and can then be combined to provide a standard time for specific work tasks. The first PMTS, called **motion time analysis**, was developed in 1927, and others appeared in the United States during the 1930s. Interest in the use of PMTS increased during and after the second world war. The most widely used system is *methods-time measurement*. *Abbr* **PMTS**

predictive maintenance *Ops* a set of techniques used to manage the *maintenance* of high-cost equipment that experiences extremely low failure rates. Statistical techniques for predicting service before failure are not effective for equipment with extremely low failure rates. Predictive maintenance uses the techniques of surveillance, diagnosis, and remedy to manage the maintenance of such equipment. It is based on the premise that most equipment will give indications of impending failure well in advance of it actually happening.

pre-employment screening *HR see health screening*

pre-emptive right *Fin* the right of a stockholder to maintain proportional ownership in a corporation by purchasing newly issued stock

preference shares *Fin* shares that entitle the owner to preference in the distribution of dividends and the proceeds of liquidation in the event of bankruptcy. *US term preferred stock*

preferential creditor *Fin* a creditor who is entitled to payment, especially from a bankrupt, before other creditors

preferential form *Fin see pink form*

preferential issue *Fin* an issue of stock available only to designated buyers

preferential payment *Fin* a payment to a preferential creditor

preferred position *Fin* the particular position in which an advertiser wants an advertisement to appear, for example, in a publication or on a website

preferred risk *Fin* somebody considered by an insurance company to be less likely to collect on a policy than the average person, for example, a non-smoker

preferred stock *(US) Fin = preference shares*

pre-financing *Fin* the practice of arranging funding for a project before the project begins

prelaunch *Mkting* the activities that precede the launch of a new product

preliminary prospectus *Fin* a document issued prior to a share issue that gives details of the shares available

premarket *Fin* used to describe transactions between market members carried out prior to the official opening of the market. *Also known as pretrading*

premature retirement *HR see early retirement*

Premiers' Conference *Gen Mgt* an annual meeting at which the premiers of the states and territories of Australia meet with the federal government to discuss their funding allocations

premium 1. *Fin* the price a purchaser of an option pays to its writer **2.** *Fin* the difference between the futures price and the cash price of an underlying asset **3.** *Fin* the consideration for a contract of insurance or assurance **4.** *Gen Mgt* a higher price paid for a scarce product or service **5.** *Gen Mgt* a pricing method that uses high price to indicate high quality

at a premium *Fin* **1.** of a fixed interest security, at an issue price above its par value **2.** of a new issue, at a trading price above the one offered to investors **3.** at a price that is considered expensive in relation to others

Premium Bond *Fin* in the United Kingdom, a non-marketable security issued by National Savings at £1 each that pays no interest but is entered into a draw every month to win prizes from £50 to £1 million. There are many lower value prizes, but only one £1 million prize. The bonds are repayable upon demand.

premium income *Fin* the income earned by a life company or insurance company from premiums

premium offer *Mkting* a sales promotion technique in which customers are offered a free gift

premium pay plan *HR* an enhanced pay scale for high performing employees. A premium pay plan can be offered as an incentive to motivate employees, rewarding such achievements as high productivity, long service, or completion of training with increased pay.

The only conclusive evidence of a man's sincerity is that he gave himself *for a principle.*
James Russell Lowell

premium pricing *Mkting* the deliberate setting of high prices for a product or service to emphasise its quality or exclusiveness. *Also known as* **prestige pricing**

prepackaged choice *Gen Mgt* a package of multimedia computer material that cannot be customised by the user

prepaid interest *Fin* interest paid. in advance of its due date

prepayment *Fin* the payment of a debt, for example, a payment on a mortgage or other loan, before it is due to be paid

prepayment penalty (*US*) *Fin* a charge that may be levied against somebody who makes a payment before its due date. The penalty compensates the lender or seller for potential lost interest.

prepayment privilege *Fin* the right to make a prepayment, for example, on a loan or mortgage, without penalty

prepayment risk *Fin* the risk that a debtor will avoid interest charges by making partial or total prepayments, especially when interest rates fall

prequalification *Mkting* a sales technique in which the potential value of a prospect is carefully evaluated through research

prescribed payments system (*ANZ*) *Fin* a system under which employers are obliged to deduct a certain amount of tax from cash payments made to casual workers. The system was introduced in Australia in 1983.

presentation *Gen Mgt* an event at which pre-planned material is shown to an audience for a specific purpose. Although a presentation is a verbal form of communication, it is often supported by other media, such as computer software, slides, printed handouts, and so on and to be successful, appropriate *body language* and good *interpersonal communication* skills are required. A presentation is normally intended to either introduce something new to the audience, to persuade them of a viewpoint, or to inform them. *Sales representatives* use presentations when introducing a product to a potential customer. Presentations are also used in *team briefing* and other business contexts.

presenteeism *HR* an employee or organisation subscribing to the view that the hours spent at work have more value than *productivity* or results. Presenteeism is often displayed by *workaholics*. At its most extreme, presenteeism can be seen in a worker who reports for work even when sick, for fear of letting the company down or of losing their job. (*slang*) *See also* **absenteeism**

present value *Fin* **1.** amount that a future interest in a financial asset is currently worth, discounted for inflation **2.** the value now of an amount of money somebody expects to receive at a future date, calculated by subtracting any interest that will accrue in the interim

preservation of capital *Fin* an approach to financial management that protects a person's or company's capital by arranging additional forms of finance

president *Gen Mgt see* **chair**

press advertising *Mkting* advertising in newspapers or magazines

press clipping (*US*) *Gen Mgt* = **press cutting**

press communications *Mkting* communications activities designed to improve press awareness and attitudes to a product or an organisation

press conference *Mkting* a meeting to which journalists are invited to hear about a new product or other news about an organisation

press cutting *Gen Mgt* a copy of a news item kept by a company because it contains important business information or is a record of news published about the company. *US term* **press clipping**

press date *Mkting* the date on which a newspaper or magazine is printed

press release *Mkting* an item of news about an organisation, its staff, products,

---

Problems are only opportunities in work clothes.   Henry J. Kaiser or services that is sent to selected members of the press

press the flesh *Gen Mgt* to shake hands with people at a business function (*slang*)

pressure group *Gen Mgt* a body of people who have banded together to campaign on one or more issues of importance to them. A pressure group usually has a formal constitution and co-ordinates its activities to influence the attitudes or activities of business or government. One area in which pressure groups operate is the environment and some large companies that have failed to practise good *environmental management* have been targeted by campaigners. Pressure groups often represent widespread views, so it is important for a company to maintain good relations with them.

prestige pricing *Mkting see premium pricing*

pre-syndicate bid *Fin* a bid made before a group of buyers can offer blocks of shares in an offering to the public

pretax *Fin* before tax is considered or paid

pretax profit *Fin* the amount of profit a company makes before taxes are deducted

pretax profit margin *Fin* the profit made by a company, calculated as a percentage of sales, before taxes are considered

pretesting *Mkting* the practice of assessing the effectiveness of an advertising campaign or marketing activity in a small sector or single region before running the full campaign

pretrading *Fin see premarket*

prevalence *Stats* a measure of the number of people with a particular quality in a statistical population

preventive maintenance *or* **preventative maintenance** *Ops* the scheduling of a programme of planned *maintenance* services or equipment overhauls. The aim of preventive maintenance is to reduce equipment failure and the need for corrective maintenance. It can be carried out at regular time intervals, after a specified amount of equipment use, when the opportunity arises, for example, at a factory's annual shutdown, or when certain pre-set conditions occur to trigger the need for action. *Also known as planned maintenance. See also reactive maintenance*

price *Fin* an amount of money that somebody charges for a good or service

price-book ratio *Fin see price-to-book ratio*

price ceiling *Fin* the highest price that a buyer is willing to pay

price competition *Gen Mgt* a form of competition based on price rather than factors such as quality or design

price control *Econ* government regulations that set maximum prices for commodities or control price levels by credit controls

price differentiation *Gen Mgt* a pricing strategy in which a company sells the same product at different prices in different markets

price discovery *Fin* the process by which price is determined by negotiation in a free market

price discrimination *Econ* the practice of selling of the same product to different buyers at different prices

price-dividend ratio *Fin* the price of a stock divided by the annual dividend paid on a share

price-earnings ratio *Fin* a company's share price divided by earnings per share (EPS).

EXAMPLE While EPS is an actual amount of money, usually expressed in pence per share, the P/E ratio has no units, it is just a number. Thus if a quoted company has a share price of £100 and EPS of £12 for the last published year, then it has a historical P/E of 8.3. If analysts are forecasting for the next year EPS of, say, £14 then the forecast P/E is 7.1.

The P/E ratio is predominantly useful

---

in comparisons with other shares rather than in isolation. For example, if the average P/E in the market is 20, there will be many shares with P/Es well above and well below this, for a variety of reasons. Similarly, in a particular sector, the P/Es will frequently vary from the sector average, even though the constituent companies may all be engaged in similar businesses. The reason is that even two businesses doing the same thing will not always be doing it as profitably as each other. One may be far more efficient, as demonstrated by a history of rising EPS compared with the flat EPS picture of the other over a series of years, and the market might recognise this by awarding the more profitable share a higher P/E.

price effect *Econ* the impact of price changes on a market or economy

price elasticity of demand *Econ* the percentage change in demand divided by the percentage change in price of a good

price elasticity of supply *Econ* the percentage change in supply divided by the percentage change in price of a good

price escalation clause *Gen Mgt* a contract provision that permits the seller to raise prices in response to increased costs

price fixing *Fin* an often illegal agreement between producers of a good or service in order to maintain prices at a particular level

price floor *Fin* the lowest price at which a seller is prepared to do business

price index *Fin* an index, such as the consumer price index, that measures inflation

price indicator *Econ* a price that is a measurable variable and can be used, for example, as an index of the cost of living

price instability *Econ* a situation in which the prices of goods alter daily or even hourly

price leadership *Mkting* the establishment of price levels in a market by a dominant company or brand

price list *Gen Mgt* a document that sets out the prices of different products or services

price range *Gen Mgt* the variety of prices at which competitive products or services are available in the market

price ring *Fin* a group of traders who make an agreement, often illegally, to maintain prices at a particular level

prices and incomes policy *Econ* a policy of using government regulations to limit price or wage increases

price-sensitive *Fin* describes a good or service for which sales fluctuate depending on its price, often because it is a non-essential item

price-sensitive information *Fin* as yet unpublished information that will affect a company's share price. For example, the implementation of a new manufacturing process that substantially cuts production costs would have a positive impact, whereas the discovery of harmful side effects from a recently launched drug would have a negative impact.

price stability *Fin* a situation in which there is little change in the price of goods or services

price support *Econ* the use of government regulations to keep market prices from falling below a minimum level

price tag *Gen Mgt* **1.** a label attached to an item being sold that shows its price **2.** the value of a person or thing

price-to-book ratio *Fin* the ratio of the value of all of a company's stock to its *book value*. Also known as *price-book ratio*

price-to-cash-flow ratio *Fin* the ratio of the value of all of a company's stock to its cash flow for the most recent complete fiscal year

price-to-sales ratio *Fin* the ratio of the value of all of a company's stock to its sales for the previous twelve months, a way of measuring the relative value of a share when compared with others.

Alignment is not about the management of quality. It is about the quality of management.
George Labovitz

EXAMPLE The P/S ratio is obtained by dividing the market capitalisation by the latest published annual sales figure. So a company with a capitalisation of £1 billion and sales of £3 billion would have a P/S ratio of 0.33.

P/S will vary with the type of industry. You would expect, for example, that many retailers and other large-scale distributors of goods would have very high sales in relation to their market capitalisations—in other words, a very low P/S. Equally, manufacturers of high-value items would generally have much lower sales figures and thus higher P/S ratios.

A company with a lower P/S is cheaper than one with a higher ratio, particularly if they are in the same sector so that a direct comparison is more appropriate. It means that each share of the lower P/S company is buying more of its sales than those of the higher P/S company.

It is important to note that a share which is cheaper only on P/S grounds is not necessarily the more attractive share. There will frequently be reasons why it has a lower ratio than another similar company, most commonly because it is less profitable.

price war *Mkting* a situation in which two or more companies each try to increase their own share of the market by lowering prices. A price war involves companies undercutting each other in an attempt to encourage more customers to buy their goods or services. In the long term, this can devalue a market and lead to loss of profits, but it can sometimes have short-term success.

price-weighted index *Fin* an index of production or market value that is adjusted for price changes

pricing *Fin* the determination of a selling price for a product or service

pricing policy *Mkting* the method of *decision-making* used for setting the prices for a company's products or services. A pricing policy is usually based on the costs of production or provision with a

margin for profit, such as, for example, *cost-plus pricing*.

primary account number *Fin* an identifier for a credit card used in secure electronic transactions

primary data *or* **primary information** *Mkting* original data derived from a new research study and collected at source, as opposed to previously published material

primary earnings per (common) share (*US*) *Fin see earnings per share*

primary liability *Fin* responsibility to pay before anyone else, for example, for damages covered by insurance

primary market *Fin* the part of the market on which securities are first offered to investors by the issuer. The money from this sale goes to the issuer, rather than to traders or investors as it does in the secondary market. *See also* **secondary market**

primary sector *Econ* the firms and corporations of the productive sector of a country's economy

prime *Fin see prime rate*

prime assets ratio *Fin* the proportion of total liabilities which Australian banks are obliged by the Reserve Bank to hold in secure assets such as cash and government securities. *Abbr* **PAR**

prime cost *Fin* the total cost of direct material, direct labour, and direct expenses

prime rate *or* **prime interest rate** *Fin* the lowest interest rate that commercial banks offer on loans

principal *Fin see mortgage*

principal budget factor *Fin* a factor which will limit the activities of an undertaking and which is often the starting-point in budget preparation

principal shareholders *Fin* the shareholders who own the largest percentage of shares in an organisation

print farming *Mkting* the management of an organisation's print requirements, including choosing printers and overseeing production

prior charge capital *Fin* capital which has a right to the receipt of interest or of preference dividends in precedence to any claim on distributable earnings on the part of the ordinary shareholders. On winding up, the claims of holders of prior charge capital also rank before those of ordinary shareholders.

prior charge percentage *Fin see priority percentage*

priority-based budgeting *Fin* a method of budgeting in which budget requests are accompanied by a statement outlining the changes which would occur if the prior period budget were to be increased or decreased by a certain amount or percentage. These changes are prioritised.

priority percentage *Fin* the proportion of a business's net profit paid in interest to preference shareholders and holders of debt capital. *Also known as* **prior charge percentage**

prior lien bond *Fin* a bond whose holder has more claim on a debtor's assets than holders of other types of bonds

privacy policy *E-com* the means by which an organisation reassures customers that personal information they supply—usually over the Internet—will be securely protected, and used only for the stated purpose.

Most customers are willing to give personal information if they know that it will benefit them. However, privacy is a major concern on the Internet, and needs to be addressed comprehensively. The use of customer information is legislated separately by individual countries, and collecting it and—in particular—moving it between countries can be very complicated, because different countries have different laws.

However, a basic principle is for an organisation to tell the individual clearly why it is collecting the information, and what that information will be used for. If

the organisation wishes to use the information for other purposes, such as sending out e-mails on special offers, or sharing with partners, the individual should be specifically informed of that intention, and given the opportunity to opt out.

It is good policy for organisations to allow individuals to check the information held on them, and to delete information if they wish to do so. A proper security procedure is essential. Internet security breaches are increasing, and hackers are particularly interested in breaking into systems that contain personal information.

private bank *Fin* **1.** a bank that is owned by a single person or a limited number of private shareholders **2.** a bank that provides banking facilities to high net worth individuals. *See also* **private banking 3.** a bank that is not state-owned in a country where most banks are owned by the government

private banking *Fin* a service offered by certain financial institutions to high net worth individuals. In addition to standard banking services, it will typically include portfolio management and advisory services on taxation, including estate planning.

private company *Fin* a company which has not been registered as a public company under the Companies Act. The major practical distinction between a private and public company is that the former may not offer its securities to the public.

private cost (*US*) *Econ* the cost incurred by individuals when they use scarce resources such as petrol

private debt *Fin* money owed by individuals and organisations other than governments

private enterprise *Econ* the parts of an economy that are controlled by companies or individuals rather than the government

Private Finance Initiative *Fin* a policy which is designed to harness private sector management and expertise in the delivery of public services. Under PFI, the public sector does not buy assets, it buys the asset-based services it requires, on contract, from the private sector, the latter having the responsibility for deciding how to supply these services, the investment required to support the services, and how to achieve the required standards. *Abbr* **PFI**

private label (*US*) *Mkting* = **own brand**

private placement (*US*) *Fin* = *private placing*

private placing *Fin* the sale of securities directly to institutions for investment rather than resale. *US term* ***private placement***

private sector *Econ* the organisations in the section of the economy that is financed and controlled by individuals or private institutions, such as companies, shareholders, or investment groups. *See also **public sector***

private sector investment *Econ* investment by the private enterprise sector of the economy

private treaty *Fin* the sale of land without an auction

privatisation *Fin* the transfer of a company from ownership by either a government or a few individuals to the public via the issuance of stock

probability *Stats* the quantitative measure of the likelihood that a given event will occur

probability distribution *Stats* a mathematical formula showing the probability for each value of a variable in a statistical study

probability plot *Stats* a graphic plot of data that compares two probability distributions

probability sample *Stats* a sample in which every individual in a finite statistical *population* has a known chance, but not necessarily an equal chance, of being included

probability sampling *Stats* sampling in which every individual in a finite *population* has a known but not necessarily equal chance of being included in the sample

probation *HR* a trial period in the first months of employment when an employer checks the suitability and capability of a person in a certain role, and takes any necessary corrective action. An employee's performance during a probation period may be evaluated informally, for example, by means of conversations with a supervisor. If a probationary period is included in a ***contract of employment***, formal documented assessment is required.

problem child 1. (*US*) *Fin* a *subsidiary company* that is not performing well or is damaging the *parent company* in some way **2.** *Mkting* a product with a low market share but high growth potential. Problem children often have good long-term prospects, but high levels of investment may be needed to realise the potential, thereby draining funds that may be needed elsewhere. *See also **Boston Consulting Group matrix***

problem-solving *Gen Mgt* a systematic approach to overcoming obstacles or problems in the management process. Problems occur when something is not behaving as it should, when something deviates from the norm, or when something goes wrong. A number of problem-solving methodologies exist, but the most widely used is that proposed by ***Charles Kepner*** and ***Benjamin Tregoe***. Steps in their problem-solving process include: recognising a problem exists and defining it; generating a range of solutions; evaluating the possible solutions and choosing the best one; implementing the solution and evaluating its effectiveness in solving the problem. Various techniques can aid problem-solving, such as ***brainstorming***, ***fishbone charts***, and **Pareto charts**.

procedure *Gen Mgt* a set of step-by-step instructions designed to ensure that a task is efficiently and consistently carried out.

Diversity is intimately linked to the possibility of self-organisation. Vandana Shiva

Procedures regulate the conduct of an organisation's activities and ensure that *decision-making* is undertaken fairly and with due consideration, as, for example, in the case of disciplinary and complaints procedures. In the context of formal quality management systems, procedures are used to control and monitor work processes and to ensure that standards are met.

procedure manual *Gen Mgt* a document containing written rules and regulations that govern the conduct of *procedures* within an organisation. Procedure manuals are often used in the induction and training of new recruits.

proceeds *Fin* the income from a transaction

process *Gen Mgt* a structured and managed set of work activities designed to produce a particular output

process box *Gen Mgt see* **flow chart**

process chart *Gen Mgt* a diagrammatic representation of the sequence of work and the nature of events in a *process*. A process chart provides the basis for visualising the different stages for evaluation and possible improvement.

process control *Ops* the inspection of work-in-progress to provide feedback on, and correct, a production process. First developed as a mechanical feedback mechanism, process control is now widely used to monitor and maintain the quality of output. *See also* **statistical process control**

process layout *Ops* a type of office or *plant layout* that groups together workstations or equipment that undertake similar processes. Within a process layout organisation, the partly finished product moves from process to process and each batch may follow a different route. *Also known as* **process-oriented layout**, **layout by function**. *See also* **product layout**

process management *Ops* the operation, *control*, evaluation, and improvement of interconnected tasks, with the aim of maximising effectiveness and efficiency

processor *E-com see* **acquirer**

process-oriented layout *Ops see* **process layout**

process production *Ops* the continuous production of a product in bulk, often by a chemical rather than mechanical *process*

process time *Gen Mgt* the period which elapses between the start and finish of one process or stage of a process

procurement *Gen Mgt see* **purchasing**

procurement exchange *E-com* a group of companies that act together to buy products or services they need at lower prices

procurement manager *Gen Mgt see* **purchasing manager**

procurement portal *E-com see* **online catalogue**

producer price index *Econ* a statistical measure, the weighted average of the prices of commodities that firms buy from other firms

producibility engineering *Ops see* **design for manufacturability**

product *Mkting* anything that is offered to a market that customers can acquire, use, interact with, experience, or consume, to satisfy a want or need. Early *marketing* tended to focus on tangible physical goods and these were distinguished from *services*. More recently, however, the distinction between products and services has blurred, and the concept of the product has been expanded so that in its widest sense it can now be said to cover any tangible or intangible thing that satisfies the consumer. Products that are marketed can include services, people, places, and ideas.

product abandonment *Mkting* the ending of the manufacture and sale of a product. Products are abandoned for many reasons. The market may be saturated or declining, the product may be superseded by another, costs of production may become too high, or a product may simply become unprofitable. Product abandonment usually occurs during the decline phase of the *product life cycle*.

product assortment *Mkting see product mix*

product bundling *Fin* a form of discounting in which a group of related products is sold at a price which is lower than that obtainable by the consumer were the products to be purchased separately

product churning *Gen Mgt* the flooding of a market with new products in the hope that one of them will become successful. Product churning is especially prevalent in Japan, where pre-launch *test marketing* is often replaced by multiple product launches. Most of these products will decline and disappear, but one or more of the new products churned out may become profitable.

product development *Mkting* the revitalisation of a product through the introduction of a new concept or consumer benefit. Product development is part of the *product life cycle*. The concepts or benefits that can be implemented range from modification of the product to simply introducing new packaging.

product development cycle *Mkting see new product development*

product differentiation *Mkting* a marketing technique that promotes and emphasises a product's difference from other products of a similar nature. Product differentiation is one of the aspects of *Michael Porter*'s *generic strategy* theory and it has been described by *Anita Roddick* as being the key to the success of the Body Shop. *Also known as differentiation*

product family *Mkting* a group of products or services that meet a similar need in the market

production *Ops* the processes and techniques used in making a product. *Also known as manufacturing*

production control *Ops* the control of all aspects of *production*, according to a predetermined production plan. *Production planning* and production control are closely linked, and sometimes the terms are used interchangeably. Nevertheless, they differ in focus: production planning focuses on the scheduling of the production process; production control focuses on the application of the plan which results from the production planning. Computerised techniques, such as material requirements planning and *optimised production technology* combine elements of planning and control.

production cost *Fin* prime cost plus absorbed production overhead

production levelling *Ops see production smoothing*

production management *Ops* the management of those resources and activities of a business that are required to produce goods for sale to consumers or to other organisations. Production management is concerned with the manufacturing industry. The growing interest in the production management task in service industries has led to the use of *operations management* as a more general term. *Also known as manufacturing management*

production planning *or* **production scheduling** *Ops* the process of producing a specification or chart of the manufacturing operations to be carried out by different functions and workstations over a particular time period. Production scheduling takes account of factors such as the availability of plant and materials, customer delivery requirements, and maintenance schedules.

production smoothing *Ops* the smoothing, or levelling, of *production scheduling* so that mix and volume are even over time. Production smoothing is an important condition for production by *kanban*, and is key to the *Toyota production system*. The aim is to minimise idle time. *Also known as production levelling*

---

production versus purchasing *Ops see purchasing versus production*

productive capacity *Ops* the maximum amount of output that an organisation or company can generate at any one time

productivity *Gen Mgt, Ops* a measurement of the efficiency of production, taking the form of a ratio of the output of goods and services to the input of factors of production. **Labour productivity** takes account of inputs of employee hours worked; **capital productivity** takes account of inputs of machines or land; and **marginal productivity** measures the additional output gained from an additional unit of input. Techniques to improve productivity include greater use of new technology, altered working practices, and improved training of the workforce.

productivity agreement *HR see productivity bargaining*

productivity bargaining *HR* a form of *collective bargaining* leading to a **productivity agreement** in which management offers a pay rise in exchange for alterations to employee working practices designed to increase *productivity*

product launch *Mkting* the introduction of a new product to a market. A product launch progresses through a number of important stages: internal communication, which encourages high levels of awareness and commitment to the new product; pre-launch activity, which secures distribution and makes sure that retailers have the resources and knowledge to market the product; launch events at national, regional, or local level; post-event activity, which helps salesforce and retailers make the most of the event; and launch advertising and other forms of customer communication.

product layout *Ops* the organisation of a factory or office so that the position of the *workstations* is optimised to suit the product. Product layout ensures that products follow an *assembly line* where the different operations are undertaken in a logical sequence. *Also known as* **product-oriented layout**. *See also* **process layout**

product leader *Mkting see* **brand leader**

product liability *Mkting* a manufacturer's, producer's, or service provider's obligation to accept responsibility for defects in their products or services. Faulty products may result in personal injury or damage to property, in which case product liability may result in the payment of compensation to the purchaser.

product life cycle *Mkting* the life span of a product from development, through testing, promotion, growth, and maturity, to decline and perhaps regeneration. A new product is first developed and then introduced to the market. Once the introduction is successful, a growth period follows with wider awareness of the product and increasing sales. The product enters maturity when sales stop growing and demand stabilises. Eventually, sales may decline until the product is finally withdrawn from the market or redeveloped.

product line *Mkting* a family of related products. Products within a line may be the same type of product, they may be sold to the same type of customer, or through similar outlets, or they may all be within a certain price range.

product management *Mkting* a system for the co-ordination of all the stages through which a product passes during its life cycle. Product management involves control of a product from its innovation and development to its decline. The process is co-ordinated by a **product manager** who focuses on the marketing of the product but may also be responsible for pricing, packaging, branding, research and development, production, distribution, sales targets, and product performance appraisal. This cross-departmental approach is based on the theory that a dedicated product management system will lead to tighter control over the product, and thus higher sales and profits. A **brand manager** fulfils a similar function to a product manager, concentrating on products within one brand.

product market *Mkting* the *market* in which products are sold, usually to organisations rather than consumers. The product market is concerned with *purchasing* by organisations for their own use, and includes such items as raw materials, machinery, and equipment which may in turn be used to manufacture items for the consumer market.

product mix *Mkting* the range of product lines that a company produces, or that a retailer stocks. Product mix usually refers to the length (the number of products in the product line), breadth (the number of product lines that a company offers), depth (the different varieties of product in the product line), and consistency (the relationship between products in their final destination) of product lines. Product mix is sometimes called **product assortment**.

product-oriented layout *Ops* see *product layout*

product placement *Mkting* a form of advertising in which an identifiable branded product is seen by the audience during a film or television programme

product portfolio *Mkting* a range of products manufactured or supplied by an organisation

product positioning *Mkting* see *brand positioning*

product range *Mkting* all of the types of product made by one company

product recall *Ops* the removal from sale of products that may constitute a risk to consumers because of contamination, *sabotage*, or faults in the production process. A product recall usually originates from the product manufacturer but retailers may act autonomously, especially if they believe their outlets are at particular risk. *See brand positioning*

product-sustaining activities *Fin* activities undertaken in support of production, the costs of which are linked to the number of separate products produced rather than to the volume of output. Engineering

change is a product-sustaining activity. *See hierarchy of activities*

profession *HR* an occupational group characterised by extensive education and specialised training, the use of skills based on theoretical knowledge, a *code of conduct*, and an association that organises its members. Members of a profession are normally well paid and derive social status and prestige from their occupation. They have substantial autonomy and tend to be highly resistant to control or interference in their affairs by outside groups. As many professionals now work within organisations rather than independently, there may be a conflict of interests between professional and corporate values, and between professional autonomy and bureaucratic direction.

professional 1. *Gen Mgt* somebody who shows a high level of skill or *competence* **2.** *HR* a member of a particular *profession* **3.** *HR* somebody paid to do a job, rather than working as a volunteer or pursuing a hobby

professionalism *HR* the skill, *competence*, or standards expected of a member of a *profession*

profile *Fin* a description of a company, including its products and finances

profile method *HR* an analytical form of *job evaluation* used by management consultants. The most well-known version of the profile method is the Hay Guide Chart and Profile Methodology.

profitability index *Fin* the present value of the money an investment will earn divided by the amount of the investment

profitability threshold *Fin* the point at which a business begins to make profits

profitable *Fin* used to refer to a product, service, or organisation which makes money

profit and loss *Fin* the difference between a company's income and its costs

profit and loss account or **profit and loss statement** *Fin* the summary record of a company's sales revenues and expenses over a period, providing a calculation of profits or losses during that time. *Abbr* **P & L**

EXAMPLE Companies typically issue P&L reports monthly. It is customary for the reports to include year-to-date figures, as well as corresponding year-earlier figures to allow for comparisons and analysis.

There are two P&L formats, multiple-step and single-step. Both follow a standard set of rules known as *Generally Accepted Accounting Principles* (GAAP). These rules generally adhere to requirements established by governments to track receipts, expenses, and profits for tax purposes. They also allow the financial reports of two different companies to be compared.

The multiple-step format is much more common, because it includes a larger number of details and is thus more useful.

It deducts costs from revenues in a series of steps, allowing for closer analysis. Revenues appear first, then expenses, each in as much detail as management desires. Sales may be broken down by product line or location, while expenses such as salaries may be broken down into base salaries and commissions.

Expenses are then subtracted from revenues to show profit (or loss). A basic multiple-step P&L looks like the table below.

P&Ls of public companies may also report income on the basis of earnings per share. For example, if the company issuing this statement had 12,000 shares outstanding, earnings per share would be £5.12, that is, £61,440 divided by 12,000 shares.

profit before tax *Fin* the amount that a company or investor has made, without taking taxes into account

MULTIPLE-STEP PROFIT & LOSS ACCOUNT		(£)
NET SALES	750,000	
Less: cost of goods sold	450,000	
Gross profit		300,000
LESS: OPERATING EXPENSES		
Selling expenses		
Salaries & commissions	54,000	
Advertising	37,500	
Delivery/transportation	12,000	
Depreciation/store equipment	7,500	
Other selling expenses	5,000	
Total selling expenses		116,000
General & administrative expenses		
Administrative/office salaries	74,000	
Utilities	2,500	
Depreciation/structure	2,400	
Misc. other expenses	3,100	
Total general & admin expenses		82,000
Total operating expenses		198,000
OPERATING INCOME		102,000
LESS (ADD): NON-OPERATING ITEMS		
Interest expenses	11,000	
Interest income earned	(2,800)	8,200
Income before taxes		93,800
Income taxes		32,360
Net Income		**61,440**

The will to win is nothing without the will to prepare. *Juma Ikangaa*

profit centre *Gen Mgt* a person, unit, or department within an organisation that is considered separately when calculating profit. Profit centres are used as part of *management control systems*. They operate with a degree of autonomy with regard to marketing and pricing, and have responsibility for their own costs, revenues, and profits.

profit distribution *Fin* the allocation of profits to different recipients such as shareholders and owners, or for different purposes such as research or investment

profit from ordinary activities *Fin* profits earned in the normal course of business, as opposed to profits from extraordinary sources such as windfall payments

profit margin *Gen Mgt* the amount by which income exceeds expenditure. The profit margin of an individual product is the sale price minus the cost of production and associated costs such as *distribution* and *advertising*. On a larger scale, the profit margin is an accounting ratio of company income compared with sales. The profit margin ratio can be used to compare the efficiency and profitability of a company over a number of years, or to compare different companies. The **gross profit margin** or **operating margin** of a company is its operating, or gross, profit divided by total sales. The **net profit margin** or **return on sales** is net income after taxes divided by total sales.

profit motive *Fin* the desire of a business or service provider to make profit

profit per employee *Fin* an indication of the effectiveness of the employment of staff. When there are full- and part-time employees, full-time equivalents should be used. It is calculated as follows:

Profit for the year before interest and tax / Average number of employees

See also sales per employee

profit-related pay *HR* a *profit sharing* scheme, approved by the Inland Revenue, in which employees received tax-free payments in addition to their basic salary.

Profit-related pay was phased out during 2000.

profit retained for the year *Fin* non-distributed profit retained as a distributable reserve

profit sharing *HR* a scheme giving *employees* a payment that is conditional on the company's profits. Profit sharing takes the form of a *share incentive scheme*, or a pay *bonus*. The purpose of relating payment to company performance is to increase *employee commitment* and *motivation*.

profit-sharing debenture *Fin* a debenture, held by an employee, whose payouts depend on the company's financial success

profits tax *Fin* a tax on profits, for example, corporation tax (*slang*)

profit–volume/contribution graph *Fin* a graph showing the effect on contribution and on overall profit of changes in sales volume or value

profit warning *Fin* a statement by a company's executives that the company may realise less profit in a coming quarter than investors expect

pro-forma *Gen Mgt* a document issued before all relevant details are known, usually followed by a final version

pro-forma financial statement *Fin* a projection showing a business's financial statements after the completion of a planned transaction

pro-forma invoice *Fin* an invoice that does not include all the details of a transaction, often sent before goods are supplied and followed by a final detailed invoice

program *E-com* a set of instructions for a computer to act upon

programme trading *Fin* the trading of securities electronically, by sending messages from the investor's computer to a market

programming *Fin see* *dynamic programming, linear programming, non-linear programming*

The goals on which hope are based have to be realistic.   *Arthur Lydiard*

progressive tax *Fin* a tax with a rate that increases proportionately with taxable income. *See also* **proportional tax**, **regressive tax**

project *Gen Mgt* a set of activities designed to achieve a specified goal, within a given period of time. Projects focus on activities outside the routine operations of an organisation. They vary immensely in size, scope, and complexity and often involve drawing together resources from different parts of an organisation for the duration of the project. The process of planning and completing projects is known as *project management*.

project costing *Fin see* **costing**, **contract costing**

project finance *Fin* money, usually nonrecourse finance, raised for a specific self-contained venture, usually a construction or development project

projection *Fin* an expected future trend pattern obtained by extrapolation. It is principally concerned with quantitative factors, whereas a forecast includes judgments.

project management *Gen Mgt* the coordination of resources to ensure the achievement of a *project*. Project management includes the planning and allocation of financial, material, and human resources and the organisation of the work needed to complete a project. Formal, structured approaches to project management began to emerge in the late 1950s in the construction and military industries, where methods such as **PRINCE**—PRojects IN Controlled Environments—developed to facilitate the process.

promissory note *Fin* a contract to pay money to a person or organisation for a good or service received

promotion 1. *HR* the award to an employee of a job at a higher grade, usually offering greater responsibility and more money **2.** *Mkting see* **sales promotion**

proof-of-purchase *Mkting* a sales receipt or other document that can be used to show that someone has bought a product

property *Fin* assets, such as land or goods, that somebody owns

property bond *Fin* a bond, especially a bail bond, for which a property is collateral

property damage insurance *Fin* insurance against the risk of damage to property

proportional tax *Fin* a tax whose amount is strictly proportional to the value of the item being taxed, especially income. *See also* **progressive tax**, **regressive tax**

proprietary ordering system *E-com* a family of computer programs, usually interactive and online, that is developed and owned by a supplier and made available to its customers to facilitate ordering

ProShare *Fin* a group that acts in the interests of private investors in securities of the London Stock Exchange

prospect *Mkting* a person or organisation considered likely to buy a product or service

prospecting *Mkting* the process of identifying people or organisations that are likely to buy a product or service

prospectus *Fin* a document that sets out corporate and financial information for prospective shareholders. A prospectus is usually issued when a company is offering new shares to the market.

prosuming *Gen Mgt* acting both as producer and consumer, as, for example, when a person plays an interactive computer game (*slang*)

protected class *HR* an employee with skills that are currently in short supply (*slang*)

protectionism *Econ* a government economic policy of restricting the level of

---

We feel the spear of the marketplace in our back.   *Tony O'Reilly*

imports by using measures such as tariffs and *NTBs*

protective put buying *Fin* the purchase of *puts* for stocks already owned

protective tariff *Econ* a tariff imposed to restrict imports into a country

protocol *Fin* a set of rules that govern and regulate a process

prototype *Gen Mgt* an initial version or working model of a new product or invention. A prototype is constructed and tested in order to evaluate the feasibility of a design and to identify problems that need to be corrected. Building a prototype is a key stage in *new product development*.

provision *Fin* a sum set aside in the accounts of an organisation in anticipation of a future expense, often for doubtful debts. *See also* **bad debt**

provisional tax *Fin* tax paid in advance on the following year's income, the amount being based on the actual income from the preceding year

proxy *Gen Mgt* somebody who votes on behalf of another person at a company meeting

proxy fight *Fin* the use of proxy votes to settle a contentious issue at a company meeting

proxy server *E-com* a program added to an intranet to provide one-way (outward) access to the Internet. In addition to providing Internet access for those within the intranet, the proxy server creates a *firewall* to prevent external users from accessing the private network.

proxy statement *Fin* a notice that a company sends to stockholders allowing them to vote and giving them all the information they need to vote in an informed way

PSBR *abbr Econ* Public Sector Borrowing Requirement

psychic income *HR* the level of satisfaction derived from a job rather than the salary earned doing it (*slang*)

psychological contract *HR* the set of unwritten expectations concerning the relationship between an *employee* and an *employer*. The psychological contract addresses factors that are not defined in a written *contract of employment* such as levels of *employee commitment*, *productivity*, *quality of working life*, *job satisfaction*, attitudes to *flexible working*, and the provision and take-up of suitable training. Expectations from both employer and employee can change, so the psychological contract must be re-evaluated at intervals to minimise misunderstandings.

psychometric test *HR* a series of questions, problems, or practical tasks that provide a measurement of aspects of somebody's personality, knowledge, ability, or experience. There are three main categories of psychometric test: ability or *aptitude tests*, *achievement tests*, and *personality tests*. A test should be both valid—it should measure what it says it measures—and reliable—it should give consistent scores. However, no test can ever be 100% accurate, and should be viewed more as a useful indicator than a definitive verdict on a person's skills or potential. Tests are used in *recruitment*, to ascertain whether or not a candidate is likely to be a good fit for a job, and in *employee development*, and their administration and interpretation must be carried out by qualified people. Tests are increasingly taken, scored, and interpreted with the aid of computer-based systems. A test may also be referred to as an **instrument**, and tests can be grouped into a **test battery**.

Pty *abbr* (*S Africa*) *Fin* used in company names to indicate a private limited liability company

public corporation *Fin* a state owned organisation established to provide a particular service, for example, the British Broadcasting Corporation. *See also* **corporation**

public debt *Fin* the money that a government or a set of governments owes

---

Experience is a dim lamp, which only lights the one who bears it.   Louis-Ferdinand Céline

public deposits *Fin* in the United Kingdom, the government's credit monies held at the Bank of England

public expenditure *Econ* spending by the government of a country on things such as pension provision and infrastructure enhancement

public finance law *Fin* legislation relating to the financial activities of government or public sector organisations

public issue *Fin* a way of making a new issue of shares by offering it for sale to the public. An issue of this type is often advertised in the press. *See also* **offer for sale**, **offer by prospectus**

public-liability insurance *Fin* insurance against the risk of being held financially liable for injury to somebody

public limited company *Gen Mgt* a company in the United Kingdom that is required to have a minimum authorised capital of £50,000 and to offer its shares to the public. A public limited company has the letters 'plc' after its name. In the United Kingdom, only public limited companies can be listed on the London Stock Exchange. *Abbr* **plc** or **PLC.** *US term* **publicly held corporation**

publicly held corporation (*US*) = **public limited company**

public monopoly *Gen Mgt* a situation of limited competition in the public sector, usually relating to nationalised industries

public offering *Fin* a method of raising money used by a company in which it invites the public to apply for shares

public placing *Fin* placing shares in a public company. *See also* **private placing**

public relations *Mkting see* **PR**

public relations consultancy *Mkting* an organisation specialising in planning and implementing public relations strategies

public sector *Gen Mgt* the organisations in the section of the economy that is financed and controlled by central government, local authorities, and publicly funded corporations. *See also* **private sector**

public sector borrowing requirement *Fin abbr* **PSBR**. *See* **public sector cash requirement**

public sector cash requirement *Econ* the difference between the income and the expenditure of the public sector. It was formerly called the **public sector borrowing requirement**.

public servant *Gen Mgt* a person employed by a government department or agency

public service *Gen Mgt* the various departments and agencies that carry out government policies and provide government-funded services

public spending *Econ* spending by the government of a country on publicly-provided goods and services

public training programme *HR see* **in-company training**

published accounts *Fin* a company's financial statements that must by law be published. *US term* **earnings report**

puff *Fin* to overstate the virtues of a product, especially a stock (*slang*)

puffery *Mkting* exaggerated claims made for a product or service. In general, puffery does not constitute false advertising under law. (*slang*)

puff piece *Mkting* an article in a newspaper or magazine promoting a product, person, or service (*slang*)

pull strategy *Mkting see* **push and pull strategies**

pull system *Ops* a production planning and control system in which the specification and pace of output of a delivery, or supplier, workstation is set by the receiving, or customer, *workstation*. In pull systems, the customer acts as the only trigger for movement. The supplier workstation can only produce output on the instructions of the customer for delivery when the customer is ready to receive it.

Demand is therefore transferred down through the stages of production from the order placed by an end customer. Pull systems are far less likely to result in work-in-progress inventory, and are favoured by just-in-time or *lean production* systems. *See also push system*

pull technology *E-com* technology that enables users to seek out and then pull in information, rather than having it pushed their way. Understanding the 'pull' nature of the Internet is often considered to be one of the key factors in determining a website's success. The Internet is essentially a pull technology, though direct outbound e-mail can be classified as a **push technology**.

pull the plug on something *Gen Mgt* to bring something such as a business project to an end, especially by cutting off its financial support (*slang*)

pump priming *Gen Mgt* the injection of further investment in order to revitalise a company in stagnation, or to help a *start-up* over a critical period. Pump priming has a similar effect to the provision of *seed capital*.

punt (*US & Canada*) *Gen Mgt* to stop trying to accomplish something and just try to avoid losing any more resources (*slang*)

purchase contract *Fin* a form of agreement to buy specified products at an agreed price

purchase history *Mkting* a record of a customer's transactions with an organisation

purchase ledger *Gen Mgt* a record of all purchases made by an organisation

purchase money mortgage (*US*) *Fin* a mortgage whose proceeds the borrower uses to buy the property that is collateral for the loan

purchase order *Gen Mgt* a document that authorises a person or an organisation to deliver goods or perform a service and that guarantees payment

purchase price *Fin* the price that somebody pays to buy a good or service

purchase requisition *Gen Mgt* an internal instruction to a buying office to purchase goods or services, stating their quantity and description and generating a purchase order

purchasing *Gen Mgt* the acquisition of goods and services needed to support the various activities of an organisation, at the optimum cost and from reliable suppliers. Purchasing involves defining the need for goods and services; identifying and comparing available supplies and suppliers; negotiating terms for price, quantity, and delivery; agreeing contracts and placing orders; receiving and accepting delivery; and authorising the payment for goods and services. *Also known as procurement*

purchasing by contract *Ops see contract purchasing*

purchasing manager *Gen Mgt* an individual with responsibility for all activities concerned with *purchasing*. The responsibilities of a purchasing manager can include ordering, commercial negotiations, and delivery chasing. *Also known as buying manager, procurement manager*

purchasing power *Gen Mgt* a measure of the ability of a person, organisation, or sector to buy goods and services

purchasing power parity *Econ* a theory stating that the exchange rate between two currencies is in equilibrium when the purchasing power of currency is the same in each country. If a basket of goods costs £100 in the United Kingdom and $150 for an equivalent in the United States, for equilibrium to exist, the exchange rate would be expected to be £1 = $1.50. If this were not the case, **arbitrage** would be expected to take place until equilibrium was restored.

purchasing versus production *Ops* a decision on whether to produce goods internally or to buy them in from outside the organisation. The aim of purchasing versus production is to secure needed items at the best possible cost, while making optimum use of the resources of the organisation. Factors influencing the decision may include: cost, spare **capacity** within the organisation, the need for tight quality and scheduling control, flexibility, the enhancement of skills that can then be used in other ways, volume and economies of scale, utilisation of existing personnel, the need for secrecy, capital and financing requirements, and the potential reliability of supply. *Also known as* **buy or make**, **make or buy**, **internal versus external sourcing**

pure competition *Fin* a situation in which there are many sellers in a market and there is free flow of information

pure endowment *Fin* a gift whose use is fully prescribed by the donor

pure play *E-com* a company that conducts business only over the Internet, provides only Internet services, or sells only to other Internet companies (*slang*)

Purple Book *Fin* a book which sets out the regulations for admission to, and continuing membership of the official list of quoted companies on the London Stock Exchange (*slang*)

purpose credit *Fin* credit used for trade in securities

push and pull strategies *Mkting* approaches used as part of a marketing strategy to encourage customers to purchase a product or service. Push and pull strategies are contrasting approaches and tend to target different types of consumer. A **pull strategy** targets the end consumer, using *advertising*, *sales promotions*, and *direct response marketing* to pull the customer in. This approach is common in consumer markets. A **push strategy** targets members of the *distribution channel*, such as *wholesalers* and *retailers*, to push the promotion up through the channel to the consumers. This approach is more common in industrial markets.

push system *Ops* a *production control* and planning system in which demand is predicted centrally and each *workstation* pushes work out without considering if the next station is ready for it. While the central control aspect of a push system can achieve a balance across workstations, in practice a particular station can suffer from any one of a number of problems that delays work flow, so affecting the whole system. Push systems are characterised by work-in-progress inventory, queues, and idle time. *See also* **pull system**

push technology *E-com see* **pull technology**

push the envelope *Gen Mgt* to exceed normal limits. Pushing the envelope is a term adapted from aviation. The term implies a sense of risk at transcending normal safe limits of operation.

put *or* **put option** *Fin* an option to sell stock within a specified time at a specified price

pyramid selling *Mkting* the sale of the right to sell products or services to distributors who in turn recruit other distributors. Sometimes ending with no final buyer, pyramid selling is a form of multi-level marketing, and often involves a system of franchises. It is similar to *network marketing*, but in many cases no end products are actually sold. Unscrupulous instigators of a pyramid marketing scheme profit from the initial fees paid to them by distributors in advance of promised sales income. Pyramid selling is now illegal in the United Kingdom.

QFD *abbr Ops* quality function deployment

qualification payment *(ANZ) Gen Mgt* an additional payment sometimes made to employees of New Zealand companies, who have gained an academic qualification relevant to their job

qualified auditor's report *Fin see* *adverse opinion*

qualified lead *Fin* a sales prospect whose potential value has been carefully researched

qualified listed security *Fin* a security that is eligible for purchase by a regulated entity such as a trust

qualitative analysis *Fin* the subjective appraisal of a project or investment for which there is no quantifiable data. *See also* *chartist*, *fundamental analysis*, *quantitative analysis*, *technical analysis*

qualitative factors *Fin* factors which are relevant to a decision, but which are not expressed numerically

qualitative lending guideline *Fin* a rule for evaluating creditworthiness that is not objective

qualitative research *Mkting* research that focuses on 'soft' data, for example, attitude research or focus groups. *See also* *quantitative research*

quality *Gen Mgt* all the features and characteristics of a product or service that affect its ability to meet stated or implied needs. Quality can be assessed in terms of conforming to specification, being fit for purpose, having zero defects, and producing *customer satisfaction*. Quality can be managed through *total quality management*, *quality standards*, and *performance indicators*.

quality assurance *Gen Mgt* all the methods used to ensure compliance with a *quality standard*. Quality assurance is recognised by the international standard *ISO 9000*.

quality audit *Gen Mgt* an independent and systematic examination to establish whether quality activities and related results comply with planned arrangements. A quality audit is a form of internal *audit* useful in the maintenance of *quality control*. A quality audit needs to look at effective implementation of quality arrangements and whether they are suitable for the achievement of objectives. It is an integral part of working towards a *quality standard* or a *quality award*.

quality award *Gen Mgt* a formal recognition of quality and business *excellence*. The best-known quality awards include the *Malcolm Baldrige National Quality Award*, the *Deming Prize*, and the *EFQM Excellence Model*.

quality bond *Fin* a bond issued by an organisation that has an excellent credit rating

quality circle *Gen Mgt* a group of employees who meet voluntarily and on a regular basis to discuss performance and problems evident in their working environment. A quality circle is usually made up of employees from the shop floor, led by a supervisor. The group has responsibility for implementing solutions to identified problems. Participants are trained in the necessary leadership, *problem-solving*, and *decision-making* skills to enable them to contribute fully to the group. The quality circle is a form of *employee involvement* derived from a Japanese idea widely adopted in the United Kingdom in the late 1970s. By the end of the 1980s, however, many organisations had abandoned the idea.

quality control *Gen Mgt* an inspection system for ensuring that pre-determined *quality standards* are being met. Quality control measures the progress of an activity by means of a quality inspection checking for and identifying

---

Consultants eventually leave, which makes them excellent scapegoats for major management blunders.
Scott Adams

non-conformance. *Also known as* **quality inspection**

quality control plan *Ops* a means of setting out practices, resources, and sequences of activities relevant to the *quality control* of a particular product, service, contract, or project

quality costs *Gen Mgt* costs associated with the failure to achieve conformance to requirements. Quality costs accrue when organisations waste large sums of money because of carrying out the wrong tasks, or failing to carry out the right tasks *right first time*. *Also known as non-conformance costs*

quality equity *Fin* an equity with a good track record of earnings and dividends. *See also* **blue chip**

quality function deployment *Ops* a *quality* technique used to design services or products based on customer expectations. Quality function deployment is an approach that sees quality as something that can be designed into a product or service at an early stage. It involves converting customers' demands into quality characteristics of the finished product. The four phases of the approach are design or *house of quality*, detail, process, and production. Each phase helps to steer a design team towards *customer satisfaction*. Quality function deployment is based on methods developed by *Genichi Taguchi*. *Abbr* **QFD**

quality inspection *Gen Mgt see* **quality control**

quality loss *Ops see* **Taguchi methods**

quality management *Gen Mgt* the use of a programme to ensure the production of high-quality products. *See also* **total quality management**

quality manual *Gen Mgt* a document containing the quality policy, quality objectives, structure chart, and description of the quality system of an organisation. A quality manual often explains how the requirements of a *quality standard* are to be met and identifies the person

responsible for *quality management* functions.

quality of design *Ops* the degree to which the design of a product or service meets its purpose. Quality of design is an important factor in *customer satisfaction*.

quality of life *HR* **1.** at a personal level, the degree of enjoyment and satisfaction experienced in everyday life, embracing health, personal relationships, the environment, *quality of working life*, social life, and leisure time **2.** at community level, a set of social indicators such as nutrition, air quality, incidence of disease, crime rates, health care, educational services, and divorce rates

quality of working life *HR* the degree of personal satisfaction experienced at work. Quality of working life is dependent on the extent to which an employee feels valued, rewarded, motivated, consulted, and empowered. It is also influenced by factors such as job security, opportunities for *career development*, work patterns, and *work-life balance*.

quality standard *Gen Mgt* a framework for achieving a recognised level of *quality* within an organisation. Achievement of a quality standard demonstrates that an organisation has met the requirements laid out by a certifying body. Quality standards recognised on an international basis include *ISO 9000* and *ISO 14000*.

quality table *Ops see* **house of quality**

quality time *Gen Mgt* time that is set aside for activities which you consider important, for example, time spent with your family (*slang*)

quango *Fin* in the United Kingdom, an acronym derived from quasi-autonomous non-governmental organisation. Established by the government and answerable to a government minister, some, but not all, are staffed by civil servants and some have statutory powers in a specified field.

quantitative analysis *Fin* the appraisal of a project or investment using econometric, mathematical, and statistical

---

techniques. *See also chartist, fundamental analysis, qualitative analysis, technical analysis*

quantitative factors *Fin* factors which are relevant to a decision and which are expressed numerically

quantitative research *Fin* the gathering and analysis of data that can be expressed in numerical form. Quantitative research involves data that is measurable and can include statistical results, financial data, or demographic data. *See also qualitative research*

quantum meruit *Fin* a Latin phrase meaning 'as much as has been earned'

quarterback (*US*) (*Canada*) *Gen Mgt* to give directions on a project (*slang*)

quarterly report *Fin see interim statement*

quartile *Stats* any of the values in a frequency or probability distribution that divide it into four equal parts

quasi-contract *Fin* a decree by a UK court stipulating that one party has a legal obligation to another, even though there is no legally binding contract between the two parties

quasi-loan *Fin* an arrangement whereby one party pays the debts of another, on the condition that the sum of the debts will be reimbursed by the indebted party at some later date

quasi-money *Fin see near money*

quasi-public corporation (*US*) *Gen Mgt* an organisation that is owned partly by private or public shareholders and partly by the government

quasi-rent *Econ* the short-run excess earnings made by a firm, the difference between production cost (the cost of labour and materials) and selling cost

question mark company *Gen Mgt see Boston Box*

questionnaire *Gen Mgt* a collection of structured questions designed to elicit information for a specific purpose. Questionnaires are commonly used in *market research* and make use of two types of question: multiple choice questions, which are designed to produce a limited response, and open questions, which allow respondents the opportunity to air their views freely.

queuing theory *Gen Mgt* techniques developed by the study of people waiting in queues to determine the optimum level of service provision. In queuing theory, mathematical formulae, or *simulations*, are used to calculate variables such as length of time spent waiting in queues and average service time, which depend on the frequency and number of arrivals and the facilities available. The results enable decisions to be made on the most cost-effective level of facilities and the most efficient organisation of the process. Early developments in queuing theory were applied to the provision of telephone switching equipment but the techniques are now used in a wide variety of contexts, including machine maintenance, production lines, and air transport.

queuing time *Fin* the time between the arrival of material at a workstation and the start of work on it

quick asset *Fin see near money*

quick ratio *Fin* **1.** a measure of the amount of cash a potential borrower can acquire in a short time, used in evaluating creditworthiness **2.** the ratio of liquid assets to current debts

quid pro quo *Fin* a Latin phrase meaning 'something for something'

quorum *Fin* the minimum number of people required in a meeting for it to be able to make decisions that are binding on the organisation. For a company, this is stated in its Articles of Association, for a partnership, in its partnership agreement.

quota *Fin* **1.** the maximum sum to be contributed by each party in a joint venture or joint business undertaking **2.** the maximum number of investments that may be purchased and sold in a given situation or market **3.** the maximum amount of a particular commodity, product, or service that can be imported into or exported out of a country

quote *Fin* a statement of what a person is willing to accept when selling, or willing to pay when buying

quoted company *Fin* a company whose shares are listed on a stock exchange

quote driven *Fin* used to describe a share dealing system where prices are initially generated by dealers' and market makers' quotes before market forces come into play and prices are determined by the interaction of supply and demand. The London Stock Exchange's dealing system, as well as those of many over-the-counter markets, have quote driven systems.

quoted securities *Fin* securities or shares that are listed on a stock exchange

---

The task of the leader is to get people from where they are to where they have not been.
Henry Kissinger

R150 Bond *Fin* the benchmark South African government bond which has a fixed interest rate of 12% and matures in 2005

racial discrimination *HR* the practice of making unfavourable distinctions between the members of different groups of people on the grounds of colour, race, nationality, or ethnic origin. In the United Kingdom, anti-discrimination law is provided by the Race Relations Act 1976. The Act established the Commission for Racial Equality to work towards the elimination of racial discrimination by promoting equality of opportunity and race relations. In 1999, measures to combat institutional racism, especially in the police force, were recommended in a report on the murder of a black student, Stephen Lawrence. *See also* **indirect discrimination**

radio button *Gen Mgt* a device on a computer screen that can be used to select an option from a list

raid *Fin* the illegal practice of selling shares short to drive the price down. *Also known as* **bear raid**

raider *Fin* a person or company that makes hostile takeover bids

rainmaker *HR* somebody, especially a lawyer, who procures clients who spend a lot of money on their firm's business

rake it in *Fin* to make a great deal of money (*slang*)

rake-off *Fin* commission (*slang*)

rally *Fin* a rise in share prices after a fall

ramp *Fin* to buy shares with the objective of raising their price. *See also* **rigged market**

rand *Fin* the South African unit of currency, equal to 100 cents

R & D *abbr Ops* research and development

Randlord *Fin* originally a Johannesburg-based mining magnate or tycoon of the late 19th or early 20th centuries, now used informally for any wealthy or powerful Johannesburg businessman

random *Stats* not part of a pattern but governed by chance

random observation method *Gen Mgt* see **activity sampling**

random sampling *Ops* an unbiased **sampling** technique in which every member of a population has an equal chance of being included in the sample. Based on probability theory, random sampling is the process of selecting and canvassing a representative group of individuals from a particular population in order to identify the attributes or attitudes of the population as a whole. Related sampling techniques include: **stratified sampling**, in which the population is divided into classes, and random samples are taken from each class; **cluster sampling**, in which a unit of the sample is a group such as a household; and **systematic sampling**, which refers to samples chosen by any system other than random selection. *See also* **non-random sampling**

range *Stats* the difference between the smallest and the largest observations in a data set

range pricing *Fin* the pricing of individual products so that their prices fit logically within a range of connected products offered by one supplier, and differentiated by a factor such as weight of pack or number of product attributes offered

ranking *Stats* the ordered arrangement of a set of variable values

ratable value *Fin* the value of something as calculated with reference to a rule

ratchet effect *Econ* the result when households adjust more easily to rising incomes than to falling incomes, as, for example, when their consumption drops by less than their income in a recession

rate cap *Fin see* ***cap***

rate of exchange *Fin see* ***exchange rate***

rate of interest *Fin* a percentage charged on a loan or paid on an investment for the use of the money

rate of return *Fin* an accounting ratio of the income from an investment to the amount of the investment, used to measure financial performance. *Also known as* *return*

EXAMPLE There is a basic formula that will serve most needs, at least initially:

[(Current value of amount invested – Original value of amount invested) / Original value of amount invested] × 100% = rate of return

If £1,000 in capital is invested in stock, and one year later the investment yields £1,100, the rate of return of the investment is calculated like this:

[(1100 – 1000) / 1000] × 100% = 100 /1000 × 100% = 10% rate of return

Now, assume £1,000 is invested again. One year later, the investment grows to £2,000 in value, but after another year the value of the investment falls to £1,200. The rate of return after the first year is:

[(2000 – 1000) / 1000] × 100% = 100%

The rate of return after the second year is:

[(1200 – 2000) / 2000] × 100% = – 40%

The average annual return for the two years (also known as average annual arithmetic return) can be calculated using this formula:

(Rate of return for Year 1 + Rate of return for Year 2) / 2 = average annual return

Accordingly:

(100% + – 40%) / 2 = 30%

The average annual rate of return is a percentage, but one that is accurate over only a short period, so this method should be used accordingly.

The geometric or compound rate of return is a better yardstick for measuring investments over the long term, and takes into account the effects of compounding. This formula is more complex and technical.

The real rate of return is the annual return realised on an investment, adjusted for changes in the price due to inflation. If 10% is earned on an investment but inflation is 2%, then the real rate of return is actually 8%.

ratings *Mkting* the proportion of a target audience who are exposed to a television or radio commercial

ratio analysis *Fin* the use of ratios to measure financial performance

ratio-delay study *Gen Mgt see* ***activity sampling***

rationalisation *Gen Mgt* the application of efficiency or effectiveness measures to an organisation. Rationalisation can occur at the onset of a downturn in an organisation's performance or results. It usually takes the form of cutbacks aimed to bring the organisation back to profitability and may involve ***redundancies***, plant closures, and cutbacks in supplies and resources. It often involves changes in ***organisation structure***, particularly in the form of ***downsizing***. The term is also used in a cynical way as a euphemism for mass redundancies.

ratio pyramid *Fin* the analysis of a primary ratio into mathematically linked secondary ratios

raw materials *Ops* items bought for use in the manufacturing or development processes of an organisation. While most often referring to bulk materials, raw materials can also include components, subassemblies, and complete products.

RBA *abbr Fin* Reserve Bank of Australia

RBNZ *abbr Fin* Reserve Bank of New Zealand

RDO *abbr* (*ANZ*) *HR* rostered day off: a day of leave allocated under certain employment agreements to staff in lieu of accumulated overtime

RDP *abbr Fin* Reconstruction and Development Program: a policy framework by means of which the South African government intends to correct

---

Minds are like parachutes. They only function when they are open.   *James Dewar*

the socio-economic imbalances caused by apartheid

RDPR *abbr Fin* refer to drawer please represent

reactive maintenance *Ops* a form of *maintenance* in which equipment and facilities are repaired only in response to a breakdown or a fault. Because of the potential for loss of production, reactive maintenance is at odds with *just-in-time*. *See also* **preventive maintenance**

readership *Mkting* a detailed profile of the readers of a newspaper or magazine

Reaganomics *Econ* the policy of former US President Reagan in the 1980s, who reduced taxes and social security support and increased the national budget deficit to an unprecedented level

real *Fin* after the effects of inflation are taken into consideration

real asset *Fin* a non-movable asset such as land or a building

real balance effect *Econ* the effect on income and employment when prices fall and consumption increases

real capital *Fin* assets that can be assigned a monetary value

real estate *(US) Gen Mgt* property consisting of land or buildings

real estate developer *(US) Gen Mgt* a person or company that develops land or buildings to increase their value

real exchange rate *Fin* an exchange rate that has been adjusted for inflation

real GDP *Econ GDP* adjusted for changes in prices

real growth *Econ* the growth of a country or a household adjusted for changes in prices

real interest rate *Fin* interest rate approximately calculated by subtracting the rate of inflation from the nominal interest rate

real investment *Fin* the purchase of assets such as land, property, and plant and machinery as opposed to the acquisition of securities

realisation concept *Fin* the principle that increases in value should only be recognised on realisation of assets by arm's-length sale to an independent purchaser

reality check *Gen Mgt* a consideration of limiting factors such as cost when discussing or contemplating an ambitious project. In other words, a test to see if something that works in theory will also work in practice. (*slang*)

real purchasing power *Econ* the purchasing power of a country or a household adjusted for changes in prices

real time company *Gen Mgt* a company that uses the Internet and other technologies to respond immediately to customer demands

real time credit card processing *E-com* the online authorisation of a credit card indicating that the credit card has been approved or rejected during the transaction

real time data *Fin* information received very soon after a company comes into existence

real time EDI *E-com* online electronic data interchange, the online transfer and processing of business data, for example, purchase orders, customer invoices, and payment receipts, between suppliers and their customers

real time manager *Gen Mgt* a manager who is responsible for delivering the immediate service that customers expect using the Internet and other technologies

real time transaction *E-com* an Internet payment transaction that is approved or rejected immediately when the customer completes the online order form

rebadge *Fin* to buy a product or service from another company and sell it as part of your own product range

rebate *Fin* **1.** money returned because a payment exceeded the amount required,

---

Companies worry too much about the cost of doing something. They should worry about the cost of not doing it.   *Philip Kotler*

for example, a tax rebate **2.** a discount **3.** of a broker, to reduce part of the commission charged to the client as a promotional offer

rebating *Mkting* a sales promotion technique in which the customer is offered a rebate for reaching volume targets

recd *abbr Fin* received

receipt *Fin* a document acknowledging that something, for example, a payment, has been received

receipts and payments account *Fin* a report of cash transactions during a period. It is used in place of an income and expenditure account when it is not considered appropriate to distinguish between capital and revenue transactions or to include accruals.

receiver *Fin* the person appointed to sell the assets of a company that is insolvent. The proceeds of the sale are used to discharge debts to creditors, with any surplus distributed to shareholders.

Receiver of Revenue *Fin* **1.** a local office of the South African Revenue Service **2.** an informal term for the South African Revenue Service as a whole

receivership *Fin* the control of a receiver, who is appointed by secured creditors or by the court to take control of company property. The most usual reason for the appointment of a receiver is the failure of a company to pay principal sums or interest due to debenture holders whose debt is secured by fixed or floating charges over the assets of the company.

recession *Econ* a stage of the *business cycle* in which economic activity is in slow decline. Recession usually follows a boom, and precedes a *depression*. It is characterised by rising unemployment and falling levels of output and investment.

recessionary gap *Econ* the shortfall in the amount of *aggregate demand* in an economy needed to create full employment

reciprocal cost allocation *Fin* a method of secondary cost allocation generally used to reallocate service department costs over the user departments. Service department costs are recharged over user departments (including other service departments) in a number of iterations until all of the service department costs have been re-charged to users.

reconciliation *Fin* adjustment of an account, such as an individual's own record of a bank account, to match more authoritative information

Reconstruction and Development Program *Fin see RDP*

record date *Gen Mgt* the date when a computer data entry or record is made

recourse *Fin* a source of redress should a debt be dishonoured at maturity

recourse agreement *Fin* an agreement in a hire purchase contract whereby the retailer repossesses the goods being purchased in the event of the hirer failing to make regular payments

recovery *Econ* the return of a country to economic health after a crash or a depression

recovery fund *Fin* a fund that invests in recovery stock

recovery stock *Fin* a share that has fallen in price because of poor business performance, but is now expected to climb due to an improvement in the company's prospects

recruitment *HR* the activity of employing workers to fill vacancies or enrolling new members. Employment recruitment is composed of several stages: verifying that a vacancy exists; drawing up a job specification; finding candidates; selecting them by *interviewing* and other means such as carrying out a *psychometric test*; and making a job offer. Effective recruitment is important in achieving high organisational performance and minimising labour turnover. Employees may be recruited either externally or internally.

recurring billing transaction *E-com* an electronic payment facility based on the automatic charging of a customer's credit card in each payment period

recurring payments *E-com* an electronic payment facility that permits a merchant to process multiple authorisations by the same customer either as multiple payments for a fixed amount or recurring billings for varying amounts

red *Fin* the colour of debit or overdrawn balances in some bank statements
in the red *Fin* in debt, or making a loss (*slang*)

Red Book *Fin* in the United Kingdom, a copy of the Chancellor of the Exchequer's speech published on the day of the Budget. It may be regarded as the country's financial statement and report.

Reddin, William James (*b.* 1930) *Gen Mgt* British-born Canadian academic. Best known for his research on *three-dimensional management*, a development of the work of *Robert Blake* and *Jane Mouton* explained in *Managerial Effectiveness* (1970).

redeemable bond *Fin see* **bond**

redeemable gilt *Fin see* **gilt-edged security**

redeemable shares *Fin* shares which are issued on terms which may require them to be bought back by the issuer at some future date, at the discretion of either the issuer or of the holder. Redemption must comply with the conditions of the Companies Act 1985.

redemption *Fin* **1.** the purchase by a company of its own shares from shareholders **2.** the repayment of a security on a specific date, usually specified when the security is issued

redemption yield *Fin* the rate of interest at which the total of the discounted values of any future payments of interest and capital is equal to the current price of a security

redeployment *HR* the movement of employees by their employer from one location or task to another. Redeployment is often used to minimise redundancies, ensure the fulfilment of a specific order, or ensure the most cost-effective use of employees.

red eye (*US*) *Fin* a pathfinder prospectus (*slang*)

redistributive effect *Fin* an effect of a progressive tax or benefit that tends to equalise people's wealth

red screen market *Fin* in the United Kingdom, a market where the prices are down and are being shown as red on the dealing screens

red tape *Fin* excessive bureaucracy (*slang*)

reducing balance depreciation *Fin see depreciation*

redundancy *HR* dismissal from work because a job ceases to exist. Redundancy occurs most frequently when an employer goes out of business, suffers a drop in business necessitating a cutback in the workforce, or relocates part, or all, of the company. Redundancy may also be due to a reduced requirement for employees to carry out work of a particular kind. Employees who are made redundant may qualify for a *redundancy payment*. If the redundancy process is handled incorrectly, the employer may be faced with claims for *unfair dismissal*. In the United Kingdom, redundancy is defined by the Employment Rights Act 1996. *US term* **layoff**

redundancy package *HR* a package of benefits that an employer gives to somebody who is made redundant. *US term severance package*

redundancy payment *HR* a one-off payment given to a worker who has been made *redundant*, usually calculated with reference to age, length of service, and weekly rate of pay. In the United Kingdom, redundancy payments are regulated by the Employment Rights Act 1996. Some redundancy payments are made in excess of the statutory minimum and also are supplemented by other benefits, such as a car and **outplacement** support. *US* term **severance pay**

redundant capacity *Ops see* **surplus capacity**

re-engineering *Gen Mgt see* **business process re-engineering**

reference 1. *HR* a statement of facts and opinions concerning the qualifications, skills, capabilities, personal qualities, conduct, and attitudes of a person, usually a job applicant. Employers supplying references have a legal obligation to take reasonable care that the information provided is accurate. **2.** *Fin see* **banker's reference**

reference population *Stats* a standard against which a statistical population under study can be compared

reference rate *Fin* a benchmark rate, for example, a bank's own base rate or LIBOR. Lending rates are often expressed as a margin over a reference rate.

reference site *E-com* a customer site where a new technology is being used successfully

referred share *Fin* a share that is ex dividend

refer to drawer *Fin* to refuse to pay a cheque because the account from which it is drawn has too little money in it

refer to drawer please represent *Fin* in the United Kingdom, written on a cheque by the paying banker to indicate that there are currently insufficient funds to meet the payment, but that the bank believes sufficient funds will be available shortly. *See also* **refer to drawer**. *Abbr* **RDPR**

refinance *Fin* to replace one loan with another, especially at a lower rate of interest

refinancing *Fin* the process of taking out a loan to pay off other loans, or loans taken out for that purpose

reflation *Econ* a government policy of reducing unemployment by increasing an economy's **aggregate demand**. *See also* **recession**

refugee capital *Fin* people and resources that come into a country because they have been forced to leave their own country for economic or political reasons

refund *Mkting* the reimbursement of the purchase price of a good or service, for reasons such as faults in manufacturing or dissatisfaction with the service provided

regeneration *Gen Mgt* the redevelopment of industrial or business areas that have suffered decline, in order to increase employment and business activity

regional fund *Fin* a unit trust that invests in the markets of a geographical region

registered bond *Fin* a bond whose ownership is recorded on the books of the issuer

registered broker *Fin* a broker registered on a particular exchange

registered capital *Fin see* **authorised capital**

registered company *Gen Mgt* in the United Kingdom, a company that has lodged official documents with the **Registrar of Companies** at Companies House. A registered company is obliged to conduct itself in accordance with company law. All organisations must register in order to become companies.

registered name *Fin* in the United Kingdom, the name of a company as it is registered at Companies House. It must appear, along with the company's registered number and office on all its letterheads and orders. *See also* **company**, **corporation**

registered number *Fin* in the United Kingdom, a unique number assigned to a company registered at Companies House. It must appear, along with the company's registered name and office on all its letterheads and orders. *See also **company**, corporation*

registered office *Gen Mgt* the official address of a company, which is reproduced on its letterheads and lodged with Companies House, to which all legal correspondence and documents must be delivered

registered security *Fin* a security where the holder's name is recorded in the books of the issuer. *See also **nominee name***

registered share *Fin* a share the ownership of which is recorded on the books of the issuer

registered share capital *Fin* see *authorised share capital*

registered trademark *Gen Mgt* see *trademark*

register of companies *Fin* in the United Kingdom, the list of companies maintained at Companies House. *See also **company**, corporation*

register of directors and secretaries *Fin* in the United Kingdom, a record that every registered company must maintain of the names and residential addresses of directors and the company secretary together with their nationality, occupation, and details of other directorships held. Public companies must also record the date of birth of their directors. The record must be kept at the company's registered office and be available for inspection by shareholders without charge and by members of the public for a nominal fee.

register of directors' interests *Fin* in the United Kingdom, a record that every registered company must maintain of the shares and other securities that have been issued by the company and are held by its directors. It has to be made available for inspection during the company's Annual General Meeting.

Registrar of Companies *Gen Mgt* the official charged with the duty of holding and registering the official start-up and constitutional documents of all *registered companies* in the United Kingdom

registration statement *Fin* in the United States, a document that corporations planning to issue securities to the public have to submit to the Securities and Exchange Commission. It features details of the issuer's management, financial status, and activities, and the purpose of the issue. *See also **shelf registration***

regression analysis *Gen Mgt* a *forecasting* technique used to establish the relationship between quantifiable variables. In regression analysis, data on dependent and independent variables is plotted on a scatter graph or diagram and trends are indicated through a line of best fit. The use of a single independent variable is known as **simple regression analysis**, while the use of two or more independent variables is called **multiple regression analysis**.

regressive tax *Fin* a tax whose percentage falls as the value of the item being taxed, especially income, rises. *See also progressive tax, proportional tax*

regulated price *Fin* a selling price set within guidelines laid down by a regulatory authority, normally governmental

regulated superannuation fund *(ANZ) Fin* an Australian superannuation fund that is regulated by legislation and therefore qualifies for tax concessions. To attain this status, a fund must show that its main function is the provision of pensions, or adopt a corporate trustee structure.

regulation *Fin* laws or rules stipulated by a government or regulatory body, such as the Financial Services Authority or the Securities and Exchange Commission, to provide orderly procedures and to protect consumers and investors

regulator *Gen Mgt* an official or body that monitors the behaviour of companies and the level of competition in particular markets, for example, telecommunications or energy

regulatory body *Fin, Gen Mgt* an independent organisation, usually set up

---

Some people use research like a drunkard uses a lampost: for support not illumination.
David Ogily

by government, that regulates the activities of all companies in an industry

regulatory framework *Fin* the set of legal and professional requirements with which the financial statements of a company must comply. Company reporting is influenced by the requirements of law, of the accountancy profession, and of the stock exchange (for listed companies).

regulatory pricing risk *Fin* the risk an insurance company faces that a government will regulate the prices it can charge

reinsurance *Fin* a method of reducing risk by transferring all or part of an insurance policy to another insurer

reintermediation *E-com* the reintroduction of intermediaries found in traditional retail channels. *See also* **disintermediation**

reinvestment rate *Fin* the interest rate at which an investor is able to reinvest income received from another investment

reinvestment risk *Fin* the risk that it will not be possible to invest the proceeds of an investment at as high a rate as they earned

reinvestment unit trust *Fin* a unit trust that uses dividends to buy more shares in the company issuing them

rejects *Ops* units of output which fail a set quality standard and are subsequently rectified, sold as sub-standard, or disposed of as scrap

relational database *Gen Mgt* a computer database in which different types of data are linked for analysis

relationship management *Mkting* the process of fostering good relations with customers to build loyalty and increase sales

relative income hypothesis *Econ* the theory that consumers are concerned less with their absolute living standards than with consumption relative to other consumers

relaxation allowance *Gen Mgt see* **standard time**

release *E-com* a version of a software program that has been modified. Release 1.0 would be followed by release 1.1 after minor modification, or release 2.0 after major changes to the program.

relevancy concept *Fin* the principle that management accounting must ensure that flexibility is maintained in assembling and interpreting information. This facilitates the exploration and presentation, in a clear, understandable, and timely manner, of as many alternatives as are necessary for impartial and confident decisions to be taken. The process is essentially forward-looking and dynamic. Therefore, the information must satisfy the criteria of being applicable and appropriate.

relevant costs/revenues *Fin* costs and revenues appropriate to a specific management decision. These are represented by future cash flows whose magnitude will vary depending upon the outcome of the management decision made. If stock is sold by a retailer, the relevant cost, used in the determination of the profitability of the transaction, would be the cost of replacing the stock, not its original purchase price, which is a sunk cost. Abandonment analysis, based on relevant cost and revenues, is the process of determining whether or not it is more profitable to discontinue a product or service than to continue it.

relevant interest *(ANZ) Fin* the legal status held by share investors who can legally dispose of, or influence the disposal of, shares

relevant range *Fin* the activity levels within which assumptions about cost behaviour in breakeven analysis remain valid

reliability *Gen Mgt* the quality of being fit for an intended purpose over a continued period of time

reliability-centred maintenance *Ops* a *maintenance* system that focuses on ensuring equipment is always functioning reliably. Reliability-centred maintenance involves assessing each piece of equipment or other asset individually and in the context of how it is being used, for example, frequency of use and volume of output. Analysis is made of its weak points and a *preventive maintenance* schedule is drawn up taking them into account.

reliability concept *Fin* the principle that management accounting information must be of such quality that confidence can be placed in it. Its reliability to the user is dependent on its source, integrity, and comprehensiveness.

relocation *Gen Mgt* the transfer of a business from one location to another. Relocation occurs for a variety of reasons, including the need for more space, the desire to centralise operations, or to be nearer to suppliers, customers, or raw materials.

remuneration *HR see* **earnings**

remuneration package *HR* the salary, pension contributions, bonuses, and other forms of payment or benefit that make up an employee's remuneration

renounceable document *Fin* written proof of ownership for a limited period, for example, a letter of allotment. *See also letter of renunciation*

renting back *Fin see* **sale and leaseback**

renunciation *Fin see* **letter of renunciation**

reorder level *Ops* a level of stock at which a replenishment order should be placed. Traditional 'optimising' systems use a variation on the following computation, which builds in a measure of safety stock and minimises the likelihood of a stock out.

reorganisation bond *Fin* in the United States, a bond issued to creditors of a business that is undergoing a Chapter 11 form of reorganisation. Interest is normally only paid when the company can make the payments from its earnings.

repayment mortgage *Fin* a long-term loan, usually for the purchase of a property, in which the borrower makes monthly payments, part of which cover the interest on the loan and part of which cover the repayment of the principal (see *mortgage*). In the early years, the greater proportion of the payment is used to cover the interest charged but, as the principal is gradually repaid, the interest portion diminishes and the repayment portion increases. *See also* **mortgage**

repeat business *Mkting* the placing of order after order with the same supplier. Repeat business can be implemented by an agreement between the customer and supplier for purchase on a regular basis. It is often used where there are small numbers of customers, or high volumes per product and low product variety. There is only market competition for the first order, and customisation is usually only available for the initial purchase. Sales and marketing have a diminished role once the business has been gained.

repertory grid *Gen Mgt* a technique for gathering information on an individual's personal constructs or perceptions of their environment through mapping interview responses to a matrix. The repertory grid was initially used and developed by clinical psychologists in the 1930s. It has business applications in job analysis, performance measurement, *evaluation of training*, questionnaire design, and *market research*.

repetitive strain injury *Gen Mgt* damage caused to muscles or tendons as the result of prolonged repetitive movements or actions. Repetitive strain injury is most commonly associated with injury to the wrist or arms through the use of computer keyboards. *Abbr* **RSI**

replacement cost *Fin* the cost of replacing an asset or service with its current equivalent

replacement cost accounting *Fin* a method of valuing company assets based on their replacement cost

---

replacement price *Fin* the price at which identical goods or capital equipment could be purchased at the date of valuation

replacement ratio *Econ* the ratio of the total resources received when unemployed to those received when in employment

replenishment system *Ops* an inventory control system that relies on accurate estimates of usage rates and delivery lead times to allow orders to be completed and to ensure stock does not run out. The timing of a replenishment order is crucial, as *buffer stock* should not be allowed to run out during the time it takes for a delivery to arrive.

repo *Fin* **1.** repurchase agreement (*slang*) **2.** in the United States, an open market operation undertaken by the Federal Reserve to purchase securities and agree to sell them back at a stated price on a future date

report *Gen Mgt* a written or verbal statement analysing a particular issue, incident, or state of affairs, usually with some form of recommendations for future action

repositioning *Mkting* a marketing strategy that changes aspects of a product or brand in order to change *market position* and alter consumer perceptions

repossession *Fin* the return of goods bought on hire purchase when the purchaser fails to make the required regular payments. *Also known as **foreclosure**. See also **recourse agreement***

repudiation *Fin* a refusal to pay or acknowledge a debt

repurchase *Fin* of a fund manager, to buy the units in a unit trust when an investor sells

repurchase agreement *Fin* in the bond and money markets, a spot sale of a security combined with its repurchase at a later date and pre-agreed price. In effect, the buyer is lending money to the seller for the duration of the transaction and using the security as collateral. Dealers finance their positions by using repurchase agreements. *Also known as **repo***

request form *E-com* an interactive web page that accepts user-provided data, for example, name, address, or shipping information, that can be saved for recurring use or sent by e-mail to the page owner

required rate of return *Fin* the minimum return for a proposed project investment to be acceptable. *See also **discounted cash flow***

required reserves (*US*) *Fin* the minimum reserves that member banks of the Federal Reserve System have to maintain

requisition *Fin* an official order form used by companies when purchasing a product or service

resale price maintenance *Mkting* an agreement between suppliers or manufacturers and retailers, restricting the price that retailers can ask for a product or service. Resale price maintenance was designed to enable all retailers to make a profit. The Resale Prices Act now prevents this practice on the grounds that it is uncompetitive. Now, unless they can prove that resale price maintenance is in the public interest, manufacturers can only recommend a retail price. *Abbr* **RPM**

research *Fin* the examination of statistics and other information regarding past, present, and future trends or performance that enables analysts to recommend to investors which shares to buy or sell in order to maximise their return and minimise their risk. It may be used either in the top-down approach (where the investor evaluates a market, then an industry, and finally a specific company) or the bottom-up approach (where the investor selects a company and confirms his or her findings by evaluating the company's sector and then its market). Careful research is likely to help investors find the best deals, in particular *value shares* or *growth equities*. *See also **fundamental analysis**, **technical analysis***

In adversity a man is saved by hope.   *Menander*

research and development *Ops* the pursuit of new knowledge and ideas and the application of that knowledge to exploit new opportunities to the commercial advantage of a business. The research and development functions are often grouped together to form a division or department within an organisation. *Abbr* **R & D**

research park (*US*) *Gen Mgt* = *science park*

reserve account *E-com see* **holdback**

reserve bank *Fin* a bank such as a US Federal Reserve Bank that holds the reserves of other banks

Reserve Bank of Australia *Fin* Australia's central bank, which is responsible for managing the Commonwealth's monetary policy, ensuring financial stability, and printing and distributing currency. *Abbr* **RBA**

Reserve Bank of New Zealand *Fin* New Zealand's central bank, which is responsible for managing the government's monetary policy, ensuring financial stability, and printing and distributing currency. *Abbr* **RBNZ**

reserve currency *Fin* foreign currency that a central bank holds for use in international trade

reserve for fluctuations *Fin* money set aside to allow for changes in the values of currencies

reserve price *Fin* a price for a particular lot, set by the vendor, below which an auctioneer may not sell

reserve ratio *Fin* the proportion of a bank's deposits that must be kept in reserve.

EXAMPLE In the United Kingdom and in certain European countries, there is no compulsory ratio, although banks will have their own internal measures and targets to be able to repay customer deposits as they forecast they will be required. In the United States, specified percentages of deposits—established by the Federal Reserve Board—must be kept

by banks in a non-interest-bearing account at one of the twelve Federal Reserve Banks located throughout the country.

In Europe, the reserve requirement of an institution is calculated by multiplying the reserve ratio for each category of items in the reserve base, set by the European Central Bank, with the amount of those items in the institution's balance sheets. These figures vary according to the institution.

The required reserve ratio in the United States is set by federal law, and depends on the amount of checkable deposits a bank holds. The first $44.3 million of deposits are subject to a 3% reserve requirement. Deposits in excess of $44.3 million are subject to 10% reserve requirement. These breakpoints are reviewed annually in accordance with money supply growth. No reserves are required against certificates of deposit or savings accounts.

The reserve ratio requirement limits a bank's lending to a certain fraction of its demand deposits. The current rule allows a bank to issue loans in an amount equal to 90% of such deposits, holding 10% in reserve. The reserves can be held in any combination of till money and deposit at a Federal Reserve Bank.

reserve requirements *Fin* the requirements an agency levies on a nation's banks to hold reserves

reserves *Fin* the money that a bank holds to ensure that it can satisfy its depositors' demands for withdrawals

residual income *Fin* pretax profits less an imputed interest charge for invested capital. Used to assess divisional performance.

residuary legatee *Fin* the person to whom a testator's estate is left after specific bequests have been made

resignation *HR* the act of voluntarily leaving a job. Resignation is normally signalled by a formal letter of resignation. On acceptance, a *notice period* is usually served before the employee can leave.

The strategist's method is very simply to challenge the prevailing assumptions with a single question: Why?
       Kenichi Ohmae

resizing *HR see downsizing*

resolution *Fin* a proposal put to a meeting, for example, an Annual General Meeting of shareholders, on which those present and eligible can vote. *See also* **extraordinary resolution, special resolution**

resource allocation *Ops* the process of assigning human and material resources to projects to ensure that they are used in the optimum way. Resource allocation is used in conjunction with **network analysis** techniques such as **critical-path method**. Basic data assembled for a project is displayed as a **bar chart** with start and finish times and resources required for each day of the project being easily identifiable. If there is a mismatch between planned resources and those available, resources can be reallocated or smoothed by manipulating start and finish times, or changing activities around. Resource allocation is usually computerised.

resource driver *Gen Mgt see cost driver*

resource productivity *Gen Mgt* an environmentally-friendly approach to production based on increasing the productivity of resources to reduce waste

resources *Ops* anything that is available to an organisation to help it achieve its purpose. Resources are often categorised into finance, property, premises, equipment, people, and raw materials.

response bias *Stats* the disparity between information that a survey respondent provides and data analysis, for example, a person claiming to watch little television but giving answers showing 30 hours' weekly viewing

response level *Mkting* a measurement of response to an advertising or marketing campaign

response marketing *E-com* in e-marketing, the process of managing responses or leads from the time they are received through to conversion to sale

response mechanism *Mkting* a means of reply such as a coupon or reply card in

an advertisement or mail shot by which customers can request further information

response rate *Stats* the proportion of subjects in a statistical study who respond to a researcher's questionnaire

response surface methodology *Stats* mathematical and statistical techniques that are used to improve product design systems

responsibility *Gen Mgt* the duty to carry out certain activities and be accountable for them to others

responsibility accounting *Fin* the keeping of financial records with an emphasis on who is responsible for each item

responsibility centre *Fin* a department or organisational function whose performance is the direct responsibility of a specific manager

restated balance sheet *Fin* a balance sheet reframed to serve a particular purpose, such as highlighting depreciation on assets

rest break *HR* a period of time during the working day when an employee is allowed to be away from their workstation for a rest or meal break. Many countries have statutory regulations governing the frequency and length of rest breaks related to the hours worked in a day. Regulations also may cover the requirement for a **rest period** over a working week or month.

rest period *HR* the length of time between periods of work that an employee is entitled to have for rest. Many countries have statutory regulations governing the rights of employees to periods of rest over daily, weekly, and, sometimes, monthly timescales. Different allowances may be given to younger workers. In addition, employees may be entitled to **rest breaks** during the working day.

restraint of trade *Gen Mgt, HR* a term in a contract of employment that restricts a person from carrying on their trade or profession if they leave an organisation. Generally illegal, it is usually intended to prevent key employees from leaving an organisation to set up in competition.

restricted tender *Fin* an offer to buy shares only under specified conditions

restructuring *Gen Mgt see* **corporate restructuring**

result-driven *Gen Mgt* relating to a form of **corporate strategy** focused on outcomes and achievements. A result-driven organisation concentrates on meeting objectives, delivering to the required time, cost, and quality, and holds performance to be more important than **procedures**.

résumé *(US) HR* = **CV**

retail banking *Fin* services provided by commercial banks to individuals as opposed to business customers, that include current accounts, deposit and savings accounts, as well as credit cards, mortgages, and investments. In the United Kingdom, although this service was traditionally provided by high street banks, separate organisations, albeit offshoots of established financial institutions, are now providing Internet and telephone banking services.

retail co-operative *Gen Mgt* a concern for the collective purchase and sale of goods by a group who share profits or benefits.

Retail co-operatives were the first offshoot of the **co-operative movement** and profits were originally shared among members through dividend payments proportionate to a member's purchases.

retailer *Mkting, Ops* an outlet through which products or services are sold to customers. Retailers can be put into three broad groups: independent traders, multiple stores, or **retail co-operatives**.

retail investor *Fin* an investor who buys and sells shares in retail organisations

retail management *Mkting* marketing or financial support aimed at improving the performance of retail outlets

retail price *Mkting* a price charged to customers who buy in limited quantities

retail price index *Econ* a listing of the average levels of prices charged by retailers for goods or services. The retail price index is calculated on a set range of items, and usually excludes luxury goods. It is updated monthly, and provides a running indicator of changing costs. *Abbr* **RPI**

retained profits *or* **retained earnings** *Fin* the amount of profit remaining after tax and distribution to shareholders that is retained in a business and used as a reserve or as a means of financing expansion or investment. *Also known as* **earnings retained**

retention money or payments withheld *Fin* an agreed proportion of a contract price withheld for a specified period after contract completion as security for fulfilment of obligations

retirement *HR* the voluntary or forced termination of employment because of age, illness, or disability. **Retirement age** is often stipulated in the **contract of employment**. Differences between the retirement ages of men and women are no longer allowed in many countries. Employees may take **early retirement** from their employer, or may, with the agreement of their employer, take gradual, or **phased retirement**. A **pension** may be drawn on reaching retirement age. The current policy of a national retirement age, when a statutory pension entitlement is drawn, is under debate in the United Kingdom.

retirement age *HR see* **retirement**

retirement pension *Fin see* **pension**

retraining *HR* **training** designed to enable employees to perform a job that their previous training has not equipped them for or to adapt to changes in the workplace. Retraining may be needed when new methods or equipment are introduced or when jobs for which employees have trained are phased out. It may also be provided by employers or governments for employees who have been made **redundant** and are no longer able to find employment using the skills they already possess. The need for retraining may arise because of a decline in a particular industry sector or because of rapid technological change.

retrenchment *Fin* the reduction of costs in order to improve profitability

retrospective study *Stats* a study that examines data collected before it began, for example, to measure the risk factors that predispose people to disease

return *Fin* 1. the income derived from an activity 2. *see* **rate of return** 3. *see* **tax return**

return on assets *Fin* a measure of profitability calculated by expressing a company's net income as a percentage of total assets.

EXAMPLE Because the ROA formula reflects total revenue, total cost, and assets deployed, the ratio itself reflects a management's ability to generate income during the course of a given period, usually a year.

To calculate ROA, net income is divided by total assets, then multiplied by 100 to express the figure as a percentage:

Net income / total assets × 100 = ROA

If net income is £30, and total assets are £420, the ROA is:

30 / 420 = 0.0714 × 100 = 7.14 %

A variation of this formula can be used to calculate return on net assets (RONA):

Net income / fixed assets + working capital = RONA

And, on occasion, the formula will separate after-tax interest expense from net income:

Net income + interest expense / total assets = ROA

It is therefore important to understand what each component of the formula actually represents.

Some experts recommend using the net income value at the end of the given period, and the assets value from beginning of the period or an average value taken over the complete period, rather than an end-of-the-period value; otherwise, the calculation will include assets that have accumulated during the year, which can be misleading.

return on capital *Fin* a ratio of the profit made in a financial year as a percentage of the capital employed

return on capital employed *Fin* indicates the productivity of capital employed.

The denominator is normally calculated as the average of the capital employed at the beginning and end of year. Problems of seasonality, new capital introduced, or other factors may necessitate taking the average of a number of periods within the year. The ROCE is known as the primary ratio in a ratio pyramid. *See also* **capital employed**

return on equity *Fin* the ratio of a company's net income as a percentage of shareholders' funds.

Return on equity (ROE) is easy to calculate and is applicable to a majority of industries. It is probably the most widely used measure of how well a company is performing for its shareholders.

It is calculated by dividing the net income shown on the income statement (usually of the past year) by shareholders' equity, which appears on the balance sheet:

Net income / owners' equity × 100% = return on equity

For example, if net income is £450 and equity is £2,500, then:

450 / 2,500 = 0.18 × 100% = 18 % return on equity

Return on equity for most companies should be in double figures; investors often look for 15% or higher, while a return of 20% or more is considered excellent. Seasoned investors also review five-year average ROE, to gauge consistency.

return on investment *Fin* a ratio of the profit made in a financial year as a percentage of an investment

EXAMPLE The most basic expression of ROI can be found by dividing a company's net profit (also called net earnings) by the total investment (total debt plus total equity), then multiplying by 100 to arrive at a percentage:

Net profit / Total investment × 100 = ROI

If, say, net profit is £30 and total investment is £250, the ROI is:

30 / 250 = 0.12 × 100 = 12%

A more complex variation of ROI is an equation known as the Du Pont formula:

(Net profit after taxes / Total assets) = (Net profit after taxes / Sales) × Sales / Total assets

If, for example, net profit after taxes is £30, total assets are £250, and sales are £500, then:

30 / 250 = 30 / 500 × 500 / 250 =12% = 6% × 2 = 12%

Champions of this formula, which was developed by the Du Pont Company in the 1920s, say that it helps reveal how a company has both deployed its assets and controlled its costs, and how it can achieve the same percentage return in different ways.

For shareholders, the variation of the basic ROI formula used by investors is:

Net income + (current value – original value) /original value × 100 = ROI

If, for example, somebody invests £5,000 in a company and a year later has earned £100 in dividends, while the value of the shares is £5,200, the return on investment would be:

100 + (5,200 – 5,000) / 5,000 × 100 = (100 + 200) /5,000 × 100 = 300 / 5,000 =.06 × 100 = 6% ROI

It is vital to understand exactly what a return on investment measures, for example, assets, equity, or sales. Without this understanding, comparisons may be misleading. It is also important to establish whether the net profit figure used is before or after provision for taxes.

return on net assets *Fin* a ratio of the profit made in a financial year as a percentage of the assets of a company

return on sales *Fin* a company's operating profit or loss as a percentage of total sales for a given period, typically a year. *See also profit margin*

EXAMPLE Return on sales shows how efficiently management uses the sales income, thus reflecting its ability to manage costs and overheads and operate efficiently. It also indicates a firm's ability to withstand adverse conditions such as falling prices, rising costs, or declining sales. The higher the figure, the better a company is able to endure price wars and falling prices. It is calculated using the basic formula:

Operating profit / total sales × 100 = Percentage return on sales

So, if a company earns £30 on sales of £400, its return on sales is:

30 / 400 = 0.075 × 100 = 7.5%

Some calculations use operating profit before subtracting interest and taxes; others use after-tax income. Either figure is acceptable as long as ROS comparisons are consistent. Using income before interest and taxes will produce a higher ratio.

Return on sales has its limits, since it sheds no light on the overall cost of sales or the four factors that contribute to it: materials, labour, production overheads, and administrative and selling overheads.

returns to scale *Econ* the proportionate increase in a country's or firm's output as a result of proportionate increases in all its inputs

revaluation *Econ* the restoration of the value of a country's depreciated currency, for example, by encouraging exports to increase foreign exchange

revaluation of currency *Fin* an increase in the value of a currency in relation to others. In situations where there is a floating exchange rate, a currency will normally find its own level automatically but this will not happen if there is a fixed exchange rate. Should a government have persistent balance of payment surpluses, it may exceptionally decide to revalue its currency, making imports cheaper but its exports more expensive.

revaluation reserve *Fin* money set aside to account for the fact that the values of assets may vary due to accounting in different currencies

revalue *Fin* to change the exchange rate of a currency

Revans, Reginald William (1907–2003) *Gen Mgt* British educator and academic. Originator of *action learning*, explained in the book of the same name (1980), which rejected the traditional approach to *management education* in favour of learning from sharing problems with others.

revenue *Fin* the income generated by a product or service over a period of time

revenue anticipation note *Fin* a government-issued debt instrument for which expected income from taxation is collateral

revenue bond *Fin* a bond that a government issues, to be repaid from the money made from the project financed with it

revenue centre *Fin* a centre devoted to raising revenue with no responsibility for costs, for example, a sales centre

revenue ledger *Fin* a record of all income received by an organisation

revenue sharing *Fin* **1.** distribution to states by the US federal government of money that it collects in taxes **2.** the distribution of income within limited partnerships

revenue stamp *Fin* a stamp that a government issues to certify that somebody has paid a tax

revenue tariff *Fin* a tax levied on imports or exports to raise revenue for a national government

reversal stop *Fin* a price at which a trader stops buying and starts selling a security, or vice-versa

reverse bear hug *Gen Mgt see* **bear hug**

reverse commuter *Gen Mgt* a commuter who travels to work in the opposite direction to the majority of people (*slang*)

reverse engineering *Ops* the taking apart of a product to establish how it was put together. Reverse engineering enables a company to redesign a product. It also enables competitors to analyse the composition, technology, and development of rival products. *Also known as* **decompilation**

reverse leverage *Fin* the negative flow of cash, or borrowing money at a rate of interest higher than the expected rate of return on investing the money borrowed

reverse mortgage *Fin* a financial arrangement in which a lender such as a bank takes over a mortgage then pays an annuity to the homeowner

reverse split *Fin* the issuing to shareholders of a fraction of one share for every share that they own. *See also* **split**

reverse takeover *Gen Mgt* the *takeover* of a large company by a smaller one, or the takeover of a public company by a private one

revolving charge account *Fin* a charge account with a company for use in buying that company's goods with *revolving credit*

revolving credit *Fin* a credit facility which allows the borrower, within an overall credit limit and for a set period, to borrow or repay debt as required

revolving fund *Fin* a fund the resources of which are replenished from the revenue of the projects that it finances

revolving loan *Fin* a loan facility where the borrower can choose the number and timing of withdrawals against their bank loan and where any money repaid may be reborrowed at a future date. Such loans are available both to businesses and personal customers.

reward management *HR* the establishment, maintenance, and development of a system that rewards the work done by employees. Reward management involves offering not only *basic pay*, but also an *incentive scheme* and *fringe benefits*. Levels of reward may be based on different criteria. Some involve

---

To invent, you need a good imagination and a pile of junk.   *Thomas Edison*

performance appraisal to determine whether an employee merits a certain reward, while others may be dependent on length of service, type of job, or team or company performance. The notion of a reward system is gradually replacing the traditional idea of a standard pay system, as it incorporates all aspects of employee compensation into one package.

Ricardo, David (1772–1823) *Gen Mgt* British economist. Developer of the concept of *comparative advantage*, as explained in his book *Principles of Political Economy* (1820).

rich media *E-com* technology that can integrate audio, video, and high-resolution graphics

Ridderstråle, Jonas (*b.* 1966) *Gen Mgt* Swedish academic. See **Nordström, Kjell**

ride the curve *E-com* to take advantage of rapid growth in demand for a new technology as it becomes widely adopted (*slang*)

rigged market *Fin* a market where two or more parties are buying and selling securities among themselves to give the impression of active trading with the intention of attracting investors to purchase the shares. This practice is illegal in the majority of jurisdictions.

right first time *Ops* a concept integral to *total quality management*, where there is a commitment to customers not to make mistakes. The approach requires employees at all levels to commit to, and take responsibility for, achieving this goal. *Quality circles* are sometimes used as a method to help in this process.

rights issue *Fin* an issue of new shares to existing holders who have the right to buy them at a discount

rightsizing *Gen Mgt* **corporate re-structuring**, or **rationalisation**, with the aim of reducing costs and improving efficiency and effectiveness. Rightsizing is often used as a euphemism for *downsizing*, or *delayering*, with the suggestion that it is not as far-reaching. Rightsizing

can also be used to describe increasing the size of an organisation, perhaps as an attempt to correct a previous downsizing, or delayering, exercise.

rights letter *Fin see **letter of allotment***

rights offer *Fin see **rights issue***

rights offering *Fin* an offering for sale of a *rights issue*

ring *Fin* **1.** a trading pit **2.** a concert party **3.** a trading session on the London Metal Exchange

ring-fence *Fin* **1.** to set aside a sum of money for a specific project **2.** to allow one company within a group to go into liquidation without affecting the viability of the group as a whole or any other company within it

ring member *Fin* a member of the London Metal Exchange

ring trading *Fin* business conducted in a trading pit

rising bottoms *Fin* a pattern on a graph of the price of a security or commodity against time that shows an upward price movement following a period of low prices (*slang*) See also **chartist**

risk *Gen Mgt* the possibility of suffering damage or loss in the face of uncertainty about the outcome of actions, future events, or circumstances. Organisations are exposed to various types of risk including damage to property, injury to personnel, financial loss, and legal liability. These may affect profitability, hinder the achievement of objectives, or lead to business interruption or failure. Risk may be deemed high or low depending on the probability of an adverse outcome. Risks that can be quantified on the basis of past experience are insurable and those that cannot be calculated are uninsurable.

risk-adjusted return on capital *Fin* return on capital calculated in a way that takes into account the risks associated with income.

EXAMPLE Being able to compare a high-risk, potentially high-return investment with a low-risk, lower-return investment helps answer a key question that confronts every investor: is it worth the risk?

There are several ways to calculate risk-adjusted return. Each has its strengths and shortcomings. All require particular data, such as an investment's rate of return, the risk-free return rate for a given period, and a market's performance and its standard deviation.

The choice of calculation depends on an investor's focus: whether it is on upside gains or downside losses.

Perhaps the most widely used is the **Sharpe ratio**. This measures the potential impact of return volatility on expected return and the amount of return earned per unit of risk. The higher a fund's Sharpe ratio, the better its historical risk-adjusted performance, and the higher the number the greater the return per unit of risk. The formula is:

(Portfolio return – Risk-free return) / Std deviation of portfolio return = Sharpe ratio

Take, for example, two investments, one returning 54%, the other 26%. At first glance, the higher figure clearly looks like the better choice, but because of its high volatility it has a Sharpe ratio of .279, while the investment with a lower return has a ratio of .910. On a risk-adjusted basis the latter would be the wiser choice.

The Treynor ratio also measures the excess of return per unit of risk. Its formula is:

(Portfolio return – Risk-free return) / Portfolio's beta = Treynor ratio

In this formula (and others that follow), **beta** is a separately calculated figure that describes the tendency of an investment to respond to marketplace swings. The higher beta the greater the volatility, and vice versa.

A third formula, Jensen's measure, is often used to rate a money manager's performance against a market index, and whether or not a investment's risk was worth its reward. The formula is:

(Portfolio return – Risk-free return) – Portfolio beta × (Benchmark return – Risk-free return) = Jensen's measure

risk analysis *Gen Mgt* the identification of risks to which an organisation is exposed and the assessment of the potential impact of those risks on the organisation. The aim of risk analysis is to identify and measure the risks associated with different courses of action in order to inform the *decision-making* process. In the context of business decision-making, risk analysis is especially used in investment decisions and capital investment appraisal. Techniques used in risk analysis include sensitivity analysis, probability analysis, *simulation*, and modelling. Risk analysis may be used to develop an organisational *risk profile*, and also may be the first stage in a *risk management* programme.

risk arbitrage *Fin arbitrage* without certainty of profit

risk assessment *Gen Mgt* the determination of the level of risk in a particular course of action. Risk assessments are an important tool in areas such as *health and safety* management and *environmental management*. Results of a risk assessment can be used, for example, to identify areas in which safety can be improved. Risk assessment can also be used to determine more intangible forms of risk, including economic and social risk, and can inform the *scenario planning* process. The amount of risk involved in a particular course of action is compared to its expected benefits to provide evidence for decision-making.

risk-bearing economy of scale *Fin* conducting business on such a large scale that the risk of loss is reduced because it is spread over so many independent events, as in the issuance of insurance policies

risk capital *Fin see venture capital*

risk factor *Gen Mgt* the degree of risk in a project or other business activity

risk-free return *Fin* the profit made from an investment that involves no risk

risk management *Gen Mgt* the range of activities undertaken by an organisation to control and minimise threats to the continuing efficiency, profitability, and success of its operations. The process of risk management includes the identification and analysis of risks to which the organisation is exposed, the assessment of potential impacts on the business, and deciding what action can be taken to eliminate or reduce risk and deal with the impact of unpredictable events causing loss or damage. Risk management strategies include taking out insurance against financial loss or legal liability and introducing safety or security measures.

risk profile *Gen Mgt* **1.** an outline of the risks to which an organisation is exposed. An organisational risk profile may be developed in the course of **risk analysis** and used for **risk management**. It examines the nature of the threats faced by an organisation, the likelihood of adverse effects occurring, and the level of disruption and costs associated with each type of risk. **2.** an analysis of the willingness of individuals or organisations to take risks. A risk profile describes the level of risk considered acceptable by an individual or by the leaders of an organisation, and considers how this will affect **decision-making** and **corporate strategy**.

ROA *abbr Fin* return on assets

robot *Ops* a programmable machine equipped with sensing capabilities used in **production** environments. Robots are used in automatic assembly and **automated handling** situations.

robotics *Gen Mgt* the industrial use of robots to perform repetitive tasks. Robotics is an application of artificial intelligence.

rocket scientist *Fin* an employee of a financial institution who creates innovative securities that usually include derivatives (*slang*)

Roddick, Anita Lucia (*b.* 1942) *Gen Mgt* British business executive. Founder of the Body Shop, whose principles, reflected in the company's **core values** of **social responsibility** and care for the environment, are explained in her autobiography *Business as Unusual* (2000).

rodo kinko *Fin* in Japan, a financial institution specialising in providing credit for small businesses

ROE *abbr Fin* return on equity

Roethlisberger, Fritz Jules (1898–1974) *Gen Mgt* US academic. Collaborated with **Elton Mayo** in the **Hawthorne experiments**, leading the research and data analysis and publicising the findings in *Management and the Worker* (1939).

rogue trader *Fin* a dealer in stocks and shares who uses illegal methods to make profits

ROI *abbr Fin* return on investment

role ambiguity *Gen Mgt* a lack of clarity on the part of an employee about the expectations of colleagues concerning his or her role within an organisation. Role ambiguity may occur in newly created posts or in positions that are undergoing change. When role ambiguity extends to responsibilities or priorities it can lead to **role conflict**.

role conflict *Gen Mgt* a situation in which two or more job requirements are incompatible. Role conflict can arise from others' misperceptions of what the priorities of a role holder should be. It may also be caused by a division of loyalties between departmental peers and the organisation, or between personal professional ethics and those of the organisation.

role culture *Gen Mgt* a style of **corporate culture**, identified by **Charles Handy**, which assumes that employees are rational and that roles can be defined and discharged within clearly defined procedures. An organisation with a role culture is believed to be generally very stable but poor at implementing **change management**.

role playing *HR* performing either as yourself in a contrived situation, in order to analyse how you react, or in the manner expected of another person. The role playing technique is a useful **training** tool, as it enables trainees to gain a better understanding of themselves, other people, new situations, and different jobs.

rolling budget *Fin* a budget continuously updated by adding a further accounting period (month or quarter) when the earliest accounting period has expired. Its use is particularly beneficial where future costs and/or activities cannot be forecast accurately. *Also known as* **continuous budget**

rolling forecast *Fin* a continuously updated forecast whereby each time actual results are reported, a further forecast period is added and intermediate period forecasts are updated

roll-out *Mkting* the full-scale implementation of an advertising campaign or marketing programme

roll up *Fin* the addition of interest amounts to principal in loan repayments

root cause analysis *Gen Mgt* a technique used in **problem-solving** to identify the underlying reason why something has gone wrong or why a difficulty has arisen. The root cause of a problem may be identified by repeatedly asking the question 'Why?', by examining relationships of cause and effect, or by defining the distinctive features of the problem and developing a number of hypotheses that can be tested. Root cause analysis has been criticised on the grounds that it presupposes a single source for a problem, while in reality the situation may be more complex.

rootless capitalism *Gen Mgt* a form of capitalism that is not tied to a specific country or economy

rort *(ANZ) Gen Mgt* an illegal or underhand strategy

ROS *abbr Fin* return on sales

RosettaNet *E-com* a consortium focusing on the development of e-business interfaces and a common global business language that would permit sharing of efficient e-business processes, for example, manufacturing, distribution, and sales

rostered day off *HR see* RDO

ROTFL *abbr Gen Mgt* rolling on the floor laughing (*slang*)

round figures *Fin* figures that have been adjusted up or down to the nearest 10, 100, 1,000, and so on

rounding *Stats* the practice of reducing the number of significant digits in a number, for example, expressing a figure that has four decimal places with only two decimal places

router *Gen Mgt* a telecommunications device used to transfer calls to an alternative network that may offer cheaper rates

routing number *(US) Fin* = **sort code**

royalties *Fin* a proportion of the income from the sale of a product paid to its creator, for example, an inventor, author, or composer

RPI *abbr Econ* retail price index

RPIX *Fin* an index based on the Retail Price Index that excludes mortgage interest payments and is commonly referred to as the underlying rate of inflation

RPIY *Fin* an index based on the Retail Price Index that excludes mortgage interest payments and indirect taxation

RPM *abbr Mkting* resale price maintenance

RSI *abbr Gen Mgt* repetitive strain injury

RTM *abbr Gen Mgt* read the manual (*slang*)

RTSC *abbr Gen Mgt* read the source code (*slang*)

RUBBY *Mkting* Rich Urban Biker (*slang*)

Rucker plan *Ops* a type of **gain sharing** scheme that is concerned with the value added by labour. The Rucker plan was developed in the 1950s by Allen Rucker. A typical Rucker plan includes a **suggestion scheme**, a committee system, and a **bonus** formula, based on **value added**. It assesses the relationship between the value added to goods as they pass through

---

the manufacturing process, and the total labour costs. Bonuses are earned when the current ratio is better than the base ratio over a given time period. A Rucker plan usually has a far less elaborate structure than the similar *Scanlon plan*.

rule of 78 *Fin* a method used to calculate the rebate on a loan with front-loaded interest that has been repaid early. It takes into account the fact that as the loan is repaid, the share of each monthly payment related to interest decreases, while the share related to repayment increases.

rumortrage (*US*) *Fin* speculation in securities issued by companies that are rumoured to be the target of an imminent takeover attempt (*slang*)

run 1. *Fin* an incidence of bank customers en masse and simultaneously withdrawing their entire funds because of a lack of confidence in the institution **2.** *Fin* an incidence of owners of holdings in a particular currency selling en masse and simultaneously usually because of a lack of confidence in the currency **3.** *Stats* an uninterrupted sequence of the same value in a statistical series

running account credit *Fin* an overdraft facility, credit card, or similar system that allows customers to borrow up to a specific limit and reborrow sums previously repaid by either writing a cheque or using their card

running yield *Fin see yield*

run with something *Gen Mgt* to pursue an idea or project (*slang*)

rust belt (*US*) *Gen Mgt* the manufacturing areas in the US Midwest that have experienced severe decline following the move away from manufacturing to service industries (*slang*)

S

SA *abbr Fin* Société Anonyme, Sociedad Anónima, Sociedade Anónima

sabbatical *HR* a period of *special leave*, traditionally a year, granted to an employee for the purpose of study, work experience, or travel

sabotage *Gen Mgt* a deliberate action to damage property or equipment. In an industrial context sabotage may be undertaken by employees who have a grievance against an employer in order to halt production or undermine the efficiency of an organisation. Sabotage of this type may include time wasting or other measures designed to reduce *productivity*. Sabotage against organisations is also undertaken by terrorist or political groups in protest against their actions or policies. Security measures may be necessary to prevent sabotage.

SADC *abbr Fin* Southern African Development Community: an organisation that aims to harmonise economic development in countries of Southern Africa. Member countries are Angola, Botswana, Democratic Republic of Congo, Lesotho, Malawi, Mauritius, Mozambique, Namibia, South Africa, Seychelles, Swaziland, Tanzania, Zambia, Zimbabwe.

safe custody *Fin see safe keeping*

safe hands *Fin* **1.** investors who buy securities and are unlikely to sell in the short- to medium-term **2.** securities held by friendly investors

safe keeping *Fin* the holding of share certificates, deeds, wills, or a locked deed box on behalf of customers by a financial institution. Securities are often held under the customer's name in a locked cabinet in the vault so that if the customer wishes to sell, the bank can forward the relevant certificate to the broker. A will is also normally held in this way so that it may be handed to the executor on the customer's death. Deed boxes are always described as 'contents unknown to the bank'. Most institutions charge a fee for this service. *Also known as* **safe custody**

safety stock *Fin* the quantity of stocks of raw materials, work in progress, and finished goods which are carried in excess of the expected usage during the lead time of an activity. The safety stock reduces the probability of operations having to be suspended due to running out of stocks.

salad
let's toss it around and see if it makes a salad *Gen Mgt* let's try this idea and see if it is successful (*slang*)

salaried partner *Fin* a partner, often a junior one, who receives a regular salary, detailed in the partnership agreement

salary *HR* a form of *pay* given to employees at regular intervals in exchange for the work they have done. Traditionally, a salary is a form of remuneration given to professional employees on a monthly basis. In modern usage, the word refers to any form of pay that employees receive on a regular basis, and it is often used interchangeably with the term *wages*. A salary is normally paid straight into an employee's account.

salary ceiling *HR* **1.** the highest level on a *pay scale* that a particular employee can achieve under their contract **2.** an upper limit on *pay* imposed by government or according to *trade union* and employer agreements

salary review *HR* a reassessment of an individual employee's rate of *pay*, usually carried out on an annual basis

salary scale *HR see pay scale*

sale and leaseback *Fin* the sale of an asset, usually buildings, to a third party that then leases it back to the owner. It is used by a company as a way of raising finance. *Also known as* **renting back**

sale by instalments *Fin see hire purchase*

---

sale by tender *Fin* the sale of an asset to interested parties who have been invited to make an offer. It is sold to the party that makes the highest offer. *See also* **issue by tender**

sales *Mkting* the activity of selling a company's products or services, the income generated by this, or the department that deals with selling

sales channel *Gen Mgt* a means of distributing products to the marketplace, either directly to the end customer, or indirectly through intermediaries such as retailers or dealers

sales conference *Mkting* a conference at which the members of a sales team are brought together for a review or a significant announcement, such as a product launch.

Sales conferences are also useful for ensuring that sales representatives are fully aware of company policies, products, and support; without these, time spent with customers may be unproductive. They also play a key role in motivating sales teams and building team spirit, an important factor for people who spend most of their time working alone. In addition, conferences can be used to reward high achievement. Many organisations run annual incentive and recognition programmes for sales employees, and using a national conference as the occasion for the award ceremony can confer real status on the winner and raise the profile of the programme among the whole salesforce, encouraging high levels of participation and effort.

sales contest *Mkting* a prize competition for salespeople, often part of an *incentive scheme*, designed to increase sales. A sales contest winner is usually the person who has achieved the most sales for a particular time period.

salesforce *Mkting* a group of salespeople or sales representatives responsible for the sales of either a single product or the entire range of an organisation's products. A salesforce normally reports to a **sales manager**. *Also known as* **sales team**

salesforce communications *Mkting* communications aimed at improving the performance and market awareness of a salesforce

sales forecast *Mkting* a prediction of future sales, based mainly on past sales performance. Sales forecasting takes into account the economic climate, current sales trends, company capacity for production, *company policy*, and *market research*. A sales forecast can be a good indicator of future sales in stable market conditions, but may be less reliable in times of rapid market change.

sales manager *Mkting* the manager directly responsible for the planning, organisation, and performance of the **salesforce**

sales network *Mkting* the distribution network by which goods and services are sold. A sales network will include both independent agents and retailers.

sales office *Mkting* the department responsible for selling a company's products or services, or the office in the company's premises that this department occupies

sales order *Fin* an acknowledgement by a supplier of a purchase order. It may contain terms which override those of the purchaser.

sales outlet *Mkting* a company's office that deals with customers in a particular region or country

sales per employee *Fin* an indicator of labour productivity. *See also* **profit per employee**

sales plan *Gen Mgt* the development of the future objectives of a sales department in order to improve performance and increase sales. A sales plan is a form of *business plan* that sets out the short- and long-term opportunities for the sales department, concentrating on building on the department's strengths and analysing and avoiding weaknesses. It also includes the setting of future sales objectives, based on realistic projections, looking at future costs, and taking into account the objectives of other departments.

sales presentation *Mkting* a structured product presentation using a binder, flipchart, or laptop computer

sales promotion *Mkting* activities, usually short-term, designed to attract attention to a particular product and to increase its sales using *advertising* and publicity. Sales promotion usually runs in conjunction with an advertising campaign that offers free samples or money-off coupons. During the period of a sales promotion, the product may be offered at a reduced price and the campaign may be supported by additional telephone or door-to-door selling or by competitions. *Also known as* **promotion**

sales promotion agency *Mkting* an organisation that specialises in planning, creating, and implementing sales promotion activities

sales quota *Gen Mgt* a target set for the *salesforce* stating the number and range of products or services that should be sold

sales representative *Mkting* a salesperson selling the products or services of a particular organisation or manufacturer. Sales representatives are sometimes employed directly by a company as part of the *salesforce*, or they may work independently and be employed by contract. Sales representatives are often paid on a commission basis.

sales resistance *Mkting* a potential customer's refusal to allow a *sales representative's* sales pitch to persuade them to buy. Sales resistance may be caused, for example, by lack of interest in, or determined dislike of, the product or service offered.

sales statistics *Mkting* data relating to the sales of a particular *product*, service, or *brand*. Sales statistics include numbers and types of products sold, areas where they are sold, calls and visits made, contacts established, categories of customers, costs and time spent on sales activities, and administration. These statistics are often used in conjunction with the *sales*

plan and for sales forecasting. They can also be used to identify areas of weakness in sales support staff and to identify areas for training. Statistics can also contribute to the identification of profitable product lines or products to *abandon*.

sales team *Mkting see* **salesforce**

sales territory *Mkting* a defined area within which a designated salesperson is responsible for selling a product or service. A sales territory is usually organised along geographical lines, for example, counties or regions, but it can also be defined by *market sector* or by product group.

sales turnover *Mkting* the total amount sold within a specified time period, usually a year. Sales turnover is often expressed in monetary terms but can also be expressed in terms of the total amount of stock or products sold.

salmon day *Gen Mgt* a day spent making a great deal of effort to achieve something but getting nowhere (*slang*)

sample *Stats* a subset of a population in a statistical study chosen so that selected properties of the overall population can be investigated

sample size *Stats* the number of individuals included in a statistical survey

sample survey *Stats* a statistical study of a sample of individuals designed to collect information on specific subjects such as buying habits or voting behaviour

sampling 1. *Mkting* a sales promotion technique in which customers and prospects are offered a free sample of a product **2.** *Ops* the selection of a small proportion of a set of items being studied, from which valid inferences about the whole set or population can be made. Sampling makes it possible to obtain valid research results when it is impracticable to survey the whole population. The size of the sample needed for valid results depends on a number of factors, including the uniformity of the population being studied and the level of accuracy

---

Good order is the foundation of all good things. *Edmund Burke*

required. The technique is based on the laws of probability, and a number of different sampling methods can be used, including *random sampling* and *non-random sampling*. Specialised applications of sampling include *activity sampling*, *acceptance sampling*, and *attribute sampling*.

sampling design *Stats* the procedure by which a particular sample is chosen from a population

sampling error *Stats* the difference between the population characteristic being estimated in a statistical study and the result produced by the sample investigated

sampling units *Stats* the elements chosen to be sampled by a sampling design

sampling variation *Stats* variation between different samples of the same size taken from the same population

samurai bond *Fin* a bond issue denominated in yen and issued in Japan by a foreign institution

sandbag *Fin* in a hostile *takeover* situation, to enter into talks with the bidder and attempt to prolong them as long as possible, in the hope that a white *knight* will appear and rescue the target company (*slang*)

S&L *abbr Fin* savings and loan association

S&P 500 *abbr Fin* Standard & Poor's Composite 500 Stock Index

S&P Index *abbr Fin* Standard & Poor's Composite 500 Index

sanity check *Gen Mgt* a check to verify that no obvious mistakes have been made (*slang*)

Santa Claus rally (*US*) *Fin* a rise in stock prices in the last week of the year

sarakin *Fin* the Japanese term for a finance company that charges high interest rates to personal customers

SARL *abbr Fin* Société à responsabilité limitée

SARS *abbr Fin* South African Revenue Service

SAS *abbr Fin* Statement of Auditing Standards

satellite centre *Gen Mgt* a *telecentre* that houses employees from a single organisation

save as you earn *HR* a system for saving on a regular basis that is encouraged by the government through tax concessions. *Abbr* **SAYE**

savings *Fin* money set aside by consumers for a particular purpose, to meet contingencies, or to provide an income during retirement. Savings, money in deposit and savings accounts, differ from investments, for example, on the stock market, in that they are not subject to price fluctuations and are thus considered safer.

savings account *Fin* an account with a financial institution that pays interest. *See also fixed rate, gross interest, net interest*

savings and loan association *Fin* a chartered bank that offers savings accounts, pays dividends, and invests in new mortgages. *See also thrift institution*

savings bank *Fin* a bank that specialises in managing small investments. *See also thrift institution*

savings bond *Fin* a US bond that an individual buys from the federal government

savings certificate *Fin see National Savings Certificate*

savings function *Econ* an expression of the extent to which people save money instead of spending it

savings ratio *Econ* the proportion of the income of a country or household that is saved in a particular period

SAYE *abbr HR* save as you earn

SC *abbr Fin* Securities Commission

scaleability *E-com* the capability of the hardware and software that support an e-business to grow in capacity as transaction demand increases

Scanlon plan *HR* a type of *gain sharing* plan that pays a *bonus* to employees for incremental improvements. The Scanlon plan was developed by Joseph Scanlon in the 1930s. A typical Scanlon plan includes an employee *suggestion scheme*, a committee system, and a formula-based bonus system. The simplest formula is: base ratio = HR payroll costs divided by net sales or production value. A Scanlon organisation is characterised by *teamwork* and *employee participation*. A bonus is paid when the current ratio is better than that of the base period. A Scanlon plan focuses attention on the variables over which the organisation and its employees have some control. *See also Rucker plan*

scatter *Stats* the amount by which a set of observations deviates from its mean

scatter chart *or* **scatter diagram** *Stats* a chart or diagram that plots a sample of bivariate observations in two dimensions

scenario *Gen Mgt* a possible future state of affairs or sequence of events. Scenarios are imagined or projected on the basis of current circumstances and trends and expectations of change in the future.

scenario planning *Gen Mgt* a technique that requires the use of a scenario in the process of *strategic planning* to aid the development of *corporate strategy* in the face of uncertainty about the future. Scenario planning was developed in a military context during the 1940s. Its use in a business context was pioneered at Royal Dutch Shell during the 1960s and increased after the 1972 oil crisis. The process of identifying alternative scenarios of the future, based on a range of differing assumptions, can help managers anticipate changes in the business environment and raise awareness of the frame of reference within which they are operating. The scenarios are then used to assist in both the development of strategies for dealing with unexpected events

and the choice between alternative strategic options.

Schein, Edgar (*b.* 1928) *Gen Mgt* US academic. The first to define *corporate culture* in *Organizational Culture and Leadership* (1985), and the developer of the notion of the *psychological contract*, originated by *Chris Argyris*.

Schein completed a PhD in social psychology at Harvard and, after graduating in 1952, carried out research into leadership as part of the Army Program. He joined MIT in 1956 and has remained there ever since. At MIT Schein researched the similarities between the brainwashing of POWs and the techniques of indoctrination used by corporations. Out of this came Schein's book *Coercive Persuasion*. His subsequent work and writing has mainly been on organisational culture, organisation development, and career development.

schmooze *Gen Mgt* to behave flatteringly during a social event towards somebody who might be in a position to benefit your career (*slang*)

Schön, Donald (1931–97) *Gen Mgt* US academic. Co-author, with Chris Argyris, of *Organizational Learning* (1978). *See also Argyris, Christopher*

Schonberger, Richard (*b.* 1937) *Gen Mgt* US industrial engineer and writer. Known for showing how techniques such as *total quality management* and *just-in-time* can be used to achieve *world class manufacturing*. Author of *World Class Manufacturing* (1986).

Schumacher, Ernst Friedrich (1911–77) *Gen Mgt* German economist. Author of *Small is Beautiful* (1973), a counterblast to the dominance of big companies. Schumacher developed his people-centred approach to life and business working alongside *Reg Revans*.

science park *Gen Mgt* an area developed as a location for high-tech or research-based companies. Usually developed by a university or local authority, a science park is often in the same locality as a higher education establishment. *US term* ***research park***

scientific management *Gen Mgt, HR* an analytical approach to managing activities by optimising efficiency and ***productivity*** through measurement and control. Scientific management theories, attributed to ***Frederick Winslow Taylor***, dominated the 20th century, and many management techniques such as ***benchmarking***, ***total quality management***, and ***business process re-engineering*** result from a scientific management approach. Other figures such as ***Henry Gantt*** and ***Frank*** and ***Lillian Gilbreth*** were firmly in the scientific school and furthered its influence, particularly through the ***time and motion study***. Such was the dominance of Taylor's influence that scientific management is also known as Taylorism. The main criticism of Taylorism is that it degenerated into an inhumane and mechanistic approach to working, treating people like machines.

scorched earth policy *Gen Mgt* destructive actions taken by an organisation in defence against a hostile ***takeover***. Extreme actions under a scorched earth policy may include voluntary liquidation or selling off critical assets. A scorched earth policy may come into play if the value of the company to be acquired exceeds the value of the company making a hostile bid. (*slang*)

scrap *Fin* discarded material that has some value

screen-based activity *Gen Mgt* a task that requires access to a computer

screening study *Stats* a medical statistical study of a population carried out to investigate the prevalence of a disease

screen popping *Gen Mgt see* ***computer telephony integration*** (*slang*)

screensaver *E-com* a program that displays a series of moving images, designed to prevent a static image being burnt into the phosphor monitor screen when a computer is idle

scrip dividend *Fin* a dividend that shareholders can accept in the form of possibly fractional shares of the company instead of cash

scrip issue *Fin* a proportional issue of free shares to existing shareholders. *US term* ***stock split***. *Also known as* ***bonus shares***, ***share split***

scripophily *Fin* the collection of valueless share or bond certificates

scroll bar *E-com* a bar at the right-hand side and/or bottom of a window that enables users to view more information on a web page

SCUM *abbr Gen Mgt* Self-Centred Urban Male (*slang*)

Sdn *abbr Fin* Sendirian

seagull manager *HR* a manager who is brought in to deal with a project, makes a lot of fuss, achieves nothing, and then leaves (*slang*)

SEAQ *abbr Fin* Stock Exchange Automated Quotations System: the London Stock Exchange's system for UK securities. It is a continuously updated computer database containing quotations that also records prices at which transactions have been struck.

SEAQ International *abbr Fin* Stock Exchange Automated Quotations System International: the London Stock Exchange's system for overseas securities. It is a continuously updated computer database containing quotations that also records prices at which transactions have been struck.

search *E-com* the facility that enables visitors to a website to look for the information they want.

Search is one of the most common activities that people carry out on a website, and therefore needs to be prominently displayed—preferably on every page, near the top. There are essentially two approaches to website search: basic search, suitable for small websites of 50 pages or under, and advanced search, for larger websites, which allows a user to refine their search on the basis of various parameters.

In either case, because search is an exclusively functional activity, the search results should be very clear and contain no distractions. Each set of results should include: the title of the web page that it refers to, shown in bold type and hyperlinked to that page; a two-line summary describing the content on that page; the URL for the page, and its date of publication.

search engine *E-com* a website that enables users to conduct **keyword** searches of indexed information on its database

search engine registration *E-com* the process of enlisting a website with a **search engine**, so that the website is selected when a user requests a search. The process involves choosing the right **keywords** and **metadata** for the documents, in order for them to be selected in as many appropriate circumstances as possible.

When registering a website with search engines, it is important to consider which will be of most benefit. Of the hundreds of search engines and directories, only a few really matter in terms of mass appeal— such as Yahoo, Google, and Alta Vista. However, there may well be specialist search engines for your particular industry, which should be on your list. All search engines used to be free to register with, but many are now charging, so consider whether they are worth the fee. An increasing number sell special placements in their search results: you choose a keyword, and when that keyword is input by a searcher, a short promotion for your website will appear. Search engines also need to be monitored regularly, as they can change the rules by which search results are presented. If your website is dropping down the results page, you may need to re-register.

seasonal adjustment *Fin* an adjustment made to accounts to allow for any short-term seasonal factors, such as Christmas sales, that may distort the figures

seasonal business *Fin* trade that is affected by seasonal factors, for example, trade in goods such as suntan products or Christmas trees

seasonal products *Mkting* products that are only marketed at particular times of the year, for example, Christmas trees or fireworks

seasonal variation *Stats* the variation of data according to particular times of the year such as winter months or a tourist season

seasoned equity *Fin* shares that have traded long enough to have a well-established value

seasoned issue *Fin* an issue for which there is a pre-existing market. *See also* **unseasoned issue**

SEATS *Fin* Stock Exchange Automatic Trading System, the electronic screen-trading system operated by the Australian Stock Exchange. It was introduced in 1987.

SEC *abbr Fin* Securities and Exchange Commission

secondary issue *Fin* an offer of listed shares that have not previously been publicly traded

secondary market *Fin* a market that trades in existing shares rather than new share issues, for example, a stock exchange. The money earned from these sales goes to the dealer or investor, not to the issuer.

secondary offering *Fin* an offering of securities of a kind that is already on the market

secondary sector *Econ* the sector of the labour force with employment options other than the wage earned in the market, consisting of married women, the semi-retired, and young people

Secondary Tax on Companies *(S Africa) Fin see* **STC**.

secondment *HR* a UK term for the temporary transfer of a member of staff to another organisation for a defined length of time, usually for a specific purpose. Secondment has grown in popularity in recent years, primarily for *career development* purposes. Secondments have been carried out between the public and private sectors as a mechanism to share management techniques and to disseminate *best practice*.

second mortgage *Fin* a loan, that uses the equity on a mortgaged property as security, taken out with a different lender than the first mortgage. As the first mortgagee holds the deeds, the second mortgagee has to register its interest with the Land Registry and cannot foreclose without the first mortgagee's permission.

second-tier market *Fin* a market in stocks and shares where the listing requirements are less onerous than for the main market, as in, for example, London's Alternative Investment Market

secretary of the board *Gen Mgt see company secretary*

Section 21 Company (*S Africa*) *Fin* a company established as a *non-profit organisation*

sector index *Fin* an index of companies in particular parts of a market whose shares are listed on a general or specialist stock exchange

secular trend *Stats* the underlying smooth movement of a *time series* over a time period of several years

secured *Fin* **1.** used to describe borrowing when the lender has a charge over an asset or assets of the borrower, for example, a mortgage or floating charge **2.** used to describe a creditor who has a charge over an asset or assets of the borrower, for example, a mortgage or floating charge. *See also collateral, security*

secured bond *Fin* a collateralised bond

secured creditors *Fin* creditors whose claims are wholly or partly secured on the assets of a business

secured debenture *Fin see debenture*

secure electronic transaction protocol *E-com see SET*

secure server *E-com* a combination of hardware and software that secures e-commerce credit card transactions so that there is no risk of unauthorised people gaining access to credit card details online

secure sockets layer *E-com see SSL*

securities account *Fin* an account that shows the value of financial assets held by a person or organisation

securities analyst *Fin* a professional person who studies the performance of securities and the companies that issue them

Securities and Exchange Commission *Fin* the US government agency responsible for establishing standards of financial reporting and accounting for public companies. *Abbr* **SEC**

Securities and Futures Authority *Fin* a self-regulatory organisation responsible for supervising the activities of institutions advising on corporate finance activity, or dealing, or facilitating deals, in securities or derivatives. *Abbr* **SFA**

Securities and Investment Board *Fin* a private company, limited by guarantee, which, along with the Bank of England, is responsible for regulating the conduct of a wide range of investment activities under the 1986 Financial Services Act. These responsibilities have been delegated to a number of self-regulatory organisations whose effectiveness is monitored by the SIB. *Abbr* **SIB**

Securities Commission *Fin* a statutory body responsible for monitoring standards in the New Zealand securities markets and for promoting investment in New Zealand. *Abbr* **SC**

securities deposit account *Fin* a brokerage account into which securities are deposited electronically

Securities Institute of Australia *Fin* a national professional body that represents people involved in the Australian securities and financial services industry. *Abbr* **SIA**

Securities Investor Protection Corporation *Fin* in the United States, a corporation created by Congress in 1970 that is a mutual insurance fund established to protect clients of securities firms. In the event of a firm being closed because of bankruptcy or financial difficulties, the SIPC will step in to recover clients' cash and securities held by the firm. The corporation's reserves are available to satisfy cash and securities that cannot be recovered up to a maximum of US$500,000, including a maximum of US$100,000 on cash claims. *Abbr* **SIPC**

securities lending *Fin* the loan of securities to those who have **sold short**

securitised paper *Fin* the **bond** or **promissory note** resulting from securitisation

security *Fin* **1.** a tradable financial asset, for example, a bond, stock, a share, or a warrant **2.** the collateral for a loan or other borrowing

security deposit *Fin* an amount of money paid before a transaction occurs to provide the seller with recourse in the event that the transaction is not concluded and this is the buyer's fault

security investment company *Fin* a financial institution that specialises in the analysis and trading of securities

seed capital *Gen Mgt* a usually modest amount of money used to convert an idea into a viable business. Seed capital is a form of *venture capital*. *US term* **seed money**

seed money (*US*) *Gen Mgt* = **seed capital**

segmentation *Stats* the division of the data in a study into regions

selection bias *Stats* the effect on a statistical or clinical trial of unmeasured variables that are unknown to the researcher

selection board *HR see* **panel interview**

selection instrument *HR see* **psychometric test**

selection interviewing *HR see* **interviewing**

selection of personnel *HR see* **recruitment**

selection test *HR see* **psychometric test**

selective pricing *Fin* setting different prices for the same product or service in different markets. This practice can be broken down as follows: category pricing, which involves cosmetically modifying a product such that the variations allow it to sell in a number of price categories, as where a range of brands is based on a common product; customer group pricing, which involves modifying the price of a product or service so that different groups of consumers pay different prices; peak pricing, setting a price which varies according to the level of demand; and service level pricing, setting a price based on the particular level of service chosen from a range.

self-actualisation *HR* the maximisation of your skills and talents. Self-actualisation was considered by *Abraham Maslow* as the pinnacle of his hierarchy of needs. *Also known as* **self-fulfilment**

self-appraisal *HR* an assessment carried out by an individual on his or her own ability or understanding. Self-appraisal is sometimes part of the *performance appraisal* process but is also carried out as part of *continuing professional development* or *career development*.

self-assessment 1. *Ops* a systematic and regular review of the activities of an organisation and the referencing of the results against a model of *excellence* that is carried out by the organisation itself. Self-assessment allows an organisation to identify its strengths and weaknesses and to plan improvement activities. The technique came to prominence with the spread of the *EFQM Excellence Model*. **2.** *Fin* in the United Kingdom, a system that enables taxpayers to assess their own income tax and capital gains tax payments for the fiscal year

self-certification *HR* in the United Kingdom, the notification and recording of the first seven days of an employee's *sick leave*. Self-certification requires the completion of a form by the employee on their return to work, indicating the nature and duration of their illness and counter-signed by a manager.

self-development *HR see personal development*

self-directed team *HR see autonomous work group*

self-employment *HR* being in business on one's own account, either on a *freelance* basis, or by reason of owning a business, and not being engaged as an *employee* under a *contract of employment*. The distinction between the self-employed and the employed is not always clear in law, but has a crucial bearing on matters such as the tax treatment of pay and the applicability of *employment protection*. A self-employed person may be an *employer* of others.

self-fulfilment *HR see self-actualisation*

self-insurance *Fin* the practice of saving money to pay for a possible loss rather than taking out an insurance policy against it

self-liquidating *Fin* providing enough income to pay off the amount borrowed for financing

self-liquidating premium *Mkting* a sales promotion technique that pays for itself, in which customers send money and vouchers or proof of purchase to obtain a premium gift

self-liquidating promotion *Mkting* a sales promotion in which the cost of the campaign is covered by the incremental revenue generated by the promotion

self-managed team *HR see autonomous work group*

self-managed work team *HR see autonomous work group*

self-managing team *HR see autonomous work group*

self-regulatory organisation *Gen Mgt* an organisation that polices its members, for example, an exchange

self-tender *Fin* in the United States, the repurchase by a corporation of its stock by way of a tender

sell and build *Gen Mgt* an approach to manufacturing in which the producer builds only when a customer has placed an order and paid for it, rather than building products for stock

seller's market *Fin* a market in which sellers can dictate prices, typically because demand is high or there is a product shortage

selling cost *Fin* cost incurred in securing orders, usually including salaries, commissions, and travelling expenses

selling season *Fin* a period in which market conditions are favourable to sellers

sell short *Fin* to sell commodities, currencies, or securities that one does not own in the expectation that prices will fall before delivery to the seller's profit. *See also bear*

seminar *Gen Mgt* a small business meeting at which participants present information or exchange ideas

semi-variable cost/semi-fixed cost/mixed cost *Fin* a cost that contains both fixed and variable components and is thus partly affected by a change in the level of activity

Semler, Ricardo (*b.* 1957) *Gen Mgt* Brazilian business executive. Owner of Semco, which he *turned around*, using three main strategies: *employee democracy, open-book management*, and self-setting salaries. His methods were written up in *Maverick!* (1993).

Sendirian *Gen Mgt* Malay term for 'limited'. Companies can use 'sendirian berhad' or 'Sdn Bhd' in their name instead of 'Pte Ltd'. *Abbr* **Sdn**

Senge, Peter (*b.* 1947) *Gen Mgt* US academic. Popularised the theory of the *learning organisation*, first suggested by **Chris Argyris** and **Donald Schön**. Senge studied how organisations develop adaptive capabilities in a world of increasing complexity and change. His work culminated in the publication of *The Fifth Discipline: The Art and Practice of the Learning Organization* (1990).

Senge studied engineering at Stanford before doing a PhD on social systems modelling at the Massachusetts Institute of Technology. He is currently director of the Center for Organizational Learning at MIT, and is also a founding partner of the training and consulting company, Innovation Associates, now part of Arthur D. Little.

senior debt *Fin* a debt whose holder has more claim on the debtor's assets than the holder of another debt. *See also junior debt*

senior management *Gen Mgt* the managers and executives at the highest level of an organisation. Senior management includes the *board of directors*. Senior management has responsibility for *corporate governance*, *corporate strategy*, and the interests of all the organisation's *stakeholders*. *Also known as management team*

senior mortgage *Fin* a mortgage whose holder has more claim on the debtor's assets than the holder of another mortgage. *See also junior mortgage*

sensitivity analysis *Fin* a modelling and risk assessment procedure in which changes are made to significant variables in order to determine the effect of these changes on the planned outcome. Particular attention is thereafter paid to variables identified as being of special significance.

sensitivity training *HR* group-based training designed to help participants develop interpersonal skills (see *interpersonal communication*). Sensitivity training is a form of human relations training, and was developed by *Kurt Lewin*, and others at the National Training Laboratory in the United States during the 1940s. The format most commonly used is a **training group**, or **T-Group**, consisting of between 7 and 12 people who meet together over a period of about two weeks, normally at a residential training centre. The aims are to develop sensitivity and awareness of participants' own feelings and reactions, to increase their understanding of *group dynamics*, and to help them learn to adapt their behaviour in appropriate ways. Group activities may include discussion, games, and exercises but may also be relatively unstructured. The provision of *feedback* is a key feature. This type of training has been controversial, as the group interactions can be confrontational, and some have suggested that participants could suffer emotional harm. The popularity of T-Groups has declined since the 1960s and 1970s. Sensitivity training can also be known as **laboratory training**. This term emphasises the way participants are placed in an environment in which different ways of interacting can be tried out. Lewin's early work in this field was developed at the National Training Laboratories, founded in 1947, in the United States.

separation *HR* a term used mainly in the United States to refer to *termination of service* or *resignation*

serial entrepreneur *Gen Mgt* an *entrepreneur* who sets up a string of new ventures, one after the other

seriation *Stats* the process of arranging a set of objects in a series on the basis of similarities or dissimilarities

SERPS *abbr Fin* State Earnings-Related Pension Scheme: in the United Kingdom, a state scheme designed to pay retired employees an additional pension to the standard state pension. Contributions, collected through National Insurance payments, and benefits are related to earnings. Individuals may opt out of SERPS and have their contributions directed to an occupational or personal pension.

server *E-com* a computer that provides services to another computer. Typically, a server stores data to be shared over a computer network. The computers receiving services are called **clients**.

server farm *E-com* a place where a number of server computers are located, usually providing server functions for a number of different organisations

server log *E-com see* **web log**

service *Mkting* any activity with a mix of tangible and intangible outcomes that is offered to a market with the aim of satisfying a customer's need or desire. Early **marketing** tended to distinguish a service from a physical good, but more recently these two have been seen as interrelated because service delivery frequently has physical aspects. For example, in a restaurant, service is provided by a waiter but physical goods, such as the food and the dining room, are also involved. In modern marketing, all forms of services and goods can be seen as **products**.

service charge 1. *Fin* a fee for any service provided, or additional fee for any enhancements to an existing service. For example, banks may charge a fee for obtaining foreign currency for customers. Residents in blocks of flats may pay an annual maintenance fee that is also referred to as a service charge. **2.** *Mkting* a gratuity usually paid in restaurants and hotels. A service charge may be voluntary or may be added as a percentage to the bill.

service contract *HR* a **contract of employment** for **executive directors** which lays down the **conditions of employment** and details of any **bonus** which may be paid, and outlines the procedure for **termination of service**

service cost centre *Fin* a cost centre providing services to other cost centres. When the output of an organisation is a service, rather than goods, an alternative name is normally used, for example, support cost centre or utility cost centre.

service/function costing *Fin* cost accounting for services or functions, for example, canteens, maintenance, personnel

service level agreement *Mkting* an agreement drawn up between a customer or client and the provider of a service or product. A service level agreement can cover a straightforward provision of a service, for example, office cleaning, or the provision of a complete function such as the **outsourcing** of the administration of a payroll or the maintenance of plant and equipment for a large company. The agreement lays down the detailed specification for the level and quality of the service to be provided. The agreement is essentially a legally binding contract.

services *Fin* value-creating activities which in themselves do not involve the supply of a physical product. Service provision may be subdivided into: pure services, where there is no physical product, such as consultancy; services with a product attached, such as the design and installation of a computer network; and products with services attached, such as the purchase of a computer with a maintenance contract.

servicing borrowing *Fin* paying the interest due on a loan

SET *abbr E-com* secure electronic transaction protocol: a payment protocol that permits secure credit card transactions over open networks such as the Internet, developed by Visa and MasterCard

set-off *Fin* an agreement between two parties to balance one debt against another or a loss against a gain

set the bar *HR* to motivate staff by setting targets that are above their current level of achievement

settlement 1. *E-com* the portion of an electronic transaction during which the customer's credit card is charged for the transaction and the proceeds are deposited into the merchant account by the acquirer **2.** *Fin* the payment of a debt or charge

settlement date *Fin* the date on which an outstanding debt or charge is due to be paid

---

set-up costs *Gen Mgt* the costs associated with making a workstation or equipment available for use. Set-up costs include the personnel needed to set up the equipment, the cost of down time during a new set-up, and the resources and time needed to test the new set-up to achieve the specification of the parts or materials produced.

set-up fees *E-com* the costs associated with establishing a *merchant account*, for example, application and software licensing fees and point-of-sale equipment purchases

set-up time *Ops* the time it takes to prepare, calibrate, and test a piece of equipment to produce a required output

set-up time reduction *Ops see single minute exchange of dies*

seven-day money *Fin* funds that have been placed on the money market for a term of seven days

severance package (*US*) *HR* = *redundancy package*

severance pay (*US*) *HR* = *redundancy payment*

sexual discrimination *HR* unfavourable treatment or *discrimination*, especially in employment, based on prejudice against a person's sex. Legislation against sexual discrimination is in place in many countries and many organisations have specific *personnel policies* to prevent sexual discrimination in the workplace.

sexual harassment *HR* a form of *discrimination* through the unwelcome and unwanted sexual conduct of one employee towards another. Most of the victims of sexual harassment are women, and the most common forms are physical, verbal, suggestive gesturing, written messages, graphic or pictorial displays, or the emotional isolation of an individual. The effective promotion of a policy to protect employees and customers from such harassment is good organisational practice.

SFA *abbr Fin* Securities and Futures Authority

SFAS *abbr Fin* Statement of Financial Accounting Standards

SFE *abbr Fin* Sydney Futures Exchange

SGX *abbr Fin* Singapore Exchange

shadow market *Gen Mgt see* **black market**

shadow price *Fin* an increase in value which would be created by having available one additional unit of a limiting resource at its original cost. This represents the opportunity cost of not having the use of the one extra unit. This information is routinely produced when mathematical programming (especially linear programming) is used to model activity.

shakeout *Fin* the elimination of weak or cautious investors during a crisis in the financial market (*slang*)

shamrock organisation *Gen Mgt* a form of *organisation structure* with three bases on which people can be employed and on which organisations can be linked to each other. The shamrock organisation was identified by **Charles Handy**. The three bases or groups are professional managers, contracted specialists such as advertising, computing, or catering personnel, and a flexible labour force discharging part-time, temporary, or seasonal roles. *See also* **Handy, Charles**

shape up or ship out (*US*) *HR* an order to improve your performance at work or else be fired (*slang*)

share *Fin* any of the equal parts into which a company's capital stock is divided, whose owners are entitled to a proportionate share of the company's profits

share account *Fin* **1.** in the United Kingdom, an account at a building society where the account holder is a member of the society. Building societies usually offer another type of account, a deposit account, where the account holder is not a member. A share account is generally paid a better rate of interest but, in the event of the society going into liquidation, deposit account holders are given preference. **2.** in the United States, an account with a credit union that pays dividends rather than interest

share capital *Fin* the amount of capital that a company raises by issuing shares

share certificate *Fin* a document that certifies ownership of a share in a company. *US term* **stock certificate**

shared drop *Mkting* a sales promotion technique in which a number of promotional offers are delivered by hand to *prospects* at the same time

shared services *Fin* a business strategy which involves centralising certain business activities such as accounting and other transaction-oriented activities in order to reduce costs and provide better customer service

shared values *Gen Mgt see* **core values**

share exchange *Fin* a service provided by certain collective investment schemes whereby they exchange investors' existing individual shareholdings for units or shares in their funds. This saves the investor the expense of selling holdings, which can be uneconomical when dealing with small shareholdings.

share-for-share offer *Fin* a *takeover bid* where the bidder offers its own shares, or a combination of cash and shares, for the target company

shareholder *Fin* a person or organisation that owns shares in a limited company or partnership. A shareholder has a stake in the company and becomes a member of it, with rights to attend the *annual general meeting*. Since shareholders have invested money in a company, they have a vested interest in its performance, can be a powerful influence on company policy, and should consequently be considered *stakeholders* as well as shareholders. Some *pressure groups* have sought to exploit this by becoming shareholders in order to get a particular viewpoint or message across. At the same time,

managers must, in order to maintain or increase the company's market value, consider their responsibility to shareholders when formulating strategy. It has been argued that on some occasions the desire to make profits to raise returns for shareholders has damaged companies because it has limited the amount of money spent in other areas, such as the development of facilities or health and safety.

shareholders' equity *Fin* a company's share capital and reserves

shareholders' perks *Fin* benefits offered to shareholders in addition to dividends, often in the form of discounts on the company's products and services

shareholder value *Fin* total return to the shareholders in terms of both dividends and share price growth, calculated as the present value of future free cash flows of the business discounted at the weighted average cost of the capital of the business less the market value of its debt

shareholder value analysis *Gen Mgt* a calculation of the value of a company by looking at the returns it gives to its shareholders. Shareholder value analysis, like the *economic theory of the firm*, assumes that the objective of a company director is to maximise the wealth of the company's shareholders. It is based on the premise that discounted cash flow principles can be applied to the business as a whole. SVA is calculated by estimating the total net value of a company and dividing this figure by the value of shares. Shareholder value analysis can be applied to assess the contribution of a business unit or to evaluate individual projects. *Abbr* **SVA**

shareholding *Fin* the shares in a limited company owned by a shareholder. *US term* **stockholding**

share incentive scheme *HR* a type of financial *incentive scheme* in which employees can acquire shares in the company in which they work and so have an interest in its financial performance. A share incentive scheme is a type of *employee share scheme*, in which employees may be given shares by their employer, or shares may be offered for purchase at an advantageous price, as a reward for personal or group performance. A *share option* is a type of share incentive scheme.

share index *Fin see index*

share issue *Fin* an occasion when shares in a business are offered for sale. The *capital* derived from share issues can be used for investment in the core business or for expansion into new commercial ventures.

share of voice *Mkting* an individual company's proportion of the total advertising expenditure in a sector

share option *Fin, HR* a type of *share incentive scheme* in which an employee is given the option to buy a specified number of shares at a future date, at a price agreed at the present time. Share options provide a financial benefit to the recipient only if the share price rises over the period the option is available. If the share price falls over the period, the employee is under no obligation to buy the shares. There may be a tax advantage to the employees who participate in such a scheme. Share options may be available to all employees or operated on a discretionary basis.

shareowner *Fin* somebody who owns a share of stock

share premium *Fin* **1.** the amount by which the price at which a company sells a share exceeds its par value **2.** the amount payable for a share above its nominal value. Most shares are issued at a premium to their nominal value. Share premiums are credited to the company's *share premium account.*

share premium account *Fin* the special reserve in a company's balance sheet to which *share premiums* are credited. Expenses associated with the issue of shares may be written off to this account.

share register *Fin* a list of the shareholders in a particular company

share shop *Fin* the name given by some financial institutions to the office open to the public where shares may be bought and sold

share split *Fin see scrip issue*

Share Transactions Totally Electronic (*S Africa*) *Fin see* **STATE**

shareware *E-com* software distributed free of charge, but usually with a request that users pay a small fee if they like the program

shark repellent *Gen Mgt* provisions in a company's bye-laws that make it more difficult for a proposition such as a change of status or the acceptance of a hostile *takeover* bid to succeed. Elements of shark repellent may include: requiring a vote that is substantially higher than that required by law; creating different voting rights attached to different stocks; very long notice for special business meetings; or requiring certain shareholders to waive rights to any capital gains resulting from a takeover. (*slang*)

shark watcher *Fin* in the United States, a firm specialising in monitoring the stock market for potential takeover activity (*slang*)

Sharpe ratio *Fin see risk-adjusted return on capital*

shelf registration *Fin* a registration statement, lodged with the Securities and Exchange Commission two years before a corporation issues securities to the public. The statement, which has to be updated periodically, allows the corporation to act quickly when it considers that the market conditions are right without having to start the registration procedure from scratch.

shelfspace *Mkting* the amount of space allocated to a product in a retail outlet

shell company *Fin* a company that has ceased to trade but is still registered, especially one sold to enable the buyer to begin trading without having to set up a new company

Shewhart, Walter Andrew (1891–1967) *Gen Mgt* US statistician. Pioneer of the development and application of statistical techniques for the control of variation in industrial production, in particular *statistical process control*. Mentor of *W. Edwards Deming*.

shibosai *Fin* the Japanese term for a private placing

shibosai bond *Fin* a *samurai bond* sold direct to investors by the issuing company as opposed to being sold via a financial institution

shift *HR* **1.** a designated period during a working day when a group of employees work continuously. Shifts are arranged in a variety of different patterns during a day or over a week or month, to enable a business to make more effective use of its equipment, and to enable a greater level of output to be achieved. **2.** a group of employees working for a designated period during a working day. Where a shift pattern changes, the hours of work for the whole group of employees alters.

shift differential *HR* payment made to employees over and above their basic rate to compensate them for the inconvenience of the pattern of *shiftwork*. A shift differential usually takes account of the time of day when the shift is worked, the duration of the shift, the extent to which weekend working is involved, and the speed of rotation within the shift.

shiftwork *HR* an arrangement whereby the working day is divided into a number of *shifts*, and a separate group of employees works for each period

shingle
hang out your shingle (*US*) *Gen Mgt* to start a business or announce the start-up of a new business (*slang*)

Shingo, Shigeo (1909–90) *Gen Mgt* Japanese researcher and consultant. Inventor of the *single minute exchange of dies* and a developer of the *Toyota production system*. Methods to achieve *zero defects* were explained in *Zero Quality Control* (1985).

shinyo kinku *Fin* in Japan, a financial institution that provides financing for small businesses

shinyo kumiai *Fin* in Japan, a credit union that provides financing for small businesses

shipping confirmation *E-com* an e-mail message informing the purchaser that an order has been shipped

shogun bond *Fin* a bond denominated in a currency other than the yen that is sold on the Japanese market by a non-Japanese financial institution. *Also known as geisha bond. See also samurai bond*

shopbot *E-com* an automated means of searching the Internet for particular products or services, allowing the user to compare prices or specifications

shopping cart *or* **shopping basket** *E-com* a software package that collects and records items selected for purchase along with associated data, for example, item price and quantity desired, during shopping at an electronic store. *Also known as shopping trolley*

shopping experience *E-com* the virtual environment in which a customer visits an e-merchant's website, selects items and places them in an electronic *shopping cart*, and notifies the merchant of the order. The experience does not include a payment transaction, which is initiated by a message generated to the point-of-sale program when the customer signals the experience is completed.

shopping trolley *E-com see shopping cart*

shop steward *HR* a representative elected by *trade union* members within an office or factory to represent their feelings, wishes, and grievances to management. A shop steward is often the first point of contact for supervisors and personnel officers in their industrial relations dealings with an outside trade union.

shop window website *E-com* a website which provides information about an organisation and its products, but without

---

Never talk defeat. Use words like hope, belief, faith, victory.   **Brendan Kennelly**

encouraging any significant visitor inter-action—rather like an online company brochure

short *Fin* **1.** a short-dated gilt (*slang*) **2.** an asset in which a dealer has a short position

short covering *Fin* the purchase of foreign exchange, commodities, or securities by a firm or individual that has been *selling short*. Such purchases are undertaken when the market has begun to move upwards, or when it is thought to be about to do so.

short-dated gilt *Fin see gilt-edged security*

shorthand *Gen Mgt* a system of rapid note-taking, using abbreviations and symbols to represent words and phrases

shorting *Fin* the act of *selling short*

short-interval scheduling *Ops* a technique for assigning a planned quantity of work to a workstation, to be completed in a specific time. Short-interval scheduling was pioneered during the 1930s by large mail-order houses in the United States and was widely used in the 1950s to provide greater control of routine and semi-routine processes through regular checks of individual performance over short spans of time. Short-interval scheduling enables *productivity* to be improved, as all delays can be identified and corrected at an early stage.

short messaging service *E-com see SMS*

short-run production *Ops* a production system designed to produce one-off or small batches of a product

short selling *Fin see sell short*

short-term bond *Fin* a bond on the corporate bond market that has an initial maturity of less than two years

short-term capital *Fin* funds raised for a period of less than 12 months. *See also working capital*

short-term debt *Fin* debt with a term of one year or less

short-term economic policy *Fin* an economic policy with objectives that can be met within a period of months or a few years

short-termism *Gen Mgt* an approach to business that concentrates on short-term results rather than long-term objectives

shovelware *E-com* a derogatory term for the materials produced by converting existing materials from a traditional medium, for example, a catalogue, without taking advantage of the digital medium's audiovisual and linking possibilities (*slang*)

show stopper *Fin* another form of *poison pill*

shrink wrap agreement *or* **shrink wrap licence** *E-com see click wrap agreement*

shutdown of production *Ops* the action of stopping production due to a lack of resources or components, equipment failure or installation, or *industrial action* by workers. Shutdown of production may also be instigated by management to reduce output. A shutdown can be a temporary measure, for example, in holiday periods, but it can also be permanent, for example, when a manufacturing company closes down after *business failure*.

SIA *abbr Fin* Securities Institute of Australia

SIB *abbr Fin* Securities and Investment Board

sickie *HR* a day of sick leave, often implying that the sickness is not genuine (*slang*)

sick leave *or* **sickness absence** *HR* absence from work caused by illness

sickness and accident insurance *Fin* a form of permanent health insurance that may be sold with some form of credit, for example a credit card or personal loan. In the event of the borrower being unable to work because of accident or illness, the policy covers the regular payments to the credit card company or lender.

sickout (*US*) *HR* a form of protest by a group of employees who attempt to

---

A man always has two reasons for what he does—a good one and the real one. **J.P. Morgan**

achieve their demands by absenting themselves from work on the grounds of ill-health (*slang*)

sight bill *Fin* a bill of exchange payable on sight

sight deposit *Fin* a bank deposit against which the depositor can immediately draw

sight draft *Fin* a bill of exchange that is payable on delivery. *See also* **time draft**

signature *E-com* the name, position, and full contact details of the sender of an e-mail, added to the end of a business message. Some e-mail programs enable users to automatically add a signature to all sent messages.

signature guarantee *Fin* a stamp or seal, usually from a bank or a broker, that vouches for the authenticity of a signature

signature loan *Fin see* **unsecured loan**

silent partner (*US*) *Fin* = **sleeping partner**

silversurfer *E-com* an Internet user aged between 45 and 65 (*slang*)

silvertail (*ANZ*) *Gen Mgt* a wealthy person of high social standing (*slang*)

Simon, Herbert (1916–2001) *Gen Mgt* US economist, and political and social scientist. Respected for his work on **problem-solving**, **decision-making**, and **artificial intelligence**. He began developing his ideas in *Administrative Behavior* (1946).

simple interest *Fin* interest charged simply as a constant percentage of principal and not compounded. *See also* **compound interest**

simple mail transfer protocol *E-com see* **SMTP**

simple moving average *Stats* the selection of units from a population in such a way that every possible combination of selected units is equally likely to be in the sample chosen

simple regression analysis *Gen Mgt see* **regression analysis**

simulation *Gen Mgt* the construction of a mathematical model to imitate the behaviour of a real-world situation or system in order to test the outcomes of alternative courses of action. Simulation was used in a military context by the Chinese as many as 5,000 years ago and has applications in the fields of science, research and development, economics, and business systems. The use of simulation has become more widespread since the development of computers in the 1950s, which facilitated the manipulation of large quantities of data and made it possible to model more complex systems. Simulation techniques are used in situations where real-life experimentation would be impossible, costly, or dangerous, and for training purposes.

simulation game *Gen Mgt* an interactive game based on a simulation of a real-life situation, where participants role-play, make decisions, and receive **feedback** on the results of their actions. A simulation game is used for training purposes and enables trainees to put theory into practice in a risk-free environment. Simulation games are used to increase business awareness and develop management skills such as **decision-making**, **problem-solving**, and team working. An element of competition between individuals or teams of players is normally involved. Formats used include board games and computer-based simulations of the running of a business.

simulation model *Gen Mgt* a mathematical representation of the essential characteristics of a real-world system or situation, which can be used to predict future behaviour under a variety of different conditions. The process of developing a simulation model involves defining the situation or system to be analysed, identifying the associated variables, and describing the relationships between them as accurately as possible.

simultaneous engineering *Ops see* **concurrent engineering**

simultaneous management *Gen Mgt* a *management style* in which managers organise competing demands in an integrated way, rather than sequentially. Simultaneous management reflects the increasingly rapid changes of the business environment, which create conflicting demands on a manager's attention. It involves integrating tasks, people, and procedures and handling them in an interactive way, rather than tackling problems individually and one at a time.

SINBAD *abbr Mkting* Single Income, No Boyfriend, And Absolutely Desperate: one of many humorous acronyms used in UK advertising to help define the market of a product or service (*slang*)

Singapore dollar *Fin* Singapore's unit of currency, whose exchange rate is quoted as S$ per US$

Singapore Exchange *Fin* a merger of the Stock Exchange of Singapore and the Singapore International Monetary Exchange, established in 1999. It provides securities and derivatives trading, securities clearing and depository, and derivatives clearing services. *Abbr* **SGX**

Singapore Immigration and Registration *Gen Mgt* the department responsible for all entry and immigration issues relating to Singapore. *Abbr* **SIR**

single currency *Fin* denominated entirely in one currency

single customs document *Fin* a standard universally used form for the passage of goods through customs

single-employer bargaining *HR see* **collective bargaining**

single entry *Fin* a type of bookkeeping where only one entry, reflecting both a credit to one account and a debit to another, is made for each transaction

single market *Fin see* **EU**

single minute exchange of dies *Ops* a technique for reducing the *set-up times* of equipment. Single minute exchange of dies was developed by *Shigeo Shingo* to improve set-up times in the *Toyota production system*. It is a simple technique that divides the elements of a set-up task into internal activities (those that can only be carried out when the machine is stopped) and external activities (those that can be carried out in advance). Single minute refers to making the changes in less than ten minutes, while exchange of dies comes from the steel presses that were the focus of Shingo's attention. By converting as many internal activities to external activities as possible, Shingo was able to reduce a four-hour set-up time on a large press to less than ten minutes. *Abbr* **SMED**

single-payment bond *Fin* a bond redeemed with a single payment combining principal and interest at maturity

single premium assurance *Fin* life cover where the premium is paid in one lump sum when the policy is taken out, rather than in monthly instalments

single premium deferred annuity *Fin* an annuity that gives tax advantage, paid for with a single payment at inception, and paying returns regularly after a set date

single sourcing *Ops* the *purchasing* policy of using one supplier for a particular component or service. Single sourcing can result in higher quality and a greater level of co-operation in *product development* than the traditional Western approach of *multiple sourcing*. Single sourcing has risen in prominence in the West following the introduction of Japanese production techniques, particularly *just-in-time*, which encourage manufacturers to establish closer relationships with a smaller number of suppliers.

single tax *Fin* a tax that supplies all revenue, especially on land

SINK *abbr Mkting* Single, Independent, No Kids (*slang*)

SIPC *abbr Fin* Securities Investor Protection Corporation

SIR *abbr Gen Mgt* Singapore Immigration and Registration

SIS *abbr Gen Mgt* strategic information systems

site analysis *E-com* analysis of information about a website stored on web servers. Typically, this information details how many page views they serve, as well as more specific data about the site's performance such as how long visitors stayed on the site and which pages they looked at when they were there.

situational interview *HR see interviewing*

six-month money *Fin* funds invested on the money market for a period of six months

Six Sigma *Ops* a data-driven method for achieving near perfect quality. Sigma is the Greek letter used to denote *standard deviation*, or the measure of variation from the mean, which in production terms is used to imply a defect. The greater the number of sigmas, the fewer the defects. In true Six Sigma environments, companies operate at a quality level of six standard deviations from the mean, or at a defect level of 3.4 per million. Six Sigma analysis can be focused upon any part of production or service activities, and has a strong emphasis on statistical analysis in design, manufacturing, and customer-oriented activities. It is based on statistical tools and techniques of quality management developed by *Joseph Juran*.

size of firm *Gen Mgt* method of categorising companies according to size for the purposes of government statistics. Divisions are typically *microbusiness*, *small business*, *medium-sized business*, and *large-sized business*.

skeleton staff *HR* the minimum number of employees needed to keep a business running, for example, during a holiday period

skewness *Stats* a lack of symmetry in a probability distribution

skill *HR* the ability to do something well, gained through training and experience. *See also **competence***

skills analysis *HR* the process of obtaining information on employees' technical and behavioural *skills*. Skills analysis is used to define the skills or *competencies* required in a particular job. It is also used to identify those skills that are not being deployed at all or could be utilised by another part of the organisation. *Also known as **skills mapping***

skills mapping *HR see skills analysis*

skills shortage *HR* a shortfall in the number of workers with the *skills* needed to fill the jobs currently available. A skills shortage may be caused by a lack of education and *vocational training*, or by wider social and economic factors such as new technological developments. A skills shortage may affect a region, an industry, or a whole country. Skills shortages of this type need to be addressed at national level through effective *manpower planning* and the development of strategies for adult education and vocational training. An organisation may suffer from a skills shortage as a result of poor *recruitment* and employee retention policies, or through inadequate provision of training and employee development opportunities.

skunkworks (*US*) *Gen Mgt* a fast-moving group, working at the edge of the *organisation structure*, which aims to accelerate the *innovation* process without the restrictions of organisational policies and procedures. Skunkworks can operate unknown to an organisation, or with its tacit acceptance. With the organisation's acceptance, skunkworks are an extreme form of *intrapreneurialism*. The term skunkworks was popularised by *Tom Peters* and *Bob Waterman* in *A Passion for Excellence* (1984).

slack variables *Fin* the amount of each resource which will be unused if a specific linear programming solution is implemented

sleeping partner *Gen Mgt* a person or organisation that invests money in a company but takes no active part in the management of the business. Although a sleeping partner is inactive in the operation of the business, they have legal obligations and benefits of ownership and are therefore fully liable for any debts. *US term **silent partner***

Sloan, Alfred Pritchard (1875–1966) *Gen Mgt* US industrialist. Chairman and CEO of General Motors, which he built into the largest company in the world by developing ***decentralised organisation structure*** and adopting the theories of **Henri Fayol**. Sloan's divisional structure, which became the model for organising large business, is described in *My Years with General Motors* (1963).

slowdown *Econ* a fall in demand that causes a lowering of economic activity, less severe than a ***recession*** or ***slump***

slump *Econ* a severe downturn phase in the business cycle

slumpflation *Econ* a collapse in all economic activity accompanied by wage and price inflation. This happened, for example, in the United States and Europe in 1929. (*slang*)

slush fund *Fin* a fund used by a company for illegal purposes such as bribing officials to obtain preferential treatment for planned work or expansion

small and medium-sized enterprises *Gen Mgt* organisations that are in the ***start-up*** or growth phase of development and have between 10 and 500 employees. This definition of small and medium-sized enterprises is the one adopted by the United Kingdom's Department of Trade and Industry for statistical purposes. *Abbr* **SME**

small business *Gen Mgt* an organisation that is small in relation to the potential market size, managed by its owners, and not part of a larger organisation. There is no single official definition of what constitutes a small business. A standard definition for the size of small business, adopted by the UK Department of Trade

and Industry for purposes of examining trends and for distinguishing from **micro-business**, **medium-sized business**, and **large-sized business**, is an organisation of between 10 and 99 employees.

small change *Fin* a quantity of coins that a person might carry with them

Small Order Execution System *Fin* on the NASDAQ, an automated execution system for bypassing brokers when processing small order agency executions of Nasdaq securities up to 1,000 shares

small print *Gen Mgt* details in an official document such as a contract that are usually printed in a smaller size than the rest of the text and, while often important, may be overlooked. Items often referred to as 'small print' can include terms and conditions or penalty clauses.

smart card *E-com* a small plastic card containing a microprocessor that can store and process transactions and maintain a bank balance, thus providing a secure, portable medium for electronic money. Financial details and personal data stored on the card can be updated each time the card is used.

smart market *E-com* a market in which all transactions are carried out electronically using network communications

smartsizing *HR* the process of reducing the size of a company by laying off employees on the basis of incompetence and inefficiency (*slang*)

SME *abbr Gen Mgt* small and medium-sized enterprises

SMED *abbr Ops* single minute exchange of dies

Smith, Adam (1723–90) *Gen Mgt* Scottish political economist and philosopher. Author of *The Wealth of Nations* (1776), one of the most influential books written about political economy, Smith did much to promulgate the theory of free trade in a society based on **mercantilism**. He is recognised for his use of the expression 'the invisible hand', which he used to describe

---

Bankers are like everybody else, except richer.

Ogden Nash

the important role of self-interest in a free market.

smoking memo *Gen Mgt* a memo, letter, or e-mail message containing evidence of a corporate crime (*slang*)

smoko (*ANZ*) *Gen Mgt* a break taken by employees during working hours, traditionally to smoke cigarettes but often to take tea or other refreshments (*slang*)

smoothing methods *Stats* procedures used in fitting a model to a set of statistical observations in a study, often by graphing the data to highlight its characteristics

SMS *abbr E-com* short messaging service: the system used to send text messages via mobile phone networks

SMTP *abbr E-com* simple mail transfer protocol: an e-mail protocol used to help pass messages along their route. SMTP is understood by e-mail software and by the server computers that each e-mail message passes.

snail mail *E-com* a derogatory term for the off-line postal service, viewed as slow in comparison to e-mail

snowball sampling *Stats* a form of sampling in which existing sample members suggest potential new sample members, for example, personal acquaintances

snowflake *Stats* a graph that shows *multivariate data*

SO *abbr Gen Mgt* significant other (*slang*)

social audit *Gen Mgt* a process for evaluating, reporting on, and improving an organisation's performance and behaviour, and for measuring its effects on society. The social audit can be used to produce a measure of the *social responsibility* of an organisation. It takes into account any internal *code of conduct* as well as the views of all *stakeholders* and draws on *best practice* factors of *total quality management* and human resource development. Like *internal auditing*, social auditing requires an organisation to identify what it is seeking to achieve, who the stakeholders are, and how it wants to measure performance.

social capital *Gen Mgt* the asset to an organisation produced by the cumulative social skills of its employees. Social capital, like *intellectual* and *emotional capital*, is intangible and resides in the employees of the organisation. It is a form of capital produced by good interpersonal skills (see *interpersonal communication*), which can be considered an asset as they are an important factor in organisational success. Key components of social capital include: trust; a sense of community and belonging; unrestricted and participative communication; democratic decision-making; and a sense of collective responsibility. Evidence of social capital can be seen, for example, in trust relationships, in the establishment of effective personal networks, in efficient *teamwork*, and in an organisation's exercise of *social responsibility*.

social cost *Fin* tangible and intangible costs and losses sustained by third parties or the general public as a result of economic activity, for example, pollution by industrial effluent

socialism *Econ* a way of organising society in which the use and production of goods are in collective (usually government) ownership

socially-conscious investing *Fin see ethical investment*

social marginal cost *Econ* the additional cost to a society of a change in an economic variable, for example, the price of petrol or bread

social responsibility *Gen Mgt* the approach of an organisation to managing the impact it has on society. Social responsibility involves behaving within certain socially acceptable limits. These limits may not always take the form of written laws or regulations but they amount to an accepted organisation-wide moral or ethical code. Organisations that transgress this code are viewed as irresponsible. In order to determine levels of social responsibility, organisations may choose to undertake a *social audit* or more specifically an *environmental* *audit*. Social responsibility, along with *business ethics*, has grown as a strategic issue as *empowerment* and the *flat organisation* have pushed decision-making down to a wider range of employees at the same time as green or caring consumers are becoming a more powerful market segment.

social responsibility accounting *Fin* the identification, measurement, and reporting of the social costs and benefits resulting from economic activities

Sociedad Anónima *Fin* the Spanish equivalent of a private limited company. *Abbr* **SA**

Sociedade Anónima *Fin* the Portuguese equivalent of a private limited company. *Abbr* **SA**

Società a responsabilità limitata *Fin* an Italian limited liability company that is unlisted. *Abbr* **Srl**

Società per azioni *Fin* an Italian public limited company. *Abbr* **Spa**

Société anonyme *Fin* the French equivalent of a private limited company. *Abbr* **SA**

Société à responsabilité limitée *Fin* a French limited liability company that is unlisted. *Abbr* **SARL**

Société d'investissement à capital variable *Fin* the French term for collective investment. *Abbr* **SICAV**

Society for Worldwide Interbank Financial Telecommunication *Fin see* **SWIFT**

socio-cultural research *Mkting* exploration of social and cultural trends which identifies how they are likely to impact on different *market sectors*

socio-economic *Econ* involving both social and economic factors. Structural unemployment, for example, has socio-economic causes.

socio-economic environment *Gen Mgt* the combination of external social and economic conditions that influence the operation and performance of an organisation. The socio-economic environment is part of the overall business environment.

socio-economic segmentation *Mkting* the division of a market by socio-economic categories

Sod's Law *Fin* the principle that if something can go wrong, it will. *US term* **Murphy's Law**

soft benefits *HR* non-monetary benefits offered to employees (*slang*)

soft commissions *Fin* brokerage commissions that are rebated to an institutional customer in the form of, or to pay for, research or other services

soft commodities *Fin* commodities, such as foodstuffs, that are neither metals nor other solid raw materials. *Also known as* **softs**. *See also* **future**, **hard commodities**

soft-core radicalism *Mkting* a marketing technique that plays on people's concerns about environmental and ethical issues in order to sell them a product (*slang*)

soft currency *Fin* a currency that is weak, usually because there is an excess of supply and a belief that its value will fall in relation to others. *See also* **hard currency**

soft landing *Econ* a situation in which a country's economic activity slows down but demand does not fall far enough or rapidly enough to cause a recession

soft loan *Fin* a loan on exceptionally favourable terms, for example, for a project that a government considers worthy

soft market *Fin* a market in which prices are falling

softs *Fin see* **soft commodities**

soft systems *Gen Mgt see* **systems method**

software *E-com see* **hardware**

sole practitioner *Gen Mgt* the sole proprietor of a professional practice

---

sole proprietor *Gen Mgt* somebody who owns and runs an unincorporated business by themselves. In the United Kingdom, a sole proprietor does not have to register the company or publish annual accounts and is taxed as an individual. They are personally liable, however, for all business losses or debts and in the event of *bankruptcy* personal possessions may be forfeited. *Also known as* **sole trader**

sole trader *Fin* a person carrying on business with total legal responsibility for his/her actions, neither in partnership nor as a company

solus position *Mkting* the condition of being the only advertisement to appear on a page

solution brand *Gen Mgt* a combination of products and related services, for example, a computer system with pre-sales consultancy, installation, and maintenance, that meets a customer's needs more effectively than a product alone

solvency margin *Fin* **1.** a business's liquid assets that are in excess of those required to meet its liabilities **2.** in the United Kingdom, the extent to which an insurance company's assets exceed its liabilities

solvency ratio *Fin* **1.** a ratio of assets to liabilities, used to measure a company's ability to meet its debts **2.** in the United Kingdom, the ratio of an insurance company's net assets to its non-life premium income

solvent *Fin* able to pay off all debts

sort code *Fin* a combination of numbers that identifies a bank branch on official documentation, such as bank statements and cheques. *US term* **routing number**

sort field *E-com* a computer field used to identify data in such a way that it can be easily categorised and arranged in sequence

source and application of funds statement *Fin see* **cash-flow statement**

source document *Fin* a document upon which details of transactions or accounting events are recorded and from which information is extracted to be subsequently entered into the internal accounting system of an organisation, for example, a sales invoice or credit note

sources and uses of funds statement *Fin see* **cash-flow statement**

Southern African Development Community *Fin see* **SADC**

sovereign loan *Fin* a loan by a financial institution to an overseas government, usually of a developing country. *See also* **sovereign risk**

sovereign risk *Fin* the risk that an overseas government may refuse to repay or may default on a **sovereign loan**

Spa *abbr Fin* Società per azioni

spam 1. *E-com* unsolicited bulk e-mail, usually sent for commercial purposes. Spam is used by some companies as a cheap form of advertising, although it is generally considered offensive and unwelcome by the Internet community. Sending spam is regarded as unethical because the cost is paid by the recipient's site or server, not the sender's. Various Internet bodies campaign against spam and those individuals or organisations accused of spamming. The term originates from a sketch in an episode of *Monty Python* in which customers at a 'greasy spoon' café are served the tinned meat Spam with everything, regardless of whether it was part of their order. **2.** *Mkting see* **direct mail**

spamkiller software *E-com* software that can block e-mail messages from companies sending unsolicited commercial e-mail

span of control *Gen Mgt* the number and range of subordinates for whom a manager is responsible. The span of control can be calculated by various methods which take into account such factors as whether those supervised are doing the same or different jobs and their levels of seniority, *empowerment*, experience, and qualification.

spare parts *Ops* a stock of components of machinery or plant held in store in case of breakdown

spatial data *Stats* variables that are measured at different locations to illustrate the spatial organisation of data

SPC *abbr Ops* statistical process control

speako *Gen Mgt* a mistake made by a computer while using a speech-recognition program (*slang*)

spear carrier *HR* somebody who is in the second tier of command in an organisation and is responsible for carrying out the commands and communicating the messages of the top-level executives (*slang*)

special clearing *Fin see special presentation*

special deposit *Fin* an amount of money set aside for the rehabilitation of a mortgaged house

special leave *HR* exceptional *leave* that may be granted to an *employee*. Special leave includes *sabbaticals*, leave granted for study (also known as *educational leave*), leave for jury service, for volunteer forces training, leave granted to candidates for local or national elections, or for trade union duties and activities, and for *community involvement* purposes. Special leave can also refer to *maternity leave* and *paternity leave*.

special presentation *Fin* the sending of a cheque directly to the paying banker rather than through the clearing system. *Also known as special clearing. See also advice of fate*

special purpose bond *Fin* a bond for one particular project, financed by levies on the people who benefit from the project

special resolution *Fin see extraordinary resolution*

specie *Fin* coins, as opposed to banknotes, that are legal tender

specification *Ops* documentation relating to the required quantity and quality of materials, and the order of the work to be carried out to complete a task

specific charge *Fin* a fixed charge as opposed to a floating charge

specific order costing *Fin* the basic cost accounting method applicable where work consists of separately identifiable contracts, jobs, or batches

speculation *Fin* a purchase made solely to make a profit when the price or value increases

speech *Gen Mgt* a formal spoken address made to an audience by a speaker. Speeches are made in the context of a meeting or conference or on other occasions such as after a business dinner. The aim of a speech may be to motivate, inspire, or entertain as well as to inform. In contrast to *presentations*, speeches are a form of public speaking normally made without the assistance of audio-visual aids, and may be wide-ranging rather than focusing on a well-defined topic or proposal. Jokes, humorous anecdotes, and quotations are frequently used in speeches. To give a speech successfully requires good *communication skills*.

spider food *E-com* words that are embedded in a web page to attract search engines

spiffs (*US*) *Mkting* gifts or money offered to store managers in exchange for promoting a product (*slang*)

spin-off *Gen Mgt* a company or subsidiary formed by splitting away from a parent company. A spin-off company can, for example, be created when research and development yields a new product that does not fit into the company's current portfolio, or when a company wants to explore a new venture related to its current activities. It can also be formed from a demerger, in which acquired companies or parts of a business are separated in order to create a more streamlined parent organisation. A spin-off is often entrepreneurial in spirit, but the backing of the parent company can provide financial stability.

splash page *E-com* an introductory or initial page, usually containing advertisements, presented to visitors to a website before they get to the *homepage*

split *Fin* an issuance to shareholders of more than one share for every share owned. *See also reverse split*. US term **stock split**

split-capital investment trust *Fin* an investment trust set up for a specific timescale where the shares are divided at launch into two different classes: income shares and capital shares. Income shareholders receive all or most of the income generated by the trust and a predetermined sum at liquidation, while capital shareholders receive no interest but the remainder of the capital at liquidation. *Also known as* **split-level trust, split trust**

split commission *Fin commission* that is divided between two or more parties in a transaction

split coupon bond *Fin see zero coupon bond*

split-level trust *Fin see split-capital investment trust*

split trust *Fin see split-capital investment trust*

sponsorship *Mkting* a form of advertising in which an organisation provides funds for something such as a television programme, music concert, or sports event in return for exposure to a target audience

Spoornet *Gen Mgt* the rail division of the state-owned South African transport company, Transnet Ltd

spot *Mkting* a TV or radio commercial (*slang*)

spot colour *Mkting* single colour overprinted on a black-and-white advertisement

spot exchange rate *Fin* the exchange rate used for immediate currency transactions

spot goods *Fin* a commodity traded on the spot market

spot interest rate *Fin* an interest rate that is determined when a loan is made

spot market *Fin* a market that deals in commodities or foreign exchange for immediate rather than future delivery

spot month *Fin see nearby month*

spot price *Fin* the price for immediate delivery of commodities or foreign exchange

spot transaction *Fin* a transaction in commodities or foreign exchange for immediate delivery

spread *Fin* **1.** the difference between the buying and selling price of a share on a stock exchange **2.** the range of investments in a portfolio

spreadsheet *Fin* a computer program that provides a series of ruled columns in which data can be entered and analysed

sprinkling trust *Fin* a trust with multiple beneficiaries whose distributions occur at the trustee's total discretion

spruik (*ANZ*) *Gen Mgt* to publicise goods or services, typically by standing at the door of a shop and addressing passersby using a microphone (*slang*)

squatter (*ANZ*) *Gen Mgt* a wealthy landowner (*slang*)

squattocracy (*ANZ*) *Gen Mgt* a derogatory term for wealthy landowners, who are considered a powerful social class (*slang*)

squeaky wheel *Gen Mgt* somebody who gets good results by being extremely assertive in their dealings with other people (*slang*)

squeeze *Econ* a government policy of restriction, commonly affecting the availability of credit in an economy

squirt the bird *Gen Mgt* to transmit a signal to a satellite (*slang*)

Bury your ego. Don't be the star. Be the star maker! — *Bud Hadfield*

Srl *abbr Fin* Società a responsabilità limitata

SSADM *abbr Gen Mgt* structured systems analysis and design method

SSAP *abbr Fin* Statement of Standard Accounting Practice

SSL *abbr E-com* secure sockets layer: a widely used protocol for encrypting data that permits the transmission of credit card transactions in a secure fashion

stabilisation fund *Econ* a fund created by a government as an emergency savings account for international financial support

staff costs *Fin* the costs of employment which include gross pay, paid holidays, and employer's contributions to national insurance, pension schemes, sickness benefit schemes, and other benefits, for example, protective clothing and canteen subsidies

staffing level *HR* the number and type of personnel employed by an organisation for the performance of a given workload. The ideal staffing level for an organisation depends on the amount of work to be done and the skills required to do it. If the number and quality of staff employed are greater than necessary for the workload, an organisation may be deemed to be over-staffed; if the number of staff is insufficient for the workload, an organisation is deemed to be under-staffed. Effective *human resource planning* will determine the appropriate staffing level for an organisation at any given point in time.

stage-gate model *Mkting see new product development*

stagflation *Econ* the result when both inflation and unemployment exist at the same time in an economy. There was stagflation in the United Kingdom in the 1970s, for example.

stakeholder *Gen Mgt* a person or organisation with a vested interest in the successful operation of a company or organisation. A stakeholder may be an employee, customer, supplier, partner, or even the local community within which an organisation operates.

stakeholder pension *Fin, HR* a pension, bought from a private company, in which the retirement income depends on the level of contributions made during a person's working life. Stakeholder pensions are designed for people without access to an *occupational pension scheme*, and are intended to provide a low-cost supplement to the state earnings related pension scheme. A stakeholder pension scheme can either be trust-based, like an occupational pension scheme, or contract-based, similar to a personal pension. Subject to certain exceptions, employers must provide access to a stakeholder pension scheme for employees, although they are not required to establish a stakeholder pension scheme themselves. Membership of a stakeholder pension scheme is voluntary. *See also Keough Plan*

stakeholder theory *Gen Mgt* the theory that an organisation can enhance the interests of its shareholders without damaging the interests of its wider *stakeholders*. Stakeholder theory grew in response to the *economic theory of the firm*, and contrasts with *Theory E*. One of the difficulties of stakeholder theory is allocating importance to the values of different groups of stakeholders, and a solution to this is proposed by *stakeholder value analysis*.

stakeholder value analysis *Gen Mgt* a method of determining the values of all *stakeholders* within an organisation for the purposes of making strategic and operational decisions. Stakeholder value analysis is one method of justifying an approach based on *stakeholder theory* rather than the *economic theory of the firm*. It involves identifying groups of stakeholders and eliciting their views on particular issues in order that these views may be taken into account when making decisions.

stamp duty *Fin* in the United Kingdom, a duty that is payable on some legal documents and is shown to have been paid by a stamp being fixed to the document

standard *Fin* a benchmark measurement of resource usage, set in defined conditions.

Standards can be set on the following bases: an ex ante estimate of expected performance; an ex post estimate of attainable performance; a prior period level of performance by the same organisation; the level of performance achieved by comparable organisations; and the level of performance required to meet organisational objectives.

Standards may also be set at attainable levels which assume efficient levels of operation, but which include allowances for normal loss, waste, and machine downtime, or at ideal levels, which make no allowance for the above losses and are only attainable under the most favourable conditions.

Standard 8 *Fin* a standard used in Internet commerce

Standard & Poor's 500 *Fin* a US index of 500 general share prices selected by the Standard & Poor agency. *Abbr* **S&P 500, S&P index**

Standard & Poor's rating *Fin* a share rating service provided by the US agency Standard & Poor

standard business transaction *E-com* any business procedure conducted between trading partners, characterised by a paper document or its equivalent EDI transaction set or message

standard cost *Fin* the planned unit cost of the products, components, or services produced in a period. The main uses of standard costs are in performance measurement, control, stock valuation, and in the establishment of selling prices.

standard cost card *Fin* a document or other record detailing, for each individual product, the standard inputs required for production as well as the standard selling price. Inputs are normally divided into material, labour, and overhead categories,

and both price and quantity information is shown for each.

standard costing *Fin* a control technique which compares standard costs and revenues with actual results to obtain variances which are used to stimulate improved performance

standard deviation *Ops* a measure of how dispersed a set of numbers are around their mean

standard direct labour cost *Fin* the planned average cost of direct labour

standard of living *Econ* a measure of economic well-being based on the ability of people to buy the goods and services they desire

standard performance–labour *Fin* the level of efficiency which appropriately trained, motivated, and resourced employees can achieve in the long run

standard time *Gen Mgt* **1.** the length of time taken by a worker to complete a particular motion, such as reaching or grasping **2.** the total time required to complete a specific task for an employee working at the expected rate. The standard time for any particular task is derived through *work measurement* and *time study* techniques, and takes into account **relaxation allowances**, which allow employees time to recover from the psychological or physiological effects of carrying out a task, and **contingency allowances**, which recognise that there may be legitimate causes of delay before a task can be completed. *Predetermined motion-time systems* may be used to help determine a standard time.

standby credit *Econ* credit drawing rights given to a developing country by an international financial institution, to fund industrialisation or other growth policies

standby loan *Econ* a loan given to a developing country by an international financial institution, to fund technology hardware purchase or other important growth policies

stand down (*ANZ*) *HR* to suspend an employee without pay (*slang*)

standing instructions *Fin* instructions, that may be revoked at any time, for a particular procedure to be carried out in the event of a certain occurrence, for example, for the monies from a fixed term account that has just matured to be placed on deposit for a further fixed period

standing order *Fin* an instruction given by an account holder to a bank to make regular payments on given dates to the same payee. *US term* **automatic debit**

standing room only *Mkting* a sales technique whereby customers are given the impression that there are many other people waiting to buy the same product at the same time (*slang*)

staple commodities *Fin* basic food or raw materials that are important in a country's economy

star 1. *Gen Mgt see* **Boston Box 2.** *Fin* an investment that is performing extremely well (*slang*)

start-up *Gen Mgt* a relatively new, usually small business, particularly one supported by venture capital and within those sectors closely linked to new technologies

start-up costs *Fin* the initial sum required to establish a business or to get a project underway. The costs will include the capital expenditure and related expenses before the business or project generates revenue.

start-up model *Gen Mgt* a business model based on rapid short-term success. Typically, the aim is to acquire venture capital, grow rapidly, and float or sell off quickly, generating profit for the founders but not necessarily for the business.

state bank *Fin* a bank chartered by a state of the United States

state capitalism *Econ* a way of organising society in which the state controls most of a country's means of production and capital

State Earnings-Related Pension Scheme *Fin see* **SERPS**

state enterprise *Gen Mgt* an organisation in which the government or state has a controlling interest

statement of account *Fin* a list of sums due, usually relating to unpaid invoices, items paid on account but not offset against particular invoices, credit notes, debit notes, and discounts

statement of affairs *Fin* a statement, usually prepared by a receiver, in a prescribed form, showing the estimated financial position of a debtor or of a company which may be unable to meet its debts. It contains a summary of the debtor's assets and liabilities. The assets are shown at their estimated realisable values. The various classes of creditors, such as preferential, secured, partly secured, and unsecured, are shown separately.

Statement of Auditing Standards *Fin* an auditing standard, issued by the Auditing Practices Board, containing prescriptions as to the basic principles and practices which members of the UK accountancy bodies are expected to follow in the course of an audit. *Abbr* **SAS**

statement of cash flows *Fin* a statement that documents actual receipts and expenditures of cash

statement-of-cash-flows method *Fin* a method of accounting that is based on flows of cash rather than balances on accounts

statement of changes in financial position *Fin* a financial report of a company's incomes and outflows during a period, usually a year or a quarter

Statement of Financial Accounting Standards *Fin* in the United States, a statement detailing the standards to be adopted for the preparation of financial statements. *Abbr* **SFAS**

statement of source and application of funds *Fin see* **cash-flow statement**

Statement of Standard Accounting Practice *Fin* an accounting standard issued by the Accounting Standards Committee (ASC). *Abbr* **SSAP**

state of balance *Gen Mgt* an approach to capitalism that balances ecological and economic priorities

state planning *Econ* the regulation of a sector of an economy by administrators rather than by the price system

statistic *Fin* a piece of information in numerical form

statistical expert system *Stats* a computer program used to conduct a statistical analysis of a set of data

statistical model *Stats* the particular methods used to investigate the data in a statistical study

statistical process control *Ops* a means of monitoring a *process* to assist in identifying causes of variation with the aim of improving process performance. Statistical process control consists of three elements: data gathering; determining control limits; and variation reduction. The tools used include process *flow charts*, tally charts, histograms, graphs, *fishbone charts*, and control charts. The thinking behind SPC has been attributed to *Walter Shewhart* in the 1920s. *Abbr* **SPC**

statistical quality control *Stats* the process of inspecting samples of a product to check for consistent quality according to given parameters

statistical significance *Fin* the level of importance at which an event influences a set of *statistics*

statistics *Fin* information in numerical form and its collection, analysis, and presentation

statute-barred debt *Fin* a debt that cannot be pursued as the time limit laid down by law has expired

statutory auditor *Fin* a professional person qualified to carry out an audit required by the Companies Act

statutory body *Fin* an entity formed by Act of Parliament

STC *abbr* (*S Africa*) *Fin* Secondary Tax on Companies: a secondary tax levied on corporate dividends

STEP analysis *Gen Mgt see* **PEST analysis**

Stewart, Rosemary Gordon *Gen Mgt* British academic. Respected for her research on managerial work and behaviour, including the essential aspects of becoming an effective manager, published in *The Reality of Management* (1963).

Stewart, Thomas (*b.* 1948) *Gen Mgt* US publisher and writer. A leader in the *knowledge management* debate who, in *Intellectual Capital: The New Wealth of Organizations* (1997), encouraged organisations to exploit their untapped knowledge.

stickiness *E-com* a website's ability to hold visitors and to keep them coming back

stick to the knitting *Gen Mgt* an exhortation to organisations to concentrate on the activities, products, and services that are key to their *core business* and consequently to their success. Stick to the knitting was popularised by *Tom Peters* and *Bob Waterman* in their book *In Search of Excellence* (1984).

sticky site *E-com* a website that holds the interest of visitors for a substantial amount of time and is therefore effective as a marketing vehicle (*slang*) *Also known as heavy site*

stipend *HR* a regular remuneration or allowance paid to an individual holding a particular office

stock *Fin* **1.** a form of security that offers fixed interest **2.** the *capital* made available to an organisation after a *share issue*

stockbroker *Fin* somebody who arranges the sale and purchase of stocks

stock certificate (*US*) *Fin* = *share certificate*

---

stock control *Fin see **inventory***

stockcount *Fin* profit gained from ownership of a stock or share

stock exchange *Fin* an organisation that maintains a market for the trading of stock

Stock Exchange Automated Quotations System *Fin see SEAQ*

Stock Exchange Automated Quotations System International *Fin see SEAQ International*

Stock Exchange Automatic Trading System *Fin see SEATS*

stockholding (US) *Fin = **shareholding***

stock market *Fin* the trading of stocks, or a place where this occurs

stock option *Fin* 1. *see **option*** 2. *see employee share ownership plan*

stockout *Ops* the situation where the stock of a particular component or part has been used up and has not yet been replenished. Stockouts result from poor inventory control or the failure of a *just-in-time* supply system. They can result in delays in the delivery of customer orders and can damage the reputation of the business.

stock split (US) *Fin = **scrip issue***

stock symbol *Fin* a shortened version of a company's name, usually made up of two to four letters, used in screen-based trading systems

stocktaking *Ops* the process of measuring the quantities of stock held by an organisation. Stock, or *inventory*, can be held both in stores and within the processes of the operation. Better *materials management* and inventory systems have made annual stocktaking less important.

stock turns *or* **stock turnover** *Ops see inventory turnover*

stokvel (S Africa) *Fin* an informal, widely-used co-operative savings scheme that provides small-scale loans

stop-go *Econ* the alternate tightening and loosening of fiscal and monetary policies. This characterised the UK economy in the 1960s and 1970s.

stop limit order *Fin* in the United States, an order to trade only if and when a security reaches a specified price

stop loss *Fin* an order to trade only if and when a security falls to a specified price

stop order *Fin* in the United States, an order to trade only if and when a security rises above or falls below its current price

stop-work meeting (ANZ) *HR* a meeting held by employees during working hours to discuss issues such as wage claims and working conditions with union representatives or management

stores requisition *Fin see materials requisition*

story stock *Fin* a stock that is the subject of a press or financial community story that may affect its price

straight-line depreciation *Fin* a form of depreciation in which the cost of a fixed asset is spread equally over each year of its anticipated lifetime

Straits Times Industrial Index *Fin* an index of 30 Singapore stocks, the most commonly quoted indicator of stock market activity in Singapore

strata title (ANZ) *Gen Mgt* a system for registering ownership of space within a multilevel building, under which a title applies to the space and a proportion of the common property

strata unit (ANZ) *Gen Mgt* an apartment or office within a multilevel building that has been registered under the *strata title* system

STRATE (S Africa) *Fin* Share Transactions Totally Electronic: the electronic share transactions system of the Johannesburg Stock Exchange

strategic alignment *Gen Mgt see strategic fit*

strategic alliance *Gen Mgt* an agreement between two or more organisations to co-operate in a specific business activity, so that each benefits from the strengths of the other, and gains *competitive advantage*. The formation of strategic alliances has been seen as a response to *globalisation* and increasing uncertainty and complexity in the business environment. Strategic alliances involve the sharing of knowledge and expertise between partners as well as the reduction of risk and costs in areas such as relationships with suppliers and the development of new products and technologies. A strategic alliance is sometimes equated with a *joint venture*, but an alliance may involve competitors, and generally has a shorter life span. *Strategic partnering* is a closely related concept.

strategic analysis *Gen Mgt* the process of conducting researching on the business environment within which an organisation operates and the organisation itself, in order to formulate *strategy*. A number of tools are used in the process of strategic analysis, including *PEST*, *SWOT analysis*, and *Michael Porter*'s five forces model.

strategic business unit *Fin* a section within a larger organisation, responsible for planning, developing, producing, and marketing its own products or services

strategic financial management *Fin* the identification of the possible strategies capable of maximising an organisation's net present value, the allocation of scarce capital resources among the competing opportunities, and the implementation and monitoring of the chosen strategy so as to achieve stated objectives

strategic fit *Gen Mgt* the extent to which the activities of a single organisation or of organisations working in partnership complement each other in such a way as to contribute to *competitive advantage*. The benefits of good strategic fit include cost reduction, due to economies of scale, and the transfer of knowledge and skills. The success of a *merger*, *joint venture*, or *strategic alliance* may be affected by the degree of strategic fit between the organ-isations involved. Similarly, the strategic fit of one organisation with another is often a factor in decisions about acquisitions, mergers, *diversification*, or *divestment*. *Also known as* **strategic alignment**

strategic goal *Gen Mgt* the overall aim of an organisation in terms of its market position in the medium or long-term. A strategic goal forms part of an organisation's *corporate strategy* and should act as a motivating force as well as a measure of performance and achievement for those working in an organisation.

strategic inflection point *Gen Mgt* the time at which an organisation takes a decision to change its *corporate strategy* to pursue a different direction and avoid the risk of decline. The term was coined by *Andy Grove* of Intel to describe the period of change that affects an organisation's competitive position. It also concerns the ability of organisations to recognise and adapt to change factors of major significance.

strategic information systems *Gen Mgt* an information system established with the aim of creating *competitive advantage* and improving the competitive position of an organisation. A strategic information system supports and shapes the *corporate strategy* of an organisation, often leading to innovation in the way the organisation conducts its business, the creation of new business opportunities, or the development of products and services based on information technology. Strategic information systems represent a development in organisational use of information systems, following in the wake of *MISs*, *EISs*, and *decision support systems*.

strategic investment appraisal *Fin* a method of investment appraisal which allows the inclusion of both financial and non-financial factors. Project benefits are appraised in terms of their contribution to the strategies of the organisation, either by their financial contribution or, for non-financial benefits, by the use of index numbers or other means.

---

strategic management *Gen Mgt* the development of *corporate strategy*, and the management of an organisation according to that strategy. Strategic management focuses on achieving and maintaining a strong *competitive advantage*. It involves the application of corporate strategy to all aspects of the organisation, and especially to *decision-making*. As a discipline, strategic management developed in the 1970s, but it has evolved in response to changes in *organisation structure* and *corporate culture*. With greater *empowerment*, strategy has become the concern not just of directors but also of employees at all levels of the organisation.

strategic management accounting *Fin* a form of management accounting in which emphasis is placed on information which relates to factors external to the firm, as well as non-financial information and internally generated information

strategic marketing *Mkting* a method of selling products directly to customers, bypassing traditional retailers or distributors

strategic partnering *Gen Mgt* structured collaboration between organisations to take joint advantage of market opportunities, or to respond to customers more effectively than could be achieved in isolation. Strategic partnering occurs both in and between the public and private sectors. Besides allowing information, skills, and resources to be shared, a strategic partnership also permits the partners to share risk. *See also* **strategic alliance**

strategic plan *Fin* a statement of long-term goals along with a definition of the strategies and policies which will ensure achievement of these goals

strategic planning *Gen Mgt see* **planning**

strategy *Gen Mgt, HR* a planned course of action undertaken to achieve the aims and objectives of an organisation. The term was originally used in the context of

warfare to describe the overall planning of a campaign as opposed to tactics, which enable the achievement of specific short-term objectives. The overall strategy of an organisation is known as *corporate strategy*, but strategy may also be developed for any aspect of an organisation's activities such as *environmental management* or production and manufacturing strategy.

stratified sampling *Ops see* **random sampling**

straw man *Gen Mgt* a first proposal for a solution to a problem, offered more as a place to start looking for a solution than as a serious suggestion for final action

streaming *E-com* Web technology used for simultaneous downloading and viewing of large amounts of material. For example, with a *multimedia* file, the user can download just enough of the file to start viewing or listening to it, while the rest of the file is downloaded in the background, reducing, but not eliminating, download time.

street (*US*) *Fin* used to describe somebody who is considered to be well informed about the market (*slang*)

street name (*US*) *Fin* a broker who holds a customer's security in the broking house's name to facilitate transactions

stress *HR* the psychological and physical state that results when perceived demands exceed an individual's ability to cope with them

stress puppy (*US*) *HR* somebody who complains a lot and seems to enjoy being stressed (*slang*)

strike *HR* a concerted refusal to work by employees, with the aim of improving wages or employment conditions, voicing a grievance, making a protest, or supporting other workers in such an endeavour. A strike is a form of *industrial action*.

strike pay *or* **strike benefit** *HR* a benefit or allowance paid by a *trade union* to its members during the course of official *strike* action to help offset loss of earnings. *Also known as* **dispute benefit**

strike price *Fin* the price for a security or commodity that underlies an option

stripped bond *Fin* a bond that can be divided into separate zero-coupon bonds to represent its principal repayment and its interest

stripped stock *Fin* stock whose rights to dividends have been separated and sold

strips *Fin* the parts of a bond that entitle the owner only to interest payments or only to the repayment of principal

structural change *Econ* a change in the composition of output in an economy that means that resources have to be reallocated

structural inflation *Fin* inflation that naturally occurs in an economy, without any particular triggering event

structural unemployment *Econ* the situation where demand or technology changes so that there is too much labour in particular locations or skills areas

structured interview *HR see* **interviewing**

structured systems analysis and design method *Gen Mgt* a technique for the analysis and design of computer systems. The structured systems analysis and design method was developed by the Central Computer and Telecommunications Agency in the United Kingdom in the early 1980s. The technique adopts a structured methodology towards systems development through the use of data flow, logical data, and entity event modelling. Core development stages include: *feasibility study*; requirements analysis; requirements specification; logical system specification; and physical design. All the steps and tasks within each stage must be complete before subsequent stages can begin. *Abbr* **SSADM**

stub equity *Fin* the money raised through the sale of high risk bonds in large amounts or quantities, as in a leveraged takeover or a leveraged buy-out

subcontract *Gen Mgt* a **contract** under which all, or part, of the work specified in an existing contract is delegated to another person or organisation

subcontracting *Gen Mgt, Ops* the delegation to a third party of some, or all, of the work that one has **contracted** to do. Subcontracting usually occurs where the contracted work, for example, the construction of a building, requires a variety of skills. Responsibility for the fulfilment of the original **contract** remains with the original contracting party. Where the fulfilment of a contract depends on the skills of the person who has entered into the contract, for example, in the painting of a portrait, then the work cannot be subcontracted to a third party. The term subcontracting is sometimes used to describe **outsourcing** arrangements.

subject line *E-com* the field at the top of an e-mail template in which the title or subject of the e-mail can be typed. The subject line is the only part of the e-mail—apart from the name of the sender—which can be read immediately by the recipient. It is important to have a strong subject line, particularly if using e-mail for advertising or promotional purposes, or the recipient may well simply delete the e-mail.

subject to collection *Fin* dependent upon the ability to collect the amount owed

subliminal advertising *Mkting* advertising intended to influence an audience subconsciously, especially through images shown very briefly on a film or television screen

subordinated debt *Fin see* **junior debt**

subordinated loan *Fin* a loan that ranks below all other borrowings with regard to both the payment of interest and repayment of the principal. *See also* **pari passu**

subscribed share capital *Fin see* **issued share capital**

subscriber *Fin* **1.** a buyer, especially one who buys shares in a new company or new issues **2.** a person who signs a company's Memorandum of Association

subscription-based publishing *E-com* content or a selection of content from a website, magazine, book, or other publication, delivered regularly by e-mail or other means to a group of people who have subscribed to received this content

subscription process *E-com* the means by which users of a website sign up to receive specific information, content, or services via that website. Someone may become a subscriber as a result of giving personal information such as an e-mail address, or of making a payment if the subscription service is directly revenue-generating.

The early Internet promoted a culture that encouraged the free transfer of information, so subscription processes were relatively rare. However, it is becoming clear that, in general, websites must pay for themselves, either directly through subscription or advertising revenues, or indirectly by delivering valuable information that will further the organisation's objectives. As the Internet evolves, many more websites will become subscription based.

Subscription processes are also used to limit access to certain information. An extranet, for example, may contain confidential material, and a subscription process will be required to ensure that the right people have access to the right information.

subscription share *Fin* a share purchased by a subscriber when a new company is formed

subsidiary account *Fin* an account for one of the individual people or organisations that jointly hold another account

subsidiary company *Gen Mgt* a company that is controlled by another. A subsidiary company operates under the control of a parent or *holding company*, which may have a majority on the subsidiary's *board of directors*, or a majority shareholding in the subsidiary, giving it majority voting rights, or it may be named

in a contract as having control of the subsidiary. If all of the stock in a company is owned by its parent, it is known as a *wholly-owned subsidiary*. A subsidiary that is located in a different country from the parent is a **foreign subsidiary company**.

subsistence allowance *HR expenses* paid by an *employer*, usually within preset limits, to cover the cost of accommodation, meals, and incidental expenses incurred by employees when away on business

subtreasury *Fin* a place where some of a nation's money is held

succession planning *Gen Mgt* the preparation for the replacement of one postholder by another, usually prompted by *retirement* or *resignation*. Succession planning involves preparing the new postholder before the old one leaves, possibly with training or through work shadowing. At a senior level, **management succession** should be accomplished as smoothly as possible in order to avoid organisational crises caused by absent or inadequate top management. General Electric is held to be an exemplar of succession planning for its preparation for the retirement of *Jack Welch*.

suggestion scheme *HR* a policy designed to encourage employees to generate ideas or proposals that improve work processes, for which they receive a gift or cash reward. The objective of a suggestion scheme is to promote *employee involvement*, creative thinking, and continuous improvement. Its success can be evaluated in terms of the participation rate or by the level of cost savings, but there may be an incalculable beneficial effect on sales, customer loyalty, retention of employees, and *motivation*.

suit *Gen Mgt* somebody who works for a large corporation and is required to wear a suit for work (*slang*)

sum *Fin* an amount or total of any given item, such as money, stocks, or securities

sum at risk *Fin* an amount of any given item, such as money, stocks, or securities that an investor may lose

sum insured *Fin* the maximum amount that an insurance company will pay out in the event of a claim

sum-of-the-year's-digits depreciation *Fin* accelerated depreciation, conferring tax advantage by assuming more rapid depreciation when an asset is new

Sunday night syndrome *Gen Mgt* feelings of depression experienced by employees when they consider their return to work on Monday morning

sunshine law *Fin* a law that requires public disclosure of a government act

Sun Tzu (*b.* uncertain) *Gen Mgt* Chinese general. Although he lived over 2,400 years ago, he is said to have an influence on modern business thinking, based on his thoughts on *strategy* recorded in *The Art of War* (various translations).

super (*ANZ*) *Fin* an informal term for superannuation (*slang*)

superannuation plan *HR* a pension plan in Australia

superannuation scheme *HR* a pension plan in New Zealand

superindustrial society *Gen Mgt* a society in which technology dominates both the personal and working lives of its members

superstitial *E-com* a form of web-based advertisement that is run while new web pages are loading onto a user's computer. Unlike *interstitials*, superstitials are loaded onto the computer using a 'cache-and-play' delivery system that works while the Internet user is browsing the Web. Superstitials are mainly used during business-to-consumer advertising campaigns.

supervisor *Gen Mgt, HR* an employee who is given authority and responsibility for planning and controlling the work of a group through close contact. A supervisor is the first level of management in an organisation. The subordinates he or she controls are usually at a non-managerial level and the supervisor is wholly responsible for their work.

supervisory management *Gen Mgt, HR* the most junior level of management within an organisation. Supervisory management activities include staff *recruitment*, handling day-to-day grievances and staff discipline, and ensuring that quality and production targets are met. *Also known as first-line management*

supplier *HR, Ops* an organisation that delivers materials, components, goods, or services to another organisation

supplier appraisal *Ops* see *vendor rating*

supplier development *HR* the development of close and long-term relationships between a customer and a *supplier*. Supplier development tends to be associated with *Japanese management* practices and has only recently been introduced to the West. Various approaches to customer-supplier relations have emerged, including co-makership, partnership sourcing, collaborative sourcing, and co-operative sourcing. All these forms of supplier development are characterised by a long-term commitment, an integration of key functions and activities, a structured framework for determining price and sharing cost and profit, a proactive approach to *problem-solving*, and the adoption of both a win-win philosophy and a culture of continuous improvement.

supplier evaluation *Ops* the process of screening and evaluating potential suppliers of materials, goods, or services. Supplier evaluation involves establishing a set of requirements, which may include basic business robustness, performance elements specific to the product or service, and the key order winning criteria for final selection. Existing and potential suppliers are screened against these criteria, prior to placing a new order. When this process is undertaken after the fulfilment of an order, it is known as *vendor rating*.

He who buys what he needs not, sells what he needs.   *Japanese proverb*

supplier rating *Ops see vendor rating*

supply and demand *Gen Mgt, Ops* the quantity of goods available for sale at a given price, and the level of consumer need for those goods at a given price. The balance of supply and demand fluctuates as external economic factors such as the cost of materials and the level of competition in the marketplace influence the level of demand from consumers and the desire and ability of producers to supply the goods. Supply and demand is recognised as an economic principle, and is often referred to as the **law of supply and demand**.

supply chain *Gen Mgt, Ops* the network of *manufacturers*, *wholesalers*, distributors, and *retailers*, who turn *raw materials* into *finished goods* and services and deliver them to *consumers*. Supply chains are increasingly being seen as integrated entities, and closer relationships between the organisations throughout the chain can bring *competitive advantage*, reduce costs, and help to maintain a loyal customer base.

supply chain management *Ops* the management of the movement of goods and flow of information between an organisation and its *suppliers* and *customers*, to achieve strategic advantage. Supply chain management covers the processes of *materials management*, *logistics*, *physical distribution management*, and *purchasing*, as well as *information management*.

supply-side economics *Econ* the study of how economic agents behave when supply is affected by changing price

support *Mkting* help, advice, and services offered to customers by a seller after a sale

support price *Econ* the price of a product that is fixed or stabilised by a government so that it cannot fall below a certain level

surety *Fin* **1.** a guarantor **2.** the collateral given as security when borrowing

surplus *Fin see budget surplus*

surplus capacity *Ops* the capability of a factory or workstation to produce output over and above the level required by consumers or subsequent processes. Surplus capacity is a product of materials, personnel, and equipment that are superfluous, or not working to maximum *capacity*. Some surplus capacity is required in any production system to deal with fluctuations in demand, and as a backup in case of failure. Excessive surplus capacity, however, adds to the cost of the production process as work-in-progress inventory or finished-goods storage increases, and can result in *overcapacity*. If a workstation has no surplus capacity its workloads cannot be increased, so it is at risk of becoming a *bottleneck*. *Also known as redundant capacity*

surrender value *Fin* the sum of money offered by an insurance company to somebody who cancels a policy before it has completed its full term

surtax *Fin* a tax paid in addition to another tax, typically levied on an a corporation with very high income

survey *Stats* the collection of data from a given population for the purpose of analysis of a particular issue. Data is often collected only from a sample of a population, and this is known as a *sample survey*. Surveys are used widely in research, especially in *market research*.

survivalist enterprise (*S Africa*) *Gen Mgt* a business that has no paid employees, generates income below the poverty line, and is considered the lowest level of micro-enterprise

sushi bond *Fin* a derogatory name for a bond that is not denominated in yen and is issued in any market by a Japanese financial institution. This type of bond is often bought by Japanese institutional investors.

sustainable advantage *Gen Mgt* a competitive advantage that can be maintained over the long term, as opposed to one resulting from a short-term tactical promotion

---

A radical is a man with both feet firmly planted in the air. Franklin D. Roosevelt

sustainable development *Gen Mgt* development that meets the needs of the present without compromising the ability of future generations to meet their own needs. The concept of sustainable development was introduced by the Brundtland Report, the first report of the World Commission on Environment and Development, set up by the United Nations in 1983. It advocates the integration of social, economic, and environmental considerations into policy decisions by business and government. Particular emphasis is given to social, cultural, and ethical implications of development. Sustainable development can be achieved through *environmental management* and is a feature of a socially responsible business.

SVA *abbr Gen Mgt* shareholder value analysis

swap *Fin* an exchange of credits or liabilities. *See also asset swap, bond swap, interest rate swap*

swap book *Fin* a broker's list of stocks or securities that clients wish to swap

swaption *Fin* an option to enter into a *swap* contract (*slang*)

sweat equity *Gen Mgt* an investment of labour rather than cash in a business enterprise (*slang*)

sweep facility *Fin* the automatic transfer of sums from a current account to a deposit account, or from any low interest account to a higher one. For example, a personal customer may have the balance transferred just before receipt of their monthly salary, or a business may stipulate that when a balance exceeds a certain sum, the excess is to be transferred.

sweetener **1.** *Gen Mgt* an incentive offered to somebody to take a particular course of action **2.** *Fin* a feature added to a security to make it more attractive to investors **3.** *Fin* a security with a high yield that has been added to a portfolio to improve its overall return. *See also kicker*

sweetheart agreement (*ANZ*) *HR* an agreement reached between employees and their employer without recourse to arbitration

SWELL *abbr Mkting* Single Woman Earning Lots in London (*slang*)

SWIFT *abbr Fin* Society for Worldwide Interbank Financial Telecommunication: a non-profit cooperative organisation whose mission is to create a shared worldwide data processing and communications link and a common language for international financial transactions. Established in Brussels in 1973 with the support of 239 banks in 15 countries, it now has over 7,000 live users in 192 countries, exchanging millions of messages valued in trillions of dollars every business day.

swing trading *Fin* the trading of stock by individuals that takes advantage of sudden price movements that occur especially when large numbers of traders have to cover short sales

swipe box *E-com* an electronic device used for reading the magnetic data on a credit card during a card-present transaction

switch *Fin* **1.** to exchange a specific security with another within a portfolio, usually because the investor's objectives have changed **2.** a swap exchange rate. *See also swap* **3.** to move a commodity from one location to another

Switch *Fin* a debit card widely used in the United Kingdom

switching *Fin* the simultaneous sale and purchase of contracts in futures with different expiration dates, for example, when a business decides that it would like to take delivery of a commodity earlier or later than originally contracted

switching discount *Fin* the discount available to holders of collective investments who move from one fund to another offered by the same fund manager. This is usually a lower initial charge compared to the one made to new investors or when existing investors make a further investment.

I never hesitated to promote someone I didn't like.　　　　*Thomas J. Watson Jr*

SWOT analysis *Gen Mgt* an assessment of Strengths, Weaknesses, Opportunities, and Threats. SWOT analysis is used within organisations in the early stages of strategic and *marketing planning*. It is also used in *problem-solving*, *decision-making*, or for making staff aware of the need for change. It can be used at a personal level when examining your *career path* or determining possible *career development*.

Sydney Futures Exchange *Fin* the principal market in Australia for trading financial and commodity futures. It was set up in 1962 as a wool futures market, the Sydney Greasy Wool Futures Exchange, but adopted its current name in 1972 to reflect its widening role. *Abbr* **SFE**

symmetrical distribution *Stats* a distribution of statistical data that is symmetrical about a central value

syndicated research *Mkting* trend data supplied by research agencies from their regularly operated retail audits or consumer panels

sysop *E-com* systems operator, somebody who manages a website or bulletin board (*slang*)

systematic sampling *Ops see random sampling*

system attack *E-com* a deliberate attack on an e-mail system, usually in the form of a barrage of messages sent to one address simultaneously

systems administrator *E-com* the person responsible for the management of an e-mail system

systems analysis *Gen Mgt* the examination and evaluation of an operation or task in order to identify and implement more efficient methods, usually through the use of computers. Systems analysis can be broken down into three main areas: the production of a statement of objectives; determination of the methods of best achieving these objectives in a cost-effective and efficient way; and the preparation of a *feasibility study*. Also known as *systems planning*

systems approach *Gen Mgt* a technique employed for organisational *decision-making* and *problem-solving* involving the use of computer systems.

The systems approach uses *systems analysis* to examine the interdependency, interconnections, and interrelations of a system's components. When working in synergy, these components produce an effect greater than the sum effects of the parts. System components might comprise departments or functions of an organisation or business which work together for an overall objective.

systems audit *Gen Mgt* an approach to *auditing* which utilises the *systems method*. By using a systems audit to assess the internal control system of an organisation, it is possible to assess the quality of the accounting system and the level of testing required from the financial statements. One shortcoming of systems audit is that it does not consider audit *risk*. Consequently, risk-based audit is now considered more effective.

systems design *Gen Mgt* the creation of a computer program to meet predetermined functional, operational, and personnel specifications. The systems design process involves the use of *systems analysis* and flow-charting of organisational functions and operations. It can be split into four stages: definition of the system's goals; preparation of a conceptual model of how these goals will be achieved; development of a physical design; and preparation of a system specification.

systems dynamics *Gen Mgt* a computer-based tool, developed at the Massachusetts Institute of Technology, designed to model the behaviour of constantly changing systems. Systems dynamics investigates the combined effects of individual changes made at different points in a system, and uses *simulation* to design information feedback structures.

systems engineering *Gen Mgt* the process of planning, designing, creating,

---

There is a misconception that small is always more beautiful than big.   **Lou Gerstner**

testing, and operating complex systems. Systems engineering can be viewed as a continuous cycle, aimed at developing alternative strategies for effective systems utilisation. It is concerned with the definition, planning, and deployment of future systems.

systems method *Gen Mgt* a widely used group of methodologies which explore the nature of complex business situations by mapping activities in a model. The systems method can be applied to systems that are either **hard systems**, where precise objectives are expressed in mathematical terms, or **soft systems**, where a human factor is involved and situations often do not involve such precise objectives. A range of *systems approaches* are available including *operational research*, *systems analysis*, and *systems dynamics*.

systems planning *Gen Mgt see* *systems analysis*

T+ *Fin* an expression of the number of days allowed for settlement of a transaction

TA *abbr Gen Mgt* transactional analysis

tacit knowledge *Gen Mgt see* **knowledge**

tactical campaign *Mkting* a series of marketing activities designed to achieve short-term targets

tactical plan *Gen Mgt* a short-term plan for achieving an entity's objectives

TAFN *abbr Gen Mgt* that's all for now (*slang*)

Taguchi, Genichi (*b.* 1924) *Gen Mgt* Japanese academic and consultant. Known for his contribution to quality engineering and founder of the *Taguchi method*, which seeks to integrate **quality control** into product design using experiment and statistical analysis. His concepts, including quality loss (see *Taguchi methods*), are explained in publications such as *Introduction to Quality Engineering* (1986).

Taguchi methods *Ops* the pioneering techniques of **quality control** developed by **Genichi Taguchi**, which focus on improving the quality of a product or process at the design stage rather than after manufacture or delivery. Taguchi's philosophy is that a quality approach that focuses on the parameters or factors of design produces a design that is more robust and is capable of withstanding variations from unwanted sources in the production or delivery process. He developed methods for both offline (design) and online (production) quality control. He developed the concepts of **quality loss** and the signal to noise ratio, and a product design improvement process based on three steps: system design, parameter design, and tolerance design.

tailgating *Fin* the practice of buying or selling a security by a broker, immediately after a client's transaction, in order to take advantage of the impact of the client's deal

tailormade promotion *Mkting* a promotional campaign that is customised for a particular customer

take a flyer *Fin* to speculate (*slang*)

take a hit *Fin* to make a loss on an investment (*slang*)

takeaway *Gen Mgt* the impressions that a consumer forms about a product or service

take-home pay *HR* the amount of **pay** an employee receives after all deductions, such as income tax, national insurance, or pension contributions. *Also known as* **net pay**

takeout financing *Fin* loans used to replace bridge financing

takeover *Fin* the acquisition by a company of a controlling interest in the voting share capital of another company, usually achieved by the purchase of a majority of the voting shares

takeover approach *Fin* the price at which a suitor offers to buy a corporation's shares. *US term* **tender offer**

takeover battle *Fin* the result of a hostile takeover bid. The bidder may raise the offer price and write to the shareholders extolling the benefits of the takeover. The board may contact other companies in the same line of business hoping that a white knight may appear. It could also take action to make the company less desirable to the bidder. *See also* **poison pill**

takeover bid *Mkting* an attempt by one company to acquire another. A takeover bid can be made either by a person or an organisation, and usually takes the form of an approach to **shareholders** with an offer to purchase. The bidding stage is often difficult and fraught with politics, and various forms of **knight** may be involved.

I shall find a way or make one.

takeover ratio *Fin* the book value of a company divided by its market capitalisation. If the resulting figure is greater than one, then the company is a candidate for a takeover. *See also* **appreciation**, **asset-stripping**

taker *Fin* **1.** the buyer of an option **2.** a borrower

takings *Fin* a retailer's net receipts

talent *HR* people with exceptional abilities, especially a company's most valued employees (*slang*)

talk offline *Gen Mgt* **1.** to continue a particular line of discussion outside the original context. A person may wish to talk offline about an issue tangential to the current discussion, or may carry on that branch of the conversation at a later time, using different media. (*slang*) **2.** to express an opinion in opposition to an employing organisation's official position

tall organisation *Gen Mgt* an **organisation structure** with many levels of management. A tall organisation contrasts with a **flat organisation**, since it has an extended vertical structure with well-defined but long reporting lines. The number of different levels may cause **communication** problems and slow **decision-making**. It is for this reason that many companies are converting to flatter structures more suited to the fast responses needed in a rapidly changing business environment.

tall poppy (*ANZ*) *Gen Mgt* a prominent member of society (*slang*)

tall poppy syndrome (*ANZ*) *Gen Mgt* an inclination in the media and among the general public to belittle the achievements of prominent people (*slang*)

talon *Fin* a form attached to a bearer bond that the holder of the bond uses when the coupons attached to the bond have been depleted to order new coupons

tangible assets *Fin* assets that are physical, such as buildings, cash and stock, as opposed to intangible assets. Leases and securities, although not physical, are classed as tangible assets because the underlying assets are physical.

tangible book value *Fin* the book value of a company after intangible assets, patents, trademarks, and the value of research and development have been subtracted

tangible fixed asset statement *Fin* a summary of the opening and closing balances for tangible fixed assets and acquisitions, disposals, and depreciation in the period

tank *Fin* to fall precipitously. This term is used especially in reference to stock prices. (*slang*)

tap CD *Fin* the issue of certificates of deposit, normally in large denominations, when required by a specific investor

tape
don't fight the tape *Fin* don't go against the direction of the market (*slang*)

target *Gen Mgt see* **objective**

target audience *Mkting* a group of people considered likely to buy a product or service

target cash balance *Fin* the amount of cash that a company would like to have in hand

target company *Fin* a company that is the object of a takeover bid

target cost *Fin* a product cost estimate derived by subtracting a desired profit margin from a competitive market price. This may be less than the planned initial product cost, but will be expected to be achieved by the time the product reaches the mature production stage.

targeted repurchase *Fin* a company's purchase of its own shares from somebody attempting to buy the company

target population *Stats* the collection of individuals or regions that are to be investigated in a statistical study

target savings motive *Econ* the motive that people have not to save when their families are growing up but to save when they are in middle age and trying to build up a pension

target stock level *Ops* the level of *inventory* that is needed to satisfy all demand for a product or component over a specified period

tariff 1. *Econ* a government duty imposed on imports or exports to stimulate or dampen economic activity **2.** *Fin* a list of prices at which goods or services are supplied

Tariff Concession Scheme *Fin* a system operated by the Australian government in which imported goods that have no locally produced equivalent attract reduced duties. *Abbr* **TCS**

tariff office *Fin* an insurance company whose premiums are determined according to a scale set collectively by several companies

task analysis *HR* a methodology for identifying and examining the jobs performed by users when interacting with computerised, or non-computerised, systems. Task analysis employs a range of techniques to help analysts collect information, organise it, and use it to integrate the human element in systems. It assists in the achievement of higher safety, *productivity*, and maintenance standards.

task culture *Gen Mgt* a form of *corporate culture* based on individual projects carried out by small teams. Task culture was identified by *Charles Handy*. It draws resources from different parts of the organisation to form study groups, working parties, and ad hoc committees to take on problems, projects, and initiatives as they arise.

task group *HR* a group of employees temporarily brought together to complete a specific project or task. A task group can take the form of an *autonomous work group* if it is responsible for its own management.

taste space *Mkting* a community of consumers identified as having similar tastes

or interests, for example, in music or books, enabling companies to recommend purchases or target advertising at them (*slang*)

tax *Fin* a governmental charge that is not a price for a good or service

taxability *Fin* the extent to which a good or individual is subject to a tax

taxable *Fin* subject to a tax

taxable base *Fin* the amount subject to taxation

taxable income *Fin* income that is subject to taxes

taxable matters *Fin* goods or services that can be taxed

tax and price index *Econ* an index number measuring the percentage change in gross income that taxpayers need if they are to maintain their real disposable income

tax avoidance *Fin* strategies to ensure the payment of as little in taxes as is legally possible. *See also tax evasion*

tax bracket *Fin* a range of income levels subject to marginal tax at the same rate

tax break *Fin* an investment that is tax efficient or a legal arrangement that reduces the liability to tax. *See also tax avoidance, tax shelter*

tax consultant *Fin* a professional who advises on all aspects of taxation from tax avoidance to estate planning

tax-deductible *Fin* able to be subtracted from taxable income before tax is paid

tax-deductible public debt *Fin* debt instruments exempt from US federal income tax

tax-deferred *Fin* not to be taxed until a later time

tax domicile *Fin* a place that a government levying a tax considers to be a person's home

tax-efficient *Fin* financially advantageous by leading to a reduction of taxes to be paid

tax evasion *Fin* the illegal practice of paying less money in taxes than is due. *See also tax avoidance*

tax evasion amnesty *Fin* a governmental measure that affords those who have evaded a tax in some specified way freedom from punishment for their violation of the tax law

tax-exempt *Fin* not subject to tax

Tax Exempt Special Savings Account *Fin* a UK savings account in which investors could save up to £9,000 over a period of five years and not pay any tax provided they made no withdrawals over that time. The advent of the ISA in 1999 meant that no new accounts of this type could be opened, but those opened prior to 1999 will continue under their original premise until their expiry date. *Abbr* **TESSA**

tax exile *Fin* a person or business that leaves a country to avoid paying taxes, or the condition of having done this

tax-favoured asset *Fin* an asset that receives more favourable tax treatment than some other asset

tax file number *Fin* an identification number assigned to each taxpayer in Australia. *Abbr* **TFN**

tax-free *Fin* not subject to tax

tax harmonization *Fin* the enactment of taxation laws in different jurisdictions, such as neighbouring countries, provinces, or states of the United States, that are consistent with one another

tax haven *Fin* a country that has generous tax laws, especially one that encourages non-citizens to base operations in the country to avoid higher taxes in their home countries

tax holiday *Fin* an exemption from tax granted for a specified period of time. *See also tax subsidy*

taxi industry *Fin* the privately owned minibus taxi services, which constitute the largest sector of public transport in South Africa

tax incentive *Fin* a tax reduction afforded to people for particular purposes, for example, sending their children to college

tax inspector *Fin* a government employee who investigates taxpayers' declarations

tax invoice (*ANZ*) *Fin* a document issued by a supplier which stipulates the amount charged for goods or services as well as the amount of **GST** payable

tax law *Fin* the body of laws on taxation, or one such law

tax loophole *Fin* a provision in a tax law that permits some individuals and companies to avoid or reduce taxes

tax loss *Fin* a loss of money that can serve to reduce tax liabilities

tax loss carry-back *Fin* the reduction of taxes in a previous year by subtraction from income for that year of losses suffered in the current year

tax loss carry-forward *Fin* the reduction of taxes in a future year by subtraction from income for that year of losses suffered in the current year

tax obligation *Fin* the amount of tax a person or company owes

tax on capital income *Fin* a tax on the income from sales of capital assets

tax payable *Fin* the amount of tax a person or company has to pay

taxpayer *Fin* an individual or corporation who pays a tax

tax rate *Fin* a percentage of a taxable amount that is due to be paid in taxes

tax refund *Fin* an amount that a government gives back to a taxpayer who has paid more taxes than were due

tax relief *Fin* **1.** the reduction in the amount of taxes payable, for example, on capital goods a company has purchased **2.** (*US*) money given to a certain group of people by a government in the form of a reduction of taxes

tax return *Fin* an official form on which a company or individual enters details of income and expenses, used to assess tax liability. *Also known as* **return**

tax revenue *Fin* money that a government receives in taxes

tax sale (*US*) *Fin* a sale of an item by a government to recover overdue taxes on a taxable item

tax shelter *Fin* a financial arrangement designed to reduce tax liability. *See also* **abusive tax shelter**

tax subsidy *Fin* a tax reduction given by a government to a business for a particular purpose, usually to create jobs. *See also* **tax holiday**

tax system *Fin* the system of taxation adopted by a country

tax treaty *Fin* an international treaty that deals with taxes, especially taxes by several countries on the same individuals

tax year *Fin* a period covered by a statement about taxes

Taylor, Frederick Winslow (1856–1917) *Gen Mgt* US engineer. Acknowledged as the father of *scientific management*, which is sometimes referred to as 'Taylorism'. Taylor's methods, recorded in *The Principles of Scientific Management* (1911), have been criticised as too mechanistic, treating people like machines rather than human beings to be motivated. They were later counterbalanced by the *human relations* school of management.

Taylor grew up in an affluent Philadelphia family. He worked as chief engineer at the Midvale Steel Company, and later became general manager of the Manufacturing Investment Company's paper mills in Maine. In 1893 he moved to New York and began business as a consulting engineer.

T-bill *abbr Fin* Treasury bill

TCO *abbr Gen Mgt* total cost of ownership

T-commerce *E-com* business that is conducted by means of interactive television (*slang*)

TCP/IP *abbr E-com* transmission control protocol/Internet protocol: the combination of protocols that enables the Internet to function. TCP deals with the process of sending packets of information from one computer to another. IP is the process of passing each packet between computers until it reaches its intended destination.

TCS *abbr Fin* Tariff Concession Scheme

TDB *abbr Fin* Trade Development Board

team briefing *HR* a regular meeting between managers or supervisors and their teams to exchange information and ideas. The idea of team briefing evolved from the concept of **briefing groups** which was developed in the United Kingdom in the 1960s and promoted by the Industrial Society as a means of communicating systematically with managers and employees throughout an organisation. The aim was to reduce misunderstandings and rumours and increase co-operation, *employee commitment*, and *team building*. Team briefings are characterised as being regular face-to-face meetings of small teams which are led by a team leader and are relevant to the work of the group, providing an opportunity for questions.

team building *Gen Mgt* the selection and grouping of a mix of people and the development of skills required within the group to achieve agreed objectives. Effective team building can be achieved through a number of models, one of the most established of which was created by *R. Meredith Belbin*.

team management *Gen Mgt see Managerial Grid*™

Team Management Wheel™ *Gen Mgt* a visual aid for the efficient co-ordination of *teamwork*, which can be used to analyse how teams work together, assist in *team building*, and aid self-development and training. The Team Management Wheel outlines eight main team roles. Team members can determine the main functions of their jobs (what they have to do), by using the 'Types of Work Index', and can determine their own work preferences (what they want to do), using the 'Team Management Index'. They are then assigned one major role and two minor roles on the Team Management Wheel. At the centre of the Wheel are the linking skills common to all team members. The Team Management Wheel was developed by *Charles Margerison* and *Dick McCann* in 1984.

team player *Gen Mgt* somebody who works well within a team (*slang*)

teamwork *Gen Mgt* collaboration by a group of people to achieve a common purpose. Teamwork is often a feature of day-to-day working, and is increasingly used to accomplish specific projects, in which case it may bring together people from different functions, departments, or disciplines. A team should ideally consist of people with complementary skills; *R. Meredith Belbin* has established nine personality types that are needed in every team. One tool aimed at effective *team building* is the *Team Management Wheel*™. There are various types of teamworking, including the *autonomous work group* and the *virtual team*.

teaser rate *Fin* a temporary concessionary interest rate offered on mortgages, credit cards, or savings accounts in order to attract new customers

technical analysis *Fin* the analysis of past movements in the prices of financial instruments, currencies, commodities, etc., with a view to predicting future price movements by applying analytical techniques. *See also fundamental analysis*

technical rally *Fin* a temporary rise in security or commodity prices while the market is in a general decline. This may be because investors are seeking bargains, or because analysts have noted a support level.

technical reserves *Fin* the assets that an insurance company maintains to meet future claims

technocracy *Gen Mgt* an organisation controlled by technical experts. *See also bureaucracy*

techno-determinist *Gen Mgt* somebody who believes that technological progress is inevitable

technographics *Gen Mgt* a research process that evaluates the attitudes of consumers towards technology. The process was introduced by Forrester Research.

technological risk *Fin* the risk that a newly designed plant will not operate to specification

technology adoption life cycle *Gen Mgt* a model used to describe the adoption of new technologies, typically including the stages of innovators, early adopters, early majority, late majority, and *technology laggards*

Technology and Human Resources for Industry Programme (*S Africa*) *Fin see THRIP*

technology laggard *Gen Mgt* an organisation that is very slow or reluctant to adopt new technology

technology stock *Fin* stock issued by a company that is involved in new technology

teeming and lading *Fin* a fraud based on a continuous cycle of stealing and later replacing assets (generally cash), each theft being used in part, or in full, to repay a previous theft in order to avoid detection

telcos (*ANZ*) *Gen Mgt* an informal term for telecommunications companies (*slang*)

telebanking *Fin* electronic banking carried out by using a telephone line to communicate with a bank

telecentre *Gen Mgt* a building offering office space and facilities outside the home but away from the main workplace to enable remote working. A telecentre

I love deadlines. I especially like the whooshing sound they make as they go flying by.
Douglas Adams

may be owned by one employer—in which case it is known as a **satellite centre**—or may be independently run on behalf of a number of organisations. Employees avoid long commuting times but work in an office rather than at home; employers avoid having to equip several homes with expensive office equipment. *Also known as* **telecottage**

telecommute *Gen Mgt* to work without leaving your home by using telephone lines to carry data between your home and your employer's place of business

telecommuter *Gen Mgt see* **teleworker**

telecommuting *Gen Mgt see* **teleworking**

teleconferencing *Gen Mgt* the use of telephone or television channels to connect people in different locations in order to conduct group discussions, meetings, conferences, or courses

telecottage *Gen Mgt see* **telecentre**

telegraphic transfer *Fin* a method of transferring funds from a bank to a financial institution overseas using telegraphs. *Abbr* **TT**

telemarketing *Mkting see* **telephone selling**

telephone banking *Fin* a system in which customers can access their accounts and a range of banking services up to 24 hours a day by telephone. Apart from convenience, customers usually benefit from higher interest rates on savings accounts and lower interest when borrowing as providers of telephone banking have lower overheads than traditional high street banks.

telephone interview survey *Stats* a method of sampling a population by telephoning its members

telephone number salary *HR* a six- or seven-figure salary (*slang*)

telephone selling *Mkting* the sale of products or services to customers over the telephone. Telephone selling may be used as an alternative, cheaper, method than door-to-door selling, or may be used to

obtain an initial appointment for a salesperson to visit a potential customer. *Also known as* **telemarketing**, **telesales**

telephone survey *Mkting* a research technique in which members of the public are asked a series of questions on the telephone

telephone switching *Fin* the process of connecting telephones to one another

telephone tag *Gen Mgt* the reciprocal calling and leaving of messages by two people who wish to speak to each other but are never available to speak on their telephones when the other calls (*slang*)

telesales *Mkting see* **telephone selling**

teleshopping *E-com* the use of telecommunications and computers to shop for and purchase goods and services

television audience measurement *Mkting* the recording of the viewing patterns of a sample of the population, used as the basis for estimating national viewing figures for individual programmes

teleworker *Gen Mgt* an employee who spends a substantial amount of working time away from the employer's main premises and communicates with the organisation through the use of computing and telecommunications equipment. A teleworker may be based at home, in which case the worker is known as a **homeworker**, or in a **telecentre**, or on a variety of sites, in which case he or she may be known as a **mobile worker**. *Also known as* **telecommuter**

teleworking *Gen Mgt* a geographically dispersed work environment where workers can work at home on a computer and transmit data and documents to a central office via telephone lines. As people become accustomed to working via e-mail and the Internet, teleworking is proving ever more popular.

The advantages of teleworking are considerable, offering as it does an excellent compromise between the security of fulltime employment and the liberty and privacy of self-employment. However, it also has disadvantages—the most important of which is the danger of being left behind, forgotten, or overlooked when new assignments or promotions come up within the organisation. It is therefore supremely important for teleworkers to build a plan for staying visible and connected with the people they work with, even if they spend much of their working life in their home office. *Also known as telecommuting*

teller *Fin* a bank cashier

tender 1. *Fin* to bid for securities at auction. The securities are allocated according to the method adopted by the issuer. In the standard auction style, the investor receives the security at the price they tendered. In a Dutch style auction, the issuer announces a strike price after all the tenders have been examined. This is set at a level where all the issue is sold. Investors who submitted a tender above the strike price only pay the strike price. The Dutch style of auction is increasingly being adopted in the United Kingdom. US Treasury Bills are also sold using the Dutch system. *See also* **offer for sale, sale by tender 2.** *Gen Mgt* to make or submit a bid to undertake work or supply goods at a stated price. A tender is usually submitted in response to an invitation to bid for a work contract in competition with other suppliers.

tender offer *(US) Fin* = **takeover approach**

tenor *Fin* the period of time that has to elapse before a bill of exchange becomes payable

term *Fin* the period of time that has to elapse from the date of the initial investment before a security, or other investment such as a term deposit or endowment assurance, becomes redeemable or reaches its maturity date

term assurance *Fin* a life policy that will pay out upon the death of the life assured or in the event of the death of the first life assured with a joint life assurance

term bill *Fin see* **period bill**

term deposit *Fin* a deposit account held for a fixed period. Withdrawals are either not allowed during this period, or they involve a fee payable by the depositor.

terminal date *Fin* the day on which a futures contract expires

terminal identification number *E-com see* **TIN**

terminal market *Fin* an exchange on which futures contracts or spot deals for commodities are traded

termination interview *HR* a meeting between an employee and a management representative in order to *dismiss* the employee. A termination interview should be brief, explaining the reasons for the dismissal, and giving details of whether a *notice period* should be worked, and whether, especially in the case of *redundancy*, additional assistance will be forthcoming from the employer.

termination of service *HR* the ending of an employee's *contract of employment* for a reason such as *redundancy*, employer *insolvency*, or *dismissal*

term insurance *Fin* insurance, especially life assurance, that is in effect for a specified period of time

term loan *Fin* a loan for a fixed period, usually called a personal loan when it is for non-business purposes. While a personal loan is normally at a fixed rate of interest, a term loan to a business may be at either a fixed or variable rate. Term loans may be either secured or unsecured. An early repayment fee is usually payable when such a loan is repaid before the end of the term. *See also* **balloon loan, bullet loan**

term shares *Fin* in the United Kingdom, a share account in a building society that is for a fixed period of time. Withdrawals are usually not allowed during this period. However, if they are, then a fee is normally payable by the account holder.

terms of trade *Econ* a ratio to determine whether the conditions under which a country conducts its trade are favourable or unfavourable

terotechnology *Ops* a multidisciplinary technique that combines the areas of management, finance, and engineering with the aim of optimising life-cycle costs for physical assets and technologies. Terotechnology is concerned with acquiring and caring for physical assets. It covers the specification and design for the reliability and maintainability of plant, machinery, equipment, buildings, and structures, including the installation, commissioning, maintenance, and replacement of this plant, and also incorporates the feedback of information on design, performance, and costs.

tertiary sector *Econ* the part of the economy made up of non-profit organisations such as consumer associations and self-help groups

TESSA *abbr Fin* Tax Exempt Special Savings Account

testacy *Fin* the legal position of a person who has died leaving a valid will

testate *Fin* used to refer to a person who has died leaving a valid will

testator *Fin* a man who has made a valid will

testatrix *Fin* a woman who has made a valid will

test battery *HR see* **psychometric test**

testimonial advertising *Mkting* advertising in which customers or celebrities recommend the product

test marketing *Mkting* the use of a small-scale version of a **marketing plan**, usually in a restricted area or with a small group, to test the marketing strategy for a new product. Test marketing gauges both the success of the marketing strategy and the reactions of consumers to a new product by giving an indication of the potential response to a product nationwide. Test marketing avoids the costs of a full-scale launch of an untested product, but a drawback is that both the product and marketing plan are exposed to competitors.

TFN *abbr Fin* tax file number

TFN Withholding Tax (*ANZ*) *Fin* Tax File Number Withholding Tax: a levy imposed on financial transactions involving an individual who has not disclosed his or her tax file number

TGIF *abbr Gen Mgt* thank God it's Friday (*slang*)

T-Group *HR see* **sensitivity training**

Theory E *Gen Mgt* a mechanism for bringing about change in an organisation through the creation of economic value and improved profits for the shareholders. Theory E has the single goal of satisfying the financial markets with a **top-down approach** style of **leadership** from the **chief executive**. Theory E contrasts with **Theory O**, which involves employee **empowerment** and **employee participation** in leadership. *See also* **alphabet theories of management**

Theory J *Gen Mgt* the **Japanese** form of management. Theory J is closely related to **Theory Z**, and was expounded by **William Ouchi**. *See also* **alphabet theories of management**

Theory O *Gen Mgt* a mechanism for organisational **change** based on developing **corporate culture** and human capability through personal and **organisational learning**. Theory O involves fostering a culture that encourages employees to find their own solutions to problems through **empowerment** and participative **leadership**. Theory O contrasts with **Theory E**, which involves a **top-down approach** style of leadership rather than **employee participation**. *See also* **alphabet theories of management**

theory of constraints *Fin* an approach to production management which aims to maximise sales revenue less material and variable overhead cost. It focuses on factors such as bottlenecks which act as constraints to this maximisation. *Abbr* **TOC**

theory of the horizontal fast track *Gen Mgt* a variation of **fast track** coined by **Charles Handy**. The theory of the horizontal fast track describes the development of talented people who are moved around from task to task to test and develop their capability in different working situations.

Theory W *Gen Mgt* an extreme extension of **Douglas McGregor**'s **Theory X**, which proposes that not only should employees be coerced into action but that force is often required. Theory W is a humorous contribution to the **alphabet theories of management**. Theory W stands for Theory Whiplash.

Theory X *Gen Mgt* a management theory based on the assumption that most people are naturally reluctant to work and need discipline, direction, and close control if they are to meet work requirements. Theory X was coined by **Douglas McGregor** in *The Human Side of Enterprise*, and it was considered by him to be an implicit basis for traditional hierarchical management. McGregor rejected Theory X as an appropriate management style and favoured instead his proposed alternative, **Theory Y**. *See also* **alphabet theories of management**

Theory Y *Gen Mgt* a management theory based on the assumption that employees want to work, achieve, and take responsibility for meeting their work requirements. Theory Y was coined by **Douglas McGregor** in *The Human Side of Enterprise*. Although he recognised that Theory Y could not solve all human resource management (see **HRM**) problems, McGregor favoured it over his **Theory X**, which required an autocratic management style. *See also* **alphabet theories of management**

Theory Z *Gen Mgt* a management theory based on the assumption that greater employee involvement leads to greater productivity. Theory Z was proposed by **Douglas McGregor** shortly before his death in an attempt to address the criticisms of his **Theory X** and **Theory Y**. McGregor's ideas were expanded by **William Ouchi** in his book *Theory Z*, reflecting the Japanese approach to human resource management (see **HRM**). Theory Z advocates greater **employee participation** in management, greater recognition of employees' contributions, better career prospects and security of employment, and greater mutual respect between employees and managers. *See also* **alphabet theories of management**

think tank *Gen Mgt* an organisation or group of experts researching and advising on issues of society, science, technology, industry, or business

thin market *Fin* a market where the trading volume is low. A characteristic of such a market is a wide spread of bid and offer prices.

third market *Fin* a market other than the main stock exchange in which stocks are traded

third-party network *or* **third-party service provider** *E-com see* **value-added network**

third-party service provider *E-com see* **value-added network**

third sector *HR see* **non-profit organisation**

Thorsrud, Einar (1923–85) *Gen Mgt* Norwegian academic. Researcher at the Tavistock Institute of Human Relations and collaborator with **Fred Emery**. Thorsrud set up an institute in Oslo which became the centre of Scandinavian exploration of the concept of **industrial democracy**.

three-dimensional management *or* **3-D management** *Gen Mgt* a theory outlining eight **management styles** that differ in effectiveness. Three-dimensional management was coined by **Bill Reddin** and was a development of the work of **Robert Blake** and **Jane Mouton**. Reddin described four managerial styles that he considered effective, and four that he considered less effective. These can be plotted in grids, showing how each style approaches relationships and tasks. The least effective type of manager is called the Deserter, the

Every really new idea looks crazy at first.   A.N. Whitehead

most effective is the Executive. Reddin believed that different styles are used in different types of work settings and that managers modify their style to suit different circumstances.

three generic strategies *Fin* strategies of differentiation, focus, and overall cost leadership outlined by Porter as offering possible means of outperforming competitors within an industry, and of coping with the five competitive forces

three martini lunch (*US*) *Gen Mgt* a business lunch involving a lot of alcohol to relax the client (*slang*)

three Ps *Gen Mgt* a model proposed by **Sumantra Ghoshal** to succeed the **three Ss**, which refers to the three foundations of today's leading companies: purpose, process, and people

360 degree appraisal *HR* the **management style** adopted depending on the location of a manager on the **Managerial Grid**™, indicating a preference for focusing on the task or people side of management

360 degree branding *Mkting* taking an inclusive approach in branding a product by bringing the brand to all points of consumer contact

three Ss *Gen Mgt* a classification of **decision-making** relating to strategy, structure, and systems. **Sumantra Ghoshal** has suggested replacing the three Ss model with the **three Ps**.

three steps and a stumble *Fin* a rule of thumb used on the US stock market that if the Federal Reserve increases interest rates three times consecutively, stock market prices will go down (*slang*)

threshold company *Gen Mgt* a company that is on the verge of becoming well established in the business world (*slang*)

thrift institution *or* **thrift** *Fin* a bank that offers savings accounts. *See also* **savings and loan association**, **savings bank**

THRIP *abbr* (*S Africa*) *Fin* Technology and Human Resources for Industry Pro-

gramme: a collaborative programme involving industry, government, and educational and research institutions that supports research and development in technology, science, and engineering

throughput accounting *Fin* a management accounting system which focuses on ways by which the maximum return per unit of bottleneck activity can be achieved

throw somebody a curve ball (*US*) *Gen Mgt* to do or say something unexpected, for example during a meeting or a project. The metaphor is from baseball. (*slang*)

TIBOR *abbr Fin* Tokyo Inter Bank Offered Rate

Tichy, Noel *Gen Mgt* US academic. Known for his research on the **transformational theory of leadership**, which developed the work of **James Burns**. See *The Transformational Leader* (1986, co-author).

tick *Fin* the least amount by which a value such as the price of a stock or a rate of interest can rise or fall. This could be, for example, a hundredth of a percentage point.

have ticks in all the right boxes *Gen Mgt* to be on course to meet a series of objectives (*slang*)

tied loan *Fin* a loan made by one national government to another on the condition that the funds are used to purchase goods from the lending nation

tie-in *Mkting* an advertising campaign in which two or more companies share the costs by combining their products or services (*slang*)

tigers *Fin* the most important markets in the Pacific Basin region, excluding Japan, including Hong Kong, South Korea, Singapore, and Taiwan

tight money *Econ* a situation where it is expensive to borrow because of restrictive government policy or high demand

TILA *abbr Fin* Truth in Lending Act

time and material pricing *Fin* a form of cost plus pricing in which price is determined by reference to the cost of the labour and material inputs to the product/service

time and motion study *HR* the measurement and analysis of the motions or steps involved in a particular task and the time taken to complete each one. Time and motion study can be broken down into two distinct techniques: *method study*, the analysis of how people work and how jobs are performed, and *work measurement*, the time taken to complete each job. It can be used to set job standards, simplify work, and check and improve the efficiency of workers. Time and motion study is similar to the broader concept of *work study*.

time bargain *Fin* a stock market transaction in which the securities are deliverable at a future date beyond the exchange's normal settlement day

time deposit *Fin* a US savings account or a certificate of deposit, issued by a financial institution. While the savings account is for a fixed term, deposits are accepted with the understanding that withdrawals may be made subject to a period of notice. Banks are authorised to require at least 30 days' notice. While a certificate of deposit is equivalent to a term account, passbook accounts are generally regarded as funds readily available to the account holder.

time draft *Fin* a bill of exchange drawn on and accepted by a US bank. It is either an after date or after sight bill.

time keeping *HR* the activity of recording the amount of time an employee works. Time keeping may involve a formal *clock in* system or it may be an informal arrangement based on trust.

time management *Gen Mgt* conscious control of the amount of time spent on work activities, in order to maximise personal efficiency. Time management involves analysing how time is spent, and then prioritising different work tasks. Activities can be reorganised to concentrate on those that are most important.

Various techniques can be of help in carrying out tasks more quickly and efficiently: information handling skills; verbal and written communication skills; *delegation*; and daily time planning. Time management is an important tool in avoiding *information overload*.

time off in lieu *HR leave* given to compensate an employee for additional hours worked. Time off in lieu is often given instead of a payment for *overtime*. *Abbr* **TOIL**

timeous (*S Africa*) *Gen Mgt* done or happening in good time

time series *Gen Mgt* a series of measurements, observations, and recordings of a set of variables at successive points in time. The time series forecasting technique is commonly used to track long-term trends and seasonal fluctuations and variations in data or statistics. It can be applied in an economic context in the review of sales, production, and investment performance, or in a sociological context in the compilation of census or panel study statistics. It can include the use of input-output analysis and *exponential smoothing*.

time sovereignty *Gen Mgt* control over the way you spend your time. Time sovereignty gives employees the ability to arrange their working lives to suit their own situations. It involves handing decisions on working hours to employees, enabling them to work flexibly, so that they can better juggle the *work-life balance*. Time sovereignty is more than just good *time management*, as it gives people control over the way they arrange their lives, rather than having to manage time within the decreed hours. It has been argued that rather than viewing work and home as separate lives, employees should see that they are living just one life that integrates both parts. Time sovereignty gives mastery over managing life as a whole.

time span of discretion *HR* the time between starting and completing the longest task within a job, used as a measure of the level of a job within an organisation. The time span of discretion was originated by *Elliot Jaques* as part of the *Glacier studies*. He saw two components to any job: prescribed and discretionary. The time span of the discretionary component refers to the longest span of time that employees spend working on a task on their own initiative, and often unsupervised. This reflects the amount of responsibility an individual has, and Jaques found that the time span of discretion rises steadily with the position of an employee in the company hierarchy. An hourly worker may have a one-hour time span of discretion, a middle manager may have one year, and a chief executive of a large company may have 20 years.

time spread *Fin* the purchase and sale of options in the same commodity or security with the same price and different maturities

time study *Gen Mgt* a *work measurement* technique designed to establish the time taken to complete work tasks in order to set a *standard time* for each task

time value *Fin* the premium at which an option is trading relative to its *intrinsic value*

timing difference *Fin* a difference between the balances held on related accounts which is caused by differences in the timing of the input of common transactions. For example, a direct debit will appear on the bank statement before it is entered into the bank account. Knowledge of the timing difference allows the balances on the two accounts to be reconciled.

TIN *abbr E-com* terminal identification number: a bank-provided identification number that uniquely identifies a merchant for point-of-sale transactions

tip *Fin* a piece of useful expert information. Used in the sense of a 'share tip', it is a share recommendation published in the financial press, usually based on research published by a financial institution.

tip-off *Fin* a warning based on confidential information. *See also* **insider trading**, **money laundering**

TISA *abbr Fin* TESSA Individual Savings Account. *See* **TESSA**

title *Fin* a legal term meaning ownership. Deeds to land are sometimes referred to as title deeds. If a person has good title to a property, their proof of ownership is beyond any doubt.

title inflation *HR* the practice of giving an employee a job title that implies status and importance. Title inflation renames an employee's job with a title that sounds more elevated or grand than the old one even though the nature of the job has not changed. This is sometimes used as a form of *motivation* or incentive to make employees feel rewarded and more valued.

TLS *abbr E-com* transaction layer security: a payment protocol based on *SSL* that offers improved security for credit card transactions

TNA *abbr HR* training needs analysis

toasted *Fin* used to refer to someone or something that has lost money (*slang*)

TOC *abbr Fin* theory of constraints

toehold (*US*) *Fin* a stake in a corporation built-up by a potential bidder which is less than 5 per cent of the corporation's stock. It is only when a 5 per cent stake is reached that the holder has to make a declaration to the Securities and Exchange Commission.

Toffler, Alvin (*b*. 1928) *Gen Mgt* US futurist and social commentator. Known for his analyses of the future which embraced the impact of the Information Society and the wired age, and the knowledge economy. His first book was *Future Shock* (1970).

Toffler studied English at New York University. In the early stages of his journalistic career, he was commissioned by IBM to write a report on the long-term social and organisational implications of the computer. He worked as Washington correspondent for a Pennsylvania

---

newspaper and as associate editor of *Fortune* before being employed as a visiting professor at Cornell University, a visiting scholar at the Russell Sage Foundation, and a teacher at the New School for Social Research.

TOIL *abbr HR* time off in lieu

Tokyo Inter Bank Offered Rate *Fin* on the Japanese money markets, the rate at which banks will offer to make deposits in yen from each other, often used as a reference rate. The deposits are for terms from overnight up to five years. *Abbr* **TIBOR**

tombstone *Fin* a notice in the financial press giving details of a large lending facility to a business. It may relate to a management buyout or to a package that may include interest rate cap and collars to finance a specific package. More than one bank may be involved. Although it may appear to be an advertisement, technically in most jurisdictions it is regarded as a statement of fact and therefore falls outside the advertisement regulations. The borrower generally pays for the advertisement, though it is the financial institutions that derive the most benefit.

top-down approach *Gen Mgt* an autocratic style of *leadership* in which strategies and solutions are identified by *senior management* and then cascaded down through the organisation. The top-down approach can be considered a feature of large *bureaucracies* and is associated with a *command and control approach* to management. A number of management gurus, particularly *Gary Hamel*, have criticised it as an out-of-date style that leads to stagnation and *business failure*. It is the opposite of a *bottom-up approach*.

top-down budget *Fin see imposed budget*

top level domain *E-com* the concluding part of a domain name, for example, the .com, .net, or .co.uk suffixes.

top management *HR* an informal term for *senior management* or a *board of directors*

top slicing *Fin* **1.** selling part of a shareholding that will realise a sum that is equal to the original cost of the investment. What remains therefore represents potential pure profit. **2.** in the United Kingdom, a complex method used by the Inland Revenue for assessing what tax, if any, is paid when certain investment bonds or endowment policies mature or are cashed in early

total absorption costing *Fin* a method used by a cost accountant to price goods and services, allocating both direct and indirect costs. Although this method is designed so that all of an organisation's costs are covered, it may result in opportunities being missed because of high prices. Consequently sales may be lost that could contribute to overheads. *See also* **marginal costing**

total assets *Fin* the total net book value of all assets

total asset turnover ratio *Fin* a measure of the use a business makes of all its assets. It is calculated by dividing sales by total assets.

total cost of ownership *Gen Mgt* a structured approach to calculating the *costs* associated with buying and using a product or service. Total cost of ownership takes the purchase cost of an item into account but also considers related costs such as ordering, delivery, subsequent usage and maintenance, supplier costs, and after-delivery costs. Originally designed as a process for measuring IT expense after implementation, total cost of ownership considers only financial expenses and excludes any *cost-benefit analysis*. *Abbr* **TCO**

total-debt-to-total-assets *Fin* the premium at which an option is trading relative to its *intrinsic value*

total environmental management *Gen Mgt see environmental management*

total loss control *Gen Mgt* the implementation of safety procedures to prevent or limit the impact of a complete or partial loss of an organisation's physical assets. Total loss control is based on safety audit and prevention techniques. It is concerned with reduction or elimination of losses caused by accidents and occupational ill health. The extent to which it is implemented is usually decided by calculating the total organisational asset cost and weighing this against the likelihood of failure and its worst possible effects on the organisation. Total loss control was developed in the 1960s as an approach to *risk management*.

total productive maintenance *Ops* a Japanese approach to maximising the effectiveness of facilities used within a business. Total productive maintenance, or TPM, aims to improve the condition and performance of particular facilities through simple, repetitive maintenance activities. Based on a culture of teamworking and consensus, TPM teams are encouraged to take a proactive approach to maintenance. A team is made up of operators and those involved in the setting up and maintenance of the facilities. TPM can be compared to *reliability-centred maintenance*. *Abbr* **TPM**

total quality management *Gen Mgt* a philosophy and style of management that gives everyone in an organisation responsibility for delivering quality to the customer. Total quality management views each task in the organisation as a process that is in a customer/supplier relationship with the next process. The aim at each stage is to define and meet the customer's requirements in order to maximise the satisfaction of the final consumer at the lowest possible cost. Total quality management constitutes a challenge to organisations that have to manage the conflict between *cost-cutting* and the commitment of employees to *continuous improvement*. Achievement of quality can be assessed by *quality awards* and *quality standards*. *Abbr* **TQM**

total return *Gen Mgt* the total percentage change in the value of an investment over a specified time period, including capital gains, dividends, and the investment's appreciation or depreciation

EXAMPLE The total return formula reflects all the ways in which an investment may earn or lose money, resulting in an increase or decrease in the investment's net asset value (NAV):

(Dividends + Capital gains distributions +/- Change in NAV) / Beginning NAV = Total return × 100%

If, for instance, you buy a stock with an initial NAV of £40, and after one year it pays an income dividend of £2 per share and a capital gains distribution of £1, and its NAV has increased to £42, then the stock's total return would be:

(2 + 1 + 2) / 40 = 5 / 40 = 0.125 × 100% = 12.5%

The total return time frame is usually one year, and it assumes that dividends have been reinvested. It does not take into account any sales charges that an investor paid to invest in a fund, or taxes they might owe on the income dividends and capital gains distributions received.

touch *Fin* the difference between the best bid and the best offer price quoted by all market makers for a particular security, the narrowest spread

touchdown centre (*US*) *Gen Mgt* a centre where business people can make calls and use computers and the Internet whilst travelling (*slang*)

touch price *Fin* the best bid and offer price available

tourist *HR* somebody who takes a training course in order to get away from his or her job (*slang*)

Townsend, Robert (*b.* 1920) *Gen Mgt* US business executive. One time chairman of Avis Rent-a-car, who built up the company into an international organisation. Best known for his book *Up the Organization* (1970), a humorous A-Z of management practices.

toxic employee *HR* a disgruntled and resentful employee who spreads discontent within a company or department (*slang*)

Toyota production system *Ops* a *manufacturing system*, developed by Toyota in Japan after the second world war, which aims to increase production efficiency by the elimination of waste in all its forms. The Toyota production system was invented, and made to work, by *Taiichi Ohno*. Japan's fledgling car-making industry was suffering from poor *productivity*, and Ohno was brought into Toyota with an initial assignment of catching up with the productivity levels of Ford's car plants. In analysing the problem, he decided that although Japanese workers must be working at the same rate as their American counterparts, waste and inefficiency were the main causes of their different productivity levels. Ohno identified waste in a number of forms, including over-production, waiting time, transportation problems, inefficient processing, *inventory*, and defective products. The philosophy of TPS is to remove or minimise the influence of all these elements. In order to achieve this, TPS evolved to operate under *lean production* conditions. It is made up of soft or cultural aspects, such as automation with the human touch— *autonomation*—and hard, or technical, aspects, which include *just-in-time*, *kanban*, and *production smoothing*. Each aspect is equally important and complementary. TPS has proved itself to be one of the most efficient manufacturing systems in the world but although leading companies have adopted it in one form or another, few have been able to replicate the success of Toyota. *Abbr* **TPS**

TPM *abbr Ops* total productive maintenance

TPS *abbr Ops* Toyota production system

TQM *abbr Gen Mgt* total quality management

tracker fund *Fin see index fund*

tracking *Mkting* research designed to monitor changes in the public perception of a product or organisation over a period of time

tracking error *Fin* the deviation by which an index fund fails to replicate the index it is aiming to mirror

tracking stock *Fin* a stock whose dividends are tied to the performance of a subsidiary of the corporation that owns it

trade balance *Fin see balance of trade*

trade barrier *Econ* a condition imposed by a government to limit free exchange of goods internationally. **NTBs**, safety standards, and tariffs are typical trade barriers.

trade bill *Fin* a bill of exchange between two businesses that trade with each other. *See also acceptance credit*

trade credit *Fin* credit offered by one business when trading with another. Typically this is for one month from the date of the invoice, but it could be for a shorter or longer period.

trade creditors *Fin* money owed to suppliers for goods and services. Other money owed, including employers' national insurance and taxation, is to be shown under the heading other creditors.

trade debt *Fin* a debt that originates during the normal course of trade

trade delegation *Mkting* a group of manufacturers or suppliers who visit another country to increase export business

Trade Development Board *Fin* a government agency that was established in 1983 to promote trade and explore new markets for Singapore products, and offers various schemes of assistance to companies. *Abbr* **TDB**

traded option *Fin* an option that is traded on an exchange that is different from the one on which the asset underlying the option is traded

tradefair *Mkting* a commercial exhibition designed to bring together buyers and sellers from a particular market sector. For the publishing industry, for example, the annual Frankfurt Book Fair is a key trade fair.

trade gap *Fin* a balance of payments deficit

trade investment *Fin* the action or process of one business making a loan to another, or buying shares in another. The latter may be the first stages of a friendly takeover.

trademark *Gen Mgt* an identifiable mark on a product that may be a symbol, words, or both, that connects the product to the trader or producer of that product. In the United Kingdom, a trademark can be registered at the Register of Trademarks, giving the producer or trader protection from fraudulent use. Any use of the trademark without permission gives the owner the right to sue for damages.

trade mission *Fin* a visit by businessmen from one country to another for the purpose of discussing trade between their respective nations

trade name *Mkting* the proprietary name given by the producer or manufacturer to a product or service. A trade name occasionally becomes the generic name for products of a similar nature, for example, 'Thermos' is often applied to all insulated flasks, and 'Hoover' to all vacuum cleaners.

Tradenet *Gen Mgt* an electronic system for applying for import or export licences from *Trade Development Boards*

TRADENZ *abbr Fin* New Zealand Trade Development Board

trade-off analysis *Gen Mgt see conjoint analysis*

trade point *Fin* a stock exchange that is less formal than the major exchanges

trade press *Mkting* specialist publications aimed at people in particular industries or business sectors

trades and labour council *(ANZ) HR* a collective organisation that represents unions at a level such as that of a state or territory

trade union *Gen Mgt, HR* an organisation of *employees* within a trade or profession that has the objective of representing its members' interests, primarily through improving pay and conditions, and provides a variety of services. *US term labor union*

trade union recognition *HR* the acknowledgment by an *employer* of the right of a *trade union* to conduct *collective bargaining* on behalf of *employees* in a particular bargaining unit. The Employment Relations Act 1999 grants a statutory right to recognition under certain conditions.

trade war *Econ* competition between two or more countries for a share of international or domestic trade

trade-weighted index *Econ* an index that measures the value of a country's currency in relation to the currencies of its trading partners

trading account *Fin see profit and loss account*

trading halt *Fin* a stoppage of trading in a stock on an exchange, usually in response to information about a company, or concern about rapid movement of the share price

trading partner *E-com* the merchant, customer, or financial institution with whom an EDI (*electronic data interchange*) transaction takes place. Transactions can be either between senders and receivers of EDI messages or within distribution channels in an industry, for example, financial institutions or wholesalers.

trading pit *Fin see pit*

trading profit *Fin see gross profit*

trading, profit and loss account *Fin* an account which shows the gross profit or loss generated by an entity for a period (trading account), and after adding other income and deducting various expenses shows the profit or loss of the business (the profit and loss account). Some small entities combine the two accounts.

The great discoveries are usually obvious.   *Philip B. Crosby*

traffic *E-com* the number of visitors to a website measured in any of several ways, for example, *click-throughs*, hits, or page views

traffic builder *Mkting* a marketing promotion that is designed to generate an increase in customers (*slang*)

training *HR* activities designed to facilitate the learning and development of new and existing skills, and to improve the performance of specific tasks or roles. Training may involve structured programmes or more informal and interactive activities, such as group discussion or *role playing*, which promote *experiential learning*. A wide range of activities, including classroom-based courses, *on-the-job training*, and business or *simulation games*, are used for training. Audio-visual and multimedia aids such as videos and CD-ROMs may also be employed. Training may be carried out by an internal training officer or department, or by external training organisations. The effectiveness of training can be maximised by conducting a *training needs analysis* beforehand, and following up with *evaluation of training*. Training should result in individual learning and enhanced organisational performance.

training group *HR see sensitivity training*

training needs *HR* a shortage of skills or abilities which could be reduced or eliminated by means of training and development. Training needs hinder employees in the fulfilment of their job responsibilities and prevent an organisation from achieving its objectives. They may be caused by a lack of skills, knowledge, or understanding, or arise from changes in the workplace. Training needs are identified through *training needs analysis*.

training needs analysis *HR* the identification of *training needs* at employee, departmental, or organisational level, in order for the organisation to perform effectively. The aim of training needs analysis is to ensure that training addresses existing problems, is tailored to organisational objectives, and is delivered in an effective and cost-efficient manner. Training needs analysis involves: monitoring current performance using techniques such as observation, interviews, and questionnaires; anticipating future shortfalls or problems; identifying the type and level of training required; and analysing how this can best be provided. *Abbr* **TNA**

trait theory *Gen Mgt* the belief that all leaders display the same key personality traits. Trait theory developed from the *great man theory* of leadership as researchers attempted to identify universally applicable characteristics that distinguish leaders from other people. During the 1920s and 1930s, theorists compiled lists of traits, but these were often contradictory and no single trait was consistently identified with good leadership.

tranche CD *Fin* one of a series of certificates of deposit that are sold by the issuing bank over time. Each tranche CD has a common maturity date.

transaction 1. *E-com* any item or collection of sequential items of business that are enclosed in encrypted form in an electronic envelope and transmitted between trading partners **2.** *Fin* a trade of a security

transactional analysis *Gen Mgt* a theory that describes sets of feelings, thoughts, and behaviour or ego-states that influence how individuals interact, communicate, and relate with each other. The theories of transactional analysis were developed between the 1950s and 1970s by Eric Berne, a US psychiatrist who studied the behaviour patterns of his patients. Berne identified three ego states, parent, adult, and child, and examined how these affected interactions or transactions between individuals. Transactional analysis is used in psychotherapy but also has applications in education and training. In *human relations* training, transactional analysis is used to help people understand and adapt their behaviour and develop more effective ways of communicating. *Abbr* **TA**

transactional theory of leadership *Gen Mgt* the idea that effective *leadership* is based on a reciprocal exchange between leaders and followers. Transactional leadership involves giving employees something in return for their compliance and acceptance of authority, usually in the form of incentives such as pay rises or an increase in status. The theory was propounded by *James MacGregor Burns*, and is closely linked with his *transformational theory of leadership*, which involves moral, rather than tangible, rewards for compliance.

transaction e-commerce *E-com* the electronic sale of goods and services, either business-to-business or business-to-customer

transaction exposure *Fin* the susceptibility of an organisation to the effect of foreign exchange rate changes during the transaction cycle associated with the export/import of goods or services. Transaction exposure is present from the time a price is agreed until the payment has been made/received in the domestic currency.

transaction file *Ops see inventory record*

transaction history *Fin* a record of all of an investor's transactions with a broker

transaction layer security *E-com see* **TLS**

transaction message *or* **transaction set** *E-com* the EDI (*electronic data interchange*) equivalent of a paper document, exchanged as part of an e-commerce transaction, comprising at least one data segment representing the document sandwiched between a header and a trailer. It is called a transaction message within the *UN/EDIFACT* protocol and a transaction set within the ANSI X.12 protocol.

transactions motive *Econ* the motive that consumers have to hold money for

their likely purchases in the immediate future

transfer *Fin* **1.** the movement of money from one account to another at the same branch of the same bank **2.** the movement of money through the domestic or international banking system. *See also* **BACS**, **Fedwire**, **SWIFT** **3.** the change of ownership of an asset

transferable skill *HR* a skill typically considered as not specifically related to a particular job or task. Transferable skills are usually those related to relationship, leadership, communication, critical thinking, analysis, and organisation.

transfer of training *HR* the appropriate and continued application of skills learned during a training course to the working environment. A measure of the transfer of training should form part of any *evaluation of training* carried out, as it can help demonstrate the cost-effectiveness of a training programme. It is normally measured between three to six months after the training course in order to allow trainees to apply their newly learned skills in the workplace.

transfer of value *Fin see chargeable transfer*

transferor *Fin* a person who transfers an asset to another person

transfer-out fee *Fin* a fee for closing an account with a broker

transfer price *Fin* the price at which goods or services are transferred between different units of the same company. If those units are located within different countries, the term **international transfer pricing** is used.

The extent to which the transfer price covers costs and contributes to (internal) profit is a matter of policy. A transfer price may, for example, be based upon marginal cost, full cost, market price or negotiation. Where the transferred products cross national boundaries, the transfer prices used may have to be agreed with the governments of the countries concerned.

---

transfer pricing *Mkting* a pricing method used when supplying products or services from one part of an organisation to another. The transfer pricing method can be used to supply goods either at cost or at profit if profit targets are to be achieved. This can cause difficulties if an internal customer can buy more cheaply outside the organisation. Multinational businesses have been known to take advantage of this pricing policy by transferring products from one country to another in order for profits to be higher in the country where corporation tax is lower.

transfer stamp *Fin* the mark embossed onto transfer deeds to signify that stamp duty has been paid

transfer value *Fin* the value of an individual's rights in a pension when they are lost in preference to rights in a new pension. *See also **vested rights***

transformational theory of leadership *Gen Mgt* the idea that effective *leadership* is based on inspiring and enthusing subordinates with a *corporate vision* in order to gain their commitment. Transformational leadership theory was developed by *James MacGregor Burns*, and is similar to his *transactional theory of leadership*. Both involve an exchange between leaders and followers, but while the transactional leader offers tangible rewards for compliance, the transformational leader offers moral rewards.

transformative potential *Gen Mgt* the ability of a force such as information technology to transform the economy, society, and business

transit time *Fin* the period between the completion of an operation and the availability of the material at the succeeding workstation

translation *Fin see **foreign currency translation***

translation exposure *Fin* the susceptibility of the balance sheet and income statement to the effect of foreign exchange rate changes

transmission *E-com* digital data sent electronically from one trading partner to another, or from a trading partner to a *value-added network*

transmission control protocol *E-com see **TCP/IP***

transmission control standards *E-com* the defined format by which to address the *electronic envelopes* used by trading partners to exchange business data

Transnet *Gen Mgt* a state-owned holding company that controls the main South African transport networks

transparency *Fin* a situation where nothing is hidden. This is an essential situation for a free market in securities. Prices, the volume of trading, and factual information must be available to all.

travel accident insurance *Fin* a form of insurance cover offered by some credit card companies when the whole or part of a travel arrangement is paid for with the card. In the event of death resulting from an accident in the course of travel, or the loss of eyesight or a limb, the credit card company will pay the cardholder or his or her estate a pre-stipulated sum. *See also travel insurance*

travel insurance *Fin* a form of insurance cover that provides medical cover while abroad as well as covering the policyholder's possessions and money while travelling. Many travel insurance policies also reimburse the policyholder if a holiday has to be cancelled and pay compensation for delayed journeys. *See also **travel accident insurance***

treasurer *Fin* somebody who is responsible for an organisation's funds

Treasurer *(ANZ) Fin* the minister responsible for financial and economic matters in a national, state, or territory government

treasuries *Fin* the generic name for negotiable debt instruments issued by the US government. *See also **Treasury bill**, **Treasury bond**, **Treasury note***

treasury *Fin* **1. Treasury** in some countries, the government department responsible for the nation's financial policies as well as the management of the economy **2.** the department of a company or corporation headed by the treasurer

Treasury bill *Fin* a short-term security issued by the government. *Also known as* **T-bill**

Treasury bill rate *Fin* the rate of interest obtainable by holding a treasury bill. Although Treasury bills are non-interest bearing, by purchasing them at a discount and holding them to redemption, the discount is effectively the interest earned by holding these instruments. The Treasury bill rate is the discount expressed as a percentage of the issue price. It is annualised to give a rate per annum.

Treasury bond *Fin* a long-term bond issued by the US government that bears interest

treasury management *Gen Mgt* the management functions responsible for the custody and investment of money, cashflow forecasting, capital provision, credit management, **risk management**, and the collection of accounts. Treasury management has a strategic role in the management of an organisation's finances.

Treasury note *Fin* **1.** a note issued by the US government **2.** a short-term debt instrument issued by the Australian federal government. Treasury notes are issued on a tender basis for periods of 13 and 26 weeks.

treaty *Fin* **1.** a written agreement between nations, such as the Treaty of Rome that was the foundation of the European Union **2.** a contract between an insurer and the reinsurer whereby the latter is to accept risks from the insurer **3.** *see* **private treaty**

Tregoe, Benjamin Bainbridge (*b.* 1927) *Gen Mgt* US manager and consultant. *See* **Kepner, Charles Higgins**

trend *Stats* the movement in a particular direction of the values of a variable in a statistical study over a period of time

trendline *Stats* the tendency to move in a particular direction shown by data variables over a period of time such as a month or year

Treynor ratio *Fin* see **risk-adjusted return on capital**

trial balance *Fin* a list of account balances in a double-entry accounting system. If the records have been correctly maintained, the sum of the debit balances will equal the sum of the credit balances, although certain errors such as the omission of a transaction or erroneous entries will not be disclosed by a trial balance.

trickle-down theory *Econ* the theory that if markets are open and programmes exist to improve basic health and education, growth will extend from successful parts of a developing country's economy to the rest

triple I organisation *Gen Mgt* a type of **corporate culture** identified by **Charles Handy** in which the focus is on three areas: Information, Intelligence, and Ideas. The triple I organisation recognises the value of information and learning. It minimises the distinction between managers and workers, concentrating instead on people and the need to pursue learning, both personal, **lifelong learning**, and **organisational learning**, in order to keep up with the pace of change.

triple tax exempt (*US*) *Fin* exempt from federal, state, and local income taxes

Trist, Eric Lansdown (1909–93) *Gen Mgt* British social psychologist. Known for research into socio-technical systems, particularly in the UK coal-mining industry, with associates such as **Fred Emery**, at the Tavistock Institute of Human Relations.

Trojan horse *E-com* a computer **virus** that pretends to serve a useful function, such as a screen saver. However, as soon as it is run, it carries out its true purpose, which can be anything from using the computer as a host to infect other computers to wiping the entire hard drive of the computer.

troll *Gen Mgt* a posting on a website that is designed to provoke a large number of responses, especially from inexperienced Internet users (*slang*)

trolling (*US*) *Mkting* making cold calls in an effort to solicit new business (*slang*)

Trompenaars, Fons (*b.* 1952) *Gen Mgt* Dutch academic. Known for his research into how national cultures influence *corporate cultures*. His work owes much to that of **Geert Hofstede**, and is published in *Riding the Waves of Culture* (1993).

trophy wife *Gen Mgt* the young wife of an older executive (*slang*)

troy ounce *Fin* the traditional unit used when weighing precious metals such as gold or silver. It is equal to approximately 1.097 ounces avoirdupois or 31.22 grams.

true interest cost *Fin* the effective rate of interest paid by the issuer on a debt security that is sold at a discount

trump *Mkting* to make something such as a competitor's product appear useless because what you have is so much better (*slang*)

trust 1. *Econ* a company that has a **monopoly 2.** *Fin* a collection of assets held by somebody for another person's benefit

trust account *Fin* a bank account that is held in trust for somebody else

trust bank *Fin* a Japanese bank that acts commercially in the sense of accepting deposits and making loans and also in the capacity of a trustee

trust company *Fin* a company whose business is administering trusts

trust corporation *Fin* a US state-chartered institution that may also undertake banking activities. A trust corporation is sometimes known as a non-bank bank.

Trusted Third Party *E-com see* **TTP**

trustee *Fin* somebody who holds assets in trust

trustee in bankruptcy *Fin* somebody appointed by a court to manage the finances of a bankrupt person or company

trustee investment *Fin* an investment that is made by a trustee and is subject to legal restrictions

trusteeship *Fin* the holding of a trust, or the term of such a holding

trust fund *Fin* assets held in trust by a trustee for the trust's beneficiaries

trust officer *Fin* somebody who manages the assets of a trust, especially for a bank that is acting as a trustee

Truth in Lending Act *Fin* in the United States, a law requiring lenders to disclose the terms of their credit offers accurately so that consumers are not misled and are able to compare the various credit terms available. The Truth in Lending Act requires lenders to disclose the terms and costs of all loan plans, including the following: annual percentage rate, points and fees; the total of the principal amount being financed; payment due date and terms, including any balloon payment where applicable and late payment fees; features of variable-rate loans, including the highest rate the lender would charge, how it is calculated and the resulting monthly payment; total finance charges; whether the loan is assumable; application fee; annual or one-time service fees; pre-payment penalties; and, where applicable, confirm the address of the property securing the loan.

tshayile time (*S Africa*) *Gen Mgt* an informal term for the end of the working day (*slang*)

TT *abbr Fin* telegraphic transfer

TTFN *abbr Gen Mgt* ta ta for now (*slang*)

TTP *abbr E-com* Trusted Third Party: an independent, trustworthy organisation that verifies individuals, companies, and organisations over the Internet

Tulgan, Bruce Lorin (*b.* 1967) *Gen Mgt* US lawyer, writer, and consultant. Pioneer of the concept that young people have a different attitude to work than their forebears and need to be managed differently. He explores this in *Managing Generation X* (1995).

turbulence *Gen Mgt* unpredictable and swift changes in an organisation's external or internal environments which affect its performance. The late 20th century was considered a turbulent environment for business because of the rapid growth in technology and globalisation, and the frequency of restructuring and merger activity.

turkey *Fin* a poorly performing investment or business (*slang*)

turkey trot (*US*) *HR* the practice of transferring a difficult, incompetent, or nonessential employee from one department to another (*slang*)

turn *Fin* the difference between a market maker's bid and offer prices

turnaround management *Gen Mgt* the implementation of a set of actions required to save an organisation from **business failure** and return it to operational normality and financial solvency. Turnaround management usually requires strong **leadership** and can include **corporate restructuring** and **redundancies**, an investigation of the root causes of failure, and long-term programmes to revitalise the organisation.

turnkey contract *Gen Mgt* an agreement in which a contractor designs, constructs, and manages a **project** until it is ready to be handed over to the client and operation can begin immediately

turnover ratio *Fin* stock or inventory turnover ratio, a measure of the number of times in a year that a business's stock or inventory is turned over. It is calculated as the cost of sales divided by the average book value of inventory/stock.

24 *E-com* the American National Standards Institute accepted protocol for the electronic interchange of business transactions

24/7 *Gen Mgt* twenty-four hours a day, seven days a week. Businesses often advertise themselves as being 'open 24/7'. (*slang*)

2L8 *abbr Gen Mgt* too late (*slang*)

twenty-four hour trading *Fin* the possibility of trading in currencies or securities at any time of day or night. It is not a reference to one trading floor being continually open, but instead refers to operations being undertaken at different locations in different time zones. A financial institution with offices in the Far East, Europe, and the United States can offer its clients 24-hour trading either by the client contacting their offices in each area, or by the customer's local office passing the orders on to another centre.

two-tier tender offer *Fin* in the United States, a takeover bid in which the acquirer offers to pay more for shares bought in order to gain control than for those acquired at a later date. The ploy is to encourage shareholders to accept the offer. Bidding of this type is outlawed in some jurisdictions, including the United Kingdom.

type I error *Stats* an error arising from incorrectly rejecting the null hypothesis in a statistical study

type II error *Stats* an error arising from incorrectly accepting the null hypothesis in a statistical study

tyrekicker (*US*) *Mkting* a prospective customer who asks for a lot of information and requires a lot of attention but does not actually buy anything (*slang*)

The best minute I spend is the one I invest in people.   *Kenneth Blanchard*

UCE *abbr E-com* unsolicited commercial e-mail: the official term for *spam*

UIF *abbr (S Africa) Fin* Unemployment Insurance Fund: a system administered through payroll deductions that insures employees against loss of earnings through being made unemployed by such causes as retrenchment, illness, or maternity

UITF *abbr Fin* Urgent Issues Task Force

ultra vires activity *Fin* an act that is not permitted by applicable rules, such as a corporate charter. Such acts may lead to contracts being void.

unbalanced growth *Econ* the result when not all sectors of an economy can grow at the same rate

unbundling *Fin* dividing a company into separate constituent companies, often to sell all or some of them after a takeover

uncalled share capital *Fin* the amount of the nominal value of a share which is unpaid and has not been called up by the company

uncertainty *Fin* the inability to predict the outcome from an activity due to a lack of information about the required input/output relationships or about the environment within which the activity takes place

uncertainty analysis *Stats* a study designed to assess the extent to which the variability in an outcome variable is caused by uncertainty at the time of estimating the input parameters of the study

uncollected funds *Fin* money deriving from the deposit of an instrument that a bank has not been able to negotiate

uncollected trade bill *Fin* an account with an outstanding balance for purchases made from the company that holds it

unconditional bid *Fin* in a takeover battle, a situation in which a bidder will pay the offered price irrespective of how many shares are acquired

unconsolidated *Fin* not grouped together, as of shares or holdings

uncontested bid *Fin* an offering of a contract by a government or other organisation to one bidder only, without competition

UNCTAD *abbr Fin* United Nations Conference on Trade and Development: the focal point within the UN system for the integrated treatment of development and interrelated issues in trade, finance, technology, and investment

underbanked *Fin* without enough brokers to sell a new issue

underlying asset *Fin* an asset that is the subject of an option

underlying inflation *Fin* the rate of inflation that does not take mortgage costs into account

underlying security *Fin* a security that is the subject of an option

undermargined account *Fin* an account that does not have enough money to cover its margin requirements, resulting in a margin call

undervalued *Fin* used to describe an asset that is available for purchase at a price lower than its worth

undervalued currency *Fin* a currency that costs less to buy with another currency than its worth in goods

underwrite *Fin* to assume risk, especially for a new issue or an insurance policy

underwriter *Fin* a person or organisation that buys an issue from a corporation and sells it to investors

underwriters' syndicate *Fin* a group of organisations that buys an issue from a corporation and sells it to investors

---

Be nice to people on your way up because you'll meet 'em on your way down. Wilson Mizner

underwriting *Fin* the buying of an issue from a corporation for the purpose of selling it to investors

underwriting income *Fin* the money that an insurance company makes because the premiums it collects exceed the claims it pays out

underwriting spread *Fin* an amount that is the difference between what an organisation pays for an issue and what it receives when it sells the issue to investors

undistributable reserves *Fin* in the United Kingdom, reserves that are not legally available for distribution to shareholders as dividends according to the Companies Act (1985)

UNDP *abbr Fin* United Nations Development Programme: the world's largest source of grants for sustainable human development. Its aims include the elimination of poverty, environmental regeneration, job creation, and advancement of women.

unearned income *Fin* income received from sources other than employment

unearned increment *Fin* an increase in the value of a property that arises from causes other than the owner's improvements or expenditure

unearned premium *Fin* the amount of premiums paid on a policy that an insurance company refunds when the policy is terminated

uneconomic *Econ* not profitable for a country, firm, or investor in the short or long term

UN/EDIFACT *E-com* a standard for *electronic data interchange* widely used in Western Europe and very similar to the *ANSI X.12 standard*. *Also known as EDI-FACT, EDI For Administration, Commerce, and Trade*

unemployment *Econ* the situation when some members of a country's labour force are willing to work but cannot find employment

Unemployment Insurance Fund *(S Africa) Fin see* **UIF**

uneven playing field *Mkting* a situation in which some competitors have an unfair advantage over others *(slang)*

unfair dismissal *HR* the *dismissal* of an *employee* that cannot be shown to be fair by the *employer*. An employee has the right not to be unfairly dismissed, and to bring a claim to an industrial tribunal provided he or she has one year's *continuous service*, although there are certain reasons for dismissal that are automatically unfair. If a finding of unfair dismissal is reached, a tribunal can make a re-instatement or re-engagement order, or it can order a basic and compensatory award to be paid. Statutory protection does not apply to members of certain groups of employees, such as the police.

unfranked investment income *Fin* amounts received by a company net of basic rate tax, for example, patent royalties

unfunded debt *Fin* short-term debt requiring repayment within a year from issuance

ungluing *Gen Mgt* the process of breaking up traditional supply chains or groups of co-operating organisations by taking control of the element of mutual interest that holds the partners together

unhappy camper *HR* somebody who has grievances against his or her employer *(slang)*

uniform accounting *Fin* a system by which different organisations in the same industry adopt common concepts, principles, and assumptions in order to facilitate interfirm comparison, or a system of classifying financial accounts in a similar manner within defined business sectors of a national economy, to ensure comparability

uniform costing *Fin* the use by several undertakings of the same costing methods, principles, and techniques

---

You can eat an elephant one bit at a time.   *Mary Kay Ash*

uniform resource locator *E-com see* **URL**

unimodal *Stats* describes a frequency or probability distribution that has only one mode

uninstalled *HR* dismissed from employment (*slang*)

uninsurable *Fin* considered unsuitable for insurance, especially because of being a poor risk

unique selling point *or* **unique selling proposition** *Mkting, Ops* a specific feature that differentiates a product from similar products. *Abbr* **USP**

unique visitor *E-com* somebody who visits a website more than once within a specified period of time. Tracking software that monitors site traffic can distinguish between visitors who only visit the site once and unique visitors who return to the site. Unique visitor statistics are considered to be the most accurate measurement of a website's popularity because they reflect the number of people who want to be there rather than those who have arrived there by accident. Furthermore, unlike hits (which are measured by the number of files that are requested from a site) unique visitors are measured according to their unique *IP addresses*. This means that no matter how many times they visit the site, they are only counted once.

unissued share capital *Fin* stock that is authorised but has not been issued. *US term* **unissued stock**

unissued stock (*US*) *Fin* = **unissued share capital**

unit *Fin* a collection of securities traded together as one item

unit cost *Fin* the cost to a company of producing one item that it markets

United Nations Conference on Trade and Development *Fin see* **UNCTAD**

United Nations Development Programme *Fin see* **UNDP**

unit of account *Econ* a unit of a country's currency that can be used in payment for goods or in a firm's accounting

unit of trade *Fin* the smallest amount that can be bought or sold of a share of stock, or a contract included in an option

unit trust *Fin* an investment company that sells shares to investors and invests for their benefit. *US term* **mutual fund**

universe *Mkting* the total market for a product or service

unlimited liability *Fin* full responsibility for the obligations of a general partnership

unlisted *Fin* used to refer to security that is not traded on an exchange

unlisted securities market *Fin* a market for stocks that are not listed on an exchange. *Abbr* **USM** *See also* **AIM**

unofficial strike *HR* a *strike* that is called without the approval or recognition of a trade union. An unofficial strike, also known as a **wildcat strike**, is a form of *industrial action* often associated with the activities of shop stewards. Any workers involved do not receive *strike pay*.

unquoted *Fin* having no publicly stated price, usually referring to an unlisted security

unrealised capital gain *or* **unrealized gain** *Fin* a profit from the holding of an asset worth more than its purchase price, but not yet sold

unrealised profit/loss *Fin* a profit or loss that need not be reported as income, for example, deriving from the holding of an asset worth more/less than its purchase price, but not yet sold

unreason *Gen Mgt* the process of thinking the unlikely and doing the unreasonable that can be a means by which an organisation or individual achieves success

unremittable gain *Fin* a capital gain that cannot be imported into the taxpayer's country, especially because of currency restrictions

---

You're either part of the solution or part of the problem.   *Eldridge Cleaver*

unseasoned issue *Fin* an issue of shares or bonds for which there is no existing market. *See also* **seasoned issue**

unsecured *Fin* used to refer to something without collateral

unsecured debt *Fin* money borrowed without supplying collateral

unsecured loan *Fin* a loan made with no collateral. *Also known as* **signature loan**

unsocial hours *HR* the working hours of an employee outside the socially recognised working day, for which an additional payment is sometimes made

unsolicited commercial e-mail *E-com* see *UCE*

unstable equilibrium *Econ* a market situation in which if there is a movement (of price or quantity) away from the equilibrium, existing forces will push the price even further away

upsell *Mkting* to sell customers a higher-priced version of a product they have bought previously

upsizing *HR see* **downsizing**

upstairs market *Fin* the place where traders for major brokerages and institutions do business at an exchange

upstream progress *Gen Mgt* advancement against opposition or in difficult conditions. A company or project can make upstream progress if it moves towards achieving its objectives despite impediments. *See also* **downstream progress**

Urgent Issues Task Force *Fin* in the United Kingdom, an organisation whose aim is to assist the ASB in areas where

unsatisfactory or conflicting interpretations of an accounting standard have developed, or seem likely to develop. *Abbr* **UITF**

URL *abbr E-com* uniform resource locator: a full web address, for example, http://www.yahoo.com

Urwick, Lyndall Fownes (1891–1983) *Gen Mgt* British educator and consultant. Promulgator of the theories of *Frederick Winslow Taylor* and *Henri Fayol*, which he developed in *Elements of Administration* (1944). Urwick was a founder of the British Institute of Management (1947), and of the management consultancy firm, Urwick Orr (1934).

usability *E-com* the suitability of a website design from the user's perspective. The term has been popularised by web design guru Jakob Nielsen who has stressed that a website must be simple to use. One of the main points of usability relates to download times. For Nielsen, 'fast response times are the most important criterion for web pages'. Nielsen also believes usability involves a human approach. He states that 'what constitutes a good site relates to the core basis of human nature and not to technology'.

usenet *E-com* the vast information space encompassed by the thousands of publicly available newsgroups

USM *abbr Fin* unlisted securities market

USP *Mkting, Ops see* **unique selling point**

utopian socialism *Econ* a form of socialism in which the use and production of all services and goods are held collectively by the group or community, rather than by a central government

---

My rule is always to do the business of the day in the day.   *Arthur Wellesley Wellington*

vacation (*US*) *HR* = *holiday*

valence *HR see* **expectancy theory**

value added *Gen Mgt* **1.** originally, the difference between the cost of bought-in materials and the eventual selling price of the finished product **2.** loosely, the features that differentiate one product or service from another and thus create value for the customer. Value added is a customer perception of what makes a product or service desirable over others and worth a higher price. Value added is more difficult to measure without a physical end product, but value can be added to services as well as physical goods, through the process of *value engineering*. *Also known as* **added value**

value-added network *E-com* an organisation that provides messaging-related functions and EDI communications services, for example, protocol matching and line-speed conversion, between trading partners. *Abbr* **VAN**. *Also known as* **third-party network**, **third-party service provider**

value-added reseller *Fin* a merchant who buys products at retail and packages them with additional items for sale to customers. *Abbr* **VAR**

value-added services *Mkting* services that enhance a basic product, such as the design in engineering components or technical support for software

value-added tax *Fin see* **VAT**

value-adding intermediary *Gen Mgt* a distributor who adds value to a product before selling it to a customer, for example, by installing software or a modem in a computer

value analysis *Ops* a cost reduction and *problem-solving* technique that analyses an existing product or service in order to reduce or eliminate any costs that do not contribute to value or performance. Value analysis usually focuses on design issues

relating to the function of a product or service, looking at the properties that make it work, or which are *unique selling points*.

value-based management *Fin* a management team preoccupation with searching for and implementing the activities which will contribute most to increases in shareholder value

value chain 1. *Gen Mgt* the sequence of activities a company performs in order to design, produce, market, deliver, and support its product or service. The concept of the value chain was first suggested by *Michael Porter* in 1985, to demonstrate how value for the customer accumulates along the chain of organisational activities that make up the final customer product or service. Porter describes two different types of business activity: primary and secondary. Primary activities are concerned principally with transforming inputs, such as raw materials, into outputs, in the form of products or services, delivery, and after-sales support. Secondary activities support the primary activities and include procurement, technology development, and human resource management. All of these activities form part of the value chain and can be analysed to assess where opportunities for *competitive advantage* may lie. To survive competition and supply what customers want to buy, the firm has to ensure that all value chain activities link together, even if some of the activities take place outside the organisation. **2.** *HR* the most traditional approach to exploring career prospects, which involves identifying the next, most obvious, move in a career path. The next step is usually assumed to be the role occupied by a manager.

value engineering *Ops* the practice of designing a product or service so that it gives as much value as possible to the consumer. Value engineering analyses a developing product so that the focus is on

---

The manager does things right; the leader does the right thing. Warren Bennis

those attributes that make the product appeal to the consumer over competing items and produce *customer satisfaction*. Value engineering also concentrates on eliminating costs that do not contribute to the creation of customer value.

value for customs purposes only *Fin* what somebody importing something into the United States declares that it is worth

value for money audit *Fin* an investigation into whether proper arrangements have been made for securing economy, efficiency, and effectiveness in the use of resources. *Abbr* **VFM**. *Also known as comprehensive auditing*

value innovation *Gen Mgt* a strategic approach to business growth, involving a shift away from a focus on the existing competition to one of trying to create entirely new markets. Value innovation can be achieved by implementing a focus on *innovation* and creation of new marketspace. The term was coined by *W. Chan Kim* and *Renée Mauborgne* in 1997.

value map *Gen Mgt* the level of value that the market recognises in a product or service and that helps to differentiate it from competitors

value mesh *HR* an expanded look at the positioning of a job in the overall marketplace. Seen as a way of helping employees identify their next move, a value mesh encourages them to consider all opportunities within their organisation and others.

value proposition 1. *Mkting* a statement by an organisation of the way in which it can provide value for a prospective customer. A value proposition is a marketing tool that explains why customers can benefit from a company's products or services. It can also be created for *recruitment* purposes, to show applicants the value of becoming an employee of the company. **2.** *Gen Mgt* a proposed scheme for making a profit (*slang*)

value share *Fin* a share that is considered to be currently underpriced by the

market and therefore an attractive investment prospect

value to the business *or* **value to the owner** *Fin see deprival value*

VAN *abbr E-com* value-added network

VAR *abbr Fin* value-added reseller

variable *Stats* an element of data whose changes are the object of a statistical study

variable annuity *Fin* an annuity whose payments depend either on the success of investments that underlie it, or on the value of an index

variable cost *Fin see cost behaviour*

variable costing *Fin see marginal costing*

variable cost of sales *Fin* the sum of direct materials, direct wages, variable production overhead, and variable selling and distribution overhead

variable interest rate *Fin* an interest rate that changes, usually in relation to a standard index, during the period of a loan

variable rate note *Fin* a note the interest rate of which is tied to an index, such as the prime rate in the United States or the London InterBank Offering Rate (LIBOR) in the United Kingdom. *Abbr* **VRN**

variance *Ops* a measure of the difference between actual performance and forecast, or standard, performance. Variance is a key measure in *statistical process control*.

variance accounting *Fin* a method of accounting by means of which planned activities (quantified through budgets and standard costs and revenues) are compared with actual results. It provides information for *variance analysis*.

variance analysis *Fin* a standard costing technique involving the comparison, calculation, and explanation of *variances* between actual and standard costs. Variance analysis is used to evaluate success in conforming to plans and budgets.

Unless your ideas are ridiculed by experts, they are worth nothing.   *Reg Revans*

variance components *Stats* the changes in random effect terms such as error terms in a linear statistical model

variety reduction *Ops* the process of controlling and minimising the range of new parts, equipment, materials, methods, and procedures that are used to produce goods or services. Variety reduction aims to minimise the variety of all elements in the production or service delivery process. Variety adds costs to any organisation and variety management and reduction can immediately benefit profitability. The main techniques of variety reduction are simplification, standardisation, and specialisation.

VAT *abbr Fin* value added tax: a tax added at each stage in the manufacture of a product. It acts as a replacement for a sales tax in almost every industrialised country outside North America. It is levied on selected goods and services, paid by organisations on items they buy and then charged to customers.

VAT collected *Fin* with the VAT already collected by a taxing authority

VAT paid *Fin* with the VAT already paid

VAT receivable *Fin* with the VAT for an item not yet collected by a taxing authority

VAT registration *Fin* listing with a European government as a company eligible for return of VAT in certain cases

VCM *abbr Fin* Venture Capital Market

velocity of circulation of money *Fin* the rate at which money circulates in an economy

vendor placing *Fin* the practice of issuing shares to acquire a business, where an agreement has been made to allow the vendor of the business to place the shares with investors for cash

vendor rating *Ops* a system for recording and ranking the performance of a supplier in terms of a range of issues, which may include delivery performance and the quality of the items. A process of vendor rating is essential to effective *purchasing*. When carried out before an order is placed, it is known as *supplier evaluation*. When undertaken after the fulfilment of an order, it is called **supplier rating**, or **supplier appraisal**.

Venn diagram *Stats* a diagram in which overlapping circles are used to show how two or more items in a statistical study are mutually inclusive or exclusive

venture capital *Fin* **1.** money used to finance new companies or projects, especially those with high earning potential and high risk. *Also known as* **risk capital** **2.** the money invested in a new company or business venture

Venture Capital Market *Fin* a sector on the *JSE* Securities Exchange for listing smaller developing companies. Criteria for listing in the VCM sector are less stringent than for the DCM (*Development Capital Market*) sector. *See also* **Development Capital Market**. *Abbr* **VCM**

venture funding *Fin* the round of funding for a new company that follows seed funding, provided by venture capitalists

venture management *Gen Mgt* the collaboration of various sections within an organisation to encourage an *entrepreneurial* spirit, increase *innovation*, and produce successful *new products* more quickly. Venture management is used within large organisations to create a small-firm, entrepreneurial atmosphere, releasing innovation and talent from promising employees. It cuts out *bureaucracy* and bypasses traditional management systems. The collaboration is generally between research and development, corporate planning, marketing, finance, and purchasing functions.

venturer *Fin* one of the parties involved in a *joint venture*

verbal contract *Gen Mgt* an agreement that is oral and not written down. It remains legally enforceable by the parties who have agreed to it.

verification *Fin* in an audit, a substantive test of the existence, ownership, and valuation of a company's assets and liabilities

versioning *Mkting* the practice of offering information to customers in different versions to suit particular customer groups (*slang*)

vertical diversification *Gen Mgt see* *diversification*

vertical equity *Fin* the principle that people with different incomes should pay different rates of tax

vertical form *Fin* the presentation of a financial statement in which the debits and credits are shown in one column of figures

vertical integration *Gen Mgt* the practice of combining some or all of the sequential operations of the *supply chain* between the sourcing of *raw materials* and sale of the final product. Vertical integration can be pursued as a strategy through the acquisition of *suppliers*, *wholesalers*, and *retailers* to increase control and reliability. It can also be achieved when a company gains strong control over suppliers or distributors, usually by exercising purchasing power.

vertical keiretsu *Gen Mgt see* *keiretsu*

vertical linkage analysis *Gen Mgt* a tool that enables analysis of the *value chain* in order to determine where opportunities for enhancing *competitive advantage* may lie. Vertical linkage analysis extends the value chain beyond the organisation to incorporate the suppliers and users who are at either end of the chain. This maximises the number of locations where value can be created for customers. Vertical linkage analysis incorporates three steps: working out the value chain for the industry and costing value-creating activities; determining cost drivers for each of these activities; and evaluating opportunities for competitive advantage.

vertical market *E-com* a market that is oriented to one particular speciality, for example, plastics manufacturing or transportation engineering

vertical merger *Gen Mgt see* *merger*

vertical thinking *Gen Mgt see* *lateral thinking*

vested employee benefits *Fin* employee benefits that are not conditional on future employment

vested rights *Fin* the value of somebody's rights in a pension in the United States if he or she leaves a job

VFM *abbr Fin* value for money audit

v-form *Fin* a graphic representation that something had been falling in value and is now rising

videoconferencing *Gen Mgt* the use of a live video link to connect people in different locations so that they can see and hear one another and conduct real-time *meetings*. Videoconferencing is a useful tool for managing *communication* with remote workers, between staff at geographically dispersed offices, including those who form a *virtual team*, or with clients at remote locations. It is also used in *distance learning* courses.

There are two basic options for videoconferencing. The more expensive option is full-blown videoconferencing using *ISDN* lines, dedicated equipment, and large screens, which guarantee a higher quality experience. Cheaper and more common is the PC/web-based videoconferencing, which piggybacks on existing PC and Internet technology, and occupies a small box window on a PC. However, it is less reliable, and still requires an ISDN line to achieve any degree of quality.

viewing figures *Mkting* the number of people who watch a particular television programme or channel

viewtime *E-com* the length of time an advertising banner is visible on a web page

viral marketing *Mkting* the rapid spread of a message about a new product or service, in a similar way to the spread of a virus. Viral marketing can be by word of mouth, but it is particularly common on the Internet, where messages can be spread easily and quickly to reach millions of people. Products can become household names in this way with very little advertising expenditure.

Viral marketing works well in the following circumstances: when a product is genuinely new and different, and it is something that opinion leaders want to associate with; when the benefits of the product are real; when the product is relevant to a large number of people, and the benefits are easy to communicate.

Some viral marketing campaigns use an incentive-based approach, rewarding people if, for example, they inform their friends and a percentage of these friends make a purchase. Because the Internet is perceived as an information resource, it is also useful to publish on a website information that users are allowed to quote and redistribute, perhaps by means of an 'e-mail-to-a-friend' button. *Linking* is also an effective viral marketing tool, as is the provision of free products or services. The Hotmail free e-mail service, for example, grew quickly with little marketing spend.

virement *Fin* authority to apply saving under one subhead to meet excesses on others

virtual hosting *E-com* a type of *hosting option*, suitable for small and medium-sized businesses, in which the customer uses space on a network vendor's server that is also used by other organisations. The hosting company agrees to deliver minimum access speeds and *data transfer* rates, and to carry out basic hardware maintenance, but the customer is responsible for managing the content and software.

virtualisation *Gen Mgt* the creation of a product, service, or organisation that has an electronic rather than a physical existence

virtual office *Gen Mgt* a workplace that is not based in one physical location but consists of employees working remotely by using *information and communications technologies*. A virtual office is characterised by the use of *teleworkers*, *telecentres*, *mobile workers*, *hot-desking*, and *hotelling*, and promotes the use of *virtual teams*. A virtual office can increase an organisation's flexibility, cost effectiveness, and efficiency.

virtual organisation *Ops* a temporary network of companies, suppliers, customers, or employees, linked by *information and communications technologies*, with the purpose of delivering a service or product. A virtual organisation can bring together companies in *strategic partnering* or *outsourcing* arrangements, enabling them to share expertise, resources, and cost savings until objectives are met and the network is dissolved. Such organisations are virtual not only in the sense that they exist largely in cyberspace, but also that they employ various forms of flexibility unconstrained by the traditional barriers of time and place, such as *virtual teams*. A greater level of trust is required between employer and employee or co-workers, or partner organisations, because they will be working out of one another's sight for the majority of the time. *See also network organisation*

virtual team *Gen Mgt* a group of employees using *information and communications technologies* to collaborate from different work bases. Members of a virtual team may work in different parts of the same building or may be scattered across a country or around the world. The team can be connected by technology such as *groupware*, e-mail, an *intranet*, or *videoconferencing* and can be said to inhabit a *virtual office*. Although virtual teams can work efficiently, occasional face-to-face meetings can be important to avoid feelings of isolation and to enable *team building*.

virus *E-com* a computer program designed to damage or destroy computer systems and the information contained within them. The fact that extremely destructive viruses can be attached to, and even embedded within, e-mail messages means that anyone with an e-mail account is a potential target. Although there is no single foolproof way to eradicate the risk of viruses, the threat they pose can be reduced in a number of ways. The main precaution that should be taken is to invest in anti-virus software that can check e-mail messages and attachments automatically.

visible trade *Econ* trade in physical goods and merchandise

vision statement *Gen Mgt* a statement giving a broad, aspirational image of the future that an organisation is aiming to achieve. Vision statements express *corporate vision*. They are related to *mission statements*.

visit *E-com* the first entry in a given time period into a website by a web user as identified by a unique web address. A visit is considered to be concluded when the user has not viewed any page at the website in a given time period.

vocational qualification *HR* a qualification awarded after a period of *vocational training* has been successfully completed. Vocational qualifications provide the knowledge and skills for a particular trade or profession and may lead to full membership of a professional body. In the United Kingdom, a Scottish or *National Vocational Qualification* is the most common form of vocational qualification.

vocational training *HR training* that equips somebody for a specific trade or profession. Vocational training may lead to a recognised *vocational qualification*, or it may form part of in-company *employee development*. It might take the form of a short course, practical training, or part-time or full-time study at a college or university.

voetstoots (*S Africa*) *Fin* purchased at the buyer's risk or without warranty

volume of retail sales *Econ* the amount of trade in goods carried out in the retail sector of an economy in a particular period

volume variances *Fin* differences in costs or revenues compared with budgeted amounts, caused by differences between actual and budgeted levels of activity

voluntary arrangement *Fin* an agreement the terms of which are not legally binding on the parties

voluntary bankruptcy *Gen Mgt see* **bankruptcy**

voluntary liquidation *Fin* liquidation of a solvent company that is supported by the shareholders

voluntary registration *Fin* in the United Kingdom, registration for *VAT* by a trader whose turnover is below the registration threshold. This is usually done in order to reclaim tax on inputs.

vortal *E-com* a portal website devoted to one specific industry. These sites enable business-to-business e-commerce transactions by bringing businesses at different points of the supply chain together. Vortal is formed from 'vertical portal'.

vostro account *Fin* an account held by a local bank on behalf of a foreign bank

votes on account *Fin* in the United Kingdom, money granted by Parliament in order to continue spending in a fiscal year before final authorisation of the totals for the year

voting shares *Fin* shares whose owners have voting rights. *US term* **voting stock**

voting stock (*US*) *Fin* = *voting shares*

voting trust *Fin* a group of individuals who have collectively received voting rights from shareholders

voucher *Fin* documentary evidence supporting an accounting entry

vouching *Fin* an auditing process in which documentary evidence is matched with the details recorded in accounting records in order to check for validity and accuracy

Vredeling Directive *Fin* a proposal, presented to the European Council of Ministers in 1980, for obligatory information, consultation, and participation of workers at headquarters level in multinational enterprises

VRN *abbr Fin* variable rate note

Vroom, Victor Harold (*b.* 1932) *Gen Mgt* Canadian academic. An authority on the psychological analysis of behaviour in organisations, whose work includes contributions on *motivation*, *leadership* styles and *decision-making*. He described his *expectancy theory* in *Work and Motivation* (1964).

Vulcan nerve pinch *Gen Mgt* the uncomfortable hand position required to reach all the keys for certain computer commands (*slang*)

vulture capitalist *Fin* a venture capitalist who structures deals on behalf of an entrepreneur in such a way that the investors benefit rather than the entrepreneur (*slang*)

wage earner *HR* a person in paid employment

wage freeze *HR* government policy of preventing *pay* rises in order to combat inflation

wage incentive *HR* a monetary benefit offered as a reward to those employees who perform well in a specified area

wages *HR* a form of *pay* given to employees in exchange for the work they have done. Traditionally, the term wages applied to the weekly pay of manual, or non-professional workers. In modern usage, the term is often used interchangeably with *salary*.

wage scale *HR see pay scale*

waiting time *Fin* the period for which an operator is available for production but is prevented from working by shortage of material or tooling, or by machine breakdown

waiver of premium *Fin* a provision of an insurance policy that suspends payment of premiums, for example, if the insured suffers disabling injury

walk *(US) Gen Mgt* to resign from a job *(slang)*

wall
let's throw it at the wall and see if it sticks *Gen Mgt* let's try this idea and see if it is successful *(slang)*

walled garden *E-com* an environment on the Internet in which customers can access only e-merchants selected by the owner of the environment *(slang)*

wallet technology *E-com* a software package providing *digital wallets* or purses on the computers of merchants and customers to facilitate payment by digital cash

Wall Street *Fin* the US financial industry, or the area of New York City where much of its business is done

WAN *E-com see network*

WAP *abbr E-com* wireless application protocol: the mobile equivalent of **HTML**, enabling websites to be accessed via mobile devices

warehousing *Ops* the storage and protection of *raw materials* and *finished goods* in a dedicated building or room

war for talent *Gen Mgt* competition between organisations to attract and retain the most able employees

warrants risk warning notice *Fin* a statement that a broker gives to clients to alert them to the risks inherent in trading in options

waste *Fin* discarded material having no value

waste management *or* **waste control** *Gen Mgt* a sustainable process for reducing the environmental impact of the disposal of all types of materials used by businesses. Waste management aims to avoid excessive use of resources and damage to the environment and may be carried out through processes such as recycling. It focuses on efficiency in the use of materials and on disposing of rubbish in the least harmful way. Waste management also involves compliance with the legislation and regulations covering this area.

wasting asset *Fin* an asset that will cease to have any value at all at a date in the future, such as an option or a short-term lease

water
let's put it in the water and see if it floats *Gen Mgt* let's try this idea and see if it is successful *(slang)*

Waterman, Robert *(b.* 1936) *Gen Mgt* US consultant. Former McKinsey consultant, who, with **Tom Peters**, wrote the bestselling work *In Search of Excellence* (1984).

I buy when other people are selling.

J. Paul Getty

Watson, Jr, Thomas (1914–93) *Gen Mgt* US industrialist. CEO of IBM, 1956–70, who gave the company a strong core philosophy and led it through a period of complete domination of the computer industry. His beliefs, which centred on consideration for the employee, care for the customer, and taking time to get things right, are described in *A Business and its Beliefs: The Ideas that Helped Build IBM* (1963).

wealth *Econ* physical assets such as a house or financial assets such as stocks and shares that can yield an income for their holder

wealth tax *Fin* a tax on somebody's accumulated wealth, as opposed to their income

wear a hat *Gen Mgt* to fulfil a specified role at a particular moment in time. Somebody may be required to wear several hats within the same company. (*slang*)

wear and tear *Fin* the deterioration of a tangible fixed asset as a result of normal use. This is recognised for accounting purposes by *depreciation*.

web bug *E-com* a small file sent to reside in a website user's browser, in order to track that consumer the next time he or she visits the website—in much the same manner as a *cookie*.

Web bugs, however, are not generally detectable by standard browsers, although there is software that can be downloaded to spot them. They are therefore controversial, as their very design reflects a desire not to let a person know that they are being tracked, and they have sometimes been used in a surreptitious manner. This has added fuel to the fear that people's privacy rights are being abused on the Internet.

webcast *E-com* use of the Web to broadcast information. A webcast event is intended to be viewed simultaneously by numerous people connecting to the same website. Webcast events often use *rich media* technology.

web commerce *E-com see* *e-commerce*

Weber, Max (1864–1920) *Gen Mgt* German sociologist. Remembered for his work on *power* and *authority*, published in *Theory of Social and Economic Organization* (1924), where he proposed *bureaucracy* as the most efficient form of *organisation*.

After studying legal and economic history, Weber was a law professor at the University of Freiburg and later at the University of Heidelberg. He studied the sociology of religion and in this area he produced his best-known work, *The Protestant Work Ethic and the Spirit of Capitalism*. In political sociology he examined the relationship between social and economic organisations. Towards the end of his life, Weber developed his political interests and was on the committee that drafted the constitution of the Weimar Republic in 1918.

web form *E-com* a means of collecting information from a visitor to a website in a structured manner. Once the consumer has filled in the form, it is usually returned to the owner of the website via e-mail.

There are several golden rules to follow when designing a web form. It should be short or, if necessary, split into clear sections. Mandatory fields—such as e-mail addresses—should be clearly marked, conventionally with red type or red asterisks. Consumers should always be given an alternative for information they cannot give—for example: 'If you don't have a ZIP code, please write "None".' Errors should be isolated: if the consumer makes an error in the form, they should be asked to correct that specific error, not simply have the form returned to them. Fields should be of sufficient size for all the requested information. Alternative means of providing the information should be made available for people with disabilities.

web log *E-com* a means of tracking activity on a website or computer system. It can provide important marketing information such as how many users are visiting the site, how they behave, and what they are interested in, as well as highlighting useful technical issues such as whether there are page errors occurring, or whether spikes in visitor behaviour are causing **bandwidth** shortages. *Also called* **server log**

web marketing *E-com* the process of creating, developing, and enhancing a website in order to increase the number of visits by potential customers

web marketplace *E-com* a business-to-business web community that brings business buyers and sellers together. Although their exact nature can vary considerably, there are essentially three types of web-based B2B marketplace: *online catalogues*, *auctions*, and *exchanges*.

webmaster *E-com* the person responsible for managing the content of a website and monitoring traffic through the site. The role of webmaster may be shared between numerous individuals within an organisation.

web response form *E-com see* **WRF**

web server *E-com* **1.** the physical computer that supports a website **2.** the software that runs on web servers. Web server software delivers web pages to browsers on Internet-based computers.

website classification *E-com* the organisation of content on a website into different categories, so that it can be identified and found easily by a user. Classification is a particularly important form of **metadata**, as a website with poor classification will be difficult to navigate and of little use to the visitor.

The top-level classification of a website expresses, in the fewest and simplest words possible, the nature of the business. For example, is it selling 'products', 'services', or 'solutions'? Are its customers 'home users', 'small businesses', 'large businesses'? It is important, if possible, to avoid going more than five levels deep in further classification. The more levels there are, the more clicks will be required from visitors to find what they are looking

for. It is also best to avoid having too many documents under one classification: more than 50 becomes confusing, and it would probably be better to break down the classification further.

weighted average *Stats* an average of quantities that have been adjusted by the addition of a statistical value to allow for their relative importance in a data set

weighted average number of ordinary shares *Fin* the number of ordinary shares at the beginning of a period, adjusted for shares cancelled, bought back, or issued during the period, multiplied by a time-weighting factor. This number is used in the calculation of **earnings per share**.

weighting *Stats* the assigning of greater importance to particular items in a data set

weightlessness *Gen Mgt* a quality considered to characterise an economy that is based on knowledge or other intangibles rather than on physical assets

Welch, Jack (*b*. 1935) *Gen Mgt* US business executive. Turned around General Electric in the 1980s by making **redundancies**, **divesting** and acquiring (see **merger**) businesses, and introducing 'Work-Out', a programme centred on **communication** and **innovation**.

welfare *HR* the physical and mental well-being of employees, and the provision of help for those in need of assistance. Welfare embraces: **physical working conditions**, such as hygiene, sanitation, temperature, humidity, ventilation, lighting, physical comfort, and refreshments; **occupational health** or wellness promotion; **counselling** and advice on personal problems, such as bereavement, drug abuse, or **stress**; and working time, covering matters such as **hours of work**, rest periods, paid holidays, and **shiftwork**. **Employee assistance programmes** are a modern form of welfare policy, although not common outside the United States.

well
let's drop it down the well and see what

Brain cells create ideas. Stress kills brain cell. Stress is not a good idea.   Doug Hall

kind of splash it makes *Gen Mgt* let's try this idea and see if it is successful (*slang*)

wellness program (*US*) *HR* a company programme offering benefits, activities, or training, to improve and promote employees' health and fitness. A wellness programme can include **wellness benefits** such as fitness training, company sponsored athletics and sports teams, health education, and life improvement classes. It also includes prevention of mental health problems by *stress* management.

wet signature *Gen Mgt* a signature on paper rather than a faxed or e-mailed copy (*slang*)

wharfie (*ANZ*) *Gen Mgt* a docker (*slang*)

Wheat Report *Fin* a report produced by a committee in 1972 that set out to examine the principles and methods of accounting in the United States. Its publication led to the establishment of the Financial Accounting Standards Board.

whisper stock *Fin* a stock about which there is talk of a likely change in value, usually upwards and often related to a takeover

whistle
blow the whistle on somebody or something *Gen Mgt* to speak out publicly about malpractice or incompetence within an organisation

whistleblowing *Gen Mgt* speaking out to the media or the public on malpractice, misconduct, corruption, or mismanagement witnessed in an organisation. Whistleblowing is usually undertaken on the grounds of morality or conscience or because of a failure of *business ethics* on the part of the organisation being reported.

white coat rule *Mkting* a US Federal Trade Commission rule prohibiting the use of actors dressed as doctors to promote a product in TV commercials (*slang*)

white-collar crime *Gen Mgt* a crime committed by somebody doing a white-collar job

white-collar job *HR* a position that does not involve physical labour. *See also* **blue-collar job**

white-collar worker *HR* an office worker. Office workers traditionally wore a white shirt and a tie.

white goods *Mkting* large household electrical appliances such as cookers, fridges, and freezers

white knight *Fin see* **knight**

white squire *Gen Mgt* a *shareholder* who purchases a significant, but not controlling, number of shares in order to prevent a *takeover bid* from succeeding. A white squire is often invited to purchase the shares by the company to be acquired, and may be required to sign an agreement to prevent them from later becoming a black *knight*.

whizz kid *Fin* a young, exceptionally successful person, especially one who makes a lot of money in large financial transactions, including takeovers

wholesale price *Fin* a price charged to customers who buy large quantities of an item for resale in smaller quantities to others

wholesale price index *Fin* a government-calculated index of wholesale prices, indicative of inflation in an economy

wholesaler *Mkting, Ops* an intermediary who buys in bulk from manufacturers for resale to *retailers* or other traders. Some wholesalers sell directly to the public. One type of wholesaler is a **cash and carry**, which offers discounted prices for bulk purchases that are paid for and taken away at the time of sale. Cash and carries traditionally serve the business community, but many now allow the general public to buy from them.

wholesale trade *Fin* trade at wholesale prices

wholly-owned subsidiary *Fin* a company that is completely owned by another company. A wholly-owned subsidiary is a *registered company* with board members who all represent one *holding company* or corporation. Board members may be directly from the holding company or acting as its nominees, or they may be from other wholly-owned subsidiaries of the holding company.

Whyte, William Hollingsworth (1917–99) *Gen Mgt* US urban theorist. Author of *The Organization Man* (1956), a study of the impact of the power of *corporate culture* on individuals from the suburban middle class.

Wickens, Peter (*b.* 1938) *Gen Mgt* British business executive. Personnel director at Nissan UK, where he helped to introduce Japanese working practices, such as *continuous improvement*, into the UK car industry. Wickens's employee relations philosophy at Nissan was based on job flexibility, *single status*, and a single union deal. His book, *The Ascendant Organisation* (1995), brings together his experience and knowledge of *best practice*.

widow-and-orphan stock (*US*) *Fin* a stock considered extremely safe as an investment

wiggle room *Gen Mgt* flexibility in matters relating to contracts or deadlines (*slang*)

wildcat strike *HR see* **unofficial strike**

Willie Sutton rule *Gen Mgt* the maxim that it is most logical to concentrate on areas that yield most profit. The Willie Sutton rule is based on an alleged remark made by bank robber Willie Sutton. He was reputedly asked why he robbed banks and replied 'Because that's where the money is'. A person or organisation following this rule will focus their effort on those activities that give the greatest return.

windfall gains and losses *Fin* unexpected gains and losses

windfall profit *Fin* a sudden large profit, subject to extra tax

windfall tax *Fin* the tax a government levies on a company that makes extraordinarily large profits in times of unusual circumstances, for example, during a war

winding-up *Fin* the legal process of closing down a company

winding-up petition *Fin* a formal request to a court for the compulsory liquidation of a company

window dressing *Fin* a creative accounting practice in which changes in short-term funding have the effect of disguising or improving the reported liquidity position of the reporting organisation

win win situation *Gen Mgt* a business situation in which all parties stand to gain something (*slang*)

WIP *abbr Fin* work in progress

wired company *Gen Mgt* a company that makes full use of information technology to run its business (*slang*)

wireless application protocol *E-com see* **WAP**

witching hour (*US*) *Fin* the time when a type of derivative financial instrument such as a *put*, a *call*, or a contract for advance sale becomes due (*slang*)

withdrawal *Fin* regular disbursements of dividend or capital gain income from an open-end unit trust

withholding tax *Fin* **1.** in the United States, the money that an employer pays directly to the government as a payment of the income tax on the employee **2.** the money deducted from a dividend or interest payment that a financial institution pays directly to the government as a payment of the income tax on the recipient

WOMBAT *abbr Gen Mgt* waste of money, brains, and time (*slang*)

wood
put wood behind the arrow *Gen Mgt* to provide resources or money for a project or enterprise (*slang*)

Stretch and discipline are the yin and yang of business.   *Christopher Bartlett*

Woodward, Joan (1916–71) *Gen Mgt* British academic. Originator of what subsequently became known as the **contingency theory** of organisations, based on research inspired by **Elton Mayo** and which was written up in *Industrial Organization* (1965).

word of mouse *E-com* word-of-mouth publicity on the Internet. Owing to the fast-paced and interactive nature of online markets, word of mouse can spread much faster than its off-line counterpart. (*slang*)

work *Gen Mgt* the expenditure of physical or mental energy to achieve a purposeful task. Work is usually performed by **employees** within organisations, where it involves completion of a particular activity that contributes to the achievement of organisational goals.

workaholic *HR* somebody who is addicted to working. A workaholic spends long hours in the workplace and probably suffers from **presenteeism**. While workaholics may be very productive, workaholism is sometimes a sign of **stress** or personal problems. The term was coined in the 1960s.

work cell *Fin* a group of employees or machines dedicated to performing a specific manufacturing task or a group of related tasks

worker control *Gen Mgt* participation by employees in the management of an organisation. Worker control can involve **worker directors**, **works councils**, or a **management buy-out**.

worker director *HR* an **employee** raised to executive status within an organisation, usually as part of a structured programme of **employee participation** in management. A worker director usually represents the views of staff at board level.

workers' co-operative *Gen Mgt see* **industrial co-operative**

work ethic *Gen Mgt* the belief that **work** itself is as important and fulfilling as the end result. The work ethic originated among Protestants and was central to the

views of Martin Luther and John Calvin. It played an important role in the achievements of the Industrial Revolution.

work experience *HR* the temporary placement of young people in organisations to give them a taste of the work environment. Successful work experience programmes require adequate preparation by schools and employing organisations, together with follow-up activities to monitor the outcomes of a placement.

work flow *Gen Mgt see* **office design**

workforce *HR* the whole body of employees, either in an organisation or across an industry

working capital *Fin* the funds that are readily available to operate a business.
| EXAMPLE | Working capital comprises the total net current assets of a business minus its liabilities.

Current assets – current liabilities

Current assets are cash and assets that can be converted to cash within one year or a normal operating cycle; current liabilities are monies owed that are due within one year.

If a company's current assets total £300,000 and its current liabilities total £160,000, its working capital is:

$$£300,000 - £160,000 = £140,000$$

working capital cycle *Fin* the period of time which elapses between the point at which cash begins to be expended on the production of a product, and the collection of cash from the purchaser

working capital ratio *Fin see* **current ratio**

working hours *HR see* **hours of work**

working lunch *Gen Mgt* a lunchtime meal during which business is transacted. A working lunch can occur either when an employee continues to work through their lunch hour, or when clients or colleagues are entertained and business is conducted at the same time, when it is also known as a **power lunch**.

The key is not in spending time, but using it.							*Arthur Bryan*

work in process (*US*) *Fin* = *work in progress*

work in progress *Fin* products that are in the process of being made. They are included in stocks and usually valued according to their production costs. *US term **work in process***

work-life balance *HR* the equilibrium between the amount of time and effort somebody devotes to work and that given to other aspects of life. Work-life balance is the subject of widespread public debate on how to allow *employees* more control over their working arrangements in order to better accommodate other aspects of their lives, while still benefiting their organisations. The agenda consists primarily of *flexible working* practices and *family-friendly policies*, although good practice demonstrates that flexibility should be open to all, including those without caring responsibilities. The work-life balance debate has arisen through social and economic changes, such as greater numbers of women in the workforce, the expectations of the younger *Generation X*, a growing reluctance to accept the longer hours culture, the rise of the 24/7 society, and technological advancements. It has been supported by government and by organisations which see it as a means of aiding *recruitment* and employee retention.

work measurement *Gen Mgt* the establishment of *standard times* for the completion of particular work tasks to a particular level of performance. In work measurement, tasks are broken down into elements. The time required for each is established and an assessment of relaxation and contingency allowances is made. Work measurement forms part of *work study* and is normally carried out subsequent to *method study* with the aim of increasing efficiency and *productivity*. Work measurement was developed in the context of industrial *production management* but has recently become more widely used. *Time study* and *predetermined motion-time systems* are used in work measurement.

work permit *HR* a licence granted to a foreign national in order that they may perform a specific job for a limited period. A work permit scheme is intended to safeguard the interests of the resident labour force while enabling employers to recruit or transfer skilled workers from abroad. It is the responsibility of the employing organisation to obtain permits from its national government.

workplace bullying *HR* persistent intimidation or harassment at work which demoralises and humiliates a person or group. There are no universally agreed definitions of what constitutes workplace bullying, as there are many kinds of bullying behaviour or tactics. As a general guideline to distinguish between workplace bullying and legitimate criticism, comments should follow the principles for offering *feedback*: it should be properly conducted, non-personal, and constructive, and should not be abusive, aiming to help people to improve their behaviour or performance rather than cause them anxiety or distress.

work profiling *HR see profile method*

work rage *Gen Mgt* an expression of irrational anger felt by an employee in the workplace (*slang*)

Worksafe Australia *HR see National Occupational Health and Safety Commission*

work sampling *Gen Mgt see activity sampling*

works council *HR* a body of representatives of management and employees who meet to exchange opinions, information and advice on matters concerning the efficiency of the organisation and the interests of staff. A works council is a form of joint consultation, or *employee participation*. The idea was first introduced by *Wilfred Brown* at the *Glacier Metal Company* as a genuine attempt at *industrial democracy*. The European Works Council Directive, approved in 1994, makes it compulsory for larger employers in Europe to implement a European works council, or EWC, if operations span two or more countries. An EWC enables employees to be informed and consulted across national boundaries.

work shadow *HR* somebody who observes a jobholder in action with the aim of learning something about how that role is performed. Work shadowing has traditionally been seen as a way of giving *work experience* to school students or graduates but it is also a means of offering employees the opportunity to find out more about other jobs within their own or other organisations. It can be used, for example, as a form of *secondment*, or as a preliminary to a sideways move for somebody experiencing *plateauing*.

work simplification *Gen Mgt* an idea pioneered by *Frank* and *Lillian Gilbreth* and favoured by practitioners of *scientific management*. Any work that does not add value to an idea or process is seen as reducible waste. Tasks in a procedure are analysed to see if unnecessary steps can be eliminated, thereby reducing complexity as much as possible. This should enable workers to complete tasks more quickly. Work simplification is most suited to manufacturing processes and low-skilled jobs. It can lead to cost savings and better use of resources but it has been criticised for resulting in workers specialising in only one task and for making work repetitive and monotonous.

works manager *HR* the person in charge of a factory, plant, or area of operations in a manufacturing company. A works manager is usually a *general manager*, with responsibility not just for the manufacturing operation but also for personnel, finance, marketing, etc.

workstation 1. *E-com* a powerful, single-user computer. A workstation is like a personal computer, but it has a more powerful microprocessor and a higher-quality monitor. 2. *Gen Mgt* the place where a person or small group carries out their particular work tasks. A workstation might take the form of an individual unit where a stage of the manufacturing process is carried out. A factory may contain many workstations, organised to optimise the production process. In an office environment, a workstation may refer to a desk with a computer, telephone, and other equipment at which one person sits.

work structuring *HR* the design of work processes. Work structuring involves arranging the factors that make up employees' jobs in the most efficient way. Factors to be engineered include *hours of work*, duties performed, and level of *empowerment*. Work structuring can make use of practices such as *flexible working*, *teamwork*, job enrichment, *job enlargement*, and *job rotation*. It is similar to *job design*.

work study *Gen Mgt, HR, Ops* the analysis of activities of employees within an organisational context. Work study comprises a set of techniques that are used to examine a work process and determine where improvements can be made. It usually involves *method study* followed by *work measurement*, and is an important tool in *total quality management*. It is similar to *time and motion study*.

work-to-rule *HR* a form of *industrial action* in which employees work strictly according to the terms of their *contract of employment*. A work-to-rule usually involves refusal to do any extra tasks and an overtime ban, causing production to slow down.

world class manufacturing *Ops* the capability of a manufacturer to compete with any other manufacturing organisation in a chosen market, with the aspiration of achieving world-beating standards in all organisational aspects. World class manufacturing encompasses the practices of *total quality management*, *continuous improvement*, international *benchmarking*, and *flexible working*.

world economy *Econ* the global marketplace that has grown up since the 1970s in which goods can be produced wherever production cost is cheapest

wrap fund (*S Africa*) *Fin* a registered fund, not itself a unit trust but with similar status to that of a stockbroker's portfolio, which invests in a range of underlying unit trusts, each of which is treated as a discrete holding

WRF *abbr E-com* web response form: a web-based form designed to collect site-visitor contact and other information. A WRF often forms part of a landing page or termination point of a website address intended to funnel response not just from a website but also from traditional direct marketing material.

Wright, T.P. (1895–1970) *Gen Mgt* originator of a mathematical model describing a *learning curve*, introduced in an article entitled 'Factors Affecting the Cost of Airplanes' in *the Journal of Aeronautical Science* (February 1936)

write-down *Fin* a reduction in the recorded value of an asset to comply with the concept of prudence. The valuation of stock at the lower of cost or net realisable value may require the values of some stock to be written down.

write off *Fin* a reduction in the recorded value of an asset, usually to zero

writing down allowances *Fin* in the United Kingdom, the annual depreciation of fixed assets for tax purposes. These allowances form part of the capital allowance system.

written-down value *Fin see* **net book value**

wrongful trading *Fin* the continuation of trading when a company's directors know that it cannot avoid insolvent liquidation

WRT *abbr Gen Mgt* with respect to (*slang*)

WYSIWYG *abbr E-com* what you see is what you get: refers to web creation software that enables users to design content on their computer that will look exactly the same when transferred to the Web. Before the advent of the Internet, the term was also used in reference to word processing software that allowed the user to see exactly how a document would look when it was printed.

X.12 *E-com see ANSI X.12 standard*

XBRL *abbr E-com, Fin* Extensible Business Reporting Language: a computer language for financial reporting. It allows companies to publish, extract, and exchange financial information through the internet and other electronic means.

XML *E-com* extensible mark-up language, a meta-language that describes rules for defining tagged mark-up languages. XML is similar to *HTML*, except that it is intended to deliver data to a variety of applications and is designed to be read by the applications run by a system, whereas HTML is intended to be read from a web browser by a person.

XML is an emerging world standard for *metadata*, delivering a common approach by which metadata for content is collected. So in order to achieve a common standard, organisations in a particular industry would agree to structure their documents in the same way. For example, finance companies would agree to use the same methods of creating documentation such as morning notes, which are short analyses issued daily. The morning notes would all use the same layout structure, and have the same metadata such as author name, date, ticker symbols, buy, and sell rating. Because of this common structure, anyone receiving these morning notes would be able to search and interrogate them in a far more comprehensive manner.

Nothing will ever be attempted, if all possible objections must first be overcome.
                                                                    Samuel Johnson

Y2K-compliant *Gen Mgt see* **millennium bug**

yakka *(ANZ) HR* an informal term for work

Yankee bond *Fin* a bond issued in the US domestic market by a non-US company

YAPPY *abbr Mkting* Young Affluent Parent *(slang)*

year-end *Fin* relating to the end of a financial or fiscal (tax) year

year-end closing *Fin* the financial statements issued at the end of a company's fiscal (tax) year

Yellow Book *Fin see* **Purple Book**

yield *Fin* a percentage of the amount invested that is the annual income from an investment.

It is calculated by dividing the annual cash return by the current share price and expressing that as a percentage.

Yields can be compared against the market average or against a sector average, which in turn gives an idea of the relative value of the share against its peers. Other things being equal, a higher yield share is preferable to that of an identical company with a lower yield.

An additional feature of the yield (unlike many of the other share analysis ratios), is that it enables comparison with cash. Cash placed in an interest-bearing source like a bank account or a government stock, produces a yield—the annual interest payable. This is usually a safe investment. The yield from this cash investment can be compared with the yield on shares, which are far riskier. This produces a valuable basis for share evaluation.

Share yield is less reliable than bank interest or government stock interest yield, because unlike banks paying interest, companies are under no obligation at all to pay dividends. Frequently, if they go through a bad patch, even the largest companies will cut dividends or abandon paying them altogether.

yield curve *Fin* a representation of relative interest rates of short- and long-term bonds. It may be normal, flat, or inverted.

yield gap *Fin* an amount representing the difference between the yield on a very safe investment and the yield on a riskier one

yield to call *Fin* the yield on a bond at a date when the bond can be called.

Bond issuers reserve the right to 'call', or redeem, the bond before the maturity date, at certain times and at a certain price. Issuers often do this if interest rates fall and they can issue new bonds at a lower rate. Bond buyers should obtain the yield-to-call rate, which may, in fact, be a more realistic indicator of the return expected.

yield to maturity *(US) Fin* = **gross yield to redemption**

YK *abbr Fin* yugen kaisha

young old *Mkting* the group of people aged between 55 and 75

yugen kaisha *Fin* in Japan, a private limited liability corporation. Usually, the number of shareholders must be less than 50. The minimum capital of a limited liability corporation is 3,000,000 yen. The par value of each share must be 50,000 yen or more. *Abbr* **YK**

YUPPY *abbr Gen Mgt* Young Urban Professional *(slang)*

Z

zaibatsu *Gen Mgt* Japanese mining-to-manufacture conglomerates dating from before the second world war. At the end of the second world war, zaibatsu were disbanded because of their involvement in the war effort. When post-war restrictions were relaxed, these groups of companies reformed as *keiretsu*.

Zaleznik, Abraham (*b*. 1924) *Gen Mgt* US academic. Author of the landmark article *Managers and Leaders: Are They Different?* published in the 'Harvard Business Review' (1977), which influenced the ideas of **Warren Bennis** on the key elements found in effective *leaders*.

ZBB *abbr Fin* zero-based budgeting

Z bond *Fin* a bond whose holder receives no accrued interest until all of the holders of other bonds in the same series have received theirs

zero-balance account *Fin* a bank account that does not hold funds continuously, but has money automatically transferred into it from another account when claims arise against it

zero-based budgeting *Fin* a method of budgeting which requires each cost element to be specifically justified, as though the activities to which the budget relates were being undertaken for the first time. Without approval, the budget allowance is zero. *Abbr* **ZBB**

zero coupon bond *Fin* a bond that pays no interest and is sold at a large discount.
Zero coupon bonds increase in value until maturity. A buyer might pay £3,000 for a 25-year zero bond with a face value of £10,000. This bond will simply accrue value each year, and at maturity will be worth £10,000, thus earning £7,000. These are high-risk investments, however, especially if they must be sold on the open market amid rising interest rates. *Also known as* **accrual bond**

zero defects *Ops* a *quality* philosophy according to which organisations aim to produce goods that are 100% perfect. Zero defects was developed during the early 1960s in the United States by **Philip Crosby** while he was working for the Martin-Marietta Corporation. The aim is to eliminate the smallest defects at each process stage. It requires a high level of *employee participation*. When introduced in Japan it merged with *quality circle* concepts.

zero fund *Gen Mgt* to assign no money to a business project without actually cancelling it (*slang*)

zero growth *Econ* a fall in output for two successive quarters

zero out *Gen Mgt* to dial zero when using an automated call system in the hope of finding a live person to speak to (*slang*)

zero-rated supplies *or* **zero-rated goods and services** *Fin* in the United Kingdom, taxable items or services on which VAT is charged at zero rate, such as food, books, public transport, and children's clothes

Z score *Fin* a single figure, produced by a financial model, which combines a number of variables (generally financial statements ratios), whose magnitude is intended to aid the prediction of failure. A Z score model may predict that a company with a score of 1.8 or less is likely to fail within 12 months. Individual companies are scored against this benchmark.